RACIAL CONFLICT, DISCRIMINATION, & POWER

RACIAL CONFLICT, DISCRIMINATION, & POWER:

Historical & Contemporary Studies

Edited by
William Barclay
Krishna Kumar
Ruth P. Simms

With a Foreword by James B. McKee

AMS Press
New York

Library of Congress Cataloging in Publication Data
Main entry under title:

Racial conflict, discrimination, and power.

    Includes bibliographies.
    1. Race problems—Addresses, essays, lectures. 2. Discrimination—Addresses, essays, lectures. 3. Race problems—Case studies—Addresses, essays, lectures.
I. Barclay, William, 1944-   II. Kumar, Krishna.
III. Simms, Ruth P.
HT1521.R27   301.45'1'042   75-11964
ISBN 0-404-13140-9
      0-404-13144-1 (pb)

TABLE OF CONTENTS

Foreword

On the study of race relations, a seemingly endless number of books and articles, and of collections of such exist. Why, then, another? Quite simply, because there is still a need for perspective and framework that most work in race relations fails to provide.

For many years now American sociologists have criticized their own work in race relations as too parochial and too atheoretical, although they rarely asked themselves what social and ideological factors would account for the kind of work they were doing. Since then, being "comparative" has become fashionable, but such efforts only sort out some differences—measurable as variables—which set off one society's race relations from another. That race relations vary in detail from one society to another is hardly a significant finding. Indeed, sociologists are often so anxious to compare national differences that the study of race relations becomes theoretically subordinated to the historically particular structure of national societies.

What William Barclay, Krishna Kumar and Ruth P. Simms have done is provide a frame of reference for the study of race relations which delineates the basic historical context out of which race relations have emerged: the expansion of Europe from the fifteenth century. This transnational process molded a basic pattern of white and non-white inequalities always evident, though in national and cultural variation, throughout the world.

Perhaps one of the most grievous deficiencies in all the modern social sciences is their inability to capture a conceptual ordering of phenomena that transcends those structural unities that are culturally and politically national. Political scientists study the nation-state, sociologists the modern society, which is also a nation, and economists the national market whose total output is measured as gross *national* product. The modern nation, then, is the fundamental unit of social reality for social science. Everything else—everything cultural, psychological, and structural—is perceived as a subunit.

To be sure, national societies do not live in isolation (there are international relations and international differences) and their interaction is the basis of whatever is comparative in social science. However, there is a *world* history, a larger pattern of events and human interactions, of which nations are but one outcome. The flow of human populations across long-established territorial boundaries, and the expansion and colonization by Europeans of almost all the non-European world from the fifteenth century on, is a basic pattern out of which race relations—and much else— emerges. It is the strength of the editors' work that they recognize this basic process, and their readings and accompanying readings explicate it for us.

This book does do more than that. It demonstrates how such past historical processes and the structural inequalities they established requires an appropriate paradigm which stresses power relations and social conflict. Race, then, is not just a liberal problem about prejudiced people and dysfunctional discriminations, but one basic aspect of international stratification and a salient component of the struggle between developing and developed peoples. The editors have gone to the literature on development to find works that help us understand these fundamental sources of struggle and conflict.

The need for a new perspective in social science which takes into account processes not restricted to nations alone, but that emphasize a common set of world developments involving all nations and that are set in a pattern of power and conflict, is here set forth for one central issue: the struggle between whites and non-whites. As the twentieth century comes to an end, the world does indeed become a small planet, a vastly troubled and endangered one. It is work such as this that breaks new ground in finding the necessary world perspective for a social science that can begin to make sense of it.

—James B. McKee

Introduction

Three features of this book distinguish it from most earlier work in the field of race relations.

First, we argue that modern race relations have their origins in, and cannot be understood apart from, the global expansion of Western Europe that began in the fifteenth century. This expansionary thrust was pioneered by the Atlantic and Iberian nations and continued by their offspring, particularly the United States. This thrust formed the content of world history from the fifteenth through the nineteenth centuries. These centuries of expansion incorporated more of the world and remolded more thoroughly the social orders of non-European peoples than any previous empire, with two significant results. First, an unequal relationship emerged between white and non-white peoples which generated deep rooted conflict, prejudices, and stereotypes. Most importantly, however, it also created a global distribution of power and privilege along the lines of color which lies at the base of much current national and international conflict.

Second, we present some emerging theoretical approaches to the study of race relations which are part of what is known as the power/conflict paradigm. These approaches stress the primacy of the economic and political dimensions of race relations instead of the cultural and psychological ones. Racial cleavages and conflicts are seen as arising from and sustained by structural inequalities. Thus, we have included selections that emphasize constructs like marginal class, internal colony, and imperialism in the analysis of race relations in widely dispersed areas of the world.

Finally, we make race and color an important dimension in the analysis of the contemporary international stratification system. We stress the link between our approach to race relations, the historical analysis of international racial conflict and expansion, and the theories of international dependency developed by a new generation of social scientists. (These latter two approaches of analysis complement each other.) Dependency theory serves as a necessary corrective to isolated comparative work on race, while the study of race relations provides a dimension often missing in the field of international dependency. Thus, our unifying themes are the historical process of white expansion and the racial conflict and power differentials which were at the base of this process. We argue that these forces which shaped the past are part of the structure of the present.

Our point of departure, then, is the expansion of the West European metropoles. It is important to understand that, despite many common features, the dynamics of expansion were not uniform. Thus, distinct systems of race relations emerged. First, the specific goals of expansion shaped the social relations linking white and nonwhite peoples. The dream of conquest had a different outcome than the labor of colonization. For example, the administrative colonialism of the Spanish in the New World created a system of race relations which differs from that produced by the settlement colonialism of the British in North America. Second, expansion under the stimulus of mercantilism by the Portuguese in Brazil, produced a different structure of race relations than the industrially based expansion of Britain in South Africa. Third, the nature of the hinterland societies into which expansion occurred was also a determinant of the system of race relations that developed. Thus, contact with the commercially advanced societies of the East, the conquest of the Amerindian empires of Central America, and the slave trade with African kingdoms created different linkages and systems within a common process of conflict and domination. It is essential to recognize the difficulty if not the impossibility of approaching the comparative study of race relations without a framework that explicitly recognizes that nations are not independent units. They are part of an international social system and the dynamics of that larger system are crucial for understanding the patterns of individual nations.

The first two sections of this book develop in some detail these dual themes of conflict and expansion. Section I contrasts the conflict approach to race relations with more traditional forms of analysis: Section II contains readings on the history of white expansion. Both sections provide the larger framework which has directed our later selections in this book. We have not attempted to be exhaustive but have instead chosen four regions which demonstrate both the variety and the commonality of modern race relations. In Section III, we examine Great Britain, one of the original white metropoles. Despite its encroachments into territories occupied by non-whites—the British soil on which the sun never sets was, after all, largely inhabited by non-whites—Great Britain itself remained racially homogeous until recent times. During the 1960's increasing racial conflict has occurred between newly arriving non-white immigrants and white Britishers. The British government has now moved to restrict this immigration. These immigrants, however, have appeared as a direct outgrowth of past expansion. The overwhelming majority of immigrants come from lands once belonging to the British Empire. Former imperial rule has not only established the social, political, and economic links which have made the recent immigration possible, it also oriented the immigrants from subordinated lands towards the British metropole. The resulting racial conflict demonstrates that the effort to draw the veil of commonwealth over the structure of empire requires more than a simple change in rhetoric.

The selections in Section IV examine the United States and those in Section V focus on the Union of South Africa. The society of the United States was the product of British expansion during the mercantile era and broke from the British metropole at an early date. South Africa, in contrast, was shaped by the expansion of an industrializing Britain during the nineteenth century. Its formal break with Britain was recent and peaceful despite heated diplomatic exchanges. In both societies the history of surplus appropriation from non-white labor also demonstrates distinct patterns. The United States imported slaves from Africa, for use in agriculture, thus laying the basis for its current racial conflict, while virtually eliminating the indigenous peoples, the native American Indians, as a distinct racial group. South Africa, while destroying the autonomy of the indigenous population, has used its forced labor in industrial development. Consequently, in the United States, nonwhites are a subordinated minority while in South Africa they are a subordinated majority. This basic distinction is probably the major source of the apparently greater resistance to change found in South Africa, although it remains unclear to what extent the system of racial domination in the U.S. has been altered. The U.S. southern system of segregation has been decisively undermined by law as have most of its colonial counterparts abroad, but the potential for a neo-colonial consolidation of white power remains appreciable. In a situation of minority settlement colonialism, South African whites have been unwilling to consider even desegregation.

Despite real differences, South Africa and the United States can best be seen as representing two points on a continuum. Historically, both societies bear the imprint of British expansion and settlement, although the Dutch also played an important role in South Africa. In both societies, sufficient immigration by white families occurred to create a system of settlement colonialism which displaced part or all of the indigenous population. Both societies made considerable use of non-white labor in their economic development while limiting the benefits accruing to non-whites as a return for this labor. The socially defined distinctions between racial groups, particularly that between whites and non-whites, remain rigid in both societies and allows a minimum of movement across racial categories. Finally, the course of past history may be shaping a perhaps reluctant alliance in the present. In refusing to vote in favor of United Nations sanctions for South Africa, the United States is perhaps recognizing a commonality of interest. After all, if race relations in South Africa is a matter of international concern, could not race relations in the United States become a matter of concern to the United Nations?

Central America is examined in Section VI. During the last several years racial conflict has not been as marked there as in the other three areas and again, the roots of this difference lie in the historical specifics of our global theme. The thrust for Spanish expansion was plunder and commerce, along with some religious conversion in an area where the population was smaller than that of Great Britain. Thus, the Spanish impact on the New World shows sharp differences when compared with the British in North America. The Spanish drive for precious metals quickly destroyed the empires of the indigenous peoples, but despite a sharp reduction in numbers, these peoples were incorporated into various systems of forced labor. The outcome was a system of administrative colonialism with limited Spanish immigration in which an intermediate group of mestizos emerged from the licit and illicit sexual relations between the Spaniards and the indigenous population. The modern system of racial domination which developed is based on cultural rather than skin color distinctions. It also seems to have some long-run possibilities of peaceful resolution not to be found in South Africa or perhaps in the United States.

In the final section of this book, we return to many of the issues raised by the approach to race relations outlined in Sections I and II. These selections sketch the international structure of racial stratification which has been the product of the racial conflict and expansion of past centuries. The national systems of racial domination analyzed in Sections III-VI are simply parts of this larger system.

The documents found at the end of each section are chosen to sharpen points made in the readings and to stimulate further discussion. We have also included short annotated bibliographies.

Finally, we wish to acknowledge our gratitude to the Department of Racial and Ethnic Studies and to the College of Urban Development of Michigan State University for their resources and support in the preparation of this book. Professors Jack Bain, Robert L. Green and James B. McKee provided valuable support at different stages of the study. Learthen Dorsey helped in preparing bibliographies. Victoria Arcega, Teddy Gamso, and Parizad Tahbazzadeh read some of the introductions and offered valuable suggestions. Quess Barclay with whom we discussed every part of the book was especially helpful, and Theresa Daman and Pamela Reitz who spent many hours providing typing and clerical assistance were indespensible during the preparation of the manuscript for publication.

I.
CONCEPTUAL
AND
THEORETICAL
PERSPECTIVES

INTRODUCTION

The sociological perspective treats race as essentially a social category and analyzes race relations with reference to social structures and processes. Sociologists, however, have elaborated two conceptual approaches which show marked variance.

One approach seeks to explain racial identities and stratification with reference to the prevailing norms and values of a society. It has been argued that once institutionalized, racial norms and structures gather momentum of their own. Individuals and groups are automatically socialized to accept them and to interact accordingly. Thus the emphasis is on the cultural dimension, and the exponents of this view are sometimes known as "cultural pluralists."

The other approach marks a significant departure from the above view; it sees racial cleavages and structures as arising out of the struggle for limited economic resources and political power. This view implies that different racial groups compete for power, domination and economic resources, and use racial factors to maintain and articulate their interests. Racial conflict is viewed in the context of wider conflicts in the society. Thus the emphasis shifts from cultural to economic and political dimensions of race relations.

These two conceptual approaches to the study of race relations are rooted in two different sociological traditions which, in fact, represent two competitive paradigms for analyzing social reality. In social sciences, they are generally known as "consensus" vs. "conflict", "integration" vs. "coercion", "structural-functional" vs. "dialectic" and "social system" vs. "power-conflict" metatheories of society. A familiarity with the main premises, beliefs and intellectual concerns of the two paradigms is helpful for understanding these two sociological approaches to race relations.

The social system paradigm has dominated the thinking of the liberal social scientists in Western democracies. The focus of this paradigm has been on the functioning of societies as a whole, and it seeks to explain their constituents—individuals and groups—mainly with reference to their relationship to the total social system. Perhaps the most articulate spokesman for this metatheory has been Harvard sociologist Talcott Parsons. A number of his disciples like Robert Merton, Marion Levy, Kingsley Davis and Wilbert Moore have also helped to refine and develop it further.

The basic premise of the social system paradigm is that societies are maintained because their needs are met by their elements. These needs, known as "functional requisites", include provision for biological survival, sexual activity and reproduction, shared goals and values, socialization, communication, and general regulation of social activity. Talcott Parsons has placed them under four broad categories: adoptive, goal-attainment, integrative, and pattern maintenance and tension management.(1)

Obviously, these functional needs of the social system cannot be fulfilled in the absence of concrete social structures. Thus, functionalists insist that social structures arise out of the needs of the system. However, the concept of social structure as developed by the theorists of this paradigm, especially Talcott Parsons, has a distinct meaning. They view social structures as constellations of roles which are stable and recurrent patterns of behavior in a social situation. Such behaviors are oriented towards one another in a social situation and involve elements of mutual expectations and patterns of evaluation. They revolve around shared norms and underlying values. In this sense, roles are normative categories.

According to functionalists, social structures are essentially normative arrangements. Thus, Talcott Parsons has scrupulously avoided the incorporation of ecological or technological variables in his conceptualization of social structure. This limited view of the construct is perhaps the outcome of an insistence that sociological categories should be differentiated from the non-sociological ones. Perhaps it would be accurate to say that the social system conception of social structure is analogous to the Marxian notion of "super-structure".

In the entire scheme of social system analysis, equilibrium is one of the most crucial constructs. Equilibrium does not mean *status quo*; it means balancing of all the inputs and outputs of the four sub-systems which revolve around the four functional needs of the system. The notion that all the sub-systems should function in close harmony appears to be a logical necessity once one accepts the system analogy. A social system maintains equilibrium only when a broad consensus exists among its members on its underlying values. Consensus of values does not mean that each sub-system of the social system should have identical value systems. It only implies that the values pervading the different sub-systems should be mutually compatible with one another. The Parsonian scheme of pattern variables is designed to suggest the compatibility or incompatibility of the different values of the subsystem of a social system.

Two implications of the social system paradigm bear special relevance to the subject of race relations. These relate to the treatment of power and to social inequality.

Power is treated by system theorists as a facility; it enables social transactions which are essential for the survival of the society. It is the output of political sub-system just as wealth is of economic sub-system. Talcott Parsons defines it as follows:

> Power we may define as the realistic capacity of the system unit to actualize its interests (attain goals, prevent undesired interferences, command respect,

control possessions, etc.) within the context of system interaction and in this sense to exert influence on processes in the system.(2)

Rejecting what he calls the "zero sum" concept of power, Parsons sees it as a function of variables like the valuation of the unit according to the societal value standards, the degree of legitimation associated with the authority, and the willing loyalty of those subject to it. Such a diffuse notion of power minimizes, if not ignores its role in the distribution of limited resources.

Social system analysts have also stressed the functional importance of social inequality. Every society, they stress, must distribute its members to different societal positions. However, a problem arises because these positions vary in terms of their perceived utility and the degree of skills and training required to perform them. Under these conditions, the society must offer differential rewards to motivate individuals to assume certain positions and continue to keep them. Therefore, the positions which are highly important to society and suffer from shortage of qualified personnel, carry the highest rewards and vice versa. In fact, rewards are attached to or built into positions. Thus Davis and Moore, who have developed a functional theory of social inequality, observe:

> Social inequality is thus an unconsciously evolved device by which societies insure that most important jobs are consciously filled by the most qualified persons.(3)

Parsons views the stratification system as the expression of the values of society. A society distributes rewards according to the qualities, performance and possessions of an individual as measured in terms of societal standards and values. And since individuals differ in these attributes, social inequality is an essential feature of social existence.

The emphasis shifts from shared goals to scarce means in the case of power-conflict paradigm. The reality of life in a power-conflict paradigm is the scarcity of means to achieve shared goals and values. Material goods and services are limited; everyone cannot get what he or she needs or wants. However, certain individuals and groups who have access to economic and political power, are able to obtain a relatively large portion of valued goods and services at the expense of others. This is the basis of a struggle between those with power and those in subordinate roles; the former want to preserve the *status quo*, while the latter seek to change it. The notion of a functional system where all elements work in close reciprocal relationship does not fit this line of reasoning. Societies are seen as having internal contradictions and conflicts which bring about their transformations and evolutions.

The power-conflict theorists treat differential access to economic resources and political power as providing the conceptual basis for the identification of different groups or classes. Karl Marx, for example, developed a model of capitalist society with a tendency towards polarization between those owning means of production and those selling their labor. In his view, the interests of these two classes are mutually antagonistic, since the former thrives on the exploitation of the latter. The Italian of the growth of parliamentary democracy, the separation of capitalists from the masses.(4) However, while Marx used his theory as a justification for the establishment of classless society, Pareto and Mosca did not share such concerns. These early conflict models of society have undergone significant changes in the hands of modern social thinkers.

German sociologist Ralf Dahrendorf, for example, has extended the notion of class conflict to include all forms of authority conflicts.(5) He insists that as a result of the growth of parliamentary democracy, the separation of capitalists from managers, the rapid expansion of the middle class, and the emergence of mass consumption society, the idea of class conflicts based on economic interests alone no longer describes the contradictions of industrialized societies. Cooperation between the two classes has been increasing instead of decreasing; the laboring and capitalist classes do not view their interests as antagonistic but complementary. Under these conditions, he suggests conflict between those who occupy authority positions and those subject to it as the focus of sociological analysis.

Several social thinkers have further developed the conflict analysis by focusing on intra-unit and inter-unit relationships at the same time.(6) They argue that while every society or collectivity has at least two or more groups or classes with conflicting interests, the relationship between them is also influenced by the interaction of the collectivities with one another. If this relationship is unequal, as is often the case, the worst sufferers are the masses in the subordinate collectivity. The benefits of this unequal relationship are shared, not only by the elites of the two collectivities, but also, to a small extent, by the masses in the dominant collectivity. Such an analysis has been used to explain the lack of class consciousness in the highly industrialized nations that gain from the domination of the less developed countries. This formulation is relevant to race relations; it has been suggested that the same relationship operates within a society when it comes to racial cleavages. Both the elites and the working classes of the dominant racial group benefit, although not in the same manner or to the same extent from the exploitation of the subordinate group.

Conflict theorists view the dominant values not as independent variables but as manifestations of objective conditions. In a passage that has become a classic statement of this position, Karl Marx says:

> The modes of production in material life determines the general character of the social, political and spiritual processes of life. It is not the consciousness of men that determines their being, but, on the contrary, their social beings determines their consciousness.(7)

The concept "modes of production" has wider meaning in Marxian sociology than mere technology. It refers to the existing state of science and technology, the modes of organization of production and even the physical and psychological skills of men. Marx insists that different human constellations in history have had different values systems depending upon the modes of production. Values, then, are not the prime movers of history; they are its product.

This view also implies that values do not have their origin in the moral identity of man but in the structured interests of a particular class or group in a society. Even if one does not subscribe to the Marxian perspective, one must concede that economic and political elites play a critical role in the imposition and institutionalization of social values. Both coercive and noncoercive measures—mass media, civil and criminal codes, educational systems, direct and indirect economic incentives, etc.,—define and institutionalize values. Is it unreasonable to suggest, the conflict theorists point out, that the elites would promote those values which are congruent with their own interests? Thus the conflict theorists take the position that the prevalent values often represent the interests of the dominant class or group rather than those of the rest of the population.

Thus the power-conflict paradigm suggests that constraint and not consensus aptly describes the social reality. The essence of this constraint is not the overt use of force under every circumstance but the imposition and perpetuation of an exploitative system that serves the interests of a specific group or class at the expense of general masses by both covert and overt means.

Our first approach to race relations—the social system approach—stresses the underlying cultural dimension of racial divisions and identities. The essence of the problem according to this approach lies in the institutionalization of racial norms and values, which come to generate their own momentum. Once institutionalized, they are learned by the members of racial groups in the way other social norms and values are acquired in a society.

The exponents of this approach do not deny the existence of economic and political discrimination and exploitation. They are not seen as the decisive variables, but are regarded as consequence rather than cause.

Often the social scientist working within this framework is inclined to study the subordinate racial group to find out the main cause for racial conflicts. In the United States, for example, studies have been undertaken which deal with the family life, community organizations, or working conditions of blacks in order to identify the cause of the alleged nonparticipation of blacks in the mainstream of American life. A good example is *Beyond the Melting Pot* by Nathan Glazer and Daniel Patrick Moynihan.(8)

Such studies have definite policy implications. Since the crux of the racial problem is seen to lie in cultural norms and values, the remedy lies in their eradication and their replacement by new values. Thus education, communication, mass media, etc., are regarded as the main instruments of eliminating racial discrimination and prejudice from the society.

The exponents of the power-conflict approach view racial cleavages and identities as mainly the function of differential access to economic resources and political power; these do not arise in a vacuum but have historical roots in the conquest and subordination of one racial group by another. It is also argued that once a group manages to occupy a privileged position, it strives to maintain it. It seeks legitimation on every possible religious, moral, or cultural ground. Racial prejudices and stereotypes are the consequence rather than the cause of individual or institutional racism. The subordinate racial group strives to change the situation. Thus the essence of the conflict is seen in the underlying struggle for scarce economic resources and political power.

The notion implicit in the power-conflict approach that racial cleavages and identities represent class rather than caste interests should be interpreted with great caution. For example, barring a few exceptions, the exponents of the power-conflict approach do not suggest that the interests of the working classes belonging to different racial groups are always identical or that the working classes of the dominant groups do not get some fringe benefits out of the exploitation of the subordinate racial minority. The main idea of the power-conflict perspective is that the relationship between racial groups is such that one derives unjustified benefits out of the exploitation of another, although these may be distributed differentially within the dominant group.

The policy implications of the power-conflict approach would obviously involve the reconstruction and reorganization of the economic and political structures of the wider society.

These two approaches to race relations are not always mutually antagonistic or exclusive. They may converge on some points. Our emphasis in this book, however, is on the power-conflict approach. The subject of race relations has recently been explored mainly through social system analysis. Although some excellent material on the implications of the power-conflict paradigm exists, it has not attracted the attention it deserves.

The selections present the broad implications of the power-conflict paradigm for the subject of race relations. Robert E. Klitgaard distinguishes three kinds of racism—irrational, economically rational-irrational, and finally, rational racism. The merit of his article lies in the demonstration that individual prejudices are not necessarily the cause or even the sustaining mechanism of racial discrimination. John Horton's article is a brilliant application of what he calls "order" and "conflict" paradigms to the study of deviance and race relations; he not only identifies conceptual differences between the two but also their different policy implications. Dale L. Johnson explains the distinction between the constructs or marginal class and internal colonies; both of these concepts are useful for the conflict paradigm analysis of race relations. Frantz Fanon discusses the relationship between racism, culture, and colonialism. He views racial prejudices as psychological rationalizations for ruling the colonial people. William Ryan analyzes the changing nature of racial ideology in the United States where race relations are shifting. Finally, Donald L. Noel's article presents a theoretical analysis of ethnic stratification.

The United Nations Educational, Scientific and Cultural Organization (UNESCO) has done a remarkable service in demolishing the myth that race determines mental aptitudes, temperment or social behavior. So far it has issued four statements bearing on the subject. The first statement was issued in July 1950 and was signed by a small number of distinguished scientists representing the fields of genetics, general biology, social psychology, sociology and economics. After its publication, it was felt that the physical anthropologists and geneticists were not adequately represented in the drafting of the statement. A second conference consisting of seven physical anthropologists and five geneticists was called in August 1951 to revise the statement. The second statement thus represents a revised version of the first statement. UNESCO called a third conference in 1964 to examine the biological aspect of the issue. The conference issued its statement in August 1964. The last statement was issued in September 1967.

NOTES

(1) Parsons, Talcott, *The Social System*, The Free Press of Glencoe, 1951, see especially pp. 3-67.

(2) Parsons, Talcott, "Essays in Sociological Theory," New York: Free Press, 1964, p. 391.

(3) Davis, Kingsley and Wilbert E. Moore, reprinted from *American Sociological Review*, Vol. X, 1945, No. 2, p. 243.

(4) See, Wilfredo Pareto: *The Mind and Society*, New York: Harcourt, Brace and World, 1935; Mosca Gaetano, *The Ruling Class*, New York: McGraw-Hill, 1939.

(5) Dahrendrof. Ralf, *Class and Class Conflict in Industrial Society*, Stanford: Stanford University Press, 1959.

(6) See Johan Galtung, *Structural Theory of Imperialism*, in the last section.

(7) Preface to a contribution to the critique of *Political Economy*.

(8) Cambridge: MIT Press, 1963.

INSTITUTIONALIZED RACISM:
AN ANALYTIC APPROACH

Robert E. Kiltgaard

. . . Now no one wishes to deny that racist bigotry exists, nor that it is a tangible problem in the United States. But we must not overlook the different *kinds* of racism, and the 'rationality' of some so-called racist actions. Otherwise, the long-overlooked machinery of the separate and unequal societies is covered over with the blanket charge of 'irrationality'. We must understand 'racism' in its many aspects. It is toward this enlightened descriptive picture that this paper aims.

What we shall call 'irrational racism' is that attitude familiar to us all, at least in stereotype, by which one prejudges and dehumanizes all those of another race. It is the bigotry which makes skin-color or some other racial feature a crucial aspect in the determination of political and economic rights. Such irrational racism hurts the black man in the U.S. today. It keeps him from jobs, proper housing, adequate schools, and human dignity.

What is often overlooked about irrational racism is that it hurts the white man economically, too. In a competitive economy, it is clear that turning down an economically qualified man for a job or a house for extraneous reasons forces a drop away from the competitive equilibrium. In the process, total productivity and total profit are reduced via a lowering in utilized factors of production. In general, behavior which is not motivated by economic considerations—rational from the point of view of maximizing profits—will be costly to the person exhibiting that behavior. Thus, irrational racism hurts the irrational racist economically.(1)

Why, then, do racists exist in significant numbers? It seems plausible to assume that if one's profits were hurt by being an irrational racist, there would be a strong incentive to stop being irrational. The invisible hand should wipe racism out, it seems.

Attractive as this argument is, it not only makes the mistake of presupposing that irrational racism is the main problem: it overlooks how irrational racism can be self-enforcing. In fact, racist behavior can be 'rational' in certain situations.

Suppose we have fifty whites living in a community. Let us posit the following:

each is an economically rational human being (that is, no one believes that non-economic motives should enter into their thinking), yet each individual thinks that everyone else is an irrational racist. In this community, then, no one really is an irrational racist: yet everyone thinks that his neighbors are.(2)

Now let us suppose that a Negro enters the community and wishes to obtain an apartment from Mr. White, one of our original fifty. Mr. White has a vacancy, in fact, and his first impulse (guided by the invisible hand) is to rent the apartment to the newcomer. But then he thinks: all the rest of my tenants are irrational racists; they will dislike my new customer merely because of the color of his skin, perhaps enough so that they will move out and live elsewhere; and that would occasion such a loss of profit that it would be irrational for me to rent to this Negro. Renting to a Negro in this community would be economically unwise (not rational), for since the others are perceived to be racists, they would hurt the landlord economically by avoiding his other rental units.

If our Negro attempts to obtain employment in the community, a similar response is likely. Mr. Lilly, for instance, may have a job opening for which the new person is qualified. But Mr. Lilly may consider that, since the rest of the community with whom he does business are racists, it would be economically unwise to hire the Negro. The rest, he figures, will not want to do business with a company which hires 'inferior' or 'unclean' help.

Therefore, thinking that others are racists can make it economically rational to take actions which seem to be those of an irrational racist.

This is not all. Not only would a member of this community have his actions determined by these perceptions that others are irrational racists, he would himself contribute by his own actions to the belief by others that he is an irrational racist (though by hypothesis he is not). 'Well,' another employer or landlord would say, 'Mr. White wouldn't rent an apartment to a black and Mr. Lilly wouldn't hire one; that just goes to show that they are racists like the others.' And in subsequent decisions similar to the ones Mr. White and Mr. Lilly made, this information will help weight against renting or hiring a Negro.

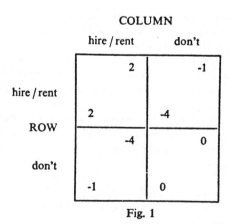

Fig. 1

The situation can be represented for two white players by the matrix shown in Fig. 1. Here is a cooperative game with Column's pay-offs indicated in the upper right of each box and Row's in the lower left.(3) It is clear that if each player knew the structure of the other's *real* preferences, an optimal equilibrium could be reached in the upper left box, where both choose to hire/rent to the black. (This is optimal because of the full use of available factors of production.) In the case of our white community, however, both Row and Column believe that the other player is an irrational racist, that the other will choose 'Don't' regardless of economic consequences. Thus each will be led to choose 'Don't' in order to avoid the -4 pay-off which would be forthcoming should they 'Hire/Rent' while the other chooses 'Don't'. (The -4 pay-off refers to the lost customers). In this fashion a stable but non-optimal equilibrium is established at 0,0.

Notice here that what matters are the players' *perceptions* of the pay-offs and choices, not the real facts. If each player knew the truth about the other's pay-off structure, it would no longer be rational to choose 'Don't' and the optimal equilibrium point would be reached. Thus, it is clear that mistaken beliefs about other people's irrationalities is what keeps this sort of irrational racism alive. The fact that Row believes Column is a racist makes it rational for Row to act like one, too; and vice versa. And it is likely that a new player (a new white member of the community) would perceive the choices of both Row and Column and conclude that they were irrational bigots. In this sense the situation is self-confirming: one mistaken perception implies another one.

The game is probably self-enforcing, too. It would seem that all a new player or a courageous old one would need to do to break the non-optimal vicious circle would be to describe what is going on. Just explaining to everyone that each citizen is 'really' not a racist would seemingly explode the myth which perpetuates the chain of mistaken perceptions. The truth, however, might be prohibitively costly to pronounce: to acknowledge that one is not an irrational racist, even if one person has said that no one in the community is, would run the risk of alienating all one's customers whose past actions have seemed so bigoted. Thus, to agree after everyone has admitted they are *not* racists is easy; to be among the first to admit it is to risk a possibly great economic loss. Even in the event of a 'first-mover', one who calls the true facts to the attention of the community, there is little to be said for being the first one to agree. And if everyone waits for everyone else to agree, no one agrees; and the myth is perpetuated. It becomes rational to be an irrational racist.

But this only scratches the surface of the real problem facing the U.S.: fully rational 'racism'.

Philosophers, especially in ethics, and social scientists seem to have more trouble with respect to the term 'rationality' than with perhaps any other extant term (now that 'God' is dead).(4) Making sense of how an action is or is not 'rational' is clearly of no small importance in our present task of understanding racist behavior. Thus, it behooves us to care for a distinction between two perfectly good meanings of the term: rationality as maximizing and rationality as deducing.

Rationality as *maximizing* can be described by the mathematical maximization of certain goods along one or more given scales. That is, given a certain ends-means relation, rationality is defined in terms of efficiency. An end in itself is not rational in this first sense; this meaning (hereafter 'rationality-1') refers to the efficacious relationship of the means chosen to the given end. Thus, rationality-1 in microeconomics is how efficiently money is made (maximizing profits): in game-theory, maximizing one's pay-offs; in utilitarian ethics, maximizing utility. Although substantive problems accrue in the choice and operational explanation of the scales of maximization involved, what is crucial for our purposes in that rationality-1 is defined in terms of efficient relationships between chosen means and given ends.

Rationality as *deducing* (hereafter 'rationality-2') is quite different. The standard for rational behavior becomes whether or not one's choices correspond with deductions drawn from certain given norms. A rational act is one which is a valid instance of an accepted universal norm. Its rationality consists not in the action's efficiency but in its validity.

These two types of rationality are not necessarily inconsistent, but quite often they come into conflict. When they do, it makes little sense merely to call an action 'irrational'. Instead, one must examine the givens—the ends in rationality-1 and the norms in rationality-2—and formulate one's objections at that level.

Let us apply this to our example of the 'rationally' racist community. The analysis showed that mere adherence to economic rationality does not guarantee the elimination of irrational racism. But, the question arises, is such adherence really 'rational'? Isn't rationality-1 a narrow way of describing the actions U.S. principles would imply in such a situation? What are the universals of U.S. rationality-2?

The United States' norms, insofar as these can be generalized, seem to focus around the principle of individual freedom, that each man should be allowed to maximize as he sees fit, given certain constraints of individual rights and equality of opportunity.(5) The individual rights constraint assures that neither another individual nor the state may interfere with certain sorts of individual activity. This constraint implies that even if some sort of economic efficiency argument could be given that some man's freedoms be curtailed, such interference would not be allowed, because such freedoms have a value in themselves. The equality of opportunity constraint assures that the optimal competitive equilibrium guaranteed by the classical Liberal analysis of social welfare will not be disturbed by irrelevant initial endowments and prejudices. That is, since all men are created equal in the eyes of God and the law, each should be given an equal chance at society's goods: and this will also lead to an optimal socio-economic equilibrium.

Such principles cannot, it would seem, imply racism. They may yield poverty and a Jeffersonian elite, but, given the fact that there are no innately superior races, they cannot yield racial poverty. The principles are color-blind, just as they ignore birth, socio-economic class, color of eyes, and so forth. Therefore, one is tempted to conclude that if the policy-maker would follow the American ideals of liberty and equality of opportunity, the problem of irrational racism would disappear.

But there are the familiar problems with the classical Liberal equilibrium—externalities, market imperfections, economies of scale, hereditary wealth, and so forth —which have led to many attacks on the principles. And in addition, the original assumption of the equality of the races' initial endowments (in terms of education, skills, 'culture', and opportunity) *on the basis of which* the whole political theory predicted racial justice, the equality is empirically non-existent. The principles guarantee just distribution among the races only on the assumption of equal initial endowments, but these equalities just do not exist today. *Why* they don't is an historical question; the important thing is how this inequality, once given, affects the outcome of the political system under the present principles.

What we wish to show is that either sort of rationality—the rationality-1 of personal welfare maximization or the rationality-2 of acting in accordance with the norms of equal opportunity and personal freedom—leads to what appear to be irrational racist acts, given the present inequality. The problem is not overcoming irrational racist hate, nor is it escaping the profit motive to rationality-2: the dilemma is that both economic maximization and U.S. principles are unable to ensure racial justice, starting from the present unequal positions of the two races.

To demonstrate all this, let us examine the case of black housing in the U.S. There is no question that the Negro in the U.S. cannot attain adequate housing as easily as the white man. In part this is because irrational bigots exist; in part it is because there are communities like the one we described above, where people are not racists but perceive that they live in a racist culture, and thus rationally-1 become irrational racists.

But let us take a further case. Take the person who is not an irrational racist and furthermore does not perceive that he lives in a community of such racists. Let us assume he is an economic man, living by rationality-1, concerned only with his own welfare. (This welfare need not be interpreted as pure selfishness, of course, for perhaps our individual acts for the good of his family or gives his profits to starving Biafrans).

Situation A — Our person owns an apartment which he wishes to rent. While believing that the Negro is innately his equal, he perceives, quite correctly, that the average Negro is not his equal according to his economic and cultural values—because of, he admits, past injustices. He will not rent an apartment to a man who is inferior in these respects, be he white or black: he says it does not maximize his or his neighborhood's welfare, and so he won't sell. (We can assume that his other tenants, who have similar beliefs, will move out if such a person white or black, is admitted.) The odds are then that a white will be accepted as a tenant far more often than will a black. In other words, the Negro's position today, that of inequality because of past injustices, which in a real sense is neither the Negro's fault nor our economic man's, makes it rational-1 for 'our' white not to sell him the house. It is not because he is black, but because, on the average, he is empirically, economically inferior at the time in question.

Thus, given many Situation A's and many economic men, while some blacks who do 'measure up' will be admitted, more blacks than whites will be excluded. This gives the appearance of irrational racism (6)

Situation B — Our economic man does not wish to rent his apartment, but his next-door neighbor wishes to rent his—to a black. Our man doesn't dislike the black person for his skin, he is not an irrational racist, yet he does everything in his power to make certain that the black does not live next door. Why? Because it is factually true that the Negro's presence will tend to lower his land's value, raise the crime rate, and make his neighborhood dirtier.(7) All the other economic men in his neighborhood will be motivated to do the same—rationality-1.

In this fashion the interesting process called 'tipping' can ensue. If the seller is not worried about adjacent land values, his neighbor's wrath, or anything else but the purchase price, and if he sells to a Negro, 'tipping' may begin. It is similar to a run on a bank: the others fear that more owners will sell, thus worsening their position even more (as the land value gets even lower, the crime rate goes up, and so forth), and it will thus be to their advantage to sell as quickly as possible. This perceived advantage will increase as the fear of others' selling increases—one Negro neighbor may not begin the chain reaction, but if a few more white neighbors sell, our economic man would realize what other economic men would be thinking, and he will feel the pressure to sell, too. The rationale shifts from Situation B's 'get blackie out' (not because he's *black*. . .) to 'get the hell out'. The matrix in Fig. 2 represents the situation.

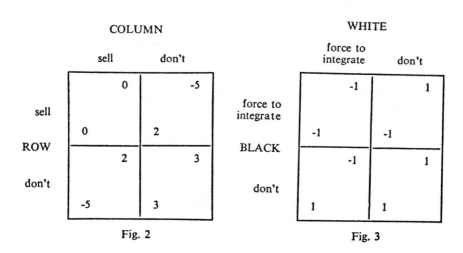

Fig. 2   Fig. 3

The optimal equilibrium for white economic men is if no one sells, the lower right box. This is the rationality-1 behind Situation A—no one wishes to sell for reasons of self-interest. Once someone does sell, however, both Row and Column fear that the other will sell, too, which would give them a -5 pay-off in lost land value, etc. The amount of the negative pay-off is partly a function of the player's fear that the other(s) will sell; and as this fear increases with each sale to a Negro, the player will be moved to protect himself from the undesirable lower left (for Row) and upper right (for Column) boxes by selling. In other words, fear will make Row assume that Column is going to sell; and thus his choice is between 0 and -5, so he will rationally-1 sell, too. His fear is economically, not racially, motivated. It is through this sort of process that an all-white neighborhood can suddenly become all black.(8)

In these two cases there was no irrational bigotry, nor were there mistaken perceptions that one's neighbors were irrational racists, although tipping is often exacerbated by these factors. Nonetheless, we saw how the profit motive can lead to segregation—either by keeping the Negro out of white neighborhoods or by abandoning them once a black moves in. It seems that conformity with rationality-1 will not solve the problem; will consistency with rationality-2?

To find out, let us investigate a further case. Here we posit an economically-disinterested, white principle-follower. This is a rational-2 person — whose actions are in accordance with whatever deductions can be drawn from the American principles of individual liberty and equal opportunity. He is emphatically not an irrational racist, nor is he the type of person, let us assume, who would subordinate his principles to the economic consideration of Fig. 2.

Now, what does such an individual say about renting or selling to a black? What does he recommend in order to solve the problem? On one hand he reaffirms that the Negro must have equal opportunity to buy a house or rent an apartment where he pleases (it follows from his principles). But suppose our economic man in Situation A says to him, 'I have a right to maximize as I wish, and in this case, it is an integral part of my liberty that I be allowed to rent my apartment to whom I please. If a man is not free to rent or sell his house as he sees fit, what becomes of the principle of individual freedom?' Our rational-2 man is faced with a dilemma. The principles of liberty and equality of opportunity cut both ways in this case. In order to give the black man the opportunity to live where he wishes and in order to stop 'tipping', one must deprive the white man of the chance to live where *he* wishes. It seems clear that any move to increase the Negro's freedom will be at the expense of the white's, while maintaining the present situation seems to legitimate racism.

The dilemma is caused by the fact that the rational-2 man's principles guarantee racial justice only given assumptions of equal initial endowments. They are designed to preserve a given equality, a status quo of an optimal social equilibrium and of racial parity. The problem is that the U.S. status quo is not one of freedom for all, as the theory assumes. A racial injustice has occurred in fact, and now the Negro's liberty is impinged by his lack of training, education, and other environmental advantages. The principles do not consider that liberty and opportunity are functions of different social/economic/cultural endowments, since in these areas they assume equality among races. Therefore, the principles can only preserve the status quo or contradict themselves.

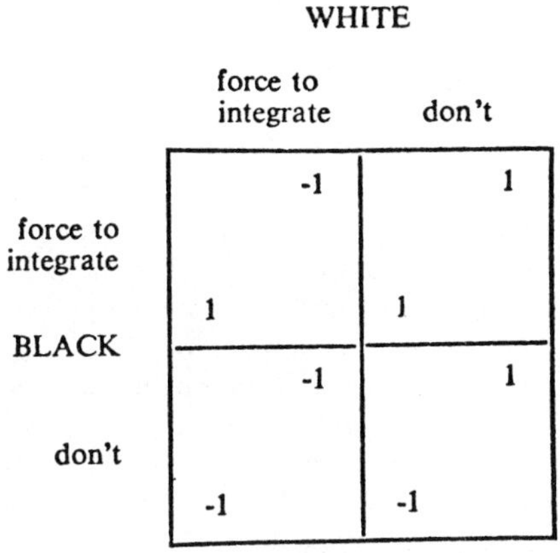

WHITE

Fig. 4

The principles assume that the matrix in Fig. 3 holds. All pay-offs are in 'freedom units' only, for to the principle-follower, these units are the only ones which enter his utility function. *Any* loss of freedom by *anyone* is a negative pay-off. Therefore, any forced integration will limit the freedom of white and black.

But this ideal matrix overlooks the fact that forced integration may be necessary in order to attain the economic prerequisites for the Negro's freedom in this unequal world. Thus, a matrix representing the actual situation would look like Fig. 4. Fig. 3 leads to a stable, optimal equilibrium at the lower right, and thus the rational-2 individual, be he black or white, would be opposed to forced integration. But Fig. 4 is far more interesting analytically, as well as being more realistic. There is a conflict of rights — the black man can only gain freedom, in one sense, via forced integration, while this will destroy the white man's. So, the black man who acts in behalf of his own freedom will opt for forced integration, while the white man protects his liberty by opposing integration.

WHITE

	force to integrate	don't
force to integrate	1,-1	1,-1
BLACK	1,-1	1,-1
don't	1,-1	1,-1
	1,-1	1,-1

Fig. 5

But our rational-2 white man will also value the black man's practical necessities of freedom; and a rational-2 black man will see the loss of white's freedom which forced integration implies. This leads to a confused situation, depicted in Fig. 5. Here there is no proper strategy for our principle-followers. There is only confusion and contradiction. The principles of individual liberty and equality of opportunity, even when followed strictly and with consideration for the other person's rights, lead to contradiction in this case. They cannot solve the present problem of racisim in housing, even if they supervene rationality-1 completely.

The economic man (rational-1) will see that the quality of education is indeed lowered by the introduction of Negroes into his children's schools (because, for example, the Negro child may lag two years behind in average reading level.) Even though our man realizes that the Negro child's lacks are environmental and 'not his fault', it is rational for him to oppose integrating his children's school for his children's sake. If Negroes are allowed to enter, and the decline in educational and cultural standards is perceived to be great enough, it may be rational-1 to withdraw his children and send them to an all-white school.

An interesting further dynamic may occur in the case of school desegregation. No school wishes to be the first to desegregate, nor to have any more Negroes than other schools: for then not only will there be an absolute decline in the quality of education, there will be a relative decline vis-a vis other schools. The white child in an integrated school will be at a competitive disadvantage compared with his counterparts at segregated schools or at schools with fewer blacks. It follows that a decentralized school system, such as the one in the United States, will face additional dynamic incentive to remain segregated apart from those a national school system would have.

The rational-2 individual will realize the fact that a Negro is not being given an equal educational opportunity. Yet he will also affirm that it is his neighbor's right to determine where and how his child is educated. The quandary of Fig. 5 is reached again.

It is clear that the logic of employment will follow that of renting a house, except that instead of being 'culturally' undesirable as a neighbor or tenant, the average Negro will be less skilled for the job than the average white. In some cases, such as high-level management positions, qualified Negroes may actually be unavailable due to past discrimination which has denied blacks requisite experience and training. Thus, even a color-blind, rational-1 man will hire proportionally less Negroes than whites and appear to be a racist.

The rational-2 man will be caught between two conflicting tendencies of his principles—the right of the employer to hire and fire according to the principle of profit maximization and the right of the Negro to a decent job—and will most likely arrive at Fig. 5 once more.

Black militant groups can gain some headlay against the racism of the economic-1 man because they can make threats. Such an organization can force the employer, for instance, to choose between hiring a less qualified black (with his resultant loss in profits) and having his business burned down. Faced with such a choice, he will hire the Negro, since ashes wholesale cheaply. One might therefore conclude that militant organizations can help bring about long-run racial equality.

Unfortunately, such militant groups often use means which easily become perverted for completely non-functional, often criminal ends. Furthermore, they tend to generate militant counter-measures, which can then lead to increasing racial tensions, even to the creation of irrational bigotry and hate. By forcing the rational-1 man to hire blacks through threats of violence, as in our example, a militant organization may turn him into an irrational racist.

For the rational-2 man a dilemma arises once more. While he defends the militants' rights of free speech and assembly, and although he may even agree with some of their arguments, he must loathe the lawlessness and revolutionary actions which the groups threaten. He faces the difficult prospect of defending, in the name of his principles, words and actions which threaten those principles' very existence.(9)

NOTES

(1) A good sample of the quantitative evidence may be found in Kain, J. F. (ed.) 1969: *Race and poverty: the economics of discrimination*. Prentice-Hall, Englewood Cliffs, N. J.

(2) There are many non-competitive situations where this is not so, of course. Exclusionary union practices can, for example, artificially enhance the privileged group's wages. Interesting further examples may be gleaned from Doeringer, P. B. & M. J. Piore 1971: *Internal labor markets and manpower analysis*. D.C. Heath, Lexington, Mass.

(3) The pay-off numbers should merely be taken as intuitive indicators of the utility gained or lost as a result of a particular action. For a detailed discussion of pay-off numbers, see Marschak, J. 1964: Scaling of utilities and probability, in M.

Shubik (ed.): *Game theory and related approaches to social behavior.* Wiley, N.Y., pp. 95-109.

(4) See, for example, the discussions in Bennett, J. 1965: *Nationality* (Routledge and Kegan Paul, London), and Sen. A.K. 1970: *Collective choice and social welfare* (Holden-Day, San Francisco).

(5) These norms are very complex and probably inconsistent. See, for example, Dahl, R.A. 1965: *A preface to democratic theory* (University of Chicago Press). What concerns us here is to see that enforcing the principles does not necessarily solve the problem of irrational racism, not (just) because these principles are self-contradictory, but because America's present objective situation forces these principles to yield a racist society.

(6) If race has this objective correlation with undesirable properties, a further phenomenon may occur: race may be used as a cheap screening device where other information is costly. See McCall, J.J. 1970: *Racial discrimination in the job market: the role of information and search,* (Memorandum RM-6162-OEO, The RAND Corporation, January 1970).

(7) These statements are not always true, and sometimes they are only true because irrational racists exist.

(8) A fascinating analytic treatment of this phenomenon is contained in Schelling, T.C. 1969 Neighborhood tipping (Harvard Institute of Economic Research Discussion Paper No. 100, December 1969).

(9) Many of these examples also apply to other forms of discrimination, such as 'sexism'. (The problem is not just one of 'irrational misogynists'.)

This selection is an abridgment from Robert E. Kiltgaard, "Institutional Racism: An Analytical Approach," *Journal of Peace Research,* 1972, No. 1, pp. 41-49, Published by Universitets Forlaget, Oslo 3, Norway.

ORDER AND CONFLICT
PARADIGMS OF RACE RELATIONS

John Horton

One of the tasks of the sociologist is to recognize his own perspective and to locate this and competing perspectives in time and social structure. In this he can use Weber, Mills, and the sociology of knowledge as guides. Following Weber's work, he might argue that in so far as we are able to theorize about the social world, we must use the vocabularies of explanation actually current in social life.(1) This insight has been expanded by C.W. Mills and applied to theorizing in general and to the character of American theorizing in particular. The key words in Mills's approach to theorizing are "situated actions" and "vocabularies of motive." His position is that theories of social behavior can be understood sociologically as typical symbolic explanations associated with historically situated actions.(2) Thus, Mills argues that the Freudian terminology of motives is that of an upper-bourgeois patriarchal group with a strong sexual and individualistic orientation. Likewise explanations current in American sociology reflect the social experience and social motives of the American sociologist. Mills contends that for a period before 1940, a single vocabulary of explanation was current in the American sociologist's analysis of social problems and that these motives expressed a small town (and essentially rural) bias.(3) He interpreted the contemporary sociological vocabulary as a symbolic expression of a bureaucratic and administrative experience in life and work.(4)

Continuing in the tradition of Weber and Mills, I attempt to do the following: propose a method of classifying current normative theories of deviant behavior and social problems; discuss liberal and sociological approaches to the race question as an example of one of these theories; and point out the implications of the normative character of theory for sociology. My general discussion of competing theories will be an elaboration of several assumptions:

1. All definitions and theories of deviation and social problems are normative. They define and explain behavior from socially situated value positions.

2. Existing normative theories can be classified into a limited number of typical vocabularies of explanation. Contemporary sociological theories of deviation are

adaptations of two fundamental models of analysis rooted in nineteenth-century history and social thought. These are *order* and *conflict* models of society. Order models imply an *anomy* theory of societal discontent and an *adjustment* definition of social deviation. Conflict models imply an *alienation* theory of discontent and a *growth* definition of deviation.

3. In general, a liberalized version of order theory pervades the American sociological approach to racial conflict, juvenile delinquency, and other social problems. I use the term "liberal" because the sociological and the politically liberal vocabularies are essentially the same. Both employ an order model of society; both are conservative in their commitment to the existing social order.

4. Alternatives to the liberal order approach exist both within the context of sociological theory and in the contemporary social and political fabric of American society. More radical versions of order models have been used by European sociologists such as Emile Durkheim; radical versions of order models are presently being used in American society by political rightists. The conflict vocabulary has been most clearly identified with Karl Marx and continues today in the social analysis of socialists and communists, while an anarchistic version of conflict theory pervades the politics of the so-called new left.

5. Current vocabularies for the explanation of social problems can be located within the social organization of sociology and the broader society. As a generalization, groups or individuals committed to the maintenance of the social status quo employ order models of society and equate deviation with non-conformity to institutionalized norms. Dissident groups, striving to institutionalize new claims, favor a conflict analysis of society and an alienation theory of their own discontents. For example, this social basis of preference for one model is clear in even the most superficial analysis of stands taken on civil rights demonstrations by civil rights activists and members of the Southern establishment. For Governor Wallace of Alabama, the 1965 Selma-Montgomery march was a negative expression of anomy; for Martin Luther King it was a positive and legitimate response to alienation. King argues that the Southern system is maladaptive to certain human demands; Wallace that the demands of the demonstrators are dysfunctional to the South. However, if one considers their perspectives in relationship to the more powerful Northern establishment, King and not Wallace is the order theorist. . .

Order theories have in common an image of society as a system of action unified at the most general level by shared culture, by agreement on values (or at least on modes) of communication and political organization. System analysis is synonymous with structural-functional analysis. System analysis consists of *statics*—the classification of structural regularities in social relations (dominant role and status clusters, institutions, etc.)—and *dynamics*—the study of the intrasystem processes: strategies of goal definition, socialization, and other functions which maintain system balance. A key concept in the analysis of system problems (social problems, deviation, conflict) is anomy. Social problems both result from and promote anomy. Anomy means system imbalance or social disorganization—a lack of or breakdown in social organization reflected in weakened social control, inadequate institutionalization of goals, inadequate means to achieve system goals, inadequate socialization, etc. At a social psychological level of analysis, anomy results in the failure of individuals to meet the maintenance needs of the social system.

Order theories imply consensual and adjustment definitions of social health and pathology, of conformity and deviation. The standards for defining health are the legitimate values of the social system and its requisites for goal attainment and maintenance. Deviation is the opposite of social conformity and means the failure of individuals to perform their legitimate social roles; deviants are out of adjustment.

A contemporary example of an order approach to society and an adjustment interpretation of health and pathology has been clearly stated in Talcott Parsons' definition of mental health and pathology:

> Health may be defined as the state of optimum *capacity* of an individual for the effective performance of the roles and tasks for which he has been socialized. It is thus defined with reference to the individual's participation in the social system. It is also defined as *relative* to his "status" in the society, i. e., to differentiated type of role and corresponding task structure, e. g., by sex or age, and by level of education which he has attained and the like.(5)

THE CONFLICT VOCABULARY

Conflict theorists are alike in their rejection of the order model of contemporary society. They interpret order analysis as the strategy of a ruling group, a reification of their values and motivations, a rationalization for more effective social control. Society is a natural system for the order analyst; for the conflict theorist it is a continually contested political struggle between groups with opposing goals and world views. As an anarchist, the conflict theorist may oppose any notion of stable order and authority. As a committed Marxist, he may project the notion of order into the future. Order is won, not through the extension of social control, but through the radical reorganization of social life; order follows from the condition of social organization and not from the state of cultural integration.

Conflict analysis is synonymous with historical analysis: the interpretation of intersystem processes bringing about the transformation of social relations. A key concept in the analysis of historical and social change (as new behavior rather than deviant behavior) is alienation—separation, not from the social system as defined by dominant groups, but separation from man's universal nature or a desired state of affairs. Change is the progressive response to alienation; concepts of disorganization and deviation have no real meaning within the conflict vocabulary; they are properly part of the vocabulary of order theory where they have negative connotations as the opposites of the supreme values of order and stability. Within the conflict framework, the question of normality and health is ultimately a practical one resolved in the struggle to overcome alienation.

Conflict theory, nevertheless, implies a particular definition of health, but the values underlying this definition refer to what is required to grow and change, rather than to adjust to existing practices and hypothesized requirements for the maintenance of the social system. Health and pathology are defined in terms of postulated requirements for individual or social growth and adaptation. Social problems and social change arise from the exploitive and alienating practices of dominant groups; they are responses to the discrepancy between what is and what is in the process of becoming. Social problems, therefore, reflect, not the administrative problems of the social system, nor the failure of individuals to perform their system roles as in the order explanation, but the adaptive failure of society to meet changing individual needs.

In order more sharply to compare order and conflict models in terms of their implications for explanations of deviation and social problems, essential differences can be summarized along a number of parallel dimensions. These dimensions are dichotomized into order and conflict categories. The resulting paradigm can be used as a preliminary guide for the content analysis of contemporary as well as classical studies of social problems.

ORDER PERSPECTIVE   CONFLICT PERSPECTIVE

1. UNDERLYING SOCIAL PERSPECTIVE AND VALUE POSITIONS (IDEAL)

a. *Image of man and society*

Society as a natural boundary-maintaining system of action	Society as a contested struggle between groups with opposed aims and perspectives
Transcendent nature of society, an entity *sui generis*, greater than and different from the sum of its parts; lack of transcendence as lack of social control means anomy	Immanent conception of society and the social relationship; men are society; society is the extension of man, the indwelling of man; the transcendence of society is tantamount to the alienation of man from his own social nature
Positive attitude toward the maintenance of social institutions	Positive attitude toward change

b. *Human Nature*

Homo duplex, man half egoistic (self-nature), half altruistic (socialized nature), ever in need of restraints for the collective good	*Homo laborans* existential man, the active creator of himself and society through practical and autonomous social action

or

Tabula rasa, man equated with the socialization process

or

Homo damnatus, the division into morally superior and morally inferior men

c. *Values*

The social good: balance, stability, authority, order, quantitative growth ("moving equilibrium")	Freedom as autonomy, change, action, qualitative growth

2. MODES OF "SCIENTIFIC" ANALYSIS

Natural science model: quest for general and universal laws and repeated patterns gleaned through empirical research Structural-functional analysis	Historical model: quest for understanding (Verstehen) through historical analysis of unique and changing events; possible use of ideal type of generalization based on historically

Multiple causality; theory characterized by high level of abstraction, but empirical studies marked by low level of generalization (separation of theory from application)

Conditions of objectivity: accurate correspondence of concepts to facts; rigid separation of observer and facts observed—passive, receptive theory of knowledge

Analysis begins with culture as major determinant of order and structure and proceeds to personality and social organization

Dominant concepts: ahistorical; high level of generality; holistic; supra-individual concepts; ultimate referent for concepts—system needs considered universally (i.e., the functional prerequisites of any social system) or relativistically (i.e., present maintenance requirements of a particular social system)

specific patterns.

Unicausality; high or low level of theoretical generalization; union of theory and practice in social research and social action

Utility in terms of observer's interests: objectivity discussed in the context of subjectivity—activistic theory of knowledge

Analysis begins with organization of social activities or with growth and maintenance needs of man and proceeds to culture

Historical, dynamic; low level of generality and high level of historical specificity; ultimate referent for concepts—human needs considered universally (i.e., man's species nature) or relativistically (demands of particular contenders for power); referent often the future or an unrealized state of affairs

3. ORDER AND CONFLICT THEORIES OF SOCIAL PROBLEMS AND DEVIATION

a. Standards for the definition of health and pathology

Health equated with existing values of a postulated society (or a dominant group in the society), ideological definition

Health equated with unrealized standards (the aspirations of subordinate but rising groups), utopian definition

b. Evaluation of deviant behavior

Pathological to the functioning of the social system

Possibly progressive to the necessary transformation of existing relationships

c. Explanation of deviation or a social problem

A problem of anomy in adequate control over competing groups in the social system; disequilibrium in the existing society

A problem of self-alienation, being thwarted in the realization of individual and group goals; a problem of illegitimate social control and exploitation

d. Implied ameliorative action

Extension of social control (further and more efficient institutionalization of social system values); adjustment of individuals to system needs; working within

Rupture of social control; radical transformation of existing patterns of interaction; revolutionary change of the social system

the system; administrative solution

4. ORDER AND CONFLICT THEORIES AS SOCIALLY SITUATED VOCABULARIES

Dominant groups: the establishment and administrators of the establishment	Subordinate groups aspiring for greater power
Contemporary representatives: Parsonian and Mertonian approach to social problems as a liberal variant of order models; politically conservative approaches	C.W. Mills, new left (SNCC, SDS, etc.) approaches an old left (socialistic and communistic)

The order and conflict models as outlined represent polar ideal types which are not consistently found in the inconsistent ideologies of actual social research and political practice. If the models have any utility to social scientists, it will be in making more explicit and systematic the usually implicit value assumptions which underlie their categories of thinking. In this paper as an exercise in the use of conflict-order models, I examine some of the normative assumptions which can be found in the approach of the sociologist and the political liberal to the Negro question. My thinking is intentionally speculative. I am not trying to summarize the vast literature on race relations, but merely showing the existence of an order pattern.

LIBERALS AND SOCIOLOGISTS ON THE AMERICAN NEGRO

Contemporary liberalism has been popularly associated with a conflict model of society; actually it is a variant of conservative order theory. Within the model, conflict is translated to mean institutionalized (reconciled) conflict or competition for similar goals within the same system. Conflict as confrontation of opposed groups and values, conflict as a movement toward basic change of goals and social structures is anathema.

The liberal tendency of American sociology and the essentially conservative character of contemporary liberalism are particularly marked in the sociological analysis of the Negro question. In the field of race relations, an order model can be detected in 1. consensual assumptions about man and society: the "over-socialized'" man and the plural society; 2. a selective pattern of interpretation which follows from these assumptions: (a) the explanation of the problem as a moral dilemma and and its solution as one requiring adjustment through socialization and social control; (b) the explanation of the minority group as a reaction-formation to exclusion from middle-class life; (c) an emphasis on concepts useful in the explanation of order (shared values as opposed to economic and political differences); an emphasis on concepts useful in the explanation of disorder or anomy within an accepted order (status competition rather than class conclict, problems of inadequate means rather than conflicting goals).

THE LIBERAL VIEW OF MAN

No one can see an ideological assumption as clearly as a political opponent. Rightist and leftist alike have attacked the liberal concept of man implicit in the analysis of the Negro question: conservatives because it is egalitarian, radicals because it is elitist and equated with a dominant ideology. The rightist believes in natural inequality; the leftist in positive, historical differences between men; the liberal believes in the power of socialization and conversion.

A certain egalitarianism is indeed implied in at least two liberal assertations: 1. Negroes along with other men share a common human nature socializable to the conditions of society; 2. their low position and general inability to compete reflect unequal opportunity and inadequate socialization to whatever is required to succeed within the American system. These assertations are, in a sense, basically opposed to the elitist-conservative argument that the Negro has failed to compete because he is naturally different or has voluntarily failed to take full advantage of existing opportunities.(6)

The conservative, however, exaggerates liberal egalitarianism; it is tempered with elitism. Equality is won by conformity to a dominant set of values and behavior. Equality means equal opportunity to achieve the same American values; in other words, equality is gained by losing one identity and conforming at some level to another demanded by a dominant group. As a leftist, J.P. Sartre has summarized this liberal view of man, both egalitarian and elitist. What he has termed the "democratic" attitude toward the Jew applies well to the American "liberal" view of the Negro:

> The Democrat, like the scientist, fails to see the particular case; to him the individual is only an ensemble of universal traits. It follows that his defense of the Jew saves the latter as a man and annihilates him as a Jew . . . he fears that the Jew will acquire a consciousness of Jewish collectivity . . . "There are no Jews," he says, "there is no Jewish question." This means that he wants to separate the Jew from his religion, from his family, from his ethnic community, in order to plunge him into the democratic crucible whence he will emerge naked and alone, an individual and solitary particle like all other particles.(7)

The conservative would preserve a Negro identity by pronouncing the Negro different (inferior), the radical by proclaiming him part of the superior vanguard of the future society; but the liberal would transform him altogether by turning him into another American, another individual competing in an orderly fashion for cars, television sets, and identification with the American Creed. In their attack on the liberal definition of man, the conservative and leftist agree on one thing: the liberal seems to deny basic differences between groups. At least differences are reconcilable within a consensual society.

THE LIBERAL SOCIETY

Thus, the liberal fate of minorities, including Negroes, is basically containment through socialization to dominant values. Supposedly this occurs in a plural society where some differences are maintained. But liberal pluralism like liberal egalitarianism allows differences only within a consensual framework. This applies both to the liberal ideal and the sociological description: the plural-democratic society *is* the present society.

This consensual pluralism should be carefully distinguished from the conflict variety. J.S. Furnivall has called the once colonially dominated societies of tropical Asia plural in the latter sense:

> In Burma, as in Java, probably the first thing that strikes the visitor is the medley of peoples—European, Chinese, Indian, native. It is in the strictest sense a medley, for they mix but do not combine. Each group holds to its own religion, its own culture and language, its own ideas and ways. As individuals they meet, but only in the marketplace, in buying and selling. There is a plural society, with different sections of the community living side by side, but separately, within the same political unit. Even in the economic sphere there is a division along racial lines.(8)

For Furnivall, a plural society has no common will, no common culture. Order rests on political force and economic expediency. For liberals and sociologists, American society has a common social will (the American Creed). Order rests on legitimate authority and consensus. The whole analysis of the Negro question has generally been predicated on this belief that American society, however plural, is united by consensus on certain values. Gunnar Myrdal's influential interpretation of the Negro question has epitomized the social will thesis:

> Americans of all national origins, classes, regions, creeds, and colors, have something in common: a social ethos, a political creed ... When the American Creed is once detected the cacophony becomes a melody ... as principles which ought to rule, the Creed has been made conscious to everyone in American society ... America is continuously struggling for its soul. The cultural unity of the nation is sharing of both the consciousness of sin and the devotion to high ideals.(9)

In what sense can a consensual society be plural? It cannot tolerate the existence of separate cultural segments. Robin M. Williams in a recent book on race relations writes: "The United States is a plural society which cannot settle for a mosaic of separate cultural segments, nor for a caste system."(10) Norman Podhoretz, a political liberal who has written often on the Negro question has stated the issue more bluntly. In his review of Ralph Ellison's *Shadow and the Act*, a series of essays which poses a threat of conflict pluralism by asserting the positive and different "cultural" characteristics of Negroes, Podhoretz states his consensual realism:

> The vision of a world in which many different groups live together on a footing of legal and social equality, each partaking of a broad general culture and yet maintaining its own distinctive identity: this is one of the noble dreams of the liberal tradition. Yet the hard truth is that very little evidence exists to suggest that such a pluralistic order is possible. Most societies throughout history have simply been unable to suffer the presence of distinctive minority groups among them; and the fate of minorities has generally been to disappear, either through being assimilated into the majority, or through being expelled, or through being murdered.(11)

The liberal and the sociologist operating with an order ideology positively fear the conflict type of pluralism. As Sartre rightly observed, the liberal who is 'himself identified with the establishment, although avowedly the friend of the minority, suspects any sign of militant minority consciousness. He wants the minority to share in American human nature and compete like an individual along with other individuals for the same values.

As Podhoretz has observed, pluralism never really meant the co-existence of quite different groups:

> For the traditional liberal mentality conceives of society as being made up not of competing economic classes and ethnic groups, but rather of competing *individuals* who confront a neutral body of law and a neutral institutional complex.(12)

How then can ethnic groups be discussed within the plural but consensual framework? They must be seen as separate but assimilated (contained) social structures. Among sociologists, Milton Gordon has been most precise about this pluralism as a description of ethnic groups in American society.

> Behavioral assimilation or acculturation has taken place in America to a considerable degree ... Structural assimilation, then, has turned out to be the rock on which the ships of Anglo-conformity and the melting pot have foundered. To understand the behavioral assimilation (or acculturation) without massive structural intermingling in primary relationships has been the dominant motif in the American experience of creating and developing a nation out of diverse peoples is to comprehend the most essential sociological fact of that experience. It is against the background of "structural pluralism" that strategies of strengthening intergroup harmony, reducing ethnic discrimination and prejudice, and maintaining the rights of both those who stay within and those who venture beyond their ethnic boundaries must be thoughtfully devised.(13)

Clearly then the liberal vocabulary of race relations is predicated on consensual assumptions about the nature of man and society. The order explanation of the Negro problem and its solution may be summarized as follows:

1. *An order or consensual model of society.*—American society is interpreted as a social system unified at its most general level by acceptance of certain central political, social, economic values. Thus, the Negro population is said to have been acculturated to a somewhat vaguely defined American tradition; at the most, Negro society is a variant or a reaction to that primary tradition.

2. *Social problems as moral problems of anomy or social disorganization within the American system.*—Social problems and deviant behavior arise from an imbalance between goals and means. The problems of the Negro are created by unethical exclusion from equal competition for American goals.

3. *The response to anomy: social amelioration as adjustment and extension of social control.*—Liberal solutions imply further institutionalization of the American Creed in the opportunity structure of society and, therefore, the adjustment of the deviant to legitimate social roles.

THE RACE QUESTION AS A MORAL DILEMMA

A familiar expression of liberal-consensualism is Gunnar Myrdal's interpretation of the American race question as a moral dilemma. According to this thesis, racial discrimination and its varied effects on the Negro—the development of plural social structures, high rates of social deviation, etc.—reflect a kind of anomy in the relationship between the American Creed and social structure. Anomy means a moral crisis arising from an incongruity between legitimate and ethical social goals (for example, success and equality of opportunity) and socially available opportunities to achieve these goals. American society is good and ethical, but anomic because the American Creed of equality has not been fully institutionalized; the ethic is widely accepted in theory but not in practice.

Sidney Hook as a political liberal has likewise insisted that American society is essentially ethical and that the Negro problem should be discussed in these ethical terms:

> Of course, no society has historically been organized on the basis of ethical principles, but I don't think we can understand how any society functions without observing the operation of the ethical principles within it. And if we examine the development of American society, we certainly can say that we have made *some* progress, to be sure, but progress nevertheless—by virtue of the extension of our ethical principles to institutional life. If we want to explain the progress that has been made in the last twenty years by minority groups in this country—not only the Negroes, but other groups as well—I believe we have to take into account the effect of our commitment to democracy, imperfect though it may be.(14)

THE SOLUTION: WORKING WITHIN THE SYSTEM

The liberal solution to the racial question follows from the American dilemma thesis: the belief in the ethical nature and basic legitimacy of American institutions. Amelioration, therefore, becomes exclusively a question of adjustment within the system; it calls for administrative action: how to attack anomy as the imbalance of goals and means. The administrator accepts the goals of his organization and treats all problems as errors in administration, errors which can be rectified without changing the basic framework of the organization. Karl Mannheim has aptly characterized the bureaucratic and administrative approach to social problems. What he says about the perspective of the Prussian bureaucrat applies only too well to his counterpart in American society:

> The attempt to hide all problems of politics under the cover of administration may be explained by the fact that the sphere of activity of the official exists only within the limits of laws already formulated. Hence the genesis or the development of law falls outside the scope of his activity. As a result of his socially limited horizon, the functionary fails to see that behind every law that has been made there lie the socially fashioned interests and the *Weltanschauungen* of a specific social group. He takes it for granted that the specific order prescribed by the concrete law is equivalent to order in general. He does not understand that every rationalized order is only one of many forms in which socially conflicting irrational forces are reconciled.(15)

The liberal administrator's solution to the Negro question entails the expansion of opportunities for mobility within the society and socialization of the deviant (the Negro and the anti-Negro) to expanding opportunities. Hence, the importance of education and job training; they are prime means to success and higher status.

Given the assumption that the American Creed is formally embodied in the political structure, the liberal also looks to legislation as an important and perhaps sole means of reenforcing the Creed by legitimizing changes in the American opportunity structure.

Another important deduction has followed from the assumption of the political and cultural assimilation of the American Negro: whatever is different or distinct in his life style represents a kind of negative reaction to exclusion from the white society. The Negro is the creation of the white. Like the criminal he is a pathology, a reaction-formation to the problem of inadequate opportunities to achieve and to compete in the American system.

Myrdal states:

> The Negro's entire life and, consequently, also his opinions on the Negro problem are, in the main, to be considered as secondary reactions to more primary pressures from the side of the dominant white majority.(16)

More recently Leonard Broom has echoed the same opinion:

> Negro life was dominated by the need to adjust to white men and to take them into account at every turn . . . Taken as a whole, the two cultures have more common than distinctive elements. Over the long run, their convergence would seem inevitable . . . Because Negro life is so much affected by poverty and subservience, it is hard to find distinctive characteristics that can be positively evaluated. In the stereotype, whatever is admirable in Negro life is assumed to have been adopted from the white man, while whatever is reprehensible is assumed to be inherently Negro.(17)

A liberal order model—consensual pluralism, with its corollary approach to the race question as moral dilemma and reaction-formation—colors the sociological analysis of the race question. It is interesting that the fundamental assumption about consensus on the American Creed has rarely been subjected to adequate empirical test.(18) Lacking any convincing evidence for the order thesis, I can only wonder who the sociologist is speaking for. He may be speaking for himself in that his paradigm answers the question of how to solve the Negro problem without changing basic economic and political institutions. He probably speaks least of all for the Negro. The liberal sociologists will have some difficulty describing the world from the viewpoint of Negro "rioters" in Los Angeles and other cities. In any case, he will not agree with anyone who believes (in fact or in ideology) that the Negro may have a separate and self-determining identity. Such a view suggests conflict and would throw doubt on the fixations of consensus, anomy, and reaction-formation.

Conflict interpretations are minority interpretations by definition. They are rarely expressed either by sociologists or by ethnic minorities. However, a few such interpretations can be mentioned to imply that the end of ideology and, therefore, the agreement on total ideology has not yet arrived.

Ralph Ellison, speaking from a conflict and nationalistic perspective, has made several salient criticisms of the liberal American dilemma thesis. He has argued that Myrdal's long discussion of American values and conclusion of multiple causality have conveniently avoided the inconvenient question of power and control in American society.

All this, of course, avoids the question of power *and* the question of who manipulates that power. Which to us seems more of a stylistic maneuver than a scientific judgment . . . Myrdal's stylistic method is admirable. In presenting his findings he uses the American ethos brilliantly to disarm all American social groupings, by appealing to their stake in the American Creed, and to locate the psychological barriers between them. But he also uses it to deny the existence of an American class struggle, and with facile economy it allows him to avoid admitting that actually there exist two American moralities, kept in balance by social science.(19)

Doubting the thesis of consensus, Ellison is also in a position to attack Myrdal's interpretation of the American Negro as a reaction-formation, and assimilation to the superior white society as his only solution.

But can a people (its faith in an idealized American Creed notwithstanding) live and develop for over three hundred years simply by reacting? Are American Negroes simply the creation of white men, or have they at least helped to create themselves out of what they found around them? Men have made a way of life in caves and upon cliffs, why cannot Negroes have made a life upon the horns of the white men's dilemma?

Mydral sees Negro culture and personality simply as the product of a "social pathology." Thus he assumes that "it is to the advantage of American Negroes as individuals and as a group to become assimilated into American culture, to acquire the traits held in esteem by the dominant white American." This, he admits, contains the value premise that "*here in America*, American culture is 'highest' in the pragmatic sense. . ." Which aside from implying that Negro culture is not also American, assumes that Negroes should desire nothing better than what whites consider highest. But in the "pragmatic" sense lynching and Hollywood, fadism and radio advertising are products of "higher" culture, and the Negro might ask, "Why, if my culture is pathological, must I exchange it for these?" . . . What is needed in our country is not an exchange of pathologies, but a change of the basis of society.(20)

CONCLUSION

The hostile action of Negro masses destroying white property is perhaps a more convincing demonstration of conflict theory than the hopes of Negro intellectuals. But as a sociologist I am not really interested in raising the question of whether a conflict definition of the race question is more correct than the more familiar order model. Each view is correct in a normative and practical sense insofar as it conforms to a viable political and social experience. What indeed is a correct interpretation of the Negro problem or any social problem? The answer has as much to do with consensus as with correspondence to the facts. Normative theories are not necessarily affected by empirical evidence because they seek to change or to maintain the world, not describe it.

Whenever there is genuine conflict between groups and interpretations, correctness clearly becomes a practical matter of power and political persuasion. This seems to be the situation today, and one can expect more heated debate. If conflict continues to increase between whites and Negroes in the United States, the liberal sociologist studying the "Negro problem" had better arm himself with more than his questionnaire. A militant Negro respondent may take him for the social problem, the sociologist as an agent of white society and the scientific purveyor of order theory and containment policy.

This clash of perspectives would be an illustration of my general argument: explanations of the Negro question or any other social problem invariably involve normative theory, values, ideologies, or whatever one may care to call the subjective categories of our thinking about society. Concepts of deviation and social problems can be discussed only in the context of some social (and therefore contestable) standard of health, conformity, and the good society. Terms like "moral dilemma," "pluralism," assimilation," "integration" describe motives for desirable action: they are definitions placed on human action, not the action itself independent of social values.

The error of the sociologist is not that he thinks politically and liberally about his society, but that he is not aware of it. Awareness may help him avoid some of the gross errors of myopia: 1. mistaking his own normative categories for "objective" fact; thus, the liberal sociologist may mistake his belief in the consensual society for actual consensus; 2. projecting a normative theory appropriate to the experience of one group on to another group; this is what Ellison means when he says that the liberal sociologist is not necessarily speaking for the Negro. Indeed, the errors of myopia are perhaps greatest whenever the middle-class sociologist presumes to describe the world and motivation of persons in lower status. Seeing the lower class Negro within a white liberal vocabulary may be very realistic politics, but it is not very accurate sociology.

Once the sociologist is involved in the study of anything that matters, he has the unavoidable obligation of at least distinguishing his vocabulary from that of the groups he is supposedly observing rather than converting. As a scientist, he must find out what perspectives are being employed, where they are operating in the society, and with what effect. Perhaps this awareness of competing perspective occurs only in the actual process of conflict and debate. Unfortunately, this is not always the situation within an increasingly professionalized sociology. The more professionalized the field, the more standardized the thinking of sociologists and the greater the danger of internal myopia passing for objectivity. But outside sociology debate is far from closed; conflict and order perspectives are simultaneously active on every controversial social issue. The liberal order model may not long enjoy uncontested supremacy.

NOTES

(1) For Weber's discussion of explanation in the social sciences see *Max Weber: The Theory of Social and Economic Organization*, trans. A.M. Henderson and Talcott Parsons (Glencoe, Ill.: Free Press, 1947), pp. 87-114.

(2) C. Wright Mills, "Situated Actions and Vocabularies of Motive," *American Sociological Review*, V (December, 1940), 904-13.

(3) C. Wright Mills, "The Professional Ideology of the Social Pathologists," *American Journal of Sociology*, XLIX (September, 1942), 165-80.

(4) C. Wright Mills, *The Sociological Imagination* (New York: Oxford University Press, 1959).

(5) Talcott Parsons, "Definitions of Health and Illness in the Light of American Values and Social Structure," in E. Gartley Jaco (ed.), *Patients, Physicians and Illness* (Glencoe, Ill.: Free Press, 1963), p. 176.

(6) For a conservative argument, see, among many others, Carleton Putnam, *Race and Reason* (Washington, D.C.: Public Affairs Press, 1961).

(7) Jean-Paul Sartre, *Anti-Semite and Jew*, trans. George J. Becker (New York:

Grove Press, 1962), pp. 56-57.

(8) J.S. Furnivall, *Colonial Policy and Practice* (London: Cambridge University Press, 1948), p. 304.

(9) Gunnar Myrdal, *An American Dilemma* (New York: Harper & Bros., 1944, pp. 3-4.

(10) Robin M. Williams, Jr., *Strangers Next Door* (Englewood Cliffs, N.J.: Prentice-Hall, Inc., 1964), p. 386.

(11) Norman Podhoretz, "The Melting-Pot Blues," *Washington Post*, October 5, 1964.

(12) Norman Podhoretz, as quoted in "Liberalism and the American Negro — a Round-Table Discussion" with James Baldwin, Nathan Glazer, Sidney Hook, Gunnar Myrdal, and Norman Podhoretz (moderator), *Commentary* XXXVII (March, 1964), 25-26.

(13) Milton Gordon, "Assimilation in America: Theory and Reality," *Daedalus*, XC (Spring, 1961), 280, 283.

(14) Sidney Hook, "Liberalism and the American Negro — a Round-Table Discussion," *Commentary*, XXXVII (March, 1964), p. 31.

(15) Karl Mannheim, *Ideology and Utopia* (New York: Harcourt, Brace & World, 1936), p. 118.

(16) Gunnar Myrdal as quoted by Ralph Ellison, "An American Dilemma: A Review," in *Shadow and the Act* (New York: Random House, 1964), p. 315.

(17) Leonard Broom, *The Transformation of the American Negro* (New York: Harper & Row, 1965), pp. 22-23.

(18) For a recent attempt to test the American dilemma thesis see Frank R. Westie, "The American Dilemma: An Empirical Test," *American Sociological Review*, XXX (August, 1965), 527-38.

(19) Ralph Ellison, *Shadow and the Act, op. cit.*, p. 315.

(20) *Ibid.*, pp. 316-17.

This selection is an abridgment from John Horton, "Order and Conflict Theories of Social Problems as Compelling Ideologies," *American Journal of Sociology*, May 1966, pp. 701-713. ©1966 by the University of Chicago. All rights reserved.

MARGINAL CLASSES, INTERNAL COLONIES AND SOCIAL CHANGE

Dale L. Johnson

The social change involved in development has meant that some human beings are constantly reshuffled into different social classes. Peasants become industrial workers, sons of workers become white-collar workers, sons of white-collar workers become technicians and professionals. But development has also meant that some classes change their function without changing their position at the bottom of the economic and social pile: black slaves became sharecroppers and sharecroppers became unskilled laborers and urban service workers. The blacks have been denied whatever benefits come from being reshuffled upward in the class structure over time. And the march of labor-displacing technology in the modern world, unparalleled in historical experience since the Industrial Revolution, appears to practically assure, short of revolutionary changes in society, that blacks will remain at the bottom; so too will Latin American Indians, peasants, and ex-peasants. In general, rural inhabitants and the urban poor throughout the capitalist world are likely to find themselves the more or less permanent *objects* of technological and social-political forces over which they have no control — until, that is, they and we say in all the world's languages, ENOUGH!

The term "development" has always implied a process of economic and social change for the better. Few analysts have stopped to ask themselves if these changes could be for the worse, or if changes could be better for some sectors of society and worse for other sectors.

It is useful to retain the positive value placed on the term *development*, and to formulate the proposition that *development is first of all the development of man out of conditions of exploitation, poverty, and oppression.*

The concept is thus based on the philosophical principles of humanism. But it also needs to be firmly grounded in social scientific theory. The second proposition, then, is that *development always involves changes in the basic institutions and structures of society.* Clearly, development is not simply a *continuous* expansion upon a previous base, such as an annual growth of national product of 2-3 percent; a steady increase in the rate of social structure that tends toward greater pluralization and authority, and social structure that tends toward greater pluralization and democratization of society. Development may, however, bring about a situation in which these desirable evolutionary changes in economic, social, and political spheres may occur. Development is basically a *discontinuous* process that involves changes in the fundamental institutions and structures of economy and society.

Not all structural changes, however, are necessarily developmental when development is seen from the humanist perspective that focuses upon the situation of man.(1) For example, changes in rural areas and the rapid industrialization of Lima have liberated thousands and thousands of Peruvian Indians from the shackles of essentially colonial domination by the landowners and their *mestizo* intermediaries. These Indians have been integrated into urban economic and social structures (and marginalized from others) in such a way that it is difficult to say they are any better off than before leaving the land. What has occurred in this situation is a basic structural shift from domination of an oppressed class by means of colonial relations to domination by means of class relations. The humanist postulate stated here permits the social scientist to analyze structural changes that are not developmental change — that is, those changes that do not necessarily improve the situation of man: *Development is the happy coincidence of structural change and improvement in the human condition.*

Marginality(2) and marginal underclasses are relatively new concepts that have their origin in the age-old concern for the plight of the poor urban classes uprooted from rural subsistence by economic forces and subjected to the vicissitudes of life as "lumpen proletariat," "masses," "surplus population," or as members of a "reserve army of the unemployed."(3) "The poor," "lumpen proletariat," and "surplus population" are descriptive terms without a great deal of analytical value. The term "masses" is very ambiguous, as it is sometimes used to refer to those at the very bottom of the social pile and at other times to everyone not of elite status. "Reserve army of the unemployed" is an analytical concept drawn from classical economics. Its value lies primarily in the implication that the process of economic change creates a class that performs certain functions within a capitalist economic and social order. While 'a reserve army of the unemployed is functional for dominant interests in a capitalist system, marginal underclasses can be afunctional or dysfunctional for the system as a whole. Unemployed labor is a factor in depressing wages in certain sectors and acts as a reserve for increases in demand for labor in periods of economic expansion without the consequence of bidding up the price of labor to "excessive" levels. Unemployment also gives employers a range of choice in investment in capital-intensive or labor-intensive technologies. Nevertheless, adoption of labor-displacing technology tends to march hand in hand with the inevitable process of increasing economic concentration. The consequences are the growth of afunctional (i.e., marginal) labor forces. Afunctional labor forces become dysfunctional for the system when it becomes necessary to divert resources for the subsistence of these unproductive populations and to strengthen the means of social control to deal with political instability caused by their revolt.

The problem is one of putting economic processes in a sociological context emphasizing class and power relations. Peruvian sociologist Anibal Quijano has defined "social marginality" as ". . . a limited mode or inconsistent structuring of belonging and participation in the general structure of society, whether with respect to the total of structures in whole or in institutional sectors.(4)

Of course, in modern nation states no class of people is excluded from society, nor are we dealing with "dual societies." The problem has rather to do with the character and quality of participation in society by members of certain structural groupings created by economic changes. Marginal underclasses are excluded from participation, only minimally participate, or participate under discriminatory conditions in certain institutions, such as the political and educational. At the same time, participation in other institutions, such as the economy, is irregular and/or only yields minimal social rewards for roles performed. Moreover, marginal underclasses cannot claim, or find difficult access to, certain privileges, advantages, or opportunities built into the social structure of society that accrue to members of other social classes.

This conception is exceedingly broad, and it is useful to limit the scope of the definition of marginality so as to refer to concrete social phenomena, such as the position vis-à-vis institutions and class structures of the poorest urban classes (the "underclasses") in racially and culturally(5) *homogeneus* societies. The position of peasants or of subordinated races in ethnically dual or plural societies is structurally distinct from that of urban underclasses, and different concepts may be useful in the analysis of the dynamics of relations between these classes and the institutions and dominant classes of society. "Internal colony" is one such concept that leads to new perspectives on the position of underdeveloped regions within a national society and on national minorities.

Marginal underclasses, then, are those populations that have not been integrated, or have been integrated under highly disadvantageous conditions, into the institutions of society, but are not located in what will be termed "regionally based internal colonies" or of allegedly "inferior" racial or cultural origins. Categorized by the character of participation in the economy, these include the hard-core unemployed, those employed in low-wage sectors of the urban economy operating with labor-intensive technologies, and, the most important category, those whose skills are superfluous to a technologically geared society.(6) A marginal underclass would include some but not all of the aged and those deprived of regular or above-subsistence income because of physical or mental incapacity.

The concept of internal colony has its principal origin in two independent sources: the work of certain Latin American intellectuals,(7) and the black liberation movement in the United States. Economically, internal colonies can be conceptualized as those populations who produce primary commodities for markets in metropolitan centers, who constitute a source of cheap labor for enterprises controlled from the metropolitan centers, and/or who constitute a market for the products and services of the centers. The colonized are excluded from participation or suffer discriminatory participation in the political, cultural, and other institutions of the dominant society. An internal colony constitutes a society within a society based upon racial, linguistic, and/or marked cultural differences as well as differences of social class. It is subject to political and administrative control by the dominant classes and institutions of the metropolis. Defined in this way, internal colonies can exist on a geographical basis or on a racial or cultural basis in ethnically or culturally dual or plural societies. (Not all of these criteria need apply in order to classify a population as an internal colony.)

The Northeast of Brazil; the Sierra region of Peru, rural areas of Guatemala, the Appalachia region and rural South of the United States, the southern region of Italy, all have one thing in common: They are underdeveloped regions functioning as internal colonies in relation to urban metropolitan centers.

An internal colony is first an economic phenomenon. The operation of the economic system generates colonies that function as satellites to national metropoles (and subsequently international metropoles, in the case of underdeveloped countries). The mass of the colonial population produce for subsistence and export primary products to the metropolis for which they receive an exceedingly low proportion of the value of the products in the form of wages or wage substitutes. Profits from economic activity in the satellite are transferred to the metropolis or are reinvested principally in production of primary goods. Institutionally, the appropriation of wealth generated in the satellite takes place directly through capital transfers by landowners (often absentee) or mineowners to metropolitan centers (national and international) or indirectly through the terms of trade between products of the satellite and products of the metropolis and through metropolitan control of the commercial and financial sectors. There is little opportunity for capital accumulation by indigenous, nonoligarchic entrepreneurs.

At the same time, the economic system generates a rigid and polarized class structure in the satellite in which the owners of the means of primary production and a merchant and/or moneylending class are integrated into the upper ranks of a national class structure. The dominant class in the colony enjoys the privileges of participation in national institutions and a national class structure, while the mass of the colony are marginalized from participation in the benefits distributed among the classes of the metropolitan society. In conventional sociological terms, "the division between city and country dwellers is more pointedly a rift between 'classes' that inhabit the cities and 'masses' of disenfranchized peasants and rural laborers who live in the countryside."(8) (Recent urban developments have meant, of course, that the peasant mass is now located in both city and country.) The proposition that has been drawn from this conception is essentially correct with respect to the rural (and new urban) mass: ". . . instead of the classical Marxist or European pattern of struggle between classes, a struggle between class and mass takes place. . ."(9)

In this situation, change is not developmental change, even though it may involve economic growth or transformation of structures. The process of economic change means a continuing, even sharpened, process of colonization. Economic transformations almost always mean increasing control of the satellite economics directly from the national (and subsequently international) metropolitan centers. Elements of the business classes of the satellites become absentee owners residing most of the year in the principal city, gradually expanding and diversifying their investments. Constant rationalization of marketing gives metropolitan merchants greater control over supplies and prices. Credit markets in the satellites disappear or are taken over by national banks. The class structure ossifies as an oligarchy-mass dichotomy. A process Frank has termed the "development of underdevelopment" occurs.(10)

American blacks, Chicanos, and Puerto Ricans; the blacks of South Africa; French Canadians; (11) the Catholics of Northern Ireland; and certain other racial and cultural minorities in different parts of the world can also be viewed as internal colonies. (12) In Mesoamerica and the Andean countries, Indians are colonized racially and geographically.

Racially and culturally based internal colonies have a number of characteristics in common with marginal underclasses, particularly in the industrially advanced countries. Internal colonies are marginal with respect to participation in the institutions and class privileges of the dominant society in much the same way as underclasses. Both populations endure similarly severe social conditions. Both underclasses and internal colonies are predominantly classes of unskilled laborers. However, internal colonies possess a more differentiated social structure. The colony normally has a class of religious figures and political leaders, professionals and entrepreneurs (a "black bourgeoisie," for example) whose activities are usually confined to the colony, and often a *comprador* class carefully cultivated by the dominant society to administer the colony in the interests of the dominant powers of society. Both groupings are characterized by a "culture of poverty," but colonies possess a culture distinctive to the race that transcends the boundaries of class cultures.

The distinction between marginal underclasses and internal colonies is particularly crucial in examining power relations. The major differences in the relations between the dominant classes and institutions of society and marginal underclasses on the one hand, and internal colonies on the other hand, revolve around different institutionalized practices of domination and different means of social control.

It is important to emphasize that *all* the classes of the dominant society rest upon the colonial population. Stavenhagen, González Casanova, and Cotler, among others, have described the manner in which the privileges and livelihood of the Ladino and mestizo populations depend upon domination and exploitation of the Indians of Mesoamerica and Peru.

> Ladinos and Indians hold different positions in the stratification scale, according to such well-known variables as income, property, degree of education, standard of living, etc. . . . Ladinos hold a higher position not only in the objective scale of socioeconomic characteristics, but they also consider themselves, *qua* Ladinos, as being superior to the Indians. They are contemptuous of the Indian as such. The latter, on the other hand, are conscious of their social and economic inferiority. . .(13)

The economic exploitation inherent in these patterns of stratification are made clear by González Casanova: .

> An exploitation of the Indian population by the different social classes of the Ladino population exists . . . The characteristic of these social classes is the fact that they rest on the exploitation of the Indian as a worker or producer. The exploitation is combined—a mixture of feudalism, slavery, capitalism, forced and salaried work, partnerships, peonage, and gratuitous "free" domestic services.(14)

The population of internal colonies is subject to discriminatory practices over and above those characteristic of relations between dominant classes and underclasses. The colonized, very often including the *comprador* class, are discriminated against in the opportunity to participate in all institutional spheres. Institutionalized discriminatory practices create rationalizations of a normative character that place sanctions upon behavior contrary to the norms on the part of either the colonized or members of the dominant society. Racist ideologies evolve. The dominated adopt submissive attitudes and usually become subservient. Sectors of the business classes of society and the privileged sectors of the working classes are, or believe themselves to be, materially advantaged by the maintenance of internal colonies. Persons located in different strata in the social structure of the dominant society are motivated to move up the social hierarchy and are fearful of moving down. The ethnic pariah population at the bottom serves as a vent for the frustrations and personal hostilities of all the strata, especially those from the middle downward. This pattern is functional, in a kind of sociological "divide and rule" sense, for the dominant class in its power and status relations with the working and middle classes.

Individuals within the marginal underclass have opportunities for social mobility, depending upon opportunity structures, to the limited degree that they can shake off their class origins and become socialized into the skills, values, and attitudes of the mainstream society. The opportunities for social mobility for individuals within an internal colony are more sharply circumscribed. The colonized can be mobile within the stratification system of the colony or, with difficulty, pass one foot into the class structure of the dominant society while the other foot remains implanted in the colony. The individual is mobile under conditions strictly defined by the dominant society. He becomes stripped of his culture and values, losing his identity with the class of origin, but remaining uncomfortably "marginal" (to use the concept in the way that American sociologists have used it) in the dominant society. This is the case of the black bourgeoisie in the United States or the *cholo* of Peru.(15)

The institutionalization of dependence relations are a principal mechanism of domination. Dependence is a severe limitation of choices available to the dominated, regulated by alternatives set ultimately by the dominant group.

In the industrial countries, personal dependence relations are not a principal mechanism of domination over internal colonies (but impersonal institutionalized dependencies are severe). The degree of dependence of the dominated upon the dominant is highly conditioned by the range of choice open to the dominated. Unlike what is common in underdeveloped societies, the industrial society is characterized by an urban existential environment in which the oppressed individual can sometimes choose between various options that are institutionally created. The colonial subject in the advanced nations (much like marginal underclasses in underdeveloped countries) is dependent upon institutions — job markets, law-enforcement and probation agencies, welfare, etc. — rather than upon power figures of the dominant population.

Because mechanisms of domination over internal colonies are usually (but not always) less subtle than the mechanism of class relations, social control over the colony involves liberal application of force and repression. Extreme measures of social control of the colonial population come easier than control measures over marginal underclasses, because of racist sentiments widespread among the population of the dominant society. The danger of violent repression is particularly acute when colonies have lost many of their economic functions, such as provision of cheap labor to large enterprises. In this case, total containment, or the genocidal solution, is always an option in an extreme situation. Of course, the essentially functionless nature of marginal underclasses may also make extreme measures of social control possible when the marginals become defined as dysfunctional.

The dominant society attempts to impose its religion upon the colonized and to use it as an instrument of domination. Priests and ministers of colonial origin are assimilated into the *comprador* class and aid in the direct social control of the colony by the dominant powers. The socialization function of religion subordinates worldly consciousness of exploitation to other-worldly visions of the good life.

The colonized population is highly mobile, moving from rural areas and regional colonies to industrializing metropolitan centers. In the process of migration, colonies are ghettoized. *The change from rural to urban life suggests a structural shift from colonial to underclass status with urbanization.* It may very well be the case that black and mixed-blood migrants from the Northeast of Brazil to Rio and São Paulo represent a shift from internal colonial to marginal underclass status. This, however, does not seem invariably to be the case, as the situation of American blacks, who remain colonized in urban ghettos, suggests.

American blacks have always constituted a colonial population: first as plantation slave labor, later as agricultural labor within the southern colony of the United States, and subsequently as unskilled labor in technologically backward sectors of the urban economy and as a reserve army of the unemployed and underemployed for the industrial sector. The great migration of blacks from the rural South to the nation's urban centers in the past three decades has an entirely different character than the earlier immigration to American cities. Successive waves of immigrants to the United States in the late nineteenth and early twentieth centuries provided cheap labor for the nation's expanding assembly lines, sweatshops, the elaborate distribution network, and an expanding service sector. The Irish, Italians, Poles, and other immigrants were never marginal classes and internal colonies except, if at all, for limited periods. During and after the Second World War blacks and browns from the rural backwaters of the South and Mexico came by the millions to northern and western industrial cities. But the era of increasing absorption of unskilled and semiskilled labor into the industrial system, and thereby into the mainstream of the class society, was rapidly drawing to a close. Blacks and browns were relegated to employment in the most technologically backward or labor-intensive sectors (menial services, construction labor, corporate agriculture) and to unemployment, the squalor of ghetto life, and welfare handouts. Today, the black, Chicano, and Puerto Rican colonies remain indispensable sources of cheap labor for the technologically backward and labor-intensive sectors. They also provide a servant class to relieve the affluent of the chores of ordinary living and to enhance their status and feelings of superiority. For the highly technological corporate and the rapidly expanding public sectors which require high skill levels, however, the minorities have become superfluous labor. Moreover, the minorities do not constitute an extensive and expanding market in a mass consumer economy — even subtracting from the buying power of the working and middle classes, who bear the tax burden for welfare.

Because minorities do not perform the traditional colonial functions as sources of cheap labor and markets for cheap manufactures to the benefit of the plantation owners or big corporations, does not mean that American minorities have entirely lost their character as internal colonies, though on the surface they appear more and more as urban marginals. The majority of the minorities serve local and regional enterprises and interests: the Mexican agricultural laborer's product is appropriated by the corporate farm (and indirectly by the supermarket and the suburban housewife), the denominational hospital squeezes the black orderly, the slumlord and ghetto merchant gouge the ghetto dweller, the white worker still can feel superior to someone, etc. In short, the ghetto is functional for a wide assortment of local interests that dominate local affairs. The American class structure does give rise to a pluralist set of interests operating on national, regional, and local levels. The corporate liberals of Domhoff's "Governing Class"(16) govern only at the national level, leaving local and regional vested interests firmly in control of urban and state politics and administration. These are the interests for whom cheap black and brown labor is by no means superfluous. Also, the means of social control remain essentially colonial in character. As nationalistic liberation movements gain strength, the institutions and power centers of the dominant center tighten control. As a matter of fact, *ghetto riots and the black liberation movement have generated very similar policies that U.S. corporations and the American government employ in their relations with external colonial dependencies when nationalist and revolutionary sentiments crystalize:* a combination of corporate investment in the colony, government aid and development programs (always designed as instruments of control), and custodial-counterinsurgent policies of repression.(17)

In Latin America rapid urbanization has brought disastrous human consequences for the internal colonies and marginal underclasses of the region. Latin American economies show high rates of technological advance, and the rate of labor productivity climbs faster than the rate of absorption of new workers into the productive labor force. The economies are less expansive than the U.S. economy: Argentina, Uruguay, and Chile, three of the most advanced countries, have been virtually stagnant for fifteen years. The problem is also acute in countries experiencing economic growth, such as Brazil, Peru, Colombia, and Mexico. Being poor, the Latin American countries cannot even provide for minimal subsistence and services (generally available to the American poor) to the growing urban mass of superfluous unskilled laborers. The polarization of society into a participant stable working class (or "labor aristocracy," more narrowly defined) and the entrenched middle class in alignment with the dominant class, as against the marginalized and colonized populations, accelerates each year.(18)

It is important to analyze change in the position of marginal underclasses and internal colonies from three perspectives: 1. that of the oppressed classes themselves, 2. that of the dominant powers who must respond to the ferment for change, and 3. that of the principal ideological currents that structure the consciousness of all parties affected by, or involved in, the process of change.

In the analysis of the problem and in the search for solutions, social science theory can ill afford to neglect the way in which underclasses and internal colonies themselves define their structural position in society and the strategies and tactics they evolve in attempting to change their situation. As is well known, the demands of urban underclasses have been for provision of those rudimentary social services that other classes enjoy and for access to the institutions of the larger society. These are reformist demands that have revolutionary implications if pushed long enough and far enough, because structurally the larger societies have not incorporated and, within the limits of the present system, probably cannot incorporate large numbers of new aspirants into the mainstream of society.

In many respects, the demands of internal colonies have been different from those of underclasses. The typical reaction to domination on the part of oppressed races is a "nationals" revolutionary movement demanding self-determination, as among American blacks, French Canadians, and certain Indian movements in Latin America. Regional internal colonies sometimes demand secession, as in the independent peasant "red republics" of Colombia.

"National" revolutionary movements have a strong cultural basis. The culture of the colonized has a quality lacking in underclass class culture: a sense of community and individual identity that can, under certain circumstances, give rise to racial consciousness and pride, the formulation of assertive ideologies, and action for change.

In general, the pattern of change in class relations within ethnically homogeneous stratified populations (and *within* the class systems of the dominant population of ethnically dual or plural societies) is toward those changes that involve the least disruption of existing structures and institutions, namely, toward incorporation of sectors of the previously marginalized classes and their "neutralization" through extension of relative rewards and privileges. When groups of the powerless succeed in organizing themselves to provoke the power structure, the response is often to co-opt the moderate leaders into official structures, isolating them from their base, to repress the militant leaders, and to yield to the masses something of what they want: wage increases, city services, measured relief from police or administrative oppression. . . . These benefits are often transitory, however, and the struggle is continual and positive response reluctant.

In most cases, however, the ability of dominant institutions and classes to incorporate and reward new entrants to the system is sharply limited by more or less "objective" conditions (i.e., technological developments, the operation of the economic system) and by subjective inhibitions (i.e., vested interests and reactionary consciousness). When "incorporation" and "neutralization" are structurally impossible or politically unfeasible, as is often the case, the response is violent repression.

. . . Finally, the possibility of developmental change must be considered from the perspectives of different ideological currents that define the limits of imagination, and therefore of the possible.

On the most obvious level, to use concept of marginal underclass implies that the strategy of liberation is the uplifting and integration of the marginal class into the mainstream of society. That is the liberal, social democratic, and Christian corporativist solution, as, for example, is implicit in the work of Goldrich, *et al.*(19) and DESAL(20) or the corporativist policies explicit in the programs of Promoción Popular in Chile under the Christian Democrats,(21) and some programs of the War on Poverty in the United States. There is also the nationalist revolutionary solution. To use the concept of internal colony automatically implies a strategy of "national" liberation. In practice, this means an attempt to build a more or less autonomous community within a larger society that can deal on a level of greater equality of power with established institutions and centers of power in the larger society in which the colony is doomed to be inextricably bound (secession from the mother country is rarely a viable alternative).

The liberal solution to the oppression of underclasses is a practical one if all that is required is a qualitative change in domination based upon class relations. Historically, the process of development has often permitted the incorporation of newly generated underclasses into the working class and the rights of citizenship.(22) Incorporation can be accomplished through extension of civil rights and political representation, by expanding job opportunities for unskilled or semiskilled labor, or by programs of qualifying unskilled labor such as extending educational opportunities or using the military or other institutions as an agency of socialization into appropriate skills, motivations, and attitudes. These are examples of policies that *act upon the situation* of marginal underclasses without necessarily implying basic changes in the institutions or social structures of society. The march of technology in the modern world, however, and the relative strength of the forces of domination (who normally use the extension of civil rights and provision of opportunities to participate as instruments of individual co-optation rather than for class incorporation) seem to suggest that incorporation of marginal classes implies the necessity of profound structural changes in institutions and stratification systems and the system of domination they reflect.

The problem is that it is precisely in the functioning of institutions and the dynamics of class relations in which marginal underclasses and internal colonies are generated. The system of domination functions to maintain, or even extend, the subordination of the classes in question. This is a particularly important problem when the most powerful groups in society *directly* derive their wealth and power from total domination of internal colonies.

Liberal reformist schemes of incorporation of marginal underclasses, and especially of internal colonies, are not likely to be viable solutions in any of the situations described above. The revolutionary solutions, on the other hand, are difficult to realize, to say the least.

The logical revolutionary strategy of marginal underclasses is sustained class struggle leading to a revolutionary seizure of power and a total transformation of society. Studies of Latin American underclasses have revealed the enormous obstacles that stand in the way of the development of revolutionary consciousness and action. Conditions of life among the underclasses are such that it is probable that underclasses will never form the vanguard of the revolution.

The organization and mobilization of underclasses is central to revolutionary strategy. Yet, the revolutionary movement in Latin America, which is largely based upon students, intellectuals, assorted malcontents of the middle class, and the organized working class, has generally failed to direct its efforts toward the underclasses. Traditional Marxists have tended to concentrate their efforts in trade unionism among relatively privileged workers and electoral politics while the *Fidelista* forces, until very recently, plotted insurrectional movements in the countryside and urban disruptions lacking a mass base. This is now changing in countries like Chile and Colombia where it is still possible, though difficult, for revolutionaries to work aboveground among urban marginals and peasants. Nor do the present insurrectional movements in Uruguay and Brazil ignore the role of underclasses in making the revolution.

In the industrial countries, the immediate possibilities for revolutionary *action* (not revolution) seem to stem from oppressed races and cultural minorities, as well as an alienated class of youth, spun off the class society, who voluntarily marginalize themselves from the system rather than let themselves be channeled into roles they have no taste for. The concept of internal colony as a principal ingredient in an ideology of change propagated among racial minorities is most useful as a consciousness-building device. (Class consciousness among underclasses is difficult to generate, in part, because of the absence of a racial or cultural basis for community and solidarity that are actual or latent in colonies.) A conception of themselves as an internal colony by oppressed minorities normally comes about only after a "civil rights" struggle, as in United States ghettos and barrios, French Canada, and Northern Ireland, and readily becomes integrated into more sophisticated nationalist perspectives when it is perceived that extensions of civil rights do not end in social and economic equality.

Fervent nationalism, however, can lead to the adoption of self-defeating strategies of change and to serious tactical errors if the over-all aim of the movement is to force basic structural changes in society. If American blacks were to lock themselves into a ghetto and the only "white" faces there were policemen (even if the policemen were black), their basic *structural* position would not necessarily change. Certainly, it is foolish and dangerous to believe that American blacks or Central American Indians could achieve a genuinely autonomous community within the wider society, though it may be possible to achieve concessions and partially control excesses of repression. At best, the demand for self-government in the ghetto can loosen the grip of the dominant institutions and power centers and force changes in power relations within the dominant society itself. The point is that raising demands for self-determination in the colony weakens the institutional mechanisms of domination through achieving concessions or by forcing the dominant to rely upon naked coercion, which may have the effect of further developing consciousness among the oppressed. The demands also generate the momentum for change in the dominant society. Ghetto insurrections and the black liberation movement in the United States have had these effects. This can also be seen at the level of particular institutions. The struggle, for example, of black students for autonomous black studies centers in American colleges and universities has illuminated the nature of power relations for all parties. Where the struggle has failed, authority retains less than its previous legitimacy. To the degree that black university students gain even partial self-determination and control over their education, the point is not lost on white students who create their own demands for control and institutional democratization.

In Latin America the colonized Indians have barely begun to assert themselves, though peasant (primarily Indians) revolts in the 1960s in Peru were a significant factor behind the military coup of 1968 and the reformist programs of the regime that followed the coup. Latin American peasant movements, rising out of the colonized status of rural areas, in general have picked up considerable momentum during the past decade. Anibal Quijano has analyzed traditional peasant revolts, messianic movements, and social banditry as these movements have evolved over time into modern reformist-agrarianism, political banditry, and revolutionary agrarianism.(23) While rural trade unionism and peasant activities in alignment with class forces and political parties of the cities is common, advanced forms of peasant movements also act in an anticolonial manner by demanding a kind of internal independence. Quijano notes that "their strategies are mostly direct and often illegal including the seizure of land, the physical and social elimination of landlords, the destruction of the local political apparatus which is replaced by another power, and finally, armed defense or reprisal against the reaction of the landlord or the state."(24)

NOTES

(1) The humanist definition of development is essentially a postulate from which to begin an analysis of development. The proposition that development always involves structural change has more the character of an empirical generalization, as economists from Schumpeter to Hirschman to the UN's Economic Commission for Latin America and sociologists from Marx to Barrington Moore have persuasively argued.

(2) The concept of marginality does not have the meaning given to it by Robert Park, "Human Migration and Marginal Man," *American Journal of Sociology* XXXIII (May 1928), pp. 881-93; or Everett Stonequist, *The Marginal Man: A Study in Personality and Culture* (New York: Charles Scribner's Sons, 1937), or the literature on "status inconsistency" that has followed. As far as I know, this chapter represents the first time the concept of "marginal" has been combined with "underclass."

(3) For a clarification of concepts from traditional political economy, especially Marxism, see Jose Nun, *Superpoblacion relativa, ejercito industrial de reserva y masa marginal* (Buenos Aires: Instituto di Tella, 1969). It is a sad commentary on contemporary social science that "marginality" represents practically the first attempt in a century to develop a concept that is capable of theoretically analyzing (not just describing) the structural position of that sector of the population conventionally referred to as "the poor."

(4) Aníbal Quijano Obregon, *Notas sobre el concepto de marginalidad social* (Santiago, Chile: CEPAL, División de Asuntos Sociales, 1966). On clarification of the concept see also Jose Nun, Juan Carlos Marín y Miguel Murmis, *La marginalidad en América Latina* (Santiago, Chile: Documento de Trabajo #2, 1967) and Nun, *ibid.*

(5) "Culturally" homogeneous meaning the absence of linguistic or religious communities with a culture markedly different from the dominant culture.

(6) An excellent portrayal of the enormity of the problem in Latin America is André G. Frank, *Urban Poverty in Latin America* (New Brunswick, N.J.: Rutgers University Monograph Series "Studies in Comparative International Development," II, No. 5, 1966); see also Richard Morse, "Recent Research on Latin American Urbanization: A Selective Survey with Commentary," *Latin American Research Review I* (1965), pp. 35-74.

(7) Pablo González Casanova, *Internal Colonialism and National Development* (New Brunswick, N.J.: Rutgers University Monograph Series "Studies in Comparative International Development," I, No. 4, 1965); and *La democracia en México* (México, D.F.: Era, 1965); Rudolfo Stavenhagen, *Classes, Colonialism, and Acculturation* ("Studies in Comparative International Development," I, No. 6, 1965); and Julio Cotler, *The Mechanics of Internal Domination and Social Change in Peru* ("Studies in Comparative International Development," III, No. 12, 1967-68).

(8) Irving Louis Horowitz, "Electoral Politics, Urbanization, and Social Development in Latin America," Glenn H. Beyer (ed.), *The Urban Explosion in Latin America* (Ithaca, New York: Cornell University Press, 1967), p. 216.

(9) *Ibid.*, p. 243.

(10) Frank has elaborated on metropolitan-satellite relations in his *Capitalism and Underdevelopment in Latin America* (New York Monthly Review Press, 1967); on regional internal colonies and Latin American Indian populations.

(11) "This is to say that French Canadian society was always a *minor society*, an inferiorized society; a colonial society where the role of colonizer was played first by England then by English Canada. . . . Collectively, we have never known freedom; we have always been a dependent, colonized people. We have never had a history. . . . This condition of being colonized and of being a minority has made of us what we are, and it is in this condition that we are able to discover the first reason of our alienation." Parti pris, *Les Québéçois* (Paris: François Maspero, 1967), p. 87.

(12) There are difficulties in retaining the concept of internal colony when the empirical referent is both an underdeveloped region whose resources are systematically appropriated by metropolis and the underclasses of ethnically or culturally dual or plural societies. Thus, in the United States, poor whites of Appalachia, the white Crackers of rural Georgia, the Puerto Ricans of New York, the Chicanos of the Southwest, and urban and rural blacks are colonized populations. There is a serious question whether the concept may not be overinclusive. In Mesoamerica and the Andean regions the correspondence between regional colonies and Indian colonies is very high; presumably, poor mestizos and acculturated Indians of the urban areas have been mobile into the marginal underclasses. But what of Brazil, where racism and institutionalized discrimination (other than class prejudice and discrimination) are less institutionalized than in the United States, and the Indian countries of Central and South America? Are the blacks and Indians of Rio *favelas* colonial populations, while fellow *favela* dwellers of mixed racial origin and white complexion members of a marginal underclass? Probably not. In short, the concept does present some difficulties. Nevertheless, I believe the concept is worth retaining. Conceptual difficulties can be overcome by simply recognizing that the presence of racial minorities in a society does not necessarily mean the establishment of colonial relations and that each country has historically handled its "race problem" in distinct ways.

(13) Stavenhagen, *op. cit.*, p. 67.

(14) González Casanova, *op. cit.*, 1965, pp. 34-35; on Peruvian Indians see Cotler, *op. cit.*

(15) On the *cholo*, see Cotler, *op. cit.*, and Aníbal Quijano, *"La emergencia del grupo cholo y sus implicaciones en la sociedad Peruana"* (Lima: Universidad de San Marcos, Facultad de Letras, *tesis doctoral,* 1965).

(16) William Domhoff, *Who Rules America?* (Englewood Cliffs, New Jersey: Prentice Hall, 1967).

(17) Beverly Leman, "Social Control of the American Ghetto," Michael Klare, "Urban Counterinsurgency," and Jill Hamberg and David Smith, "The Urban League in Action—Boston," all in *Viet-Report III* (Summer 1968).

(18) See Glaucio Ary Dillon Soares, "The New Industrialization and the Brazilian Political System," James Petras and Maurice Zeitlin, *Latin America: Reform or Revolution?* (New York: Fawcett, 1968).

(19) Daniel Goldrich, *et. al., Political Integration of Lower-Class Urban Settlements in Chile and Peru* (New Brunswick, N.J.: Rutgers University Monograph Series "Studies in Comparative International Development," III, No. 1, 1967-68).

(20) Centro para el Desarrollo Económico y Social de América Latina (DESAL), *América Latina y Desarrollo Social* (Santiago, Chile: DESAL, 1966, Tomos I y II); DESAL, *Seminarios de Promoción Popular* (Santiago, Chile: DESAL, 1966).

(21) On corporativist policies in Chile, see James Petras, *Chilean Christian Democracy: Politics and Social Forces* (Berkeley: Institute of International Studies, University of California, 1967) and his *Politics and Social Forces in Chilean Development* (Berkeley: University of California Press, 1969).

(22) T.H. Marshall, *Citizenship and Social Class* (New York: Anchor, 1964) and Reinhard Bendix, *Nation-Building and Citizenship* (New York: Wiley, 1964). Both of these books deal theoretically with the integration of new groups thrown up by industrialization into society.

(23) Aníbal Quijano Obregón, "Contemporary Peasant Movements," in Seymour Martin Lipset and Aldo Solari (eds.), *Elites in Latin America* (New York: Oxford University Press, 1967). Quijano, the author of an excellent paper on marginality, *op. cit.*, applies a class analysis framework to peasant movements and does not adopt a colonial analogy.

(24) *Ibid.*, p. 311.

This selection is a highly abridged version of the Chapter on "Oppressed Classes", from *Dependence and Underdevelopment*, James D. Cockcroft, Andre Gunder Frank and Dale L. Johnson (editors), Anchor Books, Doubleday and Company, 1972.

RACISM AND CULTURE

Frantz Fanon

The unilaterally decreed normative value of certain cultures deserves our careful attention. One of the paradoxes immediately encountered is the rebound of egocentric, sociocentric definitions.

There is first affirmed the existence of human groups having no culture; then of a hierarchy of cultures; and finally, the concept of cultural relativity.

We have here the whole range from overall negation to singular and specific recognition. It is precisely this fragmented and bloody history that we must sketch on the level of cultural anthropology.

There are, we may say, certain constellations of institutions, established by particular men, in the framework of precise geographical areas, which at a given moment have undergone a direct and sudden assault of different cultural patterns. The technical, generally advanced development of the social group that has thus appeared enables it to set up an organized domination. The enterprise of deculturation turns out to be the negative of a more gigantic work of economic, and even biological, enslavement.

The doctrine of cultural hierarchy is thus but one aspect of a systematized hierarchization implacably pursued.

The modern theory of the absence of cortical integration of colonial peoples is the anatomic-physiological counterpart of this doctrine. The apparition of racism is not fundamentally determining. Racism is not the whole but the most visible, the most day-to-day and, not to mince matters, the crudest element of a given structure.

To study the relations of racism and culture is to raise the question of their reciprocal action. If culture is the combination of motor and mental behavior patterns arising from the encounter of man with nature and with his fellow-man, it can be said that racism is indeed a cultural element. There are thus cultures with racism and cultures without racism.

This precise cultural element, however, has not become encysted. Racism has not managed to harden. It has had to renew itself, to adapt itself, to change its appearance. It has had to undergo the fate of the cultural whole that informed it.

The vulgar, primitive, over-simple racism purported to find in biology — the Scriptures having proved insufficient — the material basis of the doctrine. It would be tedious to recall the efforts then undertaken: the comparative form of the skulls, the quantity and the configuration of the folds of the brain, the characteristics of the cell layers of the cortex, the dimensions of the vertebrae, the microscopic appearance of the epiderm, etc. . . .

Intellectual and emotional primitivism appeared as a banal consequence, a recognition of existence.

Such affirmations, crude and massive, give way to a more refined argument. Here and there, however, an occasional relapse is to be noted. Thus the "emotional instability of the Negro," the "subcritical integration of the Arab," the "quasi-generic culpability of the Jew" are data that one comes upon among a few contemporary writers. The monograph by J. Carothers, for example, sponsored by the World Health Organization, invokes "scientific arguments" in support of a physiological lobotomy of the African Negro.

These old-fashioned positions tend in any case to disappear. This racism that aspires to be rational, individual, genotypically and phenotypically determined, becomes transformed into cultural racism. The object of racism is no longer the individual man but a certain form of existing. At the extreme, such terms as "message" and "cultural style" are resorted to. "Occidental values" oddly blend with the already famous appeal to the fight of the "cross against the crescent."

The morphological equation, to be sure, has not totally disappeared, but events of the past thirty years have shaken the most solidly anchored convictions, upset the checkerboard, restructured a great number of relationships.

The memory of Nazism, the common wretchedness of different men, the common enslavement of extensive social groups, the apparition of "European colonies," in other words the institution of a colonial system in the very heart of Europe, the growing awareness of workers in the colonizing and racist countries, the evolution of techniques, all this has deeply modified the problem and the manner of approaching it.

We must look for the consequences of this racism on the cultural level.

Racism, as we have seen, is only one element of a vaster whole: that of the systematized oppression of a people. How does an oppressing people behave? Here we rediscover constants.

We witness the destruction of cultural values, of ways of life. Language, dress, techniques, are devalorized. How can one account for this constant? Psychologists, who tend to explain everything by movements of the psyche, claim to discover this behavior on the level of contacts between individuals: the criticism of an original hat, of a way of speaking, of walking. . .

Such attempts deliberately leave out of account the special character of the colonial situation. In reality the nations that undertake a colonial war have no concern for the confrontation of cultures. War is a gigantic business and every approach must be governed by this datum. The enslavement, in the strictest sense, of the native population is the prime necessity.

For this its systems of reference have to be broken. Expropriation, spoliation, raids, objective murder, are matched by the sacking of cultural patterns, or at least condition such sacking. The social panorama is destructured; values are flaunted, crushed, emptied.

The lines of force, having crumbled, no longer give direction. In their stead a new system of values is imposed, not proposed but affirmed, by the heavy weight of cannons and sabers.

The setting up of the colonial system does not of itself bring about the death of the native culture. Historic observation reveals, on the contrary, that the aim sought is rather a continued agony than a total disappearance of the pre-existing culture. This culture, once living and open to the future, becomes closed, fixed in the colonial status, caught in the yoke of oppression. Both present and mummified, it testifies against its members. It defines them in fact without appeal. The cultural mummification leads to a mummification of individual thinking. The apathy so universally noted among colonial peoples is but the logical consequence of this operation. The reproach of inertia constantly directed at "the native" is utterly dishonest. As though it were possible for a man to evolve otherwise than within the framework of a culture that recognizes him and that he decides to assume.

Thus we witness the setting up of archaic, inert institutions, functioning under the oppressor's supervision and patterned like a caricature of formerly fertile institutions. . .

These bodies appear to embody respect for the tradition, the cultural specificities, the personality of the subjugated people. This pseudo-respect in fact is tantamount to the most utter contempt, to the most elaborate sadism. The characteristic of a culture is to be open, permeated by spontaneous, generous, fertile lines of force. The appointment of "reliable men" to execute certain gestures is a deception that deceives no one. Thus the Kabyle *djemaas* named by the French authority are not recognized by the natives. They are matched by another *djemaa* democratically elected. And naturally the second as a rule dictates to the first what his conduct should be.

The constantly affirmed concern with "respecting the culture of the native populations" accordingly does not signify taking into consideration the values borne by the culture, incarnated by men. Rather, this behavior betrays a determination to objectify, to confine, to imprison, to harden. Phrases such as "I know them," "that's the way they are," show this maximum objectification successfully achieved. I can think of gestures and thoughts that define these men.

Exoticism is one of the forms of this simplification. It allows no cultural confrontation. There is on the one hand a culture in which qualities of dynamism, of growth, of depth can be recognized. As against this, we find characteristics, curiosities, things, never a structure.

Thus in an initial phase the occupant establishes his domination, massively affirms his superiority. The social group, militarily and economically subjugated, is dehumanized in accordance with a polydimensional method.

Exploitation, tortures, raids, racism, collective liquidations, rational oppression take turns at different levels in order literally to make of the native an object in the hands of the occupying nation.

This object man, without means of existing, without a *raison d'etre*, is broken in the very depth of his substance. The desire to live, to continue, becomes more and more indecisive, more and more phantom-like. It is at this stage that the well-known guilt complex appears. In his first novels, Wright gives a very detailed description of it.

Progressively, however, the evolution of techniques of production, the industrialization, limited though it is, of the subjugated countries, the increasingly necessary existence of collaborators, impose a new attitude upon the occupant. The complexity of the means of production, the evolution of economic relations inevitably involving the evolution of ideologies, unbalance the system. Vulgar racism in its biological form corresponds to the period of crude exploitation of man's arms and legs. The perfecting of the means of production inevitably brings about the camouflage of the techniques by which man is exploited, hence of the forms of racism.

It is therefore not as a result of the evolution of people's minds that racism loses its virulence. No inner revolution can explain this necessity for racism to seek more subtle forms, to evolve. On all sides men become free, putting an end to the lethargy to which oppression and racism had condemned them.

In the very heart of the "civilized nations" the workers finally discover that the exploitation of man, at the root of a system, assumes different faces. At this stage racism no longer dares appear without disguise. It is unsure of itself. In an ever greater number of circumstances the racist takes to cover. He who claimed to "sense," to "see through" those others, finds himself to be a target, looked at, judged. The racist's purpose has become a purpose haunted by bad conscience. He can find salvation only in a passion-driven commitment such as is found in certain psychoses. And having defined the symptomatology of such passion-charged deliria is not the least of Professor Baruk's merits.

Racism is never a super-added element discovered by chance in the course of the investigation of the cultural data of a group. The social constellation, the cultural whole, are deeply modified by the existence of racism.

It is a common saying nowadays that racism is a plague of humanity. But we must not content ourselves with such a phrase. We must tirelessly look for the repercussions of racism at all levels of sociability. The importance of the racist problem in contemporary American literature is significant. The Negro in motion pictures, the Negro and folklore, the Jew and children's stories, the Jew in the cafe, are inexhaustible themes.

Racism, to come back to America, haunts and vitiates American culture. And this dialectical gangrene is exacerbated by the coming to awareness and the determination of millions of Negroes and Jews to fight this racism by which they are victimized.

This passion-charged, irrational, groundless phase, when one examines it, reveals a frightful visage. The movement of groups, the liberation, in certain parts of the world, of men previously kept down, make for a more and more precarious equilibrium. Rather unexpectedly, the racist group points accusingly to a manifestation of racism among the oppressed. The "intellectual primitivism" of the period of exploitation gives way to the "medieval, in fact prehistoric fanaticism" of the period of the liberation.

For a time it looked as though racism had disappeared. This soul-soothing, unreal impression was simply the consequence of the evolution of forms of exploitation. Psychologists spoke of a prejudice having become unconscious. The truth is that the rigor of the system made the daily affirmation of a superiority superfluous. The need to appeal to various degrees of approval and support, to the native's cooperation, modified relations in a less crude, more subtle, more "cultivated" direction. It was not rare, in fact, to see a "democratic and humane" ideology at this stage. The commercial undertaking of enslavement, of cultural destruction, progressively gave way to a verbal mystification.

The interesting thing about this evolution is that racism was taken as a topic of meditation, sometimes even as a publicity technique.

Thus the blues — "the black slave lament" — was offered up for the admiration of the oppressors. This modicum of stylized oppression is the exploiter's and the racist's rightful due. Without oppression and without racism you have no blues. The end of racism would sound the knell of great Negro music. . .

As the all-too-famous Toynbee might say, the blues are the slave's response to the challenge of oppression.

Still today, for many men, even colored, Armstrong's music has a real meaning only in this perspective.

Racism bloats and disfigures the face of the culture that practices it. Literature, the plastic arts, songs for shopgirls, proverbs, habits, patterns, whether they set out to attack it or to vulgarize it, restore racism. This means that a social group, a country, a civilization, cannot be unconsciously racist.

We say once again that racism is not an accidental discovery. It is not a hidden, dissimulated element. No superhuman efforts are needed to bring it out.

Racism stares one in the face for it so happens that it belongs in a characteristic whole: that of the shameless exploitation of one group of men by another which has reached a higher stage of technical development. This is why military and economic oppression generally precedes, makes possible, and legitimizes racism.

The habit of considering racism as a mental quirk, as a psychological flaw, must be abandoned.

But the men who are a prey to racism, the enslaved, exploited, weakened social group — how do they behave? What are their defense mechanisms?

What attitudes do we discover here?

In an initial phase we have seen the occupying power legitimizing its domination by scientific arguments, the "inferior race" being denied on the basis of race. Because no other solution is left it, the racialized social group tries to imitate the oppressor and thereby to deracialize itself. The "inferior race" denies itself as a different race. It shares with the "superior race" the convictions, doctrines, and other attitudes concerning it.

Having witnessed the liquidation of its systems of reference, the collapse of its cultural patterns, the native can only recognize with the occupant that "God is not on his side." The oppressor, through the inclusive and frightening character of his authority, manages to impose on the native new ways of seeing, and in particular a pejorative judgment with respect to his original forms of existing.

This event, which is commonly designated as alienation, is naturally very important. It is found in the official texts under the name of assimilation.

Now this alienation is never wholly successful. Whether or not it is because the oppressor quantitatively and qualitatively limits the evolution, unforeseen, disparate phenomena manifest themselves.

The inferiorized group had admitted, since the force of reasoning was implacable, that its misfortunes resulted directly from its racial and cultural characteristics.

Guilt and inferiority are the usual consequences of this dialectic. The oppressed then tries to escape these, on the one hand by proclaiming his total and unconditional adoption of the new cultural models, and on the other, by pronouncing an irreversible condemnation of his own cultural style. (A little-studied phenomenon sometimes apprears at this stage. Intellectuals, students, belonging to the dominant group, make "scientific" studies of the dominated society, its art, its ethical universe. In the universities the rare colonized intellectuals find their own cultural system being revealed to them. It even happens that scholars of the colonizing countries grow enthusiastic over this or that specific feature. The concepts of purity, naïveté, innocence appear. The native intellectual's vigilance must here be doubly on the alert.)

Yet the necessity that the oppressor encounters at a given point to dissimulate the forms of exploitation does not lead to the disappearance of this exploitation. The more elaborate, less crude economic relations require a daily coating, but the alienation at this level remains frightful.

Having judged, condemned, abandoned his cultural forms, his language, his food habits, his sexual behavior, his way of sitting down, of resting, of laughing, of enjoying himself, the oppressed *flings himself* upon the imposed culture with the desperation of a drowning man.

Developing his technical knowledge in contact with more and more perfected machines, entering into the dynamic circuit of industrial production, meeting men from remote regions in the framework of the concentration of capital, that is to say, on the job, discovering the assembly line, the team, production "time," in other words yield per hour, the oppressed is shocked to find that he continues to be the object of racism and contempt.

It is at this level that racism is treated as a question of persons. "There are a few hopeless racists, but you must admit that on the whole the population likes. . ."

With time all this will disappear.

This is the country where there is the least amount of race prejudice. . .

At the United Nations there is a commission to fight race prejudice.

Films on race prejudice, poems on race prejudice, messages on race prejudice. . .

Spectacular and futile condemnations of race prejudice. In reality, a colonial country is a racist country. If in England, in Belgium, or in France, despite the democratic principles affirmed by these respective nations, there are still racists, it is these racists who, in their opposition to the country as a whole, are logically consistent.

It is not possible to enslave men without logically making them inferior through and through. And racism is only the emotional, affective, sometimes intellectual explanation of this inferiorization.

The racist in a culture with racism is therefore normal. He has achieved a perfect harmony of economic relations and ideology. The idea that one forms of man, to be sure, is never totally dependent on economic relations, in other words — and this must not be forgotten — on relations existing historically and geographically among men and groups. An ever greater number of members belonging to racist societies are taking a position. They are dedicating themselves to a world in which racism would be impossible. But everyone is not up to this kind of objectivity, this abstraction, this solemn commitment. One cannot with impunity require of a man that he be against "the prejudices of his group."

And, we repeat, every colonialist group is racist.

"Acculturized" and deculturized at one and the same time, the oppressed continues to come up against racism. He finds this sequel illogical, what he has left behind him inexplicable, without motive, incorrect. His knowledge, the appropriation of precise and complicated techniques, sometimes his intellectual superiority as compared to a great number of racists, lead him to qualify the racist world as passion-charged. He perceives that the racist atmosphere impregnates all the elements of the social life. The sense of an overwhelming injustice is correspondingly very strong. Forgetting racism as a consequence, one concentrates on racism as cause. Campaigns of deintoxication are launched. Appeal is made to the sense of humanity, to love, to respect for the supreme values. . .

Race prejudice in fact obeys a flawless logic. A country that lives, draws its substance from the exploitation of other peoples, makes those peoples inferior. Race prejudice applied to those peoples is normal.

Racism is therefore not a constant of the human spirit.

It is, as we have seen, a disposition fitting into a well-defined system. And anti-Jewish prejudice is no different from anti-Negro prejudice. A society has race prejudice or it has not. There are no degrees of prejudice. One cannot say that a given country is racist but that lynchings or extermination camps are not to be found there. The truth is that all that and still other things exist on the horizon. These virtualities, these latencies circulate, carried by the life-stream of psycho-affective, economic relations. . .

Discovering the futility of his alienation, his progressive deprivation, the inferiorized individual, after this phase of deculturation, of extraneousness, comes back to his original positions.

This culture, abandoned, sloughed off, rejected, despised, becomes for the inferiorized an object of passionate attachment. There is a very marked kind of overvaluation that is psychologically closely linked to the craving for forgiveness.

But behind this simplifying analysis there is indeed the intuition experienced by the inferiorized of having discovered a spontaneous truth. This is a psychological datum that is part of the texture of History and of Truth.

Because the inferiorized rediscovers a style that had once been devalorized, what he does is in fact to cultivate culture. Such a caricature of cultural existence would indicate, if it were necessary, that culture must be lived, and cannot be fragmented. It cannot had piecemeal.

Yet the oppressed goes into ecstasies over each rediscovery. The wonder is permanent. Having formerly emigrated from his culture, the native today explores it with ardor. It is a continual honeymoon. Formerly inferiorized, he is now in a state of grace.

Not with impunity, however, does one undergo domination. The culture of the enslaved people is sclerosed, dying. No life any longer circulates in it. Or more precisely, the only existing life is dissimulated. The population that normally assumes here and there a few fragments of life, which continues to attach dynamic meanings to institutions, is an anonymous population. In a colonial system these are the traditionalists.

The former emigre, by the sudden ambiguity of his behavior, causes consternation. To the anonymity of the traditionalist he opposes a vehement and aggressive exhibitionism.

The state of grace and aggressiveness are the two constants found at this stage. Aggressiveness being the passion-charged mechanism making it possible to escape the sting of paradox.

Because the former emigre is in possession of precise techniques, because his level of action is in the framework of relations that are already complex, these rediscoveries assume an irrational aspect. There is an hiatus, a discrepancy between intellectual development, technical appropriation, highly differentiated modes of thinking and of logic, on the one hand, and a "simple, pure" emotional basis on the other. . .

Rediscovering tradition, living it as a defense mechanism, as a symbol of purity, of salvation, the decultured individual leaves the impression that the mediation takes vengeance by substantializing itself. This falling back on archaic positions having no relation to technical development is paradoxical. The institutions thus valorized no longer correspond to the elaborate methods of action already mastered.

The culture put into capsules, which has vegetated since the foreign domination, is revalorized. It is not reconceived, grasped anew, dynamized from within. It is shouted. And this headlong, unstructured, verbal revalorization conceals paradoxical attitudes.

It is at this point that the incorrigible character of the inferiorized is brought out for mention. Arab doctors sleep on the ground, spit all over the place, etc. . . .

Negro intellectuals consult a sorcerer before making decisions, etc. . . .

"Collaborating" intellectuals try to justify their new attitude. The customs, traditions, beliefs, formerly denied and passed over in silence are violently valorized and affirmed.

Tradition is no longer scoffed at by the group. The group no longer runs away from itself. The sense of the past is rediscovered, the worship of ancestors resumed. . . .

The past, becoming henceforth a constellation of values, becomes identified with the Truth.

This rediscovery, this absolute valorization almost in defiance of reality, objectively indefensible, assumes an incomparable and subjective importance. On emerging from these passionate espousals, the native will have decided, "with full knowledge of what is involved," to fight all forms of exploitation and of alienation of man. At this same time, the occupant, on the other hand, multiples appeals to assimilation, then to integration, to community.

The native's hand-to-hand struggle with his culture is too solemn, too abrupt an operation to tolerate the slightest slip-up. No neologism can mask the new certainty: the plunge into the chasm of the past is the condition and the source of freedom.

The logical end of this will to struggle is the total liberation of the national territory. In order to achieve this liberation, the inferiorized man brings all his resources into play, all his acquisitions, the old and the new, his own and those of the occupant.

The struggle is at once total, absolute. But then race prejudice is hardly found to appear.

At the time of imposing his domination, in order to justify slavery, the oppressor had invoked scientific argument. There is nothing of the kind here.

A people that undertakes a struggle for liberation rarely legitimizes race prejudice. Even in the course of acute periods of insurrectional armed struggle one never witnesses the recourse to biological justifications.

The struggle of the inferiorized is situated on a markedly more human level. The perspectives are radically new. The opposition is the henceforth classical one of the struggles of conquest and of liberation.

In the course of struggle the dominating nation tries to revive racist arguments but the elaboration of racism proves more and more ineffective. There is talk of fanaticism, of primitive attitudes in the face of death, but once again the now crumbling mechanism no longer responds. Those who were once unbudgeable, the constitutional cowards, the timid, the eternally inferiorized, stiffen and emerge bristling.

The occupant is bewildered.

The end of race prejudice begins with a sudden incomprehension.

The occupant's spasmed and rigid culture, now liberated, opens at last to the culture of people who have really become brothers. The two cultures can affront each other, enrich each other.

In conclusion, universality resides in this decision to recognize and accept the reciprocal relativism of different cultures, once the colonial status is irreversibly excluded.

BLAMING THE VICTIM, THE CURRENT IDEOLOGY OF UNITED STATES RACISM

William Ryan

Blaming the Victim is an ideological process, which is to say that it is a set of ideas and concepts deriving from systematically motivated, but *unintended*, distortions of reality. In the sense that Karl Mannheim(1) used the term, an ideology develops from the "collective unconscious" of a group or class and is rooted in a class-based interest in maintaining the *status quo* (as contrasted with what he calls a *utopia*, a set of ideas rooted in a class-based interest in *changing the status quo*). An ideology, then, has several components: First, there is the belief system itself, the way of looking at the world, the set of ideas and concepts. Second, there is the systematic distortion of reality reflected in those ideas. Third is the condition that the distortion must not be a conscious, intentional process. Finally though they are not intentional, the ideas must serve a specific function: maintaining the *status quo* in the interest of a specific group. Blaming the Victim fits this definition on all counts, as I will attempt to show in detail in the following material. Most particularly, it is important to realize that Blaming the Victim is not a process of *intentional* distortion although it does serve the class interests of those who practice it. And it has a rich ancestry in American thought about social problems and how to deal with them.

Thinking about social problems is especially susceptible to ideological influences since, as John Seeley has pointed out,(2) defining a social problem is not so simple. "What is a social problem?" may seem an ingenuous question until one turns to confront its opposite: "What human problem is *not* a social problem?" Since any problem in which people are involved is social, why do we reserve the label for some problems in which people are involved and withhold it from others? To use Seeley's example, why is crime called a social problem when university administration is not? The phenomena we look at are bounded by the act of definition. They become social problems only by being so considered. In Seeley's words, "*naming* it as a problem, after naming it as a *problem*."

It is only recently, for example, that we have begun to *name* the rather large quantity of people on earth as the *problem* of overpopulation, or the population explosion. Such phenomena often become proper predicaments for certain solutions, certain treatments. Before the 1930s, the most anti-Semitic German was unaware that Germany had a "Jewish problem." It took the Nazis to *name* the simple existence of Jews in the Third Reich as a "social problem," and that act of definition helped to shape the final solution.

We have removed "immigration" from our list of social problems (after executing a solution—choking off the flow of immigrants) and have added "urbanization." Nowadays, we define the situation of men out of work as the social problem of "unemployment" rather than, as in Elizabethan times, that of "idleness." (The McCone Commission, investigating the Watts Riot of 1966, showed how hard old ideologies die; it specified both unemployment *and* idleness as causes of the disorder.) In the near future, if we are to credit the prophets of automation, the label "unemployment" will fade away and "idleness," now renamed the "leisure-time problem," will begin again to raise its lazy head. We have been comfortable for years with the "Negro problem," a term that clearly implies that the existence of Negroes is somehow a problematic fact. *Ebony* Magazine turned the tables recently and renamed the phenomenon as "The White Problem in America," which may be a good deal more accurate.

We must particularly ask, "To whom are social problems a problem?" And usually, if truth were to be told, we would have to admit that we mean they are a problem to those of us who are outside the boundaries of what we have defined as the problem. Negroes are a problem to racist whites, welfare is a problem to stingy taxpayers, delinquency is a problem to nervous property owners.

Now, if this is the quality of our assumptions about social problems, we are led unerringly to certain beliefs about the causes of these problems. We cannot comfortably believe that *we* are the cause of that which is problematic to us; therefore, we are almost compelled to believe that *they* — the problematic ones — are the cause and this immediately prompts us to search for deviance. Identification of the deviance as the cause of the problem is a simple step that ordinarily does not even require evidence. . . .

. . . If one is to think about ideologies in America in 1970, one must be prepared to consider the possibility that a body of ideas that might seem almost self-evident is, in fact, highly distorted and highly selective; one must allow that the inclusion of a specific formulation in every freshman sociology text does not guarantee that the particular formulation represents abstract Truth rather than group interest. It is important not to delude ourselves into thinking that ideological monstrosities were constructed by monsters. They were not; they are not. They are developed through a process that shows every sign of being valid scholarship, complete with tables of numbers, copious footnotes, and scientific terminology. Ideologies are quite often academically and socially respectable and in many instances hold positions of exclusive validity, so that disagreement is considered unrespectable or radical and risks being labeled as irresponsible, unenlightened, or trashy.

Blaming the Victim holds such a position. It is central in the mainstream of contemporary American social thought, and its ideas pervade our most crucial assumptions so thoroughly that they are hardly noticed. Moreover, the fruits of this ideology appear to be fraught with altruism and humanitarianism, so it is hard to believe that it has principally functioned to block social change.

A major pharmaceutical manufacturer, as an act of humanitarian concern, has distributed copies of a large poster warning "LEAD PAINT CAN KILL!" The poster, featuring a photograph of the face of a charming little girl, goes on to explain that if children *eat* lead paint, it can poison them, they can develop serious symptoms, suffer permanent brain damage, even die. The health department of a major American city has put out a coloring book that provides the same information. While the poster urges parents to prevent their children from eating paint, the coloring book is more vivid. It labels as neglectful and thoughtless the mother who does not keep her infant under constant surveillance to keep it from eating paint chips.

Now, no one would argue against the idea that it is important to spread knowledge about the danger of eating paint in order that parents might act to forestall their children from doing so. But to campaign against lead paint *only* in these terms is destructive and misleading and, in a sense, an effective way to support and agree with slum landlords—who define the problem of lead poisoning in precisely these terms.

This is an example of applying an exceptionalistic solution to a universalistic problem. It is not accurate to say that lead poisoning results from the actions of individual neglectful mothers. Rather, lead poisoning is a social phenomenon supported by a number of social mechanisms, one of the most tragic by-products of the systematic toleration of slum housing. In New Haven, which has the highest reported rate of lead poisoning in the country, several small children have died and many others have incurred irreparable brain damage as a result of eating peeling paint. In several cases, when the landlord failed to make repairs, poisonings have occurred time and again through a succession of tenancies. And the major reason for the landlord's neglect of this problem was that the city agency responsible for enforcing the housing code did nothing to make him correct this dangerous condition.

The cause of the poisoning is the lead in the paint on the walls of the apartment in which the children live. The presence of lead is illegal. To use lead paint in a residence is illegal; to permit lead paint to be exposed in a residence is illegal. It is not only illegal, it is potentially criminal since the housing code does provide for criminal penalties. The general problem of lead poisoning then, is more accurately analyzed as the result of a systematic program of lawbreaking by one interest group in the community, with the toleration and encouragement of the public authority charged with enforcing that law. To ignore these continued and repeated law violations, to ignore the fact that the supposed law enforcer actually cooperates in lawbreaking, and then to load a burden of guilt on the mother of a dead or dangerously-ill child is an egregious distortion of reality. And to do so under the guise of public-spirited and humanitarian service to the community is intolerable.

But this is how Blaming the Victim works. The righteous humanitarian concern displayed by the drug company, with its poster, and the health department, with its coloring book, is a genuine concern, and this is a typical feature of Blaming the Victim. Also typical is the swerving away from the central target that requires systematic chane and, instead, focusing in on the individual affected. The ultimate effect is always to distract attention from the basic causes and to leave the primary social injustice untouched. And, most telling, the proposed remedy for the problem is, of course, to work on the victim himself. Prescriptions for cure . . . are inariably conceived to revamp and revise the victim, never to change the surrounding circumstances. They want to change his attitudes, alter his values, fill up his cultural deficits, energize his apathetic soul, cure his character deficits, energize his social injustice untouched. And, most telling, the propsoed remedy for the problem is, of course, to work on the victim himself. Prescriptions for cure ... are invariably conceived to revamp and revise the victim, never to change the surrounding circumstances. They want to change his attitudes, alter his values, fill up his cultural deficits, energize his apathetic soul, cure his character defects, train him and polish him and woo him from his savage ways.

Isn't all of this more subtle and sophisticated than such old-fashioned ideologies as Social Darwinism? Doesn't the change from brutal ideas about survival of the fit (and the expiration of the unfit) to kindly concern about characterological defects (brought about by stigmas of social origin) seem like a substantial step forward? Hardly. It is only a substitution of terms. The old, reactionary exceptionalistic formulations are replaced by new progressive, humanitarian exceptionalistic formulations. In education, the outmoded and unacceptable concept of racial or class differences in basic inherited intellectual ability simply gives way to the new notion of cultural deprivation: there is very little functional difference between these two ideas. In taking a look at the phenomenon of poverty, the old concept of unfitness or idleness or laziness is replaced by the newfangled theory of the culture of poverty. In race relations, plain Negro inferiority—which was good enough for old-fashioned conservatives — is pushed aside by fancy conceits about the crumbling Negro family. With regard to illegitimacy, we are not so crass as to concern ourselves with immorality and vice, as in the old days; we settle benignly on the explanation of the "lower-class pattern of sexual behavior," which no one condemns as evil, but which is, in fact, simply a variation of the old explanatory idea. Mental illness is no longer defined as the result of hereditary taint or congenital character flaw; now we have new causal hypotheses regarding the ego-damaging emotional experiences that are supposed to be the inevitable consequence of the deplorable child-rearing practices of the poor.

In each case, of course, we are persuaded to ignore the obvious: the continued blatant discrimination against the Negro, the gross deprivation of contraceptive and adoption services to the poor, the heavy stresses endemic in the life of the poor. And almost all our make-believe liberal programs aimed at correcting our urban problems are off target; they are designed either to change the poor man or to cool him out.

NOTES

(1) Karl Mannheim, *Ideology and Utopia*, trans. Louis Wirth and Edward Shils (New York: Harcourt, Brace & World, Inc., A Harvest Book, 1936). First published in German in 1929.

(2) John Seeley, "The Problem of Social Problems," *Indian Sociological Bulletin*, II, No. 3 (April, 1965). Reprinted as Chapter Ten in *The Americanization of The Unconscious* (New York: International Science Press, 1967), pp. 142-48.

A THEORY OF THE ORIGIN
OF ETHNIC STRATIFICATION

Donald L. Noel

While a great deal has been written about the nature and consequences of ethnic stratification, there have been few theoretical or empirical contributions regarding the causes of ethnic stratification.(1) It is the purpose of this paper to state a theory of the origin of ethnic stratification and then test it by applying the theory to an analysis of the origin of slavery in the United States. A number of recent contributions have clarified our knowledge of early Negro-white stratification(2) but there has been no attempt to analyze slavery's origin from the standpoint of a general theoretical framework. The present attempt focuses upon ethnocentrism, competition, and differential power as the key variables which together constitute the necessary and sufficient basis for the emergence and initial stabilization of ethnic stratification.

Ethnic stratification is, of course, only one type of stratification. Social stratification as a generic form of social organization is a structure of social inequality manifested via differences in prestige, power, and/or economic rewards. Ethnic stratification is a system of stratification wherein some relatively fixed group membership (e.g., race, religion, or nationality) is utilized as a major criterion for assigning social positions with their attendant differential rewards.

Prior to the emergence of ethnic stratification there must be a period of recurrent or continuous contact between the members of two or more distinct ethnic groups. This contact is an obvious requisite of ethnic stratification, but it is equally a requisite of equalitarian intergroup relations. Hence, intergroup contact is assumed as given and not treated as a theoretical element because in itself it does not provide a basis for predicting whether ethnic relations will be equalitarian or inequalitarian (i.e., stratified). Distinct ethnic groups can interact and form a stable pattern of relations without super-subordination.(3) Factors such as the nature of the groups prior to contact, the agents of contact, and the objectives of the contacting parties affect the likelihood of an equalitarian or inequalitarian outcome but only as they are expressed through the necessary and sufficient variables.(4)

THE THEORY AND ITS ELEMENTS

In contrast to intergroup contact *per se*, the presence of ethnocentrism, competition, and differential power provides a firm basis for predicting the emergence of ethnic stratification. Conversely, the absence of any one or more of these three elements means that ethnic stratification will not emerge. This is the essence of our theory. Each of the three elements is a variable but for present purposes they will be treated as attributes because our knowledge is not sufficiently precise to allow us to say what degrees of ethnocentrism, competition, and differential power are necessary to generate ethnic stratification. Recognition of the crucial importance of the three may stimulate greater efforts to precisely measure each of them. We shall examine each in turn.

Ethnocentrism is a universal characteristic of autonomous societies or ethnic groups. As introduced by Sumner the concept refers to that ". . . view of things in which one's own group is the center of everything, and all others are scaled and rated with reference to it."(5) From this perspective the values of the in-group are equated with abstract, universal standards of morality and the practices of the in-group are exalted as better or more "natural" than those of any out-group. Such an orientation is essentially a matter of in-group glorification and not of hostility toward any specific out-group. Nevertheless, an inevitable consequence of ethnocentrism is the rejection or downgrading of all out-groups to a greater or lesser degree as a function of the extent to which they differ from the in-group. The greater the difference the lower will be the relative rank of any given out-group, but any difference at all is grounds for negative evaluation.(6) Hence, English and Canadian immigrants rank very high relative to other outgroups in American society *but* they still rank below old American WASPs.(7)

Ethnocentrism is expressed in a variety of ways including mythology, condescension, and a double standard of morality in social relations. Becker has labeled this double standard a "dual ethic" in which in-group standards apply only to transactions with members of the in-group.(8) The outsider is viewed as fair game. Hence, intergroup economic relations are characterized by exploitation. Similarly, sexual relations between members of different groups are commonplace even when intermarriage is rare or prohibited entirely. The practice of endogamy is itself a manifestation of and, simultaneously, a means of reinforcing ethnocentrism. Endogamy is, indeed, an indication that ethnocentrism is present in sufficient degree for ethnic stratification to emerge.(9)

Insofar as distinct ethnic groups maintain their autonomy, mutual ethnocentrism will be preserved. Thus Indians in the Americas did not automatically surrender their ethnocentrism in the face of European technological and scientific superiority. Indeed, if the cultural strengths (including technology) of the out-group are not relevant to the values and goals of the in-group they will, by the very nature of ethnocentrism, be negatively defined. This is well illustrated in the reply (allegedly) addressed to the Virginia Commission in 1744 when it offered to educate six Indian youths at William and Mary:

> Several of our young people were formerly brought up at Colleges of the Northern Provinces; they were instructed in all your sciences; but when they came back to us, they were bad runners, ignorant of every means of living in the woods, unable to bear either cold or hunger, knew neither how to build a cabin, take a deer, or kill an enemy, spoke our language imperfectly, were

therefore neither fit for hunters, warriors, or counsellors; they were totally good for nothing. We are, however, not the less obliged by your kind offer, though we decline accepting it; and to show our grateful Sense of it, if the Gentlemen of Virginia will send us a Dozen of their Sons we will take great care of their education, instruct them in all we know, and make Men of them.(10)

Ethnocentrism in itself need not lead to either interethnic conflict or ethnic stratification, however. The Tungus and Cossacks have lived in peace as politically independent but economically interdependent societies for several centuries. The groups remain racially and culturally dissimilar and each is characterized by a general ethnocentric preference for the in-group. This conflict potential is neutralized by mutual respect and admission by each that the other is superior in certain specific respects, by the existence of some shared values and interests, and by the absence of competition due to economic complementarity and low population density.(11)

The presence of competition, structured along ethnic lines, is an additional prerequisite for the emergence of ethnic stratification. Antonovsky has suggested that a discriminatory system of social relations requires both shared goals and scarcity of rewards,(12) and competition here refers to the interaction between two or more social units striving to achieve *the same scarce goal* (e.g., land or prestige). In the absence of shared goals members of the various ethnic groups involved in the contact situation would have, in the extreme case, mutually exclusive or nonoverlapping value hierarchies. If one group is not striving for a given goal, this reduces the likelihood of discrimination partly because members of that group are unlikely to be perceived as competitors for the goal. In addition, the indifference of one group toward the goal in effect reduces scarcity — i.e., fewer seekers enhance the probability of goal attainment by any one seeker. However, if the goal is still defined as scarce by members of one group they may seek to establish ethnic stratification in order to effectively exploit the labor of the indifferent group and thereby maximize goal attainment. In such a situation the labor (or other utility) of the indifferent group may be said to be the real object of competition. In any event the perceived scarcity of a socially valued goal is crucial and will stimulate the emergence of ethnic stratification *unless* each group perceives the other as: disinterested in the relevant goal, *and* nonutilitarian with respect to its own attainment of the goal.

In actuality the various goals of two groups involved in stable, complex interaction will invariably overlap to some degree and hence the likelihood of ethnic stratification is a function of the arena of competition. The arena includes the shared object(s) sought, the terms of the competition, and the relative adaptability of the groups involved.(13) Regarding the objects (or goals) of competition the greater the number of objects subject to competition, the more intense the competition. Moreover, as Wagley and Harris observe, "It is important to know the objects of competition, for it would seem that the more vital or valuable the resource over which there is competition, the more intense is the conflict between the groups."(14) Barring total annihilation of one of the groups, these points can be extended to state that the more intense the competition or conflict the greater the likelihood — other things being equal — that it will culminate in a system of ethnic stratification. In other words, the number and significance of the scarce, common goals sought determine the degree of competition which in turn significantly affects the probability that ethnic stratification will emerge.

The terms of the competition may greatly alter the probability of ethnic stratification, however, regardless of the intensity of the competition. The retention of a set of values or rules which effectively regulates—or moderates — ethnic interrelations is of particularly crucial significance. If a framework of regulative values fails to emerge, or breaks down, each group may seek to deny the others the right to compete with the result that overt conflict emerges and culminates in annihilation, expulsion, or total subjugation of the less powerful group. If, in contrast, regulative values develop and are retained, competition even for vital goals need not result in ethnic stratification — or at least the span of stratification may be considerably constricted.(15)

Even where the groups involved are quite dissimilar culturally, the sharing of certain crucial values (e.g., religion or freedom, individualism, and equality) may be significant in preventing ethnic stratification. This appears to have been one factor in the enduring harmonious relations between the Cossacks and the Tungus. The influence of the regulative values upon the span of ethnic stratification is well illustrated by Tannenbaum's thesis regarding the differences between North American and Latin American slavery.(16) In the absence of a tradition of slavery the English had no established code prescribing the rights and duties of slaves and the racist ideology which evolved achieved its ultimate expression in the Dred Scott decision of 1857. This decision was highly consistent with the then widely held belief that the Negro "had no rights which the white man was bound to respect. . . ." By contrast the Iberian code accorded certain rights to the Latin American slave (including the right to own property and to purchase his freedom) which greatly restricted the extent of inequality between free man and slave.(17)

In addition to the regulative values, the structural opportunities for or barriers to upward mobility which are present in the society may affect the emergence and span of ethnic stratification. Social structural barriers such as a static, nonexpanding economy are a significant part of the terms of competition and they may be more decisive than the regulative values as regards the duration of the system. Finally, along with the goals and the terms of competition, the relative adaptive capacity of the groups involved is an aspect of competition which significantly affects the emergence of ethnic stratification.

Wagley and Harris assume that ethnic stratification is given and focus their analysis on the adaptive capacity of *the minority group* in terms of its effect upon the span and the duration of ethnic stratification. Thus they view adaptive capacity as:

> . . . those elements of a minority's cultural heritage which provide it with a basis for competing more or less effectively with the dominant group, which afford protection against exploitation, which stimulate or retard its adaptation to the total social environment, and which facilitate or hinder its upward advance through the socio-economic hierarchy.(18)

We shall apply the concept to an earlier point in the intergroup process — i.e., prior to the mergence of ethnic stratification — by broadening it to refer to those aspects of any ethnic group's sociocultural heritage which affect its adjustment to a given social and physical environment. The group with the greater adaptive capacity is apt to emerge as the dominant group(19) while the other groups are subordinated to a greater or lesser degree — i.e., the span of the stratification system will be great or slight — dependent upon the extent of their adaptive capacity relative to that of the emergent dominant group.

The duration, as well as the origin and span, of ethnic stratification will be markedly influenced by adaptive capacity. Once a people have become a minority, flexibility on their part is essential if they are to efficiently adjust and effectively compete within the established system of ethnic stratification and thereby facilitate achievement of equality. Sociocultural patterns are invariably altered by changing life conditions. However, groups vary in the alacrity with which they respond to changing conditions. A flexible minority group may facilitate the achievement of equality or even dominance by readily accepting modifications of their heritage which will promote efficient adaptation to their subordination *and* to subsequent changes in life conditions.

Competition and ethnocentrism do not provide a sufficient explanation for the emergence of ethnic stratification. Highly ethnocentric groups involved in competition for vital objects will not generate ethnic stratification *unless* they are of such unequal power that one is able to impose its will upon the other.(20) Inequality of power is the defining characteristic of dominant and minority groups, and Lenski maintains that differential power is the foundation element in the genesis of any stratification system.(21) In any event differential power is absolutely essential to the emergence of ethnic stratification and the greater the differential the greater the span and durability of the system, other things being equal.

Technically, power is a component of adaptive capacity as Wagley and Harris imply in their definition by referring to "protection against exploitation." Nevertheless, differential power exerts an effect independent of adaptive capacity in general and is of such crucial relevance for ethnic stratification as to warrant its being singled out as a third major causal variable. The necessity of treating it as a distinct variable is amply demonstrated by consideration of those historical cases where one group has the greater adaptive capacity in general but is subordinated because another group has greater (military) power. The Dravidians overrun by the Aryans in ancient India and the Manchu conquest of China are illustrative cases.(22)

Unless the ethnic groups involved are unequal in power, intergroup relations will be characterized by conflict, symbiosis, or a pluralist equilibrium. Given intergroup competition, however, symbiosis is unlikely and conflict and pluralism are inevitably unstable. Any slight change in the existing balance of power may be sufficient to establish the temporary dominance of one group and this can be utilized to allow the emerging dominant group to perpetuate and enhance its position.(23) Once dominance is established the group in power takes all necessary steps to restrict the now subordinated groups, thereby hampering their effectiveness as competitors,(24) and to institutionalize the emerging distribution of rewards and opportunities. Hence, since power tends to beget power, a slight initial alteration in the distribution of power can become the basis of a stable inequalitarian system.

We have now elaborated the central concepts and propositions of a theory of the emergence and initial stabilization of ethnic stratification. The theory can be summarized as follows. When distinct ethnic groups are brought into sustained contact (via migration, the emergence and expansion of the state, or internal differentiation of a previously homogeneous group), ethnic stratification will invariably follow if — and only if — the groups are characterized by a significant degree of ethnocentrism, competition, *and* differential power. Without ethnocentrism the groups would quickly merge and competition would not be structured along ethnic lines. Without competition there would be no motivation or rationale for instituting stratification along ethnic lines. Without differential power it would simply be impossible for one group to achieve dominance and impose subordination to its will and ideals upon the other(s).

The necessity of differential power is incontestable but it could be argued that either competition or ethnocentrism is dispensable. For example, perhaps extreme ethnocentrism independent of competition is sufficient motive for seeking to impose ethnic stratification. Certainly ethnocentrism could encourage efforts to promote continued sharp differentiation, but it would not by itself motivate stratification unless we assume the existence of a *need* for dominance or aggression. Conversely, given sociocultural differences, one group may be better prepared for and therefore able to more effectively exploit a given environment. Hence, this group would become economically dominant and might then perceive and pursue the advantages (especially economic) of ethnic stratification quite independent of ethnocentrism. On the other hand, while differential power and competition alone are clearly sufficient to generate stratification, a low degree of ethnocentrism could readily forestall *ethnic* stratification by permitting assimilation and thereby eliminating differential adaptive capacity. Ethnocentrism undeniably heightens awareness of ethnicity and thereby promotes the formation and retention of ethnic competition, but the crucial question is whether or not some specified degree of ethnocentrism is *essential* to the emergence of ethnic stratification. Since autonomous ethnic groups are invariably ethnocentric, the answer awaits more precise measures of ethnocentrism which will allow us to test hypothese specifying the necessary degree of ethnocentrism.(25)...

... Ethnocentrism, competition, and differential power provide a comprehensive explanation of the origin of slavery in the seventeenth century English colonies. The Negroes were clearly more different from the English colonists than any other group (*except* the Indians) by almost any criterion, physical or cultural, that might be selected as a basis of social differentiation. Hence, the Negroes were the object of a relatively intense ethnocentric rejection from the beginning. The opportunity for great mobility characteristic of a frontier society created an arena of competition which dovetailed with this ethnocentrism. Labor, utilized to achieve wealth, and prestige were the primary objects of this competition. These goals were particularly manifest in the Southern colonies, but our analysis provides a rationale for the operation of the same goals as sources of motivation to institutionalize slavery in the Northern colonies also.

The terms of the competition for the Negro's labor are implicit in the evolving pattern of differential treatment of white and Negro bondsmen prior to slavery and in the precarious position of free Negroes. As slavery became institutionalized the moral, religious, and legal values of the society were increasingly integrated to form a highly consistent complex which acknowledged no evil in "the peculiar institution."(26) Simultaneously, Negroes were denied any opportunity to escape their position of lifetime, inheritable servitude. Only by the grace of a generous master, not by any act of his own, could a slave achieve freedom and, moreover, there were "various legal strictures aimed at impeding or discouraging the process of private manumission."(27) The rigidity of "the peculiar institution" was fixed before the Negroes acquired sufficient common culture, sense of shared fate, and identity to be able to effectively challenge the system. This lack of unity was a major determinant of the Africans' poor adaptive capacity as a group. They lacked the social solidarity and common cultural resources essential to organized resistance and thus in the absence of intervention by a powerful external ally they were highly vulnerable to exploitation.

The operation of the three key factors is well summarized by Stampp:

> Neither the provisions of their charters nor the policy of the English government limited the power of colonial legislatures to control Negro labor as they saw fit. . . . Their unprotected condition encouraged the trend toward special treatment, and their physical and cultural differences provided handy excuses to justify it. . . . The landholders' growing appreciation of the advantages of slavery over the older forms of servitude gave a powerful impetus to the growth of the new labor system.(28)

In short, the present theory stresses that *given* ethnocentrism, the Negroes' lack of power, and the dynamic arena of competition in which they were located, their ultimate enslavement was inevitable. The next task is to test the theory further, incorporating modifications as necessary, by analyzing subsequent accommodations in the pattern of race relations in the United States and by analyzing the emergence of various patterns of ethnic stratification in other places and eras.

NOTES

(1) The same observation regarding social stratification in general has recently been made by Gerhard Lenski, *Power and Privilege*, New York: McGraw-Hill, 1966, p. ix.

(2) See Joseph Boskin, "Race Relations in Seventeenth Century America: The Problem of the Origins of Negro Slavery," *Sociology and Social Research*, 49 (July, 1965), pp. 446-455, including references cited therein; and David B. Davis, *The Problem of Slavery in Western Culture*, Ithaca: Cornell U., 1966.

(3) A classic example is provided by Ethel John Lindgren, "An Example of Culture Contact Without Conflict: Reindeer Tungus and Cossacks of Northwest Manchuria," *American Anthropologist*, 40 (October-December, 1938), pp. 605-621.

(4) The relevance of precontact and of the nature and objectives of the contacting agents for the course of intergroup relations has been discussed by various scholars including Edward B. Reuter in his editor's "Introduction" to *Race and Culture Contacts*, New York: McGraw-Hill, 1934, pp. 1-18; and Clarence E. Glick, "Social Roles and Types in Race Relations," in Andrew W. Lind, editor, *Race Relations in World Perspective*, Honolulu: U. of Hawaii, 1955, pp. 239-262.

(5) William G. Sumner, *Folkways*, Boston: Ginn, 1940, p. 13. The essence of ethnocentrism is well conveyed by Catton's observation that "Ethnocentrism makes us see out-group behavior as deviation from in-group mores rather than as adherence to out-group mores." William R. Catton, Jr., "The Development of Sociological Thought" in Robert E. L. Faris, editor, *Handbook of Modern Sociology*, Chicago: Rand McNally, 1964, p. 930.

(6) Williams observes that "in various *particular* ways an out-group may be seen as superior" insofar as its members excel in performance vis-a-vis certain norms that the two groups hold in common (e.g., sobriety or craftsmanship in the production of a particular commodity). Robin M. Williams, Jr., *Strangers Next Door*, Englewood Cliffs, N.J.: Prentice-Hall, 1964, p. 22 (emphasis added). A similar point is made by Marc J. Swartz, "Negative Ethnocentrism," *Journal of Conflict Resolution*, 5 (March, 1961), pp. 75-81. It is highly unlikely, however, that the out-group will be so consistently objectively superior in the realm of shared values as to be seen as generally superior to the in-group unless the in-group is subordinate to or highly

dependent upon the out-group.

(7) Emory S. Bogardus, *Social Distance*, Yellow Springs: Antioch, 1959.

(8) Howard P. Becker, *Man in Reciprocity*, New York: Praeger, 1956, Ch. 15.

(9) Endogamy is an overly stringent index of the degree of ethnocentrism essential to ethnic stratification and is not itself a prerequisite of the emergence of ethnic stratification. However, where endogamy does not precede ethnic stratification, it is a seemingly invariable consequence. Compare this position with that of Charles Wagley and Marvin Harris who treat ethnocentrism and endogamy as independent structural requisites of intergroup hostility and conflict. See *Minorities in the New World*, New York: Columbia, 1958, pp. 256-263.

(10) Quoted in T. Walter Wallbank and Alastair M. Taylor, *Civilization: Past and Present*, Chicago: Scott, Foresman, 1949, rev. ed., Vol. 1, pp. 559-560. The offer and counter-offer also provide an excellent illustration of mutual ethnocentrism.

(11) Lindgren, *op. cit.*

(12) Aaron Antonovsky, "The Social Meaning of Discrimination," *Phylon*, 21 (Spring, 1960), pp. 81-95.

(13) This analysis of the arena of competition is a modification of the analysis by Wagley and Harris, *op. cit.*, esp. pp. 263-264. These authors limit the concept "arena" to the objects sought *and* the regulative values which determine opportunity to compete and then partly confound their components by including the regulative values, along with adaptive capacity and the instruments necessary to compete, as part of the "terms" of competition.

(14) *Ibid.*, p. 263. They suggest that competition for scarce subsistence goals will produce more intense conflict than competition for prestige symbols or other culturally defined goals.

(15) Discussing the ideological aspect of intergroup relations, Wagley and Harris note that equalitarian creeds have generally not been effective in *preventing* ethnic stratification. *Ibid.*, pp. 280 ff. The operation of ethnocentrism makes it very easy for the boundaries of the in-group to become the boundaries of adherence to group values.

(16) Frank Tannenbaum, *Slave and Citizen: The Negro in the Americas*, New York: Random House, 1963.

(17) *Ibid.*, esp. pp. 49 ff. Marvin Harris has criticized Tannenbaum's thesis arguing that the rights prescribed by the Iberian code were largely illusory and that there is no certainty that *slaves* were treated better in Latin America. Harris in turn provides a functional (economic necessity) explanation for the historical difference in treatment of *free* Negroes in the two continents. See Marvin Harris, *Patterns of Race in the Americas*, New York: Walker, 1964, esp. Chs. 6 and 7.

(18) Wagley and Harris, *Op. cit.*, p. 264.

(19) This point is explicitly made by Tamotsu Shibutani and Kian M. Kwan, *Ethnic Stratification: A Comparative Approach*, New York: Macmillan, 1965, p. 147; see also Ch. 9.

(20) This point is made by Antonovsky, *op. cit.*, esp. p. 82, and implied by Wagley and Harris in their discussion of the role of the state in the formation of minority groups, *op. cit.*, esp. pp. 240-244. Stanley Lieberson's recent modication of Park's cycle theory of race relations also emphasizes the importance of differential power as a determinant of the outcome of intergroup contacts. See "A Societal Theory of Race and Ethnic Relations," *American Sociological Review*, 26 (December, 1961), pp. 902-910.

(21) Lenski, *op. cit.*, esp. Ch. 3.

(22) See Wallbank and Taylor, *op. cit.*, p. 95; and Shibutani and Kwan, *op. cit.*, pp. 129-130.

(23) See *ibid.*, esp. Chs. 6, 9, and 12; and Richard A Schermerhorn, *Society and Power*, New York: Random House, 1961, pp. 18-26.

(24) Shibutani and Kwan observe that dominance rests upon victory in the competitive process and that competition between groups is eliminated or greatly reduced once a system of ethnic stratification is stabilized, *op. cit.*, pp. 146 and 235, and Ch. 12. The extent to which competition is actually stifled is highly variable, however, as Wagley and Harris note in their discussion of minority adaptive capacity and the terms of competition, *op. cit.*, pp. 263 ff.

(25) The issue is further complicated by the fact that the necessary degree of any one of the three elements may vary as a function of the other two.

(26) Davis asserts that while slavery has always been a source of tension, "in Western culture it was associated with certain religious and philosophical doctrines that gave it the highest sanction." *Op. cit.*, p. ix.

(27) Wagley and Harris, *op. cit.*, p. 124.

(28) Stampp, *op. cit.*, p. 22.

This selection is abridged from, "A Theory of the Origin of Ethnic Stratification," *Social Problems*, 16 (Fall, 1968), pp. 157-72, published by the Society for the Study of Social Problems. The author and Ernest Barth have contributed to the development of a general theory of ethnic stratification in their article on "Conceptual Frameworks for the Analysis of Race Relations: An Evaluation" which appeared in *Social Forces*, 50 (March, 1972), pp. 333-348.

document

SECOND STATEMENT ON RACE

UNESCO

1. Scientists are generally agreed that all men living today belong to a single species, *Homo sapiens*, and are derived from a common stock, even though there is some dispute as to when and how different human groups diverged from this common stock.

The concept of race is unanimously regarded by anthropologists as a classificatory device providing a zoological frame within which the various groups of mankind may be arranged and by means of which studies of evolutionary processes can be facilitated. In its anthropological sense, the word "race" should be reserved for groups of mankind possessing well-developed and primarily heritable physical differences from other groups. Many populations can be so classified but, because of the complexity of human history, there are also many populations which cannot easily be fitted into a racial classification.

2. Some of the physical differences between human groups are due to differences in hereditary constitution and some to differences in the environments in which they have been brought up. In most cases, both influences have been at work. The science of genetics suggests that the hereditary differences among populations of a single species are the results of the action of two sets of processes. On the one hand, the genetic composition of isolated populations is constantly but gradually being altered by natural selection and by occasional changes (mutations) in the material particles (genes) which control heredity. Populations are also affected by fortuitous changes in gene frequency and by marriage customs. On the other hand, crossing is constantly breaking down the differentiations so set up. The new mixed populations, in so far as they, in turn, become isolated, are subject to the same processes, and these may lead to further changes. Existing races are merely the result, considered at a particular moment in time, of the total effect of such processes on the human species. The hereditary characters to be used in the classification of human groups, the limits of their variation within these groups, and thus the extent of the classificatory sub-

divisions adopted may legitimately differ according to the scientific purpose in view.

3. National, religious, geographical, linguistic and cultural groups do not necessarily coincide with racial groups; and the cultural traits of such groups have no demonstrated connexion with racial traits. Americans are not a race, nor are Frenchmen, nor Germans; nor *ipso facto* is any other national group. Moslems and Jews are no more races than are Roman Catholics and Protestants; nor are people who live in Iceland or Britain or India, or who speak English or any other language, or who are culturally Turkish or Chinese and the like, thereby describable as races. The use of the term "race" in speaking of such groups may be a serious error, but it is one which is habitually committed.

4. Human races can be, and have been classified in different ways by different anthropologists. Most of them agree in classifying the greater part of existing mankind into at least three large units, which may be called major groups (in French *grand-races*, in German *Hauptrassen*). Such a classification does not depend on any single physical character, nor does for example, skin colour by itself necessarily distinguish one major group from another. Furthermore, so far as it has been possible to analyse them, the differences in physical structure which distinguish one major group from another give no support to popular notions of any general "superiority" or "inferiority" which are sometimes implied in referring to these groups.

Broadly speaking, individuals belonging to different major groups of mankind are distinguishable by virtue of their physical characters, but individual members, or small groups belonging to different races within the same major group are usually not so distinguishable. Even the major groups grade into each other, and the physical traits by which they and the races within them are characterized overlap considerably. With respect to most, if not all, measurable characters, the differences among individuals belonging to the same race are greater than the differences that occur between the observed averages for two or more races within the same major group.

5. Most anthropologists do not include mental characteristics in their classification of human races. Studies within a single race have shown that both innate capacity and environmental opportunity determine the results of tests of intelligence and temperament, though their relative importance is disputed.

When intelligence tests, even non-verbal, are made on a group of non-literate people, their scores are usually lower than those of more civilized people. It has been recorded that different groups of the same race occupying similarly high levels of civilization may yield considerable differences in intelligence tests. When, however, the two groups have been brought up from childhood in similar environments, the differences are usually very slight. Moreover, there is good evidence that, given similar opportunities, the average performance (that is to say, the performance of the individual who is representative because he is surpassed by as many as he surpasses), and the variation round it, do not differ appreciably from one race to another.

Even those psychologists who claim to have found the greatest differences in intelligence between groups of different racial origin and have contended that they are hereditary, always report that some members of the group of inferior performance surpass not merely the lowest ranking member of the superior group but also the average of its members. In any case, it has never been possible to separate members of two groups on the basis of mental capacity, as they can often be separated on a basis of religion, skin colour hair form or language. It is possible, though not proved, that some types of innate-capacity for intellectual and emotional responses are commoner in one human group than in another, but it is certain that, within a single group, innate capacities vary as much as, if not more than, they do between different groups.

The study of the heredity of psychological characteristics is beset with difficulties. We know that certain mental diseases and defects are transmitted from one generation to the next, but we are less familiar with the part played by heredity in the mental life of normal individuals. The normal individual, irrespective of race, is essentially educable. It follows that his intellectual and moral life is largely conditioned by his training and by his physical and social environment.

It often happens that a national group may appear to be characterized by particular psychological attributes. The superficial view would be that this is due to race. Scientifically, however, we realize that any common psychological attribute is more likely to be due to a common historical and social background, and that such attributes may obscure the fact that, within different populations consisting of many human types, one will find approximately the same range of temperament and intelligence.

6. The scientific material available to us at present does not justify the conclusion that inherited genetic differences are a major factor in producing the differences between the cultures and cultural achievements of different peoples or groups. It does indicate, on the contrary, that a major factor in explaining such differences is the cultural experience which each group has undergone.

7. There is no evidence for the existence of so-called "pure" races. Skeletal remains provide the basis of our limited knowledge about earlier races. In regard to race mixture, the evidence points to the fact that human hybridization has been going on for an indefinite but considerable time. Indeed, one of the processes of race formation and race extinction or absorption is by means of hybridization between races. As there is no reliable evidence that disadvantageous effects are produced thereby, no biological justification exists for prohibiting intermarriage between persons of different races.

8. We now have to consider the bearing of these statements on the problem of human equality. We wish to emphasize that equality of opportunity and equality in law in no way depend, as ethical principles, upon the assertion that human beings are in fact equal in endowment.

9. We have thought it worth while to set out in a formal manner what is at present scientifically established concerning individual and group differences:

> In matters of race, the only characteristics which anthropologists have so far been able to use effectively as a basis for classification are physical (anatomical and physiological).
>
> Available scientific knowledge provides no basis for believing that the groups of mankind differ in their innate capacity for intellectual and emotional development.
>
> Some biological differences between human beings within a single race may be as great as, or greater than, the same biological differences between races.
>
> Vast social changes have occurred that have not been connected in any way with changes in racial type. Historical and sociological studies thus support the view that genetic differences are of little significance in determining the social and cultural differences between different groups of men.
>
> There is no evidence that race mixture produces disadvantageous results

from a biological point of view. The social results of race mixture, whether for good or ill, can generally be traced to social factors.

This document is published from *Race Concept: Results of an Inquiry*. Series: "The Race Question in Modern Science" by permission of UNESCO, ©UNESCO 1951.

document

THIRD STATEMENT ON RACE

UNESCO

All men living today belong to a single species, *Homo sapiens*, and are derived from a common stock. There are differences of opinion regarding how and when different human groups diverged from this common stock.

Biological differences between human beings are due to differences in hereditary constitution and to the influence of the environment on this genetic potential. In most cases, those differences are due to the interaction of these two sets of factors.

There is great genetic diversity within all human populations. Pure races — in the sense of genetically homogeneous populations — do not exist in the human species.

There are obvious physical differences between populations living in different geographical areas of the world, in their average appearance. Many of these differences have a genetic component.

Most often the latter consist in differences in the frequency of the same hereditary characters.

Different classifications of mankind into major stocks, and of those into more restricted categories (races, which are groups of populations, or single populations) have been proposed on the basis of hereditary physical traits. Nearly all classifications recognize at least three major stocks.

Since the pattern of geographic variation of the characteristics used in racial classification is a complex one, and since this pattern does not present any major discontinuity, these classifications, whatever they are, cannot claim to classify mankind into clearcut categories; moreover, on account of the complexities of human history, it is difficult to determine the place of certain groups within these racial classifications, in particular that of certain intermediate populations.

Many anthropologists, while stressing the importance of human variation, believe that the scientific interest of these classifications is limited, and even that they carry the risk of inviting abusive generalizations.

Differences between individuals within a race or within a population are often greater than the average differences between races or populations.

Some of the variable distinctive traits which are generally chosen as criteria to characterize a race are either independently inherited or show only varying degrees of association between them within each population. Therefore, the combination of these traits in most individuals does not correspond to the typological racial characterization.

In man as well as in animals, the genetic composition of each population is subject to the modifying influence of diverse factors: natural selection, tending towards adaptation to the environment, fortuitous mutations which lead to modifications of the molecules of deoxyribonucleic acid which determine heredity, or random modifications in the frequency of qualitative hereditary characters, to an extent dependent on the patterns of mating and the size of populations.

Certain physical characters have a universal biological value for the survival of the human species, irrespective of the environment. The differences on which racial classifications are based do not affect these characters, and therefore, it is not possible from the biological point of view to speak in any way whatsoever of a general inferiority or superiority of this or that race.

Human evolution presents attributes of capital importance which are specific to the species.

The human species which is now spread over the whole world, has a past rich in migrations, in territorial expansions and contractions.

As a consequence, general adaptability to the most diverse environments is in man more pronounced than his adaptation to specific environments.

For long millenniums progress made by man, in any field, seems to have been increasingly, if not exclusively, based on culture and the transmission of cultural achievements and not on the transmission of genetic endowment. This implies a modification in the role of natural selection in man today.

On account of the mobility of human populations and of social factors, mating between members of different human groups which tend to mitigate the differentiations acquired, has played a much more important role in human history than in that of animals. The history of any human population or of any human race, is rich in instances of hybridization and those tend to become more and more numerous.

For man, the obstacles to interbreeding are geographical as well as social and cultural.

At all times, the hereditary characteristics of the human populations are in dynamic equilibrium as a result of this interbreeding and of the differentiation mechanisms which were mentioned before. As entities defined by sets of distinctive traits, human races are at any time in a process of emergence and dissolution.

Human races in general present a far less clearcut characterization than many animal races and they cannot be compared at all to races of domestic animals, these being the result of heightened selection for special purposes.

It has never been proved that interbreeding has biological disadvantages for mankind as a whole.

On the contrary, it contributes to the maintenance of biological ties between human groups and thus to the unity of the species in its diversity.

The biological consequences of a marriage depend only on the individual genetic make-up of the couple and not on their race.

Therefore, no biological justification exists for prohibiting intermarriage between persons of different races, or for advising against it on racial grounds.

Man since his origin has at his disposal ever more efficient cultural means of nongenetic adaptation.

Those cultural factors which break social and geographic barriers, enlarge the size of the breeding populations and so act upon their genetic structure by diminishing the random fluctuations (genetic drift).

As a rule, the major stocks extend over vast territories encompassing many diverse populations which differ in language, economy, culture, etc.

There is no national, religious, geographic, linguistic, or cultural group which constitutes a race *ipso facto*; the concept of race is purely biological.

However, human beings who speak the same language and share the same culture have a tendency to intermarry, and often there is as a result a certain degree of coincidence between physical traits on the one hand, and linguistic and cultural traits on the other. But there is no known causal nexus between these and therefore it is not justifiable to attribute cultural characteristics to the influence of the genetic inheritance.

Most racial classifications of mankind do not include mental traits or attributes as a taxonomic criterion.

Heredity may have an influence in the variability shown by individuals within a given population in their responses to the psychological tests currently applied.

However, no difference has ever been detected convincingly in the hereditary endowments of human groups in regard to what is measured by these tests. On the other hand, ample evidence attests to the influence of physical, cultural and social environment on differences in response to these tests.

The study of this question is hampered by the very great difficulty of determining what part heredity plays in the average differences observed in so-called tests of over-all intelligence between populations of different cultures.

The genetic capacity for intellectual development, like certain major anatomical traits peculiar to the species, is one of the biological traits essential for its survival in any natural or social environment.

The peoples of the world today appear to possess equal biological potentialities for attaining any civilizational level. Differences in the achievements of different peoples must be attributed solely to their cultural history.

Certain psychological traits are at times attributed to particular peoples. Whether or not such assertions are valid, we do not find any basis for ascribing such traits to hereditary factors, until proof to the contrary is given.

Neither in the field of hereditary potentialities concerning the overall intelligence and the capacity for cultural development, nor in that of physical traits, is there any justification for the concept of 'inferior' and 'superior' races.

The biological data given above stand in open contradiction to the tenets of racism. Racist theories can in no way pretend to have any scientific foundation and the anthropologists should endeavour to prevent the results of their researches from being used in such a biased way that they would serve non-scientific ends.

This document is reprinted from *Four Statements on the Race Question*, UNESCO, ©UNESCO, 1969.

BIBLIOGRAPHY

Parsons(7) and Demerath & Peterson(2) are recommended for a simple treatment of the social system paradigm. Lenski (5) and Dahrendorf (1) present thought-provoking analyses of the power-conflict paradigm. Lenski has summarized the two traditions and has made an attempt to reconcile them. He regards the notion of surplus as crucial to his theory of social stratification. Dahrendorf has presented a cogent criticism of Marx and has developed his own theory of class conflict with reference to modern industrial societies. A capsule version of the two paradigms as they impinge upon race relations, has been presented by Schermerhorn (8) in his first chapter. Glazer and Moynihan (4) is interesting insofar as it illustrates the case of the cultural pluralist. Van den Berghe (9) has made a significant contribution to the interpretation of the pluralist's approach. In fact, he has tried to incorporate some of the features of power-conflict paradigm in his theoretical framework. Magubane (6) has presented an excellent criticism of cultural pluralists with reference to African realities. Finally, one strongly recommends Fanon (3) who has discussed the effects of colonial rule upon the personality structures of the subject people.

(1) Dahrendorf, Ralf. *Class and Class Conflict in Industrial Society*, Stanford: Stanford University Press, 1959.

(2) Demerath III, N.J. and Richard A. Peterson (eds.). *System, Change and Conflict*, New York: Free Press, 1967.

(3) Fanon, Frantz. *The Wretched of the Earth*, New York: Monthly Review Press, 1965.

(4) Glazer, Nathan and Daniel P. Moynihan. *Beyond the Melting Pot*, Cambridge: MIT Press, 1963.

(5) Lenski, Gerhard. *Power and Privilege: A Theory of Social Stratification*, New York: McGraw-Hill, 1966.

(6) Magubane, Ben. "Pluralism and Conflict Situations in Africa: A New Look." *African Social Research* 7, 1969, pp. 529-54.

(7) Parsons, Talcott. *Social Systems*, Glencoe: The Free Press, 1951.

(8) Schermerhorn, R.A. *Comparative Ethnic Relations: A Framework for Theory and Research*, New York: Random House, 1970.

(9) Van den Berghe, Pierre L. *Race and Racism: A Comparative Perspective*, New York: John Wiley, 1967.

II.
THE HISTORICAL ORIGINS OF MODERN RACE RELATIONS

INTRODUCTION

The world-wide interaction between whites and non-whites is a fundamental theme in the long sweep of modern history from the earliest efforts of Portugal to reach the East to the partition of Africa in the late nineteenth century. As John Horton has suggested, the conflict model of race relations emphasizes historical analysis. We can then differentiate the changing forms of race relations, such as slavery and debt peonage, from the continuity of racial domination and subordination. From this perspective, we intend to sketch the broad historical outlines of the origins of modern race relations. This section provides an historical background and a framework of analysis for the sections on Great Britain, the United States, South Africa, and the Andean Region of Central America.

The expansion of the Roman Empire engulfed the peoples of Western Europe into the stream of modern history. With the disintegration of that Empire, Western Europe turned inward, becoming an object of history for Arab, Mongol, and Norse invaders. Its largely self-contained economy and society changed slowly, and its population generally remained unaware of the flourishing civilizations on other continents. Yet within the social structure of Western Europe, forces were at work which would transform this area and would shape world history for centuries.

It was as if the Medieval Era represented an internal gathering of energies in Western Europe which was followed by an outward thrust unprecedented in scope and duration. By the twelfth century, Western Europe's isolation was ending. The mercantile interests of Genoa, Venice, and Milan had established links with the East and were prospering as the middlemen of a long distance trade. In the early fifteenth century, Portugal attempted to challenge the Italian city states' grip on the Western Europe/East nexus by sailing around the continent of Africa. In 1415, the Portuguese captured the Moorish stronghold of Ceuta in Northern Africa, and twenty-six years later, a Portuguese ship captain, Antam Goncalvez, returned to Lisbon with a dozen slaves from the African coast. The direct Western European slave traffic with Africa had begun.(1)

Portugal continued its efforts to get to the East but was soon challenged by Spain. In turn, the trade of the two Iberian nations was overtaken by England, France, and Holland during the next century. The competition for leadership continued, and much of history from the fifteenth to the nineteenth century is a continuing conflict among these five nations concerning the expansion of each. The age of exploration and discovery was a five-nation struggle for control of parts of Asia, Africa, and the New World. The inter-European wars from the sixteenth to the eighteenth century represented the continuing politics of expansion by other means, while the Pax Britannica of the nineteenth century was the peace imposed on Europe by a successful imperial power.

Certainly expansion and the creation of empire were not unusual in history. Nor was the looting of lands and the enslavement of peoples violently incorporated into these empires unprecedented. Yet some unique features, associated with the expansion of Western Europe, laid the foundation for the system of modern race relations. First, the area that Western Europe came to control was greater than any area previously conquered. The influence of the Western European empires was more *extensive* than that of any previous empires, including the Roman Empire. Generally, Western Europe laid the basis for a world-wide system of stratification. Second, the way Western Europe used conquered lands and peoples enabled several nations to escape, for some time, the stagnation and decline which beset most earlier empires fairly rapidly.(2) Third, through either formal political control or informal economic dominance, the structural evolution of most of the non-European world was shaped by Western Europe for several hundred years. Consequently, the influence of the Western European empires was more *intensive* than that of previous empires. Finally, and perhaps most significantly, the skin color of Western Europeans differed from that of most of the peoples they conquered. Thus, the world stratification system created by the new empires was affected by racial differences, for Western Europe was a white world expanding into a non-white world. It is only in light of that expansion that the terms "white" and "non-white," as distinct from, say, "yellow" and non-yellow, have the meaning they do. Although skin color distinctions have served in other parts of the world as the basis of social differentiation,(3) they have not had the determinate impact on world history and the lives of so many people as the Western European expansion had between 1400 and 1900. This historical legacy provides the context for W.E.B. DuBois's prophetic remark: "the color line is the problem of the twentieth century."

What was the connection between Western Europe's development and its pacification of more and more areas outside of Europe? What did the non-white world contribute to the development of the European white world? Finally, what impact did the expansion of the white world have on the non-white one? Answers lie in the relationship linking these two worlds, a relationship which changed in form but which in content—the appropriation of lands and peoples from Asia, Africa, and the New World—remained constant.

Land would produce what European markets needed: precious metals, spices, and sugar. One problem remained: how to make the land yield its wealth. Labor was needed to work the land, and it was difficult to get enough white Europeans to travel several thousand miles to work long hours for someone else. Europeans had plenty of opportunity to work in England, France, or Spain. It would have been equally difficult to get the non-white peoples of Africa, Asia, and the New World to work if they had been given a choice, but the only choice involved was the decision of the white conquerors as to whom was able-bodied enough to work. Thus, Western Europe began to incorporate its extended empire into its own growth and to move beyond a period of plundering to a period of colonization. The forms of colonialism varied. In some areas the indigenous non-white peoples were destroyed or pushed aside as "new societies" based on European immigrations were created; in other areas, a minority of whites administered non-white colonies; in a few instances, control was informal rather than formal. In all cases, however, in the racial content of the stratification system, the lighter skinned population dominated the system.

For years, many historians have argued that the United States was unique, because it was the first new nation founded as a result of an anti-colonial revolution; as such, it represented a break from the Western European past.(4) Nevertheless, in terms of expansion and racial differentiation, the United States merely represented a national variation of the international theme of white expansion and appropriation of a non-white world. The United States is almost the paradigm case: the Indians had the land that the whites wanted, and the whites took it in ways that paralleled the Western European conquests in Asia, Africa, and Latin America.

The slave trade and slave labor were part of the development of both North and South in the United States. The cotton trade, based on the labor of slaves, provided much of the capital which was central to the timing and pace of Northern industrialization during the first forty years of the nineteenth century.(5) Nothing in the definition of colonial expansion requires crossing an ocean. "Manifest Destiny" is simply the United States' version of the "white man's burden," an ideology justifying the creation of a system of racial stratification which incorporated, at a national level, the same social relationships that were in the international structure of the Western European empires.

What was the ideology that accompanied the social relationships of Western Europe and United States expansion? From the sixteenth century priest, Gaines de Sepulveda, to the nineteenth century British poet, Rudyard Kipling, to the French nobleman, Count Arthur de Gobineau, to the U.S. Senator Albert J. Beveridge, the explanations evolved around race. Racial though served to justify white dominance of non-whites in the name of the long-run interests of both. Racism consequently justified pillage, plunder, and profit planned or nature would determine the civilizing and Christianization of the non-white world.

Some elements of racial thought did exist prior to the expansion of Western Europe, but the expansion and the social relationships of the modern empires created a world system that provided the necessary structure to support the elaboration of racial thought. Racism, as distinct from prejudice, is best understood as an ideology, a set of social relationships of dominance and subordination in which the inferiority of some people is inferred from perceived physical characteristics.(6) The Western European world chose skin color as the crucial characteristic at an early stage. The strength of racism as a system of thought arose because it seemed to explain the real power relationships that emerged during the fifteenth century. The real conflict benefits resulting from these racial categorizations, if they were acknowledged at all, were only incidental compensation for the burden assumed by white peoples. As one English historian phrased it, "We seem, as it were, to have conquered and peopled half the world in a fit of absence of mind.(7) Today, the categorizations involve humanistic concern, cultural exchange, economic benevolence to explain white domination in the world. Only with the rise of non-white nations to world power, including military victories and the recent trade agreements on oil, has the international structure of racism been challenged substantially.

Beginning, then, around the fifteenth century, the world was increasingly divided into subjects and objects, those who made history and those who had to respond to it. If we were to draw a line around the small group of Western European nations and the Eastern half of the North American continent, we would effectively outline the elite of the worl stratification system, the creation and maintenance of which formed the content of history for more than four centureis. It is the current operation of that stratification and its contradictions that provide the focus of study of modern race relations.

Approaching the study of race relations requires an effort to synthesize the factors of race and class. Each of the authors in this section makes that effort, and each would probably have some disagreements with the others. Together, the selections suggest some of the excitement and power of the history and conflict in race relations. The first selection provides a general view of modern race relations similar to that sketched in this Introduction. Although Oliver Cox's work is over twenty years old, it has until recently been largely overlooked by social scientists. In an excerpt from his brilliant analysis of the Western European and African trade, Basil Davidson traces the impact of the slave trade on the attitudes of the white traders. The shift from an egalitarian relationship to slave trading also brought about a negative shift in European attitudes. In a selection from his classic work,- *Capitalism and Slavery*, Eric Williams argues strongly that resources from abroad were important in the development of England. Although his thesis has been attacked since the book was published, it has found persuasive defenders, most recently Eric Hobsbawm.(8) The selection by Samir Amin develops a typology of Western Europe upon Africa and provides a useful framework for further analysis of that impact upon Latin America and Asia.

In the documents section are excerpts from two prominent English apologias for slave trade. Especially contemporary is Postlewayt's call for balancing the right of the oppressed to continue the trading. Because the rhetoric of race and expansion in United States history is abundant, we have included only one selection by Albert Beveridge, a nationally known figure in the United States in the late nineteenth century.

NOTES

(1) See Davidson, Basil, *The African Slave Trade Precolonial History 1450-1850*, Boston: Little, Brown & Company, 1961. A selection from this work appears in this section of the book.

(2) See James O'Connor's discussion of the difference between pre-capitalist and capitalist empires in "The Meaning of Economic Imperialism," in *Imperialism and Underdevelopment*, edited by Robert I. Rhodes, New York: Monthly Review Press, 1970, pp. 102-103.

(3) van den Berghe, Pierre L., *Race and Racism*, New York: John Wiley, 1967.

(4) E.G., S.M. Lipset, *The First New Nation*, New York: Basic Books, 1963.

(5) North, Douglass C., *The Economic Growth of the United States: 1790-1860*, New York: W. W. Norton and Company, 1966, pp. 66-74. A selection

from this work appears in the section in this book on the United States.

(6) See Oliver C. Cox, *Caste, Class, and Race,* New York: Monthly Review Press, 1970, part 3, introduction and Chapter 16. A selection from this work appears in this section of the book.

(7) Seeley, J.A., "The Expansion of England, 1883," quoted in A.P. Thornton, *The Doctrines of Imperialism,* New York: John Wiley, 1965, p. 23.

(8) See Eric Hobsbawm, *Industry and Empire,* London: Weidenfeld, 1968.

THE RISE
OF MODERN RACE RELATIONS

Oliver C. Cox

In a discussion of "the origin" of race relations it should be well to determine at the outset exactly what we are looking for. We shall proceed, therefore, by first eliminating certain concepts that are commonly confused with that of race relations. These are: ethnocentrism, intolerance, and "racism."

Ethnocentrism, as the sociologists conceive of it, is a social attitude which expresses a community of feeling in any group—the "we" feeling as over against the "others." This attitude seems to be a function of group solidarity, which is not necessarily a racial phenomenon. Neither is social intolerance racial antagonism, for social intolerance is social displeasure or resentment against that group which refuses to conform to the established practices and beliefs of the society. Finally, the term "racism" as it has been recently employed in the literature seems to refer to a philosophy of racial antipathy. Studies on the origin of racism involve the study of the development of an ideology, an approach which usually results in the substitution of the history of a system of rationalization for that of a material social fact.(1) Indeed, it is likely to be an accumulation of an erratic pattern of verbalizations cut free from any on-going social system. . . .

. . . Probably a realization of no single fact is of such crucial significance for an understanding of racial antagonism as that the phenomenon had its rise only in modern times.(2) In a previous study on "the origin of caste" we have attempted to show that race conflict did not exist among the early Aryans in India, and we do not find it in other ancient civilizations. Our hypothesis is that racial exploitation and race prejudice developed among Europeans with the rise of capitalism and nationalism, and that because of the world-wide ramifications of capitalism, all racial antagonisms can be traced to the policies and attitudes of the leading capitalist people, the white people of Europe and North America.

By way of demonstrating this hypothesis we shall review briefly some well-known historical situations. In tracing the rise of the Anglo-Saxons to their position as the master race of the world(3) we shall omit consideration of the great Eastern civilizations from which Greece took a significant cultural heritage. There seems to be no basis for imputing racial antagonism to the Egyptians, Babylonians, or Persians. At any rate, the Greeks were the first European people to enter the stream of eastern Mediterranean civilization, and the possibility of racial exploitation did not really occur until the Macedonian conquest. Our point here is, however, that we do not find race prejudice even in the great Hellenistic empire which extended deeper into the territories of colored people than any other European empire up to the end of the fifteenth century.

The Hellenic Greeks had a cultural, not a racial, standard of belonging, so that their basic division of the peoples of the world were Greeks and barbarians—the barbarians having been all those persons who did not possess the Greek culture, especially its language. This is not surprising, for the culture of peoples is always a matter of great moment to them. But the people of the Greek city-states, who founded colonies among the barbarians on the shores of the Black Sea and of the Mediterranean, welcomed those barbarians to the extent that they were able to participate in Greek culture, and intermarried freely with them. The Greeks knew that they had a superior culture to those of the barbarians, but they included Europeans, Africans, and Asiatics in the concept Hellas as these peoples acquired a working knowledge of the Greek culture.

The experience of the later Hellenistic empire of Alexander tended to be the direct contrary of modern racial antagonism. The narrow patriotism of the city-states was given up for a new cosmopolitanism. Every effort was made to assimilate the barbarians to Greek culture, and in the process a new Greco-Oriental culture with a Greco-Oriental ruling class came into being. Alexander himself took a Persian princess for his wife and encouraged his men to intermarry with the native population.(4) In this empire there was an estate, not a racial, distinction between the rulers and the un-Hellenized natives.

Moreover, the inclination of Alexander to disregard even cultural differences in his policy toward the peoples of his empire seemed to have stimulated one of the most remarkable philosophies of all time: that of the fundamental equality of all human beings. In Athens, in about 300 B.C., Zeno developed a system of thought called stoicism which held in part that "all men should be fellow citizens; and there should be one life and order, as of a flock pasturing together, which feeds together by a common law." This doctrine was not a reaction to race prejudice but rather to certain invidious cultural distinctions among the peoples of the time; and the idea has come down to us by way of the Roman law, the preaching of St. Paul, and the writings of the philosophers of the Enlightenment. It has been given a democratic emphasis in the American Declaration of Independence and in amendments to the Constitution of the United States.

The next great organization of peoples about the Mediterranean Sea — and insofar as European civilization is concerned this may be thought of as constituting the whole world — was the Roman Empire. In this civilization also we do not find racial antagonism, for the norm of superiority in the Roman system remained a cultural-class attribute. The basic distinction was Roman citizenship, and gradually this was extended to all freeborn persons in the municipalities of the empire. Slaves came from every province, and there was no racial distinction among them. Sometimes the slaves, especially the Greeks, were the teachers of their masters; indeed, very much of the cultural enlightenment of the Romans came through slaves from the East. Because slavery was not a racial stigma, educated freedmen, who were granted citizenship upon emancipation, might rise to high positions in government or industry. There were no interracial laws governing the relationship of the great mass of obscure common people of different origin. Moreover, the aristocracy of the empire, the senators and *equites*, was constituted largely from responsible provincials in the imperial administration.

One should not mistake the social relationship among the various social estates of the Greek and Roman world for race relations. The Spartiates, *Perioikoi*, and Helots of Laconia, for instance, were not races but social estates; neither did the *Metics*,(5) the alien residents of Periclean Athens, constitute a race. In early republican Rome intermarriage was forbidden between the privileged patrician class and the plebian mass, but this was a social-estate partition rather than a racial accommodation.

If we have not discovered interracial antagonism in ancient Greece and Rome, the chances of discovering it in the system which succeeded the fall of the Roman Empire are even more remote. With the rise of the politico-religious system of Christianity, Western culture may be thought of as having entered its long period of gestation. Its first signs of parturition were the Crusades. But during all this time and even after the Renaissance the nature of the movement and of the social contact of peoples in this area precluded the possibility of the development of race prejudice. . . .

. . . One aspect of this era of barbarian invasion, the movement of Asiatics into Europe, is of especial significance. The Asiatics were better warriors than rulers. We may say rather conclusively that the white man's rise to superiority over the colored peoples of the other continents is based pivotally on his superiority as a fighter. This is, however, a rather recent achievement. In the Middle Ages the Asiatics outfought him. The Huns, Saracens, Moors, Seljuk Turks, Ottoman Turks, Tartars — all went deep into Europe, subjugated and sometimes enslaved white peoples who today are highly race-prejudiced. At any rate, we shall not find racial antagonism among these invaders. . . .

. . . In Europe itself the policies of the Roman Catholic Church presented a bar to the development of racial antagonism. The Church, which gradually attained more or less religious, economic, and ideological dominance, had a folk and personal — not a territorial or racial — norm of belonging. The fundamental division of human beings was Christian and non-Christian. Among the non-Christians the heathen, the infidel, and the heretic were recognized by differential negative attitudes; however, as a means of entering the Christian community, conversion or recantation was freely allowed and even sought after. . . .

. . . In the Middle Ages, then, we find no racial antagonism in Europe; in fact, Europeans were, at this time, more isolated and ignorant about foreign peoples and world geography than the Romans and Greeks were.

But gradually, under a commercial and religious impulse, Europe began to awaken and to journey toward strange lands. The First Crusade may be taken as the starting point which finally led to world dominance by Europeans. When after their travels in the last quarter of the thirteenth century the Polos returned from the court of the great Kublai Khan in China to tell Europeans a story of fabulous wealth and luxury, the astonished people could hardly believe what they heard. Yet Marco Polo's memoirs were a great stimulant to traders. It was not until the discovery of America and the circumnavigation of the globe, however, that the movement assumed a decidedly irreversible trend. The period between the First Crusade and the discovery of America continued to be characterized by the religious view of world order; but it set a pattern of dealing with non-Christian peoples which was to be continued, minus only its religious characteristics, to this day. To the extent that the religious controls remained effective, racial antagonism did not develop; what really developed was a Jew-heathen-infidel antagonistic complex which was to color European thought for some centuries. . . .

. . . In fact, it was this need for trade with the East, especially by the Italian, Spanish, and Portuguese merchants, and its obstruction by the Mohammedans whose country lay across their path in the Near East, which induced the Portuguese in the fifteenth century, to feel their way down the African coast in the hope of sailing around this continent to the East Indies. Here began the great drama that was, in a few hundred years, to turn over the destiny of the world to the decisions of businessmen. But our concern at this point is to indicate that racial antagonism had not yet developed among the Europeans.

In the first place, the geography of the world was still a mystery, and some of the most fantastic tales about its peoples were believed. Stories of the splendor, luxury, and wisdom of the peoples of the East held all Europe in constant wonderment. No one would have been surprised if some traveler had returned from the heart of Africa to break the news that he had found a black monarch ruling over a kingdom surpassing in grandeur and power any that had then existed in Europe. In short, the white man had no conception of himself as being capable of developing *the* superior culture of the world — the concept "white man" had not yet its significant social definition — the Anglo-Saxon, the modern master race, was then not even in the picture.

But when the Portuguese began to inch their way down the African coast they knew that the Moors and heathens whom they encountered were inferior to them both as fighters and as culture builders.(6) This, however, led to no conclusions about racial superiority. Henry the Navigator, himself, sought in those parts a Christian prince, Prester John, with whom he planned to form an alliance "against the enemies of the faith." All through the latter half of the fifteenth century the Portuguese sailors and explorers kept up this search for the kingdom of the lost black prince.

Of more significance still is the fact that there was as yet no belief in any cultural incapacity of these colored people. Their conversion to Christianity was sought with enthusiasm, and this transformation was supposed to make the Africans the human equals of all other Christians. The Portuguese historian, Gomes Eannes de Azurara, writing in the middle of the fifteenth century, gives us some idea of the religious motives for Prince Henry's exploits among the peoples on the West African coast. One reason for the Navigator's slave raids:

. . . was his great desire to make increase in the faith or our lord Jesus Christ and to bring to him all souls that should be saved,—understanding that all the mystery of the Incarnation, Death, and Passion of our Lord Jesus Christ was for this sole end — namely the salvation of lost souls, whom the said Lord Infant [Henry] by his travail and spending would fain bring into the true faith. For he perceived that no better offering could be made unto the Lord than this. For if God promised to return one hundred goods for one, we may justly believe that for such great benefits, that is to say, for so many souls as were saved by the efforts of this Lord, he will have so many hundreds of guerdons in the Kingdom of God, by which his spirit may be glorified after this life in the celestial realm. For I that wrote this history saw so many men and women of those parts turned to the holy faith, that even if the Infant had been a heathen, their prayers would have been enough to have obtained this salvation. And not only did I see the first captives, but their children and grandchildren as true Christians as if the Divine grace breathed in them and imparted them a clear knowledge of itself.(7)

This matter of cultural conversion is crucial for our understanding of the development of racial antagonism. For the full profitable exploitation of a people, the dominant group must devise ways and means of limiting that people's cultural assimilation. So long as the Portuguese and Spaniards continued to accept the religious definition of human equality, so long also the development of race prejudice was inhibited. Although it is true that the forays on the African coast were exceedingly ruthless, the Portuguese did not rationalize the fact with a racial argument. To kill or to take into slavery the heathen or infidel was to serve the highest purpose of God. As Azurara pointed out: ". . . though their bodies were now brought into subjection, that was a small matter in comparison to their souls, which would now possess true freedom for evermore."(8) In granting to Prince Henry a "plenary indulgence," Pope Eugenius IV gave "to each and all those who shall be engaged in the said war [slave raids], complete forgiveness of all their sins." (9)...

. . . The next era in the history of race relations commenced with the discovery of America. If we see that race prejudice is an attitudinal instrument of modern human, economic exploitation, the question as to whether race prejudice was found among the primitive peoples of the world will not arise. It would be, for instance, a ridiculous inversion of thought to expect the native peoples of America to have had race prejudice for the white invaders.(10) But modern society — Western civilization — began to take on its characteristic attributes when Columbus turned the eyes and interests of the world away from the Mediterranean toward the Atlantic. The mysticism of the East soon lost its grip on human thought, and the bourgeois world got under way. The socioeconomic matrix of racial antagonism involved the commercialization of human labor in the West Indies, the East Indies, and in America, the intense competition among businessmen of different western European cities for the capitalist exploitation of resources of this area, the development of nationalism and the consolidation of European nations, and the decline of the influence of the Roman Catholic Church with its mystical inhibitions to the free exploitation of economic resources. Racial antagonism attained full maturity during the latter half of the nineteenth century, when the sun no longer set on British soil and the great nationalistic powers of Europe began to justify their economic designs upon weaker European peoples with subtle theories of racial superiority and masterhood.

It should be observed that this view is not generally agreed upon. A popular belief among writers on modern race relations is that the phenomenon has always been known among most, if not all, peoples. This approach apparently tends to give theories of race relations a "scientific" aspect, but it contributes little to an understanding of the problem.

For instance, Jacques Barzun may be misleading in his saying that "if anyone deserves burning in effigy for starting the powerful race-dogma of Nordic superiority" it is Tacitus. This is supposed to be so because Tacitus, in his admiration of the primitive "Germans," made assertions "embodying the germ of present-day Nordicism."(11) Yet it seems evident that neither Tacitus, St. Paul, Noah, nor the Rig-Vedic Aryans are responsible for the racial practices and ideologies developed among modern Europeans. Moreover, the use of the metaphor "germ" is likely to convey the idea that this excursus of Tacitus, his "noble-savage" description of the virtues of the tribal Germans, was continually built upon by them over the centuries, until at last it blossomed into nazism.

We might just as well rely upon that notable charge of Cicero to Atticus in the first century B.C., "Do not obtain your slaves from Britain because they are so stupid and so utterly incapable of being taught that they are not fit to form a part of the household of Athens," as a basis for the explanation of modern race prejudice against the British — the only difficulty being that there has never been any such prejudice.

When white scholars began their almost desperate search of the ancient archives for good reasons to explain the wonderful cultural accomplishments among the whites, European economic and military world dominance was already an actuality. Most of the discoveries which explain the racial superiority of the tall, long-headed blond may be called Hamite rationalizations or deductions from cultural situations which cannot be identified with those of modern race relations. Probably the most widely accepted of these has been the biblical story of the descendants of Ham as a people cursed forever to do the menial work of others.

When English, French, and German scholars discovered the Aryans in the Sanskrit literature of the Hindus, the Hindus themselves were unaware of the Aryans' racial potentialities. The concept "Arya" meant practically nothing to them. It remained for the nationalistic Germans to recognize that the term "Arya" designated Germans particularly and that, because of this, the right of Germans to exploit all other peoples of the world, not excluding the Hindus, was confirmed.

In the study of race relations it is of major importance to realize that their significant manifestations could not possibly have been known among the ancients. If we had to put our finger upon the year which marked the beginning of modern race relations we should select 1493-94. This is the time when total disregard for the human rights and physical power of the non-Christian peoples of the world, the colored peoples, was officially assumed by the first two great colonizing European nations. Pope Alexander VI's bull of demarcation issued under Spanish pressure on May 3, 1493, and its revision by the Treaty of Tordesillas (June 7, 1494), arrived at through diplomatic negotiations between Spain and Portugal, put all the heathen peoples and their resources — that is to say, especially the colored peoples of the world — at the disposal of Spain and Portugal.(12)

Sometimes, probably because of its very obviousness, it is not realized that the slave trade was simply a way of recruiting labor for the purpose of exploiting the great natural resources of America.(13) This trade did not develop because Indians and Negroes were red and black, or because their cranial capacity averaged a certain number of cubic centimeters; but simply because they were the best workers to be found for the heavy labor in the mines and plantations across the Atlantic.(14) If white workers were available in sufficient numbers they would have been substituted. As a matter of fact, part of the early demand for labor in the West Indies and on the mainland was filled by white servants, who were sometimes defined in exactly the same terms as those used to characterize the Africans. Although the recruitment of involuntary labor finally settled down to the African coasts, the earlier kidnappers did a brisk business in some of the most enlightened European cities. Moreover, in the process of exploiting the natural resources of the West Indies, the Spanish conquistadors literally consumed the native Indian population.

This, then, is the beginning of modern race relations. It was not an abstract, natural, immemorial feeling of mutual antipathy between groups, but rather a practical exploitative relationship with its socio-attitudinal facilitation — at that time only nascent race prejudice. Although this peculiar kind of exploitation was then in its incipiency, it had already achieved its significant characteristics.(15) As it developed and took definite capitalistic form, we could follow the white man around the world and see him repeat the process among practically every people of color. . . .

NOTES

(1) See Hannah Arendt, "Race-Thinking Before Racism," *The Review of Politics*, Vol. 6, January 1944, pp. 36-73; and Frederick G. Detweiler, "The Rise of Modern Race Antagonisms," *The American Journal of Sociology*, Vol. 37, March 1932, pp. 738-47.

(2) Cf. Ina Corine Brown, *National Survey of the Higher Education of Negroes*, U.S. Office of Education, Misc. No. 6, Vol. II, pp. 4-8.

(3) Professor G.A. Borgese makes an observation pertinent to this remark: "The English-speaking mind is not fully alive to the gravity of this issue. Unlike their German cousins and foes, the Anglo-Saxon stocks did not strive to *become* the master race or *Herrenvolk* holding sway over the world and mankind. . . . Yet, unlike their German cousins and rivals, they have succeeded in *being* a *Herrenvolk*, a race master." "Europe Wants Freedom from Shame," *Life*, March 12, 1945, pp. 41-42. (Italics Borgese's.)

"The Germans needed all of Hitler's ranting and daily doses from the Goebbels propaganda machine to persuade them that they were better than other people. Englishmen simply take it for granted and rarely waste a syllable discussing it." See John Scott, *Europe in Revolution*, p. 216.

(4) In describing the composition of Alexander's army invading India, E.R. Bevan says: ". . . mingled with Europeans were men of many nations. Here were troops of horsemen, representing the chivalry of Iran, which had followed Alexander from Bactria and beyond, Pashtus and men of the Hindu Kush with their highland-bred horses, Central-Asiatics who ride and shoot at the same time; and among the campfollowers one could find groups representing the older civilizations of the world, Phoenicians inheriting an immemorial tradition of shipcrafts and trade, bronzed Egyptians able to confront the Indians with an antiquity still longer than their own." *The Cambridge History of India*, Vol. I, p. 351.

(5) The Metics may probably be better thought of as presenting a multinationality situation. On this point Gustave Glotz, referring to the Metics of various national origins, concludes: ". . . there was formed in Greece in the fifth and sixth centuries a kind of international nation which was preparing, chiefly in economic interests but also in the domain of ideas and in the very framework of society, for the cosmopolitanism of the Hellenistic period." *Ancient Greece at Work*, p. 191.

(6) It should be noted that the Portuguese felt they were superior because they were Christians, not because they were white. In an address to his men just before they attacked an unsuspecting west-coast community, the captain of a caravel declared: ". . . although they are more in number than we by a third yet they are but Moors, and we are Christians one of whom ought to suffice for two of them. For God is He in whose power lieth victory, and He knoweth our good wills in His holy service," Azurara, *The Discovery and Conquest of Guinea*, p. 138.

(7) Op. cit., p. 29. See also C. Raymond Beazley, *Prince Henry the Navigator*.

(8) Op. cit., p. 51.

(9) Ibid., p. 53

(10) Although Columbus participated in the enslavement of the Indians of the West Indies, which finally led to their extermination, his first impression of them is well known: "They are a loving uncovitous people, so docile in all things that I do assure your Highness I believe in all the world there is not a better people or a better country; they love their neighbours as themselves, and they have the sweetest and gentlest way of speaking in the world and always with a smile." Again, "As they showed us such friendship and as I recognized they were people who would yield themselves better to the Christian faith and be converted more through love than by force, I gave them some coloured buttons and some glass beads ... and [they] became so attached to us that it was a marvel to behold." See Francis A. MacNutt, *Bartholomew De Las Casas*, pp. 18, 19.

(11) *Race, A Study of Modern Superstition*, pp. 11, 28.

(12) As early as 1455 Pope Nicholas V had granted the Portuguese exclusive right to their discoveries on the African coast, but the commerical purpose here was still very much involved with the crusading spirit.

(13) In a discussion of the arguments over slavery during the Constitutional Convention, Charles A. Beard observes: "South Carolina was particularly determined, and gave northern representatives to understand that if they wished to secure their commercial privileges, they must make concessions to the slave trade. And they were met half way. Ellsworth said: 'As slaves multiply so fast in Virginia and Maryland that it is cheaper to raise than import them, whilst in the sickly rice swamps foreign supplies are necessary, if we go no farther than is urged, we shall be unjust towards South Carolina and Georgia. Let us not intermeddle. As population increases, poor laborers will be so plenty as to render slaves useless.'" *An Economic Interpretation of the Constitution*, p. 177. Quote from Max Farrand, *Records*, Vol. II, p. 371.

(14) In a discussion of the labor situation among the early Spanish colonists in America, Professor Bailey W. Diffie observes: "One Negro was reckoned as worth two, four, or even more Indians at work production." *Latin American Civilization*, p. 206.

(15) Francis Augustus MacNutt describes the relationship in Hispaniola: "Columbus laid tribute upon the entire population of the island which required that each Indian above fourteen years of age who lived in the mining provinces was to pay a little bell filled with gold every three months; the natives of all other provinces were to pay one *arroba* of cotton. These amounts were so excessive that in 1496 it was found necessary to change the nature of the payments, and, instead of the gold and cotton required from the villages, labour was substituted, the Indians being required to lay out and work the plantations of the colonists in their vicinity." *Bartholomew De Las Casas*, p. 25.

This selection is abridged from, *Caste, Class, and Race: A Study in Social Dynamics*, New York: Monthly Review Press, 1970, pp. 321, 322-325, 325-326, 326-328, 330-333.

THE SLAVE TRADE
AND EUROPEAN ATTITUDES

Basil Davidson

European ideas about Africa, before the years of discovery, varied remarkably with time and place. In southern Europe, face to face with North African power and commerce, there was beginning to be a good deal of solid information by the year 1500. Some knowledge of the scope and wealth of the lands beyond the Sahara was getting through to influential men. Yet even the well-informed ports of the Mediterranean could yield extraordinary fluctuations of judgment; and the facts they had to go on were encased, all too often, in a lavish covering of superstitious legend.

Much of this legend was learned from the Moors — Berbers and Arabs of the Moorish states of North Africa. Seldom could Christians penetrate the African interior, and only a handful of those who did have left any trace in the records. The earliest known European traveler's memoir from "inner Africa" — and it would stand alone for many years to come — dates from 1447, and was written by an Italian called Antonio Malfante in Tuat, an oasis of the northern Sahara. Tuat in those days was an important staging-post for trans-Saharan caravans which had come from the south with African slaves, whether as victims or as porters, since times beyond recall.

Malfante picked up the caravan gossip of Tuat, and already it was rich with strange misunderstandings. He explains to a friend in Genoa that to the south of Tuat and the Great Desert there are black peoples who have "innumerable great cities and territories." But these peoples of the south "are in carnal acts like the beasts: the father has knowledge of his daughter, the son of his sister. They breed greatly, for a woman bears up to five at a birth. Nor can it be doubted that they are eaters of human flesh." Already the image of Black Africa is beginning to be the image of Caliban.

Elsewhere in Europe, especially in northern Europe, where the trade with Africa was virtually unknown, opinions could be interestingly different. Northern Europe might understand Africa no more than Africa understood northern

Europe: "Scotland," an Andalusian Arab writer had declared in 1154, "has neither dwellings, nor towns, nor villages." Yet even in remote Scotland a little was beginning to be known and thought of Africa by late medieval times; and the Scots, by the early years of the sixteenth century, had even welcomed a few visitors from Africa. Such rare "travelers" were evidently men and women taken out of Portuguese slaving ships by Scottish privateers. One or two of these visitors from the far south became famous in Edinburgh society, and not the least of these was that "black lady with the fulsome lips" of whom, in about 1460, the poet Dunbar wrote some memorable verses. . . .

. . . And if European attitudes toward Africans in those early times displayed a wide range of contrast, they were generally uniform in one important respect. They supposed no natural inferiority in Africans, no inherent failure to develop and mature. That was to be the great myth of later years: the central myth of European expansion that first took shape on the deck of a slaving ship. Race contempt crept in when free men could justify their material interests by the scorn they had for slaves — for men, that is, to whom an unnatural inferiority had given every appearance of a natural inferiority. How otherwise would so intelligent a man as Thomas Jefferson have reached the conclusions that he did?

"Comparing them [Negroes in North America] by their faculties of memory, reason and imagination," Jefferson was writing after more than a century of intensive slaving had passed by, "it appears to me that in memory they are equal to the whites; in reason much inferior, as I think one could scarcely be found capable of tracing and comprehending the investigations of Euclid; and that in imagination they are dull, tasteless, and anomalous."

An American contemporary, as it happened, gave the answer to Jefferson. "Now I beg to know," wrote Imlay White in reply, "what can be more uncertain and false than estimating and comparing the intellect and talents of two descriptions of men: one enslaved, degraded and fettered in all their acts of volition . . . the other free, independent and with the advantage of appropriating the reason and science which have been the result of the study and labours of the philosophers and sensible men for centuries back?"

Was the charge of inferiority altogether a myth? To be treated as an inferior is often to become an inferior, and it is precisely because the judgments of Europe were applied, so persistently and repeatedly, to Africans who were slaves that the writing of African history for this period must involve an analysis of the European state of mind as well as of the African condition. . . .

. . . In the early days of discovery, men in Europe believed they had found partners and allies and equals in Africa. "Let them go and do business with the King of Timbuktu and Mali," Ramusio, secretary to the rulers in Venice, was urging the merchants of Italy in 1563, "and there is no doubt they will be well received there with their ships and their goods, and treated well, and granted the favours that they ask. . . ."

Four hundred years afterwards, other men in Europe were sure that Africans had never so much as known the rudiments of political organization, let alone the means of building powerful states and operating central governments; Africans, it would be commonly said, simply lacked the faculty for growing up. "Their inherent mental inferiority, almost more marked than their physical characters," Professor

Keane was writing with assured Victorian complacency in 1896, "depends on physiological causes. . . ." Once an African grew beyond childhood, Richard Burton had decided a little earlier, "his mental development is arrested, and thenceforth he grows backwards instead of forwards." . . .

. . . In the year 1441, just half a century before Christopher Columbus crossed the Atlantic, there sailed from Portugal "a little ship" under the command of one Antam Gonçalvez. The orders of this "very young man," as he was called by Zurara, the Portuguese chronicler, were to steer southward along the western shore of Africa as other captains had done for several years before him. He was not yet to try for new discoveries but to prove his worth by shipping a cargo of skins and the oil of those "sea wolves" — sea lions — whose acquaintance the Portuguese had lately made on the Atlantic coast of Africa.

Gonçalvez and his crew took their cockleshell as far as the southern seaboard of what is now Morocco or the Spanish colony of Rio de Oro. This was a considerable achievement, for it was only seven years since the long-feared Cape Bojador had been doubled by a Portuguese ship which had then managed to return in safety. In this southward sailing it was not the going beyond Bojador that was difficult but the returning: on that coast the winds blow always from the northward. Only with their recent adaptation of the lateen sail of the eastern Mediterranean were the Portuguese capable of sailing close enough to the wind to enable them to count on getting safely back again.

Having persevered southward for as far as he judged it wise or useful to the winning of a reputation, the youthful Gonçalvez conceived the idea of pleasing his royal master, Prince Henry of Portugal, by capturing some of the inhabitants of this unknown southern land. "O how fair a thing it would be," Zurara makes him say to his crew, "if we, who have come to this land for a cargo of such petty merchandise, were to meet with the good luck to bring the first captives before the face of our Prince."

On the following night Gonçalvez went ashore with nine of his men. "When they were about a league distant from the sea they came on a path which they kept, thinking some man or woman might come by there whom they could capture; but it happened otherwise." They pushed on for another three leagues, and there they "found the footmarks of men and youths, the number of whom, according to their estimate, would be from forty to fifty, and these led the opposite way from where our men were going."

Should they persist or go back? Heat, fatigue, and thirst discouraged the raiders. They decided to give up. But while returning over the sand-warm dunes to the sea, "they saw a naked man following a camel, with two assegais in his hand, and as our men pursued him there was not one who felt aught of his great fatigue. But though he was only one, and saw the others that they were many, yet [this African] had a mind to prove those arms of his right worthily and began to defend himself as best he could, showing a bolder front than his strength warranted.

"But Affonso Goterres wounded him with a javelin, and this put the Moor in such fear that he threw down his arms like a beaten man." The Portuguese took him prisoner; then, "as they were going on their way, they saw a Black Mooress come along," and so they seized her too.

Spear to spear — such is the first recorded skirmish of Europeans and Africans south of the Sahara. The Moor was probably a Berber of the Sanhaja Tawreg of the far western desert, while the woman may have been a Negro slave in Sanhaja keeping. And this capture was otherwise no different from countless other episodes of the time, except that it was made by men from Europe, since the first thought of such raiders was to seize prisoners who might tell them the nature of the land and its people.

This need for information merged in Europe, as in Africa, with the commercial and social advantages of capturing people who could be sold as slaves. Portugal was full of Moorish captives, but the market was still a good one. The taking of prisoners for information led to kidnaping for profit. Luck had it that another Portuguese venturer, Nuño Tristão, was also on the coast. Tristao joined the little ship of Gonçalvez and, thanks again to Zurara, we have an almost direct and altogether dramatic record of what these raiders did together. The newcomer, "a youthful knight very valiant and ardent," was captain of an armed caravel with orders both to explore the coast and to take captives "as best he could." The two captains decided on a joint enterprise.

"And so it chanced that in the night" — after their landing together — "they came to where the natives lay scattered in two encampments. . . . And when our men had come nigh to them, they attacked [the natives] very lustily, shouting at the tops of their voices 'Portugal' and 'Santiago,' the fright of which so abashed the enemy that it threw them all into disorder.

"And so, all in confusion, [the natives] began to fly without any order or carefulness. Except indeed that the men made some show of defending themselves with their assegais (for they knew not the use of any other weapon), especially one of them who fought face to face with Nuño Tristão, defending himself till he received his death. And besides this one, whom Nuño Tristão slew by himself, the others killed three and took ten prisoners, what of men women and boys. And it is doubted that they would have slain and taken many more, if they had all fallen on together at the first onslaught."

These twelve captives they carried back with them to Lisbon, and one of the Africans, a man who claimed to be of chiefly birth, explained to the Portuguese what manner of land he had come from. Much encouraged, Prince Henry thereupon sent a special embassy to the Pope, explaining his plans for further raid and even conquest; and the Pope, welcoming this new crusade, granted "to all of those who shall be engaged in the said war, complete forgiveness of all their sins."

The prisoner of chiefly birth "greatly desired to be free, and often asked Gonçalvez to take him back to his country, where he declared he would give for himself five or six Black Moors." In the end he had his way. Gonçalvez sailed once more to the southward and ransomed this prisoner and another for "ten blacks, male and female, from various countries" — Negro slaves, that is, of the Sanhaja Berbers of Mauretania; and these in turn he brought back to Lisbon.

So far, the score was only twenty. Now it rose by leaps and bounds. In 1443–1444 Nuño Tristão, again far down the western coast, reached the island of Arguim, soon to become famous in Portuguese slaving annals, and seized twenty-nine men and women from canoes in which they were paddling near the shore. And now the critics at home were confounded. Many had blamed Prince Henry for incurring the expense of sending ships where nothing seemed more likely than their total loss. "And the worst of it was that besides what the vulgar said among themselves, people of more importance talked about it in a mocking manner, declaring that no profit would result from all this toil and expense.

"But when they saw the first Moorish captives brought home" from the African coast, "and the second cargo that followed these, they became already somewhat doubtful about the opinion they had at first expressed; and altogether renounced it when they saw the third consignment that Nuno Tristao brought home, captured in so short a time, and with so little trouble. . . ."

Such was the effect that so small a cargo as twenty-nine slaves could have on medieval Lisbon. The critics changed their tune, "and their covetousness now began to wax greater. And as they saw the houses of others full to overflowing of male and female slaves, and their property increasing, they thought about the whole matter and began to talk among themselves." The outcome of their talking was financial support for a large expedition of six ships under Lançarote and Gil Eannes (he who had first passed southward beyond Cape Bojador in 1434), and a small-scale war on the western coast in which one hundred and sixty-five men, women, and children were taken captive "besides those that perished and were killed."

Beating northward, Lançarote and Eannes looked for still more captives. Fifteen Portuguese were ordered to "march along the land, and look if they could see any Moors, or find any trace of them." The ships stood off from the flat coastline while boats were launched to row along the shore within sight of the marching men. "And on their way they saw the Moors flying as fast as they could; for they had already caught sight of [the Portuguese]; and at once all our men leaped on shore and began to run after them. But as yet they could not overtake the Moor men, but only the women and little children, not able to run so fast, of whom they caught seventeen or eighteen." The whole expedition reached Lagos in southern Portugal with two hundred and thirty-five captives. With this pathetic triumph the oversea slave trade may really be said to have begun. . . .

. . . Misunderstandings grew apace. Fear and ignorance quickened on either side into beliefs that were strange, but also strangely alike. There came into being a "community of legend." Nothing shows this better than the currency of thought about man-eating.

Cannibalism certainly existed in Africa. Some African peoples had long practiced the ritual eating of the flesh of their especially honored enemies. Now and then, no doubt, famine drove men to eat each other. None of this was exclusive to humanity in Africa; although at one or two points, and for reasons that were evidently not disconnected with the slave trade, cannibal habits appear to have gained a destructive hold.

Yet most Europeans who thought of Africa were convinced from early times that it was the general custom in that continent for men to eat their fellows from taste and preference. A good illustration of this fantasy may be found in Cavazzi's celebrated description of the three African kingdoms of Congo, Matamba, and Angola. The artist in that fine quarto volume, published at Bologna in 1687, gave free rein to popular belief. He offered a splendidly graphic line engraving of a cannibal scene: several Angolans butchering human limbs and cooking them on a gridiron.

Now the odd thing is that this cannibal myth worked both ways. The drawing in Cavazzi's book occurs on page 32. But a little beyond, on page 164, Cavazzi is describing how the slaves of Angola have a particular horror of being shipped away. Why? Because, he writes, they are convinced that Europeans want them, not for labor, but for turning into oil and charcoal — or simply for eating. Europeans learned with surprise that Africans generally believed them to be great and irredeemable cannibals.

Many of the old descriptions of the coast record this belief, but none better than that of Olaudah Equiano, an Ibo slave who afterwards lived in London as a free man and whose book deserves respect. Captured as a young boy in about 1756, he retained a vivid memory of his fear that the stewpot was his fate. "When I looked round the ship," he recalled of the moment when he was delivered to the European slavers, "I saw a large furnace or copper boiling, and a multitude of black people of every description chained together, every one of their countenances expressing dejection and sorrow." He "no longer doubted of his fate." He turned to his companions, newly enslaved as he was, and "asked them if we were not to be eaten by those white men with horrible looks, red faces, and long hair:" . . .

. . . By the eighteenth century this slaving mythology was in full bloom on either side. Yet it remains an interesting fact that this period of the largest extension of slaving was also the period of a revised European estimate of African society. Moreover, at about this time the "noble savage" came on stage. This is noticeable as early as 1744, when William Smith, together with his own memoirs of the coast, published the account of Charles Wheeler, an agent of the Royal African Company who had seen ten years' service, evidently at Cape Coast. Wheeler's description of African life is strong on lascivious detail and was possibly written with an indulgent eye to the eighteenth century public; but there is no doubting the idyllic note. He dwells with fond amusement on this concubine with "jetty breasts" but argues strongly for the "sexual liberty" which, he says, Africans accept. They are never, he claims, tempted to rape as European men, through constant frustration, are tempted. "All the time I liv'd there, I never once heard of those detestable and unnatural Crimes of Sodomy and Bestiality, so much practis'd among Christians."

"A Guinean," says Wheeler, "by treading in the paths prescrib'd by his ancestors, paths natural, pleasant, and diverting, is in the plain road to be a good and happy man; but the European has sought so many inventions, and has endeavour'd to put so many restrictions upon nature, that it would be next to a miracle if he were either happy or good." Not entirely a balanced view, perhaps, but certainly a new one in the literature of the coast. "And I doubt not upon an impartial examination of the premises, it would be found that we Christians have as many idle ridiculous notions and customs as the natives of Guinea have, if not more. . . ."

This note was struck repeatedly in Britain and France as the antislavery campaigns grew stronger. Long-accepted beliefs were challenged by the most unlikely observers. In 1796, for example, a pensioned officer of a brigade of Scottish mercenaries in the Dutch colonial service published his memoirs of an expedition against rebel slaves in Surinam (on the northern coast of South America) during 1772–1777. The frontispiece shows the young man, whose name was Stedman, leaning on his gun while a rebel Negro lies dead at his feet. But there is a ravaged expression on Stedman's face, and the rubric underneath has these surprising words:

"From different Parents, different Climes we came,
At different Periods:" Fate still rules the same.
Unhappy Youth, while bleeding on the ground,
'Twas *Yours* to fall—but *Mine* to feel the wound.

Some of the most useful memoirs during the eighteenth century were those of ships' doctors and surgeons, men who were trained to look facts in the face. One such writer, Thomas Winterbottom, observed of the coastal Africans of the region of Sierra Leone in 1796, that they "are in general shrewd and artful, sometimes malevolent and perfidious. Their long connection with European slave traders has tutored them in the arts of deceit, so that false weights and measures, damaged goods, and all the various cheats which the ingenuity of the more enlightened European has strained itself to invent, are now detected almost as soon as they are attempted to be put into practice. It is in great measure owing to this cause that traders who visited the coast of Africa in hopes of becoming suddenly rich, disappointed in finding the natives better acquainted with the value of their country's produce than they at first supposed, and too well instructed by dear bought experience to be so grossly imposed upon as formerly, have drawn of them so foul a picture as they could invent. . . ."

This new tone of cool inquiry, cutting through the mist of legend, was partly cause and partly effect of the antislaving agitations of the last quarter of the eighteenth century. It is of great importance in European literature about Africa. Henceforward, Europeans would be increasingly divided into two opposed views: one, the traditional, tending to hold that Africa had never possessed cultures that were worthy of respect or even of serious investigation; the other, the scientific, tending to argue the reverse.

One may reasonably think that the ending of the slave trade must have reinforced this spirit of inquiry. This happened to some extent. But the trade was followed without much interval by colonial conquest and the "scramble for Africa"; and a new spirit of obscurantist reaction soon carried all before it. Otherwise intelligent men were writing about Africa, by the beginning of the twentieth century, with much the same condescension and contempt as their predecessors of earlier times. "People more animal-like than reasonable," Cavazzi had declared of the Angolans in 1687. "Dancing among these barbarians, having no motive in the virtuous talent of displaying the movement of the body, or the agility of the feet, aims only at the vicious satisfaction of a libidinous appetite." Such words read oddly in our day; yet the records of the colonial period are full of remarks no less absurd.

By 1900 the average European opinion about Africa — though there were some memorable exceptions — showed scarcely a trace of the stubborn curiosity which men like Winterbottom had deployed a century earlier. Sir Harry Johnston is a case in point. He knew some parts of Africa fairly well; yet none of his experience stopped him from accepting the doctrines of the day. Indeed, he swallowed them whole. For him, as for others, all signs of civilization in Africa were to be attributed to outside influence. "Undoubtedly," he wrote in 1910, "the influence of the Portuguese . . . wrought some surprising movements all along the coast of West Africa and in the southern basin of the Congo, by which organised kingdoms arose which created and stimulated commerce, and which in their general effects on the people were perhaps less drearily horrible than the anarchy of cannibal savages." Yet the truth — as any diligent inquirer could have known even in 1910 — was precisely the reverse. For the kingdoms of the Congo had preceded the Portuguese; and the Portuguese, far from creating them, had in truth destroyed them.

The tide of reaction flowed far and wide; and some of its racialist inundations are mournfully with us to this day. Johnston was a man of liberal reputation in the England of his time, yet he could airily dismiss the consequences of the slave trade for Africa as small or nonexistent. No doubt unconsciously, he repeated the opinions of the Liverpool slavers of the eighteenth century who had claimed that the trade could even bring "an access of happiness" to Africa. "So far as the sum of human misery in Africa was concerned," he wrote, "it is probable that the trade in slaves between that continent and America scarcely added to it. It even to some extent mitigated the suffering of the negro in his own home; for once this trade was set on foot and it was profitable to sell a human being, many a man, woman or child who might otherwise have been killed for mere caprice, or for the love of seeing blood flow, or as a toothsome ingredient of a banquet, was sold to a slave-trader. . . ."

. Such language passed for serious comment in high colonial times. Only at the end of the imperial epoch, still many years ahead when Johnston wrote his books, would Europeans and Americans begin to look at Africa systematically, and as a subject in its own right rather than a mere object of pity, amazement, or contempt. . . .

This selection is abridged from *The African Slave Trade: Precolonial History 1450–1480*, by Basil Davidson ©1961 by Basil Davidson. Reprinted by permission of Little, Brown & Co. in association with The Atlantic Monthly Press, pp. 3-4, 5-6, 6-7, 33-37, 96-98, & 98-102.

TRADE SLAVERY AND BRITISH DEVELOPMENT

Eric Williams

According to Adam Smith, the discovery of America and the Cape route to India are "the two greatest and most important events recorded in the history of mankind." The importance of the discovery of America lay not in the precious metals it provided but in the new and inexhaustible market it afforded for European commodities. One of its principal effects was to "raise the mercantile system to a degree of splendour and glory which it could never otherwise have attained to."(1) It gave rise to an enormous increase in world trade. The seventeenth and eighteenth centuries were the centuries of trade, as the nineteenth century was the century of production. For Britain that trade was primarily the triangular trade. In 1718 William Wood said that the slave trade was "the spring and parent whence the others flow."(2) A few years later Postlethwayt described the slave trade as "the first principle and foundation of all the rest, the mainspring of the machine which sets every wheel in motion."(3)

In this triangular trade England — France and Colonial America equally — supplied the experts and the ships; Africa the human merchandise; the plantations the colonial raw materials. The slave ship sailed from the home country with a cargo of manufactured goods. These were exchanged at a profit on the coast of Africa for Negroes, who were traded on the plantations, at another profit, in exchange for a cargo of colonial produce to be taken back to the home country. As the volume of trade increased, the triangular trade was supplemented, but never supplanted, by a direct trade between home country and the West Indies, exchanging home manufactures directly for colonial produce.

The triangular trade thereby gave a triple stimulus to British industry. The Negroes were purchased with British manufactures; transported to the plantations, they produced sugar, cotton, indigo, molasses and other tropical products, the processing of which created new industries in England; while the maintenance of the Negroes and their owners on the plantations provided another market for British industry, New England agriculture and the Newfoundland fisheries. By

1750 there was hardly a trading or a manufacturing town in England which was not in some way connected with the triangular or direct colonial trade.(4) The profits obtained provided one of the main streams of that accumulation of capital in England which financed the Industrial Revolution.

The West Indian islands became the hub of the British Empire, of immense importance to the grandeur and prosperity of England. It was the Negro slaves who made these sugar colonies the most precious colonies ever recorded in the whole annals of imperialism. To Postlethwayt they were "the fundamental prop and support" of the colonies, "valuable people" whose labor supplied Britain with all plantation produce. The British Empire was "a magnificent superstructure of American commerce and naval power on an African foundation."(5)

Sir Josiah Child estimated that every Englishman in the West Indies, "with the ten blacks that work with him, accounting what they eat, use and wear, would make employment for four men in England."(6) By Davenant's computation one person in the islands, white or Negro, was as profitable as seven in England.(7) Another writer considered that every family in the West Indies gave employment to five seamen and many more artificers, manufacturers and tradesmen, and that every white person in the islands brought in ten pounds annually clear profit to England, twenty times as much as a similar person in the home country.(8) William Wood reckoned that a profit of seven shillings per head annum was sufficient to enrich a country; each white man in the colonies brought a profit of over seven pounds.(9) Sir Dalby Thomas went further — every person employed on the sugar plantations was 130 times more valuable to England than one at home.(10) Professor Pitman has estimated that in 1775 British West Indian plantations represented a valuation of fifty millions sterling,(11) and the sugar planters themselves put the figure at seventy millions in 1788.(12) In 1798 Pitt assessed the annual income from West Indian plantations at four million pounds as compared with one million from the rest of the world.(13) As Adam Smith wrote: "The profits of a sugar plantation in any of our West Indian colonies are generally much greater than those of any other cultivation that is known either in Europe or America."(14)

According to Davenant, Britain's total trade at the end of the seventeenth century brought in a profit of £2,000,000. The plantation trade accounted for £600,000; re-export of plantation goods £120,000; European, African and Levant trade £600,000; East India trade £500,000; re-export of East India goods £800,000.(15) ...

... The amazing value of these West Indian colonies can more graphically be presented by comparing individual West Indian islands with individual mainland colonies. In 1697 British imports from Barbados were five times the combined imports from the bread colonies; the exports to Barbados were slightly larger. Little Barbados, with its 166 square miles, was worth more to British capitalism than New England, New York and Pennsylvania combined. In 1773 British imports from Jamaica were more than five times the combined imports from the bread colonies; British exports to Jamaica were nearly one-third larger than those to New England and only slightly less than those to New York and Pennsylvania combined. For the years 1714–1773 British imports from Montserrat were three times the imports from Pennsylvania, imports from Nevis were almost double those from New York, imports from Antiqua were over three times those from New England. Imports from Barbados were more than twice as large as those from the bread colonies, imports from Jamaica nearly six times as large. For the same years Jamaica as an export market was as valuable as New England; Barbados and Antigua combined meant as much to British exporters as New York; Montserrat and Nevis combined were a better market than Pennsylvania. British exports to Africa during these years were only one-tenth less than those to New England, British imports from Africa one-quarter more than those from New York and more than double those from Pennsylvania.(16)

Mercantilists were enthusiastic. The triangular trade, and the associated trade with the sugar islands, because of the navigation they encouraged, were more valuable to England than her mines of tin or coal.(17) These were ideal colonies.

But for them Britain would have no gold or silver, except what she received from illicit commerce with the Spanish colonies, and an unfavorable balance of trade.(18) Their tropical products, unlike those of the northern part of the mainland, did not compete with those of the home country. They showed little sign of that industrial development which was the constant fear where the mainland was concerned. Their large black population was an effective guarantee against aspirations to independence.(19) It all combined to spell one word, sugar. "The pleasure, glory and grandeur of England," wrote Sir Dalby Thomas, "has been advanced more by sugar than by any other commodity, wool not excepted."(20) . . .

. . . This external trade naturally drew in its wake a tremendous development of shipping and shipbuilding. Not the least of the advantages of the triangular trade was its contribution to the wooden walls of England. There was less distinction between a merchant ship and a man-of-war in those days than there is today. The "long voyage" was an admirable nursery for the seamen, the merchantmen invaluable aides to the navy in time of war; and advocates of the slave trade argued that its abolition would annihilate the marine by cutting off a great source of seamen.(21) As one Liverpool slave trader wrote: "It is a matter of too much importance to this kingdom — when ever it is *abolish'd* the naval importance of this kingdom is abolish'd with it, that moment our flagg will gradually cease to ride triumphant on the seas."(22)

In 1678 the Commissioners of Customs reported that the plantation trade was one of the great nurseries of the shipping and seamen of England and one of the greatest branches of its trade.(23) Here again the sugar colonies outdistanced the bread colonies. More English ships sailed to the sugar colonies than to all the mainland colonies combined. In 1690 the sugar colonies employed 114 ships, of 13,600 tons and 1,203 seamen; the mainland colonies 111 ships, of 14,320 tons and 1,271 seamen.(24) Between 1710 and 1714, 122,000 tons of British shipping sailed to the West Indies, 112,000 tons to the mainland.(25) The West Indian trade in 1709 employed one-tenth of British shipping engaged in foreign trade.(26) Between 1709 and 1787 British shipping engaged in foreign trade quadrupled,(27) ships clearing for Africa multiplied twelve times and the tonnage eleven times.(28)

Shipbuilding in England received a direct stimulus from the triangular trade. Vessels of a particular type were constructed for the slave trade, combining capacity with speed in an effort to reduce mortality. Many shipwrights in Liverpool were themselves slave traders. The outstanding firm was Baker and Dawson, one of the largest exporters of slaves to the West Indies, and engaged, after 1783, in the supplying of slaves to the Spanish colonies. John Gorell was one of the Liverpool members of the Company of Merchants trading to Africa. So was John Okill, one of Liverpool's most successful shipbuilders, but apparently he eschewed the slave trade. In a port whose prosperity was intimately connected with the slave trade, William Rathbone was a curiosity in his refusal to supply timber for the construction of vessels to be employed in the slave trade,(29) in which half of Liverpool's sailors were engaged.(30)

The shipping industry was divided, as industry in general, on the question of the organization of the slave trade. Some sections favored the Royal African Company, others the free traders.(31) But on the question of abolition the industry presented a united front, arguing that abolition would strike at the very roots of Britain's naval and imperial supremacy. The first reaction of Liverpool to the act of 1788 regulating the capacity of slavers was that it left 22 masters of slave ships, 47 mates and 350 seamen unemployed, with their families and the tradesmen dependent more indirectly on the trade with Africa.(32)

In addition to the seamen, there were the ancillary trades. Carpenters, painters and boat-builders; tradesmen and artisans connected with repairs, equipment and lading; commissions, wages, dock duties, insurances — all depended partly on the ships trading to Africa. To supply the ships, there were in 1774 fifteen roperies in Liverpool.(33) There were few people in the town, it was claimed, who would not be affected, directly or indirectly, by abolition.(34)

The sugar islands made yet another contribution to the growth of shipping. The peculiar economy developed in the West Indies concentrated on export crops while food was imported. Most important of all the food supplies was fish, an article dear to the heart of every mercantilist, because it provided employment for ships and training for seamen. Laws were passed in England to encourage the consumption of fish. Friday and Saturday were set apart as fish days. Fish was an important item of the diet of the slaves on the plantations, and the English herring trade found its chief market in the sugar plantations.(35) The Newfoundland fishery depended to a considerable extent on the annual export of dried fish to the West Indies, the refuse or "poor John" fish, "fit for no other consumption."(36) A West Indian tradition was thereby fostered. Imported salted cod is still today a normal and favorite dish in all but the well-to-do West Indian families; whether it is still "fit for no other consumption" is not known. . . .

. . . The development of the triangular trade and of shipping and shipbuilding led to the growth of the great seaport towns. Bristol, Liverpool and Glasgow occupied, as seaports and trading centers, the position in the age of trade that Manchester, Birmingham and Sheffield occupied later in the age of industry.

It was said in 1685 that there was scarcely a shopkeeper in Bristol who had not a venture on board some ship bound for Virginia or the Antilles. Even the parsons talked of nothing but trade, and it was satirically alleged that Bristol freights were owned not by merchants but by mechanics.(37) Customs duties rose from £10,000 in 1634 to £334,000 in 1785. Wharfage dues, payable on every vessel above sixty tons, doubled between 1745 and 1775.(38)

It was the slave and sugar trades which made Bristol the second city of England for the first three-quarters of the eighteenth century. "There is not," wrote a local annalist, "a brick in the city but what is cemented with the blood of a slave. Sumptuous mansions, luxurious living, liveried menials, were the produce of the wealth made from the sufferings and groans of the slaves bought and sold by the

Bristol merchants. . . . In their childlike simplicity they could not feel the iniquity of the merchandise, but they could feel it lucrative."(39) An analysis of a committee set up in 1789 to oppose the movement for abolition of the slave trade shows that among the members elected were nine merchants at some time mayors of Bristol, five who were sheriffs, seven had been or were to be Masters of the Society of Merchant Venturers.(40)

When Bristol was outstripped in the slave trade by Liverpool, it turned its attention from the triangular trade to the direct sugar trade. Fewer Bristol ships sailed to Africa, more went directly to the Caribbean. In 1700 the port had forty-six ships in the West Indian trade.(41) In 1787 there were thirty Bristol vessels engaged in the slave trade, seventy-two in the West Indian trade; the former averaged 140 tons each, the latter 240.(42) In 1788 Bristol had as many ships in the trade to the Leeward Islands, and almost as many in the trade to Jamaica, as in the trade to Africa.(43) Nearly one-third of the tonnage which entered, more than one-third of that which sailed from, the port was engaged in the trade with the sugar colonies,(44) and it was the amiable custom in Bristol to celebrate the arrival of the first sugar ship each year by a gift of wine at the expense of the fortunate owner.(45) The West Indian trade was worth to Bristol twice as much as all her other overseas commerce combined. As late as 1830 five-eighths of its trade was with the West Indies, and it was said in 1833 that without the West Indian trade Bristol would be a fishing port.(46)

Bristol had a West Indian Society of its own. The Town Council distributed municipal funds for the relief of distress caused by fire in the sugar islands. It was customary for younger sons and junior members of West Indian firms to spend some years on the plantations before entering business at home. Bristol members of Parliament in the eighteenth century were frequently associated, in one way or another, with the sugar plantations, and so important did the islands become to Bristol that for the first half of the nineteenth century Bristol was always represented in Parliament by a West Indian — a Baillie, a Protheroe, or a Miles. James Evan Baillie exhorted his fellow citizens not to lay the axe at the root of their own prosperity by supporting the abolition of slavery in the islands.(47) His own prosperity was also at stake. The compensation paid to the family for their ownership of numerous slaves in Trinidad and British Guiana exceeded £62,000.(48) Bristol presented a determined opposition to the equalization of the sugar duties which gave the *coup de grace* to the West Indian monopoly. Thereafter Bristol's trade with the West Indies declined rapidly. In 1847 forty per cent of the port's tonnage was bound for the West Indies, and ships returning from the islands constituted less than two per cent of the arrivals. Bristol's trade with the islands did not revive until the end of the nineteenth century with the advent of the banana in the world market.(49)

What the West Indian trade did for Bristol the slave trade did for Liverpool. In 1565 Liverpool had 138 householders, seven streets only were inhabited, the port's merchant marine amounted to twelve ships of 223 tons. Until the end of the seventeenth century the only local event of importance was the siege of the town during the English Civil War.(50) In collecting ship money Strafford assessed Liverpool at fifteen pounds; Bristol paid two thousand.(51) The shipping entering Liverpool increased four and a half times between 1709 and 1771; the outward tonnage six and a half times. The number of ships owned by the port multiplied four times during the same period, the tonnage and sailors over six times.(52) Customs receipts soared from an average of £51,000 for the years 1750 to 1757 to £648,000 in 1785.(53) Dock duties increased two and a half times between 1752 and 1771.(54) The population rose from 5,000 in 1700 to 34,000 in 1773. By 1770 Liverpool had become too famous a town in the trading world for Arthur Young to pass it by on his travels over England.(55)

The abolitionist Clarkson argued that the rise of Liverpool was due to a variety of causes, among which were the salt trade, the prodigious increase of the population of Lancashire, and the rapid and great extension of the manufactures of Manchester.(56) This is a particularly flagrant case of putting the cart before the horse. It was only the capital accumulation of Liverpool which called the population of Lancashire into existence and stimulated the manufactures of Manchester. That capital accumulation came from the slave trade, whose importance was appreciated more by contemporaries than by later historians.

It was a common saying that several of the principal streets of Liverpool had been marked out by the chains, and the walls of the houses cemented by the blood, of the African slaves,(57) and one street was nicknamed "Negro Row."(58) The red brick Customs House was blazoned with Negro heads.(59) The story is told of an actor in the town, who, hissed by the audience for appearing before them, not for the first time, in a drunken condition, steadied himself and declared with offended majesty: "I have not come here to be insulted by a set of wretches, every brick in whose infernal town is cemented with an African's blood."(60)

It was estimated in 1790 that the 138 ships which sailed from Liverpool for Africa represented a capital of over a million pounds. Liverpool's own probable loss from the abolition of the slave trade was then computed at over seven and a half million pounds.(61) Abolition, it was said, would ruin the town. It would destroy the foundation of its commerce and the first cause of the national industry and wealth. "What vain pretence of liberty," it was asked in Liverpool, "can infatuate people to run into so much licentiousness as to assert a trade is unlawful which custom immemorial, and various Acts of Parliament, have ratified and given a sanction to?"(62) . . .

. . . It is necessary now to trace the industrial development in England which was stimulated directly or indirectly by the goods for the triangular trade and the processing of colonial produce.

The widespread ramifications of the slave trade in English industry are illustrated by this cargo to Africa for the year 1787: cotton and linen goods, silk handkerchiefs, coarse blue and red woolen cloths, scarlet cloth in grain, coarse and fine hats, worsted caps, guns, powder, shot, sabers, lead bars, iron bars, pewter basons, copper kettles and pans, iron pots, hardware of various kinds, earthen and glass ware, hair and gilt leather trunks, beads of various kinds, silver and gold rings and ornaments, paper, coarse and fine checks, linen ruffled shirts and caps, British and foreign spirits and tobacco.(63)

This sundry assortment was typical of the slave trader's cargo. Finery for Africans, household utensils, cloths of all kinds, iron and other metals, together with guns, handcuffs and fetters: the production of these stimulated capitalism, provided employment for British labor, and brought great profits to England.

Until the tremendous development of the cotton industry in the Industrial Revolution, wool was the spoiled child of English manufactures. It figured largely in all considerations affecting the slave trade in the century after 1680. The cargo of a slave ship was incomplete without some woolen manufactures — serges, says, perpetuanos, arrangoes and bays. Sometimes the cloth was called after the locality where it was first manufactured. Bridwaters represented Bridgewater's interest in the colonial market; Welsh Plaines, a woolen cloth of the simplest weave, was manufactured in western England and Wales.

A parliamentary committee of 1695 voiced the public sentiment that the trade to Africa was an encouragement to the woolen manufacture.(64) Among the arguments put forward to prove the importance of the slave trade, the exports of wool which that trade encouraged were always given first place. A pamphlet of 1680, illustrating the public utility and advantages of the African trade, begins with "the exportation of our native woollen and other manufactures in great abundance, most of which were imported formerly out of Holland . . . whereby the wooll of this nation is much more consumed and spent then formerly; and many thousand of the poor people imployed."(65) Similarly, the Royal African Company stated in a petition in 1696 that the slave trade should be supported by England, because of the exports it encouraged of woolen and other English manufactures.(66) . . .

. . . That woolen goods should figure so prominently in tropical markets is to be attributed to the deliberate policy of mercantilist England. It was argued in 1732, on behalf of the mainland colonies, that Pennsylvania alone consumed more woolen exports from England than all the sugar islands combined, and New York more than any sugar island except Jamaica.(67) Woolen goods were more suited for these colder climates, and the Barbadian planters preferred light calicoes which could be easily washed.(68) But wool was England's staple, and climatic considerations were too great a refinement for the mercantilist mind. Any one familiar with British West Indian society today will appreciate the strength of the tradition thereby fostered. Woolen undergarments are still common in the islands today, though more among the older generation, and suits of blue serge are still a sign of the well-dressed man. Like the Englishman and unlike the North American in the colonies, the Caribbean colored middle class today still apes the fashions of the home country in its preference for the heavier materials which are so ridiculous and uncomfortable in a tropical environment.

But cotton later superseded wool in colonial markets as it did in domestic. Of a total export of four million pounds of woolen manufactures in 1772, less than three per cent went to the West Indies and less than four per cent to Africa.(69) The best customers were Europe and America. In 1783 the woolen industry was slowly beginning its belated imitation of the technological changes which had revolutionized the cotton industry. In its progress after 1783 the triangular trade and West Indian market played no appreciable part.

What the building of ships for the transport of slaves did for eighteenth century Liverpool, the manufacture of cotton goods for the purchase of slaves did for eighteenth century Manchester. The first stimulus to the growth of Cottonopolis came from the African and West Indian markets.

The growth of Manchester was intimately associated with the growth of its outlet to the sea and the world market. The capital accumulated by Liverpool from the slave trade poured into the hinterland to fertilize the energies of Manchester; Manchester goods for Africa were taken to the coast in the Liverpool slave vessels. Lancashire's foreign market meant chiefly the West Indian plantations and Africa. The export trade was £14,000 in 1739; in 1759 it had increased nearly eight times; in 1779 it was £303,000. Up to 1770 one-third of this export went to the slave coast, one-half to the American and West Indian colonies.(70) It was this tremendous dependence on the triangular trade that made Manchester.

Light woolen goods were popular on the slave coast: so were silks, provided they were gaudy and had large flowers. But the most popular of all materials was cotton goods, as the African was already accustomed to coarse blue and white cotton cloths of his own manufacture, and from the beginning the striped loincloths called "annabasses" were a regular feature of every slave trader's cargo. Indian textiles, banned in England, soon established a monopoly of the African market. Brawls, tapsells, niccanees, cuttanees, buckshaws, nillias, salempores — these Indian cloths were highly prized, and yet another powerful vested interest was drawn into the orbit of the slave trade. Manchester tried to compete with the East India Company; bafts, for example, were cheap cotton fabrics from the East later copied in England for the African market. But the backwardness of the English dyeing process made it impossible for Manchester to get the fast red, green and yellow colors popular on the coast. Manchester proved unable to imitate the colors of these Indian cottons, and there is evidence to show that the French cotton manufacturers of Normandy were equally unsuccessful in learning the secrets of the East.

Manchester was more fortunate in its trade in cotton and linen checks, though figures for the first half of the eighteenth century are unreliable. The European and colonial wars of 1739–1748 and the reorganization which the African Company was undergoing up to 1750 caused a slump in the cotton trade to Africa, and when it revived after 1750 Indian exports were inadequate to satisfy the demand. English manufacturers made full use of this opportunity to push their own goods. In 1752 the export of cotton-linen checks alone from England was £57,000; in 1763, at the end of the Seven Years' War, it stood at the exceptionally high figure of £302,000, but after 1767 remained between £100,000 and £200,000, when Indian competition again proved formidable. . . .

. . . Between the cotton manufacturers of Manchester and the slave traders there were not the close connections that have already been noticed in the case of the shipbuilders of Liverpool. But two exceptional instances of such connections exist. Two well-known cotton manufacturers of Lancashire, Sir William Fazackerly and Samuel Touchet, were both members of the Company of Merchants trading to Africa. Fazackerly, a London dealer in fustians, presented the case of the separate traders of Bristol and Liverpool against the African Company in 1726.(71) Touchet, member of a great Manchester check-making house, represented Liverpool on the governing body of the company during the period 1753–1756. He was concerned in the equipping of the expedition which captured Senegal in 1758 and tried hard to get the contract for victualling the troops. A patron of Paul's unsuccessful spinning machine intended to revolutionize the cotton industry, accused openly of attempting to monopolize the import of raw cotton, Touchet added to his many interests a partnership, with his brothers, in about twenty ships in the West Indian trade. Touchet died, leaving a large fortune, and was described in his obituary notice as "the most considerable merchant and manufacturer in

Manchester, remarkable for great abilities and strict integrity, and for universal benevolence and usefulness to mankind." Two modern writers have left us this description of the man: "Icarus-like soaring too high," he emerges as "the first considerable financier that the Manchester trade produced, and certainly as one of the earliest cases of a Manchester man who was concerned at once in manufacturing and in large scale financial and commercial ventures in the City and abroad."(72)

Other cases emphasize the significance of Touchet's career. Robert Diggles, African slave trader of Liverpool, was the son of a Manchester linen draper and brother of another. In 1747 a Manchester man was in partnership with two Liverpool men in a voyage to Jamaica. A leading Manchester firm, the Hibberts, owned sugar plantations in Jamaica, and at one time supplied checks and imitations of Indian goods to the African Company for the slave trade.(73)

Manchester received a double stimulus from the colonial trade. If it supplied the goods needed on the slave coast and on the plantations, its manufacturers depended in turn on the supply of the raw material. Manchester's interest in the islands was two-fold.

The raw material came to England in the seventeenth and eighteenth centuries chiefly from two sources, the Levant and the West Indies. In the eighteenth century that Indian competition which proved too formidable for Manchester on the slave coast and which was threatening to swamp even the home market with Indian goods was effectively smashed, as far as England was concerned, by the prohibitive duties on Indian imports into England. The first step was thereby taken by which the motherland of cotton became in the nineteenth and twentieth centuries the chief market of Lancashire. In the eighteenth century the measure gave Manchester a monopoly of the home market, and private Indian traders began to import the raw cotton for the Lancashire factories. A competitor to the West Indian islands had arisen, to be followed later by Brazil, whose product by 1783 was recognized as clearly superior to all the other varieties. . . .

. . . The processing of colonial raw materials gave rise to new industries in England, provided further employment for shipping, and contributed to a greater extension of the world market and international trade. Of these raw materials sugar was pre-eminent, and its manufacture gave birth to the sugar refining industry. The refining process transformed the crude brown sugar manufactured on the plantations into white sugar, which was durable and capable of preservation, and could be easily handled and distributed all over the world.

The earliest reference to sugar refining in England is an order of the Privy Council in 1615 prohibiting aliens from erecting sugar houses or practising the art of refining sugar.(74) The importance of the industry increased in proportion to its production on the plantations, and as sugar became, with the spread of tea and coffee, one of the necessities of life instead of the luxury of kings.

About the middle of the eighteenth century there were 120 refineries in England. Each refinery was estimated to provide employment for about nine men. In addition the distribution of the refined product called into existence a number of subsidiary trades and required ships and wagons for the coastal and inland trade.(75)

The sugar refining industry of Bristol was one of the most important of the kingdom. It was in Bristol in 1654 that the diarist, Evelyn, saw for the first time the method of manufacturing loaf sugar,(76) and in the annals of Britsol's history sugar figures frequently as a gift to distinguished visitors to the town — Richard, son of Oliver Cromwell, and King Charles II, in return for which the king knighted four of the town's merchants.(77)

In 1799, there were twenty refineries in Bristol, and the town did more refining than London in proportion to size and population. Bristol's sugar was considered superior in quality, its proximity to the coal supplies for fuel enabled it to sell cheaper than London, while it found in Ireland, the whole of South Wales and West England the markets for which it was destined by its geographical location.(78) Sugar refining long remained one of the staples of Bristol. The refiners of the city petitioned Parliament in 1789 against the abolition of the slave trade on which "the welfare and prosperity, if not the actual existence, of the West India Islands depend."(79) In 1811 there were sixteen refineries in the town, whose connection with this industry ceased only towards the end of the nineteenth century, when bananas replaced sugar.(80)

Some of Bristol's most prominent citizens were connected with the sugar refining business. Robert Aldworth, seventeenth century alderman, was closely identified with refining, while he was at the same time a merchant who built two docks to accommodate the increased shipping.(81) William Miles was the outstanding refiner of the eighteenth century. His career is typical of many other cases. Miles came to Bristol with three half-pence in his pocket, worked as a porter, apprenticed himself to a shipbuilder, saved fifteen pounds, and sailed to Jamaica as a ship's carpenter in a merchantman. He bought a cask or two of sugar which he sold in Bristol, at a huge profit, and with the proceeds bought articles in great demand in Jamaica and repeated his former investment. Miles soon became very wealthy and settled in Bristol as a refiner. This was the humble origin of one of the greatest fortunes made in the West Indian trade. Taking his son into partnership, Miles was wealthy enough to give him a check for £100,000 to enable him to marry the daughter of an aristocratic clergyman. The elder Miles became an alderman, and died rich and honored; the younger continued as a West Indian merchant dealing chiefly in sugar and slaves, and at his death in 1848 left property valued at more than a million.(82) In 1833 he was in possession of 663 slaves in Trinidad and Jamaica, for which he received compensation in the amount of £17,850.(83)

The frequent association of Glasgow with the tobacco industry is only a part of the truth. The prosperity of the town in the eighteenth century was due at least as much to its sugar refining business. Sugar refining dated back to the second half of the seventeenth century. The Wester sugar-house was built in 1667, followed by the Easter in 1669, and shortly after the South sugar-house and another. Yet another followed in 1701. But Glasgow labored under the disadvantage that before 1707 direct trade relations with the colonies were illegal, and Glasgow's sugar refiners were forced to depend on Bristol for their raw material. By the Act of Union and a happy accident this unsatisfactory situation was brought to an end. Two Scotch officers, Colonel William Macdowall, cadet of an ancient family, and Major James Milliken, while quartered in St. Kitts, wooed and won two heiresses, the widow Tovie and her daughter, owners of great sugar plantations. The missing link had been found. The arrival of the heiresses and their husbands meant that Glasgow became one of the leading ports of entry for the cargoes of West Indian sugar. In the very year of the happy event a new refinery was set up.(84)

The majority of the refineries were located in and around the capital — eighty compared with Bristol's twenty. In 1774 there were eight refineries in Liverpool, one of them, the house of Branckers, a firm also engaged in the slave trade, being one of the most extensive in the whole kingdom.(85) There were others in Manchester, Chester, Lancashire, Whitehaven, Newcastle, Hull, Southampton and Warrington.

It may well be asked why the refining of the raw sugar was not done at the source, on the plantations. The division of labor, between the agricultural operations in the tropical climate, and the industrial operations in the temperate climate, has survived to this day. The original reason had nothing to do with the skill of labor or the presence of natural resources. It was the result of the deliberate policy of the mother country. The ban on sugar refining in the islands corresponded to the ban on iron and textile manufacture on the mainland. Should they have refiners in England or the plantations? asked Sir Thomas Clifford in 1671. "Five ships go for the blacks," was his answer, "and not above two if refined in the plantations; and so you destroy shipping, and all that belongs to it; and if you lose this advantage to England, you lose all." Hence the heavy duty placed on refined sugar imported into England, four times as much as upon the brown sugar. By this policy England was called upon for a larger number of casks for the raw sugar, more coals and victuals were consumed, and the national revenues increased.(86) Davenant's pleas for permission of colonial refining(87) fell on deaf ears.

It is significant that a similar struggle was taking place in France, resulting in a similar victory for the mercantilists. Colbert had permitted the refining of sugar in the French West Indies, and raw and refined sugar from the islands paid the same duty in France. But in 1682 the duty on refined sugar was doubled, while two years later, under penalty of a fine of 3,000 livres, it was forbidden to erect new refineries in the islands. A decree of 1698 was even more drastic. The duty on raw sugar from the West Indies was lowered from four to three livres per hundredweight, while the duty on refined sugar was increased from eight to twenty-two and a half livres. This latter figure was the same duty charged on refined sugar from foreign lands: "the drastic nature of the protection afforded the French refiners as against their compatriots in the colonies becomes apparent."(88) ....

... Yet another colonial raw material gave birth to yet another English industry. One of the important by-products of sugar is molasses, from which rum may be distilled. But rum never attained the importance of cotton, far less of sugar, as a contribution to British industry, partly, perhaps, because much rum was imported direct from the islands in its finished state. Imports from the islands increased from 58,000 gallons in 1721 to 320,000 in 1730. In 1763 the figure stood at one and a quarter million gallons and was steadily over two million between 1765 and 1779.(89)

Rum was indispensable in the fisheries and the fur trade, and as a naval ration. But its connection with the triangular trade was more direct still. Rum was an essential part of the cargo of the slave ship, particularly the colonial American slave ship. No slave trader could afford to dispense with a cargo of rum. It was profitable to spread a taste for liquor on the coast. The Negro dealers were plied with it, were induced to drink till they lost their reason, and then the bargain was struck.(90) One slave dealer, his bag full of the gold paid him for his slaves, stupidly accepted the slave captain's invitation to dinner. He was made drunk and awoke next morning to find his money gone and himself stripped, branded and enslaved with his own victims, to the great mirth of the sailors.(91) In 1765 two distilleries were established at Liverpool for the express purpose of supplying ships bound for Africa.(92) Of equal importance to the mercantilist was the fact that from molasses could be obtained, in addition to rum, brandy and low wines imported from France. The distilleries were an important evidence of Bristol's interest in the sugar plantations, and many were the jeremiads which they sent to Parliament in defence of their interests and in opposition to the importation of French brandies. Bishop Berkeley voiced the prevailing feeling when he asked acidly, in strict mercantilist language, "whether if drunkenness be a necessary evil, men may not as well get drunk with the growth of their own country?"

The eighteenth century in England was notorious for its alcoholism. The popular drink was gin, immortalized by Hogarth in his *Gin Lane*. A classic advertisement of a gin shop in Southwark read: "Drunk for a penny, dead drunk for two-pence, clean straw for nothing." Gin and rum contended for pride of place. . . .

. . . Slave trading demanded goods more gruesome though not a whit less useful than woolen and cotton manufacturers. Fetters and chains and padlocks were needed to fasten the Negroes more securely on the slave ships and thus prevent both mutiny and suicide. The practice of branding the slaves to identify them required red-hot irons. Legal regulations prescribed that on any ship designed for Africa, the East Indies, or the West Indies, "three-fourths of their proportion of beer was to be put in iron bound cask, hooped with iron hoops of good substance, and well wrought iron."(93) Iron bars were the trading medium on a large part of the African coast and were equivalent to four copper bars.(94) Iron bars constituted nearly three-quarters of the value of the cargo of the *Swallow* in 1679, nearly one-quarter of the cargo of the *Mary* in 1690, nearly one-fifth of a slave cargo in 1733.(95) In 1682 the Royal African Company was exporting about 10,000 bars of iron a year.(96) The ironmasters, too, found a useful market in Africa.

Guns formed a regular part of every African cargo. Birmingham became the center of the gun trade as Manchester was of the cotton trade. The struggle between Birmingham and London over the gun trade was merely another angle to the struggle for free trade or monopoly which he have already noticed for the slave trade in general between the capital and the outports. In 1709 and 1710 the gun makers of London petitioned in favor of the Royal African Company's monopoly. The Birmingham gun makers and iron makers threw their weight and influence against the company and the London interests. Three times, in 1708, 1709, and 1711, they petitioned against a renewal of the monopoly which had been modified in 1608.(97) Their trade had increased since then and they feared a renewal of the monopoly, which would subject their manufactures "to one buyer or to anyone monopolizing society, exclusive of all others."(98)

In the nineteenth century Birmingham guns were exchanged for African palm-oil, but the eighteenth century saw a less innocent exchange. The Birmingham guns of the eighteenth century were exchanged for men, and it was a common saying that the price of a Negro was one Birmingham gun. The African musket was an important Birmingham export, reaching a total of 100,000 to 150,000 annually. With the British government and the East India Company, Africa ranked as the most important customer of the Birmingham gunmakers.(99)

The needs of shipbuilding gave a further stimulus to heavy industry. The iron chain and anchor foundries, of which there were many in Liverpool, lived off the building of ships. Copper sheathing for the vessels gave rise to local industries in the town and adjacent districts to supply the demand. Between thirty and forty vessels were employed in transporting the copper, smelted in Lancashire and Cheshire, from the works at Holywell to the warehouses in Liverpool.(100)

The ironmaster's interest in the slave trade continued throughout the century. When the question of abolition came before Parliament, the manufacturers of and dealers in iron, copper, brass and lead in Liverpool petitioned against the project, which would affect employment in the town and send forth thousands as "solitary wanderers into the world, to seek employment in foreign climes."(101) In the same year Birmingham declared that it was dependent on the slave trade to a considerable extent for a large part of its various manufactures. Abolition would ruin the town and impoverish many of its inhabitants.(102) . . .

NOTES

(1) Adam Smith, *Wealth of Nations* (Cannan edition, New York: 1937), 415-416, 590-591.

(2) W. Wood, *A Survey of Trade* (London, 1718), Part III, 193.

(3) J.F. Rees, "The Phases of British Commercial Policy in the Eighteenth Century," *Economica* (June, 1925), 143.

(4) J. Gee, *The Trade and Navigation of Great Britain Considered* (Glasgow, 1750), 25-26

(5) M. Postlethwayt, *The African Trade, the Great Pillar and Support of the British Plantation Trade in North America* (London, 1745), 4, 6.

(6) *Cambridge History of the British Empire*, I, 565.

(7) C. Whitworth (ed.), *The Political and Commercial Works of Charles Davenant*, (London, 1781), II, 20.

(8) J. Bennett, *Two Letters and Several Calculations on the Sugar Colonies and Trade* (London, 1738), 55.

(9) Wood, *op. cit.*, 156.

(10) Sir D. Thomas, *An Historical Account of the Rise and Growth of the West India Colonies, and the Great Advantages they are to England, in respect to Trade* (London, 1690). The essay is printed is the Harleian Miscellany, II, 347.

(11) F.W. Pitman, "The Settlement and Financing of British West India Plantations in the Eighteenth Century," *Essays in Colonial History by Students of C.M. Andrews* (New Haven, 1931), 271.

(12) *Report of the Committee of Privy Council, 1788*, Part IV, No. 18, Appendix.

(13) J.H. Rose, *William Pitt and the Great War* (London, 1911), 370.

(14) Adam Smith, *op. cit.*, 366.

(15) Whitworth, *op. cit.*, II, 18.

(16) Trade figures have been compiled in Sir C. Whitworth, *State of the Trade of Great Britain in its imports and exports, progressively from the year 1697-1773* (London, 1776), Part II, pp. 1-2, 47-50, 53-72, 75-76, 78, 82-91.

In the general percentages given in the text for West Indian and mainland trade, I have included in the West Indies figures for 1714–1773 trade with minor places such as St. Croix, Monte Christi and St. Eastatius also trade with islands conquered by Britain in war but later restored — e.g., Cuba, Canada, Florida, etc.

(17) Bennett, *op. cit.*, 50, 54.

(18) L.F. Stocks (ed.) *Proceedings and Debates in the British Parliament Respecting North America* (Washington, D.C., 1924–1941), IV, 329. Sir John Barnard, March 28, 1737.

(19) Postlethwayt, *The African Trade, the Great Pillar . . .*, 13-14.

(20) E.D. Ellis, *An Introduction to the History of Sugar as a Commodity* (Philadelphia, 1905), 82.

(21)*Cobbett's Parliamentary History of England* (referred to hereafter as *Parl. Hist.*) XXIX, 343, Alderman Watson, April 18, 1791; E. Donnan (ed.) *Documents Illustrative of the History of the Slave Trade to America* (Washington, D.C., 1930–1935), II, 606.

(22) Holt and Gregson Papers (Liverpool Public Library), X, 429. Letter entitled "Commerce," in Gregson's handwriting, undated.

(23) G.L. Beer, *The Old Colonial System* (New York, 1933), I, 17.

(24) *Ibid.*, I, 43 n.

(25) Stock, *op. cit.*, III, 355.

(26) This proportion is obtained by taking the average of the 122,000 tons for the West Indies in the five years 1710–1714, and comparing it with the figure of 243,600 tons engaged in foreign trade in 1709, given in A.P. Usher, "The Growth of English Shipping, 1572–1922," *Quarterly Journal of Economics* (May, 1928), 469.

(27) Usher, *op. cit.*, 496. In 1787, 998,637 tons.

(28) F.W. Pitman, *The Development of the British West Indies, 1700-1763* (New Haven, 1917), 67.

(29) R. Stewart-Browne, *Liverpool Ships in the Eighteenth Century* (Liverpool, 1932), 117, 119, 126-127, 130. For Baker and Dawson's slave trading with the Spanish colonies, see Donnan, *op. cit.*, II, 577 n; H.H.S. Aimes, *A History of Slavery in Cuba, 1511 to 1868* (New York, 1907), 36: *Report of the Committee of Privy Council*, 1788, Part VI.

(30) W. Enfield, *An Essay Towards the History of Liverpool* (London, 1774), 26, gives 5,967 seamen in 1771. Gregson says 3,000 were employed in the slave trade. Holt & Gregson Papers (Liverpool Public Library), X, 434. Undated letter to T. Brooke, M.P.

(31) The shipping trades of London petitioned in 1708 in favor of the monopoly. Against the monopoly came two petitions from the shipowners of Whitehaven in 1709 and 1710; three petitions from the shipwrights of London and its environs in 1708 and 1710; and a petition from the shipwrights of several cities in 1709. Stock, *op. cit.*, III, 204 n, 207 n, 225 n, 226, 249, 250 n, 251.

(32) Holt and Gregson Papers, X, 375, 377.

(33) Enfield, *op. cit.*, 89.

(34) Holt and Gregson Papers, X, 435. Gregson to Brooke.

(35) C.M. MacInnes, *Bristol, A Gateway of Empire* (Bristol, 1939), 337.

(36) *Parl. Hist.*, XXIX, 343, Alderman Watson, April 18, 1791.

(37) J. Latimer, *Annals of Bristol in the Eighteenth Century* (Bristol, 1893), 6.

(38) W.N. Reid and J.E. Hicks, *Leading Events in the History of the Port of Bristol* (Bristol, n.d.), 106; J. Latimer, *Annls of Bristol in the Seventeenth Century* (Bristol, 1900), 334; W. Barrett, *The History and Antiquities of the City of Bristol* (Bristol, 1780), 186; J.A. Fraser, *Spain and the West Country* London, 1935), 254-255.

(39) J.F. Nicholls and J. Taylor, *Bristol Past and Present* (Bristol, 1881–1882), III, 165.

(40) MacInnes, *op. cit.*, 335.

(41) *Ibid.*, 202.

(42) *Ibid.*, 233.

(43) Barrett, *op. cit.*, 189.

(44) *Ibid.* Incoming ships from the West Indies amounted to 16,209 out of a total of 48,125 tons; outgoing ships to the West Indies represented 16,913 out of a total of 46,729 tons.

(45) MacInnes, *op. cit.*, 236, 367.

(46(*Ibid.*, 358, 370.

(47) *Ibid.*, 228, 230, 235, 363, 370.

(48) H. of C. *Sess. Pap.*, 1837-8, Vol. 48. The exact figure was £62,355.0.5. The family owned 954 slaves outright, and was part owner of another 456 (pages 117, 120, 132, 168).

(49) MacInnes, *op. cit.*, 371.

(50) Enfield, *op. cit.*, 11-12.

(51) P. Mantoux, *The Industrial Revolution in the Eighteenth Century* (London, 1928), 108.

(52) Enfield, *op. cit.*, 67.

(53) Fraser, *op. cit.*, 254-255.

(54) Enfield, *op. cit.*, 69.

(55) Mantoux, *op. cit.*, 109.

(56) T. Clarkson, *Essay on the Impolicy of the African Slave Trade* (London, 1788), 123-125.

(57) J. Corry, *The History of Lancashire* (London, 1825), II, 690.

(58) H. Smithers, *Liverpool, Its Commerce, Statistics and Institutions* (Liverpool, 1825), 105.

(59) A. Mackenzie-Grieve, *The Last Years of the English Slave Trade* (London, 1941), 4.

(60) G. Williams, *History of the Liverpool Privateers, with an Account of the Liverpool Slave Trade* (Liverpool, 1897), 594.

(61) Holt and Gregson Papers, X, 367, 369, 371, 373.

(62) J.A. Picton, *Memorials of Liverpool* (London, 1873), I, 256.

(63) Donnan, *op. cit.*, II, 567-568.

(64) Stock, *op. cit.*, II, 109.

(65) Donnan, *op. cit.*, I, 267.

(66) Stock, *op. cit.*, II, 179.

(67) Stock, *op. cit.*, IV, 161 n - 162 n.

(68) *Ibid.*, III, 45.

(69) J. James, *History of the Worsted Manufacture in England from the Earliest Times* (London, 1857), appendix, p. 7.

(70) A.S. Turberville, *Johnson's England* (Oxford, 1933), I, 231-232.

(71) Donnan, *op. cit.*, II, 337 n, 521-522n.

(72) A.P. Wadsworth and J. de L. Mann, *The Cotton Trade and Industrial Lancashire* (Manchester, 1931), 149, 156-157, 231, 233, 243-247, 447.

(73) *Ibid.*, 229 n, 231, 231 n.

(74) Fraser, *op cit.*, 241.

(75) Latimer, *Annals of Bristol in the Eighteenth Century*, 302; Pitman, *Development of the British West Indies*, 340.

(76) Nicholls and Taylor, *op. cit.*, III, 34.

(77) Latimer, *Annals of Bristol in the Seventeenth Century*, 280-281, 318-320.

(78) *The New Bristol Guide* (Bristol, 1799), 70.

(79) Donnan, *op. cit.*, II, 602-604.

(80) Reid and Hicks, *op. cit.*, 66; MacInnes, *op. cit.*, 371.

(81) Latimer, *Annals of Bristol in the Seventeenth Century*, 44-45, 88.

(82) H.R.F. Bourne, *English Merchants, Memoirs in Illustration of the Progress of British Commerce* (London, 1866) II, 17-18; J.B. Botsford, *English*

Society in the Eighteenth Century as Influenced from Overseas (New York, 1924), 120, 123.

(83) *H. of C. Sess. Paf.*, 1837-8, Vol. 48. The exact sum of £17,868.16.8 (pages 68-69, 167-168).

(84) G. Eyre-Todd, *History of Glasgow* (Glasgow, 1934), III, 39-40, 150-154.

(85) Enfield, *op. cit.*, 90; T. Kaye, *The Stranger in Liverpool; or an Historical and Descriptive View of the Town of Liverpool and its environs* (Liverpool, 1829), 184. For the Branckers and the slave trade, see Donnan, *op. cit.*, II, 655 n.

(86) Stock, *op. cit.*, I, 385, 390.

(87) Whitworth, *Works of Davenant*, II, 37.

(88) C.W. Cole, *French Mercantilism, 1683-1700* (New York, 1943), 87-88. The prohibition is still in operation today. See J.E. Dalton, *Sugar, A Case Study of Government Control* (New York, 1937), 265-274.

(89) Stock, *op. cit.*, IV, 132 n; L.J. Ragatz, *Statistics for the Study of British Caribbean History, 1763-1833* (London, n.d.), 17, Table XI.

(90) Saugnier and Brisson, *Voyages to the Coast of Africa* (London, 1792), 285.

(91) R. Muir, *A History of Liverpool* (London, 1907), 197.

(92) Donnan, *op. cit.*, II, 529 n.

(93) Stock, *op. cit.*, II, 264 n.

(94) Donnan, *op. cit.*, I, 234 n, 300 n.

(95) *Ibid.*, I, 256, 262; II, 445.

(96) *Ibid.*, I, 283.

(97) Stock, *op. cit.*, III, 207 n, 225 n, 278 n (Birmingham); 204 n, 228 n (London).

(98) Donnan, *op. cit.*, II, 98.

(99) W.H.B. Court, *The Rise of the Midland Industries* (Oxford, 1938), 145-146.

(100) Stewart-Browne, *op. cit.*, 52-53.

(101) Donnan, *op. cit.*, II, 610-611.

(102) *Ibid.*, II, 609.

This selection is abridged from Eric Williams, *Capitalism and Slavery* (Chapel Hill, N.C., University of North Carolina Press, 1944), pp. 51-53, 54-55, 57-59, 60-63, 65-66, 67-69, 70-72, 73-76, 78-79, 81-82, 84.

UNDERDEVELOPMENT AND DEPENDENCE IN BLACK AFRICA

Samir Amin

Contemporary Black Africa can be divided into wide regions which are clearly different from one another. But it is more difficult to pinpoint the differences, to study their nature, origin and effects than to see them.

The *unity* of Black Africa is nonetheless not without foundations. Beside the question of 'race' — which is no more homogeneous nor less mixed, since pre-historical times, than are the other 'races' (white, yellow or red) — a common or kindred cultural background and a social organization which still presents striking similarities, make a reality of Black Africa. The colonial conquest of almost the whole of this continent strengthened this feeling of unity of Black Africa. Seen from London, Paris or Lisbon, Black Africa appeared to the European observer as a homogeneous entity, just as North Americans have regarded Latin America.

From inside, however, Black Africa just as Latin America, evidently appears extremely *variegated*. The present States, which resulted from an artificial carving-up, do not constitute the sole or even essential basis of this diversity. However, this recent reality left its mark on Africa and is likely — for better or for worse — to consolidate itself. Even more of a reality are some 100 or 200 regions of varying size, crossing the frontiers of the present States. These regions constitute yet another aspect of the reality; they derive their definition not from their geographical position alone, but also and in particular because of the homogenous nature of their social, cultural, economic and even political conditions.

Between these two extremes—African unity and micro-regional variety—the continent can be divided into a few wide macro-regions. We propose to distinguish *three* such regions, and we shall discuss the basis for such a distinction.

Traditional West Africa (former French West Africa, Togo, Ghana, Nigeria, Sierra Leone, Gambia, Liberia, Guinea Bissao), Cameroon, Chad and the Sudan together constitute a first region, *Africa of the colonial economy* (Économie de traite). We shall have to give a precise definition of this concept which unfortunately is too often treated lightly. This integrated whole is clearly divisible into three sub-regions: the coastal sub-region, which is easily accessible from the outside world and which constitutes the 'rich' area; the hinterland, which mostly serves as a labour pool for the coastal areas and as a market for industries being established on the coast; and the Sudan, whose particular characteristics will be examined later.

The traditional Congo River Basin (Congo Kinshasa, Conge Brazzaville, Gabon and the Central African Republic) form a second macro-region, *Africa of the concession-owning companies*. Here also we shall have to explain how, over and above differences in policies of the French and Belgian governments and the forms these policies have taken, genuine similarities in the mode of colonial exploitation characterize the whole of the zone, justifying its demarcation.

The eastern and southern parts of the continent (Kenya, Uganda, Tanzania, Rwanda, Burundi, Zambia, Malawi, Angola, Mozambique, Zimbabwé, Botswana, Lesotho and South Africa) constitute the third macro-region, *Africa of the labour reserves*. Here also, we shall see that, apart from the varied nature of the countries, the region was developed on the basis of the policy of colonial imperialism according to the principle of 'enclosure acts' which were applied to entire peoples.

Ethiopia, Somalia, Madagascar, Réunion and Mauritius, like the Cape Verde Islands on the opposite side of the continent, do not form part of these macro-regions, although here and there one finds some aspects of one or other of the three systems. However, they were combined with another system which has played an important part in the actual development: the slavery-mercantilist system of the Cape Verde Islands, Réunion and Mauritius, the 'pseudo-feudal' systems of Ethiopia and Madagascar. Obviously, questions of frontiers between the regions remain: Katanga belongs to the area of labour reserves, Eritrea to that of the colonial trade, etc.

The proposed distinction in a definition of the periods in African history is deliberately based on the effects of the last period in Africa's history: that of *colonization*. We shall thus have to study the organization of the dialectic between the major colonial policies, here divided into three categories, and the structures inherited from previous periods. To do so, we shall have to go back in time and distinguish between four separate periods.

The *pre-mercantilist period* stretched from the beginnings until the 17th century. In the course of this long history, relations were forged between Black Africa and the rest of the old world, particularly from both ends of the Sahara, between the Savannah countries (between Dakar and the Red Sea) and the Mediterranean. Social formations emerged which cannot be understood if they are not placed within the context of all the multitude of social formations in their relationship with one another. During that period, Africa taken as a whole does not appear as weaker than the rest of the old world, also taken as whole. The unequal development within Africa was not any worse than that north of the Sahara, on both sides of the Mediterranean.

The *mercantilist period* stretches from the 17th century to 1800. It is characterized by the slave-trade, and the first retrograde steps date back to this period. Not only the coastal areas were affected by this trade: its effects spread throughout the continent through a decline in productive forces. There were two distinct slave-trading areas: the Atlantic trade, by far the most harmful due to the numbers involved, which spread from the coast to the whole of the continent, from St Louis in Senegal to Quelimane in Mozambique; and we have the oriental trade operating from Egypt, the Red Sea and Zanzibar towards the Sudan and East Africa. This second type of mercantilist trade continued after 1800 because the industrial revolution which shook the foundations of society in Europe and North America did not reach the Turkish-Arab world.

The *third period* lasted from 1800 to 1880-90. It is characterized by the attempt, at least with respect to certain regions within the area of influence of Atlantic mercantilism, to set up a new form of dependence between these regions and that part of the world where capitalism was firmly entrenched in industrialization. These attempts, however, had very limited backing and we shall see why. This period did not affect the area of influence of oriental mercantilism.

The fourth period, that of *colonization*, completed the work of the third period in the 'West', took over after oriental mercantilism in the 'East' and developed with ten-fold vigour — the present forms of dependence of the continent according to the three models mentioned above. The present throws light on the past. The completed forms of dependence, which appeared only when Africa was actually made the periphery of the world capitalist system in its imperialist stage, and was developed as such, enable us to understand by comparison the meaning of previous systems of social relations and how African social formations were linked with those of other regions of the old world with which they had contact.

Characteristic of Black Africa in the pre-mercantilist period (up to the 17th century) were complex social formations, sometimes created by the state, almost invariably based on visible social differentiations which reveal the ancient nature of the process of degradation of the primitive village community. At that time, Black Africa was not more backward than the rest of the world. The great confusion arising in discussions of traditional African society is due to at least four main reasons: 1. the scarcity of documents and remains of the past, leaving only accounts of Arab travellers, 2. the confusion between the concept of mode of production and the concept of social formation, which calls for a basic differentiation, to which we shall return, 3. the confusion between the different periods of African history, particularly between the pre-mercantilist and the following mercantilist periods; and the justifiable concern of historians to relate concrete history, which is continuous, thus enhacing this confusion; and 4. ideological prejudices against Africa, clearly connected with colonial racism. . . .

. . . In *L'Accumulation* (Amin 1970) I described the mercantilist period (1600-1800) as that which saw the emergence of the two poles of the capitalist mode of production: proletarization resulting from the decline of feudal relationships, and the accumulation of wealth in the form of money. When, during the industrial revolution, the two poles became united, money wealth turned into capital and the capitalist mode of production reached its completed stage. During this three-century long incubation period, the *American periphery* of the Western European mercantile centre played a decisive role in the accumulation of money wealth by the Western European bourgeoisie. Black Africa played a no less important role: *periphery of the periphery*. Reduced to the role of supplier of slave labour for the plantations of America, *Africa lost its autonomy*. It began to be shaped according to foreign requirements, those of mercantilism. Let us finally recall that the plantations of

America referred to, despite their slave-based form of organization, do not constitute autonomous societies (which would be slave-based). As we have mentioned before, the slave-based mode of production is here an element of a non-slave-based society, i.e. it is not the dominant feature of that society. The latter is *mercantilist*; and the trade monopoly — which under its control and for its benefit sells the products of these plantations on the European market, thus quickening the pace of disintegration of feudal relations — was the dominant feature of the plantation economy. The peripheral American society was thus an element in the world structure whose centre of gravity was in Western Europe.

The devastating effects of the mercantilist slave trade for Africa are now better known, thanks to the works of a few historians free from racist colonial prejudices. We would here like to mention one of the most recent and brilliant works in this field: 'Le royaume de Waalo 1659–1859' by Boubacar Barry,(1) from which the following is drawn.

Firstly, whilst pre-mercantile trans-Sahara trade, in which the Waalo participated, had strengthened state centralization and stimulated progress in that autonomous Senegalese Kingdom, the Atlantic trade which replaced it when the French settled in Saint-Louis (1659), did not give rise to any productive forces. On the contrary, it cause them to decrease and brought about disintegration of the society and of the Waalo-Waalo state. This is why force had to be used by the French to cutt off the Trans-Sahara links, to subjugate that region of Africa and later its external relations to suit the requirements of the French trading post of Saint-Louis. African society obviously opposed this worsening of its situation: Islam served as the basis for this opposition. Saint-Louis traders paid with weapons for the slaves they bought. All this ruptured the former balance of power between the king (the *Brak*), who maintained a permanent army of captives under crown control (the *Tyeddo*), the council of elders which nominated him (the *Seb Ak Baor*) and which had a system of prerogatives superimposed over the *lamanat* (the collective clan-ownership of lands in the village communities) and the village communities themselves, based on the *lamanat*. The customary dues paid by the traders of Saint-Louis to the *Brak* encouraged a civil war which involved the *Brak*, the *Tyeddo* and the *Kangam* (leading citizens) and a ransacking of communities to obtain slaves. The Muslim priests (marabouts) tried to organize the resistance movement of these communities. Their aim was to *stop the slave trade*, i.e. the export of the labour force — but not to put an end to internal slavery. Henceforth, Islam changed its character: from being the religion of a minority group of traders, it became a popular resistence movement. A first war waged by the marabouts (1673–1677) failed to convert the people of the 'Fleuve' region and to stop the slave trade. A century later in 1776 the *Toorodo* revolution in Toucouleur country overthrew the military aristocracy and put a stop to the slave trade. But in the Waalo Kingdom, being too near to Saint-Louis, the attempt by prophet Diile in 1830 failed in the face of French military intervention in support of the *Brak*.

Secondly, the Waalo case is of special interest because the slave trade took place parallel to the gum trade. However, the latter did not have the same effects on African society. The export of goods (instead of labour power) does not necessarily have a devastating effect and may, on the contrary, lead to progress. This type of export is not characteristic of the mercantilist period for Africa as a whole which almost exclusively supplied slaves. But here exceptionally it played an equally important role, because the slaves (like *Galam* gold) mainly followed the road to Gambia. However, gum was supplied by the Waalo but also by the Trarza Moors in particular. The latter could export it either via Saint Louis to the French alone or via Portendick which was open to competition between the English and the Dutch. To cut off the Portendick route, the French helped the Trarza to settle in the Fleuve region and to cross it during the *Gum War* (first quarter of the 18th century). Such circumstances thus introdued into the region a certain contradiction of secondary importance between the Waalo and the Trarza. It is contradiction which explains the failure of the *war of the Muslim priests* (marabouts) of the 17th century, led simultaneously by those marabouts who were hostile to the slave trade and by the Moors who put increasing pressure on the Waalo in order to monopolize the gum trade.

The mercantilist slave trade had similar devastating effects wherever in Africa it took place. From Saint-Louis to Quelimane, along the coast, it affected almost the entire continent except the north-eastern area (Sudan, Ethiopia, Somalia and East Africa). The similarity between the Waalo history and that of the Congo Kingdom should be recalled.(2) Here the slave trade also brought about the disintegration of the central authority and led to anarchy which opened the way for the Yaga raids. Such examples abound. Everywhere on the continent there were anarchy and wars, the flight of peoples towards shelter regions which were difficult to reach but also very often poor (such as the shelter zones of the paleonegritic peoples in the over-populated mountains of West Africa). It all ended with an alarming decrease in the population numbers. The processes of integration of the peoples and of the construction of large communities which began in the pre-mercantilist period were stopped. Instead there took place an incredible fragmentation, isolation and tangling which lie at the root of one of the most serious handicaps of contemporary Africa . . .

. . . The slave trade disappeared with the end of mercantilism, i.e. essentially with the advent of the industrial revolution. Capitalism in the centre then took on its complete form; the function of mercantilism — the primitive accumulation of wealth — lost its importance, the centre of gravity shifted from the merchant sector to the new industry. The old periphery — America of the plantations — and its periphery — Africa of the slave trade — had to give way to a new periphery. The function of the new periphery was to provide *products* which would tend to reduce the value of constant capital and that of variable capital used at the centre: raw materials and agricultural produce. The terms which made advantageous the exchange supplying the centre with these products are the precisely terms revealed by the theory of un-equal exchange. (See Amin 1970)

However, until the end of the 19th century central capital had only very limited means of achieving that goal. Only when monopolization appeared at the centre did large-scale exports of capital become possible; henceforth central capital had the means of organizing directly in the periphery, by modern methods, the production which suited it, under conditions which suited it. Until then it could only rely on the ability of local social formations to adjust 'spontaneously', 'by themselves', to the new requirements of the system. America could do it; in India the British colonial power could impose it as did the Dutch in Indonesia; in certain Eastern countries (Ottoman Empire and Egypt) the joint efforts of 'spontaneous internal adjustment' and external pressure produced some results. This is not the place to trace that history. Even in tropical Africa some results were obtained which were exclusively due to the internal adjustment of the African societies. There exist a number of studies which are highly informative on the mechanism of this adjustment.

The research work of Boubacar Barry is one of these. Here again we refer the reader to this exciting book. The project of establishing a colonial agricultural settlement in the Waalo region, making it plantation country (for cotton, sugar cane, tobacco etc.), first formulated at the end of the 18th century by the British Governor of Saint-Louis, was put on the agenda during the Revolution and the Empire as a consequence of the Santo Domingo slave revolt. When the Waalo was 'bought' in 1819 by Governor Schmaltz, the experiment began. Barry analyses its failure. The first cause of failure was the resistance of the village communities to their dispossession in favour of European planters, which had been agreed to by the aristocracy in return for extra 'customary' benefits. The second cause was the lack of manpower, since there was no reason why the peasants should leave their communities and become proletarians on the plantations. The Brak provided some workers which to all intents and purposes were slaves: long-term recruits (engagés à temps). But the settlement colonization could only use 'tinkering' methods. It was not until the colonial conquest that ample resources opened the way for proletarianization: taxation, pure and simple dispossession, forced labour—in short, all the methods used in Africa after 1880, very similar to those used earlier by the British in India, the Dutch in Indonesia, the French in Algeria and the Egyptians in the Sudan. The fact remains that the Waalo agricultural settlement ended in failure in 1831. But the attempt had accentuated the people's hatred of its aristocracy and prepared for its conversion to Islam: outside the official authority, Muslim communities organized themselves defensively around the Sérigne to whom they paid tithes. When Faidherbe conquered the Waalo between 1855 and 1859 with the intention of starting up the agricultural settlement again and procuring for French industry the cotton which it needed, the vanquished aristocracy embraced Islam. A new chapter opened, and we shall see later how the new production came to be organized in accordance with the requirements of the centre. Thus Islam changed its structure a second time: instead of being a resistance ideology it was to become a powerful means of integrating the new periphery and subordinating it to the project of the centre.

Other African societies made an effort to adjust themselves to this project even before they were conquered. Walter Rodney (1966) points out that throughout the Benin coast the slaves who were still raided but who could no longer be exploited were put to work inside the society to produce the export products which Europe demanded. Catherine Coquery (1971a) has analysed in these terms the prodigious development of Dahomean palm groves. Onwuka Dike (1965) shows how the Ibo society, which was unable to have recourse to slaves, nevertheless adapted itself for the production of export palm oil. Here again many more examples could be cited.

The constitution and subsequent destruction of Samory's empire reveals another aspect of integration mechanisms.(3) The collection of export products and the conveying of imports received in exchange, strengthened the position of the Dioula Moslems, a minority inherited from the remote days of pre-mercantilism. With the 'dioula revolution' they were able to set up a state which they controlled. But this late episode occurred just at the beginning of the colonial period. The state of Samory had scarcely been founded when it had to face the conquerors. The latter were to destroy that state, reorganize the channels of trade in the direction which suited them and reduce the Dioula to the subordinate functions of colonial trade.

The partitioning of the continent, complete by the end of the 19th century, multiplied the means available to the colonialists to attain the target of capital at the centre. This target was the same everywhere: to obtain cheap exports. But to achieve this, capital at the centre which had now reached the monopoly stage could organize production on the spot and there exploit both the natural resources (by wasting them or stealing them, i.e. paying a price for them which did not enable alternative activities to replace them when they were exhausted)(4) and cheap labour. Moreover, through direct and brutal political domination it could limit the incidental expenses of maintaining local social classes as conveyor-belts(5) and could use direct political methods of coercion.

However, although the target was the same everywhere, we can see that different variants of the system of colonial exploitation were developed. These variants did not depend — or depended only slightly — on the nationality of the colonizer. The contrast between direct French rule and indirect British rule, so frequent in the literature, is not very noticeable in Africa. It is true that a few differences are attributable to the nationality of the masters. British capital, being richer and more developed and having additionally acquired the 'best pieces', carried out an earlier and more thorough development than French capital.(6) Belgium, as small power which had been forced to come to terms with the great powers and had to accept the competition of foreign goods in its Congo, did not have the direct colonial monopolies which France used and abused to its advantage. Portugal similarly agreed to share its colonies with major Anglo-American capital.

In the region which we have called *Africa of the labour reserves*(7) (l'Afrique des reserves), capital at the centre needed to have a large proletariat immediately available. This was because there was great mineral wealth to be exploited (gold and diamonds in South Africa, copper in Northern Rhodesia) or an untypical settler agriculture in tropical Africa (old Boer colonization in South Africa, new British settlement of Southern Rhodesia and, in the extreme north of the region, of Kenya which until 1919 was separated from the southern part of 'labour reserve Africa' by German Tanganyika). To obtain this proletariat quickly, the colonizers dispossessed the African rural communities by violence and drove them back deliberately into small regions. Furthermore, they kept them in these poor regions with no means of modernizing and intensifying their farming. Thereby they forced the 'traditional' society to be a supplier of temporary or permanent migrants on a vast scale, thus providing a cheap proletariat for the mines, the European farms, and later for the manufacturing industries of South Africa, Rhodesia and Kenya. Henceforth we can no longer speak of a traditional society in that region of the continent, since the labour reserve society had a function which had nothing to do with 'tradition': that of supplying a migrant proletariat. The African social formations of this region, distorted and impoverished, lost even the semblance of autonomy: the unhappy Africa of the Bantustans and apartheid was born: it was to supply the greatest return to central capital. The 'economistic' ideological mythology of the 'laws of the labour market' under these circumstances, formulated by Arthur Lewis, has been subjected to merciless criticism in which Giovanni Arrighi restored political violence to its true place. (See Lewis 1954; Arrighi 1968)

Until very recently there was no known large-scale mineral wealth in West Africa likely to attract foreign capital, nor was there any settler colonialization. On the other hand the slave trade, very active on that coast, had given rise to and developed complex social structures which we have analysed above. The colonial powers were thus able to shape a structure which made possible the large-scale production of tropical agricultural products for export under the terms necessary to interest central capital in them, i. e. provided that the returns to labour they involved were so small that these products cost less than any possible substitutes produced in the centre itself.

The total of these procedures and the structures to which they gave rise constituted the colonial-type trade *(Économie de traite).*(8) These procedures were, as always, as much political as economic. The main procedures were: 1. the organization of a dominant trade monopoly, that of colonial import-export houses, and the pyramidal shape of the trade network they dominated, in which the Lebanese occupied the intermediate zones, and the former African traders were crushed and had to occupy subordinate positions; 2. the taxation of peasants in money which forced them to produce what the monopolists offered to buy; 3. political support to the social strata and classes which were allowed to appropriate de facto some of the tribal lands and the organization of internal migrations from regions which were deliberately left in their poverty so as to be used as labour reserves in the plantation zones; 4. political alliance with social groups which, in the theocratic framework of the Muslim brotherhoods (confrèries) were interested in commercializing the tribute they levied on the peasantry; and 5. when the foregoing procedures proved ineffective, recourse pure and simple to administrative coercion: forced labour. Under these circumstances the traditional society was distorted to the point of being unrecognizable: it lost its autonomy, its main function was to produce for the world market under conditions which, because they impoverished it, deprived it of any prospect of radical modernization. This 'traditional' society was not, therefore, in transition (to 'modernity'): it was *completed* as a dependent society, a peripheral one, and hence a dead end. It therefore retained certain traditional appearances which constituted its only means of survival. The colonial-type trade covered all the subordination-domination relationships between this pseudo-traditional society integrated into the world system and the central capitalist society which shaped and dominated it. Since it has too often been made commonplace, the concept of 'économie de traite' has been reduced to a mere description: the exchange of agricultural products against imported manufactured goods.(7) Yet the concept is much richer: it describes analytically the exchange of agricultural commodities provided by a peripheral society shaped in this way against the products of a central capitalist industry (imported or produced on the spot by European enterprises).

The results of the colonial-type trade have varied according to different regions of this 'Afrique de la traite'. To give honour where honour is due: it was British capital which initiated a perfectly consistent formulation of aims and procedures. When, at the beginning of colonization, Lever Brothers asked the Governor of the Gold Coast to grant concessions which would enable it to develop modern plantations, the latter refused because 'it was unnecessary'. It would be enough, he explained, to help the 'traditional' chiefs to appropriate the best lands so that these export products could be obtained without extra investment costs. Lever then approached the Belgians and obtained concessions in the Congo, we shall see why later.

We have analysed (in Amin 1970, pp. 347-48) the conditions for the success of the 'économie de traite'. These are: 1. an 'optimum' degree of hierarchization of 'traditional' society, which exactly corresponded to that of the zones formed by the slave trade; 2. an 'optimum' population density in the rural areas — 10 to 30 inhabitats per square kilometre; 3. the possibility of starting the process of proletarization by calling upon immigrants foreign to the ethnic groups of the plantation zone; 4. the choice of 'rich' crops providing a sufficient surplus per hectare and per worker at the very first stage of their development; and 5. support of the political authority and making available to the privileged minority such resources (political and economic, especially agricultural credit) as would make possible the appropriation and development of the plantations.

The complete model of the 'économie de traite' was achieved in the Gold Coast and German Togoland by the end of the 19th century, and was reproduced much later in French West Africa and French Equatorial Africa. We have explained that this lateness, which reflected that of French capitalism, was attributable to the attempts at quasi-settler colonization even under unfavourable conditions (French Planters in Ivory Coast and in Equatorial Africa.) and the corresponding maintenance of forced labour until the modern period, after World War II.(Amin 1971)

The 'économie de traite' took two main forms. Kulakization, i.e. the constitution of a class of indigenous planters of rural origin, the virtually exclusive appropriation of the land by these planters, and the employment of paid labour, was the dominant form in the Gulf of Guinea, where conditions enabled colonial-type trading to develop. On the other hand, in the savanna, from Senegal through Northern Nigeria to Sudan, the Muslim brotherhoods permitted another type of colonial trading: the organization of production and export (ground-nuts and cotton) in the context of vast areas subject to a theocratic political power — that of the Mourid brotherhoods of Senegal, the 'Sudanates' of Nigeria and Ausar and Ashiqqa in the Sudan — which kept the form of a tribute-paying social formation, but was integrated into the international system because the surplus appropriated in the form of tribute levied on the village communities was itself marketed. It was the Egyptian colonization in Sudan which created the most advanced conditions for the development of this type of organization, which in that country tended towards a latifundum system pure and simple. The British merely plucked the fruits of this evolution. The new latifundia-owners, who after 1898 accepted the colonial administration had cotton grown for the benefit of British industry. Powerful modern techniques (large-scale irrigation in the Gezira) were made available to them. But the 'second transformation of Islam' in West Africa after the colonial conquest, opened the way to the same kind of evolution, although less definite and slower. We have already seen that Islam in this region underwent a first transformation: from being the religion of a minority caste of merchants in the pre-mercantilist period integrated into an animist society (hence similar to Judaism in Europe), it became the ideology of popular resistance to the slave trade in the mercantilist period. This second transformation made Islam, 'restored' by the aristocracy and the colonial authorities, into the guiding ideology of peasant leaders for the organization of the export production which the colonizers desired. The Mourid phenomenon of Senegal is probably the most striking example of this second transformation. That the founders of the brotherhood and some short-sighted colonial administrators felt — for a time — hostile to each other does not matter. Ultimately the brotherhood proved to be the most important vector for the expansion of the groundnut economy and the submission of the peasants to the goal of this economy: to produce a large amount and to accept very low, stagnating wages despite progress in productivity.

To organize the 'économie de traite' it was necessary to destroy the pre-colonial trade and to reorganize the flows in the direction required by the externally-oriented nature of the economy. For there had been, before the conquest, regional complementarities with broad natural bases (forest-savanna), strengthened by the history of the relations between the West African societies. The domestic trade in kola and salt, trade between herdsmen and crop farmers, the outflow of exports and the dissemination of imports — all this constituted a dense and integrated network, dominated by African traders. The colonial trading houses had to gain control of these flows and direct them all towards the coast; that was why the colonial system destroyed African domestic trade and then reduced the African traders to the role of subordinate primary collectors, when it did not simply eliminate them. The destruction of the trade of Samory, like that of the people of mixed blood in Saint-Louis, Gorée and Freetown, that of the Hausa and Ashanti of Salaga and that of the Ibo of the Niger delta, bears witness to this other devastating socio-economic effect of the 'économie de traite'.(10)

Thus at regional level, the colonial trade necessarily gave rise to a polarization of dependent peripheral development. The necessary corollary of the 'wealth' of the coast was the impoverishment of the hinterland. Africa, predisposed by geography and history to a continental development, organized around the major inland river arteries (thus providing for transport, irrigation, electric power, etc.) was condemned to be 'developed' only in its narrow coastal zone. The exclusive allocation of resources to the latter zone, a planned policy of colonial trade, accentuated the regional imbalance. The mass emigration from the hinterland to the coast formed part of the logic of the system: it made (cheap) labour available to capital where capital required it, and it is only 'the ideology of universal harmony' which sees in these migrations anything other than migrations which impoverish the departure zones.(11) The culmination of the colonial trade system was balkanization, in which the 'recipient' micro-regions had no 'interest' in 'sharing' the crumbs of the colonial cake with their labour reserves.

Thus the bounties of the colonial trade were highly relative. However, it was impossible to implement this system in *Central Africa*, the third macro-region of the continent. Here, ecological conditions had to some extent protected the peoples who took refuge from the ravages of the slave trade fleeing into zones unlikely to be penetrated from the coast. The low population density and the lack of sufficient hierarchization made the colonial-trade model non-viable. Discouraged, the colonial authorities gave the country to any adventurers who would agree to try to 'get something out of it' without resources — since adventure does not attract capital. The misdeeds of the concessionary companies who, between 1890 and 1930, ravaged French Equatorial Africa with no result except a trivial profit, and those of Leopold's policy in the Congo, have been duly denounced.(12) So, in the Belgian Congo it was only after World War I when the solution was adopted of having industrial plantations established directly by the major capitalists (it will be remembered that Lever, which was not permitted to establish itself in the Gold Coast, was welcomed by the Belgians) that a small-scale 'économie de traite' infiltrated as an extension of the plantation zones belonging to foreign capital. As for French Equatorial Africa, it had to wait until the fifties before seeing the first symptoms of the 'économie de traite'. Thus the (negative) impact of the period of concessionary companies, which is still omni-present, justifies the name of *Africa of the concessionary companies* which we give to the region.

In all three cases, then, the colonial system organized the society so that it produced on the best possible terms, from the viewpoint of the mother country, exports which provided only a very low and stagnating return to labour. This goal having been achieved, it must now be analysed in theoretical terms.(13) For the present discussion, we have to conclude that there are no traditional societies in modern Africa: there are only dependent peripheral societies.

REFERENCES

Afana, O. 1966: *L'economie de L'Oquest Africain.* Paris.

Amin, S. 1967: *Le developpment du capitalisme en Cote d'lvoire.* Paris.

Amin, S. 1970: *L'accumulation a l'echelle mondiale.* Anthropos-IFAN.

Amin, S. 1971a: *L'Afrique de l'Ouest bloquee.* Paris.

Amin, S. 1971b: La politique coloniale francaise a l'egard de la bourgeoisie commercante Senegalaise, in Meillassoux (ed): *The development of indigenous trade and markets in West Africa.* Oxford.

Amin, S. 1971c: Le modele theorique de l'accumulation dans le monde contemporain, centre et peripherie. (Also in English) Mimeograph, IDEP, Dakar.

Amin S. & C. Coquery 1969: *Histoire economique du Congo 1880-1968.* IFAN-Anthropos.

Arrighi, G. 1968: *The political economy of Rhodesia.* Mouton.

Ballandier, G. 1965: *La vie quotidieune au royaume du Congo du XV-I au XV-IIIe siecle.* Paris.

Barry, B. 1971: Le royaume de Waalo, 1659-1859. Thesis, Paris.

Berg, E. J. 1965: The economics of the migrant labor system, in Kuper, H. (ed): *Urbanization and migration in West Africa.* Univ. of California.

Canale, S. 1960: *L'Afrique Noire, l'ere coloniale,* Paris.

Coquery, C. 1971a: De la traite des esclaves a l'exportation de l'huile de palme et des palmisteaux Dahomey, XIXe siecle, in Meillassoux (ed) *The development of indigenous trade and markets in West Africa.* Oxford.

Conquery, C. 1971b: Le Congo francais au temp des compagnies consessionaires 1890-1930. Thesis Paris.

Dike, K. Onwuka 1956: *Trade and politics in the Niger Delta 1830-1885.* Oxford.

Gray, R. 1961: *The two nations.* Oxford.

Horwitz, R. 1967: *The political economy of South Africa.* London.

Lewis, A. 1954: *Economic development with unlimited supplies of labour.* The Manchester School.

Merlier, R. 1965: *Le Congo, de la colonisation belge a l'independance.* Paris.

Person, J. Y. 1970: *Samori.* IFAN.

Ranger, T.O. (ed) 1968: *Aspects of Central African History,* Heinemann, London.

Rodney, W. 1966: African slavery and other forms of social oppressions on the Upper Guinea Coast in the context of the Atlantic slave trade, *Journ. African History No. 3, 1966.*

Szereszewski, R. 1965: *Structural changes in the economy of Ghana 1891-1911.* London.

Thion, S. 1969: *Le pouvoir pole.* Paris.

Vansina, J. 1962:   Long distance trade routes in Central Africa. *Journ. African History.*

Vansina, J. 1963:   Notes sur l'origine du royaume de Kongo, *Journ. African History.*

Vansina, J. 1967: *Introduction a l'ethnographie du Congo.* Brussels.

NOTES

(1) Barry 1971, mimeographed. The qualities of this research, both in rigorous method and in presentation, make it superfluous to 'summarize' this history, for which we refer the reader to the work concerned.

(2) See, inter alia, Vansina 1967, 1962, and 1963; Ballandier 1965; and Ranger 1968.

(3) Person 1970; the expression 'dioula revolution' is from Person.

(4) This problem of the looting of natural resources is beginning to be studied with the present-day awareness of 'environment problems' (although the term is ambiguous). See Amin 1970, postscript to the second edition, pp. 594–95.

(5) Hence the late development in Africa of the peripheral model of industrialization by import substitution. It was not until independence that the local elites who took over from the colonial administration constituted the first element of a domestic marked for 'luxury goods' according to the interlinkage relationships which we discuss later on (The theoretical model of accumulation in the modern world, center and periphery: Amin 1971c). Hence also the markedly bureaucratic nature of the 'privileged classes'.

(6) Thus the structures set up in the Gold Coast in 1890, which have characterized Ghana up to the present day (Szereszewski 1965), made their appearance in the Ivory Coast only from 1950, after the abolition of forced labour (Amin 1967).

(7) See Horwitz 1967; Gray 1961; Thion 1969; and above all Arrighi 1968.

(8) We have analyzed this colonial trade (Amin 1971a). See also Szereszewski 1965; Amin 1967; Afana 1966; and Vauhaeverbeke 1970.

(9) As Canale does (Canale 1960), in the chapter on the 'economie de traite'.

(10) See my contribution to the discussion of this problem in Amin 1971b.

(11) Berg 1965 reflects better than anyone else this non-scientific ideology. The conventional approach which it develops assumes that migrations 'redistribute' one factor of production (labour) which originally was unequally distributed. If that were so, migrations would tend to *equalize* the growth rates of the economies of the various regions. But we can see that they are everywhere accompanied by a growing disparity between rates of growth: the acceleration of (per capita) growth in the immigration zones and its reduction in the emigration zones.

(12) Coquery 1971b; Merlier 1965; Amin & Coquery 1969.

(13) See Amin 1971c for a further discussion.

This selection is abridged from Samir Amin, 'Underdevelopment and Dependence in Black Africa: Historical Origin," *Journal of Peace Research,* No. 2 (1972), pp. 105–119, Published by UniversitetsForlaget, Oslo 3, Norway.

document

MEMOIRS OF THE REIGN OF BOSSA AHADEE
... AND A SHORT ACCOUNT
OF THE AFRICAN SLAVE TRADE, 1789

Robert Norris

Since the labour of African slaves has been found necessary for the cultivation of the soil in the tropical climates of America, from the utter incapacity of white people to undergo that fatigue, every European nation possessing colonies there, has been solicitous to acquire a share in this traffic; nor have the most scrupulous of them entertained a doubt of their right to purchase, what the Africans exercised a right to dispose of.

Among the adventurers in this trade, the British possess, at present, the greatest share. It was during the government of the commonwealth, that Negroes were carried, in any numbers, to the British West Indies, and then, chiefly to Barbadoes: a few indeed were brought to Virginia, by a Dutch ship, as early as 1620; but it was the Royal African Company, that first carried on, from England, vigorous commerce to Africa, during the reign of Charles II. We may form an opinion of the magnitude of it, in its most flourishing state, prior to the revolution in 1688, by considering that the company employed thirty ships annually, which delivered about five thousand Negroes in the West Indies. The increase of it to its present state, may be attributed to the enterprizing spirit of the merchants; to the superior address of those employed in the executive part of it; to the opulence of the manufacturers, which enables them to extend a credit to the former, beyond what can be had in any other country; and to the annual grants of parliament, for the maintenance of several forts, and factories in Africa. From these concurring circumstances, the British planters are supplied with Negroes, on more reasonable terms than their neighbours; and a large surplus is left, which is disposed of to the French and Spaniards for specie, and other valuable commodities.

The importance of this trade to Great Britain may be determined from the following considerations: it immediately employs about one hundred ships, which sail annually for Africa, with cargoes which amount nearly to a million sterling, and which are composed of the productions of the British settlements in the East and West Indies; and of British manufactures, to the value of seven hundred thousand pounds. The circuitous returns of these cargoes are computed at a million and a half. The artificers and mechanics employed at Liverpool alone, receive one hundred thousand pounds annually for labor and materials employed in equipping the ships engaged in it; and exclusive of the large sums paid for seamen's wages, the commissions and privilege of the captains and officers amount at least to fifty thousand pounds annually; which are generally realized there, and have contributed greatly to the rapid increase of that commercial town.

The African trade, connected as it is with the West Indian commerce, and with the trade to the remaining continental colonies, and Newfoundland fishery, is of the utmost consequence to the employment of many thousands of our fellow subjects; to the naval power of Britain; and to the royal revenues; all which are conjoined by sympathetic ties. The value of three millions at least of domestic manufactures, exclusive of other merchandize, annually finds a profitable vent by means of the African and West Indian trades; and above five millions of property, arising from the labor of Negro slaves, employed in the West Indian islands, is yearly imported from thence: which contributes not less than a million and an half annually to the revenue of this kingdom. To carry on this immense traffic, and to supply these islands with lumber and provisions, from the continental colonies and Newfoundland fishery, gives constant employment to at least a thousand ships, and to above fifteen thousand mariners. To enumerate the fatal consequences that would inevitably ensue from a check given to this extensive commerce, much more the suppression of it, exceeds the present limits of this short sketch, but they shall be hinted in the sequel.

The adventurers in this trade, who have seen for near a century past, the Society for propagating Christianity, composed of the Archbishop of Canterbury, the Bishop of London, and many pious doctors of the established church, deriving, as masters, a yearly income from the labor of their Negroe slaves in the West Indies, which is appropriated to the increase of Christianity in the world, could not consider it as contrary to the spirit of the Scriptures, or to the principles of morality: nor could the adventurers regard this traffic as inconsistent with the natural rights of mankind, when they read in the statute of 9 and 10 of King William (which was made avowedly for extending the trade to Africa), *"That this trade was highly beneficial to this kingdom;"* a declaration of a king, who was the patron of liberty, and of a parliament that had vindicated the natural rights of mankind; and when they read also in the stat. of 23 Geo. II. *"That the trade to Africa is very advantageous to Great Britain, and necessary to the plantations."* Which act was made by a whig king, and a whig parliament; who, when they dissolved the late African Company, granted a large sum of money as a compensation for their rights, in order that a trade thus necessary and advantageous, might be carried on with greater energy and success.

Encouraged by these, and various other acts of parliament, which declared the African trade to be highly beneficial to this nation, many merchants engaged their fortunes in it; nor could they imagine the *purchase* of Negroes from those states of Africa (who have the same right to dispose of them as the parliament has to inflict the pains of banishment or death) or consider the *sale* of them as illegal, when they knew that many able lawyers, learned judges, and illustrious chancellors had expressly declared this purchase and sale to be lawful; and to have transferred to the master such a property as could not be affected by local changes, or subsequent baptism: and when the adventurers know also, that in conformity to the declarations of these judges and lawyers, the statute of the 5th of his late and of the 13th of his present Majesty, subjected the Negroes in the West Indian islands, as well as the lands which they laboured, to the payment of all debts, owing either to his Majesty, or to any of his subjects; and directed these Negroes to be sold, like any other chattels, for satisfaction of such debts. In consequence of which, the five hundred thousand Negroes, now belonging to the planters in those islands, are pledged by the legislature, and by the nation, for payment of the debts that are due, either to the British merchants or manufacturers, or to the subjects of foreign princes; who, by a late act of parliament, have been encouraged and enabled to lend money to these planters, on the security of their lands, and of the labour of their Negroes.

Yet this trade, so highly benefical to the adventurers, and important to the state; a trade sanctioned by the clergy supported by the judges, and authorized by the laws, has lately been condemned both in principle and practice. By the law and usage of parliament, the most trivial right of the most inconsiderable subject is never taken away, even for the public good itself, without a manifest necessity, and a full compensation. Yet an attempt has been made, and measures are unremittingly pursued, to deprive the British planters, merchants and manufacturers, of the advantage of this important traffic; and under a pretence of regulation, restrictions have already been proposed, which strike at its existence: but though the liberty of Negroes seems now to be the favorite idea, the liberty of Britons to pursue their lawful occupations should not be forgotten: for the principle which has raised the commerce and navigation of this country, and with them the landed interest and revenues of the kingdom, from inconsiderable beginnings to their present greatness, is the *right* which every man in it possesses, to carry on his own business, in the way most advantageous to himself and the society, without any sudden interruption in the pursuit of it; and the *consciousness* which he has, of the steady protection of the laws, in the prosecution of what has been shewn to be legal.

This document is reprinted from Robert Norris, *Memoirs of the Reign of Bossa Ahadee . . . and a Short Account of the African Slave Trade.* Frank Cass & Co. Ltd, 1968, pp. 161-169.

document

ON U.S. EXPANSION

Senator Albert Beveridge

It is a noble land that God has given us; a land that can feed and clothe the world; a land whose coastlines would enclose half the countries of Europe; a land set like a sentinel between the two imperial oceans of the globe, a greater England with a nobler destiny. . . .

Therefore, in this campaign, the question is larger than a party question. It is an American question. It is a world question. Shall the American people continue their march toward the commercial supremacy of the world? Shall free institutions broaden their blessed reign as the children of liberty wax in strength, until the empire of our principles is established over the hearts of all mankind?

Have we no mission to perform, no duty to discharge to our fellowman? Has God endowed us with gifts beyond our deserts and marked us as the people of His peculiar favor, merely to rot in our own selfishness, as men and nations must, who take cowardice for their companion and self for their deity — as China has, as India has, as Egypt has?

Shall we be as the man who had one talent and hid it, or as he who had ten talents and used them until they grew to riches? And shall we reap the reward that waits on our discharge of our high duty; shall we occupy new markets for what our farmers raise, our factories make, our merchants sell — aye, and, please God, new markets for what our ships shall carry?

Hawaii is ours; Porto Rico is to be ours; at the prayer of her people Cuba finally will be ours; in the islands of the East, even to the gates of Asia, coaling stations are to be ours at the very least; the flag of a liberal government is to float over the Philippines, and may it be the banner that Taylor unfurled in Texas and Fremont carried to the coast.

The Opposition tells us that we ought not to govern a people without their consent. I answer: The rule of liberty that all just government derives its authority from the consent of the governed, applies only to those who are capable of self-government. We govern the Indians without their consent, we govern our territories without their consent, we govern our children without their consent. How do they know that our government would be without their consent? . . .

The March of the Flag! . . .

Distance and oceans are no arguments. The fact that all the territory our fathers bought and seized is contiguous, is no argument. In 1819 Florida was farther from New York than Porto Rico is from Chicago to-day; Texas, farther from Washington in 1845 than Hawaii is from Boston in 1898; California more inaccessible in 1847 than the Philippines are now. Gibraltar is farther from London than Havana is from Washington; Melbourne is farther from Liverpool than Manila is from San Francisco.

The ocean does not separate us from lands of our duty and desire — the oceans join us, rivers never to be dredged, canals never to be repaired. Steam joins us; electricity joins us — the very elements are in league with our destiny. Cuba not contiguous! Porto Rico not contiguous! Hawaii and the Philippines not contiguous! The oceans make them contiguous. And our Navy will make them contiguous.

But the Opposition is right — there is a difference. We did not need the western Mississippi Valley when we acquired it, nor Florida, nor Texas, nor California, nor the royal provinces of the far northwest. We had no emigrants to people this imperial wilderness, no money to develop it, even no highways to cover it. No trade awaited us in its savage fastnesses. Our productions were not greater than our trade. There was not one reason for the land-lust of our statesmen from Jefferson to Grant, other than the prophet and the Saxon within them. But, today, we are raising more than we can consume, making more than we can use. Therefore we must find new markets for our produce. . . .

The commercial supremacy of the Republic means that this Nation is to be the sovereign factor in the peace of the world. For the conflicts of the future are to be conflicts of trade — struggles for markets — commercial wars for existence. And the golden rule of peace is impregnability of position and invincibility of preparedness. So, we see England, the greatest strategist of history, plant her flag and her cannon on Gibraltar, at Quebec, in the Bermudas, at Vancouver, everywhere.

So Hawaii furnishes us a naval base in the heart of the Pacific; the Ladrones another, a voyage further on; Manila another, at the gates of Asia — Asia, to the trade of whose hundreds of millions American merchants, manufacturers, farmers, have as good right as those of Germany or France or Russia or England; Asia, whose commerce with the United Kingdom alone amounts to hundreds of millions of dollars every year; Asia, to whom Germany looks to take her surplus products; Asia, whose doors must not be shut against American trade. Within five decades the bulk of Oriental commerce will be ours. . . .

We can not fly from our world duties; it is ours to execute the purpose of a fate that has driven us to be greater than our small intentions. We can not retreat from any soil where Providence has unfurled our banner; it is ours to save that soil for liberty and civilization. . . .

BIBLIOGRAPHY

Further reading is recommended in the excellent account of the European impact on Africa by Davidson (4) and in Williams (9) for the key role that slavery in the West Indies played in the political economy of the British Empire prior to the nineteenth century. A classic account of the white man in Africa is found in Morel (8), Brown (1) contains excerpts from several differing interpretations of slavery while Genovese (6), part one, provides an analysis of comparative slave systems and the development of capitalism. The importance of the international gap in weapons and navigational technology for the early success of European expansion is analyzed by Cippola (3). The devastating economic impact of white expansion is outlined in the introduction and first chapter of Griffin (7) with particular emphasis on Latin America. The readings in Frucht (5) span a wide period of history in the New World. This work also contains a good selective bibliography. Boxer (2) demonstrates the total inadequacy of interpretations which argue that the Portuguese Empire did not have a racial basis. Finally, the penetration of capitalist social relations into precapitalist societies and the revolutionary response of six of these societies is brilliantly discussed in Wolf (10).

(1) Brown, Richard D. (ed.). *Slavery in American Society*. Lexington, Massachusetts: D.C. Heath and Company, 1969.

(2) Boxer, C.R. *Race Relations in the Portuguese Colonial Empire*. Oxford, England: Oxford University Press, 1963.

(3) Cippola, Carlo. *Guns and Sails in the Early Phases of European Expansion*. London: Collins, 1965.

(4) Davidson, Basil. *The African Slave Trade: Precolonial History 1450-1850*. Boston: Little, Brown and Company, 1961.

(5) Frucht, Richard (ed.). *Black Society in the New World*. New York: Random House, 1971.

)6) Genovese, Eugene. *The World the Slaveholders Made: Two Essays in Interpretation*. New York: Random House, Vintage Books, 1971.

(7) Griffin, Keith. *Underdevelopment in Spanish America*. London: George Allen and Unwin, Ltd., 1969.

(8) Morel, E.D. *The Black Man's Burden: The White Man in Africa from the Fifteenth Century to World War I*. First published in 1920, reprinted; New York: Monthly Review Press, 1969.

(9) Williams, Eric. *Capitalism and Slavery*. New York: Capricorn Books edition, 1966.

(10) Wolf, Eric. *Peasant Wars of the Twentieth Century*. New York: Harper and Row, 1969.

III.
THE
BRITISH
CASE
STUDY

INTRODUCTION

Generally, social scientists studying Britain attribute that country's racial problems to the recent migrations from the Caribbean, Asia, and Africa. It has been suggested that the rapid inflow of the "colored people"(1) has created social and economic problems for immigrants themselves and has aroused resentment among the working classes who perceive the immigrants as a social threat. Although this suggestion is not without substance, it is only one aspect of a problem that is essentially rooted in Britain's history of slave trade and colonial domination.

One of the earliest contacts between the British and Africans was in 1554 when John Locke, a prosperous merchant, brought slaves from East Africa to England. Eight years later, John Hawkins shipped five hundred slaves from West Africa to the New World; (2) it was a successful undertaking which his countrymen copied for several centuries. Initially, slave trading by the British was sporadic. In the late seventeenth century, however, the West Indies were colonized.

What followed was an era of triangular trade. British ships carried manufactured goods to Africa where they would be bartered for slaves who were then shipped to the New World where they were exchanged for sugar and tobacco. Since the economic advantages from this triangular trade were enormous, whatever moral concerns or reservations the British may have had about it were of less concern than their increasing profits.

One effect of this enterprise was that Britain no longer remained a completely white nation. Sailors and ship captains brought slaves to Britain as objects of curiosity or as bounty. Within some circles, it was fashionable at private parties to display slave children wearing copper or silver collars. By 1770, about eighteen thousand slaves were in London alone; they comprised about three percent of the total population.(3)

When slavery was abolished in the latter part of the eighteenth century, the problem of racial conflict acquired new dimension as the British were concerned about the prospect of a permanent black population. The government encouraged the blacks to emigrate to Africa by providing free passage and minor financial incentives. Although this limited emigration did not solve the "colored" problem, it did result in a demographic imbalance and a decline in the black population. Britain was left with a largely black, male population; these men had little opportunity to marry black women, and consequently, future black generations were reduced in number.

Britain's active involvement in slave trading and its subsequent debate between abolitionists and non-abolitionists distorted the image of black people in that country. To the pro-slavery lobby, Africans were sub-humans, and to the abolitionists, they were simple people corrupted by European contact. Distorted images of Africans were later generalized to Asians; that generalization partly explains many of the deep-rooted racial prejudices and stereotypes that still survive among the British people.

During the nineteenth century Britain colonized parts of Asia, Africa, and the Caribbean. In spite of the vastness of the British Empire, very few colored people migrated to England until World War I. The acute shortage of manpower which developed during the war was relieved by utilizing manpower resources of the colonies. Africans and Asians were employed in ordinance factories, ports, ships, and general industries, and troops from the colonies were commanded by white officers. A similar use of colonial populations would occur again during World War II. Most colored subjects returned to their native countries after both wars, although a few went to England and settled in a few communities.

The end of World War II marked the beginning of the decolonization process. The Labor government granted independence to India and Pakistan, and later to other colonies. Under these changing conditions, the British Nationality Act of 1948 was passed, granting citizenship to all subjects of the Commonwealth irrespective of color or race. Citizens of independent Commonwealth nations thereby became British subjects with dual citizenship. With their dual citizenship, the subjects of the British Commonwealth found it easy to migrate to Britain.

Many migrants from the West Indies arrived in England during the fifties, partly due to the McCarran-Walter Act of 1952 which severely restricted immigration into the United States. As Dilip Hiro has observed:

> Having been deprived of the American outlet, the West Indies were compelled to explore other avenues for migration. And imperial Britain with its open door policy seemed a natural choice. Consequently, there was a sudden upsurge in the West Indian immigration to Britain. Nearly 11,000 West Indians came to Britain in 1954. The following year, the figure more than doubled. After that the number stabilized at about 17,000 a year until the rumors of impending restrictions on commonwealth immigrants created the 'beat the ban rush.' The peak was reached in first half of 1962 when more than 34,000 West Indians arrived as immigrants.(4)

Although Britain already had a small community of Asians, approximately 50,000 people from the middle class in India and Pakistan arrived in Britain between 1955 and 1960.(5)

Colonial immigrants became "scapegoats" in Britain for many of the country's social problems ranging from housing to crime and delinquency, and they faced discrimination and hostility everywhere. Racial riots erupted in Nottingham, Nottinghill, and London in 1958. Eventually, the government formulated a two-fold policy: on one hand, it decided to control colored immigration, and on the other, it sought to remove some of the social and economic grievances of the migrants. The Commonwealth Immigration Act of 1962 and the Race Relations Act of 1965 implemented that governmental policy.

In 1967, the racist overtones of British immigration policy surfaced again. When Kenya was granted independence, the European and Asian minorities there were given an option of becoming citizens of either Britain or Kenya. Most Europeans and 90,000 of 180,000 Asians opted for British citizenship and obtained passports.(6) Kenya, pursuing its Africanization program, was not interested in having people who turned down citizenship in the country and passed a law in 1967 stipulating that non-citizens could stay and work in Kenya only temporarily.

In Britain, neither the government nor the public relished the prospect of thousands of Asians entering the country. In addition to the Asians, the Europeans were migrating from Kenya, and no legal way had been devised to distinguish between Europeans and Asians who had British passports. To avoid overt reference to "race" or "color," the authorities decided to restrict right of entry to passport holders who had substantial connection with Britain, either by birth or their parents' or grandparents' birth. The British government did, however, agree to appraise the entry of Asians from Kenya, and during the Uganda crisis, it assumed full responsibility for Asians who were British nationals.

Approximately 595,100 immigrants were living in England and Wales in 1966,(7) a relatively small population considering the fact that there were 1.26 colored immigrants per hundred people.(8) This colored population can be classified into three broad groups: West Indians, Asians, and Africans. The West Indians comprise the largest colored minority. The total number of immigrants from India is approximately 163,600, while the Pakistanis, including Bengalis, number approximately 67,000.(9) West and East Africans comprise the smallest minority.

The constructs of "marginal subclass" and "internal colonies" can be used with few exceptions to describe the present state of immigrants in Britain. Most immigrants live in slums and ghettos which are generally organized on ethnic lines; they work at unskilled or semi-skilled jobs. Eric Butterworth notes, for example, that night shifts in many woolen mills in Yorkshire depend entirely upon immigrant labor, since the jobs involve disruption of normal life.(10) Cohen and Jenner have found that Pakistani workers, rather than white Britishers, were more willing to work in the woolen industry where working conditions are not satisfactory.(11) In addition, immigrants do not have a decisive voice in the political process. Under these conditions, the power-conflict approach can provide a useful line of analysis.

In the first selection in this section, E. J. B. Rose and his colleagues observe that a close relationship between the demand for labor and immigration has generally existed; the greater the demand for labor, the larger the immigration, and vice versa. Bob Hepple discusses racial discrimination in British industry, and Maurice Peston, discussing the effects of immigration on the British economy, suggests that immigrants have been functional for the economy and have served as a "marginal class."

NOTES

(1) By "colored people," the British mean nonwhite and they include both Asians and Africans. This usage is followed throughout this introduction.

(2) James Walvin, *The Black Presence: A Documentary History of the Negro in England, 1555-1860*, London: Orbach and Chambers Ltd., (1971), p. 8.

(3) Dilip Hiro, *Black British, White British*, London: Eyre and Spottiswoode, 1971, p. 4.

(4) Dilip Hiro, *op. cit.*, p. 3-2.

(5) E.J.B. Rose and Associates, *Color and Citizenship*, Institute of Race Relations, London: Oxford University Press, (1969), p. 83.

(6) David Steel, *No Entry*, London: C. Hurst and Company, 1969.

(7) Rose and Associates, *op. cit.*, p. 83.

(8) *Ibid.*

(9) *Ibid.*

(10) Eric Butterworth (ed.), *Immigrants in West Yorkshire*, London: Institute of Race Relations, special series, 1967.

(11) B. Cohen and P. Jenner, "The Employment of Immigrants: A Case Study within the Wool Industry," *Race*, Vol. 10., No. 1, July 1968, p. 54.

LABOR DEMAND AND MIGRATION TO BRITAIN

E. J. Rose et al.

It is popularly believed that the prime reasons for the migration from the coloured Commonwealth are the poverty, deprivation, and over-population of the sending societies as opposed to the general wealth and, in particular, the generous social services of the United Kingdom. It is also believed that once such a migration is in motion it will continue as long as the sending societies are at a lower level of material wealth than the receiving society, and thus the spectre of a Britain with standing room only is raised. This explanation does not, however, account for the reasons why the migration from the Commonwealth countries started at one particular moment in time, why the numbers of migrants arriving in the U.K. rose and fell, and why the proportions of men and women kept changing within the migration.

A detailed study made by Ceri Peach(1) of West Indian migration to Britain shows the relative influence of changing conditions in the West Indies and Britain on the migration flow. Peach studied the migration rates between 1955–61 of the various West Indian islands and British Guiana and compared these to indices of population pressure, per capita income, unemployment, economic growth, and so on, of these islands. His finding was that adverse conditions in the West Indies should be considered as a permissive and not a dynamic factor in the migration, 'they (adverse conditions in the West Indies) allow migration to take place; they do not cause it.'(2) This conclusion was based on his finding no correlation between different rates of migration from each island and conditions in these islands when comparing each island against the next.

Peach did find, however, that the rates of migration from each island tended to follow the same pattern between 1956 and 1961: migration rose in all the islands in the same year despite the fact that their rates of economic growth did not rise and fall together. This led him to the conclusion 'that trends in migration are governed by factors external to the West Indies'.(3) The external factor that determined the rise and fall in migration was the demand for labour in the United Kingdom. Using as the index of labour demand the number of outstanding vacancies in each quarter kept by the Ministry of Labour, he found a correlation between rises in labour demand and rises in the rate of migration. This correlation is derived by Ceri Peach from quarterly figures of outstanding vacancies and West Indian arrivals. The downturn in the economy from the latter half of 1956 to the end of 1958 is reflected in the lower arrival figures. It will be noted that if a lag of three months for migration is allowed for, then the directions of change of labour index and of the level of migration are in agreement.

Peach further argues that if it is labour demand that determines trends in migration then this will have the greatest effect on male immigration and least on the migration of women and children who in many cases will be joining a relative who has already migrated. He shows convincingly that throughout the period of recession, as numbers fell, the proportion of men in the migration fell, and with recovery it rose as the overall figures arose. In 1960 arrivals were the highest yet recorded and the proportion of men was the highest since the boom year of 1955.

Peach suggests that there are two types of intending migrant, firstly the solid core who would come whatever the conditions, consisting mainly of dependants, and secondly the 'floating migrants' who would respond to reports of conditions in Britain. Information about conditions would come by letter from earlier migrants and evidence is cited that from the early period of the migration the vast bulk of West Indian migrants had contacts in Britain.(4) He thus concludes 'conditions in Britain were the major determinants in the trends of that migration'.(5)

The migration of Indians and Pakistanis followed a very different pattern from that of the West Indians. The migration from India and Pakistan whilst of earlier origin did not develop into a substantial mass movement until 1961. The sudden change in migration movements in 1961, when net inflow increased nearly sixfold over the previous year, is explicable in terms of three factors affecting migration. First, there was the fear of control in Britain. This affected the organization of transport and the activities of travel agents in India and Pakistan who exploited and helped to create the demand. In turn, this led to the wide-scale avoidance and the removal of controls which had previously been imposed by the Indian and Pakistani Governments to restrict immigration to Britain. The effect of labour demand in Britain on migration before 1961 is more difficult to assess for Indians and Pakistanis, but if one allows for a greater time-lag than that shown by the West Indians then the very small net inflows in 1959 following two years of almost continuous fall in labour demand may be significant. But it was undoubtedly fear of control that completely changed the well-established pattern of migration.

Two main sets of conclusions are possible from this examination of migration from the Caribbean and Asia in the period up till the introduction of control in 1962. First, the major determinants of the migration were in Britain, but, as Peach has said, from 1961 'political forces overtook those of economics in the commanding position;'(6) secondly, the introduction of control and the political agitation that led to control distorted the pattern of migration and induced many people to migrate, at unpropitious times, who possibly would never have migrated. (Peach shows, for example, that the rise in the West Indian figures in 1961 and 1962 for the first time took place against the economic indicators.)(7) Thus one comes to the paradoxical conclusion that the most vigorous proponents of control created the very situation that they most feared by inducing a far higher rate of migration than had ever occurred before. The effect of the Commonwealth Immigrants Act was not only to increase the number of immigrants in this country, including their dependants who followed much later, but to increase the rate of arrivals to such an extent that in eighteen months the net inflow was almost as great as that of the previous five years. This massive increase was to compound the real problems which were in the United Kingdom and not at the gates.

The movement of Commonwealth immigrants into Britain in the 1950s was not a unique phenomenon when viewed against general movements into Britain. In the years immediately after the War, labour shortages in Britain were so intense that, apart from schemes for former allies and displaced persons, active recruitment was carried out by the Ministry of Labour in various parts of Europe to attract foreign workers. Between 1945 and 1957 there was a net immigration of more than 350,000 European nationals into the United Kingdom.(8) Despite this large influx and continuing migration from Eire, one of the main problems that has affected the British economy throughout the fifties and sixties has been shortages of labour. Lack of spare capacity, both labour and capital, in the economy has been blamed for the recurrent cycles of 'stop-go' that have plagued the British economy. A situation of over-full employment has meant cost inflation and balance of payment problems that have led to deflationary measures by Government.

Studies of the employment of coloured immigrant workers found that many employers only started employing coloured labour in times of great labour shortage. The works superintendent of a Midlands foundry described the position as follows: 'The big influx of labour began in 1954. At this time you couldn't get an armless, legless man never mind an able-bodied one'.(9) As we have seen, a few employers, such as London Transport, the National Health Service, and the British Hotels and Restaurants Association, made direct arrangements with the Barbados Government for the recruitment of skilled labour. These employers took initial responsibility for the accommodation and welfare of the recruits, but they were the exception, and otherwise no effort was made to match employment vacancies with the supply of migrant labour before the process of migration got underway.

Most of the European countries with high growth rates have been the recipients of migrant flows, often larger than that of Britain. The extent of the differences in culture and economic development between the receiving European Economic Community countries and the sending countries has often been comparable to the differences between Britain and the Commonwealth countries. West Germany, France, Holland, and Belgium have imported much of their labour through official and semi-official recruitment schemes which paid for the passage and undertook responsibility for initial welfare and accommodation. In contrast, Britain took in labour from the Commonwealth for which it did not have to find accommodation nor pay the costs either of recruitment or transport.

In what types of jobs and in what industries did the coloured immigrant initially find work? Usually it was in an industry that was losing ground as far as pay and status were concerned (for example, public transport), or in those jobs that were considered unpleasant by the host community (for example, in foundries), or that entailed long and awkward hours. In general, the employment most easily available for the newly-arrived coloured immigrant was the sort of employment that the English worker did not want. In times of full employment with the demand for more and more skilled and/or highly-paid labour the local labour force became more upwardly mobile. This movement upwards left a vacuum into which replacement labour had to be attracted.

We are here concerned only with the question whether to import labour from Europe and the Commonwealth was the best method of meeting the labour demands of British industry. Since 1945, it has been often alleged that British industry has been wasteful and uneconomic in its employment of labour and that the responsibility for this lies both with management and unions. It can be argued that a migrant flow of labour has delayed the much needed structural changes necessary in industry by supplying a pool of cheap, available labour, and there is undoubtedly some truth in this argument, but it fails to take into account the very varied factors peculiar to each industry in which immigrants were employed. While structural reorganization may well be an ideal long-term solution of Britain's recurring labour shortages, most employers would certainly have and did use a series of short-term measures that seemed to offer a quicker and more certain solution. In some of the industries in which immigrants found work there was little room for major redeployment of labour, and in some instances the immigrant worker was more amenable to change than the local worker. It can also be argued that if unions and management in this country had been more willing to accept a drastic re-apportioning of labour together with concomitant redundancies, there might have been less demand for immigrant labour.

There does, however, remain a hard core of jobs filled by coloured immigrants that because of their unpleasant nature, low pay, or socially arduous hours were almost impossible to fill, especially in those regions where there were many better jobs, in terms of pay, conditions, and status, and the demand for these better jobs was growing. It is unlikely, in the face of competition, at home and overseas, that wage rises sufficiently great to overcome English labour's reluctance to enter the less well-regarded jobs would have been possible in all cases.

It is possible that greater capital investment in industry might have reduced the demand for immigrant labour, but this too is open to doubt. In the one study(10) carried out in a section of the wool textile industry in Yorkshire, it was found that the employment of immigrant (Pakistani) labour had facilitated capital investment in the sample of companies studied. The reason for this was that the new machinery was so expensive that it was necessary to have some form of shift working which was in the main manned by Pakistani labour. Similar parallels probably exist in other industries where new machinery necessitates shift working and employers find it is only possible to operate this machinery by a heavy reliance on immigrant labour, due to English labour's reluctance to work at night or on changing shifts.

More efficient organization of the labour force or greater investment might have been the ideal answer to many of the problems of labour shortage. However, given the conditions existent in British industry in the 1950s or even in the present day, these methods dealing with shortages of labour supply were never the most probable. If the coloured immigrant had not come to Britain the major employers would probably have attempted to widen their area of recruitment to other parts of the U.K., Eire, and Europe. It is possible that similar schemes to those run by the European Economic Community countries would have been set up. In some cases wage rises would have attracted more labour but the scope for these increases was limited and it should be noted that the greatest demands for the type of labour the immigrant supplied were in regions like the London and Birmingham areas where the highest average pay in this country is found.

The distribution of coloured immigrants in this country has been determined by the same factors as affected their migration. In those areas where low-paid workers are moving out the immigrant has moved in to take their places. Peach has summarized the position of West Indians saying, 'they have gone to the decreasing urban cores of expanding industrial regions'.(11) This conclusion is as applicable to Indians and Pakistanis as to West Indians. They have not settled in areas of low labour demand such as Wales, Scotland, or the North-East. The industries which have offered work to the coloured immigrant are in the main the service and older manufacturing industries at the centres of the great cities and rarely the new industries in the suburbs and beyond.

NOTES

(1) G.C.K. Peach, *West Indian Migration to Britain* (London, Oxford University Press, for Institute of Race Relations, 1968); also Peach, 'West Indian Migration to Britain: the Economic Factors', *Race* (Vol. VII, no I, July 1965).

(2) Peach, *West-Indian Migration to Britain*, p. 92.

(3) Peach, *West-Indian Migration to Britain*, p. 36.

(4) G. E. Cumper, 'Employment in Barbados' *Social and Economic Studies* (Vol. 8, no. 2, 1959), p. 129, and R. B. Davison, *West-Indian Migrants* (London, Oxford University Press, for Institute of Race Relations, 1962), p. 23.

(5) Peach, *West -Indian Migration to Britain*, p. 49. See also Davison, *West Indian Migrants*, p. 23.

(6) Peach, *West-Indian Migration to Britain*, p. 49.

(7) Peach, *West-Indian Migration to Britain*, p. 46.

(8) A.T. Bouscaron, *International Migrations since 1945* (New York, Praeger, 1963). Gross figures were considerably larger but a large number returned to Europe.

(9) Quoted by Peter Wright, *The Coloured Worker in British-Industry* (London, Oxford University Press, for Institute of Race Relations, 1968). See also Sheila Patterson, *Dark Strangers* (London, Tavistock Publications, 1963).

(10) Brian Cohen and Peter Jenner, 'The Employment of Immigrants: A Case Study within the Wool Industry', *Race* (Vol. X, no. 1, July 1968).

(11) Peach, 'Factors affecting the Distribution of West Indians in Britain', *Transactions and Papers 1966*, No. 38 (Institute of British Geographers). See also Peach's analysis of the West Indian's role as a replacement population in *West -Indian Migration to Britain*.

This selection is reprinted from E. J. Rose, et. al., *Color and Citizenship: A Report on British Race Relations*. Published for the Institute of Race Relations, London by Oxford University Press, N. Y., 1969, pp. 74–81.

THE BRITISH INDUSTRIAL SYSTEM AND RACIAL DISCRIMINATION

Bob Hepple

The problem of racial discrimination in employment is one of the factors which influences the processes of absorption of immigrants (of all origins and colours) into the receiving society of Britain. It is of particular significance in relation to the status and opportunities of second and later generations of immigrant groups who have retained their ethnic and cultural distinctiveness or dark pigmentation.

In relation mainly to the first generation, empirical research in six areas in 1967(1) confirmed and elaborated the finding of several earlier local studies that there was 'substantial discrimination', largely based on colour, against coloured immigrants applying for jobs. Other, more fundamental, research has isolated several factors influencing the absorption of the first generation, such as the immigrants' educational attainments, employment experience, language ability, cultural background, motivations, and attitudes; the local labour core's economic fears, mild antipathy to all strangers, and stereotyped attitudes about coloured people from former British colonies; the status, personality, and degree of pragmatic 'business sense' of management; and, occasionally, the behaviour of customers and the public at large.

In order to comprehend all these factors, some researchers have made use of S. N. Eisenstadt's theory of absorption.(2) In the leading study, Mrs. Sheila Patterson(3) has demonstrated the development of attitudes and behaviour on the index of absorption from the level of initial contact (where management will not employ immigrants and local labour will not work alongside them) through two phases of accommodation (in which managements try various modes of selection and local labour agrees to accept them subject to such safeguards as quotas and gradually comes to regard each newcomer both as an individual and as 'one of us') to the level of assimilation (in which managements are prepared to promote immigrants and local labour, to accept them in supervisory posts). On the part of immigrants, there are corresponding levels in which, at first, they keep together in groups and later start to mingle and become capable of supervisory work. In another stage (which may be 'final' or may lead on to assimilation) described as 'pluralistic integration', managements use ethnic work-gangs and individual immigrants emerge as leaders of these gangs.

Each of these stages of industrial absorption can be found in British industry — the precise level reached in a particular firm depending on such factors as the size and 'culture' of the enterprise and the character and adaptability of the particular immigrant group involved. For example, in her study of Croydon industry (where about 4 per cent of the total labour force is immigrant and there is considerable economic expansion), Mrs. Patterson(4) found that Polish political refugees and exiles were well on the way to industrial assimilation, while the younger, British-educated workers of Polish origin were fully assimilated in a wide range of firms; at the other extreme, West Indians (the largest and most recently arrived group) were for the most part mainly in semi-skilled and unskilled work in the earlier or later phases of accommodation. Most of the West Indian second generation were still at school, and it remained to be seen whether the first-generation immigrants would have established themselves sufficiently as part of the working community to be able to sponsor their locally educated children by the time the latter entered the job market.

The majority of coloured youngsters seeking jobs in 1968 spent most of their lives in their native lands; they were less likely than their British-born contemporaries to have had grammar or technical school education, less likely to have been apprenticed or in training for skilled jobs. There is now some weight of evidence, however, to suggest that coloured school leavers have higher job expectations than whites.(5) These aspirations may be the product of the cultural alienness of children of immigrants for whom the normal process of socialization — which is said to limit aspiration to a 'realistic' level — does not work. In part at least, the higher aspirations may reflect an understanding by coloured school leavers that they must aim higher and have better qualifications than their white counterparts. To some extent these young people are creating unfavourable stereotypes, thereby affecting the chances of the 'true' second generation of those born or mainly educated in Britain.

Little is known about this second generation, but as long ago as 1947 a study in Cardiff(6) showed that few of the coloured children who grew up and sought employment there could break through the 'closed circle' created by discrimination, and they quickly lost any ambitions they may have had. Apart from racial discrimination, it is clear from another study of Moslem communities in Tyneside and Cardiff,(7) undertaken in 1949-51, that the assimilation of coloured children may be retarded by the strong controls of the young person's own culture.

Racial discrimination, then, cuts across the generations but is of primary importance only in the second.

The general model which will be used here is that of Dunlop,(8) who describes a system of industrial relations as a system of rules. 'Rules' is used as a generic term to describe all the means by which jobs are regulated. These rules are established by the actors in the system, namely, a hierarchy of managers and supervisors, a hierarchy of workers and their spokesmen, specialized government agencies and private agencies set up by the actors (e.g. trade unions, employers' bodies, and immigrant organizations). They make these rules in certain contexts which involve three determinants: 1. the technological characteristics of the work place and the work community; 2. the market or budgetary constraints which impinge on the actors;

and 3. the locus and distribution of power in the larger society. This analytical system is completed by an ideology (or 'shared understanding'), that is, a set of beliefs and ideas commonly held by the actors which helps to bind or integrate the system as an entity (e.g. in Britain, the importance attached to voluntarism).

It must be emphasized that such an industrial relations system is logically an abstraction. It is not designed to describe in factual terms the real world of time and space. It is useful simply as a tool of analysis which focuses attention on certain critical variables. This framework of theoretical analysis, although rudimentary, may help researchers to set the right questions for inquiry and statistical testing and to arrive at general propositions. It must also be made clear that this article is solely concerned with the way in which the inner structure of the industrial relations system affects ethnic minorities and the way in which their presence affects the system. But it must be remembered that an industrial relations system is no more than a sub-system of the whole social system. . . .

An attempt will be made to consider, in the light of existing research: 1. the contexts of the industrial relations system; 2. its rules; and 3. its ideology.

 ## THE CONTEXTS OF THE INDUSTRIAL RELATIONS SYSTEM

The type of work, the skill and educational levels which it requires, the degree of contact with customers that it necessitates, and the locality of the work place are among the technical contexts of the system. Clearly, these and similar matters have an important bearing on rule-making as it affects ethnic minorities in the work force.

For example, it has for long been an untested assumption that the employment of immigrant labour is associated with old, under-capitalized industries unable or unwilling to invest in new machinery. However, recent research by Brian Cohen in the wool industry in the West Riding of Yorkshire,(9) discovered that it was the new investment in high-cost machinery which led to the employment of Pakistani males. This was because the machinery required intensive working to become profitable and these men, without family commitments in England, were prepared to do night-shifts and were anxious to work long hours of overtime so as to accumulate savings. The semi-skilled nature of the work and the length of time for which it had to be undertaken determined the source of labour supply in the absence of local male labour. Dayshifts for this type of work tended to remain the prerogative of local female labour, where this was available. A change in the job content and hours of operation served to change the rule of the work place, i.e. that local female labour was normally employed. This change resulted in further rule changes about overtime and wage-fixing. Technical changes, therefore, are a dynamic element leading to changes in the complex of rules.

The contact of workers with customers affords another illustration of the impact of the technical environment on rules and is one that is particularly significant to ethnic minorities. Just as rules are fashioned to impose special standards (e.g. of dress and appearance) on workers who must have direct contact with customers, so too management takes account of the real or supposed objections of customers and the public to members of different ethnic groups. At one point this may lead to the employment of only Chinese waiters in a 'Chinese-style' restaurant; at another point, it may result in discrimination against coloured people in respect of certain 'contact' jobs. In her study of Croydon industry, Mrs. Patterson(10) found that the acceptance or non-acceptance of coloured immigrants in particular roles depended on the whole context and scope of each role, the extent to which it was regular or intermittent, intimate or distant. For example, very few objections are heard about coloured immigrants in the role of doctors, nurses, and hospital staff due to the kind of services they render, the abnormal circumstances imposed by illness and need, and the depersonalized nature of hospital relationship. The public may be less willing to accept coloured immigrants as teachers because their role is more personalized, longer sustained, and overlaps into the informal social sphere. At lower status levels, coloured immigrants were most 'acceptable' where they were identifiable by means of a uniform or badge or where the performance of their role takes place in a circumscribed area (e.g. in public) over a limited period. Examples are railwaymen, busmen, postmen, sportsmen, and entertainers. The greater degree of intimacy involved in relationships with shop assistants and waitresses makes these somewhat less acceptable roles. Most unacceptable of all are those roles which involve intrusions into the Englishman's 'castle-home', e.g. meter-readers, repairmen. The role of policemen, as guardians of public order and social norms, has made police authorities reluctant (particularly in the early years of coloured immigration) to appoint coloured policemen. In all these situations, public reaction — direct or indirect, real or imagined — affects rules.

The geographical location of the enterprise also affects its rules. In the West Riding study,(11) one of the firms not employing coloured immigrant labour was sited near a new housing estate and had an adequate supply of local labour. In Croydon, Mrs. Patterson(12) found that the difficulty which coloured immigrants had in obtaining residential accommodation in the more 'select' suburbs, limited the number of immigrant workers in employment in those areas. (Incidentally, it ought to be noted that the rules of the industrial relations system, in turn, have their effect on the housing of immigrants in 'twilight areas' or 'zones of transition': for example, the widespread operation of informal quotas in Croydon industry unintentionally regulated the build-up of immigrants in these areas; contrast this with the rapid concentration of Asians in certain areas where they are employed in local factories in ethnic work-gangs.)

These illustrations show the impact of the technical context on the substance of rules as they affect ethnic minorities. It must not be forgotten that this context also affects the hierarchies of workers and management. For example, the nature of the work may determine whether management uses an English-speaking 'go-between' to supervise Asian workers. The similarity of work done by workers in an enterprise, coupled with their strategic position, may induce a degree of solidarity which cuts across ethnic divisions. The character of the enterprise (e.g. nationalized railways as compared with municipal or private road transport) may determine the degree of State involvement in establishing fair labour practices.

The competitive structure of an industry or firm, its specialized market conditions, general economic conditions, and the state of the market for labour services, all have a vital bearing on rule-making as it affects ethnic minorities.

Research into these matters is virtually non-existent. Cohen(13) showed that in the competitive labour-intensive wool industry (consisting of many small units) the employment of immigrant labour was the almost inevitable choice of management since higher wage-rates to attract internal migrants would have made night-shifts uneconomic and would have raised prices, with some firms going out of business in the process. Increased capital investment of a labour-substitution nature has been hampered by money shortages (in turn traceable to imperfections in the money market) and bottle-necks in the production of investment goods. The rules which evolved were, accordingly, ones which favoured the employment of immigrant labour at relatively low wage-rates. Comparative research in an industry with a different wage and competitive structure, e.g. engineering, might be expected to yield a different set of rules, possibly discriminating against the employment of immigrant labour.

A striking example of the way in which specialized market conditions affect rule-making is the shipping industry. Here economic circumstances favoured the employment of lascars (sailors who are natives of India) on British ships because of their relative cheapness per head and their apparent suitability for work in the tropics. This led to racial differentiations between seamen employed on British ships, which were embodied in legislation since the early nineteenth century. This legislative discrimination persisted until its repeal in 1970. However, much customary segregation and discrimination on British merchant ships is specifically excepted from the provisions of the Race Relations Act 1968.(14)

General economic conditions have an important bearing on rule-making. The higher proportions of male and female immigrants (as a percentage of those economically active) out of employment in comparison with the corresponding proportion of the total population out of employment, as revealed by census figures, not only reflects the jobs that immigrants do but may also be due, in part, to redundancy rules which discriminate against recent immigrants ('last in, first out') or 'foreign' labour. In turn, these rules are seen by local labour as necessary protective devices against the threat of unemployment. To the extent that other rules — usually the result of national policies such as redundancy payments schemes and job security measures — cushion local labour from the effects of economic recession, ethnic minorities are indirectly protected as well.

Both the technical and market contexts determine the size of the work force in particular enterprises and this affects the rules relating to ethnic minorities. For example, large, efficient, rapidly expanding mass-production plants in the light engineering sector in Croydon(15) had developed increasingly satisfactory techniques for the selection, induction, training, and industrial integration of West Indians and other coloured workers, and, unlike some smaller firms, showed little evidence of 'favoured nation' policies which discriminate against some but not all ethnic minorities.

Thus far I have discussed the 'market' contexts in purely economic terms. But perhaps the most important 'market' is that for labour services; and it is in this connection that students of industrial relations recognize that the ethnic characteristics of the work force and the racial prejudices or antipathies of workers and managements, complicate the substance of rule-making. For example, racial myths about the 'dirty' habits of Asians may lead local English workers to demand separate toilets; objections to the wearing of beards and turbans by Sikhs may involve the managers of municipal transport departments in disputes about the interpretation of rules which require certain standards of dress or appearance; and language differences may result in the maintenance of ethnic work-units.

The 'immigrant' character of the work force, too, has significant effects on rules relating to training and discipline. For example, in his study of coloured workers in the North and Midlands, Dr. Peter Wright has shown how special demonstration techniques were evolved for immigrants and how, in some instances, complex jobs were modified.(16)

The power context is crucial in defining the status of managers, local labour core, ethnic minorities, and Government and private agencies.

For example, where a trade union exists and is active on behalf of all its members, jobs and promotion may be secured for those who allege discrimination. On the other hand, if the union is inactive or allies itself with management discrimination, advancement will be denied. Where no union exists, immigrant-based groups tend to lack the power or status to negotiate with management. Attempts to create such a power-base by forming 'immigrant' factory groups or separate unions of coloured workers have been opposed by trade unions as divisive and have not met with any noticeable response from coloured workers themselves. In fact, the policy of most immigrant and sponsor organizations has been to encourage membership in the general trade union movement. The belief of these groups is that active union participation will provide the only feasible power-base for anti-discriminatory activities. This attitude may be contrasted with the formation of separate occupational organizations by Polish immigrants which for a time reduced the frequency of contacts between Poles and British people but at the same time helped the Poles find jobs and sheltered them from discrimination.(17)

The relation of trade unions to their own members is no less important in determining the context and application of rules. For example, in a study of a strike involving 600 Punjabi workers at a Southall factory,(18) Peter Marsh found that poor communications between the administrative wing of the Transport and General Workers' Union and its members were accentuated by the fact that most of the strikers were not articulate in English or in the subtleties of local union practice. A protracted dispute between the strikers and certain officials arose over a question of the interpretation of ambiguous union rules concerning 'official support' for strike action.

The status of local managements in relation to national hierarchies of management is another feature of the power context. For example, the initiative of the Engineering Employers' Federation in negotiating with the unions a special agreement relating to racial discrimination in employment, resulted in the establishment of committees of local employers and unions to consider complaints of discrimination. These procedures, in turn, were adopted by some non-federated employers, such as Fords.(19) Weak national bodies, on the other hand, are incapable of influencing the situation in this way.

Finally, Government agencies define rules. For example, the employment services of the Department of Employment and Productivity claim to have seen encouraging results in the course of persuading employers to consider job applicants on merit alone. On the other hand, the Department's ability to affect the situation is hampered by other general rules; for example, it is not compulsory for employers to notify the Department of vacancies, and the Department faces competition from private fee-charging agencies which, prior to 1968, were free to practise discrimination. In the future, other independent agencies (created by Parliament), such as the Race Relations Board and its local conciliation committees and the Community Relations Commission and its local groups, may play a significant part in the rule-making that directly relates to ethnic minorities. It is, as yet, too early to gauge the impact of these agencies.

RULES AND IDEOLOGY OF THE INDUSTRIAL RELATIONS SYSTEM

In *Race, Jobs, and the Law in Britain*, I have described the substantive rules of industrial relations which affect persons differently on grounds of race,(20) and in the preceding discussion I have mentioned some of these by way of example.

The main point that needs to be emphasized here is that these rules are of two kinds. First there are those which form part of the *internal* system of job regulation within particular enterprises. On the other hand, there are a number of rules of an *external* nature in that they depend upon the participation and consent of persons outside the enterprise.

Examples of internal rules are: shop-floor 'understandings' about the proportion of 'foreign' or coloured workers to English or white workers to be employed in the establishment or in certain occupations; barriers against promotion; formal and informal arrangements about the sharing of overtime work; the establishment of ethnic work-units; the separation of toilet or canteen facilities; special redundancy rules. These all share the characteristic that they are settled autonomously within each enterprise.

Examples of external rules are: the policy of the Department of Employment and Productivity about discriminatory job referrals; collective labour agreements restricting or protecting foreign or coloured labour; the intervention of union officials either for or against discriminatory conduct within an enterprise; the admissions policy of trade unions and, in particular, the existence of closed shops and craft barriers; special vocational training schemes for immigrants; legal rules; the activities of bodies outside industry such as community relations groups and immigrant organizations.

In order to understand the effectiveness of measures against racial discrimination in employment, it is essential to analyse the ways in which the technical, market, and power contexts influence the development of the internal and external rules respectively. At present, the main feature of the internal rules is their discriminatory content. Indeed, discrimination (through quotas, 'favoured nation' policies, and ethnic segregation) has been used spontaneously in order to accommodate ethnic minorities. These rules are the product of such factors as the type of work involved, the degree of contact with customers required, geographical location, the economics of labour-intensive industries and general economic conditions, as well as personal psychological tensions, fear of strangers, and colour/status consciousness.

These rules will not change in themselves unless there is some fundamental change in the actors, the contexts, or the ideology. As Dunlop points out, 'industrial relations systems show considerable tenacity and persistence'.(21) The very notion of an industrial relations system implies an internal balance which is likely to be restored if that balance is temporarily displaced. For example, the temporary organization of immigrant workers (as in the Southall strike) will have no long-term effect on the rules. But a major organizational change, such as the recognition by management of a powerful shop-floor organization dedicated to racial equality or a change in personnel management, is likely to result in rule changes. Present indications are that such changes are unlikely. Indeed, such events as the London dockers' and meat porters' marches in support of Enoch Powell's anti-immigrant speech are reminders of the strong internal resistance to change. Moreover, although a limited study has shown fairly active participation by coloured workers in trade unions, these workers are not themselves at the centre of deliberations for change.(22)

It is not easy to predict what effect likely changes in the technical and market contexts will have on rules affecting ethnic minorities. But it seems improbable that automation (labour-substitution investment) will in itself favour minorities. As long as other pressures exist for racial discrimination, coloured minorities are bound to be excluded in the main from the new skilled and white-collar job opportunities which automation promises; instead they are likely to be relegated to the declining activity of manual labour.

The present direction of the internal rules, then, appears to be increasingly discriminatory.

The external rules, on the other hand, are moving in an anti-discriminatory direction. The principal feature of the traditional system of job regulation as it affected ethnic minorities, as I have said elsewhere, 'is that the competition of the labour market was restricted by rules aimed at limiting the supply of labour and the terms on which competition could take place'.(23) This was usually done on the basis of nationality (e.g. against 'foreign' workers) rather than on grounds of colour. This traditional system rested upon a set of values appropriate to the colonial era, with all its notions of national superiority.

A very significant feature of these external rules is that they were achieved almost exclusively through voluntary processes, that is they rested on social sanctions and, above all, the threat of strikes or dismissals. Apart from the shipping industry, the law played no role except in the limited form of restrictions on the right of aliens to seek and change employment, more recently extended to certain Commonwealth citizens.

The changes which are now taking place rest on the changing ideology of the system, a new set of 'shared understandings' as yet indefinite and in the process of formation. The ideas of racial equality and 'integration,' rooted in the post-colonial world and strongly influenced by world-wide movements against racial oppression and *apartheid*, are now in conflict with the older *laissez-faire* philosophy of 'freedom to discriminate' and 'freedom of contract.' At the same time, the response of successive British Governments to economic difficulties and industrial unrest is bringing about a new climate of opinion in which voluntarism and corporate autonomy, twin pillars of the traditional system, are under growing attack.

NOTES

(1) Political and Economic Planning and Research Services Ltd., *Racial Discrimination* (London, P.E.P., 1967), p. 81.

(2) S.N. Eisenstadt, *The Absorption of Immigrants* (London, Routledge & Kegan Paul, 1954).

(3) Sheila Patterson, *Immigrants in Industry* (London, Oxford University Press, for Institute of Race Relations, 1969), esp. p. 206, Table 3.

(4) op. cit., pp. 173-204.

(5) D. Beetham, *Immigrant School Leavers and the Youth Employment Service in Birmingham* (London, Institute of Race Relations Special Series, 1967); Peter Figueroa, 'School Leavers and Colour Barrier,' thesis in preparation.

(6) K. Little, *Negroes in Britain: A Study of Racial Relations in English Society* (London, Kegan Paul, 1947).

(7) S.F. Collins, 'The British-Born Colonial,' *Sociological Review* (N.S.) (Vol. 3, No. 1, 1955), p. 77.

(8) John T. Dunlop, *Industrial Relations Systems* (New York, Holt, Rinehart and Winston, 1959), esp. pp. 7-18.

(9) Brian Cohen and Peter Jenner, 'The Employment of Immigrants: A Case Study Within the Wood Industry,' *Race* (Vol. X, No. 1, July 1968), pp. 41-56.

(10) op. cit., pp. 275-80.

(11) Cohen and Jnner, op. cit.

(12) op. cit., p. 231.

(11) Cohen and Jenner, op. cit.

(14) Hepple, *Race, Jobs and the Law in Britain*, Chapters 3 and 6.

(15) Patterson, op. cit., pp. 70-4.

(16) Peter Wright, *The Coloured Worker in British Industry* (London, Oxford University Press, for Institute of Race Relations, 1968), pp. 105-9.

(17) J. Zubrzycki, *Polish Immigrants in Britain* (The Hague, Martinus Nijhoff, 1956), pp. 108, 115, 119.

(18) Peter Marsh, *Anatomy of a Strike: Unions, Employers and Panjabi Workers in a Southall Factory* (London, Institute of Race Relations Special Series, 1967), esp. pp. 87-90.

(19) This agreement was later abandoned, however, because the Confederation of Shipbuilding and Engineering Unions was not prepared to accept the system of appeals from the voluntary bodies to the Race Relations Board, provided for in the Race Relations Act of 1968.

(20) See especially Chapters 5 and 6.

(21) Dunlop, op. cit., p. 27.

(22) B. Radin, 'Coloured Workers and British Trade Unions,' *Race* (Vol. VIII, No. 2, 1966), p. 157.

(23) Hepple, op. cit., p. 156.

This selection is abridged from Simon Abbott, ed. *The Prevention of Racial Discrimination in Britain*, published for the United Nations Institute for Training and Research and the Institute of Race Relations by Oxford University Press, N.Y., 1971, pp. 155-157, 159, 160-168.

IMMIGRATION AND ITS EFFECTS ON ECONOMY

Maurice Peston

This essay stems from a concern with the costs and benefits of labour as they affect the United Kingdom. Because of the lack of appropriate empirical studies it has to be mainly analytical and speculative. Its purpose is, therefore, chiefly to consider various possibilities and to put current discussion into some sort of perspective. An attempt is made to show that certain simple views of the economic effects of immigration are probably untrue, but whilst it is easy to show that the effects of immigration on the United Kingdom are neither necessarily advantageous nor disadvantageous, it is much more difficult to estimate what may have been the actual net benefits or disbenefits during the past two decades.

Our plan will be to consider some simple hypotheses concerning the economic effects of immigration. In addition, we will discuss broadly the sort of conditions under which it is likely to be advantageous for the home population to permit the entry of labour from other countries. Before doing that, however, it is useful to mention briefly the economic causes of immigration.

Immigration can occur for a variety of reasons, many of which will be extraneous to the economic system. But the economist will emphasize that immigration is determined partly by the comparative economic conditions in the giving and receiving country and partly by transport and similar costs. In addition, however, there may be an income effect in the giving country, namely, that up to a point as incomes rise in that country immigration may *increase*, because at high income levels immigrants may be able to afford to move where previously they had been unable to do so. (There may also be increased knowledge of immigration possibilities connected with rising income.) It is also possible that up to a point immigration is self-increasing, the earlier immigrants pulling others after them.

There are certain hypotheses that have been put forward concerning the economic consequences of immigration which are worthy of consideration, either to show that they are false, or that their significance is much less than might be imagined. These are as follows: 1. immigration causes unemployment; 2. immigration reduces the rate of economic growth; 3. immigration reduces the rate of technical progress; 4. immigration leads to a deterioration in the balance of payments; and 5. immigration causes inflation.

These hypotheses are of course inter-related and are here separated out for the sake of analytical convenience. Also, in so far as they are intended to be empirical, ultimately their truth or falsity will depend on appropriate testing. This, it must be emphasized, has not yet been carried out on a large enough scale or in enough detail to decide the matter, but it does not mean that no serious discussion is possible in this field or that the issue can be regarded as entirely open.

One topic which is frequently discussed is the relationship between immigration, the tax system, and expenditure under the social services. We shall consider this chiefly under the heading of immigration and inflation, although it is, of course, true that it is somewhat broader than that.

Let us start with the question of unemployment. It may be expected that, especially in conditions of comparatively free entry to a country, immigrants themselves may expect to experience unemployment in the initial stages of looking for a job or in deciding whether a particular job is suitable. It is also likely that immigrants, as the latest arrivals, might expect to be amongst the first to be laid off in any slack conditions of trade that arise in most countries from time to time. Also, there is a tendency for immigrants to enter those occupations which experience large amounts of unemployment anyway. Putting these three factors together there is a considerable likelihood that the immigrant population would on average experience more unemployment than the population in general, and also that within the immigrant population those who arrived the longest time ago would experience less unemployment than the average. (This is, of course, not to say that *all* immigrants necessarily experience more unemployment than the population on average, but rather that the spectrum of unemployment experience of immigrants lies to the right of the spectrum of unemployment of the home population where these two are measured on a scale of increasing unemployment from left to right.) In this connexion two points emerge from the examination of immigrant unemployment: first, that the cyclical pattern of the immigrant population is much the same as that of the total population and, secondly, that immigrants form an increasing share of unemployment in the down-swing.

Further evidence on unemployment among immigrants is provided by Eric Butterworth in *Immigrants in West Yorkshire.*(1) While the data is not absolutely clear cut, it is certainly compatible with the view that immigrants experience relatively more unemployment than the domestic population, and that economic fluctuations tend to affect them disproportionately. What is not apparent from Butterworth's data, but would repay further study, is whether there is a 'settling-in effect,' so that after a point the unemployment experience of the immigrant becomes the same as that of the domestic population.

The fact that immigrants may experience more unemployment than the home population is not the same as saying that unemployment among the home population will rise as a result of immigration or even that unemployment among the total population will rise. This may be seen in a variety of ways. First, it has been argued that for an economy to work effectively in the short run, it must have a degree of slack, made up partly of physical capacity and partly of human capacity. It is likely that, to the extent that this slack is made up of immigrants, it will not be made up of the home population. As a result the effect of immigration is not to increase unemployment but merely to take over the burden of unemployment from the home population. Secondly, in the case of some countries, notably West Germany, the flow of immigration may be extremely responsive to pressures in the domestic labour market so that the pool of unemployment does not even occur in the domestic economy itself. Ceri Peach has shown that in the 1950s there was a similarly close relationship between the demand for labour in the United Kingdom and West Indian immigration.(2)

Thirdly, economic efficiency requires to some degree a willingness of the labour force to be mobile. While this mobility is partly occupational and industrial, it is also partly geographical. If the immigrant population is more mobile geographically (and that is certainly the general impression of, for example, Pakistanis given in the earlier parts of the present Report), it will happen that the same shifts in the structure of economic activities will take place with less disruption both of the home labour force and of the labour force as a whole. If the immigrants are more mobile, this enables the domestic population to be less mobile. Moreover, immigration may be partially a substitute for inter-regional migration, and may help to offset the alleged costs of inter-regional migration.

Fourthly, and this refers also to the last hypothesis on the list, some unemployment results from the central government's attempts, not always successful, to deal with the problem of inflation. If it happens that the net effect of immigration is anti-inflationary, this too may help to reduce the overall unemployment in the economy. In sum, I am not arguing that immigration necessarily leads to lower unemployment, or that it would be impossible for any person or group in the home labour force to suffer from more unemployment as a result of immigration. My point is that the view that immigration inevitably leads to more unemployment is easily criticized on theoretical grounds and is not in accordance with the facts. To take the two obvious cases, West Germany for two decades did not experience increased unemployment as a result of immigration, and United Kingdom unemployment does not correlate with immigration (indeed, Peach tends to argue that there is a positive correlation between unfilled vacancies in the United Kingdom and immigration from the West Indies.(3)

Turning now to the problem of economic growth, one difficulty is that there is not general agreement on the causes of economic growth. This, however, will not prevent us establishing the negative point that immigration is not necessarily deleterious to growth. Again, it is worth mentioning that as far as empirical work is concerned not a great deal has been done, and there are difficulties lying in the way of the potential researcher. The most obvious of these again concerns cause and effect — any positive connexion between immigration and growth might be that the first is conducive to the second, or that the second is conducive to the first.

On the theoretical side, it is possible that an economy may grow at a slower rate than otherwise because of shortage of labour in general or shortage of a particular kind of labour. This point is obviously relevant in situations of increasing marginal product of labour or where (as is remarked below) the rate of technical progress is an increasing function of the rate of growth of the labour force. While it is highly controversial, it is worth noting that Professor Kaldor's inaugural lecture, 'The Causes of the Slow Rate of Economic Growth of the United Kingdom,' would support this view as far as the United Kingdom economy is concerned.(4) If we set aside the problem of the marginal product of labour, before looking at technical progress, it is worth paying a little attention to the propensity to save.

It is usually accepted that physical capital accumulation has a positive connexion with the process of growth and at full employment can be undertaken only if firms, households, or the Government saves. Saving depends partially on the distribution of income, which aspect of the subject we shall deal with later on. At this point, we are only concerned to ask whether there is any reason to believe that the propensity to save of immigrants will be lower than comparable people born in this country. This is to some extent a psychological or sociological matter and outside the compass of a purely economic article, but it is worth mentioning that there is nothing in those other social sciences which leads to the conclusion that immigrants have a lower propensity to save. Within economics itself there is one positive point that may be noted, namely that immigrants may well own less capital than people in the home population with similar incomes, which would act as an incentive to save more. Evidence on immigrants to the United States or the United Kingdom certainly does not support the view that they have an unduly low propensity to save. In fact, it is apparent from Radburn's and Vanags's investigations that West Indians and Pakistanis in Birmingham have a higher propensity to save than the comparable domestic population, even when allowance is made for their remittances home.

As far as technical progress is concerned, it could be argued that this will be determined partly by the resources available for it, so that if immigration is conducive to growth, it is equally conducive to technical progress and thus to further growth. It is sometimes argued, however, that technical progress is increased in conditions of labour shortage, making it imperative to develop and employ new labour saving techniques. This would be slowed down by an easier availability of labour which would encourage employees to go on using old-fashioned labour intensive methods. There are two arguments to be set against this. One is that technical progress means change, and an immigrant labour force may be less well entrenched and more willing to change than the domestic population. Secondly, technically advanced equipment may be situated in unattractive places or may need to be worked continuously through the day and on every day of the year. Again, an immigrant labour force, especially if it has fewer family ties, may be more willing to work in this way. As far as the facts are concerned they do not show that those countries which have experienced the greatest labour shortage have also made the most technical progress. It is equally not true that as immigration has increased in the United Kingdom in the past fifteen years, the rate of technical progress has fallen.

It may be expected that technical progress is related not simply to the aggregate labour force but also to its structure. There may be certain sorts of labour which are conducive to technical progress because it is comprised of the kind of people who carry it out, either inventing new techniques or helping to put them into practical use. In this category would come scientists, engineers, and certain sorts of managers or entrepreneurs.

Another sort of labour may be conducive to technical progress because it is willing to work the technically advanced machines or is complementary to the labour force working on those machines. This sort of labour may not itself need to be particularly advanced, but, as has been remarked above, it may have to be sufficiently flexible to be willing to work under all sorts of adverse conditions. It should also be remembered that, for example, there may not only be a demand for multi-shift working directly on the advanced machines, but for all the other activities of the factory, including all the managerial and office staff who may have to be continuous around the clock. A person who is willing to make tea, drive a vehicle, or answer the phone at any time of the day or night is just as vital to continuous working as an actual operative.

There is ample evidence that in many industrialized countries, including the United Kingdom, immigrants have been a significant source of supply of both these types of labour. A pool of cheap immigrant labour may well have played a vital part in the technical progress of the United States or, more recently, Germany and Italy. (In the case of Italy there is every reason to treat the population movement from the extreme south to the north as a special case of immigration.) Similarly, at the top end of the spectrum, in both the United States and the United Kingdom, technically advanced industries such as chemicals have developed on the basis of immigrant labour. Once again, therefore, the conclusion must be that the hypothesis that the recent comparative technological backwardness of the United Kingdom is attributable to immigration and would be reversed by immigration control is unproven, and certainly cannot be substantiated beyond doubt by existing economic theory.

Indeed the available evidence does allow one to go considerably further on this subject. In his work, Butterworth states:

> The night shifts of many woollen mills in West Yorkshire depend on immigrant labour, illustrating that migrants are to be found in jobs which involve a good deal of disruption of normal patterns of life. The economic motivation with which migrants come makes them look for ways of supplementing income, particularly as they have been much more mobile than the bulk of the labour force, and the woollen industry provides plenty of opportunities for overtime.(5)

In their extremely important article in *Race*, Cohen and Jenner reach the following conclusion:

> The degree to which new capital investment and the employment of immigrants go together is surprising, and it would be fair to conclude that the employment of immigrants has facilitated new capital investment in the sample of firms under study. This is because new machinery is too expensive to be worked only forty or forty-eight hours a week and it must be employed as intensively as possible thus necessitating shift work. This is a trend not confined to the wool industry and may well, in the future, make headway into more white-collar occupations. It is well recognized that there is a general disinclination to work nights or changing shifts, and higher rates of pay are the general rule. The immigrant (Pakistani) workers are usually more willing to take this work than local labour. . . .(6)

It may be remarked that in this respect the domestic population are akin to the latter day Luddites whose restrictive practices and antipathy to new equipment may be undermined by the immigrants. There is, however, another side to this question of technical progress which must be mentioned. It is possible that immigration may benefit the receiving country; it is equally possible that the equivalent emigration will harm the losing country. This is particularly likely at the top end of the skill spectrum. Insofar as such people flow from poorer countries to richer ones, the technological backwardness of the former and the technological advance of the latter may both be accentuated. This possibility applies to the United Kingdom as a loss of high level manpower to the United States and the rich Commonwealth and to the poor Commonwealth as a loss of manpower to the United Kingdom. Immigration restrictions on such people may well, therefore, benefit the losing country and could be advocated on those grounds, but for the same reason they would harm the receiving country.

The effect of immigration on the balance of payments turns partly on whether the free movement of labour into the economy is inflationary. It is easy to show that it is not necessarily inflationary, and may even be anti-inflationary. It is agreed by most economists that some or all of the rise in prices and money wages that occurs from time to time (and has occurred pretty continuously in the United Kingdom for the past thirty years) is attributable to the excess pressure of demand in the labour market. The greater the shortage of labour, the more a particular demand pressure will be inflationary. The effect of immigration is to provide one additional source of supply of labour and, therefore, the outcome will be to reduce inflationary pressure rather than increase it. To quote the obvious example, the ability of West Germany to grow at an extremely fast rate with little or no unemployment and minimal price inflation is attributable in large part to the availability of immigrant labour. Inflation is also sometimes attributable to the cost pressure of trade unions. Although this is a more controversial matter, it can hardly be argued that increased immigration will add to that cost pressure. If anything, the expectation must be that it will be reduced.

A particular argument that has been presented on the subject of immigration and inflation is based on the view that immigrants typically place a greater burden on the social services than they pay in taxes. This view has been associated with E.J. Mishan and L. Needleman, although it is not unique to them and their analysis of the macro-economic effects of immigration covers a much wider field. The general idea involved here is that immigration adds less to supply than to demand, causing the general level of prices to rise, or in crude terms, that immigration has an expenditure multiplier greater than its output multiplier, both measured in approximate terms. To quote Mishan and Needleman:

> If net immigration added to the natural product without increasing effective demand, or if it increased effective demand in smaller proportions, then, whatever the other economic effects, it would contribute in the short run to a reduction of the pressure of excess aggregate demand however caused.(7)

Although the public sector side is only part of the story, the result of an excess demand for social services over tax payments would be either a decline in the quality of the social services provided or, if quality is maintained, an increase in the budget deficit which at full employment is inflationary. This argument may be criticized partly in terms of its assumptions. It is not necessarily the case that all immigrants place a greater burden on the social services than they pay in taxes, even in the short run. Secondly, even if this aspect of immigration were inflationary, it would have to be set against other aspects which may be non-inflationary. Thirdly, the point is often made that many of the social services in the United Kingdom are staffed to a considerable extent by immigrants. If those immigrants were barred from the United Kingdom, the cost of the social services would be higher, and that is certainly inflationary. A crucial piece of evidence in all of this was presented by Mrs. K. Jones in 'Immigrants and the Social Services'.(8) It seems to follow from her investigations that, presumably partly as a result of the different demographic structure of immigrants and their higher participation rates, the pressure of expenditure on the social services is less than that of the domestic population.

It is also worth noting that it is not true that the immigrants' needs are met solely by the provision of new social capital. Instead, they move to a considerable extent into the old and obsolete social capital vacated by the domestic population. A recent report from Birmingham has the following to say:

> It is difficult to give an accurate estimate of the cost of school building necessitated solely by immigration. For instance, probably, a large number of English families have moved from the city to such places as Sutton Coldfield, Milfield, Solihull, etc. which has freed places in Birmingham schools for immigrants, but it is estimated that seven schools would not have been required had there been no immigration at a cost of 991,421 pounds. In addition, two other schools would probably have been much smaller in size had it not been for immigration. Twenty three minor works at a total cost of 110,470 pounds are attributable to immigration. The cost of school building for immigrants on this basis to date is approximately 1,376,235 pounds.(9)

It is difficult to determine how many children are to be counted against this expenditure, but for 1962–8, the number of so-called non-European children in Birmingham schools has increased by 12,500 approximately. This is a capital cost of 110 pounds per child or, as an annuity over thirty years at 8% per annum, slightly more than 10 pounds per year per child. To put this into perspective, it is worth noting that a family with two children earning the average industrial wage will pay some ten to fifteen times this in rates and taxes in a year. The point may be put in another way, Studies of the incidence of taxes and social service benefits (for example, in *Economic Trends*, August 1966) show that these are redistributive towards people with lower than average incomes and larger than average families. If immigrants fall into these categories there will be a redistribution in their favour. This redistribution, however, will be mitigated in the short run at least by the lower pressure on social services of the sort indicated by Mrs. Jones. (We do not have a great deal of evidence on taxes, but note this remark of Davison: 'There were also a large number of cases where there appears to be quite genuine hardship and overpayment of tax.')(10)

It is by no means unlikely, therefore, that the efficiency of some or all the economy may rise as a result of immigration, and it is possible that inflationary pressures will be reduced. It follows that it cannot be argued with certainty that immigration will lead to a deterioration in the balance of payments. It may well lead to an improvement in the balance of payments, and in the case of West Germany most certainly has. There is, however, one special aspect of immigration which might be presumed to have a deleterious effect on the balance of payments. That is, that it is not unreasonable to argue that immigrants coming from foreign lands may have a high propensity to remit sums to their original homeland, either to raise the income levels of their poor dependants left behind or to help them meet the cost of becoming immigrants themselves. The obvious example here concerns the sums sent from the United States to Italy which, while they have been a great help to the Italian balance of payments, have been an equal hindrance to the United States! There is no doubt that West Indians, Indians, and Pakistanis remit significant sums home, although it is worth noting that these financial flows are to the Sterling Area. Even here, however, the matter is not quite as simple as all that because in these days of foreign aid it is not inconceivable that now or in the future these remittances may take the place in part of aid that would have been given by the richer country to the poorer. In other words, although there is every presumption that from this point of view the effect of immigration would be to worsen the balance of payments, the net effect may be less than the sum remitted.

If we now summarize the arguments on these major macro-hypotheses, they amount to the view that from a purely theoretical view there is no presumption that overall immigration is harmful in the sense of causing unemployment, lowering growth, adding to inflation, or worsening the balance of payments. Immigration may be benevolent, reducing unemployment, increasing growth, diminishing inflation, and even improving the balance of payments. These general considerations may, of course, be regarded as secondary to the particular conditions of the United Kingdom economy in the post-war period. On this it is impossible to pronounce with any confidence because of the lack of empirical knowledge. None the less, there is no strong evidence to support the theory that overall immigration is harmful and there are small pieces of evidence, varying from the willingness of immigrants to work in bad conditions to their staffing of the social services, that immigration has been positively beneficial to the economy. My own view on this appears at the end of this chapter. A fundamental analysis of the costs and benefits of immigration would need to consider both of these as flows over time firstly in conditions of zero or restricted immigration. Whether immigration itself has a beneficial effect is too open-ended a question; the correct approach is to compare more immigration with less and to specify all the other relevant events that would occur. In this chapter it is impossible to carry out an analysis in such fundamental terms, especially as far as its dynamic consequences are concerned. Apart from shortage of space, there is also the point that there is within economics little realistic analysis of the alternative future development paths open to an economy, especially when alternative population and manpower developments have to be taken into account. It must be appreciated, therefore, that the elementary view that we present may have to be modified later on as a result of a more sophisticated study of the subject.

The domestic population will gain in economic terms from a higher rate of immigration compared with a lower if the flow of benefits which it gains from that immigration is greater than the flow of costs. In emphasizing the flow side it is accepted that the fact that in any year the costs may exceed the benefits is not a sufficient condition for restricting immigration, or the fact that in any year the benefits may exceed the costs is equally not a sufficient condition for encouraging immigration. We also emphasize economic terms to mean that while economics is in principle an all embracing subject, what would normally be included in a cost-benefit analysis, and what is most likely to be quantifiable, might take no account of the social aspects of the matter which might be decisive in determining the total net benefits in any real case.

The net gain to the domestic population may be measured by the change in the flow of disposable real income plus the change in the flow of public consumption goods (including in these such aspects of environment as congestion, noise, smoke, and so on) accruing to them. The effect of immigration, therefore, will be economically beneficial if the increase in the flow of real national income plus the flow of economic goods not measured by real national income increases by more than the immigrants' share. This means that it is not a sufficient test of the value of immigration from the economic standpoint to inquire if real national income rises. On the one hand, part of all of the increase may accrue to the immigrants; on the other hand, economic welfare is measured only imperfectly by real national income.

In strict economic terms (which the general reader may prefer to ignore) this seems to mean that if there were diminishing marginal product of every factor of production, a given technology, no external economies and diseconomies of production or consumption, and the economy were in a state of perfectly competitive equilibrium, there would be no advantage to the domestic population from allowing immigration to occur. If, however, technical progress is speeded up, if net external effects are increased, if there are unexploited returns to scale and increasing marginal product of labour, if the frictions in adjusting to economic change are diminished, and if there already exist monopoly elements, restrictive practices, and imperfect markets, immigration could be economically beneficial to the domestic population.

Technical progress and the problem of economic adjustment have been referred to already, and it has been argued that these could well be helped by immigration, either generally or of specific kinds. As far as external economies or diseconomies are concerned, immigrants may obviously have a direct effect in so far as they add to congestion or noise. They may, however, also represent a supply of labour to certain occupations which might cut down the costs of mitigating these external economies. For example, public transport might fall in price relative to private transport as a result of immigration. (It is indeed the case that immigrants do tend to work to a disproportionate extent in transport.) In certain countries at certain times, with labour comparatively scarce compared with land and physical capital, there may be unexploited returns to scale due to shortage of labour, and increasing marginal product of labour. It is, perhaps, unlikely that this is characteristic of the United Kingdom today. At the same time, the markets for commodities and for all sorts of labour are imperfect and contain strong monopoly elements.

These phenomena are all interrelated, especially the neighbourhood effects, economies of scale, and market imperfections. To the extent that they exist in a country such as the United Kingdom, their effect will be to enable the domestic population to gain some of the increase in output resulting from the immigration. This is not to argue that an economy *must* gain from general immigration. Obviously, the closer an economy corresponds to the static perfectly competitive model mentioned earlier, the less likely the domestic population will gain. Speculation on the United Kingdom position at this point is dangerous. It would certainly seem unlikely, however, given the monopoly power of many firms and of organized labour, that the full value of their marginal product would automatically accrue to immigrants. Thus, apart from the benefits connected with the technical progress and economic adjustment, it is quite possible from the theoretical standpoint that overall the domestic population in aggregate would gain from further immigration.

This gain overall, of course, would not imply that everybody actually did benefit from immigration or that no section of society would lose. Thus, in considering the economic impact of immigration, it is important to consider what the immigrant consists of. In the simplest analysis one might assume that he consists simply of a unit of labour, and, indeed, that might have been a satisfactory assumption to deal with some of the immigration of the nineteenth century. For analysis of contemporary phenomena, however, something more sophisticated is called for. One thinks in terms of a unit of human capital, possessing a certain general education, certain particular skills, and a given expectation of working life. (He may also be accompanied by savings, i.e. command over physical capital.) As such, on arrival the immigrant will represent an addition to the supply of labour to many different occupations. He may also represent a supply of entrepreneurship to various trades and markets.

It follows that to some types of domestic labour an immigrant representing a good substitute will weaken their market position and cause their income to be lower than it otherwise would be. This substitution effect from immigration is not a trivial matter, and it will only be in extremely special cases that the immigrant does not represent a threat of this kind to somebody. An immigrant doctor or teacher is a substitute for a domestic one; an immigrant labourer is a substitute for a domestic one. More generally, immigrant labour overall is a substitute for domestic labour. At the same time, immigrant labour is complementary to some sorts of domestic labour, enabling them to carry out their function more effectively and remuneratively. An immigrant medical auxiliary will be of help to a domestic doctor, an immigrant research assistant to a domestic researcher. More generally, there may be all sorts of activities which are not carried out at all and occupations left quite empty because no one could afford them at the prices required if they were staffed by the domestic labour force. In this case, of course, the immigrant labour would be complementary to the domestic labour force.

Reference may also be made here to the upgrading of the domestic labour force as immigrants appear to take over certain low level occupations. The labour market may, indeed, be administered so that generally the existing population moves up as immigrants arrive. It should be emphasized, incidentally, that this is not necessarily a discriminatory phenomenon. On the one hand, it seems to be characteristic of immigrants all over the world, and on the other, immigrants may have less capital invested in them; in addition to which further investments in human capital may require them to move through the occupational hierarchy from the bottom up. What is true of labour is also true of capital. It has already been argued that the productivity of capital could be higher as a result of immigration. Equally, however, in certain cases it could be lower. The obvious cases concern the substitution of capital for labour because the home labour force is so expensive. Cheaper immigrant labour may in turn be a substitute for this capital. Examples would be domestic servants in place of household equipment, kitchen staff in place of kitchen equipment, teachers in place of teaching machines. It certainly does not follow *a priori* that because the immigration is of human beings the net effect will be to raise the return to capital and lower that to the home-born labour force. (Incidentally, to recall an earlier remark, it would also be necessary to state what is happening to the flow of capital anyway. It is possible that the flow of immigration would be going on at the same time as an influx of physical capital from overseas complicating the analysis still further.) Having said that, however, it would certainly be surprising if workers in the home country did not scrutinize the economic effects of immigration most carefully and did not at least start from the position that a new supply of labour, as of anything else, is a threat to the existing supply. . . .

. . . In this brief essay I have examined a number of arguments that are usually put forward in connexion with the economic effects of immigration. I have also taken into consideration whatever empirical studies have been made in this field, bearing in mind that it is early days yet and there is a great deal more sophisticated research that needs to be done before it would be possible to regard the subject as exhausted. My intention throughout has been mainly negative — to show that a number of opinions that have been expressed do not stand up to analysis and are at variance with the facts. In that way it is possible to come to the negative conclusion that it cannot be established that immigration in general or the immigration of the past decade or so has been disadvantageous to the United Kingdom economy. It, therefore, remains for those who are opposed to immigration on economic grounds to explain further what their arguments are, or to invent new arguments, or to discover and present new relevant facts.

Having reached this point, it might well be argued that as an academic one should and can go on further. One has helped to clarify the issues, and it is now up to the politicians to decide, and it is, anyway, likely that they will decide chiefly according to non-economic criteria.

My own view, however, is that one can legitimately go further than this, without offending against the tradition of pure scholarship. What follows is admittedly largely a matter of judgement, but I cannot help but conclude from my own interpretation of the available material, both theoretical and empirical, that on balance immigration has been economically beneficial to the economy, and I would add that excessive restraint on immigration might have adverse effects on the economy at large and on particular sectors. Although neither I nor anybody else has done the cost-benefit analysis which would enable us to place a precise figure on the net benefit to the domestic population, there are certain phenomena which are outstanding and tip the balance in the positive direction. I am particularly impressed by the greater mobility and flexibility of the immigrant population, the fact of its providing a pool (however temporary) of spare capacity in the labour market, its propensity to save, and its propensity to work in the social service sector of the economy while imposing a disproportionately small burden on public expenditure. For these reasons my conclusion is that immigration has been conducive to growth and has been anti-inflationary. It is reasonable to infer that it has led to a rise in the standard of living of the domestic population, and an up-grading of the domestic population in the occupational hierarchy. Even where, as in the case of dock workers, it could conceivably be a threat to the existing labour force, this is mainly because of the restrictive practices that exist and might be broken down by an alternative supply of labour.

My final conclusion, therefore, is that not only must the opponents of immigration base their case on grounds other than economic, but also they must show that the non-economic disadvantages, to the extent that they exist, offset potential economic benefits.

NOTES

(1) Eric Butterworth (ed.), *Immigrants in West Yorkshire* (London, Institute of Race Relations, Special Series, 1967).

(2) G. C. K. Peach, 'West Indian migration to Britain: the economic factors', *Race* (Vol. VII, no. 2, July 1965).

(3) *Ibid.*

(4) N. Kaldor, 'Causes of the Slow Rate of Economic Growth of the United Kingdom' (inaugural lecture, published by Cambridge University Press, 1966).

(5) Butterworth, op. cit.

(6) B. Cohen and P. Jenner, 'The Employment of Immigrants: a case study within the wool industry', *Race* (Vol. X, no. 1, July 1968), p. 54.

(7) E. J. Mishan and L. Needleman, 'Immigration, Excess Aggregate Demand and the Balance of Payments', *Economica* (May 1966).

(8) K. Jones, 'Immigrants and the Social Services', *National Institute Economic Review* (No. 41, August 1967).

(9) Report from the Finance and General Purposes Committee of the City of Birmingham, May 1968.

(10) R.B. Davison, *Black British* (London, Oxford University Press, for the Institute of Race Relations, 1966), p. 100.

This selection is abridged from E.J. Rose, et. al., *Color and Citizenship: A Report on British Race Relations*, published for the Institute of Race Relations, London by the Oxford University Press, N.Y., 1969, pp. 639–654, 654-656.

document

ON IMMIGRATION
PROBLEMS IN ENGLAND

Enoch Powell

In an earlier speech in February I had mentioned a class in a school in my constituency where there was only one white child. I mentioned it as a fact calculated to bring home to people the size and concentration of the immigrant population. Immediately, I was denounced as lying or retailing hearsay; and though the truth of what I said was confirmed in open council a few days later by the Chairman of the Education Committee, the national press refrained from reporting it and Roy Jenkins, the Chancellor of the Exchequer, in a speech at Swansea three months later, who had only to lift the telephone on his desk to ascertain the truth, preferred to brand me a liar by stating that no such school had ever been discovered. However, Nemesis had not long to wait; and in September the very newspapers which had attacked me had the ignominy of having to report the existence not only in Wolverhampton but in Birmingham of such classes, as well as the 90 per cent immigrant school in my own constituency. So quickly does the incredible turn into what everybody knew all the time.

In the context of a Bill which the native inhabitants of this country were bound to see as directed against themselves, an important part of my argument at Birmingham was the fact of reverse discrimination — that it is not the immigrant but the Briton who feels himself the 'toad beneath the harrow' in the areas where the immigrant population is spreading and taking root. This indeed was the background against which the Opposition were justifiably claiming that the Race Relations Bill would do more harm than good. To illustrate it I described the typical situation of the last and usually elderly white inhabitants of a street or area otherwise wholly occupied by immigrants, and I did so by citing an individual case from Wolverhampton in a correspondent's own words.

The outcry which followed illuminated like a lightning flash the gulf between those who do not want to know and the rest of the nation. Here were circumstances which those who know the facts know are being repeated over and over again, at this very moment, in the towns and the cities affected by immigration — often with aggravations more distressing than in the case I cited. It was ordinary, not extraordinary. Yet all at once the air was filled with denunciation: I was romancing; I had picked up a hoary, unverified legend; I had no evidence; nobody could find the old lady — no more than the class with the one white child! Where do these people live, who imagine that what I related was so remarkable and incredible that they had to conclude it was apocryphal? What do they suppose happens, or has been happening, or will be happening, as the growing immigrant numbers extend their areas of occupation? They must live either a long way off, or they must live with their eyes tight shut.

I will not betray those who write to me in confidence or expose to publicity those who understandably fear it; but as I have been traduced and defamed, I will select one out of the numerous witnesses who wrote and offered me their own evidence for the truth and typicality of what I described. It is, I repeat, not something rare, not something abnormal, but something which is part of the daily life and experience of fellow countrymen of ours who happen to be less fortunately situated than Mr. Rees-Mogg or Mr. Bernard Levin.

Dr. W. E. Bamford on 17th August writes to me from 408 Garratt Lane, S. W. 18. After describing his experiences in attending a patient aged eighty-four on the second floor of a house owned by an immigrant landlord, as a result of which 'the police have since provided me with a police escort each time I visited the patient,' he continues:

I saw her with the consultant geriatrician from St. John's Hospital on Tuesday, 13th August. His advice was that it was best to "cut one's losses" as she would eventually be intimidated out of her home. He arranged to admit her to St. John's with a view to rehabilitation and finding another home for her. It is very tragic that this poor old lady should now have to leave her home and possessions where she has spent most of her life, but there seems no other solution.

I am most reluctant to cause any racial disharmony. I have many coloured patients on my list and I believe my relations with persons of all colours have always been harmonious.

I would like to draw your attention to a few other incidents which involved my patients:

An elderly widow of 80 had the house in which she was living bought by a West Indian lady. The old lady was intimidated by having:

1. Her bell disconnected.
2. Her letters not received.
3. When she went out, she would come back to find water had been poured on her bed.
4. Her possessions were broken.
5. In the darkness when going upstairs she would receive a thump on the back.
6. She was accused of behaving immorally when she had a young technician in to do repairs to her broken possessions.

In spite of informing the police — she had no witnesses! — and the fact that I informed the M.O.H. Dr. Garland and the Health Visitor, she was intimidated out of her home eventually.

A widow with 2 young children was similarly intimidated by the knocking on the wall and the disturbance of her sleeping children at all hours of the night by West Indian neighbours. Actual damage was caused to her ceilings and walls. She had to leave in spite of appeals to the police.

A young English couple were intimidated out of their flat by their West Indian landlord by verbal abuse and filth smeared on and around their toilet.

There is just one witness, just a few examples; but let no one object that they are 'just a few'. Ask those who know and they will tell you whether all that is exceptional.

Let no one object, either, that there are bad British landlords too, that British people bully and maltreat British people, and so on. I know. I have never said or implied that immigrants are more predisposed to vicious or spiteful behaviour than the indigenous population. Though their customs and their social habits and expectations may be widely different, there is no reason to suppose they are more malevolent or more prone to wrong-doing. That is, however, not the point. With the malefactors among our own people we have got to cope; they are our own responsibility and part of our own society. It is something totally different when the same or similar activities are perpetrated by strangers, and above all when they occur in the course of an increase in the numbers of those strangers and an extension of the areas which they occupy — an increase and an extension to which the victims perceive no end in sight. Surely only very clever people could fail to understand so simple a point.

The issue is not, as some people appear to imagine, one of being nice to the immigrants or strangers in our midst, however diverse their race or culture. The issue is an issue of numbers, now and especially in the future. And so I come to the question of numbers, and of the increase in numbers; for it is the very heart of the matter. As Lord Elton once put it: 'If it were known in my home village that the Archbishop of Canterbury were coming to live there, we should undoubtedly ring a peal on the church bells. If it were known that five archbishops were coming, I should still expect to see my neighbours exchanging excited congratulations at the street corners. But if it were known that 50 archbishops were coming, there would be a riot.'

First, let us get our sense of perspective. Let us look at present numbers. There are today in this country about 1¼ million Commonwealth immigrants, though the basis of the statistics is far from perfect and the number is likely to be more rather than less. Suppose that any Government fifteen years ago had declared: it is our intention that by 1968 1¼ million Afro-Asians shall have entered this country and settled in it. People would not have believed their ears. Of course, no Government, no party would have dared to put forward such a proposal; if they had, they would have been hissed out of office. Yet the thing is no less absurd or monstrous now that it has become a reality than it would have seemed to everybody beforehand. It never was proposed or argued on grounds of supplying labour or skill. Indeed, it could not be; for that has nothing to do with immigration. The doctors, aliens as well as Commonwealth citizens, who have made it possible, by getting a few years of post-graduate experience in Britain, to expand the hospital service faster than would otherwise have been possible, have no more to do with immigration than have the *au pair* girls admitted for a year or two to give domestic help or the workers moving temporarily from one Common Market country to another. Those who still talk about needing immigrant doctors, dentists, and teachers, are not really talking about immigration at all. As for unskilled labour, the mere attempt to justify mass importation of it would have been exploded by economists and trade unions alike: the remedy for shortage of labour in a developed economy is more capital and better organisation. In short, it is only now that this has happened and the people of Britain are faced with a *fait accompli*, that all sorts of excuses are invented and we are told in terms of arrogant moral superiority that we have got a 'multi-racial society' and had better like it.

Yet if that were all, it could be endured. With their almost incredible tolerance the English — it is virtually only England which is affected — would settle down to live with what they neither asked for nor wanted nor were warned of nor understood. But the present, this 1¼ million reality — however inconceivable it would have been in prospect — this is not all. People look to the future, and, as they do so, they remember that they have been betrayed and misled in the past. It is our duty not to betray or mislead them again.

It is easy to understand how enormously strong is the temptation for all politicians to baulk at this vision of the future, and not least for my own Party, the Conservative Party, which formed the government of the country during the crucial years and would fain close its eyes and ears to the wholly unnecessary and avoidable havoc its own inaction wrought — a tragedy which need never have been enacted. If Britain had provided herself in 1956 instead of 1962 with what every other nation under the sun possesses — a law defining its own people — what a world of anguish, past and future, would never have been? Even those of us who inveighed against the British Nationality Act 1948 from the outset and who from inside and from outside government urged legislation over the years, feel an oppressive sense of guilt and humiliation. The temptation to close our eyes to the future is correspondingly strong. But it is a temptation that has to be conquered.

Even more dangerous is the too common taunt: 'You did the wrong; you have no right to talk about it now.' Woe betide the nation that will not let its rulers admit their errors and try to remedy the consequences: there is no surer way to persist on a disastrous course until it is too late than to attach the penalty of mockery to those who say: 'We have done wrong.'

Let us take as our starting point the calculation of the General Register office that by 1985 there would be in this country 3½ million coloured immigrants and their offspring — in other words, that the present number would have increased between two and threefold in the next seventeen years — on two assumptions, current rate of intake and current birthrate. I have been endlessly accused of using this figure without regard to those assumptions. I did not. In my previous speech I expressly qualified it as being 'on present trends', and to the consideration of those two assumptions I now address myself.

The first assumption is that the rate of net inflow continues as at present. It has not, indeed, diminished since the estimate was made, but I am willing to suppose that, especially with the substantially greater limitations which a Conservative Government has undertaken to apply, the rate would be markedly reduced during the period in question. For the purposes of argument I will suppose that it falls at a steady rate from 60,000 in 1968 to nil by 1985. In that case the total in the latter year would be reduced by about ½ million, that is to 3 million.

I now turn to the second and more crucial assumption, the birth rate. There are those who argue that the longer the immigrant population is resident in this country, the more closely their birth rate will approximate to that of the indigenous population, and thus, of course, to a rate of increase at which their proportion to the total would remain static. Now, I have no doubt that an immigrant element thoroughly absorbed into a host population does tend to have the same birth rate, and I have no doubt that among our Commonwealth immigrants the small minority to whom that description can be applied, may soon show evidence of this. But to suppose that the habits of the great mass of immigrants, living in their own communities, speaking their own languages and maintaining their native customs, will change appreciably in the next two or three decades is a supposition so grotesque that only those could make it who are determined not to admit what they know to be true or not to see what they fear. On the contrary, there are grounds for arguing that the immigrant birth rate is more likely to rise during the next two or three decades; for instance, the proportion of females must increase as dependants join male workers, so that a given total of immigrant population will yield more family units.

Let me take you and show you the process actually happening. In the county borough of Wolverhampton, as recently enlarged to a total population of 267,000 in 1967, the proportion of immigrants and their offspring was 5.13 per cent on the basis of the 1966 sample census, though of course, as the borough now includes large suburbs which are wholly white, this percentage gives no idea of the proportions or concentration in the inner zones of the borough. Now, the immigrant population, which forms 5.13 per cent of the whole, produces no less than 23 per cent of the births; that is, while one in twenty of the population is an immigrant, one in four of the births is an immigrant birth. I am not referring to births in maternity beds — there, the immigrant proportion is higher still, one in three — but to total births; and before anyone calls me a liar, I might mention that the figures are those of the borough Medical Officer of Health and may be found reprinted, among other places, in The Lancet for 26th October.

The procession, and the rate at which it gathers numbers year by year, can be traced as it moves upwards through the schools. Here are the percentages of immigrant children in the Wolverhampton schools last April, reading upwards: infant schools 17.1 per cent; junior and infant schools 12.7 per cent, junior schools 10.9 per cent; secondary schools 9.7 per cent. However, even those figures do not fully reflect the rate at which births have been rising hitherto, because they include not only children born to immigrants in this country but children who have immigrated when of, or under, school age — and Asian and West Indian children of school age are still arriving in Wolverhampton at the rate of eight or nine hundred a year. The idea that the size of the immigrant population, even without any net intake at all, is destined from now onwards to increase little more rapidly than that of the indigenous population, cannot seriously be sustained in the face of the sort of reality I have described. The only prudent assumption is that the present trend will continue for at least a decade or two. This is the assumption which underlies the Registrar General's projection, and gives the figure of 3 million for 1985, after allowing, as I have done, for reduction of intake. I am reassured that I am not far from the mark when I notice that a year ago the Home Office spokesman, who can hardly be accused of wanting to play the numbers up, arrived at 2½ million in 1985 as the lowest figure he could foresee after making the utmost allowance both on intake and on birth rate.

After 1985, we may perhaps allow ourselves to hope for a decline in the rate of reproduction; but if the following seventeen years, instead of multiplication by the factor of two, as between 1967 and 1985, resulted only in multiplication by a factor of 1½, the total immigrant and immigrant-descended population at the end of the century — to be precise, in 2002 — would be 4½ million, or three and a half times the present number; and that is assuming no further net immigration at all after

1985. Bearing in mind that the assumptions which produce this figure are deliberately pitched low, it will be seen that my reference at Birmingham to something 'in the region of 5–7 million' for the year 2000 'on present trends' was neither random nor ill-considered.

Now, if that minimum figure of 4½ million is expressed as a percentage of the projected population of the United Kingdom for the year 2000, it works out at a little over 6 per cent. But of course it is monstrously fallacious thus to divide the immigrant population into that of the U. K. as a whole. I do not know what would be the aspect of a United Kingdom where uniformly one in eighteen of the population — in Easington and Exeter, in Aberystwyth and Aberdeen, in Antrim and Eastbourne — was an Afro-Asian. But that is not how it would be. The very growth in numbers would increase the already striking fact of dense geographical concentration, so that the urban part of whole towns and cities in Yorkshire, the Midlands and the Home Counties would be preponderantly or exclusively Afro-Asian in population. There would be several Washingtons in England. From these whole areas the indigenous population, the people of England, who fondly imagine that this is their country and these are their home towns, would have been dislodged — I have deliberately chosen the most neutral word I could find. And here for the first time this morning I offer a subjective judgement, because in the nature of the case there can be no other and because on such a matter it is the duty of a politican to make and to declare his judgement. I do so, I hope, not unduly moved — though why should I not be moved? — by the hundreds, no, thousands of my countrymen who speak to me or write to me of their fear and foreboding: the old who rejoice that they will not live to see what is to come; the young who are determined that their children shall not grow up under the shadow of it. My judgement then is this: the people of England will not endure it. If so, it is idle to argue whether they ought to or ought not to. I do not believe it is in human nature that a country, and a country such as ours, should passively watch the transformation of whole areas which lie at the heart of it into alien territory.

On these two grounds then — the prospective growth of numbers with its physical consequences, and the unacceptability of those consequences — rests the urgency of action. We can perhaps not reduce the eventual total of the immigrant and immigrant-descended population much, if at all, below its present size: with that, and with all that implies, we and our children and our children's children will have to cope, until the slow mercy of the years absorb even that unparalleled invasion of our body politic. What I believe we can do, and therefore must do, is to avert the impending disaster of its increase.

There are two, and, so far as I can see, only two measures available to this end. Both are obvious; one is far more important, and far more difficult, than the other. If further net immigration were virtually to cease at once, that would reduce the prospective total for 1985 by a further half million, and would have a somewhat more than proportionate effect on whatever is to be the rate of increase after 1985; for, as I have pointed out, the inflow, consisting as it does mostly of dependants, forms the basis for new family units in the future. I say 'virtually cease', because of course no one would wish an absolute veto on the settlement of individual Afro-Asians in this country in future, any more than of other aliens. But let there be no prevarication about what is meant. What is meant is that we would cease to admit not only new settlers and their dependants but the dependants or remaining dependants of immigrants already here. The first half of this presents no human difficulty: if we admit no new settlers, there is no problem about their dependants. The problem attaches to the reservoir of dependants who have not yet joined immigrants already here. In this case we have to decide between two evils, the denial of entry to an immigrant's dependants and the consequences of the prospective growth in numbers. But here the minor issue merges into the major one, that of repatriation.

I have argued that on any prudent view, quite apart from any subsequent immigration, the future prospect is unacceptable. Hence the key significance of repatriation or at any rate re-emigration. A policy of assisting repatriation by payment of fares and grants is part of the official policy of the Conservative Party. It is a just, rational, and humane policy; it accepts that a wrong has unintentionally been done to the immigrant by placing him in a position where the future is as pregnant with trouble for him as for the rest of the population, and it accepts the duty of reinstating him as far as possible. As my colleague, Mr. Boyd-Carpenter, pointed out in a speech at Blackpool recently which has received too little attention, it would provide the fair answer for the immigrant here whose dependants were not permitted to join him. The question is what would be the practical scope and application of such a policy.

I believe that ignorance of the realities of Commonwealth immigration leads people seriously to underestimate the scope of the policy and thus to neglect and despise the chief key to the situation. Perhaps it is the historical associations of the word 'immigrant' which create in those remote from the facts the picture of individuals who have left their homes behind for ever to seek a new future in a far-off land, rather in the mood of those Victorian pictures of the emigrants' farewell.

Of course, there are many cases where individuals have uprooted themselves to come here; but in the mass it is much nearer the truth to think in terms of detachments from communities in the West Indies or India or Pakistan encamped in certain areas of England. They are still to a large extent a part, economically and socially, of the communities from which they have been detached and to which they regard themselves as belonging. As a recently published study of one of the West Indian islands put it:

> Migrant communities in Britain are linked to their home societies by an intricate network of ties and obligations. There are strong social pressures for members of a community to send back money to their families in the island, where most of them expect to return eventually . . . the ideology of migration and the social networks formed around it are so closely connected that it is rare for migrants to abandon one without leaving the other. Thus migrants who decide to stay permanently in Britain often cut themselves off from the others.

This description could apply, even more strongly, to the communities from India and Pakistan, whose total numbers now exceed the West Indian, and whose links with their homes are kept in being by a constant flow not only of remittances, amounting to many millions of pounds a year, but of personal visits and exchanges, the scale of which would astonish anyone not closely acquainted with the actual phenomenon of Commonwealth immigration in this country. The annual holiday 'back home' in the West Indies or in India or Pakistan is no rare feature of life in the immigrant communities.

Against this background a programme of large-scale voluntary but organised, financed, and subsidised repatriation and re-emigration becomes indeed an administrative and political task of great magnitude, but something neither absurdly impracticable nor, still less, inhuman, but on the contrary as profoundly humane as it is far-sighted. Under an agreement between Ceylon and India for the repatriation of more than half a million Indians over fifteen years, 35,000 return to India each year with their assets. The Government of Guyana is anxious to promote the re-emigration to that country of West Indians and others who can help to build up its economy and develop its resources. A cursory survey carried out by a national newspaper six months ago indicated that over 20 per cent of immigrants interviewed would contemplate availing themselves of an opportunity to go home. It need not even follow that the income from work done here in Britain would be suddenly lost to the home communities if permanent settlement of population were replaced by what many countries in Europe and elsewhere are familiar with — the temporary, albeit often long-term, intake of labour.

The resettlement of a substantial proportion of the Commonwealth immigrants in Britain is not beyond the resources and abilities of this country, if it is undertaken as a national duty, in the successful discharge of which the interests both of the immigrants themselves and of the countries from which they came are engaged. It ought to be, and it could be, organised now on the scale which the urgency of the situation demands, preferably under a special Ministry for Repatriation or other authority charged with concentrating on this task.

At present large numbers of the offspring of immigrants, even those born here in Britain, remain integrated in the immigrant community which links them with their homeland overseas. With every passing year this will diminish. Sometimes people point to the increasing proportion of immigrant offspring born in this country as if the fact contained within itself the ultimate solution. The truth is the opposite. The West Indian or Asian does not, by being born in England, become an Englishman. In law he becomes a United Kingdom citizen by birth; in fact he is a West Indian or an Asian still. Unless he be one of a small minority — for number, I repeat again and again, is of the essence — he will by the very nature of things have lost one country without gaining another, lost one nationality without acquiring a new one. Time is running against us and them. With the lapse of a generation or so we shall at last have succeeded — to the benefit of nobody — in reproducing 'in England's green and pleasant land' the haunting tragedy of the United States.

The English as a nation have their own peculiar faults. One of them is that strange passivity in the face of danger or absurdity or provocation, which has more than once in our history lured observers into false conclusions — conclusions sometimes fatal to the observers themselves — about the underlying intentions and the true determination of our people. What so far no one could accuse us of is a propensity to abandon hope in the face of severe and even seemingly insurmountable obstacles. Dejection is not one of our national traits; but we must be told the truth and shown the danger, if we are to meet it. Rightly or wrongly, I for my part believe that the time for that has come.

This is a slightly abridged version of Enoch Powell's speech on Immigrant Problems in England. This speech was delivered at the Rotary Club of London on November 16, 1968. It has been reported to be one of his detailed expositions of his views and has been reproduced extensively by his admirers in the published literature.

IV.
THE
UNITED STATES
CASE
STUDY

INTRODUCTION

The slave trade first linked Africa and the New World due to the labor demand in Spanish, Portuguese and Dutch colonies. The British were slow to become involved in the trade; only in the latter half of the sixteenth century did they raid the cargoes of established powers. Nevertheless, the first British colonists in the New World were well aware of African slaves as a source of labor.

The New World colonies were not the large sugar factories on Caribbean islands, nor were they organized around the search for precious metals as in Portuguese America. The American Indian population was less dense than that in Spanish America and was less suitable as a slave labor force. The British colonists then were unable to establish themselves as a small dominant class over a large resource of African or American Indian labor. Nevertheless, labor was an important problem for the early settlers, and they attempted a variety of solutions.

At first, the settlers used both white and black indentured labor. The first Africans brought to the British colonies — twenty people acquired by the Jamestown colony in 1619 — were probably seen more as indentured servants than as slaves. Although white indentured servants continued to supply most of the colonists' labor needs for the rest of the seventeenth century, a distinction developed between white and black servants. By the 1640's, whites served for five to seven years (or less) and were freed. Blacks were likely to serve for life. Practice preceded law, for it was not until the 1660's that the Maryland House passed a bill stating, "All Negroes and other slaves shall serve *Durante Vita* (for life.)"(1) By 1670, Virginia specified that all non-Christian slaves were to serve for life. This legislation was crucial to the future of slavery, since almost seventy percent of the slave population lived and worked in Maryland and Virginia. Thus, the white colonists had in the late seventeenth century equated Africans with slavery.

Although white immigration continued to be the basis of the system of colonial settlements in the British colonies, the institution and immigration of slaves grew in importance. The North American colonies in the British Empire, like the West

Indian sugar colonies, were closely tied to the slave trade and to an agriculture depending upon slave labor.(2) At this time, a shift in sea trading, which was to be important in the accumulation of capital for Northern industrialization had begun. The ports of New York, Boston, and Philadelphia accomodated more trade than the ports of Hampton and Charleston in the South. The North began to control trade products produced by slaves.

Slavery was not restricted to the Southern colonies. Throughout the eighteenth century, people were held as slaves in all thirteen original colonies. The pattern of race relations did not show any sharp distinction between the North and South; even slave revolts errupted in the 1740's in both New York and South Carolina. By the middle of the eighteenth century then, the role of the black population as an agrarian labor force was firmly established to contribute to the commercial and industrial development in the North.

In its effects upon race relations, the War for Independence had not been a social revolution, distinguished from other anti-colonial struggles. The Declaration of Independence had stated that "all men are created equal," but it did not state whether Jefferson and his colleagues considered blacks and American Indians as men. In practice, a slave was perhaps three-fifths of a man. Some emancipation did occur during the revolution. For example, Lord Dunmore, the British governor of Virginia, attempted to recruit blacks to the British cause by promising manumission.(3) The Continental Congress responded to Lord Dunmore's action (and to the shortage of white volunteers) by expanding recruitment to include free blacks in 1776 and slaves in 1779. Lord Dunmore's offer of manumission was matched in 1779, and approximately 5,000 blacks served in the Continental Army.

The egalitarian ideals of the revolutionary period, accompanied by the closing of foreign markets for materials and products produced with slave labor, prompted some reassessment of slavery. However, the abundance of cotton and the newly invented cotton gin provided Britain with an inexpensive way to supply raw cotton to its textile industry. Prior to the Civil War, the slave population grew rapidly, especially in the South and along the Mason-Dixon line, and increasingly an internal trading of slaves by American owners developed. There was no significant free black population. At the same time, Northern industrialization, financially supported by the cotton trade, began, while national stability was established at the expense of the black population with the Compromises of 1820 and 1850.

The large increase in cotton production brought changes for blacks. New land in Alabama, Mississippi, Louisiana, and Arkansas replaced the upper South as the major area for cotton production, thereby creating an internal, forced migration of slaves. In Maryland and Virginia, slaves were raised for export and were shipped along the coast into the deep South.

The international cotton trade continued to pace the number of black slaves in the labor system. Nationally, the free black population was never more than 2.5 percent of the total population prior to the Civil War, a sharp contrast with the slaveholding colonies of Cuba and Brazil where the free black population ranged up to 50% of the total black populations. The lack of any but a marginal position for free blacks in society before the Civil War was a major reason for the failure of the war to resolve racial problems in the United States.

The Civil War, like the War for Independence, was not a social revolution. Most Northerners, including President Lincoln, were unwilling to cope with slavery. The conflict can best be seen as a struggle over the organization of the trans-Mississippi

West and the establishment of a future course of national development.(4) The Northern "town" fought to prevent the spread of slavery and for hegemony over the Southern "countryside." The end of slavery came from the logic of the war and was understood primarily as a military tactic. Given the hesitant nature of abolition, it is not surprising that Reconstruction failed to implement the programs that would have drastically altered future race relations: land distribution, government-provided credit for farmers, equitable access to markets, and guaranteed political freedoms.

Political and economic change during Reconstruction ended with the 1877 compromise giving Rutherford B. Hayes the presidency. The next three decades are often called the "black nadir," yet to understand these years in a national context is an error. In the South the mechanisms for white control over blacks — the violence and terror, debt peonage, white monopolized ownership of productive land, segregation, and the exclusion of blacks from the political process — were only a national manifestation of an international colonial thrust. During this time, the Partition of Africa occurred, the sphere of influence politics in China began, and the United States, after defeating Spain, suppressed independence movements in the Philippines and Cuba.

While cotton remained an important export, economic growth shifted to railroads, iron and steel, and machinery. Black labor was no longer as important to the economy as it had been, and consequently the South was no longer the area of economic growth that it had been. The future lay more with the urban and industrial sectors of the economy, supplied with a labor force of immigrants, than with the rural agricultural sector where most of the black population remained.

This period of seeming stagnation in the South was deceptive. In the 1870's, blacks began leaving the South, but it was not until the 1890's that migration reached a significant level. The attraction of Northern jobs promoted by recruiters, political oppression, and the increased mechanization in Southern agriculture led to the migration. Blacks heard stories of previous migrants and about the influence of black-owned Northern newspapers. The early years of the migration to the North were crucial for the formation of a new urban settlement pattern, the black ghetto, which altered the older pattern of a more scattered distribution of population in both Northern and Southern cities.(5)

By 1940, approximately 77 percent of the black population was in the South and was more residentially segregated in urban areas than any other racial or ethnic group.(6) By the 1960's blacks had become more urban than whites, more concentrated in central cities, and were as likely to live outside the South as in it. They have the highest and longest level of residential segregation of any previous minority. Finally, the blacks had become the "last immigrants" to the American city, although they had been among the first immigrants to the British colonies.

The potential of the American city for absorbing primarily European immigrants and giving them a secure position in society had been overrated. It was a potential not widely realized until the arrival of blacks. Not only did the new migrants face institutional racism, they were also arriving in cities when unskilled jobs, those usually available to rural migrants, were declining. Between 1910 and 1940, the decline in jobs was in percentages while absolute numbers remained fairly stable After World War II when over a million blacks a year were migrating from the South, the decline in unskilled jobs in cities was absolute as well. At this time, there were no great waves of European immigrants to compete for unskilled jobs.

The political impact of the black migration began to be felt after World War II. The legal end of segregation in the South did not, despite expectations, solve American race relations. Instead, the extent of racial problems in cities began to be revealed. No longer needed in agriculture and threatened by their marginal position in the cities, the black urban rebellions in the 1960's underlined a new reality.

The selections in this section are broadly representative of the new approaches to race relations produced by American politics in the 1960's. Louis Knowles and Kenneth Pruitt provide an overview of the history of American racism. Their emphasis is on the institutional basis of racism rather than attitudes and prejudices which have been discussed in earlier work. Harold Baron focuses on the period between the Civil War and the end of World War II. He argues that the limited demand for black labor determined the position of blacks well beyond the era of slavery. William Tabb contrasts three approaches to the study of race relations. What he calls the conventional wisdom, represented by the Kerner Commission Report, has been the chief kind of analysis within the social sciences. An excerpt from that Report provides an account of the Newark rebellion.

The final two selections by Michael Reich and Barry Bluestone raise some crucial issues to the future of race relations in the United States. Reich, suggesting an alliance between black and white workers, nevertheless, neglects the problems of the accumulated gains that the working, white middle class have in the current structure of racial inequality. Bluestone discusses the issue of neo-colonialism as an outcome of current racial conflict. Ending this section is a document by Eldridge Cleaver, the black activist and theoretician, discussing the international linkages of race relations.

NOTES

(1) Thomas F. Gossett, *Race: The History of an Idea in America*, Schocken Books, New York, 1965, p. 30.

(2) Eric Williams, *Capitalism and Slavery*, New York: Capricorn Books, 1966, especially Chapter 3.

(3) Benjamin Quarles, "Lord Dunmore as Liberator," *William and Mary Quarterly*, Vol. 15, No. 4, October, 1958, pp. 494–507.

(4) See Barrington Moore, *Social Origins of Dictatorship and Democracy: Lord and Peasant in the Making of the Modern World*, Boston: Beacon Press, 1967, Chapter III.

(5) See for example, Allan H. Spear, *Black Chicago: The Making of a Negro Ghetto, 1890-1920*, Chicago: University of Chicago Press, 1967.

(6) On residential segregation, see Karl E. and Alma F. Taeuber, *Negroes in Cities*, Chicago: Aldine Publishing Company, 1965.

INSTITUTIONAL AND IDEOLOGICAL ROOTS OF RACISM

Louis L. Knowles and Kenneth Prewitt

Institutional racism is a term which describes practices in the United States nearly as old as the nation itself. The term, however, appears to be of recent coinage, possibly first used by Stokely Carmichael and Charles V. Hamilton in their widely read book, *Black Power.*(1) It is our goal to work with this term until we feel we have come to some full understanding of it, and to present an analysis of specific practices appropriately defined as "institutionally racist." Our strategy is to be self-consciously pragmatic. That is, we ask not what the motive of the individuals might be; rather we look at the consequences of the institutions they have created.

The murder by KKK members and law enforcement officials of three civil rights workers in Mississippi was an act of individual racism. That the sovereign state of Mississippi refused to indict the killers was institutional racism. The individual act by racist bigots went unpunished in Mississippi because of policies, precedents, and practices that are an integral part of that state's legal institutions. A store clerk who suspects that black children in his store are there to steal candy but white children are there to purchase candy, and who treats the children differently, the blacks as probable delinquents and the whites as probable customers, also illustrates individual racism. Unlike the Mississippi murderers, the store clerk is not a bigot and may not even consider himself prejudiced, but his behavior is shaped by racial stereotypes which have been part of his unconscious since childhood. A university admissions policy which provides for entrance only to students who score high on tests designed primarily for white suburban high schools necessarily excludes black ghetto-educated students. Unlike the legal policies of Mississippi, the university admission criteria are not intended to be racist, but the university is pursuing a course which perpetuates institutional racism. The difference, then, between individual and institutional racism is not a difference in intent or of visibility. Both the individual act of racism and the racist institutional policy may occur without the presence of conscious bigotry, and both may be masked intentionally or innocently.

In an attempt to understand "institutional racism" it is best to consider first what institutions are and what they do in a society. Institutions are fairly stable social arrangements and practices through which collective actions are taken. Medical institutions, for instance, marshal talents and resources of society so that health care can be provided. Medical institutions include hospitals, research labs, and clinics, as well as organizations of medical people such as doctors and nurses. The health of all of us is affected by general medical policies and by established practices and ethics. Business and labor, for example, determine what is to be produced, how it is to be produced, and by whom and on whose behalf products will be created. Public and private schools determine what is considered knowledge, how it is to be transmitted to new generations, and who will do the teaching. Legal and political institutions determine what laws regulate our lives, how and by whom they are enforced, and who will be prosecuted for which violations.

Institutions have great power to reward and penalize. They reward by providing career opportunities for some people and foreclosing them for others. They reward as well by the way social goods and services are distributed — by deciding who receives training and skills, medical care, formal education, political influence, moral support and self-respect, productive employment, fair treatment by the law, decent housing, self-confidence, and the promise of a secure future for self and children. No society will distribute social benefits in a perfectly equitable way. But no society need use race as a criterion to determine who will be rewarded and who punished. Any nation that permits race to affect the distribution of benefits from social policies is racist.

It is our thesis that institutional racism is deeply embedded in American society. Slavery was only the earliest and most blatant practice. Political, economic, educational, and religious policies co-operated with slaveholders to "keep the nigger in his place." Emancipation changed little. Jim Crow laws as well as residential and employment discrimination guaranteed that black citizens remained under the control of white citizens. Second-class citizenship quickly became a social fact as well as a legal status. Overt institutional racism was widely practiced throughout American society at least until World War II.

With desegregation in the armed forces and the passage of various civil rights bills, institutional racism no longer has the status of law. It is perpetuated nonetheless, sometimes by frightened and bigoted individuals, sometimes by good citizens merely carrying on "business as usual," and sometimes by well-intentioned but naive reformers. An attack on institutional racism is clearly the next task for Americans, white and black, who hope to obtain for their children a society less tense and more just than the one of the mid-1960's. It is no easy task. Individual, overt racist acts, such as the shotgun slaying of civil rights workers, are visible. Techniques of crime detection can be used to apprehend guilty parties, and, in theory, due process of law will punish them. To detect institutional racism, especially when it is unintentional or when it is disguised, is a very different task. And even when institutional racism is detected, it is seldom clear who is at fault. How can we say who is responsible for residential segregation, for poor education in ghetto schools, for extraordinarily high unemployment among black men, for racial stereotypes in history textbooks, for the concentration of political power in white society?

Our analysis begins with attention to ideological patterns in American society which historically and presently sustain practices appropriately labeled "institutionally racist." We then turn attention to the procedures of dominant American institutions: educational, economic, political, legal, and medical. It is as a result of practices within these institutions that black citizens in America are consistently penalized for reasons of color.

Quite obviously the social arrangements which fix unequal opportunities for black and white citizens can be traced back through American history — farther back, as a matter of fact, than even the beginning of slavery. Our purpose is not to rewrite American history, although that needs to be done. Rather our purpose in this limited space is to point out the historical roots of institutional racism by examining the ideology used to justify it. In understanding how deeply racist practices are embedded in the American experience and values, we can come to a fuller understanding of how contemporary social institutions have adapted to their heritage.

Some form of white supremacy, both as ideology and institutional arrangement, existed from the first day English immigrants, seeking freedom from religious intolerance, arrived on the North American continent. From the beginning, the early colonizers apparently considered themselves culturally superior to the natives they encountered. This sense of superiority over the Indians, which was fostered by the religious ideology they carried to the new land, found its expression in the self-proclaimed mission to civilize and Christianize — a mission which was to find its ultimate expression in ideas of a "manifest destiny" and a "white man's burden."

The early colonists were a deeply religious people. The church was the dominant social institution of their time, and the religious doctrines brought from England strongly influenced their contacts with the native Indians. The goals of the colonists were stated clearly:

> *Principal and Maine Ends* (of the Virginia colony) . . . were first to preach and baptize into *Christian Religion* and by propogation of the *Gospell*, to recover out of the arms of the *Divell*, a number of poore and miserable soules, wrapt up unto death, in almost invincible ignorance . . . and to add our myte to the Treasury of Heaven.(2)

Ignorance about the white man's God was sufficient proof in itself of the inferiority of the Indian and, consequently, of the superiority of the white civilization.

The mission impulse was doomed to failure. A shortage of missionaries and an unexpected resistance on the part of the Indian (who was less sure that the white man's ways were inherently superior) led to the dismantling of the few programs aimed at Christianization. It became clear that conquering was, on balance, less expensive and more efficient than "civilizing."

Thus began an extended process of genocide, giving rise to such aphorisms as "The only good Indian is a dead Indian." It was at this time that the ideology of white supremacy on the North American continent took hold. Since Indians were capable of reaching only the stage of "savage," they should not be allowed to impede the forward (westward, to be exact) progress of white civilization. The Church quickly acquiesced in this redefinition of the situation. The disappearance of the nonwhite race in the path of expansionist policies was widely interpreted as God's will. As one student of America's history has written, "It apparently never seriously occurred to (spokesmen for Christianity) that where they saw the mysterious law of God in the disappearance of the nonwhite races before the advancing Anglo-Saxon, a disappearance which apparently occurred without anyone's willing it or doing anything to bring it about, the actual process was a brutal one of oppression, dispossession, and even extermination."(3)

In short, what began as a movement to "civilize and Christianize" the indigenous native population was converted into a racist force, accompanied, as always, by a justificatory ideology. In retrospect, the result is hardly surprising. The English colonists operated from a premise which has continued to have a strong impact on American thought: the Anglo-Saxon race is culturally and religiously superior; neither the validity nor the integrity of alien cultures can be recognized. (The Indian culture, though native to the land, was considered the alien one.) When it became clear that Indians could not be "saved," the settlers concluded that the race itself was inferior. This belief was strengthened by such racist theories as the Teutonic Theory of Origins, which pointed out the superiority of the Anglo-Saxons. The institution of slavery and its accompanying justification would seem to have been products of the same mentality.

It has, of course, been the white man's relationship with the black man which has led to the most powerful expressions of institutional racism in the society. This is a history which hardly needs retelling, although it might be instructive to consider how closely related was the justification of Indian extermination to that of black slavery. It was the heathenism or savagery, so-called, of the African, just as of the Indian, which became the early rationale for enslavement. A particularly ingenious version of the rationale is best known under the popular label "Social Darwinism."

The Social Darwinian theory of evolution greatly influenced social thought, hence social institutions, in nineteenth-century America. Social Darwinists extended the concept of biological evolution in the development of man to a concept of evolution in development of societies and civilizations. The nature of a society or nation or race was presumed to be the product of natural evolutionary forces. The evolutionary process was characterized by struggle and conflict in which the "stronger, more advanced, and more civilized" would naturally triumph over the "inferior, weaker, backward, and uncivilized" peoples.

> The idea of natural selection was translated to a struggle between individual members of a society; between members of classes of society, between different nations, and between different races. This conflict, far from being an evil thing, was nature's indispensable method of producing superior men, superior nations, and superior races.(4)

Such phrases as "the struggle for existence" and "the survival of the fittest" became *lingua franca*, and white Americans had a full-blown ideology to explain their treatment of the "inferior race."

The contemporary expression of Social Darwinian thinking is less blatant but essentially the same as the arguments used in the nineteenth century. The poverty and degradation of the nonwhite races in the United States are thought to be the result of an innate lack of ability rather than anything white society has done. Thus a long line of argument reaches its most recent expression in the now famous "Moynihan Report": the focal point of the race problem is to be found in the pathology of black society.

Social Darwinism was buttressed with two other ideas widely accepted in nineteenth-century America: manifest destiny and white man's burden. Briefly stated, manifest destiny was simply the idea that white Americans were destined, either by natural forces or by Divine Right, to control at least the North American continent and, in many versions of the theory, a much greater share of the earth's surface. Many churchmen supported the idea that such expansion was the will of

God. The impact of this belief with respect to the Indians has already been noted. Let it suffice to say that manifest destiny helped provide the moral and theological justification for genocide. The belief that American expansion was a natural process was rooted in Social Darwinism. Expansionism was simply the natural growth process of a superior nation. This deterministic argument enjoyed wide popularity. Even those who were not comfortable with the overt racism of the expansionist argument were able to cooperate in policies of "liberation" in Cuba and the Philippines by emphasizing the evils of Spanish control. Many, however, felt no need to camouflage their racism. Albert J. Beveridge, Senator from Indiana, stated his position clearly:

> The American Republic is a part of the movement of a race — the most masterful race of history — and race movements are not to be stayed by the hand of man. They are mighty answers to Divine commands. Their leaders are not only statesmen of peoples — they are prophets of God. The inherent tendencies of a race are its highest law. They precede and survive all statutes, all constitutions. . . . The sovereign tendencies of our race are organization and government.(5)

In any case, if racism was not invoked as a justification for imperialist expansion in the first place, it subsequently became a justification for continued American control of the newly "acquired" territories. This was particularly true in the Philippines. "The control of one country by another and the denial of rights or citizenship to the Filipinos were difficult ideas to reconcile with the Declaration of Independence and with American institutions. In order to make these opposing ideas of government compatible at all, the proponents of the acquisition of the Philippines were forced to rely heavily on race theories."(6)

An argument commonly expressed was that the Filipinos were simply incapable of self-government. " 'The Declaration of Independence,' stated Beveridge, 'applies only to peoples capable of self-government. Otherwise, how dared we administer the affairs of the Indians? How dare we continue to govern them today?' "(7) The decision, therefore, as to who was capable of self-government and who was not so capable was left to the United States Government. The criteria were usually explicitly racist, as it was simply assumed that whites, at least Anglo-Saxons, had the "gift" of being able to govern themselves while the inferior nonwhite peoples were not so endowed.

The ideology of imperialist expansion had an easily foreseeable impact on the domestic race situation. As Ronald Segal points out in *The Race War*,

> Both North and South saw and accepted the implications. What was sauce for the Philippines, for Hawaii and Cuba, was sauce for the Southern Negro. If the stronger and cleverer race is free to impose its will upon "new-caught sullen peoples" on the other side of the globe, why not in South Carolina and Mississippi? asked the *Atlantic Monthly*. "No Republican leader," proclaimed Senator Tillman of South Carolina, " . . . will now dare to wave the bloody shirt and preach a crusade against the South's treatment of the Negro. The North has a bloody shirt of its own. Many thousands of them have been made into shrouds for murdered Filipinos, done to death because they were fighting for liberty." Throughout the United States doctrines of racial superiority received the assent of influential politicians and noted academics. The very rationalizations that had eased the conscience of the slave trade now

provided the sanction for imperial expansion.(8)

Another component of the ideology which has nurtured racist policies is that of "the white man's burden." This phrase comes from the title of a poem by Rudyard Kipling, which appeared in the United States in 1899. Whatever Kipling himself may have wished to convey, Americans soon popularized and adopted the concept as an encouragement for accepting the responsibility of looking after the affairs of the darker races. This notion of the "white man's burden" was that the white race, particularly Anglo-Saxons of Britain and America, should accept the (Christian) responsibility for helping the poor colored masses to find a better way of life.

It should be clear that this notion is no less racist than others previously mentioned. Behind the attitude lies the assumption of white supremacy. In exhorting Americans to follow British policy in this regard, the philosopher Josiah Royce stated the assumption clearly.

> . . . The Englishman, in his official and governmental dealings with backward peoples, has a great way of being superior without very often publicly saying that he is superior. You well know that in dealing, as an individual, with other individuals, trouble is seldom made by the fact that you are actually superior to another man in any respect. The trouble comes when you tell the other man, too stridently, that you are his superior. Be my superior, quietly, simply showing your superiority in your deeds, and very likely I shall love you for the very fact of your superiority. For we all love our leaders. But tell me I am your inferior, and then perhaps I may grow boyish, and may throw stones. Well, it is so with the races. Grant then that yours is the superior race. Then you can say little about the subject in your public dealings with the backward race. Superiority is best shown by good deeds and by few boasts.(9)

Both manifest destiny and the idea of a white man's burden, in disguised forms, continue to shape white America's values and policies. Manifest destiny has done much to stimulate the modern day myth that colored peoples are generally incapable of self-government. There are whites who continue to believe that black Afro-Americans are not ready to govern themselves. At best, blacks must first be "properly trained." Of course, this belief influences our relations with nonwhites in other areas of the world as well.

The authors have found the concept of manifest destiny helpful in analyzing white response to "black power." Black power is based on the belief that black people in America are capable of governing and controlling their own communities. White rejection of black power reflects, in part, the widely accepted white myth that blacks are incapable of self-government and must be controlled and governed by whites. Many whites apparently still share with Albert Beveridge the belief that "organization and government" are among the "sovereign tendencies of our race."

The belief in a "white man's burden" also has its modern-day counterpart, particularly in the attitudes and practices of so-called "white liberals" busily trying to solve "the Negro problem." The liberal often bears a strong sense of responsibility for helping the Negro find a better life. He generally characterizes the Negro as "disadvantaged," "unfortunate," or "culturally deprived." The liberal generally feels superior to the black man, although he is less likely to publicly state his sense of superiority. He may not even recognize his own racist sentiments. In any case, much like Josiah Royce, he senses that "superiority is best shown by good deeds and by few boasts." Liberal paternalism is reflected not only in individual attitudes but in the procedures and policies of institutions such as the welfare system and most "war on poverty" efforts.

It is obvious that recent reports and action plans carry on a traditional, if diversionary, view that has long been acceptable to most white Americans: that it is not white institutions but a few bigots plus the deprived status of Negroes that cause racial tension. Such a view is mythical. We are not content with "explanations" of white-black relations that are apolitical, that would reduce the causes of racial tension to the level of psychological and personal factors. Three hundred years of American history cannot e encapsulated so easily. To ignore the network of institutional controls through which social benefits are allocated may be reassuring, but it is also bad social history. America is and has long been a racist nation, because it has and has long had a racist policy. This policy is not to be understood by listening to the proclamations of intent by leading citizens and government officials; nor is it to be understood by reading off a list of compensatory programs in business, education, and welfare. The policy can be understood only when we are willing to take a hard look at the continuing and irrefutable racist consequences of the major institutions in American life. The policy will be changed when we are willing to start the difficult task of remaking our institutions.

NOTES

(1) Stokely Carmichael and Charles Hamilton, *Black Power: The Politics of Liberation in America* (New York: Vintage Books, 1967).

(2) Quoted in Thomas F. Gossett, *Race: The History of an Idea in America* (Dallas: SMU Press, 1963), p. 18.

(3) *Ibid.*, p. 196.

(4) *Ibid.*, p. 145.

(5) *Ibid.*, p. 318.

(6) *Ibid.*, p. 328.

(7) *Ibid.*, p. 329.

(8) Ronald Segal, *The Race War* (Baltimore: Penguin Books, 1967), p. 219.

(9) Gossett, p. 334.

This selection is from Louis L. Knowles and Kenneth Prewitt, Eds., *Institutional Racism in America*. © 1969, pp. 4–14. Reprinted by permission of Prentice-Hall, Inc., Englewood Cliffs, New Jersey.

THE DEMAND FOR BLACK LABOR

Harold M. Baron

The economic base of racism would have to be subjected to intensive analysis in order to get at the heart of the oppression of black people in modern America. If we employ the language of Nineteenth Century science, we can state that the economic deployment of black people has been conditioned by the operation of two sets of historical laws: the laws of capitalist development, and the laws of national liberation. These laws were operative in the slave era as well as at present. Today the characteristic forms of economic control and exploitation of black people take place within the institutional structure of a mature state capitalist system and within the demographic frame of the metropolitan centers. The economic activities of blacks are essentially those of wage (or salary) workers for the large corporate and bureaucratic structures that dominate a mature capitalist society. Thus today racial dynamics can be particularized as the working out of the laws of the maintenance of mature state capitalism and the laws of black liberation with the metropolitan enclaves (rather than a consolidated territorial area) as a base.

This essay places major emphasis on capitalist development. While attention will be paid to aspects of national liberation, it would be a very different essay if that were the main point of concentration. Further, in order to make the inquiry manageable, it concentrates on the key relationship of the demand for black labor. . . .

THE TRANSITION ERA, FIRST PHASE: 1860 TO WORLD WAR I

So far we have been establishing a comprehension of some of the underlying contradictions that frame the control of black labor by examining their origins in the slave era. Before we turn to the present period there is another set of relationships that will provide further conceptual illumination: the conditions that underlay the abolition of slavery. One set of factors lay in the world development of capitalism itself. The bourgeoisie's seizure of power in the French Revolution destabilized that nation's colonial regime and undermined the slave system by promulgating the doctrine of the rights of man as a universal dictum. In England, the expansion of its capitalist might into Asia gave rise to a powerful political interest counter to that of the West Indian planters; plus, the success of the industrial revolution created the material base for envisioning a liberal bourgeois order with thorough formal equality. In the United States, the demise of slavery occurred in the midst of a war that established the further course of capitalist development — whether it would proceed on a "Prussian model", with the planters playing the role of the Junkers, or the industrialists and little men on the make would independently establish their hegemony through an entrepreneurially-oriented state.

The other·source of abolition lay in the role of the black people in the Americas. Denied the right to reconstruct their African societies, they strove to survive and reconstitute themselves as a people. Amidst the plantations and the black quarters of the cities, a new community was formed.(1) At crucial points these black communities transcended the need for survival and struck out for liberation. While sabotage, escapes, and uprisings were consistent themes of New World slavery, the key move was the successful revolt of the black Jacobins in Haiti under the leadership of Toussaint L'Ouverture, which set an example for black and other oppressed people from that time on. By winning their freedom and defeating the most-powerful armies in the world, these revolutionaries not only forced changes in the relative relations of the forces in Europe, but also undermined much essential confidence in the continuing viability of the slave system as a whole. It was little accident that both the British and the US abolition of the slave trade followed shortly on the heels of the Haitian revolution.

In the United States, where a large white population was always close at hand, there were few important slave revolts, and even those were invariably put down before they could become well established. Black self-determination took the form of day-to-day slave resistance, and the development of an independent political line within the abolitionist movement. Most important, the role of black people in the Civil War converted it into a struggle for their own freedom. As Du Bois cogently summarizes:

> Freedom for the slave was a logical result of a crazy attempt to wage war in the midst of four million black slaves, trying the while sublimely to ignore the interests of those slaves in the outcome of the fighting. Yet these slaves had enormous power in their hands. Simply by stopping work, they could threaten the Confederacy with starvation. By walking into the Federal camps, they showed to doubting Northerners the easy possibility of using them as workers and as servants, as spies, as farmers, and finally as fighting soldiers. And not only using them thus, but by the same gesture depriving their enemies of their use in just these fields. It was the fugitive slave who made the slaveholders face the alternative of surrendering to the North or to the Negroes.(2)

The Civil War destroyed the Southern plantocracy as a major contender for the control of national power. For a decade during Reconstruction, the freedmen struggled to establish themselves as an independent yeomanry on the lands they had worked for generations. However both South and North agreed that blacks were to be subservient workers — held in that role now by the workings of "natural" economic and social laws rather than the laws of slavery. The Compromise of 1877 was the final political blow to black Reconstruction, remanding to the dominant white Southerners the regulation of the black labor force.(3)

Abolition of slavery did not mean substantive freedom to the black worker. He was basically confined to a racially-defined agrarian labor status in which he was more exploited than any class of whites, even the landless poor. White land-owners extracted an economic surplus from the labor of blacks through a variety of arrangements, including peonage, wage labor, sharecropping, and rent tenancy. Even the black owners of land were often dependent on white patronage for access to the small plots of inferior soil to which they usually held title. Profits predicated on low wages or onerous share arrangements were often augmented by long-term indebtedness at usurious rates of interest for advances of provisions and supplies. Many a sharecropper and laborer would not realize any appreciable money income for years on end.

The methods of labor control over the black peasantry did not greatly raise net labor costs over those of the slavery era. In both eras the black masses received only enough to survive and reproduce. Pressure on profits came from falling commodity prices rather than from rising labor costs. "The keynote of the Black Belt is debt. . . . " wrote W. E. B. DuBois at the turn of the century. "Not commercial credit, but debt in the sense of continued inability of the mass of the population to make income cover expenses." Of conditions in Dougherty County, Georgia he wrote:

> In the year of low-priced cotton, 1898, of 300 tenant families 175 ended their year's work in debt to the extent of $14,000; 50 cleared nothing; and the remaining 75 made a total profit of $1600. . . . In more-prosperous years the situation is far better — but on the average the majority of tenants end the year even or in debt, which means they work for board and clothes.(4)

From the obverse side white planters in racist language gave their supporting testimony to this extra economic exploitation of the black peasants. One Alabama landlord declared: "White labor is totally unsuited to our methods, our manners, and our accommodations. No other laborers (than the Negro) of whom I have knowledge would be so cheerful or so contented on four pounds of meat and a peck of meal a week, in a little log cabin 14 by 16 feet, with cracks in it large enough to afford free passage to a large-size cat." From Mississippi a planter spoke to the same theme: "Give me the nigger every time. The nigger will never 'strike' as long as you give him plenty to eat and half clothe him: He will live on less and do more hard work, when properly managed, than any other class or race of people."(5)

Black agriculturists were important to the economic development of the South and the nation. Raw cotton production tripled between 1870 and 1910. Consumption of cotton by domestic manufacturers increased six-fold from 800,000 bales in 1870 to 4,800,000 bales in 1910. Cotton continued to be the United States' leading export commodity in global trade, still accounting for a quarter of the value of all merchandise exports on the eve of World War I — in spite of the fact that prices had decreased greatly through international competition as the European powers encouraged cotton production in the overseas areas in which they were augmenting their imperial power. Such rapid growth of cotton production (and that of other farm commodities) implied a great demand for black workers in the fields. Characteristically blacks were engaged on the cotton plantations, especially those with richer lands. The form of engagement was roughly divided between sharecropping, wage labor, and rental tenancy. Between 1890 and 1910 the number of black men in agriculture increased by over half a million, or 31%. During this entire period three out of five black men were employed in agriculture.

Maintaining the semi-servile status of the black labor force required the augmentation of color-caste distinctions. Southern slavery, after all, had been more than just an economic arrangement: it was a cultural system that provided a wide range of norms congruent with plantation discipline. Slave status had served as a line of demarcation throughout the society. Therefore emancipation not only changed the economic form of planter control, but also left gaps in the social superstructure that reinforced it. Under these conditions the strengthening of racialism per se in all cultural arrangements became an imperative for any hope of continuance of the planters' hegemony over Southern society. Since racism had pervaded all major facets of social and political control. Much of the further elaboration of color-caste distinctions arose in the course of the Southern ruling class's struggles to keep the rest of the whites in line.

The road to the establishment of this new system of order in the South was by no means a smooth one. Abrogation of the slave system had made possible some new types of mobility among both blacks and whites, bringing about changes in the forms of inter-racial conflict and class conflict. Blacks were now able to move geographically, even in the face of continued legal and extra-legal restraints. The migration that took place was mainly a westerly one within the South. Inside the black community class mobility developed through the emergence of a small middle class. At the same time, there now opened up to poorer whites areas that had formerly been the preserve of slavery. During the pre-Civil War era no white would compete with a slave for his position on the plantation. Albeit when planters and slaveless small farmers did contend for land, as frequently occurred, the black slave was indirectly involved. With emancipation, racial rivalry for the soil became overt. Freedmen struggled to gain land, sometimes as owners but more frequently as indebted tenants. At the same time, many white smallholders, forced out from infertile and worn soil, sought many of the same lands. After the Civil War the white farmers increased in numbers at a greater rate than the blacks. By 1900, even as tenants, the whites were in the majority. Blacks moved from a non-competitive status in slavery (or perhaps better "concealed competition between the bond and the free"), as Rupert Vance has pointed out, to a condition of overt inter-racial competition. "As slaves Negroes were objects of race prejudice; as a new competitive group struggling for status and a place on the land Negroes found themselves potential objects of mass pressure and group conflict."(6)

Transformations also took place within the Southern ruling class. Ownership of land tended to shift out of the hands of the older planter class into those of merchants, lawyers, and in some cases Northern interests, removing many of the impediments to land-owners' making their decisions more nakedly, on the basis of pure entrepreneurial calculations. This partial unfreezing of labor and capital resources provided some important pre-conditions for the industrialization of the South. Nevertheless, the ideal for black labor in the eyes of dominant white groups was that of a contented agrarian peasantry. Paternalistic members of the Southern elite spoke of satisfied workers controlled by fair but rigidly-enforced rules. "Let the Negro become identified with and attached to the soil upon which he lives, and he himself, the land-owner, and the country alike will be advanced by his labor."(7)

In the social and political realms the conflicts inherent in the black peasantry's subjugation became intertwined with the conflicts inherent in the subordination of any potential political power in the hands of the white smallholders and landless. As things turned out, blacks were to suffer both from the control of the propertied and from the competition of the poor. The political process provided a major means by which this was carried out. "It is one of the paradoxes of Southern history," writes C. Vann Woodward, "that political democracy for the white man and racial discrimination for the black were often products of the same dynamics." The imperatives of preserving class rule supplied the basis of the paradox: "It took a lot of ritual and Jim Crow to bolster the rule of white supremacy in the bosom of a white man working for a black man's wage."(8) Functionally the poorer whites were permitted to influence the formal political process only under conditions that would not undermine the essential power and economic control of the ruling class. The execution of this strategy was completed during the defeat of the Populist movement in the 1890s by excluding the black people from politics and by heightening the color-caste distinctions through an extension of Jim Crow laws and customs. Since the black people had already been defeated through Redemption 20 years before, the moves to disfranchise black people at the turn of the century had as "the real question . . . which whites would be supreme". Ruling circles channeled disfranchisement to their own ends "as they saw in it an opportunity to establish in power 'the intelligence and wealth of the South' which could of course 'govern in the interests of all classes' ".(9) Many whites as well as blacks were denied the ballot, and the substantive differences expressed in the political process were delimited to a narrower range. Inter-class conflicts among whites were much displaced by inter-racial conflicts, and the hegemony of larger property interests was secured. . . .

Northern ruling classes were quick to accept those conditions in the South that stabilized the national political system and provided the raw commodities for their mills and markets. Therefore they supported the establishment of a subservient black peasantry, the regional rule of the Southern propertied interests, and the racial oppression that made both of these things possible. The dominant Northern interests shared the ideal of the smooth kind of racial subjugation projected by the paternalistic Southern elite, but they went along with what proved necessary. "Cotton brokers of New York and Philadelphia, and cotton manufacturers of New England . . . knew full well the importance of bringing discipline to the Southern labor force. When theories of Negro equality resulted in race conflict, and conflict in higher prices of raw cotton, manufacturers were inclined to accept the point of view of the Southern planter rather than that of the New England zealot."(10) Northern businessmen who supported black education in the South had in mind a system that would encourage the students to stay in rural areas and would train them for hard work and menial positions.(11)

Thus, through a process that Harvard's Paul Buck approvingly called *The Road to Reunion* and Howard's Rayford Logan scathingly labeled *The Betrayal of the Negro*, national political, business, and intellectual elites came to define race as a Southern question for which they would not assume any leadership. By 1900 Southern sympathizer and Northern anti-slavery man alike agreed on the rightfulness of the subjugation of the black man. It was accepted as a necessary condition for order in the American state. And order was most essential to the extraordinary expansion of the industrial system. Beyond that point the black man was ignored and considered a "nothing", especially on Northern ground. Reasons of state and racism had combined to legitimize the new form of agrarian thralldom. . . .

THE TRANSITION ERA, SECOND PHASE:
WORLD WAR I TO WORLD WAR II

The new equilibrium of racial regulation that had stabilized around tenancy agriculture as the dominant force of black exploitation received its first major disturbance from the impact of World War I. A certain irony inheres in the condition that imperialism's cataclysm should begin the break-up of agrarian thralldom within the United States. The War's effect on black people took place through the mediation of the market-place, rather than through any shake-up of political relations. Hostilities in Europe placed limitations on American industry's usual labor supply by shutting off the flow of immigration at the very time the demand for labor was increasing sharply due to a war boom and military mobilization. Competition with the Southern plantation system for black labor became one of the major means of resolving this crisis of labor demand.

The black labor reserve in the countryside that had existed essentially as a *potential* source of the industrial proletariat now became a very *active* source. Whereas in the past this industrial reserve had not been tapped in any important way except by rural-based operations such as lumbering, with the advent of the War the industrial system as a whole began drawing on it. This new demand for black workers was to set in motion three key developments: first, the dispersion of black people out of the South into Northern urban centers; second, the formation of a distinct black proletariat in the urban centers at the very heart of the corporate-capitalist process of production; third, the break-up of tenancy agriculture in the South. World War II was to repeat the process in a magnified form and to place the stamp of irreversibility upon it.

Migration out of the countryside started in 1915 and swept up to a human tide by 1917. The major movement was to Northern cities, so that between 1910 and 1920 the black population increased in Chicago from 44,000 to 109,000; in New York from 92,000 to 152,000; in Detroit from 6,000 to 41,000; and in Philadelphia from 84,000 to 134,000. That decade there was a net increase of 322,000 in the number of Southern born blacks living in the North, exceeding the aggregate increase of the preceding 40 years. A secondary movement took place to Southern cities, especially those with shipbuilding and heavy industry. . . .

. . . Labor agents sent South by railroad and steel companies initiated the migration by telling of high wages and offering transportation subsidy. In some cases whole trainloads of workers were shipped North. Though American firms had employed labor recruiters for work among the European peasantries for decades, this was the first time they went forth in any strength to bring black peasants to the city. Many Southern localities tried to protect their labor stocks by legislating proscriptions on labor agents and charging them prohibitive license fees, but on the whole recruiters played only a secondary role.(12) A more important impetus to migration came from the Northern-based black press, most notably the *Chicago Defender*, and above all from the letters and the reports of blacks who had already moved north. Successful employment served as its own advertisement, and better wages outside the South proved very attractive. During the summer of 1917 male wage-earners in the North were making $2.00 to $2.50 a day while the money wages on Mississippi farms ranged from $.75 to $1.25.(13) Early migrations to Northern cities had been from the Upper South. Now blacks came in from all over, with the

Deep South having the heaviest representation. In many cotton areas boll-weevil invasions destroyed the crop, acting as a push off the land at the same time Northern industry was providing a pull.

There was a temporary slackening of the demand for black labor when post-war demobilization caused heavy unemployment. In Chicago, where as many as 10,000 black laborers were out of work, the local Association of Commerce wired to Southern chambers of commerce: "Are you in need of Negro labor? Large surplus here, both returned soldiers and civilian Negroes ready to go to work."(14) In Detroit in 1921, black unemployment rates were five times as great as those of native white workers, and twice as great as those of the foreign-born.(15) But a strong economic recovery at the very time that restrictive immigration laws went into effect brought a second great migration out of the South in the years 1922 to 1924. The magnitude of this second movement has been estimated at slightly under a half-million persons, and may have been greater than that of the wartime movement.(16) The employers who already had a black sector in their work force were able to tap this supply with much less trouble and cost than had been incurred a few years before. As William Graves, personal assistant to Julius Rosenwald, told the Chicago Union League Club: "The Negro permanency in industry was no longer debatable."(17)

The tremendous social dislocations created by the mobilization and the wartime economic boom heightened inter-racial tensions and laid the groundwork for over 20 race riots that occurred on both sides of the Mason-Dixon Line. Careful studies of the two major race riots in Northern industrial centers (East Saint Louis in 1917 and Chicago in 1919) reveal the tremendous friction that had developed between white and black workers.(18) These hostilities were not simply an outgrowth of race prejudice, for in both cases employers had fostered competition for jobs, especially by employing blacks as strikebreakers. Conflict between working-class whites and working-class blacks was analogous in a way to the previously-discussed racial competition among tenants and smallholders for land in the South. When the conflict erupted into mass violence, the dominant whites sat back and resolved the crises in a manner that assured their continued control over both groups.

The first feature of the program that Northern industry developed in relation to the inter-racial conflicts that the riots evidenced was that the permanency of black workers in the North was conclusively established. Management accepted its interest in guaranteeing minimal survival conditions of housing, education, et cetera to perpetuate this labor force. Even during slack times business had to maintain a certain continuity of employment, especially in those jobs that functionally became "Negro jobs". Economically, even in a recession, long-run costs are reduced if something of a permanent work force is retained, for when good times return the recruitment and training of an entirely new labor force can require a great monetary outlay.(19) Thus, as the 1920s wore on, while there was a virtual cessation of articles regarding the employment of blacks in business-oriented and welfare publications, the fact that blacks *would* be employed was now accepted. The shifting of racial stereotypes to fit the new situation was indicated by a business spokesman who reported that the black man "has lost his slovenliness, lazy habits, gambling, and liquor-drinking propensities". He noted that plant superintendents in heavy industry had come to consider black workers especially tractable. "They found Negroes on the whole far more adjustable than the foreign-born. They used a common language, were loyal in times of stress, and were more co-operative in matters such as stock purchases, buying insurance, et cetera."(20)

At the same time, it has to be understood that black workers were employed on management's own terms. Sometimes these terms would involve the deliberate use of blacks to divide the work force. As a case in point, International Harvester integrated the hiring of blacks into its open-shop policies. Part of its strategy was to keep any nationality group from becoming too numerous in any one plant lest they become cohesive in labor conflicts. The decision on hiring was left up to the individual plant superintendents, some keeping their shops lily-white, others hiring large numbers of black workers. Harvester's management was caught up in a contradiction between its need for black workers, especially in the disagreeable twine mill and foundry, and its desire to keep them below 20% at any one plant.(21)

A somewhat-different approach was taken by Ford Motor Company. In the 1921 depression Henry Ford decided to maintain the black work force at the gigantic River Rouge plant in the same proportion as blacks in the total population of the Detroit area. The great majority of blacks at the River Rouge plant were employed in hot, heavy jobs in the rolling mills and foundry, but it was company policy to place a few in every major production unit and even allow a certain amount of upgrading to skilled positions. At the other Ford plants, as at the other major auto companies, black workers were confined to hard unskilled jobs. But the job concessions at Rouge became a mechanism by which Ford was able to gain considerable influence over Detroit's black community. Hiring was channeled through some preferred black ministers who agreed with Henry Ford on politics and industrial relations. Company black personnel officials were active in Republican politics and in anti-union campaigns. Ford had learned early a racial tactic that is widely employed today — that of trading concessions, relaxing economic subordination in order to increase political subordination.(22)

In industry generally the black worker was almost always deployed in job categories that effectively became designated as "Negro jobs". This classification, openly avowed in the South, was often claimed in the North to be merely the way things worked out through application of uniform standards. The superintendent of a Kentucky plough factory expressed the Southern view:

> Negroes do work white men won't do, such as common labor; heavy, hot, and dirty work; pouring crucibles; work in the grinding room; and so on. Negroes are employed because they are cheaper. . . . The Negro does a different grade of work and makes about $.10 an hour less.(23)

There was not a lot of contrast in the words of coke works foremen at a Pennsylvania steel mill: "They are well fitted for this hot work, and we keep them because we appreciate this ability in them." "The door machines and the jam cutting are the most undesirable; it is hard to get white men to do this kind of work."(24) The placement of workers in separate job categories along racial lines was so marked in Detroit that in response to a survey many employers stated that they could not make a comparison between the wages of whites and blacks because they were not working on the same jobs.(25) In the North there was some blurring of racial distinctions, but they remained strong enough to set the black labor force off quite clearly. While the pay for the same job in the same plant was usually equivalent, when blacks came to predominate in a specific job classification, the rate on it would tend to lag. White and black workers were often hired in at the same low job classification; however for the whites advancement as often possible, while the blacks soon bumped into a job ceiling. In terms of day-to-day work, white labor was given a systematic advantage over black labor and a stake in the racist practices.

Northern management's public equal-opportunity posture to preserve their black work force was expressed with clarity at a 1920 conference of officials from five Chicago firms, employing over 6,000 workers, and an official of the Chicago Urban League:

> All of these labor managers expressed the opinion that there would be no reduction in the force of Negro employees. They cited the shortage of men for heavy labor, due to the lack of immigration from abroad, and all said that their companies were eager to employ more Negroes. Equal pay for the same work to whites and to Negroes was given as general practice. General satisfaction with Negro labor was expressed, and the ability of their Negro workers is equal, they said, to that of white workers of corresponding education. All mentioned the advantage, as compared with various immigrant groups, of a common language, enabling all foremen and officers to speak directly with the men. No discrimination in use of restaurants, sanitary facilities, et cetera was reported. All testified that Negroes were given the same opportunities as white workers for advancement to higher positions. The fact that a smaller percentage of Negroes are to be found in the higher positions is due, they said, to the fact that a smaller proportion are as well educated.(26)

The amazing thing about this meeting is that if the references to the immigrants are deleted it has the sound of similar sessions that are held today — half a century later.(27)

In the South, where four-fifths of the nation's black population still lived at the end of the 1920s, the situation of black labor was to all appearances essentially unchanged. The number of black men engaged in Southern industry grew during this decade only 45% as fast as the number of whites. Black workers were concentrated in stagnant or declining plants, such as sawmills, coal mines, and cigar and tobacco factories. The increased hiring of blacks in such places was chiefly a reflection of the fact that the jobs had no future and the employers were not able to attract white workers. Black employment in textiles was severely limited, as in South Carolina, where state law forbade blacks to work in the same room, use the same stairway, or even share the same factory window as white textile workers.(28) Industry in the South, as far as black workers were concerned, still offered little competition to the dominance of agrarian tenancy.

Beneath the surface, however, significant changes were taking place in the rural South. While as late as the mid-1930s Charles S. Johnson could write of a cotton county in Alabama that "The plantation technique on the side of administration was most effective in respect to discipline and policing, and this technique has survived more or less despite the formal abolition of slavery."(29) This state of affairs was then being undermined. Cotton cultivation was moving westward, leaving many blacks in the Southeast without a market crop. Out in the new cotton lands in Texas and Oklahoma whites provided a much larger proportion of the tenants and sharecroppers. By 1930 a slight decrease was seen in the number of black farm operators and laborers. Later, the great depression of the 1930s accelerated this trend as the primary market for agricultural commodities collapsed and the acreage in cotton was halved. Black tenants were pushed off land in far greater proportions than whites. New Deal agricultural programs were very important in displacing sharecroppers and tenants, since they subsidized reductions in acreage. In the early government-support programs landlords tended to monopolize subsidy payments, diverting much of them out of tenants' pockets. When the regulations were changed in the tenants' favor, the landowner had an incentive to convert the tenants to wage laborers or dismiss them altogether so as to get the whole subsidy.(30) The great depression marked the first drastic decline in the demand for black peasants since their status had been established after the Civil War. . . .

. . . On the eve of World War II, when defense production really began to stimulate the economy, the number of jobs increased rapidly. At first, however, it was almost as if the black unemployed had to stand aside while the whites went to work. In April 1940. 22% of the blacks (about 1,250,000 persons) were employed, as were 17.7% of the white labor force. By October, employment had increased by 2,000,000 jobs, and white unemployment had declined to 13%, while black unemployment remained at the same level. Firms with tremendous labor shortages still abided by their racial definitions of jobs and refused to take on available black workers. In September 1941 a US Government survey found that of almost 300,000 job openings, over half were restricted to whites. In Indiana, Ohio, and Illinois, 80% of the openings were thus restricted.(31)

Military mobilization of much of the existing labor force and an almost 20% growth in non-farm employment from 32,000,000 in 1940 to 40,000,000 in 1942 were the pre-conditions necessary to enlarge the demand for black labor. While the President's creation of the Fair Employment Practice Committee (FEPC) under pressure from black organizations helped open up some doors, it was the logic of the labor market that shook the racial status quo. By 1942, management-oriented publications were dealing with the question of employing black workers — a topic they had not considered since the mid-1920s.

The American Mangement Association told its members: "As some shortages develop for which there is no adequate supply of labor from the usual sources, management is forced to look elsewhere. It is then that the Negro looms large as a reservoir of motive power — a source which management has hitherto given only a few furtive, experimental pokes with a long pole." Once more surveys were conducted which showed that most employers consider black workers as efficient as whites. Management reiterated statements about non-discrimination when production conditions forced them to change their racial hiring practices. *Fortune* magazine consoled its executive readers that their personal racism need not be violated: "Theoretically, management should have fewer objections to hiring colored labor than any other part of the industrial team. The employer seldom has social contact with his workers anyway, and his primary concern is production efficiency and satisfactory investment return."(32)

Nationally, the demand for black labor was tremendous. In the spring of 1942 it composed 2.5% to 3% of the war-production work force, and by the fall of 1944 this proportion had risen to 8.3%. These million and a half black war workers were concentrated in the areas of the most stringent labor shortage. Fourteen industrial centers accounted for almost half of these war workers, and of these centers only one was located in the South and only two were border cities. In areas of acute labor shortage, the absence of any white reserve of labor gave blacks much greater access to war work than in labor surplus areas. Black migration was a necessary condition for this employment, and the movement of the families out of the Southern countryside and small towns was accelerated.

The vast demand for labor in general, that had to turn itself into a demand for black labor, could only be accomplished by way of a great expansion of the black sectors of metropolitan labor markets. Training programs for upgrading to skilled and semi-skilled jobs were opened up, at first in the North and later in the South. By 1943–1944, 35% of pre-employment trainees in shipbuilding courses and 29% in aircraft were blacks. World War I had established a space for black laborers as unskilled workers in heavy industry. During World War II this space was enlarged to include a number of semi-skilled and single-skilled jobs in many industries.(33)

World War II marked the most-dramatic improvement in economic status of black people that has ever taken place in the urban industrial economy. The income of black workers increased twice as fast as that of whites. Occupationally, blacks bettered their positions in all of the preferred occupations. The biggest improvement was brought about by the migration from South to North (a net migration of 1,600,000 blacks between 1940 and 1950). However within both sections the relative proportion of blacks within skilled and semi-skilled occupations grew. In clerical and lower-level professional work, labor shortages in the government bureaucracies created a necessity for a tremendous black upgrading into posts hitherto lily-white.

During the era between the two World Wars the national aspirations of blacks worked themselves out on the base of their new material conditions — that is, those of their becoming an urban people whose masses were proletarians. Conflicting tendencies beset this movement at every stage. The dominant white society usually followed the strategy of denying the very existence of its peoplehood. The black community was considered a pathological form rather than something valid in itself. Whenever the black community did thrust itself forward, the tactics of management shifted to a balance of naked repression with co-optive channeling. Within the community there was a constant contention as to which of the class forces would dominate — the black bourgeoisie, that sector of the black working class operating under the dominance of white trade-union organizations, or a nationally-based black working class. . . .

. . . Only after the outbreak of World War II, when blacks were still being excluded from much of the rapidly-expanding economy, did a black movement set out independently from the New Deal-labor coalition and take the initiative in defining a race position on the national level. In January 1941 A. Philip Randolph, President of the Brotherhood of Sleeping Car Porters, an all-black AFL union, issued a call for a massive march on Washington to demand of the Government a greater share in the defense effort. The March on Washington Movement expressed the mood of the black community and received an upswelling of support sufficient to force President Roosevelt to establish a Fair Employment Practice Committee in return for the calling off of the projected march. Although this movement was not able to establish a firmly-organized working-class base or sustain itself for long, it foreshadowed a new stage of development for a self-conscious black working class with the appeal that "An oppressed people must accept the responsibility and take the initiative to free themselves."(34) . . .

NOTES

(1) CLR James: "The Atlantic Slave Trade and Slavery", *Amistad I* (New York, 1970), Pages 133–134. The possibility of a bourgeois mode of development of the black community in the US was cut off, although valiant efforts were made in this direction by black professional men, entrepreneurs, and craftsmen. Nineteenth

Century Pan-Africanism and black nationalism most likely had significant roots in this phenomenon.

(2) W.E.B. DuBois: *Black Reconstruction in America,* 1860–1880 (1962 Edition, Cleveland), Page 121.

(3) "The Compromise of 1877 did not restore the old order in the South, nor did it restore the South to parity with other sections. It did assure the dominant whites political autonomy and non-intervention in matters of race policy, and promised them a share in the blessings of the new economic order. In return the South became . . . a satellite of the dominant region. . . . Under the regime of the Redeemers the South became a bulwark instead of a menace to the new order." C. Vann Woodward: *Reunion and Reaction* (Second Edition, New York, 1956), Pages 266–267.

(4) *The Souls of Black Folk,* Chapter 8.

(5) Quoted in Woodward: *Origins of the New South,* Page 208.

(6) Rupert Vance: "Racial Competition for Land", in Edgar T. Thompson (editor): *Race Relations and the Race Problem* (Durham, 1939), Pages 100–104.

(7) J.B. Killebrew: *Southern States Farm Magazine* (1898), Pages 490–491, cited in Nolen (previously cited), Page 170. For a concrete explication of this approach, see Alfred Holt Stone: *Studies in the American Race Problem* (New York, 1909), Chapter 4.

(8) Woodward: *Origins of the New South,* Page 211.

(9) *Ibid.,* Pages 328–330.

(10) Paul H. Buck: *The Road to Reunion* (Boston, 1937), Pages 154–155.

(11) Carter G. Woodson: "Story of the Fund", Chapter 2, typescript, Julius Rosenwald Papers, University of Chicago Library; Louis Harland: *Separate and Unequal* (Chapel Hill, 1958), Page 77.

(12) US Labor Department: *Negro Migration in 1916–17* (Washington, 1919), Pages 22–23, 27–33, 118–122; Spear: *Black Chicago,* Pages 33–38.

(13) Charles H. Wesley, *Negro Labor in the United States, 1850–1925,* (New York, 1927), pp. 293–94; U.S. Labor Department: *Negro Migration,* pp. 125–126.

(14) William M. Tuttle Junior: *Race Riot: Chicago in the Red Summer of 1919* (New York, 1970), Pages 130–132.

(15) Herman Feldman: *Racial Factors in American Industry* (New York and London, 1931), Pages 42–43.

(16) Louise V. Kennedy: *The Negro Peasant Moves Cityward* (New York, 1930), Pages 35–36.

(17) William C. Graves: Memorandum of Address Made June 17th Before the Inter-racial Committee of the Union League Club", Julius Rosenwald Papers, University of Chicago Library.

(18) Elliot M. Rudwick: *Race Riot at East Saint Louis, July 2, 1917* (Carbondale, 1964); Tuttle: *Race Riot.*

(19) Spero and Harris: *The Black Worker,* Pages 167–168.

(20) Graves: "Memorandum of Speech Made June 17th".

(21) Robert Ozanne: *A Century of Labor-Management Relations at McCormick and International Harvester* (Madison, 1967), Pages 183–187.

(22) Bailer: "The Negro Automobile Worker", Pages 416–419; Herbert Northrup: *Organized Labor and the Negro* (New York, 1944), Pages 189–195.

(23) Spero and Harris: *The Black Worker,* Page 169.

(24) Cayton and Mitchell: *The Black Worker,* Page 31.

(25) Kennedy: *The Negro Peasant Moves Cityward,* Page 98; Feldman: *Racial Factors in American Industry,* Pages 57–58.

(26) "Conference on the Negro in Industry Held by the Committee on Industry, Chicago Commission on Race Relations, April 23, 1920", typescript, Julius Rosenwald Papers, University of Chicago Library.

(27) This writer gave such a reading to several hundred management officials at a session sponsored by the Graduate School of Management of the University of Chicago in 1969. It was an ironic success.

(28) Erwin D. Hoffman: "The Genesis of the Modern Movement for Equal Rights in South Carolina, 1930–1939", *Journal of Negro History* (October 1959), Page 347.

(29) Charles S. Johnson: *The Shadow of the Plantation* (Chicago, 1934), Page 210. For a good review of the situation of blacks in the rural South during this period, see E. Franklin Frazier: *The Negro in the United States* (New York, 1949), Chapter 10.

(30) Gunnar Myrdal: *An American Dilemma* (1964 Edition, New York, two volumes), Volume 1, Pages 256–269.

(31) "The Negro's War", *Fortune* (June 1942), Pages 76–80.

(32) *Ibid.;* American Management Association: *The Negro Worker* (Research Report Number 1, 1942), Pages 3–4 and 27–28; Nicholas S. Falcone: *The Negro Integrated* (New York, 1945).

(33) Robert Weaver: *Negro Labor, A National Problem* (New York, 1946), Pages 78-93.

(34) The standard work on the MOW movement is Herbert Garfinkel: *When Negroes March* (Glencoe, 1959). The MOW movement actually presaged two forms of future tactics. In its appeal to the masses for a black-defined program of struggle it summarized all of the decade's action for jobs on a local level and impelled them forward on a national basis. On the other hand, in that the movement failed to develop an organized working-class constituency, it foretold tactics of maneuver without mass struggle — of legislative lobbying, judicial procedures, and jockeying within the Democratic Party — which were to be pursued by the bourgeois and trade-union organizations until demonstrations and civil disobedience finally arose from below out of the civil-rights movement.

This selection is abridged from Harold M. Baron, "The Demand for Black Labor: Historical Notes on the Political Economy of Racism," *Radical America*, Vol. 5, No. 2, March-April, 1971, pp. 1–2, 10–16, 17–18, 19–20, 21–26, 27–29, 30–31, Published at 5 Upland Road, Cambridge, Massachusetts. Reprinted by permission of Harold M. Baron.

RACE RELATIONS
MODELS AND SOCIAL CHANGE

William K. Tabb

In the discussion of the structural position of black Americans in our society there appear to be two theoretical interpretations which dominate radical perspectives on the question. The first is that of the black ghetto as an internal colony set off from the rest of the society and systematically exploited in a consistent manner to maximize the well-being of the "mother country" (white America). The second view sees blacks as a marginal working class, lacking control over the means of production and who, though forced to work longer hours for less pay than other (white) workers, are essentially members of the working class. The policy implications of these two conceptual frameworks are quite different.

THE KERNER REPORT AS CONVENTIONAL WISDOM

The dominant view offered by the Kerner Commission Report is that blacks have been discriminated against, treated brutally, and excluded from their rightful place as equal citizens. This, the *Report* suggested, was the effect of "white racism" defined as the prejudiced attitudes whites showed towards blacks. By stressing these attitudes, the *Report* gave its attention to *personal* racism rather than *institutional* racism. "Thus the *Report* placed too much emphasis on changing white attitudes and underplayed the importance of changing white behavior and the basic structure of such institutions as schools, labor unions, and political parties" (Final Report of the Assembly on the Kerner Report Revisited, 1970: 3–4).

The generally uncritical acceptance and praise for the *Report* in academic circles and by the informed public is in some ways easy to understand. It is almost with a sigh of relief that Americans accepted the pious generalizations that we are all guilty, we are a racist society, white attitudes are to blame, we must do more to help the blacks.

The *Report* represents the concerned liberal viewpoint which typically:
1. stresses moral objections to racism while understanding the extent to which

racism is a structural part of American institutions, and 2. denies that the market economy — hence, employment, housing, and so on, is *structurally* exploitative. The corollary to 1. and 2. is that "we" have "options" and can "rearrange priorities" without altering the socio-economic structure.

The Kerner Commission studied black Americans — inadequacies were found in their housing, employment, education and other aspects of well-being *vis-a-vis* the majority. The *Report* did not study white society which was identified as the problem. The unanswered questions remain. Why are many white people and almost all white institutions racist? What structural changes are needed to redistribute resources, power, and wealth more evenly among classes and between races? While white society has been slow to address these questions, minority groups, especially blacks, have long been discussing the matter in ways which increasingly depart from mainstream white thinking.

As more blacks implicitly, and increasingly explicitly, come to hold essentially anti-capitalist ideology, the type of solutions to racist exploitation which they are willing to consider undergoes significant change. This expansion of options to be considered is reflected in the rise to influence of the Nation of Islam and the Black Panther Party. The separatist ideology of the muslims is not new to American black thinking, but the Panther stress on class analysis certainly is. The degree to which the strategy debates in the black community are keyed to an assessment of the possibilities inherent in the capitalist system is a subject which requires brief attention.

BLACKS AND CAPITALISM

At one pole in the discussion of the place of blacks in the American system stand men like Burkeley Burrell, currently the President of the black National Business League, an organization founded in 1900 by Booker T. Washington (financed by white corporate leaders, most prominantly John D. Rockefeller of Standard Oil and Julius Rosenwald of Sears).

> ... It is an article of faith with us that the free entrepreneuring system that is an American trademark is directly and indirectly responsible for all of the good things that have inured to our citizenry. *We want to become a truly meaningful part of that system* ... (cited in Henderson and Ledebur, 1970:51, emphasis in original).

Those who accept the desirability of participation by blacks as owners in American capitalism as a major goal include many moderates and some militants — most prominently Roy Innis of CORE.

Innis and others have been criticized in strong terms by blacks who reject American capitalism as a model of development. James Foreman and his associates for example have charged: "Ironically, some of the most militant Black nationalists, as they call themselves, have been the first to jump on the bandwagon of black capitalism. They are pimps, Black power pimps and fraudulent leaders and the people must be educated to understand that any black man or Negro who is advocating a perpetuation of capitalism inside the United States is in fact seeking not only his ultimate destruction and death, but is contributing to the continuous exploitation of black people all around the world. For it is the power of the United States government, this racist imperialist government that is choking the life of all people around the world" (Boggs, 168:1).

The distinction between the nature of capitalist and socialist solutions is pointed out even by such leaders as Ralph Abernathy of SCLC when he suggests:

> We need to organize community owned development corporations where profits will be returned to building the community. . . . We want to share in the public sector of the economy through publicly controlled non-profit institutions. . . . I don't believe in Black Capitalism. I believe in black socialism (cited in Henderson and Ledebur, 1970: 1–4).

The differences in frames of reference and with their ideological presumptions of different theories of causation have been belabored in order to stress the bias in mainstream research done by whites about blacks and to contrast them to some of the thinking being done by blacks. While generalization in this area is hazardous, all too many Americans, including I would suggest the group which has been termed concerned liberals, see the dimensions of past tragedies and foresee the possibility of still worse conflict, yet do not see racism in its institutional framework, but rather only in its individual manifestations and harmful attitudes. What alternative analyses are available to those wishing to understand the place of the black minority in the United States? Specifically, is the colonial framework referred to earlier useful in understanding the historical experience and present reality of black Americans?

THE GHETTO AS COLONY

The key relationships which must be demonstrated before the colonial analogy be accepted are the existence between two distinct and clearly separate groups of a superior-inferior status relationship encompassing both economic control and exploitation, and political dependence and subjugation. If these can be demonstrated to exist, then the case can be made that the ghetto must break the shackles imposed by colonial exploitation for meaningful long-range improvement to take place.

In defining colonialism, militants argue that the spatial separation of colony and colonial power is secondary to the existence of control of the ghetto from the outside through political and economic domination by white society. An historical comparison of the forms which colonialism has taken, and a description of the place of blacks in the American economy, make clear that internal colonialism is an apt description of the exploitation of blacks in our society.

The vast majority of colonies were established by Western powers over technologically less advanced peoples of Asia, Africa, and Latin America. Military supremacy, combined with judicious bribing of local leaders and a generous sprinkling of Christian missionaries, enabled an outside power to dominate an area spatially separate from the ruling state. In some colonies there was extensive settlement by Europeans. If the territory was relatively unpopulated (Canada, Australia, New Zealand, and the United States), a policy of genocide and exchanging land for beads allowed the settlers to gain control. When their numbers and strength grew, the settlers could demand independence from the mother country. Nationhood was usually followed by a continuing economic relationship, but on better terms than the colony had enjoyed before it became independent. In some of the cases where European settlement was large but still a small minority of the total population indigenous, often a long and bloody struggle for independence resulted. Algeria is a case in point.

The black experience in America was somewhat different. Here the colonized were brought to the "mother" country to be enslaved and exploited. Internal colonialism thus involves the conquest and subjugation of a people and their physical removal to the ruling state. The command of the resources of the captive people (their labor power) followed. One can find parallel cases in the histories of ancient Egypt, Greece, and Rome. In these nations slaves were also brought to the mother country to be exploited, to do the dirty work of these "great societies." The grandeur of the mother country was built on the backs of the exploited slaves.

In the United States an important part of the capital accumulated in the early nineteenth century also came from slave labor. North (1961) suggests that the timing and pace of an economy's development is determined by the success of its export sector and the disposition of the income received by the export sector. He argues that in the key years in which capital accumulation took place, "it was the growth of the cotton textile industry and the demand for cotton which was decisive. The vicissitudes of the cotton trade were the most important influence upon the varying rates of growth in the economy during the period" (1961:67). That New England merchants, through their control over the foreign trade and commerce of the country, and over insurance and shipping, did much of the actual accumulating should not be allowed to obscure this point. Cotton was the strategic variable. It paid for our imports, and "the demand for western foodstuffs and northeastern services and manufactures was basically dependent upon the income received from the cotton trade" (North: 1961:67). This is not an attempt to single out one factor as providing the "key" to development; but as cotton was the "carrier" industry inducing economic growth, so slavery was the basis of cotton production. Often the terrible burden of slavery is acknowledged, but rarely is the contribution of slave labor to the capital accumulation process seen as the very sizable factor in American development that it truly was.

To bring the story quickly to the present, the relevant question is: did the freeing of the slaves make a structurally significant difference in the colonial relationship? A comparison between the black ghetto as a colony within the United States today and the typical ex-colony which has gained its nominal political independence yet remains in neo-colonial subjugation suggests that in both instances formal freedom is not to be equated with real freedom.

Introductory chapters of a standard development textbook present a description of the typical less-developed country: low per capita income, high birth rate, a small, weak middle class, low rates of increase in labor productivity, in capital formation, and in domestic savings, as well as a small monetized market. The economy of such a country is heavily dependent on external markets, where its few basic exports face an inelastic demand (i.e., a demand which is relatively constant regardless of price and so expanding total output may not mean higher earnings). The international demonstration effect (the desire to consume the products which are seen generally available in the wealthier nations) works to increase the quantity of foreign goods imported to the underdeveloped country, putting pressure on their balance of payments since the value of imports exceeds the value of exports. Much of the small modern sector of the underdeveloped economy is owned by outsiders. Local entrepreneurship is limited, and in the absence of intergovernmental transfers, things might be still worse.

The economic relations of the ghetto to white America closely parallel those between third world nations and the industrially advanced countries. The ghetto also has a relatively low per capita income and a high birth rate. Its residents are for the most part unskilled. Businesses lack capital and managerial know-how. Local markets are limited. The incidence of credit default is high. Little saving takes place in the ghetto, and what is saved is usually not invested locally. Goods and services tend to be "imported" for the most part, only the simplest and the most labor-intensive are produced locally. The ghetto is dependent on one basic export — its unskilled labor power. Aggregate demand for this export does not increase to match the growth of the ghetto labor force and unemployment is prevalent. Cultural imperialism is also part of the relationship; ghetto schools traditionally teach the history of the "Mother Country" as if blacks had no part in its development, as if blacks had no identity of their own, no culture, no origins worthy of mention in the chronicles of the world's nations and peoples. The dominant culture is constantly held up as good, desirable, worthy of emulation. The destruction of the indigenous culture is an important weapon in creating dependence and reinforcing control.

Consumer goods are advertised 24 hours a day on radio and television; ghetto residents are constantly reminded of the availability of goods and services which they cannot afford to buy. Welfare payments and other governmental transfers are needed to help pay for the ghetto's requirements. Welfare, however, only reinforces the dependency relationship, reinforces the psychology of inferiority, keeping body barely together even as it gnaws at the soul, sapping militancy and independence. (It should also be said in this context that the welfare rights movement shows both a greater reservoir of strength and a political awareness of the role of welfare in attempting to perpetuate inequality.) Local businesses are owned, in large numbers, by non-residents, many of whom are white. Marginal, low-profit businesses are more likely to be owned by blacks; larger, more profitable ones are owned by whites (Heilbrun, 1970; Zweig, 1970). Important jobs in the local public economy (teachers, policemen, and postmen) are held by white outsiders. These "disparities" are not lost on area residents, many of whom see the ownership patterns, the direction and nature of capital flows, as both systematic and endemic to a system of colonialism.

It has been suggested that the distortion of the local economy caused by outside ownership can be compared to the creation of underdevelopment in external colonies through processes described by Frank (1967). In this light, the dishonest practices of ghetto merchants (Caplovitz, 1967; Sturdivant, 1969) and the crippling effects on ghetto residents (Grier and Cobbs, 1968; Clark, 1965) can be seen not as unfortunate occurrences which come about through "unfair dealings" by greedy individuals, but rather as the direct result of the unequal power relations between the internal colony and the white mother-country.

The conclusion has been drawn from the colonial model that attention should be centered on attempting to create community control over the local public economy, to encourage black ownership in the private sector, and in some cases to promote collectivization of the local economy. These political and economic programs may be seen as attempts to achieve black power. This phrase, greeted only a few years back with great horror by many whites and also some blacks, has been accepted, accommodated, and increasingly, it is charged, used by the same forces which have long controlled the destiny of the black ghettos to impose the equivalent of neo-colonialism. The objective of indirect rule can be detected in statements such as the following by Jacob Javits, the Republican Senator from New York, addressing the United States Chamber of Commerce in 1968. "American business has found that it must develop host country management and new forms of joint ownership in establishing plants in the fiercely nationalistic less-developed countries, (so too) this same kind of enlightened partnership will produce the best results in the slums of our own country" (1968:S5053). It is not only the desire to continue to do business which leads to a willingness to accept blacks as junior partners; long-range self-interest dictates such a policy on even more basic grounds of self-interest. For example, the final report from a conference for corporate executives held at the Graduate School of Business at Columbia University in January 1964 stresses that "practical businessmen must recognize that this (ghetto rebellion) is a deep-seated economic problem that threatens every business, perhaps even our business system" (Ginsberg, 1964:87). Since that meeting the corporate house organs and business community journals have been flooded with articles stressing the need for corporate involvement.

The rationale for this new found interest has not gone unnoticed by blacks, who have placed "black capitalism" and "corporate involvement" in the context of neo-colonialism. Allen (1969:187–8), for example, writes:

> . . . any black capitalist or managerial class must act, in effect, as the tacit representative of the white corporations which are sponsoring that class. The task of this class is to ease corporate penetration of the black communities and facilitate corporate planning and programming of the markets and human resources in those communities. This process occurs regardless of the personal motivations of the individuals involved, because it stems from the nature of the corporate economy itself and the dependent status of the fledgling, black capitalist-managerial class.

Increasingly even the acquiring of political control of city hall in predominantly black urban areas is a "hollow prize," since the local tax base just cannot support the programs needed by the central cities. The "independent" local political administration is dependent on "foreign aid" from the external mother country. Hence the total independence of a black nation would mean even greater poverty for blacks who would have their labor power and little else. Independence based on community control would have a less extreme, but essentially similar result, perpetuating division within the working class.

Such an analysis also suggests that black power need not finally be measured by its ability to establish black autonomy from white society. Black control over the black community brings benefits only if it is within the context of an ability to enforce demands for the transfer of significant resources. Effectiveness in this area necessitates alliances with other groups to pressure for common goals. The questions of alliance with whom and for what have generally been answered: coalition with the labor movement to redistribute resources to the working class and low income people, away from corporations and all those enjoying "unearned" income (see Rustin, 1966). While this answer appears in accord with some strands of Marxian theory, it is an answer which has been repeatedly rejected by most white workers and their union leadership.

Blauner (1969:393) has argued that the utility of the colonial analogy depends upon the distinction between "colonization as a process and colonialism as a social, economic, and political system" arguing that "Important as are economic factors, the power of race and racism cannot be sufficiently explained through class analysis" (1969:394). Blauner (1969:396) stresses the "common *process* of social oppression" which he sums up in his discussion of "the colonization complex." Blauner's distinction makes the colonial analogy a more acceptable one. At the same time it points in the direction of a wider theory of exploitation in which colonization as a process can be seen as a method of class subjugation in which part of the working class — black Americans, Puerto Ricans, and others are separated out as a distinct group from the rest of the working class to serve the function of a pariah group creating division in the working class and perpetuating division within the working class.

The reasons an alliance has been difficult to forge must be investigated in more detail in terms of the objective relations between white and black workers in the historic development of American-capitalism.

BLACKS AS A MARGINAL WORKING CLASS

Marxists have long recognized that some segments of the working class enjoy privileges and material gain at the expense of other workers (Thompson, 1964; Hammonds, 1928). Engels saw the small minority of skilled artisans in the England of 1844 as forming "an aristocracy among the working class" (a phrase appearing in the introduction to the 1892 edition of *The Conditions of the Working Class in England in 1844*). Lenin in the eighth chapter of *Imperialism* suggests that at least some segments of the working class benefit from the exploitation of colonial labor.

The marginal working class, Leggett (1968:14) has written, "refers to a sub-community of workers who belong to a subordinate ethnic or racial group which is unusually proletarianized and highly segregated. Workmen of this type fill many manual roles in heavy industry and face an inordinant amount of economic insecurity. This is evidenced by their large concentration in marginal occupational positions, their lack of formal education, and finally and most obviously, their high rate of unemployment." The isolation of the blacks is in many respects similar to that of other workers who are forced to form their own separate communities. Kerr and Siegel (1954:191) describe the coal town and the logging camp as ghetto-like, worlds unto themselves, in which a sense of group solidarity develops. "These communities," they write, "have their own codes, myths, heroes, and social standards. There are few neutrals in them to mediate the conflicts and dilute the mass . . . all the members of each of these groups have the same grievances." The strike for the isolated mining town is "a kind of colonial revolt against far removed authority, an outlet for accumulated tensions, and a substitute for occupational and social mobility" (Kerr and Siegel 1954:192). The ghetto rebellion can be described in similar terms.

The extent to which the capitalist class is able to isolate segments of the working class from each other strengthens its position. By creating a marginal working class of blacks and giving white workers a relatively more privileged position, it strengthens its control. If one group of workers are able to command higher pay, to exclude others from work, and if the other group or groups of workers are limited in their employment opportunities to the worst jobs and lowest pay, then a marginal working class has been created which benefits the labor aristocracy and to an even greater extent the capitalist class. The marginal working class produces goods which are generally available below the cost which would have been obtained if they had received wages closer to those paid to the labor aristocracy which had used its bargaining position to its own advantage. Thus Hobsbawm suggests "The aristocracy of labor arises when the economic circumstances of capitalism make it possible to grant significant concessions to the proletariate, while certain strata manage, by means of their special scarcity, skill, strategic position, organizational strength, etc., to establish notably better conditions for themselves than the rest" (1970:50). In just such a manner has black labor generally been excluded from equal status, to the benefit of white society—capitalist and worker alike.

From the time black slaves were free to sell their labor as a commodity, they came to serve both as a reserve army and as a pool of labor ready of necessity to do the "dirty work" for the society at low wages. In the first role they served as an equilibrating factor in the economy. In periods of labor shortage blacks have made important gains, but with economic downturns they have been systematically displaced. Thus the jobs that blacks were recruited for in the labor shortages of World War I and the prosperity of the twenties were taken away in the Depression. Ross (1967:15) writes: "There was widespread invasion of Negro jobs by unemployed whites, often with the assistance of employers, unions, and lawmakers. Municipal licensing ordinances were reviewed in the South in order to drive Negroes out of barbering, plumbing, and other new occupations Negroes had entered during recent years." In the second role they were restricted to the most menial, physically exhausting, and alienating labor which the white society offered. Furthermore, this allowed white society to enjoy a profusion of goods and services at prices much lower than if these commodities had been produced at prevailing white worker wages. Thus blacks served in part as the classic Marxian reserve army and also as a "non-competing group," to borrow a term from another 19th century scholar, John Cairnes.

Therefore, it is important to see that the position of blacks in the society is primarily a result of their position as a marginal working class. Under American capitalism someone has always played this role. Traditionally immigrant groups have served as the structural equivalent of the blacks, as a white marginal working class. In England, until the arrival of great numbers of Pakistanis in recent years, the Irish were the major occupants of this position.

In the United States institutionalized discrimination contributes to particular forms of poverty among blacks and enhances the privileges of many whites. Discrimination is the medium — in the context of U.S. economics and social history — by which a special kind of poverty and a special kind of labor reserve is maintained.

"As in the case of white poverty, Negro poverty — more clearly seen because of its extreme character — is a function of the industrial and economic structure. Elimination of discrimination will not eliminate such major sources of poverty as unemployment, causal and intermittent jobs and low-paid occupations" (Magdoff, 1965:75–6). It is within this structural framework that the place of blacks as a marginal working class becomes clearer. It is not only that blacks are often at the end of the hiring line, but also that to some extent they are standing in a different line.

> The manpower problems of the urban ghetto appear best defined in terms of a dual labor market: a *primary* market offering relatively high-paying, stable employment, with good working conditions, chances of advancement and equitable administration of work rules; and a *secondary* market, to which the urban poor are confined, decidedly less attractive in all of these respects and in

direct competition with welfare and crime for the attachment of the potential labor force (Piore, 1968:2–3).

The possibilities for change on a class basis are constrained by forces largely beyond the control of black Americans. Obstacles include not merely material benefits whites receive from the exploitation of blacks, but important "psychic income" as well. Whites gain in relative status if blacks are held down. Fear of blacks is an integral accompaniment to these feelings of superiority.

Whites are made to feel better off than the blacks and so less prone to demand better pay and working conditions; on the other hand, if they become militant they can be replaced by blacks who will work for less. This factor is most relevant in low wage unskilled and semi-skilled employment. An economic system based on individual competition breeds a social system based on relative income and status. One fears moving down the status hierarchy and so fears those below trying to move up. The degree to which the individual aspires to move up leads him to identify with the group above him.

> The net result of all this is that each status group has a deep-rooted psychological need to compensate for feelings of inferiority and envy toward those above by feelings of superiority and contempt for those below. It thus happens that a special pariah group at the bottom acts as a kind of lightning rod for the frustrations and hostilities of all the higher groups, the more so the nearer they are to the bottom. It may even be said that the very existence of the pariah group is a kind of harmonizer and stabilizer of the social structure — so long as the pariahs play their role passively and resignedly (Baran and Sweezy, 1970:309).

Thus the gains from racism often appear to outweigh the material losses. White workers' subjective calculations on the matter are not made without pressures of employers who encourage racism as well as union officials who do the same partly out of fear of new leadership groups emerging, and partly out of the recognition that if the employer can exploit black workers less he may seek to exploit whites more. It seems also that both workers and their union leaders are heavily conditioned by the "scarcity consciousness" bred during the Great Depression and sustained in each downturn. The supply of union workers is to be kept down.

If the costs and benefits of present racist arrangements to white workers are crucial determinants of the future of race relations, it is not the only key. The costs of perpetuating racism and the repression which accompanies this policy will be determined largely by the militancy of blacks and their white supporters. The climate will be further tempered by the type and number of jobs the economy generates. A slack labor market means more competition and racial tensions. A growing economy has greater potential to bring benefits to all and so minimize both race and class conflicts.

Another important factor is the apparent trend toward bifurcation within the black community. On the one hand, the black middle-class seems to have significantly expanded. The 1970 Census data should allow confirmation of this growth. Some commentators even speak of an emerging black "silent majority" (Hamilton, 1970). On the other hand, in the hard core urban poverty area conditions appear to be getting worse. The use of averages for all non-whites masks these counter trends. It may well be that even as more blacks reach middle-class status, the black underclass will become both objectively worse off and more volatile (Brimmer, 1970 and Hacker, 1970). The middle-class blacks assuming positions in the wider society will be increasingly called upon to keep the lid on things by whites and at the same time will be under pressure from below to identify with the continuing black struggle, or be denounced as oreos (like the cookie, black on the outside, white on the inside). Identity questions and the political dilemma of the black middle-class are likely therefore to intensify. Some significant degree of job integration may be possible for the middle-class black but for the vast majority of ghetto blacks, integration can only have less and less meaning, given population trends and the persistence of housing segregation. The recent employment gains of middle-class blacks have for the most part been outside the ghetto. Unlike the older black bourgeois who lived off of the larger black community, the additions to the black middle-class more and more work in the white world. Attempts to strengthen the traditionally small black entrepreneurial class which is seen as crucial by some policy makers if community stability is to be achieved in ghetto areas, have in spite of much publicity, not been overly successful.

Even programs of "Black Capitalism," which promise to "give them a piece of the action," as President Nixon often phrased it during the last presidential campaign, are little heard of these days. The reason is evident in government statistics. There are not many profitable honest business opportunities available in the ghetto. As the minority group program of the Small Business Administration expanded in recent years, the default rate also climbed to unacceptable rates and the program has been downgraded. Similarly job creation in the private sector has been quietly shelved as the economy has moved downward. Programs to redistribute even relatively insignificant resources to black urban poor have been interpreted as race legislation and resisted by conservatives both in and out of Congress. It is the failure of liberal solutions which is startling when contrasted with the last decade's War on Poverty and Great Society rhetoric. The failure of these approaches to date has not led to searching for more basic reforms of existing economic and social institutions. The pessimism which seems to affect a large part of those academics actively engaged in policy research seems to be well founded — the inaction of government officials except selectively in the area of the law enforcement is difficult to ignore.

How matters will develop in this area in the longer run is more difficult to envisage. A number of factors seem to be important. First, there is the question of the type of structural transformation the economy will undergo in the next decade. The rate at which unskilled low-paying jobs decrease as a proportion of total employment, the rate of increase in jobs requiring significant amounts of education, and the progress blacks make in educational attainment certainly provide one key. The growth of the number of educated blacks in white collar positions of high relative status may create resentment on the part of white blue collar workers whose relative position in the status hierarchy is diminished. They may react, especially as their numbers diminish through slower growth rates in blue collar occupations, especially in the skilled trades, by excluding the less educated blacks who cannot hope for white collar jobs but who are objectively qualified to enter these trades. The manner in which demand and supply in different occupations reach equilibrium may become more artificial as, for example, blacks become more heavily represented in government jobs and continue to be excluded from construction work. Second, the overall stability and rate of growth of the economy cannot but help influence black progress and white acceptance of black gains. White workers secure in their own positions and enjoying increases in real wages more willingly accept black gains. Also in terms of government expenditures for minority poor, spending more out of greatly expanded resources may be accompanied by a lighter tax burden, especially if war expenditures are also contained. On the other hand, a mild downturn such as the one now current accentuates racial conflicts as the competition for resources intensifies. Paradoxically, a severe downturn which was clearly induced by the Government's unwillingness to regulate the economy might lead to the imposition of social controls and government intervention and planning which would be in the interests of both the white working-class and minority groups. The potential for movement in this direction is certainly greater than in the 1930's. All of this is of course speculation. The point is that we have reached the situation in which we come to realize that our policy choices in this area are more and more conditioned by constraints originating elsewhere in the economy.

POLICY IMPLICATIONS

If blacks have historically functioned as an internal colony exploited by the white society in general and, at the same time, served as a marginal work force to the pecuniary advantage of employer groups and to the benefit of white workers who derive income but who may be suffering long-term losses from racism, then it seems that blacks and whites seeking a change in race relations must become clearer as to whom they identify as "the enemy."

Certainly the groups expressing racist views most openly are those who see themselves competing directly with blacks for jobs and status. Such racial antagonisms spring from a competitive system which pits individuals and groups against each other. To the extent to which workers come to see the commonality of their situation, this comes to be more clearly perceived.

The colonial analogy becomes misleading when it is used to suggest the possibility of meaningful black independence within the context of American society (Tabb, 1970). As the size of the black middle-class increases, the cohesiveness of common racial identity may be lessened and a long term sustained effort to achieve independence made even more difficult. At the same time strengthening the black community's economic and political power increases its bargaining position *vis-a-vis* the white society. This remains true whether seen as a step toward separatism, or as a step toward eventual integration at a future date.

The civil rights approach reached its logical end when concessions became harder to grant, and whites, especially Northern whites, perceived direct loss in proportion to black gains. It may be for this reason that in addition to separatist demands, for those concerned with racial quality to make progress, broad goals must be set which are clearly class rather than race oriented — adequate jobs, housing, incomes, and education — for all. The white workers who have a lower real income in 1971 than they had in 1965 because taxes and prices have risen faster than their pay, should not be the only group, or even the major group, to bear the burdens of redistribution. There are other possibilities, given the current situation of our cities, our environment and at the most basic levels, our society, which make fundamental change seem less utopian than it did a decade ago.

A possibility which cannot be underestimated is that the growing black middle-class may become convinced that the system is indeed flexible and willing to take talented blacks like themselves into full participation. If this transpires, American blacks will move from the unenviable position of collectively suffering racism, to the somewhat more ambiguous position where mobility is achieved for a sizable but still proportionately small part of the black people. The remainder of the black underclass may then be written off, confined to secondary labor markets, to the traditional marginal working-class role or when in too great supply, to the human scrap heap of redundant labor.

In the past an understanding of race was central to comprehension of the position of black Americans. In the future as racist barriers are overcome by a significant number of blacks, it may be that a race *and* class analysis will become more important. Such an approach would study the determinants of the willingness of white society to accept racial equality and also consider the possibility of comprehensive structural change in the economy which currently perpetuates a large underclass of predominantly black Americans.

Whether meaningful change will occur is conditioned by the degree of objective failure on the part of the economic and social system to meet the needs of Americans — black and white — and the degree of subjective awareness that other priorities and forms of organization are possible. These are topics which go beyond the scope of this paper.

REFERENCES

Allen, Robert L., 1969, Black Awakening in Capitalist America. New York: Doubleday, pp. 187-188.

Baran, Paul A. and Paul M. Sweezy, 1970, "Monopoly capitalism and race relations," in David Mermelstein, (ed.), Economics: Mainstream Readings and Radical Critiques. New York: Random House.

Blauner, Robert, 1969, "Internal colonialism and ghetto revolts." Social Problems (Spring).

Boggs, James, 1968, Manifesto for a Black Revolutionary Party. Philadelphia: Pacesetters.

Brimmer, Andrew F., 1970, "Economic progress of Negroes in the United States: The deepening schism." Presented at the Founders' Day Convocation at Tuskegee Institute. Mimeo.

Caplovitz, David, 1967, The Poor Pay More. New York: The Free Press.

Clark, Kenneth B., 1965, Dark Ghetto. New York: Harper and Row.

Frank, Andre Gunter, 1967, Capitalism and Underdevelopment in Latin America, New York: Monthly Review Press.

Ginsberg, Eli (ed.), 1964, The Negro Challenge to the Business Community. New York: McGraw-Hill.

Grier, William H. and Price M. Cobbs, 1968, Black Rage. New York: Bantam Books.

Hacker, Andrew, 1970, "The violent black minority." New York Times Magazine, May 10.

Hamilton, Charles V., 1970, "The silent black majority." New York Times Magazine, May 10.

Hammond, J.L. and Barbara, 1928, Town Laborer, 1760-1832, The New Civilization. London: Longmans Green & Co.

Heilburn, James, 1970, "Jobs in Harlem: A statistical analysis." Regional Science Association Papers.

Henderson, William L. and Larry C. Ledebur, 1970, Economic Disparity: Problems and Strategies for Black America. New York: The Free Press.

Hobsbawm, Eric, 1970, "Lenin and the 'aristocracy of labor'," in Paul M. Sweezy and Harry Magdoff, Lenin Today. New York: Monthly Review, p. 50.

Javitts, Jacob, 1968, "Remarks to the 56th annual meeting of the United States Chamber of Commerce," in United States, Congressional Record, 90th Congress, 2nd Session, May 7.

Kerr, Clark and Abraham Siegel, 1954, "The interindustry propensity to strike —An international comparison," in Arthur Kornhauser, Robert Dubin, and Arthur M. Rose, (eds.), Industrial Conflict. New York: McGraw-Hill.

Leggett, John C., 1968, Class, Race and Labor. New York: Oxford University Press.

Magdoff, Harry, 1965, "Problems of United States capitalism," in Ralph Miliband and John Saville, The Socialist Register 1965. New York: Monthly Review Press, pp. 75-6.

Meranto, Philip (3d.), 1970, The Kerner Report Revisited. University of Illinois: Institute of Government and Public Affairs, June.

North, Douglass C., 1961, The Economic Growth of the United States, 1790-1860. Englewood Cliffs, N.J.: Prentice-Hall, Inc.

Parenti, Michael, 1970, "The possibilities for political change," in Philip Meranto ed., The Kerner Commission Revisited. Urbana: University of Illinois, Institute of Government and Public Affairs.

Piore, Michael J., 1968, "Public and private responsibility in on-the-job training of disadvantaged workers." Department of Economics Working Paper, Number 23, Cambridge, Mass.: M.I.T. June.

Report of the National Advisory Commission on Civil Disorders, 1968, New York: Bantam Books.

Ross, Arthur M., 1967, "The Negro in the American economy," in Employment, Race, and Poverty, ed. Arthur M. Ross and Herbert Hill. New York: Harcourt, Brace & World.

Rustin, Bayard, 1966, "Black power and coalition politics," Commentary (September).

Sturdivant, Frederick D. (ed.), 1969, The Ghetto Marketplace. New York: The Free Press.

Tabb, William K., 1970, The Political Economy of the Black Ghetto. New York: W. W. Norton.

Thompson, E. P., 1964, The Making of the English Working Class, New York: Pantheon Books.

United States Bureau of the Census and the Bureau of Labor Statistics, 1970, The Social and Economic Status of Negroes in the United States, 1969. Washington D.C.: Government Printing Office, p. 75.

Zweig, Michael, 1970, "Black capitalism and the ownership of property in Harlem." Stony Brook Working Paper, No. 16. Stony Brook: Economic Research Bureau, State University of New York, August.

This selection is reprinted from William K. Tabb, "Race Relations Models and Social Change," *Social Problems*, Spring, 1971, pp. 431–44. Published by the Society for the Study of Social Problems. Earlier versions of this paper were presented to the meetings of the Union for Radical Political Economics, December, 1969, and before the Seventh World Congress of Sociology, September, 1970. Useful comments were made to the author following both presentations.

NEWARK: REBELLION AND REPRESSION

National Advisory Commission on Civil Disorders

Founded in 1666, the city, part of the Greater New York City port complex, rises from the salt marshes of the Passaic River. Although in 1967 Newark's population of 400,000 still ranked it thirtieth among American municipalities, for the past 20 years the white middle class had been deserting the city for the suburbs.

In the late 1950's the desertions had become a rout. Between 1960 and 1967, the city lost a net total of more than 70,000 white residents. Replacing them in vast areas of dilapidated housing where living conditions, according to a prominent member of the County Bar Association, were so bad that "people would be kinder to their pets," were Negro migrants, Cubans and Puerto Ricans. In six years the city switched from 65 percent white to 52 percent Negro and 10 percent Puerto Rican and Cuban.

The white population, nevertheless, retained political control of the city. On both the City Council and the Board of Education seven of nine members were white. On other key boards the disparity was equal or greater. In the Central Ward, where the medical college controversy raged, the Negro constituents and their white councilman found themselves on opposite sides of almost every crucial issue.

The municipal administration lacked the ability to respond quickly enough to navigate the swiftly changing currents. Even had it had great astuteness, it would have lacked the financial resources to affect significantly the course of events.

In 1962, seven-term Congressman Hugh Addonizio had forged an Italian-Negro coalition to overthrow long-time Irish control of the City Hall. A liberal in Congress, Addonizio, when he became mayor, had opened his door to all people. Negroes, who had been excluded from the previous administration, were brought into the government. The police department was integrated.

Nevertheless, progress was slow. As the Negro population increased, more and more of the politically oriented found the progress inadequate.

The Negro-Italian coaliton began to develop strains over the issue of the police. The police were largely Italian, the persons they arrested largely Negro. Community leaders agreed that, as in many police forces, there was a small minority of officers who abused their responsibility. This gave credibility to the cries of "Brutality!" voiced periodically by ghetto Negroes.

In 1965 Mayor Addonizio, acknowledged that there was "a small group of misguided individuals" in the department, declared that "it is vital to establish once and for all, in the minds of the public, that charges of alleged police brutality will be thoroughly investigated and the appropriate legal or punitive action be taken if the charges are found to be substantiated."

Pulled one way by the Negro citizens who wanted a Police Review Board, and the other by the police, who adamantly opposed it, the mayor decided to transfer "the control and investigation of complaints of police brutality out of the hands of both the police and the public and into the hands of an agency that all can support — the Federal Bureau of Investigation;" and to send "a copy of any charge of police brutality . . . directly to the Prosecutor's office." However, the FBI could act only if there had been a violation of a person's federal civil rights. No complaint was ever heard of again. . . .

When it became known that the secretary of the Board of Education intended to retire, the militants proposed for the position the city's budget director, a Negro with a master's degree in accounting. The mayor, however, had already nominated a white man. Since the white man had only a high school education, and at least 70 percent of the children in the school system were Negro, the issue of who was to obtain the secretaryship, an important and powerful position, quickly became a focal issue.

Joined with the issue of the 150-acre medical school site, the area of which had been expanded to triple the original request — an expansion regarded by the militants as an effort to dilute the black political power by moving out Negro residents — the Board of Education battle resulted in a confrontation between the mayor and the militants. Both sides refused to alter their positions. . . .

. . . The militants, led by the local CORE (Congress of Racial Equality) chapter, disrupted and took over the Board of Education meeting. The outcome was a stalemate. The incumbent secretary decided to stay on another year. No one was satisfied.

At the beginning of July there were 24,000 unemployed Negroes within the city limits. Their ranks were swelled by an estimated 20,000 teenagers, many of whom, with school out and the summer recreation program curtailed due to a lack of funds, had no place to go.

On July 8, Newark and East Orange Police attempted to disperse a group of Black Muslims. In the melee that followed, several police officers and Muslims suffered injuries necessitating medical treatment. The resulting charges and countercharges heightened the tension between police and Negroes.

Early on the evening of July 12, a cab driver named John Smith began, according to police reports, tailgating a Newark police car. Smith was an unlikely candidate to set a riot in motion. Forty years old, a Georgian by birth, he had attended college for a year before entering the Army in 1950. In 1953 he had been honorably discharged with the rank of corporal. A chess-playing trumpet player, he had worked as a musician and a factory hand before, in 1963, becoming a cab driver.

As a cab driver, he appeared to be a hazard. Within a relatively short period of time he had eight or nine accidents. His license was revoked. When, with a woman passenger in his cab, he was stopped by the police, he was in violation of that revocation.

From the high-rise towers of the Reverend William P. Hayes Housing Project, the residents can look down on the orange-red brick facade of the Fourth Precinct Police Station and observe every movement. Shortly after 9:30 P.M., people saw Smith, who either refused or was unable to walk, being dragged out of a police car and into the front door of the station.

Within a few minutes at least two civil rights leaders received calls from a hysterical woman declaring a cab driver was being beaten by the police. When one of the persons at the station notified the cab company of Smith's arrest, cab drivers all over the city began learning of it over their cab radios.

A crowd formed on the grounds of the housing project across the narrow street from the station. As more and more people arrived, the description of the beating purportedly administered to Smith became more and more exaggerated. The descriptions were supported by other complaints of police malpractice that, over the years, had been submitted for investigation — but had never been heard of again.

Several Negro community leaders, telephoned by a civil rights worker and informed of the deteriorating situation, rushed to the scene. By 10:15 P.M. the atmosphere had become so potentially explosive that Kenneth Melchior, the senior police inspector on the night watch, was called. He arrived at approximately 10:30 P.M.

Met by a delegation of civil rights leaders and militants who requested the right to see and interview Smith, Inspector Melchior acceded to their request.

When the delegation was taken to Smith, Melchior agreed with their observations that, as a result of injuries Smith had suffered, he needed to be examined by a doctor. Arrangements were made to have a police car transport him to the hospital.

Both within and outside of the police station the atmosphere was electric with hostility. Carloads of police officers arriving for the 10:45 P.M. change of shifts were subjected to a gauntlet of catcalls, taunts and curses.

Joined by Oliver Lofton, administrative director of the Newark Legal Services Project, the Negro community leaders inside the station requested an interview with Inspector Melchior. As they were talking to the inspector about initiating an investigation to determine how Smith had been injured, the crowd outside became more and more unruly. Two fo the Negro spokesmen went outside to attempt to pacify the people.

There was little reaction to the spokesmen's appeal that the people go home. The second of the two had just finished speaking from atop a car when several Molotov cocktails smashed against the wall of the police station.

With the call of "Fire!" most of those inside the station, police officers and civilians alike, rushed out of the front door. The Molotov cocktails had splattered to the ground; the fire was quickly extinguished.

Inspector Melchior had a squad of men form a line across the front of the station. The police officers and the Negroes on the other side of the street exchanged volleys of profanity.

Three of the Negro leaders, Timothy Still of the United Community Corporation, Robert Curvin of CORE, and Lofton, requested they be given another opportunity to disperse the crowd. Inspector Melchior agreed to let them try, and provided a bullhorn. It was apparent that the several hundred persons who had gathered in the street and on the grounds of the housing project were not going to disperse. Therefore, it was decided to attempt to channel the energies of the people into a nonviolent protest. While Lofton promised the crowd that a full investigation would be made of the Smith incident, the other Negro leaders urged those on the scene to form a line of march toward the city hall.

Some persons joined the line of march. Others milled about in the narrow street. From the dark grounds of the housing project came a barrage of rocks. Some of them fell among the crowd. Others hit persons in the line of march. Many smashed the windows of the police station. The rock throwing, it was believed, was the work of youngsters; approximately 2,500 children lived in the housing project.

Almost at the same time, an old car was set afire in a parking lot. The line of march began to disintegrate. The police, their heads protected by World War I-type helmets, sallied forth to disperse the crowd. A fire engine, arriving on the scene, was pelted with rocks. As police drove people away from the station, they scattered in all directions.

A few minutes later a nearby liquor store was broken into. Some persons, seeing a caravan of cabs appear at city hall to protest Smith's arrest, interpreted this as evidence that the disturbance had been organized, and generated rumors to that effect.

However, only a few stores were looted. Within a short period of time the disorder ran its course.

The next afternoon, Thursday, July 13, the mayor described it as an isolated incident. At a meeting with Negro leaders to discuss measures to defuse the situation, he agreed to appoint the first Negro police captain, and announced that he would set up a panel of citizens to investigate the Smith arrest. To one civil rights leader this sounded like "the playback of a record," and he walked out. Other observers reported that the mayor seemed unaware of the seriousness of the tensions. . . .

. . . On Thursday, inflammatory leaflets were circulated in the neighborhoods of the Fourth Precinct. A "Police Brutality Protest Rally" was announced for early evening in front of the Fourth Precinct Station. Several television stations and newspapers sent news teams to interview people. Cameras were set up. A crowd gathered.

A picket line was formed to march in front of the police station. Between 7:00 and 7:30 P.M. James Threatt, Executive Director of the Newark Human Rights Commission, arrived to announce to the people the decision of the mayor to form a citizens group to investigate the Smith incident, and to elevate a Negro to the rank of captain.

The response from the loosely milling mass of people was derisive. One youngster shouted "Black Power!" Rocks were thrown at Threatt, a Negro. The barrage of missiles that followed placed the police station under siege.

After the barrage had continued for some minutes, police came out to disperse the crowd. According to witnesses, there was little restraint of language or action by either side. A number of police officers and Negroes were injured.

As on the night before, once the people had been dispersed, reports of looting began to come in. Soon the glow of the first fire was seen.

Without enough men to establish control, the police set up a perimeter around a two-mile stretch of Springfield Avenue, one of the principal business districts, where bands of youths roamed up and down smashing windows. Grocery and liquor stores, clothing and furniture stores, drug stores and cleaners, appliance stores and pawnshops were the principal targets. Periodically police officers would appear and fire their weapons over the heads of looters and rioters. Laden with stolen goods, people began returning to the housing projects.

Near midnight, activity appeared to taper off. The Mayor told reporters the city had turned the corner. . . .

. . . During the morning the governor and the mayor, together with police and National Guard officers, made a reconnaissance of the area. The police escort guarding the officials arrested looters as they went. By early afternoon the National Guard had set up 137 roadblocks, and state police and riot teams were beginning to achieve control. Command of anti-riot operations were taken over by the governor, who decreed a "hard line" in putting down the riot.

As a result of technical difficulties, such as the fact that the city and state police did not operate on the same radio wavelengths, the three-way command structure — city police, state police and National Guard — worked poorly.

At 3:30 P.M. that afternoon, the family of Mrs. D. J. was standing near the upstairs windows of their apartment, watching looters run in and out of a furniture store on Springfield Avenue. Three carloads of police rounded the corner. As the police yelled at the looters, they began running.

The police officers opened fire. A bullet smashed the kitchen window in Mrs. D. J.'s apartment. A moment later she heard a cry from the bedroom. Her 3-year old daughter, Debbie, came running into the room. Blood was streaming down the left side of her face: the bullet had entered her eye. The child spent the next two months in the hospital. She lost the sight of her left eye and the hearing in her left ear.

Simultaneously, on the street below, Horace W. Morris, an associate director of the Washington Urban League who had been visiting relatives in Newark, was about to enter a car for the drive to Newark Airport. With him were his two brothers and his 73-year old step-father, Isaac Harrison. About 60 persons had been on the street watching the looting. As the police arrived, three of the looters cut directly in front of the group of spectators. The police fired at the looters. Bullets plowed into the spectators. Everyone began running. As Harrison, followed by the family, headed toward the apartment building in which he lived, a bullet kicked his legs out from under him. Horace Morris lifted him to his feet. Again he fell. Mr. Morris' brother, Virgil, attempted to pick the old man up. As he was doing so, he was hit in the left leg and right forearm. Mr. Morris and his other brother managed to drag the two wounded men into the vestibule of the building, jammed with 60 to 70 frightened, angry Negroes.

Bullets continued to splatter against the walls of the buildings. Finally, as the firing died down, Morris — whose stepfather died that evening — yelled to a sergeant that innocent people were being shot.

"Tell the black bastards to stop shooting at us," the sergeant, according to Morris, replied.

"They don't have guns; no one is shooting at you," Morris said.

"You shut up, there's a sniper on the roof," the sergeant yelled.

A short time later, at approximately 5:00 P.M., in the same vicinity a police detective was killed by a small caliber bullet. The origin of the shot could not be determined. Later during the riot a fireman was killed by a .30 caliber bullet. Snipers were blamed for the deaths of both.

At 5:30 P.M., on Beacon Street, W. F. told J. S., whose 1959 Pontiac he had taken to the station for inspection, that his front brake needed fixing. J.S., who had just returned from work, went to the car which was parked in the street, jacked up the front end, took the wheel off and got under the car.

The street was quiet. More than a dozen persons were sitting on porches, walking about, or shopping. None heard any shots. Suddenly several state troopers appeared at the corner of Springfield and Beacon. J. S. was startled by a shot clanging into the side of the garbage can next to his car. As he looked up he saw a state trooper with his rifle pointed at him. The next shot struck him in the right side.

At almost the same instant, K. G., standing on a porch, was struck in the right eye by a bullet. Both he and J. S. were critically injured.

At 8:00 P.M., Mrs. L. M. bundled her husband, her husband's brother, and her four sons into the family car to drive to a restaurant for dinner. On the return trip her husband, who was driving, panicked as he approached a National Guard roadblock. He slowed the car, then quickly swerved around. A shot rang out. When the family reached home, everyone began piling out of the car. Ten-year-old Eddie failed to move. Shot through the head, he was dead.

Although, by nightfall, most of the looting and burning had ended, reports of sniper fire increased. The fire was, according to New Jersey National Guard reports, "deliberately or otherwise inaccurate." Major General James F. Cantwell, Chief of Staff of the New Jersey National Guard, testified before an Armed Services Subcommittee of the House of Representatives that "there was too much firing initially against snipers" because of "confusion when we were finally called on for help and our thinking of it as a military action."

"As a matter of fact," Director of Police Spina told the Commission, "down in the Springfield Avenue area it was so bad that, in my opinion, Guardsmen were firing upon police and police were firing back at them . . . I really don't believe there was as much sniping as we thought . . . We have since compiled statistics indicating that there were 79 specified instances of sniping."

Several problems contributed to the misconceptions regarding snipers: the lack of communications; the fact that one shot might be reported half a dozen times by half a dozen different persons as it caromed and reverberated a mile or more through the city; the fact that the National Guard troops lacked riot training. They were, said a police official, "young and very scared," and had had little contact with Negroes.

Within the Guard itself contact had certainly been limited. Although, in 1949, out of a force of 12,529 men there had been 1,183 Negroes, following the integration of the Guard in the 1950's the number had declined until, by July of 1967, there were 303 Negroes in a force of 17,529 men.

On Saturday, July 15, Spina received a report of snipers in a housing project. When he arrived he saw approximately 100 National Guardsmen and police officers crouching behind vehicles, hiding in corners and lying on the ground around the edge of the courtyard.

Since everything appeared quiet and it was broad daylight, Spina walked directly down the middle of the street. Nothing happened. As he came to the last building of the complex, he heard a shot. All around him the troopers jumped, believing themselves to be under sniper fire. A moment later a young Guardsman ran from behind a building.

The director of police went over and asked him if he had fired the shot. The soldier said yes, he had fired to scare a man away from a window; that his orders were to keep everyone away from windows.

Spina said he told the soldier: "Do you know what you just did? You have now created a state of hysteria. Every Guardsman up and down this street and every State Policeman and every city policeman that is present thinks that somebody just fired a shot and that it is probably a sniper."

A short time later more "gunshots" were heard. Investigating, Spina came upon a Puerto Rican sitting on a wall. In reply to a question as to whether he knew "where the firing is coming from?" the man said:

"That's no firing. That's fireworks. If you look up to the fourth floor, you will see the people who are throwing down these cherry bombs."

By this time four truckloads of National Guardsmen had arrived and troopers and policemen were again crouched everywhere, looking for a sniper. The director of police remained at the scene for three hours, and the only shot fired was the one by the Guardsman.

Nevertheless, at six o'clock that evening two columns of National Guardsmen and state troopers were directing mass fire at the Hayes Housing Project in response to what they believed were snipers.

On the tenth floor, Eloise Spellman, the mother of several children, fell, a bullet through her neck.

Across the street a number of persons, standing in an apartment window, were watching the firing directed at the housing project. Suddenly several troopers whirled and began firing in the general direction of the spectators. Mrs. Hattie Gainer, a grandmother, sank to the floor.

A block away Rebecca Brown's 2-year old daughter was standing at the window. Mrs. Brown rushed to drag her to safety. As Mrs. Brown was, momentarily, framed in the window, a bullet spun into her back.

All three women died.

A number of eye witnesses, at varying times and places, reported seeing bottles thrown from upper story windows. As these would land at the feet of an officer he would turn and fire. Thereupon, other officers and Guardsmen up and down the street would join in.

In order to protect his property, B. W. W., the owner of a Chinese laundry, had placed a sign saying "Soul Brother" in his window. Between 1:00 and 1:30 A.M., on Sunday, July 16, he, his mother, wife, and brother, were watching television in the back room. The neighborhood had been quiet. Suddenly B. W. W. heard the sound of jeeps, then shots.

Going to an upstairs window he was able to look out into the street. There he observed several jeeps, from which soldiers and state troopers were firing into stores that had "Soul Brother" signs in the windows. During the course of three nights, according to dozens of eye witness reports, law enforcement officers shot into and smashed windows of businesses that contained signs indicating they were Negro owned.

At 11:00 P.M., on Sunday, July 16th, Mrs. Lucille Pugh looked out of the window to see if the streets were clear. She then asked her 11-year-old son, Michael, to take the garbage out. As he reached the street and was illuminated by a street light, a shot rang out. He died.

By Monday afternoon, July 17, state police and National Guard forces were withdrawn. That evening, a Catholic priest saw two Negro men walking down the street. They were carrying a case of soda and two bags of groceries. An unmarked car with five police officers pulled up beside them. Two white officers got out of the car. Accusing the Negro men of looting, the officers made them put the groceries on the sidewalk, then kicked the bags open, scattering their contents, all over the street.

Telling the men, "Get out of here," the officers drove off. The Catholic priest went across the street to help gather up the groceries. One of the men turned to him: "I've just been back from Vietnam two days," he said, "and this is what I get. I feel like going home and getting a rifle and shooting the cops."

Of the 250 fire alarms, many had been false, and 13 were considered by the city to have been "serious." Of the $10,251,000 damage total, four-fifths was due to stock loss. Damage to buildings and fixtures was less than $2 million.

Twenty-three persons were killed — a white detective, a white fireman, and 21 Negroes. One was 73-year-old Isaac Harrison. Six were women. Two were children.

This selection is abridged from *Report of the National Advisory Commission on Civil Disorders*, Bantam Books, Inc., New York: 1968, pp. 57–58, 59, 60–63, 63–64, 64–69.

THE ECONOMICS OF RACISM

Michael Reich

This paper presents a radical analysis of racism and its historical persistence in America, focusing on the effects of racism on whites. The paper contrasts the conventional approach of neoclassical economic analysis — with its optimistic conclusions concerning the possibility of eliminating racism — with a radical approach — which argues that racism is deeply rooted in the current economic institutions of America, and is likely to survive as long as they do. A statistical model and empirical evidence are presented which support the radical approach and cast doubt on the conventional approach. The specific mechanisms by which racism operates among whites are also discussed briefly.

THE PERVASIVENESS OF RACISM

When conventional economists attempt to analyze racism, they usually begin by trying to separate various forms of racial discrimination. For example, they define "pure wage discrimination" as the racial difference in wages paid to equivalent workers, i.e., those with similar years and quality of schooling, skill training, previous employment experience and seniority, age, health, job attitudes, and a host of other factors. They presume that they can analyze the sources of "pure wage discrimination" without simultaneously analyzing the extent to which discrimination also affects the factors they hold constant.

But such a technique distorts reality. The various forms of discrimination are not separable in real life. Employers' hiring and promotion practices, resource allocation in city schools, the structure of transportation systems, residential segregation and housing quality, availability of decent health care, behavior of policemen and judges, foremen's prejudices, images of blacks presented in the media and the schools, price gouging in ghetto stores — these and the other forms of social and economic discrimination interact strongly with each other in determining the occupational status and annual income, and welfare, of black people. The processes are not simply additive, but are mutually reinforcing. Often, a decrease in one narrow form of discrimination is accompanied by an increase in another form. Since all aspects of racism interact, an analysis of racism should incorporate all of its aspects in a unified manner.

No single quantitative index could adequately measure racism in all its social, cultural, psychological, and economic dimensions. But, while racism is far more than a narrow economic phenomenon, it does have very definite economic consequences: blacks have far lower incomes than whites. The ratio of median black to median white incomes thus provides a rough, but useful, quantitative index of the economic consequences of racism for blacks as it reflects the operation of racism in the schools, in residential location, in health care — as well as in the labor market itself. We shall use this index statistically to analyze the causes of racism's persistence in the United States. While this approach overemphasizes the economic aspects of racism, it is nevertheless an improvement over the narrower approach taken by conventional economists.

COMPETING EXPLANATIONS OF RACISM

How is the historical persistence of racism in the United States to be explained? The most prominent analysis of discrimination among economists was formulated in 1957 by Gary Becker in his book *The Economics of Discrimination.*(1) Racism, according to Becker, is fundamentally a problem of tastes and attitudes. Whites are defined to have a "taste for discrimination" if they are willing to forfeit income in order to be associated with other whites instead of blacks. Since white employers and employees prefer not to associate with blacks, they require a monetary compensation for the psychic cost of such association. In Becker's principal model white employers have a taste for discrimination; marginal productivity analysis is invoked to show that white employers hire fewer black workers than efficiency criteria would dictate — as a result, white employers lose (in monetary terms) while white workers gain from discrimination against blacks.

Becker does not try to explain the source of white tastes for discrimination. For him, these attitudes are determined outside of the economic system. (Racism could presumably be ended simply by changing these attitudes, perhaps by appeal to whites on moral grounds.) According to Becker's analysis, employers would find the ending of racism to be in their economic self-interest, but white workers would not. The persistence of racism is thus implicitly laid at the door of white workers. Becker suggests that longrun market forces will lead to the end of discrimination anyway — less discriminatory employers, with no "psychic costs" to enter in their accounts, will be able to operate at lower costs by hiring equivalent black workers at lower wages, thus driving the more discriminatory employers out of business.(2)

The radical approach to racism argued in this paper is entirely different. Racism is viewed as rooted in the economic system and not in "exogenously determined" attitudes. Historically, the American Empire was founded on the racist extermination of American Indians, was financed in large part by profits from slavery, and was extended by a string of interventions, beginning with the Mexican War of the 1840's, which have been at least partly justified by white supremacist ideology.

Today, transferring the locus of whites' perceptions of the source of many of their problems from capitalism and toward blacks, racism continues to serve the needs of the capitalist system. Although an individual employer might gain by refusing to discriminate and agreeing to hire blacks at above the going black wage rate, it is not true that the capitalist class as a whole would profit if racism were eliminated and labor were more efficiently allocated without regard to skin color. I will show below that the divisiveness of racism weakens workers' strength when bargaining with employers; the economic consequences of racism are not only lower incomes for blacks, but also higher incomes for the capitalist class coupled with lower incomes for white workers. Although capitalists may not have conspired consciously to create racism, and although capitalists may not be its principal perpetuators, nevertheless racism does support the continued well-being of the American capitalist system. . . .

We have, then, two alternative approaches to the analysis of racism. The first suggests that capitalists lose and white workers gain from racism. The second predicts the opposite — that capitalists gain while workers lose. The first says that racist "tastes for discrimination" are formed independently of the economic system; the second argues that racism is symbiotic with capitalistic economic institutions.

The two approaches reflect the theoretical paradigms of society from which each was developed. Becker follows the paradigm of neoclassical economics in taking "tastes" as exogenously determined and fixed, and then letting the market mechanism determine outcomes. The radical approach follows the Marxian paradigm in arguing that racial attitudes and racist institutions must be seen as part of a larger social system, in placing emphasis on conflict between classes and the use of power to determine the outcomes of such conflicts. The test as to which explanation of racism is superior is, in some ways, an illustrative test of the relative explanatory power of these competing social paradigms.

The very persistence of racism in the United States lends support to the radical approach. So do repeated instances of employers using blacks as strikebreakers, as in the massive steel strike of 1919, and employer-instigated exacerbation of racial antagonisms during that strike and many others.(3) However, the particular virulence of racism among many blue- and white-collar workers and their families seem to refute the radical approach and support Becker.

THE EMPIRICAL EVIDENCE

Which of the two models better explains reality? We have already mentioned that the radical approach predicts that capitalists gain and workers lose from racism, while the conventional Beckerian approach predicts precisely the opposite. In the latter approach racism has an equalizing effect on the white income distribution, while in the former racism has an unequalizing effect. The statistical relationship between the extent of racism and the degree of inequality among whites provides a simple, yet clear test of the two approaches. This section describes that test and its results.

First we shall need a measure of racism. The index we use, for reasons already mentioned, is the ratio of black median family income to white median family income (B/W). A low numerical value for this ratio indicates a high degree of racism. We have calculated values of this racism index, using data from the 1960 Census, for each of the largest 48 standard metropolitan statistical areas (SMSA's). It turns out there is a great deal of variation from SMSA to SMSA in the B/W index of racism, even within the North; Southern SMSA's generally demonstrated a greater degree of racism. The statistical technique we shall use exploits this variation.

We shall also need measures of inequality among whites. Two convenient measures are S_1, the percentage share of all white income which is received by the top 1 percent of white families, and G_w, the Gini coefficient of white incomes within as well as between social classes.(4)

Both of these inequality measures vary considerably among the SMSA's; there is also a substantial amount of variation in these variables within the subsample of Northern SMSA's. Therefore, it is interesting to examine whether the pattern of variation of the inequality and racism variables can be explained by causal hypotheses. This is our first statistical test.

A systematic relationship across SMSA's between racism and white inequality does exist and is highly significant: the correlation coefficient is — .47.(5) The negative sign of the correlation coefficient indicates that where racism is greater, income inequality *among whites* is also greater. This result is consistent with the radical model and is inconsistent with the predictions of Becker's model.

This evidence, however, should not be accepted too quickly. The correlations reported may not reflect actual causality, since other independent forces may be simultaneously influencing both variables in the same way. As is the case with many other statistical analyses, the model must be expanded to control for such other factors. We know from previous inter-SMSA income distribution studies that the most important additional factors that should be introduced into our model are 1. the industrial and occupational structure of the SMSA's; 2. the region in which the SMSA's are located; 3. the average income of the SMSA's; and 4. the proportion of the SMSA population which is black. These factors were introduced into the model by the technique of multiple regression analysis. Separate equations were estimated with G_w and S_1 as measures of white inequality.

In all the equations the statistical results were strikingly uniform: racism was a significantly unequalizing force on the white income distribution, even when other factors were held constant. A 1 percent increase in the ratio of black to white median incomes (i.e., a 1 percent decrease in racism) was associated with a .2 percent decrease in white inequality, as measured by the Gini coefficient. The corresponding effect on S_1 was two-and-a-half times as large, indicating that most of the inequality among whites generated by racism was associated with increased income for the richest 1 percent of white families. Further statistical investigation revealed that increases in racism had an insignificant effect on the share received by the poorest whites, and resulted in a small decrease in the income share of whites in the middle-income brackets.(6)

THE MECHANISMS OF THE RADICAL MODEL

Within the radical model, we can specify a number of mechanisms which further explain the statistical finding that racism increases inequality among whites. We shall consider two mechanisms here: total wages of white labor are reduced by racial antagonisms, in part because union growth and labor militancy are inhibited, and the supply of public services, especially in education, available to low- and middle-income whites is reduced as a result of racial antagonisms.

Wages of white labor are lessened by racism because the fear of a cheaper and underemployed black labor supply in the area is invoked by employers when labor presents its wage demands. Racial antagonisms on the shop floor deflect attention from labor grievances related to working conditions, permitting employers to cut costs. Racial divisions among labor prevent the development of united worker organizations both within the workplace and in the labor movement as a whole. As a result, union strength and union militancy will be less, the greater the extent of racism. A historical example of this process is the already mentioned use of racial and ethnic divisions to destroy the solidarity of the 1919 steel strikers. By contrast, during the 1890's, black-white class solidarity greatly aided mine-workers in building militant unions among workers in Alabama, West Virginia, Illinois, and other coalfield areas.

The above argument and examples contradict the common belief that an exclusionary racial policy will strengthen rather than weaken the bargaining power of unions. But racial exclusion increases bargaining power only when entry into an occupation or industry can be effectively limited. Industrial-type unions are much less able to restrict entry than craft unions or organizations such as the American Medical Association. This is not to deny that much of organized labor is egregiously racist.(7) But it is important to distinguish actual discrimination practice from the objective economic self-interest of union members.

The second mechanism we shall consider concerns the allocation of expenditures for public services. The most important of these services is education. Racial antagonisms dilute both the desire and the ability of poor white parents to improve educational opportunities for their children. Antagonism between blacks and poor whites drives wedges between the two groups and reduces their ability to join in a united political movement pressing for improved and more equal education. Moreover, many poor whites recognize that however inferior their own schools, black schools are even worse. This provides some degree of satisfaction and identification with the status quo, reducing the desire of poor whites to press politically for better schools in their neighborhoods. Ghettos tend to be located near poor white neighborhoods more often than near rich white neighborhoods; racism thus reduces the potential tax base of school districts containing poor whites. Also, pressure by teachers' groups to improve all poor schools is reduced by racial antagonisms between predominately white teaching staffs and black children and parents.(8)

The statistical validity of the above mechanisms can be tested in a causal model. The effect of racism on unionism is tested by estimating an equation in which the percentage of the SMSA labor force which is unionized is the dependent variable, with racism and the structural variables (such as the SMSA industrial structure) as the independent variables. The schooling mechanism is tested by estimating a similar equation in which the dependent variable is inequality in years of schooling completed among white males aged 25 to 29 years old.(9)

Once again, the results of this statistical test strongly confirm the hypotheses of the radical model. The racism variable is statistically significant in all the equations and has the predicted sign: a greater degree of racism results in lower unionization rates and greater amounts of schooling inequality among whites. This empirical evidence again suggests that racism is in the economic interests of capitalists and other rich whites and against the economic interests of poor whites and white workers.

However, a full assessment of the importance of racism for capitalism would probably conclude that the primary significance of racism is not strictly economic.

The simple economics of racism does not explain why many workers seem to be so vehemently racist, when racism is not in their economic self-interest. In extra-economic ways, racism helps to legitimize inequality, alienation, and powerlessness — legitimization which is necessary for the stability of the capitalist system as a whole. For example, many whites believe that welfare payments to blacks are a far more important factor in their high taxes than is military spending. Through racism, poor whites come to believe that their poverty is caused by blacks who are willing to take away their jobs, and at lower wages, thus concealing the fact that a substantial amount of income inequality is inevitable in a capitalist society.

Racism also provides some psychological benefits to poor and working-class whites. For example, the opportunity to participate in another's oppression may compensate for one's own misery. The parallel here is to the subjugation of women in the family: after a day of alienating labor, the tired husband can compensate by oppressing his wife. Furthermore, not being at the bottom of the heap is some solace for an unsatisfying life; this argument was successfully used by the Southern oligarchy against poor whites allied with blacks in the inter-racial Populist movement of the late nineteenth century.

In general, blacks as a group provide a convenient and visible scapegoat for problems that actually derive from the institutions of capitalism. As long as building a real alternative to capitalism does not seem feasible to most whites, we can expect that identifiable and vulnerable scapegoats will always prove functional to the status quo. These extra-economic factors thus neatly dovetail with the economic aspects of racism discussed in the main body of this paper in their mutual service to the perpetuation of capitalism.

NOTES

(1) University of Chicago Press.

(2) Some economists writing on discrimination reject Becker's "tastes" approach, but accept the marginal productivity method of analysis. See, for example, L. Thurow, *op. cit.* The main substantive difference in their conclusions is that for Thurow, the entire white "community" gains from racism; therefore, racism will be a little harder to uproot. See also A. Krueger, "The Economics of Discrimination," *Journal of Political Economy*, October, 1963.

(3) See, for example, David Brody, *Steelworkers in America: The Nonunion Era* (Cambridge: Harvard University Press, 1960); Herbert Gutman, "The Negro and the United Mineworkers," in J. Jacobson, ed., *The Negro and the American Labor Movement* (New York: Anchor, 1968); S. Spero and A. Harris, *The Black Worker* (New York: Atheneum, 1968), *passim.*

(4) The Gini coefficient varies between 0 and 1, with 0 indicating perfect equality, and 1 indicating perfect inequality. For a more complete exposition, see H. Miller, *Income Distribution in the United States* (Washington, D.C.: Government Printing Office, 1966). Data for the computation of G_w and S_1 for 48 SMSA's were taken from the 1960 Census. A full description of the computational techniques used is available in my dissertation.

(5) The correlation coefficient reported in the text is between G_w and B/W. The equivalent correlation between S_1 and B/W is $r = -.55$. A similar calculation by S. Bowles, across states instead of SMSA's, resulted in an $r = -.58$.

(6) A more rigorous presentation of these variables and the statistical results is available in my dissertation.

(7) See Herbert Hill, "The Racial Practices of Organized Labor," in J.

Jacobson, ed., *The Negro and the American Labor Movement* (N.Y.: Anchor paperback, 1968).

(8) In a similar fashion, racial antagonisms reduce the political pressure on governmental agencies to provide other public services which would have a pro-poor distributional impact. The two principal items in this category are public health services and welfare payments in the Aid to Families with Dependent Children program.

(9) These dependent variables do not perfectly represent the phenomena described, but serve as reasonable proxy variables for these purposes.

This selection is abridged from, "The Economics of Racism," by Michael Reich in David M. Gordon, (ed.), *Problems in Political Economy: An Urban Perspective*, D.C. Heath and Company, Lexington, Massachusetts: 1971, pp. 108, 109–113. Reprinted by permission of Michael Reich.

BLACK CAPITALISM: THE PATH TO BLACK LIBERATION?

Barry Bluestone

The real problem in the inner cities of America is not white faces behind drugstore counters, a phenomenon only little more than skin deep.(1) Rather the root problem is the total lack of income generating production, the obvious hallmark of a poor community. For all practical purposes the inner city is a devastated region, stifled for decades by a colonial rule which systematically, if not with malevolent intent, deprived its inhabitants of the physical and human capital needed for development. Denied the educational resources and the physical infrastructure necessary to develop technical skills and provide an efficient means of production, while at the same time denied access to the corporate sector through discriminatory practices in housing, in the schools, on the job, and in the capital market, the ghetto has been forced to rely upon its one remaining resource: cheap labor. This it exports on demand at a going rate of $1.60 an hour or less. During periods of extremely high national aggregate demand, all but 10% of such supply is bought; during periods of recession, as much as 40% is left to rot away. The ghetto is thus forced to survive on poverty wages, welfare payments, and anything it can beg, borrow, or steal.

Such an economy, lacking its own means of production and means of distribution, behaves as a sieve. Income injected into the ghetto economy quickly dissipates into outlying suburbs and outside investment. In economic terms, the inner city has a very small multiplier, approaching the value of one. Instead of remaining in the ghetto, passing from grocer to baker to candlestick-maker in return for services or goods supplied, the income dollar brought into the black community in the morning, through a small payroll or welfare check, gets spent that afternoon in a white-owned ghetto store, and leaves in the evening for the suburbs and beyond. Such an income cycle reduces considerably the real income of the community and, what is worse, prevents the accumulation of any meaningful savings which could be turned to investment. The lack of indigenous black-owned enterprise thus accounts in part for the continuing leakages of capital from the ghetto. . . .

... In response to the call for black economic development, scores of "black capitalism" schemes are unveiled each month, each with its own particular ideology and structure. Strategies range from large established corporations entering the ghetto to establishing centrally controlled subsidiaries which capitalize on surplus labor and low wages to perspectives which forsee community ownership and control of large-scale production and distribution centers, a form of "black socialism."

The simplest case is the traditional one. With a small amount of acquired capital, either saved or borrowed, private black entrepreneurs buy out individual white stores and manage them according to time-honored custom. Drugstores, grocery markets, and clothing outlets remain traditionally marginal, reaping small profit, adding only slight employment opportunity and little income to the community. The only critical difference is the black face behind the counter and the fact that the small trials and tribulations of capitalist ownership now accrue to a Negro rather than white soul. To be sure, external direct control is minimized under this plan (although the competitive marketplace continues to call the tune.) But to see in this strategy a means to economic development indicates a serious myopia, for almost by definition, the traditional scheme fails to aggregate enough capital for investment in profitable large-scale enterprise.

A significant alternative to "corner store" capitalism is posed by white corporate intervention in the ghetto economy. Consider the following:

Having already cashed in on over $13 million worth of on-the-job training programs financed from tax dollars, firms like AVCO, Raytheon, Fairchild-Hiller, Lockheed, Ling-Temco-Vought, and Aerojet-General are turning their attention to government subsidized black enterprise. In fact as early as 1966, following the Watts riot, Aerojet-General developed the Watts Manufacturing Company and placed a Negro business leader in the president's chair. William H. Zisch, Vice-chairman of Aerojet, documents their foster child's progress.(2)

> When the Company was started, we did not have any business; but we were certain that we could do more for Watts by putting a plant there than by trying to absorb 500 Watts residents into our regular work force at plants which were 20 and 30 miles away in a city which has inadequate public transportation.
>
> After considerable effort, we obtained a contract for the construction of large hospital tents for the military services. We invested a total of $1.3 million in the project. More recently we expanded our product lines to wood working and metal work. Today, Watts Manufacturing Company is a growing concern.
>
> Our company's experience leads me to conclude that in order to establish meaningful business and industry in urban poverty areas, private enterprise must go a bit beyond conventional methods. Flexibility, I think, is the name of the game we must play to be really successful in the inner city today.

While Aerojet's philanthropy created several hundred new jobs in a riot-torn city thereby providing some marginal improvement in a post-marginal condition, it has done little to realign the relationship of the black community to the white power structure. For the control of the Watts subsidiary does not emanate from the ghetto; rather the "black" company remains the child of Aerojet and it is to the father firm that WMC, Inc. pays deference, and in the long-run, possibly profits.

Beyond direct corporate intervention in the ghetto are concerted efforts to develop black corporations from within the inner city. The most famous and successful of these efforts remains the Opportunities Industrialization Center program pioneered by the Rev. Leon H. Sullivan of Philadelphia. In a recent interview, Dr. Sullivan related how he came to establish the OIC and explained its progress.(3)

> One Saturday night when I was thinking about this whole problem, I read about Jesus feeding 5,000 people with bread and fishes a little boy had given Him. The miracle, you see, was in the giving. So I decided that in my congregation we could share our resources and create a financial base on which to build housing and, ultimately, business enterprises.

Beginning with a quarter million dollars raised from his church, Sullivan invested in a million dollar apartment complex. Later "Progress Plaza," the largest black-owned shopping center in the world was established with 16 privately-owned shops on 4½ acres. Not content, Sullivan's acquired sense directed him into the aerospace industry where he created Progress Aerospace Enterprises with management borrowed from the General Electric Corporation and a G.E. subcontract for $2.5 million of component production for the U.S. moon mission. In addition, Sullivan's Zion Investment Corporation has established the Progress Garment Manufacturing Company in Philadelphia which employs seventy-five workers. Management responsiblity of the Investment Corporation rests in a Board of Directors selected by its 3,500 shareholders. The waiting list for stock ownership is in excess of 2,000 families. Philadelphia has over half a million Negroes.

The Opportunities Industrialization Center program has now spread to over 70 cities and $5 million has been raised from the private sector to initiate local projects. Even Puerto Rico, Kenya, Senegal and Nigeria are experimenting with the OIC training program, a program aimed at creating skills for use in private enterprise both in and outside the ghetto. In the United States, the OIC National Industrial Advisory Council, composed of 25 "influential" business leaders has been created by Sullivan to help sell the program to corporate heads who conceivably might give aid to newly developing black business. George Champion, chairman of the board of the Chase Manhattan Bank heads up the Advisory Council. . . .

. . . How evenly spread the benefits from Sullivan's efforts will be is yet to be seen. Whether capitalism can work for the Negro working-class as well as the bourgeousie remains a moot point. Nevertheless, it appears evident that the OIC program has gained the support of white business and thus the scarce resources of capital and technical expertise seem assured at least in the short-run. But inherent in such a strategy lingers the potential for external domination and control by an "amiable" white power structure. And thus how much of the black community can escape poverty and powerlessness in this way cannot be exactly determined, but surely the rosy beginning need not point ineluctibly to a rosy future.

Yet a fourth strategy is now being developed by a small group of black businessmen, economists, and accountants in Detroit. The Inner City Business Improvement Forum (ICBIF) was established immediately after the 1967 Detroit riot.(4) With an inventory showing less than 35% of the ghetto economic base owned by blacks, and a $50,000 gift "bribed" from Henry Ford II, ICBIF set out to build a black infrastructure within the inner city to stem the outward flow of black-earned dollars. Over the past eighteen months ICBIF's leadership has evolved a "community concept of comprehensive inner city development" which stresses the need to develop not only retail outlets controlled by the black community, but the absolute necessity of establishing a production sector and black banking system to accumulate internally generated investment funds. Shying away from the paternalistic New Detroit Committee, created even before the 1967 conflagration cooled, ICBIF has turned to individual white investors and increasingly to the government for seed capital. In 1968 *"Our" Supermarket* was established on Detroit's East side to serve a large part of the surrounding black community. ICBIF provided 10% of the funds, while a leading city bank and the Small Business Administration picked up the first and second mortgages to supply the rest of the initial capital outlay. Now one-dollar shares are being sold in the community so as to assure that profit from the supermarket goes to the community consumer rather than suburban interests. The board of directors for this supermarket and similar ventures created by ICBIF is chosen by the "block" clubs in the serviced area. This, along with a strict limit on an individual's stockholdings, ensures democratic control of each enterprise.

ICBIF has also aided traditional black retail businesses, supplying them with technical aid and seed capital in some cases. Unlike the major enterprises of ICBIF, these are left in private control along the lines of "corner store" black capitalism. With a combination of community owned and operated supermarkets and privately owned and operated small-scale retail shops, the black community in Detroit is beginning to gain some control over the estimated $750 million worth of consumer dollars which annually pass over inner city store counters. . . .

. . . Evidence from ICBIF's first year and a half of operation, Detroit appears to possess the potential for developing a semiautonomous viable inner city economy, one which could provide thousands of jobs and a large number of investment outlets. Aided initially by white business, fearing the chaos of the black ghetto, the plan envisioned by ICBIF foresees a cutting of the umbilical cord to the white community. Free of external maniupulation, black control is gained over an independent economic structure which can interact with the white-controlled economy from a position of comparative advantage rather than subservience. But whether even this scale of independent black enterprise is sufficient for economic viability, free of white support, is questionable.

To complete a typology of black business strategies, we should add those schemes which are avowedly political and only secondarily economic in nature. The economic development strategy, in essence, is no more than an organizational tool for building an indigenous inner city political base. By investing small amounts of capital, either generated internally or "hustled" from guilt-ridden whites, a nascent community-controlled black economic sector is launched, providing some new employment opportunities, but more importantly, a rallying point for community action. Profits from the enterprise are plowed back into the organization both for further business expansion and for political action. In this manner, the community organization becomes self-sufficient and free from external control. As the economic substructure expands, the political organization matures, benefitting from a well-financed base. Educational and cultural activities can be added to the political thrust of such a movement, thus creating an integrated program of community action.

By now it should be patently clear that each of the strategies outlined above can be evaluated upon two potentially conflicting criteria: first, the speed with which the plan leads to economic development as measured by rising employment, incomes, and capital outlay; and second, whether the scheme possesses a structure and dynamic conducive to economic and political liberation as measured by economic self-sufficiency and political influence. The conflict between the pace of development and self-determination arises from the scarcity of capital and expertise in the ghetto. For the inner city community to develop economically over a short period of time, much capital and talent must be imported from the white community. Inevitably, large-scale importation leads to surrendering some control over the direction of development.

Thus, while one scheme leads rapidly to investment in the ghetto by white business, it almost assuredly fails to promise radical change in the structure of power relations between white and black. On the other hand, development carried on solely by the black community may contribute some political freedom, but at the cost of continued economic stagnation. A conscious decision must then be made by the black community as to which road it chooses to travel, and indeed, how much "liberty" should be surrendered to hasten the development process. For the black community, to have their cake and eat it too will seldom be a permissible choice. . . .

. . . Why has the corporate establishment leaped enthusiastically to the aid of black capitalist development when in the recent past it was a bastion of reaction to the War on Poverty and legislation aimed at eliminating racial discrimination? Without being overly sarcastic, we would suggest that it is good practice in answering this question to look at who stands to make the profit and who the loss.

It has become increasingly clear that the growing unrest in the inner city threatens the smooth-running society. As Detroit burned, the auto plants were forced to shut down production; and when production resumed, militant black groups like DRUM, the Dodge Revolutionary Union Movement, gained new strength within the plants. Demands for greater control over jobs and the economic environment were heard not only on 12th Street but on the assembly lines at the Rouge Plant as well. Because of such developments, corporate managers have awakened to the fact that while what's good for America might not always be good for General Motors, what's bad for the American ghetto is increasingly bad for G.M. Viewed in this perspective, an explosive inner city is a menace to the corporate establishment and the interests it defends.

To those responsible for maintaining efficient production on the assembly lines of the corporate sector, black capitalism has become one possible alternative to black chaos. If black capitalism works, the hope is that the black community will turn inward toward constructing a new set of economic conditions within the inner city rather than turning outward with attempts at reconstructing the conditions of power within the white business community. And while, at present rates, welfare checks designed to diminish dissidence portend an ever expanding social expense and the training of blacks for white corporations appears at best a long-run ameliorative device, black capitalism seems to offer some relief from the immediate chaos, if not from its causes.

Increasingly management also realizes that its own autonomy can be better preserved and long-run profits augmented by reducing the role of the federal government in developing the ghetto. By forging an alliance between black capitalists and themselves and foreclosing a nascent government-black producer coalition, the corporate elite can look forward to lower input costs (in terms of intermediate goods used by large-scale industry in final goods production) and can spare themselves future competition both for government contracts and in the manufacture of some products. At the same time, such an alliance may appear to corporate management as a defense against "creeping socialism," a specter which still haunts the paranoid. Furthermore, a smaller federal role in poverty programs and a larger corporate role in developing all black subsidiaries in the inner city could lead to a reduced emphasis on legislation aimed at discriminatory policies within the corporate sector. Legislation which now prohibits the federal government from contracting with firms which fail to live up to fair practice codes might be enforced less stringently. Finally, the public relations boost derived from lending a helping hand to the poor as well as the taxsaving from discontinued Great Society programs are viewed as boons to big business.

In understanding the corporate manager's positive attitude toward black ghetto enterprise, one must realize that corporate profits will not be endangered by the introduction of the black capitalism strategy envisioned by the corporate establishment. The reason is simple: This strategy foresees the black community providing only two generalized products: retail services to fill the community's need for vegetables, meats, drugstore products, and television repair, etc., and small-scale manufacture of intermediate goods used in the industrial sector to produce automobiles, washing machines, and computers. In the first case, the corporate sector is left unharmed by black capitalism because the corporate sector sells very little at the retail level and when it does, it usually does not do it in the ghetto. The squeeze here will be on the small-time white shopkeeper; the corner grocer and the local repair shop owner.

Ghetto manufacturing firms, examples of the second case, will not only fail to deplete corporate profits, but actually will contribute to them. It is for this reason that corporations like Aerojet have spread their "philanthropy" into the ghetto. Excess profits of the largest industrial giants can be invested in the inner city (without fear of retaliation from the government anti-trust division) to establish subsidiaries which provide them with cheap parts and labor hired at less than union scale. With the business perspective of "the poverty problem is a technical problem,"(5) corporate enterprise efficiency experts can provide the cost-benefit analyses necessary to ensure profitable gain from inner city firms. For example:

It has been estimated that approximately sixty percent of the value of an American automobile is not produced by the Big Three. Rather this value is due to the literally scores of thousands of parts vendors which manufacture everything from a carburetor screw to a convertible top frame and sell them to automobile producers. In other large-scale industry, the value-added by parts suppliers is likely to be as high. Obviously, then, big business is dependent on small-scale enterprise for a large percentage of its profit. If the price of parts is reduced, the profit of the car manufacturer (or the electrical equipment firm or the television set producer, etc.) can be raised with comparative ease.

Somewhere between 75–90% of the parts vendors for the largest producing corporations are union shops. In many cases, the wage rate paid in such small plants is comparable to that paid in the leading industries. The auto companies, therefore, must pay indirectly the higher union wage of the carburetor-screw machine operator; and this, of course, becomes part of the cost of producing a car. If this wage could be reduced, the cost of the carburetor is cut; and thus the cost of producing an automobile is lower, and GM, Ford, and Chrysler make a higher profit. Multiply this by 60% of the final value of American automobiles, and the total potential profit gain is no doubt tremendous. Stockholders will be made happy and so will corporate management.

Sidestepping unions in the already organized parts supply industry is a difficult, if not risky practice. Since the 1950's, such attempts have been rare by large corporations. But now the opportunity for circumventing union power by means of coalition with the federal government and the black community has emerged. The small plant can pay half the going wage of the unionized vendor operation thereby ensuring a competitive edge over union plants, and yet still pay above the wage scale normally offered low-skilled workers in the ghetto. In this way both the ghetto and the corporation benefit. Such a symbiotic relationship between the corporate elite and the community poor at the expense of the unionized workingclass has the potential for evolving as the most exotic in a long line of techniques aimed at curbing union strength. Ford hired blacks to break unions in the twenties and now Ford has a better idea. It, like other modern corporations, has found a new, almost socially acceptable way to do the same thing in the sixties and seventies. Little wonder the AFL-CIO has vigorously attacked all black capitalism plans.

Other strategies utilizing black capitalism to produce higher white corporate profit show equal ingenuity. For example, during the short-lived period of five-year/50,000 mile automobile warranties, auto industry executives developed a scheme whereby pre-delivery automobile diagnostic centers would be established in the ghetto, using black labor and white corporate capital and expertise. Such black-owned centers, manned by trained black auto mechanics, would test new cars at company expense before delivery to their prospective buyers. In this way fewer repairs would be required at cost to the auto industry and customer satisfaction would be reinforced. However, before the diagnostic centers were financed, the shorter car warranty was reinstated by the industry. Now the auto firm is no longer responsible for repairing much of its built-in obsolescence, and consequently the industry's savings from pre-delivery diagnosis and adjustment is reduced. The upshot is that the auto executives' enthusiasm for the centers has waned considerably and the project lies on the scrap heap.

Last, but not least, mention must be made again of the profits which can be gleaned from government subsidy programs designed to induce big business participation in inner city development. With such subsidies or tax incentives as specified in the Community Self-Determination Bill, for example, little effort is required on behalf of the corporate structure to create a "ghetto-industrial" complex including cost-plus contracts and the profits they imply. We may not be very far off in concluding that it appears the corporate establishment is more than happy to help the black community — especially if it gets a little helping itself!

Business brought into the ghetto by the white corporate establishment may very well add something to the inner city environment. Some new jobs will be created, the average wage in the core city may rise a bit, and a few enterprising Negroes will no doubt reap the ability to escape the ghetto altogether. For some a new sense of pride may even develop. But what is equally true is that no black capitalism scheme which relies on the white establishment for sustenance will lead to a form of inner city economic development which in turn can lead to black socio-political liberation. To put it plainly, it is not in the interest of big business to develop a viable black economic sector, competitive in the newly evolving growth industries. At best the black community will vie with the blue collar union sector for a share of the intermediate goods market.

But if corporate intervention in the inner city will not create a viable economy, can independent private black capitalism, unaided, but also unencumbered by the mixed blessing of corporate involvement, lead the black community to freedom? The answer is probably no. Independent private black enterprise cannot serve as the catalyst for economic development and political power.

It is a sad fact that private small-scale enterprise pays extremely low wages, reaps little profit for its owner, and consequently contributes little to economic development *per se.* While black retail capitalism will boost the inner city multiplier by some small amount, the additional income thus generated will fail to raise a significant number from poverty. Consider, for instance, the average hourly wage rates paid in retail trade across the nation in the mid-1960's: (6)

Limited price variety stores	$1.31
Eating and drinking places	1.14
Drug and proprietory stores	1.56
Gasoline service stations	1.52
Apparel and accessory stores	1.70
Retail food stores	1.91

These were average rates; the inner city wage levels helped to keep them this low. In addition statistics on low-wage industry profits show that there is little room to raise these wage rates much beyond such low levels.(7) All of this is due to the high degree of business competition in the retail field, which subjects the small-scale firm to a profit and wage squeeze. Add to this the additional costs which small-scale business in the inner city must bear because of higher insurance costs, uninsured losses due to crime, and the higher cost of inner city transportation, and the picture of low wages and low profits comes sharply into focus. Hence, while the sight of black faces behind ghetto drugstore counters may be comforting psychologically, it is not economically.

A small private production sector will also fail to add much viability to the inner city economy. In the first place it is highly unlikely that individuals from the black community will have the ability to raise sufficient capital, independent of white business and government, to initiate enterprise especially in the fastest growing sectors of the economy: electronics, computers, automation equipment design, etc. To be successful in these industries requires enough capital to keep pace with rapid technological change. In addition the efficient size of manufacturing firms is usually beyond the capacity of ghetto residents with their present inadequate resources. Finally, even if the capital could be raised to develop one or two competitive production centers, the marginal addition to the welfare of a ghetto the size of Detroit's, Chicago's, New York's, Los Angeles', or even Cleveland's would be insignificant in terms of producing a catalyst for full-scale economic development.

The result, inevitably, of black entrepreneur capitalism is not the creation of an inner city economic infrastructure, but the development of a larger black bourgeoisie, which given rising income, will quickly emigrate from the ghetto taking along both a large part of the wage bill and all of the profit. The tendency toward a black class society is thereby reinforced, with continued low wages and welfare programs in the inner city and a richer, only slightly more numerous, black middle class community on the outside. Again income will flow outward in great quantity, leaving the bulk of the ghetto residents no better off, save for a few more low-wage jobs and a few more black faces across the drugstore counter. Profits are reaped by an enlarged black middle class, while the losses continue to be borne by the poor . . . democratic rule, invest in cooperative industry on a relatively large scale. Supermarkets, department stores, banks, and intermediate-size factories can be the first order of business — not corner drugstores. Creating business centers which are relatively crime-proof compared to sidewalk shops, taking full advantage of scale economies, and aggregating profits will ensure lower costs and larger reinvestment potential. As the black community "owns" the industry, the wages and dividends from such enterprise remain within the inner city. Those who choose to leave the ghetto should not be allowed to take more capital out of the community than the small amount they originally contributed (with some interest) nor should they be permitted to take part of the wage bill with them. As long as there remains unemployment in the inner city, residents who choose to emigrate must relinquish the jobs they hold in community enterprise. Escape from the ghetto remains open, but not at the expense of the majority of the ghetto community. In order to maximize reinvestment so as to build as viable and diversified an inner city economy as possible, leakages of capital and income must be kept to a minimum. Community ownership and control ensures that the route from poverty is provided the entire black underclass, not merely a chosen few. Furthermore, if a good part of black community development is to be financed by federal funds — through low-interest loans or seed grants — justice is only done if the whole community benefits and not merely a relatively small number of private entrepreneurs. Both on efficiency and equity grounds, then, black cooperative enterprise is preferable to "traditional" corner store capitalism.

Here we must add a word of caution. Despite grandiose plans and even federal support, the black community should not be hoodwinked by either the corporate establishment nor many of its own ebullient leaders into believing that "black capitalism" in any of its forms including black "socialism" can automatically lead to economic and political freedom. For no matter how important a goal, black economic self-determination will ultimately be largely an illusion. To be sure, hundreds, possibly even thousands of jobs will be created and many businesses may end up under black control; but in the final analysis, the market will determine which businesses succeed and which fail. Unlike the textbook model, the American market, manipulated in good part by the already existing corporate structure, allows few new small independent enterprises to reach the strata of "big business." The inner city, starved for capital and expertise — even with federal aid — begins far back in the field of potential money-winners. Thus mythologizing about the possibility of the black community creating through its own industry the route to equal affluence will be in vain or worse, a practice conducive to self-destructive frustration. In the context that the *goal* of economic development is the answer *per se*, the trap of "black capitalism" is laid.

Yet there exists another context in which to place black economic self-determination, and it is in this context that we find the genius of the black economic development strategy. While the creation of a black economy in the ghetto may not lead inexorably to a viable economic base — competitive with the staunchest of "white" enterprise — the act of striving toward an inner city economy yields a powerful tool for organizing the black community into a coherent political force capable of extracting concessions on jobs, housing, income, and dignity from the government and from the corporate establishment. While "black socialism" alone may not be capable of rooting out poverty, it may root out powerlessness and thus gain for the black community the indirect means to freedom from poverty and the manifestations of racism. In the striving for economic independence, not only is dependence on the white power structure for jobs and poverty incomes reduced, but the economic incentive to coalesce within the black community increases as well. Jobs and income are created within the community and it is from such a base that political and social power are born.

Black community enterprise will, in addition, have a considerable impact on the whole economy, not because it can successfully compete with white enterprise directly, but because income generated from community enterprise can be used to develop well-financed political organization, capable of confronting City Hall and Congress with a united front. If in the past, the black movement has been stifled by a lack of financial support, especially once it diverged from the strict integrationist political line, the community movement will now have a self-financed base. For while a large part of the "profit" from black community enterprise can be reinvested in expanded business projects, a part can also be earmarked specifically for political activity.

Taken in this context, black community enterprise not only places black faces behind drugstore counters, and allows a moderate scale production sector, but more importantly, it facilitates the creation of an indigenously financed, strictly independent, political force within the ghetto. Unlike "corner store" black capitalism which fails on two accounts: to create an economic infrastructure capable of pulling the black community out of poverty, and to create a meaningful community controlled power base; and unlike corporate intervention in the ghetto which adds longevity to white economic and political dominance over the black community, black community enterprise, or what we have called "black socialism" promises a new hope for political and social liberation.

While as a "goal," the black economic development strategy may be an utter failure in any of its forms, as a "means" one of its forms, "black socialism," may be judged in the future an unqualified success. The real question of black enterprise then must not be whether it succeeds on the accountant's balance sheet, but whether it succeeds ultimately in the struggle to redistribute a just share of political and social power toward the black community.

NOTES

(1) This is not to deny the psychological and cultural advantages which accrue to the black community from gaining control over its own environment.

(2) William E. Zisch, "The Private Sector's Role in the Urban Crisis," Industrial Relations Center, California Institute of Technology, Pasadena, California, 1968, pp. 10–11.

(3) *U.S. News and World Report*, " 'Black Capitalism' at Work: What's Happening in Philadelphia — An Exclusive Interview," February 17, 1969, p. 63.

(4) Information on the Inner City Business Improvement Forum (ICBIF) was obtained from an oral interview with the organization's Executive Secretary, Walter McMurtry.

(5) At a small graduate seminar in Manpower Economics held at the University of Michigan in October, 1968, Arjay Miller explained that the problem of poverty was basically a technological one. He felt the will for waging war on poverty had been mustered, and only the technical know-how of business economics was necessary now to liberate the impoverished.

(6) Barry Bluestone, "Lower-Wage Workers and Marginal Industries," in Ferman, Kornbluh, and Haber, *Poverty in America*, second edition, University of

Michigan Press, Ann Arbor, 1968.

(7) George Delehanty and Robert Evans, Jr., "Low-Wage Employment: An Inventory and an Assessment," Northwestern University, mimeo, no date.

This selection is abridged from Barry Bluestone, "Black Capitalism: The Path to Black Liberation? *The Review of Radical Political Economics*, Vol. 1, No. 1, May 1969, pp. 38–39, 40–51, 52–55.

document

DOMESTIC LAW AND
INTERNATIONAL ORDER

Eldridge Cleaver

The police department and the armed forces are the two arms of the power structure, the muscles of control and enforcement. They have deadly weapons with which to inflict pain on the human body. They know how to bring about horrible deaths. They have clubs with which to beat the body and the head. They have bullets and guns with which to tear holes in the flesh, to smash bones, to disable and kill. They use force, to make you do what the deciders have decided you must do.

Every country on earth has these agencies of force. The people everywhere fear this terror and force. To them it is like a snarling wild beast which can put an end to one's dreams. They punish. They have cells and prisons to lock you up in. They pass out sentences. They won't let you go when you want to. You have to stay put until they give the word. If your mother is dying, you can't go to her bedside to say goodbye or to her graveside to see her lowered into the earth, to see her, for the last time, swallowed up by that black hole.

The techniques of the enforcers are many: firing squads, gas chambers, electric chairs, torture chambers, the garrote, the guillotine, the tightening rope around your throat. It has been found that the death penalty is necessary to back up the law, to make it easier to enforce, to deter transgressions against the penal code. That everybody doesn't believe in the same laws is beside the point. . . .

. . . The police do on the domestic level what the armed forces do on the international level: protect the way of life of those in power. The police patrol the city, cordon off communities, blockade neighborhoods, invade homes, search for that which is hidden. The armed forces patrol the world, invade countries and continents, cordon off nations, blockade islands and whole peoples; they will also overrun villages, neighborhoods, enter homes, huts, caves, searching for that which is hidden. The policeman and the soldier will violate your person, smoke you out with various gases. Each will shoot you, beat your head and body with sticks and clubs, with rifle butts, run you through with bayonets, shoot holes in your flesh, kill you. They each have unlimited firepower. They will use all that is necessary to bring you to your knees. They won't take no for an answer. If you resist their sticks, they draw their guns. If you resist their guns, they call for reinforcements with bigger guns. Eventually they will come in tanks, in jets, in ships. They will not rest until you surrender or are killed. The policeman and the soldier will have the last word.

Both police and the armed forces follow orders. Orders. Orders flow from the top down. Up there, behind closed doors, in antechambers, in conference rooms, gavels bang on the tables, the tinkling of silver decanters can be heard as icewater is poured by well-fed, conservatively dressed men in hornrimmed glasses, fashionably dressed American widows with rejuvenated faces and tinted hair, the air permeated with the square humor of Bob Hope jokes. Here all the talking is done, all the thinking, all the deciding. Gray rabbits of men scurry forth from the conference room to spread the decisions throughout the city, as News. Carrying out orders is a job, a way of meeting the payments on the house, a way of providing for one's kiddies. In the armed forces it is also a duty, patriotism. Not to do so is treason.

Every city has its police department. No city would be complete without one. It would be sheer madness to try operating an American city without the heat, the fuzz, the man. Americans are too far gone, or else they haven't arrived yet; the center does not exist, only the extremes. Take away the cops and Americans would have a coast-to-coast free-for-all. There are, of course, a few citizens who carry their own private cops around with them, built into their souls. But there is robbery in the land, and larceny, murder, rape, burglary, theft, swindles, all brands of crime, profit, rent, interest — and these blase descendants of Pilgrims are at each other's throats. To complicate matters, there are also rich people and poor people in America. There are Negroes and whites, Indians, Puerto Ricans, Mexicans, Jews, Chinese, Arabs, Japanese — all with equal rights but unequal possessions. Some are haves and some are have-nots. All have been taught to worship at the shrine of General Motors. The whites are on top in America and they want to stay there, up there. They are also on top in the world, on the international level, and they want to stay up there, too. Everywhere there are those who want to smash this precious toy clock of a system, they want ever so much to change it, to rearrange things, to pull the whites down off their high horse and make them equal. Everywhere the whites are fighting to prolong their status, to retard the erosion of their position. In America, when everything else fails, they call out the police. On the international level, when everything else fails, they call out the armed forces.

A strange thing happened in Watts, in 1965, August. The blacks, who in this land of private property have all private and no property, got excited into an uproar because they noticed a cop before he had a chance to wash the blood off his hands. Usually the police department can handle such flare-ups. But this time it was different. Things got out of hand. The blacks were running amok, burning, shooting, breaking. The police department was powerless to control them; the chief called for reinforcements. Out came the National Guard, that ambiguous hybrid from the twilight zone where the domestic army merges with the international; that hypocritical force poised within America and capable of action on either level, capable of backing up either the police or the armed forces. Unleashing their formidable firepower, they crushed the blacks. But things will never be the same again. Too many people saw that those who turned the other cheek in Watts got their whole head blown off. At the same time, heads were being blown off in Vietnam. America was embarrassed, not by the quality of her deeds but by the surplus of publicity focused upon her negative selling points, and a little frightened because of what all those dead bodies, on two fronts, implied. Those corpses spoke eloquently of potential allies and alliances. A community of interest began to emerge, dripping with blood, out of the ashes of Watts. The blacks in Watts and all over America could now see the Viet Cong's point: both were on the receiving end of what the armed forces were dishing out.

This document is excerpted from *Soul on Ice* by Eldridge Cleaver. Copyright © 1968 by Eldridge Cleaver. Used with permission of McGraw-Hill Book Co.

BIBLIOGRAPHY

Further reading is recommended in Knowles and Prewitt (5) for a good introductory analysis of institutional racism in several areas of U.S. life. The speeches of Malcolm X collected in Breitman(2) outline much of the basis of the colonial/neocolonial analysis of U.S. race relations. Lester(6) provides a highly readable account of the civil rights movement of the early 1960's and the radicalization of many participants. The essays collected in Parsons and Clark(7) present thorough statistical documentation of the situation of black America. Allen(1) is an important work which develops the colonial/neocolonial analysis, Frazier(3) presents much information that can be interpreted within this framework. Perlo (8) remains a useful discussion of sharecropping. Spear(9) outlines the political and economic forces that created a major black urban ghetto in the North during the period of mass migration of blacks out of southern agriculture. The paper by Fusfeld(4) is a good overview of the sources of urban racial conflict and the deterioration of U.S. cities. The political economy approach to the urban ghetto in Tabb(10) is a helpful corrective to much current discussion which is cast in terms of a culture of poverty.

(1) Allen, Robert. *Black Awakening in Capitalist America*. New York: Anchor Books, 1970.

(2) Breitman, George (ed.). *The Last Year of Malcolm X: The Evolution of a Revolutionary*. New York: Schocken Books, 1967.

(3) Frazier, E. Franklin. *Black Bourgeoisie: The Rise of a New Middle Class in the United States*. New York: Collier, 1962.

(4) Fusfeld, Daniel R. "The Basic Economics of the Urban and Radical Crisis." *Conference Papers of the Union of Radical Political Economics*, December, 1968. Available as Reprint No. 1 from the Union for Radical Political Economics, Ann Arbor, Michigan.

(5) Knowles. Louis L. and Kenneth Prewitt, (eds.). *Institutional Racism in America*. Englewood Cliffs, New Jersey: Prentice-Hall, 1969.

(6) Lester, Julius. *Look Out, Whitey! Black Power's Gon' Get Your Mama*. New York: Grove Press, 1968.

(7) Parsons, Talcott and Kenneth Clark, (eds.). *The Negro American*. Boston: Beacon Press, 1967.

(8) Perlo, Victor. *The Negro in Southern Agriculture*. New York: International Publishers, 1953.

(9) Spear, Allan H. *Black Chicago: The Making of a Negro Ghetto, 1890-1920*. Chicago: University of Chicago Press, 1967.

(10) Tabb, William. *The Political Economy of the Ghetto*. New York: W.W. Norton and Company, 1970.

V.
THE
SOUTH
AFRICAN
CASE
STUDY

INTRODUCTION

South Africa is ruled by a minority of 3.7 million people of European origin who constitute less than eighteen percent of the total population. The other racial and ethnic groups are: fifteen million Africans, two million coloreds of mixed origin, and a small population of Asians who were brought there as indentured laborers by the British during the nineteenth century. The ruling class of whites has monopolized economic resources and political power, established a hierarchical, closed society based on race, and has devised a complex legal-political system which enables whites to exploit abundant, cheap African labor.

The past and present history of South Africa is a striking example of the close relationship between colonialism and racism. Although the Portuguese were the first Europeans to land in South Africa, the Dutch were the first to establish a colony. Jan van Reiburg, an official of the Dutch East India Company landed with a party of a hundred on April 6, 1652 to establish a trading station. These early settlers soon found it difficult to manage the settlement with their limited manpower. Unable to persuade native Hottentots and Bushmen to accept wages for labor, the Company decided to import slaves from East, North, and Central Africa. The first slaves arrived in 1654; in 1658, 375 slaves were imported. The use of slaves continued for almost two hundred years when slavery was abolished in 1836. The settlement became a colony in 1657 and grew as the East India Company dispatched Dutch and German immigrants for permanent residence. They were later joined by the French Huguenots fleeing religious persecution.

The gradually increasing population of the colony necessitated continuing expansion which created a conflict between the settlers and the Hottentots who resisted the former's encroachment. The Hottentots were subdued by the free burghers' superior gun power, and they were attached to their farms and encouraged to marry other Hottentots to increase the slave population. Some racial intermingling between Hottentots and the early settlers occurred and resulted in the present colored population, but the free burghers became a master class depending upon forced non-white labor, and their control has been crucial to the emergence of racism in South Africa. The historian, Leonard M. Thompson, has observed:

Therefore, the free burghers were never an autonomous community but a community dependent upon non-white labor. Like other slave-owning communities, they despised manual and domestic work as servile work; they did not generate an artisan class.(1)

After two short occupations, the British finally gained control of the colony in 1806. They tried to improve colonial administration by regularly collecting taxes and improving civil and criminal justice. They also enacted legislation to control and finally to abolish slavery in 1836. The London Missionary Society which established a branch in South Africa did a valiant job in protecting the legal rights of the slave population.

The British, however, were not averse to using a system of forced non-white labor. Although they abolished slavery, they initiated a system which forced Hottentots to work for the white population. As early as 1809, the British governor, the Earl of Caledon, issued a proclamation concerning the Hottentots who were "to be provided with an encouragement for prefering entering the service of the inhabitants to leading an indolent life." This "encouragement" denied Hottentots their right to lead a pastoral life and forced them to serve the settlers in homes, agriculture, or in industry. The proclamation was repealed in 1828 as a result of the efforts of the London Missionary Society.

The abolition of slavery by the British, and especially the low compensation provided to slave holders, infuriated the free burghers. The introduction of English as a language, the appearance of English missionairies, and English taxation increased the burghers' discontent. As a result, large numbers of free burghers left the Eastern Cape and established their settlements outside the reign of British authority. The vast areas North of the Orange River where these people and their descendants, called Trekboers or more commonly, Afrikaners, settled were already inhabited by a number of Bantu tribes divided by their own inter-tribal conflicts. Over the years through conquest, war, and massacre of the African population, the Trekboers succeeded in establishing two republics: the South African Republic and the Orange Free State Republic. These states provided the Boer population with land, cheap forced labor, and the freedom to treat slaves or "apprentices" in any way they willed.

The discovery of diamonds in Kimberley and later gold in Johannesburg changed South Africa; the colony rapidly acquired great international prominence. The British government resolved to annex the two Boer Republics, and although they resisted, the Boers were no match to British power. In 1902, a twelve-point peace treaty was signed in which one clause promised self-government to the Republic and another stipulated that the white population would be able to decide the fate of the majority of the inhabitants of the Republic.

The beginning of the twentieth century marked the drift of rural whites into the industrial centers. Unskilled and uneducated, they faced competition from Africans in the labor market and exploitation from the British. Since the Afrikaners constituted a majority in numbers among the whites, who alone had the right to exercise adult franchise, the Afrikaners could use the political structure to achieve a better position in the economic system.

The Afrikaners' Nationalist party came into power in 1948, and since then it has devised a highly exploitative political and economic system to serve the interests of the population of European origin. The guiding philosophy of the present government is generally known as apartheid.

Ideologists of apartheid emphasize two basic postulates: first, each racial group has a distinct individuality which should be preserved; second, total separation of racial groups is the only means of preserving individuality. In other words, the population of European origin is superior to others, and its superior position should be preserved at all costs.

The policy of physical separation can be seen in the establishment of the eight Bantustans, which are supposed to develop ultimately as separate sovereign states within the South African Republic. Yet these so-called Bantustans are not eight geographical entities; they are scattered over the country, often separated by white areas, and take up about thirteen percent of the total land of the country. Thus, Africans who constitute more than seventy percent of the population have access to only thirteen percent of the land. In addition, the Bantu lands are eroded and not irrigated; they have no sea ports, airports, highways, or cities.

All Africans, regardless of place of their work, must reside in one of these eight Bantustans which are under the authority of the hereditary tribal chiefs advised by a council. Of the hundred and nine members of the council, sixty are nominated by government officials. As a result, the social and political authority of tribal chiefs has been consolidated by the power and influence delegated to them by the white power structure. The chiefs therefore tend to be more responsive to their source of power than to the needs of the native population.

The absurdity of Bantustans becomes apparent when one realizes that approximately thirty six percent of the African population lives in urban areas. Thus, more Africans than whites live in white areas, and the 1970 census shows that the African population is increasing in urban areas despite the Bantustans. Under these circumstances, the assertion that all Africans will be able to permanently settle in Bantustans is hardly convincing. Should the Bantustans ever achieve complete internal autonomy, they are unlikely to be free of South African economic and political domination; they probably would become satellites of metropolitan South Africa.

Further implications of apartheid policies can be seen in labor and employment legislation. Several legislative measures have been passed which deprive non-white workers of trade union rights as well as access to skilled jobs and higher wages. The Industrial Conciliation Act, which regulates the relations between employees and employers, defines the term, "employee," to exclude persons subject to the Native Labor Regulation Act. African trade unions cannot be registered, and according to the Native Labor Act of 1953, labor conflicts involving Africans are considered illegal and criminal, while strikes by whites and colored are lawful except in some cases. Africans are legally prohibited from taking certain skilled jobs in mining and in construction. Skilled jobs are reserved for whites in railways, motor-assembling industries, and some transport services.

It is reasonable to suggest that the government has established a system of cheap labor to allow the ruling minority the enjoyment of a high standard of living. The United Nations International Labor Organization's *Ad Hoc* Committee on Forced Labor has reflected this suggestion:

. . . the Committee is convinced of the existence in the Union of South Africa of a legislative system applied only to the indigenous population and designed to maintain an insuperable barrier between these people and the inhabitants of European origin. The indirect effect of this agricultural and manual work is thus to create a permanent, abundant and cheap labor force.

Industry and agriculture in the Union depend to a large extent on the existence of this indigenous labor force whose members are obliged to live under the strict supervision and control of the state authorities.

The ultimate consequence of the system is to compel the native population to contribute, by their labor, to the implementation of the economic policies of the country, but the compulsory and the involuntary nature of this contribution results from the particular status and situatión created by special legislation applicable to the indigenous population alone, rather than from direct coercive measures designed to compel them to work, although such measures, which are the inevitable consequence of this status, were also found to exist.(2)

Racial and ethnic conflicts cannot be understood in isolation from the problems of the material means of living and systems of economic production and distribution. One can analyze South Africa as a class society of white masters and non-white servants in which the economic interests of each class condition their social and political behavior towards one another. Africans are denied political participation, because participation would abolish the present economic system which the ruling class enjoys. Alex Hepple has observed:

The strong overtones of race discrimination tend to obscure the fact that the framework of South African society is essentially class discrimination, with the whites as masters and the non-whites the servants. In all South Africa's major discriminatory laws there is economic advantage for some or other sections of the white population. This is particularly so in regard to the racial labor laws. If Africans were to be given political rights, they might force changes in the labor system and end the lucrative exploitation of their poorly paid labor.(3)

Generally, the need for cheap labor has been a significant conditioning factor in the systematic racial stratification of South Africa. Earlier, labor was provided by African slaves and native "apprentices, but now more subtle and efficient ways have been devised to use African labor paid with subsistence wages. Although the ruling minority wants abundant cheap labor to maintain its homes and to keep its agricultural, industrial, and governmental systems working, the minority does not want to provide elementary political and economic rights to black Africans, because such rights would erode the whites' position of power.

The selection in this section illuminate some crucial aspects of the South African situation. Anthony Atmore and Nancy Westlake argue that historically capitalism and racism are not as incompatible as liberal economists insist. Harold Wolpe identifies the differences between segregation and apartheid by referring to the changing modes of capitalistic and African pre-capitalistic modes of production. Edward Feit's paper presents a case study of urban revolt in South Africa. He explains how urban insurgency was organized, why its initial success was limited, and why the revolt failed. This section concludes with a document, a speech by Hendrik F. Verwoerd on the meaning of apartheid.

NOTES

(1) Leonard M. Thompson, "The South African Dilemma," in Louis Hartz (ed.) *The Founding of New Societies*, (New York: Harcourt, Brace & World, 1964), p. 45.

(2) Report on the *Ad Hoc* Committee on Forced Labor, United Nations, E/2431, paragraphs 372-374.

(3) Alex Hepple, *South Africa*, (New York: Frederick A. Praeger, 1966), p. 254.

REFLECTIONS ON THE HISTORY
OF SOUTH AFRICA

Anthony Atmore and Nancy Westlake

. . . This critique will attempt to assess, with special regard to the Oxford History, the general applicability of the two main conceptions used by liberal historians to explain the development of South African history. These notions—that of *stasis* (or stagnation) and *isolation*— first appear in Volume I with regard to the pre-colonial history of South Africa. These conceptions, in the specific context in which they appear, expose certain ideological presuppositions which, certainly despite the authors' wishes, are colonial in origin and in effect. The result extends beyond misconceptions about the nature of the pre-colonial societies; for an adequate understanding of these societies is necessary in order to comprehend the dynamic of their complex interaction with colonial groups, and the resulting complex changes in colonial society.

A number of reviewers (1) have commented upon the static and synchronic nature of some of the material in the first volume, especially in those chapters dealing with the history of the sub-continent up to the eighteenth century. At one level, this stems from the disciplinary approach of Professor Wilson, an anthropologist. But there is an element of confusion, in the reviews as well as in the chapters under review, Khoisan- and Bantu-speaking societies cannot have been as static as they are made to appear—this is largely a matter of information and the establishment of a chronology (note in this respect Gray's remarks about the 'revolutionary' nature of the advance of Iron Age agricultural technology).(2) What appears to be at issue is the nature of the structures of these societies, the way in which they worked; their immobility, and isolation are relative (and not necessarily proven). Even if we know little about them diachronically, they must have shared the common characteristic of all human societies, be they large or small 'scale'; that is that they possess an internal dynamic of change, and a structure which copes with the basically new requirements of each generation. Barrington Moore deals with this problem in the epilogue to *Social Origins of Dictatorship and Democracy:* 'The assumption of inertia that cultural and social continuity do not require explanation, obliterates the fact that both have to be recreated anew in each generation, often with great pain and suffering.(3) In this respect, in a revealing passage, Professor Wilson describes the surface of such a society, but does not thereby reveal its structural dynamic:

> One of the dominant values of Nguni society was respect for traditional customs: as so commonly in small-scale societies piety and conservatism were identified, and the chief obligation of the living was to carry out the *amasiko*, the ritual observances sanctioned by the shades. . . . Not only the symbolic idiom, but minute details of ritual observance, of marriage and family relationships, and of law described from the sixteenth century onwards are familiar to anyone acquainted with the conservative section of Mpondo or Xhosa even as late as 1930. (Monica Wilson, Vol. I, 'The Nguni People', pp. 128-9)

The concepts of isolation, continuity, and change raise problems which are not solved by description: 'Though the pace of change varied . . . there is one *consistent trend* from the sixteenth century onwards, that from isolation to wider interaction', which had wide-ranging 'implications' (p. 129, our emphasis); but this is a statement that does not pose adequate questions.

STASIS AND ISOLATION: THE AFRIKANERS

The notions of 'stasis' and 'isolation' have also been applied by liberal historians to the development of racism in South Africa. In this regard they have been used to denote 'Afrikaner', or 'platteland', society. The concepts n such a context often function as terms of condemnation. To complete their meaning, the ellipses which appear in the liberal grammar have to be filled in—i.e., isolation (from capitalism and Western civilisation), and stasis (rather than progress). As such, they denote what historians think history has been, but *ought* not to have been . . .

These conceptual presuppositions appear in Volume I, sometimes in the form of apparent inconsistencies. Thus Dr. May Katzen, in examining the origins of Boer/Afrikaner society (Volume I, 'White Settlers and the Origin of a New Society, 1652-1778'), suggests that the '*new* Cape always remained (that is, up to the end of the Netherlands period) a *genuinely colonial society*, which could not achieve the autonomy and self-sufficiency of the San and Khoikhoi societies which preceded it.' (It is tiresome to reiterate that no analytical tools are provided to compare very fruitfully the variables which might have produced these differences.) 'The settlers provided both the impetus for growth and the measure of its dependence,' and this was the case even in the interior: 'In the eighteenth century the frontiersmen begged a slow-moving, reluctant central (sic) government to extend its control over them' (p. 185, our emphasis). Dr. Katzen goes so far as to suggest that 'many of the most important features of the emergent new society at the Cape were moulded by the policies of the VOC (the Netherlands East India Company), (p. 185). Slavery, for example, was consciously promoted by VOC official policy (the monopolitic VOC—and its West Indian counterpart—was in effect the external commercial sector of the Netherlands state), as suited to the specific colonial conditions at the Cape. Although slaves were used by wealthier colonial farmers throughout the area of settlement, they were most concentrated in Cape Town itself and in the surrounding wheat and wine producing country—the 'metropolitan' district of the colony: large quantities of wine and brandy were consumed in the colony and by the crews of passing ships, so the government did well out of its monopoly; and 'the Cape supplied the whole Eastern Empire with wheat until 1781' (p, 206) and even for a time exported wheat to the Netherlands. By the middle of the eighteenth century 'trekboers' were 'apprenticing' Khoisan children, a cheap form of slavery in the outlying districts. Such evidence suggests that the presence of the mode of production involving a 'slaveocracy' and a slave class in this period can only be understood as an element within the simultaneous development of capitalism rather than as an isolated local phenomenon.

Dr. R. Katzen considers that 'despite differences in economic and political orientation between the western Cape and the frontier areas, the white colonists were essentially a single community with a common heritage' (p. 228). Unifying factors included kinship and membership of the Dutch Reformed Church. Outback people trekked great distances to the older settlements in the Western Cape for the *nagmaal* (communion) service, and so it was the church at the Cape, the metropolis, which 'was the main instrument of culture and education' (p. 230). Apart from these gatherings, the settlers were dispersed 'over vast distances', which 'tended to create a series of atomized families' (p. 232). Thus the focal point of community in the eighteenth century seems to have been those areas that had the closest contact with the European economy, culture, and government.

Yet in concluding her chapter, Dr. Katzen attempts to lay the foundation of the Boer/Afrikaner 'frontier' interpretation: 'But though . . . the Cape settler community was a "fragment" of its parent society, it also differed from it fundamentally . . . The eighteenth-century Cape Burgher community received its most distinctive features from the fact that most whites were farmers *(boers)*,' whose characteristics are spelt out (hospitality, frugality, ignorant complacency and insularity, an overwhelming individualism). '*Even* the south-west Cape farms represented large patriarchal estates where many family needs were supplied by slaves, and self-sufficiency was *even* greater in the frontier regions' (pp. 231-2). The two interpretations—of dependence and of self-sufficiency—are not of course mutually exclusive, but they do appear to rest upon unstated suppositions, one of which is isolation—or, to make this concrete (and mythical), the 'frontier'.

Influence from both the parent, Western European, metropolitan centres, and from the colonial metropolitan areas of the Western Cape, and ports such as Port Elizabeth and Durban, remained important—if not predominant—in the nineteenth century, with the South African Republic (Transvaal) attempting to replace British paramountcy with a dependence upon the Netherlands and to a lesser extent upon Germany, *Predikants*, for example, in the Orange Free State and in the South African Republic, to whom the Oxford historians give a primary role in the development of Afrikaner racist attitudes (Thompson, Vol. I, p. 428; Vol. II, pp. 334, 342; de Villiers, Vol. II, pp. 370-3), came from Scotland and the Netherlands, or from the Cape, as did the majority of the leading figures in the bureaucracy (such as it was) and the judiciary (note that the 1854 Constitution of the Orange Free State was modelled upon the U.S. constitution; Thompson, Vol. I, pp. 426-7). By the turn of the century, 'when social Darwinism pervaded the culture of the Western world,' Thompson concludes that 'Afrikaner race attitudes were not fundamentally different from the attitudes that prevailed in Europe and the United States' (Vol. II, pp. 342-3). If this were the case—and the proposition is not adequately substantiated—then the evidence suggests the necessity of considering the nature of the relationship between the ideologies prevalent in the metropolitan centres of Western Europe and North America and those on the frontier, and of examining the content and import of the concept of isolation, or, as it is more usually expressed, of the frontier, in this context.

Dr. Martin Legassick, in writing on the South African 'frontier tradition', has remarked:

... in the South African situation there has been a tendency to move between the idea of rontier as isolation from the parent society, and the frontier as meeting-place of black and white cultures, peoples, and societies. The two are not necessarily the same.

White frontiersmen expected all their dependents (save their families) to be non-white: they did not expect all non-whites to be their servants.(4)

It was on the so-called front er, according to Legassick, as opposed to the areas longer settled by 'whites', that 'non-whites' were able to profit from greater opportunity, both in terms of independence and of economic enterprise, in particular as land-holders and traders. The dichotomy 'white' and 'non-white' itself masks a large amount of intermixture between immigrants from Europe and indigenous peoples. In addition, African and Afrikaner communities on the frontier, in as much as they were autonomous, experienced parallel developments in the middle years of the nineteenth century, as both were 'small-scale', largely based upon subsistence agriculture and cattle-keeping, and both were in the process of state formation (or, at times, state disintegration).(5)

It was in the frontier regions, moreover, that colonists allied with African groups, sometimes even in opposition to other colonists (the earlier history of the settler groups in the Transvaal, such as Conraad de Buys,(6) and Joao Albasini, in the Limpopo valley, provide examples), though there are few if any cases before the Anglo-Boer war of colonists directly arming Africans for military use against fellow colonists. A possible exception to this general attitude amongst colonist communities not to use armed African forces in their own internal conflicts was in the 1870s, the first decade of the diamond extractive industry, when many thousands of Africans came to the diamond diggings and mines to earn money to purchase firearms and ammunition, which were readily available for sale. This practice was condoned by the British and Cape governments, despite protests from the republican governments (and from Natal) against the large numbers of armed Africans who entered their territories from Griqualand West. The British officials and Cape politicians appeared to have acted entirely from economic self-interest: the trade was profitable to the Cape, and it was feared (rightly) that prohibition would stop the flow of labour from the still semi-autonomous African polities to the diamond mining industry. The arming of Africans, as allies or 'loyalists', against other Africans had been common from the early years of colonial settlement up till the 1870s and 1880s, the decades when African political independence was finally broken, a process which coincided with the development of the diamond and gold mining industries.

In the light of the reappraisal of the South African frontier concept now being undertaken by Legassick and other scholars (in a somewhat belated effort to align South African historiography with North American trends, one of which has been a critique of the Turner hypothesis),(7) it is difficult to maintain, as do the Oxford historians, that racial distinctions 'transcending all other distinctions', were rigidly established in the nineteenth century.

Nor was there a rigid pattern of relationships between colonial farm masters and African servants in this period; lack of rigidity does *not* imply lack of violence in these relations. African and colonist communities up to the last quarter of the nineteenth century were relatively autonomous in terms of labour. Land was still adequate—in absolute, if not in relative terms (by the middle years of the century, there was already much speculation in land, an indication of relative land scarcity)—to the economic needs of these communities, and despite persistent demands for cheap labour from colonial farmers in all parts of South Africa, most Africans elected to work as independent subsistence or commercial farmers. The main distinction that can be drawn is between much of the Free State and Transvaal on the one hand, where the money economy had barely arrived and where the apparatus of government was minimal, and the Cape and Natal on the other, where commercial agriculture was undertaken in some favoured areas and where the administration of government was far more extensive. By the 1870s in the British colonies increasingly large numbers of Africans (and, in Natal, Indians) were involved in the commercial economy,(8) and it is perhaps in these areas of longer colonial settlement, and not on the frontiers, that the beginnings of the modern job and wage colour bars can best be sought; it was in these areas that the notion of 'kaffir work' specifically denoted the situation where those defined as whites, in general, refused to work alongside 'non-white' workers at the same task for equal pay.(9) The treatment of African and Indian labour by colonial farmers in the Cape and in Natal was often harsh, in spite of complaints about its scarcity.(10)

In those regions of South Africa not involved in commercial agriculture by the middle of the century, that is, in most of the Free State and Transvaal, as well as 'backward' parts of the Cape and Natal, wages were not offered, the requirement being for a limited number of servants rather than for an expanding labour force. In the Boer Republics, colonial farmers resorted either to a crude labour tax to compel small numbers of migrant labourers, or to 'apprenticeship' to provide servants. The methods of obtaining apprentices, and the length of the period of apprenticeship—legally to the age of twenty-one—resembled aspects of slavery, but once freed from their apprenticeship, many servants probably remained in service, forming a serf-like class.(11) It was not unusual for settler subsistence farmers or their families to work with their African servants at the same task,(12) and thus the significance of the term 'kaffir-work' was less concrete than in predominantly wage areas. The notion did have a powerful emotive import for the trekboers and their descendants, and as such was an element of the ideology that cemented Boer/Afrikaner racist attitudes, ultimately justifying colonial exploitation. But actual social relations between master and servant are better characterized by their conjunction of intimacy and violence.

We suggest that the content of master-servant relations in which the farmer maintained authority over a small number of generally permanent African labourers, who lived with their families, were allowed a slight amount of agricultural independency (as *plakkers*/squatters), and were involved in colonial family life, definitively varied from those arising in plantation and mining industries in which a small number of colonial capitalists employed a strange (in the sense of alien and migrant), large African wage labour force. Our thesis challenges that of the Oxford

History (Francis Wilson, Chapter 5; Welsh, Cahpter 7.)(13) Apartheid neither *directly* developed from, nor had *simple* origins in, the master-servant relations which predominated in the republics.

MINEOWNERS, FARMERS, AND CHEAP BLACK LABOUR

The assumption that urbanization, which was inextricably linked with the development of large-scale production and wage labour, was paramountly determined by 'feudal' relations appears untenable in the light of this assessment of the nature of pre-industrial South African societies. Kimberley, the first example of modern, rapid urbanization in South Africa (as distinct from commercial towns such as Cape Town, and other ports, and also as distinct from the Tswana towns), was the outgrowth of diamond mining, an industry controlled by English-speaking capitalists, many of them immigrants, and influenced by the political power of propertyless colonists who had failed as independent miners to keep up with the pace of accumulation of capital. Conflicts between those colonists who were unemployed or wage labourers and the capitalists were mediated by the presence in the colonial situation of an African labour force excluded from the legal political process.

Mineowners preferred easily controlled cheap 'fresh kaffir' migrants, whilst the propertyless colonists demanded positions with status and high wages. After an initial few turbulent years, the demands of the two colonial classes had very largely coalesced, formally in a series of proclamations promulgated by the British governor Sir Henry Barkly in 1872 and explicitly based upon English vagrancy laws and the Cape Seaman's Registration Act, the import of which was that African labour was thereafter to be cheap, migrant, and regimented.(14) Although these proclamations were not strictly enforced in the early period of mining industry, undoubtedly by 1876 (the year of a report of a commission upon the 'Labour Question' in Griqualand West), 'the seed of the industrial colour bar had been sown'.(15) The diamond mining industrialists were not forced, but rather actively collaborated in this process; from the start of the process, industrialization, rather than subverting a colonial labour aristocracy, changed its nature and extended it. The theme of conflict/bargain between colonial English- and Afrikaans-speaking workers, capitalists, and the state, can be traced from its origins in the last quarter of the nineteenth century through the twentieth century to the present day. At every stage of the conflict mine owners were not only under strong social and political pressures, but could expect, in return for high salaries paid to the relatively few Europeans, the backing of the government of the day and of the organized colonial workers for a large unorganized (and therefore easily controlled) and cheap migrant African labour force.

The 1913 Natives Land Act is an excellent example of the interplay of general structural determinants, and of the complex interaction of various colonial interest groups. The Land Act, which, together with the 1911 Mines and Works Act (which provided the opportunity for the formal enforcement of the job bar), was one of the first major pieces of discriminatory legislation after Union, was received by liberals in Britain, including missionary and philanthropic organizations, as a piece of legislation beneficial to African interests. According to Leo Kuper (Vol. II, p. 437) the Act maintained the 'grossly unequal division of land' which was the result of the 'Wars of Dispossession'; it was in fact an unorganized miscellany of clauses designed to solve or ameliorate the varied problems of sections of the colonial population in regard to land, labour, and political supremacy. The gist of the Act was that colonists and Africans were to become geographically and socially segregated within the total sphere of domination by the ruling colonial group, while economic intermingling was to take varied forms depending on the particular needs of the more politically influential sections within that group. None of the Oxford historians makes the vital link between the 1913 Act, which one of the African political leaders of the time (J. L. Dube) rightly predicted would lead to a further loss of African economic independency,(16) and the Land Bank Act of 1912, which provided state financial assistance for white farmers. Francis Welsh, in his chapter on farming, suggests different interpretations of the Land Act in terms of land and labour, which he appears to consider to be mutually exclusive factors. This uncertainty leads to a remarkable statement of liberal mystification: 'Looking back, the historian is tempted to interpret the Act almost exclusively as the basis of the country's future policy of apartheid, but the contemporary evidence suggests that those who agitated for the legislation were far more concerned with the problem of labour supply than with anything else' (Vol. II, p. 127). What, one may ask, was apartheid all about in the 1950s and 1960s? . . .

THE 'LOGIC' OF CAPITALISM

As we have seen, the liberal view holds that apartheid and capitalism have not only been causally unrelated, but have been, and remain, in conflict. To maintain, as does the liberal thesis, that capitalism (which itself is defined by a specific structure of social relations) successfully developed in conditions in which social relations were totally opposed to its growth is theoretically dubious. In consideration of the rapidity of industralization, which since 1933 has attained an average real growth of 5 per cent, this thesis appears even more doubtful. According to Houghton the 'real Gross Domestic Product (at 1958 prices) increased from R5,153 million to R7,426 million, an increase of 44 per cent or an average growth-rate of about 7 per cent per annum over the period 1960-66. In 1963 the real growth-rate reached 9.4 per cent' (Vol. II, p. 39). Not only domestic capital, but also international capital (the two have been increasingly intermingled) has profited from—and promoted—the continuation of apartheid. In the 1960s South Africa was one of Britain's largest earners of investment income abroad, whilst American investments have markedly increased since the war, encouraged as they have been by high profit margins, which were over 20 per cent on U.S. direct investment in 1964—making South Africa the most profitable major country for private investment in the world.(17) Houghton implicitly acknowledges the importance of the promotion of apartheid for the international investment market: 'The . . . demonstration of renewed confidence (after 1960) must be attributed to the manifest strength and growth of the South African economy and, perhaps, to *the realization that its government was unlikely to capitulate to the forces of African nationalism. Increased prosperity and expanding employment opportunities eased social tension within the country'* (Vol. II, p. 40, our emphasis).

It does appear that the concept of capitalism, in the liberal argument, has been reduced to a fixed economic determinant that is viewed as having worked in the past more or less successfully in unfavourable conditions produced by the external variant of apartheid. In his chapter 'Economic Development, 1865—1965', Houghton maintains:

> . . . some of them [Africans in the 1930s] took up their permanent abode in town bringing their families to join them there, and in spite of many hindrances imposed by Government policy, the African population of the large industrial towns rose rapidly. The majority, particularly the mine workers, were temporary migrants, circulating throughout their working lives between town and country. They have been described as 'men of two worlds', because they had close and inseparable ties both with their peasant society and with the modern industrial world. The existence of this vast army of perpetual migrants indicated an imbalance in the national economy and exercised a disturbing effect upon labour stability and the industrial wage-structure typical of a state of economic dualism as described by many writers in this field (Vol. II, p. 35).

This is not the place to examine the theory of economic dualism,(18) but the whole tenor of our argument is that it is not applicable to the South African situation. In spite of the 'disturbing effect' the economy flourished. But by the late 1960s—and therefore strictly-speaking beyond the timescope of the Oxford History—shifts in the domestic and international economic system were creating renewed doubts in the minds of liberal economists as to the capability of capitalism to continue to operate so successfully under what they conceived as the 'external restraints' of apartheid. In fact, the problems the colonial classes were facing derived from the contradictions of a capitalist economy *based* upon apartheid. In the first place, the structure of apartheid—particularly the element of cheap labour—has resulted in a high rate of exploitation of labour and a high rate of profit. These factors promoted a rapid rate of capital accumulation and industrial expansion. But apartheid has also restricted the market for the expanding production of consumer goods and, thereby, of industrial commodities. This factor has limited the realization of profits and the rate of capital expansion.(19) Secondly, the availability of cheap labour retarded the development of machine technology. In this context, skilled African labour was economically unnecessary. Since the Depression of the 1930s, there has however been an increasingly dominant counter-tendency to increase the use of machines relative to labour in order to raise productivity and profits.(20) The particular historical conjunction of these tendencies in the late 1960s produced what seems to be an economic crisis, characterized by a shortage of skilled labour, massive unemployment, and poverty, and a decreasing rate of capital expansion.(21)

The liberal economists' case is a restatement of the 'rational economy' argument: the source of South Africa's economic problems is apartheid, a system that capitalism will inevitably abolish. Heribert Adam, in a recent sociological work which analyses these economic and political processes, has argued that because 'the mounting importance of manufacturing . . . requires more job dilution and the admission of more and better trained Africans into semi-skilled and skilled positions of crucial importance for the functioning of an industrial society', the labour force will have become stabilized, 'if a sufficient productivity rate is to be achieved'. 'Manufacturing capital', asserts Adam, 'interested in a domestic market for its products presupposes also purchasing power of the local workers in contrast to the foreign market-oriented mining capital.(21)

But even if manufacturing and mining capital can be separated in this manner, the contradictions inherent in the South African economy, in actuality, present several different potential courses of capitalist development, as primarily determined by the effectiveness of political forces (colonist and African) within the state. The kind of economic projection made by Kuper (Vol. II, p. 48) does not necessarily entail a dismantling of apartheid or its disintegration; it is feasible in a rich racist society to attain a much higher, but still unequal, per capita income, and also to obtain 'unrestricted employment opportunities' through the continued operation of a wage bar—unrestricted not being synonymous with equal.(23) Increased material prosperity in the past has not eroded racism, and there is no reason why it should be expected to do so in the future.

Political power, at the level of the state, has in the past been monopolized by the colonial classes. Their most thorough-going discriminatory mechanism has been the exercise of the ideology of racism within the sphere of the colonial economy. The result has been the development of various 'colour' bars, most importantly bars relating to the level of jobs and wages. Some of the issues involved in this complex process are raised in the Oxford History, but none of the authors treat them with the critical attention they deserve. Welsh (The Growth of Towns) discusses the 'colour' bars at some length, but does not make clear the crucial distinction between job and wage bars.(24) He does, however, emphasize the critical period in the 1920s and early 1930s when the influx to the urban areas of mainly Afrikaans-speaking 'poor whites' created in the minds of the wealthier colonial groups the 'danger' that 'proletarianization might mean the rejection of traditional values, "de-nationalization", and finding common cause with non-whites in a class struggle' (Vol. II, p. 184).(25) The wage bar in particular was used to avert this 'danger'. Houghton, in his chapter on economic development (the first chapter of the second volume and surely a key one), only mentions the 'colour' bars in passing. He implicitly shares the assumptions of the industrial capitalists, namely that the job bar has had a retarding effect upon the development of industrialization, but that the wage bar has somehow been forced upon beneficient employers by the exigencies of the South African political economy. Despite the authors' intentions, the Oxford History in fact endorses the very course followed by the South African state: the adjustment of the job bars so as to permit the use of African skilled labour; the retaining of wage bars to maintain the rate of exploitation and profit.(26)

The flexibility of the job bar throughout its history is revealed in a comparison of the organization of labour in colonial agriculture and industry. In this regard, Francis Wilson considers that the 'civilized labour' policy had effectively protected colonial urban workers from competition from Africans; while the process of expropriation and urbanization of the *bywoner* from the late nineteenth century prevented this policy from being applied to the farms. Parallel expropriation (plus servile coercion) of the African gradually provided cheap labour to fill those positions previously held by colonial dependents. Francis Wilson is vague on the pace of this process—a failing, no doubt, largely due to the difficulty in obtaining evidence— but as early as 1932 there was evidence of white farmers replacing unsatisfactory white managers with Africans'. By 1960 African foremen could in 'numerous cases . . . be regarded as farm managers rather than leading labourers' (Vol. II, p. 145).(27) Indeed, 'more and more farms were being left to the sole occupancy of black employees' (p. 156), and Wilson includes a map of the southern Free State which clearly indicates the degree of 'beswarting' of the platteland in 1959. As he pertinently comments, 'black mine managers or factory managers were inconceivable . . . both in the 1930s and in the 1960s' (p. 145).

Once the *bywoner* had become largely urbanized, in the colonial agrarian sector—massively subsidized by the state, the political price for 'beswarting'—concepts of class (defined economically) and colonial status (defined racially) became indistinguishable. The inference to be drawn from this distinction between the urban and rural sectors is that the job bar was essential to the successful functioning of industrial capitalism, and that conflict within the colonial classes, in particular between the colonial proletariat and the industrial capitalists, was mitigated by the enforcement of the job bar.

The specific economic and political problems of the colonial classes in the late 1960s called for a new shift in the content of the job bar. The Physical Planning and Utilization of Resources Act of 1967 aimed to strengthen industry, especially in regard to African urbanization and its concomitant problems of control. In border industries the Act allows for a weakening of the job bars, grants exemptions to industries from minimum wage provisions and excludes trade unions. Colonial workers, in return, have been promised more extensive or more sophisticated job bars in urban areas, where the colonial workers have achieved a virtual monopoly of trade union activity. These adjustments have been accompanied by other shifts in the complex of colonial bars, especially those relating to contracts and mobility (that is, the 'pass law' controls).

In regard to the wage bar, the Oxford historians have responded very uncritically to what, with certain well-publicized exceptions, is a situation of falling real wages and impoverishment of the majority of the South African population. Monica Wilson describes in detail the growing poverty of what she terms the African peasant communities, but provides only a limited analysis of the causes of this poverty. Houghton states that the earning of urban African workers 'rose significantly' (Vol. II, p. 43), while Kuper asserts that real wages of Africans in the manufacturing industry had risen appreciably in the 1960s (Vol. II, p. 466), so much so that the suggestion is that the objective interests of both Africans and colonists are to maintain the present course of capitalist development.

Statistics are often faulty and deceptive, but even South African government sources largely belie such statements of liberal optimism. This optimism overlooks the fact that the Africans' *share* in the national wealth, which they largely create, has declined in the last decade. In 1960, Africans, who represent about 70 percent of the population received 26 per cent of the national income: and their income per head represented 11.2 per cent of the colonist income. By 1969, the Africans' percentage of the national income had fallen to 18.8 per cent; and their income per head represented only 8 per cent that of colonists'.(28) In some isolated cases African manufacturing wages may have risen, but the *gap* between colonist and African earning has been widening; in manufacturing it went from 5.1:1 in 1966 to 5.7:1 in 1970.(29) In 1969 African wages rose by 2.5 per cent while consumer prices rose by 3.4 per cent. The average income per African family living in the cities has, in the meantime, remained well below the official poverty datum line.(30) In Soweto, probably one of the most prosperous African urban areas, 68 per cent of African families lived below the P.D.L. in 1970.(31) In 1970 the infant mortality rate for urban Africans was 122 per 1,000 compared with 31 per 1,000 for colonists.(32) Standards for Africans in smaller towns, villages and rural areas have been considerably worse.(33) To anyone who has read Father Desmond's account of the effects of the African resettlement policy, liberal optimism is clearly unfounded.(34)

The policies of the Nationalist governments, then, have extended, rather than fundamentally altered, the pre-existing structure in which Africans were essentially viewed as cheap labour. Far from being anachronistic, the Nationalists have responded to colonial economic problems in a way so as to mediate between conflicting colonial groups while favouring the industrial capitalism, in as much as a 'healthy economy' is vital to maintain the present power structure, in regard to both colonial supremacy and the supremacy of certain groups among the colonists. Their political actions have encouraged capitalist development by intensifying apartheid, and have thereby aggravated colonial economic contradictions.

Heribert Adam acknowledges the 'modernizing' conjunction of capitalism and apartheid in South Africa, and realizes that although Africans may become an increasingly important component of the 'skilled' and stabilised labour force, the 'pressure' that they might be able to exercise would be nullified by 'their lack of organization in the absence of trade unions or urban political parties'. Adam concludes that the 'homeland concept' (he prefers the term to 'Bantustan')(35) could serve as 'a rallying point and organizational platform', even for urban workers, 'for emerging nations of black power and a new African nationalism in Azania . . . South Africa's political dynamic dialectically strengthens the antagonisms of white domination by the very process of their separation and exclusion until the subordinates themselves have accumulated sufficient power for their own liberation'.(36)

In this argument the analysis of the South African situation has come full circle, and Adam appears to turn the liberal ideology neatly on its head: rather than the beneficient forces of capitalism overcoming the abrasive system of apartheid, apartheid destroys itself by its own success—by creating separate and independent states. And Adam is not the only liberal academic to project this outcome.(37) It is, however, too neat. It ignores the fact that capitalism and apartheid are both features of a specific South African structure; it ignores the real nature of the dialectical process in modern (post-mineral and labour exploitation) South African history, that whilst the domination of the colonial classes does separate and exclude Africans from any share of political power, Africans are not separated and excluded from the capitalist economy. This economy—whether labour intensive or capital intensive—could not operate without the participation of African labour, and yet this dependence of the economy has not historically or at present given Africans any control over the economy, because of the political predominance of the colonial classes. The operation of the apartheid policy is an exercise in political sleight-of-hand which does not basically affect the political primacy of the colonial classes. The dialectical contradictions (note Professor Adam) relate to the nature of the political and economic structure imposed by the colonial classes, not to variations within the structure instituted by these classes . . .

The history of South Africa is dominated by its *colonial* character.(38) Although South Africa is no longer, strictly speaking, a colony, we must define the main features of this concept in order to comprehend the basic continuity of its history; this proposition does not deny that there are discontinuities in South African history, particularly between the pre-industrial and industrial periods.

'Colony' may be defined primarily as a territory over which a foreign state maintains political and economic domination. Given this definition, we may

distinguish, broadly, two types of colony:
  1. Colonies where few or no indigenous peoples existed, or where specific conditions led to their rapid annihilation. These colonies developed either a widespread capitalist mode of production, as in Australia, New Zealand, and the pampas of Argentina and Uruguay,(39) or imported a population which served primarily as slaves, as in the West Indies, the southern United States, and northeastern Brazil. The latter type developed conditions resembling the second category of colonial development; i.e.,
  2. Those colonies in which the indigenous population was, and remained, large. In regard to these, we may note as a general guideline the following basic features: (a) A struggle between modes of production and unequal strength; in particular, the struggle between the indigenous 'pre-capitalist' modes of production and the metropolitan capitalist mode of production, in which the latter mode was, in the long run, dominant. (b) A monopoly of political and military power, on the level of the state, by a class or alliance of classes, the members of which were designated as descendants of metropolitan citizens, and the origins of which were ultimately founded on the dominant mode of production. (c) The propagation, through appropriate state institutions (political, economic, legal, ideological, etc.), of modes of ideology which corresponded to the specific political and economic conditions of colonial domination.
  These features (a), (b), and (c) led to: (d) The uneven development of the economy and of social relations, whereby the capitalist economic system developed on the basis of the perpetuation (or creation) of certain aspects of 'pre-capitalist' structures; for example, systems of forced labour and servile status.(40)
  Since the seventeenth century, the history of South Africa has shown tendencies to exemplify both types of colony. There have been features in the histories of the various colonial communities which appear to be analogous with, say, the history of Canada. But to emphasize these analogies is to abstract the colonial communities from the wider, developing structure of South Africa.(41) The continued and active presence of increasing members of the indigenous population has produced a colonial situation of the second main type, whatever the pretensions of the colonists themselves might have been.
  The *forms* of colonial domination and struggle in South Africa have changed over time in accordance with relatively specific economic and political developments. The earlier political history of the Cape Colony culminated in the granting of representative government in 1853 under a franchise which, given the conditions of the time, included a small number of Africans—that is, Coloured and Mfengu—parliamentary voters. As political and demographic conditions changed, so was this franchise circumscribed, with the effect of limiting African political rights, in a series of acts—1887, 1892, 1893, and 1894, and the Act of Union of 1910, until the abolition of the Cape franchise for Africans in 1936. In the sphere of imperial politics, there were shifts following the transfer of sovereignty from the Netherlands to Britain in 1814, from the Boer republics to Britain in 1902, and from Britain to the colonists in 1910. On the imperialist economic level, in contrast, Britain extended its relations with South Africa *after* 1910, while after the Second World War, the forms of imperialist economic exploitation altered as other Western capitalist states invested in South Africa.
  Internal economic changes have included the immense leap in the late nineteenth

century from a commercial-agricultural to an industrial mining economy based initially upon domestic, colonial accumulation of capital (and only slotting into international capitalism after the process of industrialization had got under way). Internal economic changes have also included the growth of manufacturing industries since the 1920s, and especially since the Second World War; Afrikaners have been involved in the growth of manufacturing industries to a much larger extent than they were in the earlier mining industries, with important political consequences.

This economic expansion led to imperialist policies on the part of South Africa whilst its component parts were still constitutionally British colonies (or Afrikaner republics under some form of British suzerainty). Colonial conditions, especially the resistance of African modes of production and the expectation of cheap labour by the colonists, resulted in the exploitation of Indian, Chinese, and 'foreign' African labour (from Mozambique, Malawi, and Zambia) since the 1860s. And in the twentieth century, new colonial conditions led to the extension of imperialism—including 'South African' imperialism—in Africa in the form of exports of finance and commodity capital.

These specific changes of the form of domination occurred within, and did not alter, the colonial *content* of South African history. That many among the ruling population trace their ancestry in South Africa back two or three centuries, or regard South Africa as their homeland—even in the event of a successful liberation struggle (of course, for a majority of the ruling population there has already been a successful liberation struggle, namely the South African war)—does not alter the colonial structure. Whatever the attitudes of individuals or of groups, there exists, objectively, a political monopoly of state power by immigrants from the metropolitan countries or those designated as their descendants. The majority of the population, which is designated as the descendants of indigenous societies (or of imported servile labourers), have been and remain excluded from the centres of legal political power. These politically unenfranchised Africans, on the basis of some form of coercion, operate the factories, mines, farms, kitchens, and nurseries of South Africa.

This economic and political domination remains represented in the sphere of ideology as racist(42) domination. Ideology, in general, denotes the subjective acknowledgement by individuals of their objective conditions of existence. We may think of ideology simply as 'common sense.' To put it crudely, in a class society, the dominant ideology represents the complex of political and economic interests of the ruling class. The varied elements of this ideology are propagated through appropriate institutions—in modern history, mainly through state controlled education, as well as religious institutions, communications, etc. For the individual, ideology arises from an immediate (or unconscious) recognition of the appearances generated by the particular economic and political structure. The effect of ideology is to reproduce and modify its conditions of existence.(43)

In this context, the development of racism in South Africa may be explained schematically as follows. Very soon after their arrival, if not immediately, the first Dutch and North German V.O.C. officials and servants related to the indigenous societies as colonists, as a dominant class. The previous ideological history of the colonists in part derived from forms of racism that had arisen in the specific conditions of the various mercantile colonies which preceded the South African settlement, or were contemporaneous with it. Enclosed in this colonial world-view, the settlers were unable to perceive the complex nature of African societies. They immediately 'recognised' them as barbaric, and equated the notion of barbarism and certain 'obvious' physical differences. To the first settlers, and to later generations of colonists, these apparent cultural and physical differences were the *cause* and the justification of colonial domination. Through the practice of racism the settlers became the individual supports of the colonial system. Specific forms of racism have been propagated by various colonial institutions, as these developed over time in the South African situation. Such colonial institutions have been, in particular, the Christian missionary societies and their churches, the schools, and the 'native' administrative apparatus. Through these institutions, ideology—especially racism— perpetuated the original differences (real or imaginary) in colour and culture according to the specific, and uneven, course of historical development within the colonial situation.(44)

The specific forms of colonial economic, political, and ideological domination created the conditions in South Africa for a markedly inconsistent and incomplete development of capitalism and bourgeois society. The sjambok *and* contract labour, the reserves *and* compounds, have arisen out of the colonial-capitalist structure. Pre-capitalist characteristics have not merely survived as relics but, on the farms and in the cities, daily fulfil necessary functions. The impoverished peasants of the reserves, the farm labourers, the regimented factory workers, the *lumpen proletariat*, and the kitchen-maids and garden 'boys' of the suburban households, all bear the burdens of serf-like status. These 'backward' modes have been the very *basis* for the development of capitalism within the South African colonial order.

The development of industrial capitalism within this order has resulted in a complex class structure. The concept of a capitalist class is undisputed, although its nature is complex, i.e., colonial capitalist, metropolitan capitalist, small scale/large scale capitalism, English, Afrikaner, even African, capitalists. There is, however, little agreement among historians over the concept (or concepts) to delineate the labour force. The notions used in the past by South African colonists have had a highly ideological content. In the earlier stages of South African industrialization, colonial workers often used the term 'slave' to denote African workers whom they considered to be a threat to their position. The epithet 'slave' has been largely replaced by the still popular concept of 'migrant', since it has been by pointing to the existence of alternatives, both in reference to access to traditional means of production and to social and political relationships, that low wages, urban segregation, political exclusion, and other means of domination over Africans have been rationalized. It is certainly the case that certain forms of pre-capitalist and agrarian capitalist social relations of production were extended as a condition of the process of accumulation of industrial capital. But, in the course of accumulation, the lands of the great majority of Africans were expropriated, so that wage labour became, in time (as the *per capita* economic resources of the remaining African land rapidly dwindled), their major source of subsistence and urban areas their permanent homes. Uneven development retarded, but did not prevent, the formation of an *African proletariat*.

A parallel process of expropriation and urbanization led to the development among the colonists of workers dependent upon industrial wages. This *colonial proletariat* has benefited politically by means of the minority franchise, economically by means of wage and job bars, and ideologically by means of racism. As part of the *herrenvolk*, their struggles both with capitalists and the state were largely over the share of proceeds derived from colonial exploitation of the African masses. The South African class structure has, in sum, been primarily determined by colonial demarcation, and revolutionary politics have accordingly developed along nationalist lines.

The writers of South African history, whatever their intentions, inevitably play a part in this political process. Historiography, in its initial *impetus* and in its *effects*, is necessarily biased,(45) a proposition admirably expressed by Nosipho Majeke in the introduction to his incisive little book:

> For a people engaged in a liberation struggle, it is necessary to rewrite the history of the past. It is part of the very process of liberation to expose the distortions of history which are presented by the herrenvolk as truth. . . . If a ruling minority can enslave the minds of the people, control their ideas and their whole way of thinking, they have found an even more efficient weapon for subjugating them than the use of force. . . . For then the people themselves assist in their own enslavement. . . . Now we have to ask ourselves why the herrenvolk, calling in the assistance of its handmaiden, the Church, have always controlled education. . . . They must have a mighty fear of the power of ideas . . . that will stir the enslaved mind to see its own conditions and question how it came to pass. Anything that contributes to such self-knowledge is of value to him. It is part of the liberating process itself.(46)

The content of critical historiography is the final product of a process by which the historian applies his methodology to the so-called 'raw material' of history. The abstract nature of historical discourse signifies the impossibility of directly capturing the concreteness of historical events in historical narrative. In as much as the historian's conceptual apparatus is badly constructed, the quality of explanation suffers. The power of historiography depends on the precision of its concepts and the rigour of their interrelation. The murky realms of South African historiography demand elucidation.

NOTES

(1) See, for example, Shula Marks, 'African and Afrikaner History', *Journal of African History* (Vol XI, No. 3, 1970), p. 433; Richard Gray, in *Race* (Vol. XI, July 1969); Anthony Atmore, *Bulletin of the School of Oriental and African Studies* (Vol. 33, 1970), pp. 435-6.

(2) Gray, op. cit., p. 90; see also idem, in *Race* (Vol. XIV, No. 1, July 1972), p. 83.

(3) Barrington, Moore Jr., *Social Origins of Dictatorship and Democracy*, (Harmondsworth, Penguin, 1966), p. 486.

(4) Martin Legassick, 'The Frontier Tradition in South African Historiography', Institute of Commonwealth Studies, London, Collected Seminar Papers on the Societies of Southern Africa in the Nineteenth and Twentieth Centuries, Vol. 2, pp. 13, 19.

(5) This point has been made by Shula Marks in the review article 'African and Afrikaner History', *Journal of African History*, p. 439.

(6) Roger Wagner is preparing a London thesis on Conraad de Buys and the 'Buysvolk'. The history of Buys is one of the many examples of 'intermixture'. On 'intermixture' see Anna Boeseken, 'Die Verhouding tussen Blank en Nie-blank in Suid-Afrika van die haud van die Vroegste Dokumente', *South African Historical*

Journal (Vol. 2, 1970), pp. 3-18, and also G. Watson, *Passing for White* (London, Tavistock, 1970).

(7) Frederick Jackson Turner argued that the 'frontier' or 'wilderness' was the primary determinant in American History. See his collected papers *The Frontier in American History*, first published 1920, which contained an essay 'The Significance of the Frontier in American History' written in 1893. A short introduction to the case for and against is *The Turner Thesis*, ed. G. R. Taylor (Boston, D. C. Heath, 1956), and also Richard Hofstadter, 'Turner and the Frontier Myth', *American Scholar* (Vol. XVIII, October 1949), pp. 433-43. A notable work on this topic is Henry Nash Smith, *Virgin Land* (Cambridge, Mass., Harvard University Press, 1950/1970).

(8) The building of railways and harbours in the 1870s led to a marked increase in the numbers of African wage earners. For some indications of the process involved in this development, see CO 51, 178 (Appendix 1, Vol. 1), 1874 Blue Book on Native Affairs, G.27: King Williams Town Report by J. R. Innes, pp. 12-13; C. Brownlee (Sec. of Native Affairs) to Government Agents and Magistrates, 9/1/74, ca. p. 155. CO 51, 188, (App. 1, V. 1), Blue Book of Native Affairs, 1876, G. 16: Report of F. Gladwin (Acting Resident Magistrate, Port St. Johns), pp. 24-7; Indutwa Report, p. 59; East London Report, pp. 70-2. According to Government Agent C. Griffith, 15,000 passes were issued in 1875 to Sotho going to work in the Cape Colony, the Free State or on the Diamond Fields—see CO 51, 188 p. 7. The growth of this labour force was intermittent, and for an indication of the fluctuations in the numbers of African wage earners, see the monthly registration of labourers, listed by chiefdom, in the Griqualand West Government Gazette, CO 109, 1, 1876-80. With reference to the importation of Indian labour in this period, see L. M. Thompson, 'Indian Immigration into Natal, 1860-1872', *Archives Yearbook* (Vol. II, 1952), pp. 17-74; and B. A. Le Cordeu, 'The Relations between the Cape and Natal, 1846-79', ibid. (Vol. I, 1965), pp. 177-9.

(9) Anthony Trollope, *South Africa* (London, Chapman and Hall, 1878), Vol. I, pp. 102, 147.

(10) On the 'iron rod school', found mainly in the eastern Cape, see ibid., Vol. I, p. 277; Vol. II, pp. 334-6.

(11) For analysis of a serf-like status, see *A. V. Chayanov: On the Theory of Peasant Economy*, edited by D. Thorner, B. Kerblay and R. E. F. Smith (Illinois, University of Illinois Press, 1966), esp. pp. 16-28 of this neglected work.

(12) Trollope, op. cit., II, 238-40.

(13) Welsh's discussion of the urbanization of the *bywoner* (Vol. II, pp. 202-21) suggests, contrary to his conclusions, basic ideological discontinuities, and supplements our argument.

(14) Barkly, Proclamations I, II, III, August 1872. C. 732, 1873: Barkly-Kimberley, 2/8/72; 4/8/72; 3/10/72. CO. 48, 461: 8920 (85), 9412 (91). CO 48, 462: 10902 (107). See also George McCall Theal, *History of South Africa since 1795*, Vol. V (London, 1908), p. 277.

(15) Welsh, Vol. II, p. 181, closely following S. T. van der Horst, *Native Labour in South Africa*, (London, 1942 and Cass, 1971), ch. V.

(16) John L. Dube, President of the South African Native National Congress. From the *Cape Argus* (14 February 1914), in *Correspondence re. Natives Land Act, 1913* (Cd. 7508), 1914, pp. 23-4.

(17) Giovanni Arrighi and John S. Saul, 'Nationalism and Revolution in Sub-

Saharan Africa', *The Socialist Register*, eds. Ralph Miliband and John Saville (London, Merlin Press, 1969), p. 139.

(18) Houghton cites only one exponent of the economic dualist theory, namely W. A. Lewis, 'Economic Development with Unlimited Supplies of Labour', *The Manchester School* May 1954). For a critique of the theory, see G. Arrighi, 'Labour Supplies in Historical Perspective: A Study of Proletarianization of the African Peasantry in Rhodesia', *Journal of Development Studies* (Vol. IV, No. 3, April, *Review*, 67, May-June 1971.

(19) Sean Gervasi, "The Nature and Consequences of South Africa's Economic Expansion', University of London Institute of Commonwealth Studies, Collected Seminar Papers on the Societies of Southern Africa in the Nineteenth and Twentieth Centuries, Vol. 2, pp. 145-9.

(20) Martin Legassick, 'Foced Labour, Industrialization and Racial Differentiation, unpublished paper, section on 'Secondary Industrialization in a Forced Labour Economy'.

(21) The term 'skilled labour' in South African history has in general referred to social relations of production rather than to techniques of production. An analysis of recent assertions of the shortage of skilled labour (see for example Muriel Horrell, *South Africa's Workers*, Johannesburg, South African Institute of Race Relations, 1969, pp. 83-7) by capitalists and officials must consider the dual reference of the term. Legislation since 1956 (Horrell, pp. 88-93, 133), and agreements between trade unions and industrial capitalists in individual industries (Horrell, pp. 89-126), do seem to signify a technical aspect to the latest 'skilled labour' issue. For highly pertinent references to unemployment, underemployment, and 'dedevelopment' in South Africa, see Cosmas Desmond, *The Discarded People* (Harmondsworth, Penguin, 1971). For a useful summary of the economic decline of the late 1960s, see Africa Bureau, Fact Sheet 6, 1970, 'The South African Economy'.

A critical study of post war economic developments in South Africa is urgently required.

(22) Heribert Adam, *Modernizing Racial Domination: South Africa's Political Dynamics* (Berkeley and Los Angeles, University of California Press, 1971), p. 182.

(23) This argument is alluded to in several places in Frederick Johnstone, 'White Prosperity and White Supremacy in South Africa', *African Affairs* (Vol. 69, April 1970), especially p. 139.

(24) Ibid., pp. 126-30.

(25) Welsh cites G. D. Scholtz, *Het die Afrikaanse Volk 'n Toekoms?* (Johannesburg, 1953), p. 116: 'Not only did the poor white sink from the social and commercial standards of the white community, but the non-whites, as a result of these contacts and this social intimacy, lost the necessary respect for whites in general, and developed in his heart a feeling of defiance and a dangerous desire for equality with the whites.' We argue that this kind of 'intimacy' was widespread in the interior of Southern Africa *before* the beginning of the process of industrialization.

(26) The extension of South Africa imperialist policies to the rest of Africa in the last decade is a further attempt by the state to resolve economic problems (in as much as these imperialist policies have an economic as distinct from political motivation); in particular, to ease market problems and provide a further source of capital accumulation. According to Spence (Vol. II, pp. 495-6, 527), the 'outward looking policy' is premised by the economic and political solidity of apartheid. To supplement our argument as to the inherent antagonisms within the apartheid economy, and their connection with imperialism, see Gervasi, op. cit. ref. 25, and Robert Molteno, *Africa and South Africa* (London, Africa Bureau, 1971).

(27) Francis Wilson cites the South African Agricultural Union, *Memorandum for submission of Enquiry into Agriculture* (1967), p. 15.

(28) X Ray (Vol. VI, No. 2, 1/71), The Africa Bureau, London.

(29) X Ray (Vol. II, No. 6, 2/72). The source for the Bureau's statistics on wages was the Bantu Wages and Productivity Association.

(30) Ibid. Figures from Market Research Africa, 1971.

(31) X Ray (Vol. I, No. 1, 7/70). Figures from the Non-European Affairs Department of Johannesburg.

(32) X Ray (Vol. II, No. 6, 2/72). From the South Africa Institute of Medical Research Survey, 1971.

(33) Ibid. From Market Research Africa, 1971.

(34) Cosmas Desmond, The Discarded People (Harmondsworth, Penguin, 1971).

(35) Cosmas Desmond has aptly termed the policy of 'homelands' or 'Bantustans' a 'charade of double think'. Desmond, op. cit., p. 25.

(36) Adam, op. cit., pp. 182-3. There is a growing literature on the 'modernizing (aspects) of apartheid', which reaches often contradictory conclusions, cf. H. Blumer, 'Industrialisation and Race Relations' in G. Hunter, ed., Industrialisation and Race Relations (London, Oxford University Press for the Institute of Race Relations, 1965); F. Johnstone, op. cit.; Martin Legassick, 'Development and Underdevelopment in South Africa', unpublished paper, Royal Institute of International Affairs, 11 March 1961; A. W. Stadler, 'Race and Industrialisation in South Africa: a critique of the "Blumer thesis" ', unpublished paper, Royal Institute of International Affairs, 28 January 1971; Stanley Trapido, 'South Africa in a Comparative Study of Industrialization', Journal of Development Studies (Vol. VII, No. 3, 1971); Harold Wolpe, 'Industrialism and Race in South Africa', in Sami Zubaida, ed., Race and Racialism (London, Tavistock, 1970), pp. 151-79. It is interesting to compare Adam's conclusions, summarized above, with the closing remarks of his chapter, 'The South African Power Elite: A Survey of Ideological Commitment', in South Africa: Sociological Perspectives (London, Oxford University Press, 1971): 'The flexibility of the South African power elite to adapt its system of dominance to changing conditions, to strengthen it economically, and to streamline it politically by concessions towards deracialization, should not be underestimated. Ambivalent progress though it may seem to the advocates of heightened polarization, it could nevertheless prove to be the most decisive factor for future development in the South of Africa' (p. 101).

(37) Cf. Richard Gray, in a review of the second volume of the Oxford History, Race (Vol. XIV, No. 1, July 1972): 'traditional loyalties' merge, 'with other frustrated interests, into a radical, if desperate, rejection of integration and white liberalism.'

(38) Most South Africanists attempt to categorize the character of the South African situation. These categorizations have been assessed recently by Adam, in Modernizing Racial Domination. For a useful summary, see p. 17. Adam would probably agree with our emphasis upon the colonial character of South African history, although our definitions of the features of colonialism, as set out below, differ somewhat from his (p. 30). Not his term 'settler colonialism' (p. 17 and elsewhere) which is valuable, but must be clearly defined. Adam provides a useful discussion of the literature and of the concepts of pluralism (pp. 20-3). (See also J. Rex, "The Plural Society: The South African Case', Race (Vol. XII, No. 4, April 1971). The notions of pluralism pervade the Oxford History, and have been analysed, if only obliquely, in this critique.)

(39) Laclau, 'Feudalism and Capitalism in Latin America', op. cit., p. 30.

(40) This is not a theory of factors. None of these elements (economic, political, ideological—or military) can be conceived as acting in history in their 'purity'. Rather, the process by which colonial rule was established involved the inseparable

interaction of all elements. The historical content of each element, and their relations of dominance, varied given the particular historical situation. N. Majeke in *The Role of the Missionaries in Conquest* (Johannesburg, 1952), powerfully presents the mode of this interaction. His thesis is in part reductionist, but its coherent and clearly expressed principles make it excellent raw material for further work.

(41) Adam appears to be so abstracting the colonists, especially Afrikaners, in both the works referred to. See the concluding chapter of *Modernizing Racial Domination* and p. 17: 'the consideration of "pragmatic oligarchy" as a key concept in the understanding of the Apartheid system'.

(42) For some recent examples of a vast literature on 'racism', see the works of John Rex, especially 'The Concept of Race in Sociological Theory' in Sami Zubaida, ed., *Race and Racialism*, and *Race Relations in Sociological Theory* (London, Weidenfeld, 1970). Our discussion of racism contrasts with that of Rex. In *Race Relations*, Rex's approach appears to be empiricist: he accepts that the concept of 'racial differences' necessarily refers to given elements in reality—'race relations . . . have the following characteristics: they refer to situations in which two or more groups with distinct identities and recognizable characteristics are forced by economic or political circumstances to live together in a society. . . . Ascriptive allocation of roles and rights . . . are justified in terms of some kind of deterministic theory, whether that theory be of a scientific, religious, cultural, historical, ideological or sociological kind' (pp. 159-60). A concept from the sphere of racist ideology has become the first term of his own definition. Philip Mason's magisterial *Patterns of Dominance* (London, Oxford University Press for the Institute of Race Relations, 1970), describes a great range of racist situations and prescribes a grand and liberal solution. An entire issue of *Race* (Vol. XIII, No. 4, April 1972) was given over to an examination of the theoretical considerations involved in a study of racist situations. Eric Dunning, 'Dynamics of Racial Stratification: Some Preliminary Observations', briefly analyses the South African case (pp. 432-3), but assumes the antipathy between the 'industrial economy' and apartheid, which we argue to be a misconception.

(43) For some pointers towards a theory of ideology, see Louis Althusser, *For Marx* (London, Allen Lane, 1969), pp. 232-6; and *Lenin and Philosophy* (London, New Left Review Editions, 1971), the essay 'Ideology and Ideological State Apparatuses', pp. 123-73. Also Antony Cutler, 'Fascism and Political Theory'

(44) In this respect, Adam's observation that 'South Africa now displays racialism without racism' *(Sociological Perspectives, p. 79)*, denotes, if correct, a mere shift within the structure of racist ideology; its equivalent 'separate but equal' is a classic form of racism.

(45) E. H. Carr, for one, has long pointed out this home truth to historians, in *What is History?* (Harmondsworth, Ppenguin, 1961/1964), pp. 22-8.

(46) Majeke, op. cit., Introduction.

The original title of this section is "A Liberal Dilemma: A Critique of The Oxford History of South Africa," pp. 107-136. Abridged and reprinted from *Race*, XIV, 2 (October, 1972), published for the Institute of Race Relations ,London, by Oxford University Press © Institute of Race Relations, 1972.

CAPITALISM AND CHEAP LABOUR-POWER IN SOUTH AFRICA: FROM SEGREGATION TO APARTHEID

Harold Wolpe

A few exceptions apart (e.g. Legassick, 1971, 1972; Wolpe, 1970, 1971; Trapido, 1971; Johnstone, 1970) the literature—radical, liberal and racist alike (e.g. Simons and Simons, 1969; Asherson, 1969; Van der Horst 1965; Van den Berghe, 1967; Rhoodie, 1969)—analyzes and describes the society in terms of racial concepts. Even where the relationship between classes is incorporated into the discussion, race is nevertheless treated as the dominant and dynamic force (e.g. Simons and Simons, 1969: 614-15). 'Racial segregation', 'separate development', 'racial discrimination', 'racial groups' (African, White, Coloured and Asiatic), 'colour-bar', 'White ruling-class', 'race-relations', etc., etc.—these are the concepts of the analysis of South Africa. The predominance of these concepts can, no doubt, be attributed to the opaqueness of racial ideology, which is reflected, inter alia, in the formulation of laws in racial terms, in the content of the mass media, in the policies and ideological statements of all the political parties and organisatons (both black, white and also mixed) and in almost the entire intellectual product of the society.

The overwhelming importance accorded to race in these approaches is apparent, above all, in their treatment of the relationship between racially oriented action and 'the economy'. Thus, on the one hand, the content of 'Native' or 'Bantu' policy (to use the official terms) which can be found in the legislative programmes, government policies and commission reports both before and after 1948(1) is analyzed in its own terms and treated as being concerned solely with the regulation of 'race relations'. On the other hand, whether the economy is conceived of in terms of liberal economics (Van der Horst, 1965; Van den Berghe, 1967; Hutt, 1964; Horwitz, 1967) or in Marxist terms as a capitalist mode of production (Simons and Simons, 1969; Asherson, 1969), racial beliefs are treated as a force external to, but productive of, distortions in the otherwise rational economic system.(2) In its most advanced form this leads to the 'theory' of the plural society which both reflects the dominant ideology and provides an apparently scientific corroboration of it. This approach (see e.g.

Kuper and Smith, 1970; Van den Berghe, 1967) accepts, precisely by reference to the racial or ethnic content of the laws, policies and ideologies current in the society, the critical salience of race to the exclusion of the mode of production. The basic structure of the society is seen, in this and the other analyses referred to, in the relationship between a dominant White group and a dominated Black group.

It is of fundamental importance to stress that in this perspective the State of South Africa comes to be treated as the instrument of oppression of Whites over Blacks but (precisely because class relationships are not normally included in the analysis) as neutral in the relationship between classes. It in no way detracts from the conception of the State as an instrument of White domination, however, to insist that the South African state is also an instrument of class rule in a specific form of capitalist society. Indeed, while there have been, of course, variations in emphasis and detailed policy (variations which stem, in part, from the specific class composition of and alliances in the parties which have ruled from time to time, from the conflicts between class and segments of classes and from changing socio-economic conditions), nevertheless, since the establishment of the Union of South Africa in 1910 (to go back no further), the State has been utilized at all times to secure and develop the capitalist mode of production. Viewed from this standpoint racist ideology and policy and the State now not only appear as the means for the reproduction of segregation and racial discrimination generally, but also as what they really are, the means for the reproduction of a particular mode of production.(3)

It is not possible in this paper to discuss in detail the historical evidence which demonstrates this,(4) but, insofar as it is necessary the point can be sufficiently established by a brief reference to different functions the State has performed since the formation of the Union of South Africa.

Firstly, the State has acted directly through the law (e.g. Land Bank Act which provides for subsidies and grants to White farmers), through special agencies (for example, the Industrial Development Corporation which has been important in the growth of, *inter alia,* the textile industry), through the development of State enterprises and in other ways to foster capitalist development. Horwitz (1967: 355) has summed up some of the processes as follows:

> There has been a significant structural change in the South African economy in the last twenty-five years, when an increasing share of the domestic market has been secured to domestic manufacturers as a deliberate objective of state policy. The instruments employed—ranging from tariff-duty protection at higher rates, advance guarantees of tariff protection to induce large-scale, otherwise high risk investments, import controls to compel foreign manufacturers-exporters to franchise or participate in South African plants, state finance and other inducement-aids for strategic import-substitution, heavily-capitalized industries—have helped industrialize the country.

Secondly, the repressive apparatus of the State (police, army, prisons, courts, etc.) has been used broadly in two ways. First, as the occasion arose, to coerce workers, whether black or white, on behalf of or in support of employers. A small selection of the more dramatic examples of this would include the 1914 white mine-workers strike, the 1922 general strike (Rand Revolt) of white workers, the 1946 African Mine-workers strike and the 1972 Ovambo workers' strike. Second, to enforce the laws which either overtly guarantee the perpetuation of capitalism—laws such as the Industrial Conciliation Act 1924, the Masters and Servants Act, the

Native Labour (Settlement of Disputes) Act 1953, the Native Labour Regulation
Act 1911, and so on—or (as in the case of most laws affecting Africans) which co-
vertly perform the same functions—for example, the Native Lands Act 1913, and
the Native (Abolition of Passes and Co-ordination of Documents) Act 1952.

It is precisely from the racial terms that are employed in these laws that their
ideological function can be determined. The enactment of laws, the express purpose
of which is the regulation of relationships between racial groups and the ordering
of the conduct of the members of legally defined racial categories, is both an expression of racist ideology and a means of reinforcing that ideology. This is so because not only do racial laws, in common with other laws, appear as neutral to the
capitalist structure of the society by taking that structure as given, but more importantly, like other laws but in a different way, they actively operate to mask both
the capitalist nature of the society altogether and the consequences of their
provisions for the functioning of that system.

It follows from what has been argued in this Section that, in order to break
through the mask of racial ideology, it is necessary to show how these racial prescriptions articulate with the mode of production or, more precisely, the modes of production in South Africa . . .

. . . In the period under consideration the economic system or social formation
has been comprised of at least three different modes of production. The history of
South Africa(5) shows the emerging *dominance*, first through British imperialism,
and then also through internal capitalist development, of the capitalist mode of
production. The development of this dominant mode of production has been inextricably linked with two other modes of production—the African redistributive
economies and the system of labour-tenancy and crop-sharing on White farms. The
most important relationship is between capitalism and the African economics and
although it is not entirely satisfactory to do so, for reasons of space, the discussion
which follows is restricted to this relationship.

These two modes of production may be briefly characterized as follows: First,
the capitalist mode of production in which 1. the direct labourers, who do not own
the means of capitalist production, sell their labour-power to the owners of the means
of production who are non-labourers and 2. the wages the labourer receives for the
sale of his labour-power are met by only a portion of the value of the product he actually produces, the balance being appropriated as unpaid labour (surplus value) by
the owners of the productive means. Second, the mode of production in the areas of
African concentration (particularly, but not exclusively, the Reserves) in which 1.
land is held communally by the community and worked by social units based on kinship (the enlarged or extended family) and 2. the product of labour is distributed,
not by exchange, but directly by means of an allocation through the kinship units in
accordance with certain rules of distribution . . .

. . . In South Africa, the development of capitalism has been bound up with, first,
the deterioration of the productive capacity and then, with increasing rapidity, the
destruction of the pre-capitalist societies. In the earlier period of capitalism (approximately 1870 to the 1930's), the rate of surplus value and hence the rate of
capital accumulation depended above all upon the maintenance of the pre-capitalist
relations of production in the Reserve economy which provided a portion of the

means of reproduction of the migrant labour force. This relationship between the two modes of production, however, is contradictory and increasingly produces the conditions which make impossible the continuation of the pre-capitalist relations of production in the Reserves. The consequence of this is the accelerating dissolution of these relations and the development, within South Africa, towards a single, capitalist, mode of production in which more and more of the African wage-labour force (but never the whole of it) is 'freed' from productive resources in the Reserves. This results in important changes in the nature of exploitation and transfers the major contradiction from the relationship *between* different modes of production to the relations of production *within* capitalism.

Here we arrive at the critical point of articulation between ideology, racial political practice and the economic system. Whereas Segregation provided the political structure appropriate to the earlier period, Apartheid represents the attempt to maintain the rate of surplus value and accumulation in the face of the disintegration of the pre-capitalist economy. Or, to put it another way, Apartheid, including separate development, can best be understood as the *mechanism specific to South Africa* in the period of secondary industrialization, of maintaining a high rate of capitalist exploitation through a system which guarantees a cheap and controlled labour-force, under circumstances in which the conditions of reproduction (the redistributive African economy in the Reserves) of that labour-force is rapidly disintegrating.

THE AFRICAN RESERVES

Arrighi (1970), Bundy (1971) and others have shown that the processes of commercialization and accumulation were, no less than in Latin American societies, occurring in African rural economies in Rhodesia and South Africa. It is, nonetheless true, that by not later than 1920 the overwhelming economic and political power of the capitalist sector had succeeded, whether through unequal terms of trade or otherwise, in under-developing the African economy so that it no longer presented any significant competitive threat to White farmers. Production, in the African Reserves, of a marketable surplus became increasingly rare, finally disappearing altogether.(6) Unlike some other situations elsewhere, therefore, the capitalist sector was unable to extract the (non-existent) surplus product *directly* from the African pre-capitalist sector. The relations between the two sectors were, indeed '. . . reduced to the provision by the backward sector' of a supply of labour-power to the capitalist sector. The peculiar feature of this labour-force is that it is migrant and temporary, returning to the Reserves in between periods of work, and retains means of production in the African economy or has a claim on such means. The exploitation of migrant labour-power of this kind enables the capitalist sector to secure an increased rate of surplus value. How is this effected? . . .

. . . When the migrant-labourer has access to means of subsistence, outside the capitalist sector, as he does in South Africa, then the relationship between wages and the cost of the production and reproduction of labour-power is changed. That is to say, capital is able to pay the worker *below* the cost of his reproduction. In the first place, since in determining the level of wages necessary for the subsistence of the migrant worker and his family, account is taken of the fact that the family is supported, to some extent, from the product of agricultural production in the Reserves, it becomes possible to fix wages at the level of subsistence of the individual worker. Arrighi (1970) has shown this to be the basis of cheap labour in Rhodesia and Schapera (1947) has argued this for South Africa on the basis of the following quotation from the Chamber of Mines' (the largest employer of migrant labour) evidence to the Witwatersrand Native Mine Wage Commission (21/1944):

> It is clearly to the advantage of the mines that native labourers should be encouraged to return to their homes after the completion of the ordinary period of service. The maintenance of the system under which the mines are able to obtain unskilled labour at a rate less than ordinarily paid in industry depends upon this, for otherwise the subsidiary means of subsistence would disappear and the labourer would tend to become a permanent resident upon the Witwatersrand, with increased requirements . . .

In the second place, as Meillassoux (1972: 102) has pointed out:

> The agricultural self-sustaining communities, because of their comprehensiveness and their *raison d'etre* are able to fulfil functions that capitalism prefers not to assume . . . the functions of social security.

The extended family in the Reserves is able to, and does, fulfil 'social security' functions necessary for the reproduction of the migrant work force. By caring for the very young and very old, the sick, the migrant labourer in periods of 'rest', by educating the young, etc., the Reserve families relieve the capitalist sector and its State from the need to expend resources on these necessary functions.

The portion of the product of the Reserves which is thus indirectly appropriated by the capitalist sector is represented in Figure I.

Figure 1

The Relative Proportion of Surplus to Necessary Labour in the Capitalist Sector where:

(a)	(b)
The Working‑ ꞁ is Wholly dependent upon Wages fo ꞁeproduction	The Working-Class derives a portion of its means of Reproduction from the Reserve Economy

(Note: This figure is not drawn to scale)

Where S = surplus labour time/product
N = labour time/product necessary for reproduction of labour-power
N_1 = the decreased proportion of labour time/product devoted to the reproduction of labour-power by the capitalist sector where portion of the necessary means of subsistence is provided by the Reserve Economy (N_2)
S_1 = the increased surplus labour time/product.

For the product of African agricultural production to be indirectly available to the capitalist mode of production in this way, two conditions are necessary—means of subsistence must actually be produced by the non-capitalist economy and these means must be accessible to the migrant worker and his kin in the Reserves.

The accessibility to the migrant-worker of the product (and of the 'social services') of the Reserves depends upon the *conservation*, albeit in a restructured form, of the reciprocal obligations of the family. The interest of the capitalist sector in preserving the relations of the African familial communities is clear—if the network of reciprocal obligations between migrant and family were broken neither the agricultural product nor the 'social services' of the African society would be available to the worker. It is no accident that the South African State has consistently taken measures, including the recognition of much of African law and custom, the recognition of and grant of powers to chiefs, the reservation of areas of land, etc., aimed at preserving the 'tribal' communities . . .

. . . The conclusion can thus be drawn that in the early period of industrialization in South Africa (the period of gold mining) the Reserve economy provided the major portion of Africans employed in capitalist production, at any given moment, with supplementary subsistence and was thus a crucial condition of the reproduction of the migrant working-class. The crucial function thus performed by the policy of Segregation was to maintain the productive capacity of the pre-capitalist economies and the social system of the African societies in order to ensure that these societies provided portion of the means of reproduction of the migrant working-class.

THE CORROSION OF CHEAP MIGRANT LABOUR-POWER

The production and reproduction of the migrant labour-force thus depended upon the existence of a rough equilibrium between production, distribution and social obligation in the Reserves—the level of production in the Reserves together with wages being *more or less* sufficient to meet the (historically determined) subsistence requirements of migrants and their families, while land tenure and familiar community relationships ensured the appropriate distribution of the Reserve product. This equilibrium was, however, inherently fragile and subject to irresistible pressures.

Given the developed incapacity of the Reserves to generate a surplus product, the limited area of land available (fixed by the Native Land Act), the increasing pressure of population and, therefore, congestion on the land, the loss, at any given time, of a large proportion of the economically active adults to temporary employment in the capitalist sector, the relatively backward and inefficient farming methods, and the tendency (related to the traditional culture and economy) of Africans to accumulate cattle and thereby overstock the land available, the only possibility of ensuring appropriate levels of agricultural production is through investment by the capitalist sector. As the Tomlinson Commission (1956)(7) later showed, soil conservation measures, irrigation schemes, fencing, mechanisation and agricultural training require heavy outlay. Large scale investment, however, (unless it could be met from the resulting surplus, a situation which would itself create other intractable problems since it implies the development of an economically powerful class of African agricultural producers, a retardation of the flow of migrants or, at least, the severance of the economic link between Africans moving into urban industrial employment and the product in the Reserves) would negate the very purpose served by a migrant labour force. That is to say, the effect of large-scale investment in the Reserves would be to make cheap labour-power costly in the sense that the accumulation advantages to capitalism deriving from such labour-power would be lost or reduced if the surplus was utilized in the African rural areas. In fact, as was pointed out earlier, the State's expenditure on agricultural development in the Reserves has always been extremely low, increasing only marginally as conditions of production worsened. The immediate consequence of all this was a rapid decline in the agricultural product in the Reserves . . .

. . . The conclusion which emerges is that, overall, production in the Reserves provides a declining fraction of the total subsistence of migrant-labourers.

The level of production, however, is not the only relevant aspect; the way in which the product is distributed must also be considered. The important question is whether or not the family in the Reserve is able to fulfil its obligation of producing agricultural means of subsistence, for consumption in the Reserves, to supplement the wages earned by a member of the family in the capitalist sector? It was pointed out above that in the earlier period of capitalist development, the system of land tenure and the mode of distribution of the product ensured that supplementary means of subsistence were available to the migrant labour force. However, capitalist development produced further changes which had the effect of altering the pattern of distribution so that the diminishing agricultural product became more and more unequally distributed and less and less available to wage-labourers.

In the first place, the development of classes in the Reserves (or, perhaps, strata within classes), which had already begun in the nineteenth century, was intensified and broadened. At least three distinct classes have emerged.

Firstly, those who own or occupy land, and secondly, those who are both landless and who own no cattle, many of whom appear to live in rural locations and thirdly, landless rural dwellers who own cattle which are grazed on common land . . .

. . . It follows from this that a proportion of the families living in the Reserves produce either very little or, in the case of the landless and cattleless, no means of subsistence.

Thus far I have discussed the economic changes in the Reserves which undermined, to a significant degree, the economic basis of the migrant labour system and by the same token a substantial economic prop of cheap labour-power. The essence of the argument has been that the amount of subsistence available to the migrant labour force and their families in the Reserves has either diminished because the overall decline in production has resulted in a decrease in the product *per capita* or has virtually disappeared because of the partial or total loss, in the case of some families, of means of production.

This, however, is only one aspect of the process, for, in the second place, the product of the Reserves may no longer be available to the migrant as a means of subsistence for himself and his family in the Reserves by reason of the termination of the reciprocal social obligations of support between the migrant and his kin in the Reserve, even where the latter continues to produce subsistence. An important condition for this change is the permanent urbanisation of a substantial number of workers. The process of secondary industrialization and the development of the tertiary sector of the economy, provided the opportunity for the development of, and was accompanied by an ever increasing, permanently urbanized, industrial proletariat.

The first point to note is that the percentage of the African population in the urban areas increased from 12.6% in 1911 to 23.7% in 1946 and by 1971 was approximately 38% . . .

The significance of these figures derives from the fact that, in contrast to Africans employed in mining, those employed in secondary industry are not brought into employment (or returned to the Reserves) through recruiting organizations. They are, of course, subject to the pass laws and other legal provisions restricting their right of residence in urban areas, laws which have become increasingly rigorous over time. Nevertheless, employment in manufacturing coupled with residence in 'locations' and townships undoubtedly enabled large numbers of African workers to settle permanently in the urban areas and in due course to raise families there . . . there can be no doubt that . . . the number of Africans in the urban areas having no relevant links with the Reserves has grown steadily and rapidly and that they today constitute a significant, if not major, proportion of African industrial workers.

APARTHEID: THE NEW BASIS OF CHEAP LABOUR

The focus in the two previous Sections has been largely on the economic foundation. The immediate result of the decline in the productive capacity of the pre-which have continuously and to an ever increasing degree undermined this foundation. the immediate result of the decline in the productive capacity of the pre-capitalist economies was a decrease in the agricultural product of the Reserves resulting, therefore, in a decrease of the contribution of the Reserves towards the subsistence necessary for the reproduction of the labour force. This threatened to reduce the rate of surplus value through pressure on wages and posed, for capital, the problem of preventing a fall in the level of profit.

The solution, for capital, to this problem must take account of the complementary effect of the erosion of the economic foundations of cheap migrant labour-power, upon both the African rural societies and the urbanized industrial proletariat. I have already shown that the system of producing a cheap migrant labour force generated rural impoverishment, while at the same time it enabled extremely low wages to be paid to Africans in the capitalist sector. But increasing rural impoverishment, since it removes that portion of the industrial workers' subsistence which is produced and consumed in the Reserves, also intensifies urban poverty. This twofold effect of capitalist development tends to generate conflict, not only about wages, but about all aspects of urban and rural life and to bring into question the structure of the whole society. This broadening and intensification of conflict is met by political measures which in turn lead to an increasingly political reaction. Clearly, the nature, form and extent of the conflicts generated by the structural conditions will depend not only upon the measures of state control but on the complex conjuncture of political ideologies and organization, trade unions, the cohesion of the dominant sector, and so on. Although these may vary, what is continuously present, it must be stressed, is the tendency for the structural conditions to generate conflicts, in one form or another, which centre on the system of cheap labour.

This struggle began long before 1948 when the conditions discussed above began to emerge (and control measures to be taken), but the particularly rapid urbanization and industrialization fostered by the Second World War sharpened and intensified the trends we have been discussing and the resultant conflicts. The 1940s were characterized by the variety and extent of the industrial and political conflicts especially in the urban, but also in the rural areas. In the period 1940-49 1,684,915 (including the massive strike of African mineworkers in 1946) African man-hours were lost as compared with 171,088 in the period 1930-1939. Thousands of African workers participated in squatters' movements and bus boycotts. In 1946 the first steps were taken towards an alliance of African, Coloured and Indian political movements and this was followed by mass political demonstrations. Towards the end of the 1940s a new force—militant African intellectuals—appeared on the scene. There were militant rural struggles at Witzieshock and in the Transkei. These were some of the signs of the growing assault on the whole society (and the structure of cheap labour-power which underpinned it) which confronted the capitalist state in 1948 . . .

. . . the policy of Apartheid developed as a response to this urban and rural challenge to the system which emerged inexorably from the changed basis of cheap labour-power. What was at stake was nothing less than the reproduction of the labour-force, not in general, but in a specific form, in the form of cheap labour-power. Within its framework Apartheid combined both institutionalizing and legitimating mechanism and, overwhelmingly, coercive measures.

It is beyond the scope of the present paper to set out in any detail the structure of coercive control erected by the Nationalist Government. In a fuller account it would be necessary to do this and to show how Apartheid, as a response to the principal contradiction between capital and cheap African labour, ramifies out and penetrates into the secondary contradictions which in turn have, to some extent, a reciprocal effect on the system. It will be sufficient at this point to refer to three aspects of the mainly coercive mechanisms of Apartheid . . .

. . . At the most general level, that of control of the African political challenge, Apartheid entails the removal of the limited rights which Africans and Coloureds had in the Parliamentary institutions of the White State; the revision of old and the introduction of a whole complex of new repressive laws which make illegal militant organized opposition (e.g. Suppression of Communism, Unlawful Organisations and Sabotage Acts, etc.), and the building of all-powerful agencies of control—security police, Bureau of State Security, the army, and police and army civilian reserves, etc.

In the economic sphere measures have been introduced to prevent or contain the accumulation of pressure on the level of wages. Most obvious in this regard is the Natives (Settlement of Disputes) Act which makes it illegal for Africans to strike for higher wages or improved working conditions. This, coupled both with the fact that African trade unions are not legally recognized and that their organization is impeded also by other measures, has effectively prevented the emergence of an African trade union movement capable of having any significant effect on wages. The decline in industrial strikes since 1948 and the tendency of real wages for Africans to fall indicates the success of Government policy.

Less obvious, but having the same purpose of controlling the development of strong African pressure for higher wages, are the important measures introduced by the Nationalist Government relating to African job and geographical mobility. The nature and meaning of these measures has been obscured by the terms of the relevant laws and the Government's policy statements to the effect that Africans were to be regarded only as temporary migrants in the urban areas, there only as long as they ministered to White needs.

The Pass Laws and the Native Urban Areas Act 1925 which regulated the right of residence in urban areas, were, of course, available in 1948. The 'modernization' of the Pass Laws (under the Native (Abolition of Passes and Coordination of Documents Acts) and the establishment of labour bureaux which serve to direct African workers to where White employers require them has been effected through a battery of amendments to old laws and the introduction of new laws which give the State exceptionlly wide powers to order Africans out of one area and into another. There are practically no legal limitations on these powers which can be used to remove 'excess' Africans from areas where their labour is not required or 'troublesome' Africans to outlying, isolated areas where they will be politically harmless. All Africans are, legally, only temporary residents in the urban areas.

These facts have been interpreted as meaning that the Government has elaborated and perfected the migrant labour system. Control over residence and movement is clearly one essential element of a system based on a migrant labour force, but it is not the only one. Therefore, to treat the increase in the State's legal power to declare Africans temporary sojourners in the urban area and to move them as exigencies demand as constituting the 'modernization' of the system, without taking account of changes in its economic basis, is insufficient. In the present case it results in the failure to grasp the essential changes in the nature of capitalist exploitation in South Africa. It has been the main contention of this paper that in South Africa the migrant labour-force, *properly speaking*, did not mean *merely* a mobile labour force, or a labour force that could be made mobile, that is that could be directed and redirected to where it was required. Above all, a *migrant* labour-force is labour-force which is both mobile *and* which has a particular economic basis in the pre-capitalist Reserve economy. With the disappearance of that economic basis, I have argued, the problems of curtailing industrial action and of political control over Africans in the urban areas became extremely acute. That control is exercised, in part, by repressive measures including, importantly, the elaboration of the State's power over the residence and movement of labour. That is to say, the extension of the State's power over the residence and movement of the labour force, which adds to the State's repressive control over it (precisely, one feature of Apartheid) is a function of the economic changes in the Reserves which generate a threat to the cheapness of labour-power . . .

. . . There is . . . little to suggest that, in the first few years of rule, the Nationalist Party had a fully worked out policy in relation to the Reserves or one which differed significantly from that of earlier governments. There are, however, two important points to be noted.

Firstly, the Government already had clearly in mind the establishment of an apparatus of control which would be cheap to run and acceptable to the African people. The 1951 Bantu Authorities Act which strengthened the political authority of the (compliant) chiefs, subject to the control of the State—indirect rule—was the first (and, at the outset, very conflictual) step in that direction. Secondly, political control in the Reserves was obviously recognized to be no solution to the problem of the never-ending enlargement of a working-class totally removed from the Reserves. In this the Government accepted, by implication, the contention, emphasized by the Native Laws Commission (1948), that the flow of people off the land and into the urban areas was an economic process . . .

Whatever the reasons, by 1959 the Government's policy began to change in significant respects. Without attempting to set out a chronological record, I want to analyse the emergence after 1959 of separate development as the mode of maintaining cheap labour in the Reserves (complementing that in the urban areas) which takes as given the changes in the African 'tribal' economies and erects, under the overarching power of the capitalist state, an institutionalized system of partial political control by Africans. That is to say, the practice and policy of Separate Development must be seen as the attempt to retain, in a modified form, the structure of the 'traditional' societies, not, as in the past, for the purposes of ensuring an economic supplement to the wages of the migrant labour force, but for the purposes of reproducing and exercising control over a cheap African industrial labour force in or near the 'homelands', not by means of preserving the precapitalist mode of production but by the political, social, economic and ideological enforcement of low levels of subsistence.

In 1959, in the Parliamentary debate on the Promotion of Bantu Self-Government Act, the Prime Minister Dr. Verwoerd stated:

> . . . if it is within the capacity of the Bantu, and if those areas which are allocated to him for his emancipation, or rather, which are already his own, can develop *into full independence*, then it will develop in this way. (Hansard, 1959, Cols. 6520.)

This was echoed by Vorster in 1968 (Hansard Col. 3947):

> We have stated very clearly that we shall lead them to independence.

Significantly, the ideological shift from White supremacy to self-determination and independence was accompanied by a parallel alteration in the ideology of race. Thus, whereas in all its essentials Nationalist Party ideology had previously insisted upon the biological inferiority of Africans as the justification for its racialist policies, as the Government was impelled towards the Bantustan policy so it began to abandon certain of its previous ideological positions. Now the stress fell upon ethnic *differences* and the central notion became 'different but equal' . . .

. . . There is an obvious necessity for this ideological change since a policy of ethnic political independence (for each of the eight ethnic groups identified) was incompatible with an ideology of racial inferiority. Nor would the latter have facilitated the attempt to set up the complex machinery of government and administration intended, in fact, to institutionalize relations between the State and the Reserves *and* to carry out certain administrative functions necessary for economic development in the Reserves. What all this amounts to, as one writer has expressed it, is 'racialism without racism'.

The Transkei Constitution Act was passed in 1963(8) and provided for a legislative assembly to exercise control over finance, justice, interior, education, agriculture and forestry, and roads and works. The Republican Government retains control, *inter alia*, over defence, external affairs, internal security, postal and related services, railways, immigration, currency, banking and customs. It need hardly be stressed that this arrangement in no way approaches political independence. At the same time it must not be overlooked that within limits, set both by the Constitution and the available resources, the Transkeian Government exercises real administrative power. By this means the South African State is able to secure the execution of certain essential social control and administrative functions at low cost particularly as a considerable portion of Government expenditure can be obtained through increased general taxes. Thus in 1971 the Transkeian Government's budget was £18 million of which £3½ million was obtained through taxation of Transkeian citizens.

It is, however, in the sphere of economic development that the emerging role of the Reserves can be seen most clearly. I am not here referring to the rather minor role of the various development corporations (Bantu Development Corporation, Xhosa Development Corporation and so on) in fostering economic development in the Reserves. In fact, up to the present they have largely served to assist small traders and commercial interests by means of loans—that is, they appear to be instruments for the nurturing of a petit-bourgeoisie and have little to do with economic growth in the reserves. Far more important is the State's policy of industrial decentralization . . .

. . . There are three aspects of the situation which need to be stressed. Firstly, neither the provisions of the Industrial Conciliation Act nor Wages Act determinations made for other regions apply to the border industries. This is extremely important in two respects. Since the Industrial Conciliation Act is inapplicable, Section 77 which empowers the Minister of Labour to reserve certain jobs for particular racial groups also does not apply and neither do the provisions of industrial agreements which reserve the higher paid skilled jobs for White workers. This being so it becomes possible to employ Africans in jobs which, in the 'White' areas, are the exclusive preserve of white workers. The effect of this, in conjunction with the inapplicability of wage determinations for other areas, is that a totally different and much lower wage structure becomes possible and has arisen.

Secondly, as elsewhere, African trade unions are not recognized and the provisions of the Natives (Settlement of Disputes) Act apply.

The third, and in some ways perhaps the most important aspect, relates to the conditions of life of the African workers in the Border industries. Not only, as has already been indicated, is the level of subsistence extremely low in the 'homelands' but in addition there are virtually no urban areas which might tend to increase this level. The assessment by the State, employers' organizations and so on, of African subsistence requirements in the Reserves is much lower than in the main industrial centres. This fact is not altered (or, at least will not be altered for a considerable period) by the necessity of establishing townships of some kind for the housing of workers employed in industry. It is an interesting index of the State's policy that a major item of expenditure for the so-called development of the Reserves has been for town-planning . . .

. . . The towns planned will be, no doubt, simple in the extreme, supplying little in the way of the complex services and infrastructure of the 'White' urban areas. Despite the State's expenditure all the indications are that what will be established will be rural village slums(9) alleviated marginally, if the Transkei is typical, by the allocation of garden allotments for the purpose of the production of vegetables, etc., which, incidentally, will no doubt provide the rationale for lower wages . . .

CONCLUSION

The argument in this paper shows that Apartheid cannot be seen merely as a reflection of racial ideologies and nor can it be reduced to a simple extension of Segregation.

Racial ideology in South Africa must be seen as an ideology which sustains and reproduces capitalist relations of production. This ideology and the political practice in which it is reflected is in a complex, reciprocal (although asymmetrical) relationship with changing social and economic conditions. The response of the dominant classes to the changing conditions, mediated by these ideologies, produces the two faces of domination—Segregation and Apartheid.

The major contradiction of South African society between the capitalist mode of production and African pre-capitalist economies is giving way to a dominant contradiction *within* the capitalist economy. The consequences of this is to integrate race relations with capitalist relations of production to such a degree that the challenge to the one becomes of necessity a challenge to the other. Whether capitalism still has space (or time) for reform in South Africa is an issue which must be left to another occasion.

NOTES

(1) See for example: Transvaal Local Government Commission of 1922 (Stallard Commission) T.P. 1-122; Native Land Commission (Beaumont Commission) 26-1916; Native Economic Commission 1930-1932 (U.G. 22, 1932); Social and Economic Planning Council—Report No. 9: The Native Reserves and Their Place in the Economy of the Union of South Africa (U.G. 32/1946); Report of the Commission for the Socio-Economic Development of the Bantu Areas Within the Union of South Africa (Summary) (U.G. 61/1955) (Tomlinson Commission); Native Lands Act 1913; Native Trust and Lands Act 1936; Native (Urban Areas) Consolidation Act 1945 and subsequent amendments; Bantu Authorities Act 1951.

(2) For a critique of this approach see Wolpe (1970).

(3) Althusser's (1971) essay 'Ideology and Ideological State Apparatuses is relevant on this point. Althusser (p. 124) suggests that:

> ... in order to exist, every social formation must reproduce the conditions of its production at the same time as it produces, and in order to be able to produce. It must therefore reproduce: 1. the productive forces, and 2. the existing relations of production.

The reproduction of both the forces (that is, labour power) and the relations of production are secured for the most part

> ... by the exercise of State power in the State Apparatus, on the one hand the (Repressive) State Apparatus, on the other the Ideological State Apparatus. (Althusser 1971: 141.)

See also, Poulantzos, N., 'The Problem of the Capitalist State', *New Left Review*, November-December 1969, No. 58, p. 67.

(4) Considerable historical material on this point can be found in Simons and Simons (1969).

(5) For a good outline of this history see Legassick (1972).

(6) The explanation of why this occurred rather than an intensification of trade relations adverse to the Reserves is related both to the interest of mining capital in labour rather than in the agricultural product and to the utilisation of State power by Afrikaner farmers vulnerable to competition from Africans. For an elaboration of this aspect see Legassick (1972).

(7) See note 1 for the full reference. The Commission was appointed to enquire into the socio-economic development (sic) of the Reserves.

(8) Other Bantustans are in various stages of formation.

REFERENCES

Althusser, L. (1971) *Lenin and Philosophy*, London, New Left Books.

Arrighi, G. (1970), 'Labour Supplies in Historical Perspective: A study of the Proletarianization of the African Peasantry in Rhodesia', *Journal of Development Studies*, pp. 197-234.

Asherson, R. (1969) 'South Africa: Race and Politics', *New Left Review* 53, January-February 1955.

Bundy, C. (1971) 'The Response of African Peasants in the Cape to Economic Changes, 1870-1910: A Study in Growth and Decay', unpublished Seminar Paper, *Institute of Commonwealth Studies*, London.

Gervassi, S. (1970) *Industrialization, Foreign Capital and Forced Labour in South Africa*, United Nations, ST/PSCA/Set A./10.

Horwitz, R. (1967) *The Political Economy of South Africa*, London, Weidenfeld and Nicholson.

Johnstone, R. (1970) 'White Prosperity and White Supremacy in South Africa Today', *African Affairs* Vol. 69, No. 275.

Kuper, L. and Smith, M. G. (1969) *Pluralism in Africa*, University of California Press.

Legassick, M. (1971) 'Development and Underdevelopment in South Africa', unpublished Seminar Paper for the Southern Africa Group, The Royal Institute of International Affairs, Chatham House, London.

Legassick, M. (1972) 'South Africa: Forced Labour, Industrialization, and Racial Differentiation', to be published in a forthcoming volume in a series on the political economy of the Third World edited by Richard Harris.

Meilassoux, C. (1972) 'From Reproduction to Production', *Economy and Society* Vol. I, No. 1, p. 93.

Rhoodie, N.J. (1969) *Apartheid and Racial Partnership in South Africa*, Pretoria, Academica.

Schapera, I. (1947) *Migrant Labour and Tribal Life*, London, Oxford University Press.

Simons, H.J. and R.E. (1969) *Class and Colour in South Africa 1850-1950*, London, Penguin African Library.

Trapido, S. (1971) 'South Africa in a Comparative Study of Industrialization',- *Journal of Development Studies*, Vol. 7, No. 3, 309.

Van Der Horst, S. (1971) *Native Labour in South Africa*, Cass.

Van Der Horst, S. (1965) 'The Effects of Industrialization on Race Relations in South Africa', in Hunter, G. (Ed.), *Industrialization and Race Relations*, London, Oxford University Press.

Van Den Berghe, P. (1967) *South Africa: A Study in Conflict*, University of California Press.

Wilson, M. (1971) 'The Growth of Peasant Communities', in Wilson, M. and Thompson, L. (Eds.), *The Oxford History of South Africa*, Vol. II, Chapter II, London, Oxford University Press.

Wolpe, H. (1970) 'Industrialization and Race in South Africa', in Zubaida, S. (Ed.), *Race and Racialism*, London Tavistock Publications.

Wolpe, H. (1971) 'Class, Race and the Occupational Structure in South Africa', Paper delivered to the World Sociology Congress, September 1970.

URBAN REVOLT IN SOUTH AFRICA: A CASE STUDY

Edward Feit

This article has as its theme the organisation of an African urban revolt in South Africa from 1960 to 1965. Reference is made mainly to events in Port Elizabeth and its near neighbour, East London; it need hardly be added that there were similar developments in other parts of the country. The way in which the revolt was organised was little reported at the time, and the details emerged only in the verbatim court records of the trials of both leaders and followers. Press reports of these trials are scattered over a number of South African newspapers, whose reporting — while good — is not as detailed as the documents; and a few items appear in the overseas press. The importance of this revolt, which is still being waged from outside South Africa's borders, might justify an analysis of what took place in the country itself, even if the research on which it is based remains incomplete.

Few African countries can rival South Africa in the richness of available documentation, and this applies to court records particularly. Verbatim records, as public documents, are available to scholars, and provide a mine of information on African resistance to the South African Government. It is these records that form the raw material of this article. They are of value because South Africa still has an independent judiciary and its court procedures are based on the adversary system. There are no 'staged' trials with carefully rehearsed evidence, put on for propaganda purposes. As a result, court records can be used with reasonable confidence.

Court records, as research sources, have obvious advantages. They are the work of many hands. They often contain biographical details of those involved which would otherwise not be obtainable. The main body consists of questions and answers, the answers of one side being tested by the other. It ends with the summing-up of a judge, who in South Africa, as in Britain, is drawn from the ranks of lawyers with long years of court experience.

There are, however, flies in the research ointment. Using court records does, in fact, involve formidable problems of analysis, and it may be as well to summarise these briefly. Men on trial are in jeopardy. They are accused of criminal acts, carrying penalties. Even where innocent, they can hardly be expected to tell the whole truth, as this could well be damaging to their case. The witnesses called on both sides, often men who have turned State's evidence, are afraid not only of involving themselves more deeply, but also of retribution from those remaining in the organisation when the trial is over. Both are often overawed by the procedures and protocol of the courts, which are designed to be awe-inspiring.

Added to all this is the nature of the legal system itself. Evidence brought to court is selected by interested parties. It is brought to help one or the other side and to frustrate the case of the opponent. The whole evidence, in all its details, seldom sees the light of day. At the same time, the accused is brought to court on a specific charge, and anything unrelated to the charge is considered irrelevant. Thus the research worker will find that what seemed a vein of promising enquiry is shut off by a curt comment from the Bench.

These difficulties are freely admitted; but there is so much important material in these court records that their careful sifting here seems justified. To avoid prejudice, the evidence of both accused and accusers was largely ignored, and only that of witnesses considered. Witnesses in court are not, of course, completely reliable. Often they are giving evidence on events that took place months or even years earlier. Often they are inexact in recalling the times and places where events occurred, and they are not always truthful. Were one to wait for such a witness, one would have to wait a long time. What is necessary is satisfaction beyond reasonable doubt that *in its essential details* the story told was true.(1) The story must contain a hard core of evidence which remains unshaken in essence, no matter how much counsel chips away at it. Such evidence has been sought and used in this essay. The judgement of a witness's truthfulness was made easier by the number of trials, held at different times in different towns, which permitted comparison of the organisation of the African underground in various places. The evidence of one set of witnesses could, thus, be used to corroborate that of others. The picture to be presented is, in this way, perhaps as truthful a one as can be obtained.

The court cases, it should be clear, were not sought out for their legal implications, but for the purposes of understanding an urban revolt as it affected the lowest reaches of the organisation—less the leadership than the often neglected foot-soldiers. To describe the revolt in all parts of the country would be beyond the scope of a brief article. The revolt considered is that which the African National Congress and the Communist Party of South Africa organised through *Umkonto we Sizwe*— the 'Spear of the Nation'.

THE A.N.C. AND THE 'M' PLAN

Until 1944 the African National Congress had been largely an organisation of the African elite. It had confined its activities to attempts to work within the framework of the South African constitution, and to secure change by petitions and appeals. The feeling in the A.N.C. changed after the war until, with the victory of the A.N.C. Youth League in 1949, a more militant course was adopted. Militancy was, however, to be by demonstration only, and violence was expressly eschewed. Allying themselves with the South African Indian Congress, and later with a variety of other Congresses, each for one of the main racial groups in the country, which together made up the Congress Alliance, they undertook a series of campaigns which, despite some spectacular demonstrations, proved largely abortive. In 1958 the momentum of the A.N.C. seemed largely spent. The organisation split in two, with the more nationalist wing breaking away as the Pan-Africanist Congress.

The Pan-Africanist Congress, in its turn, launched a militant campaign against the 'pass' laws, which led to rioting and demonstrations all over the country, the Sharpeville incident being the most publicised. Faced with intense African unrest, the Government declared a state of emergency in April 1960, and it was illegal to belong to either the A.N.C. or the P.A.C.—whose leaders were detained—or to carry them on in any form. Both organisations, confronted with this ban, decided to go underground when the emergency was lifted and their leaders were released.

The end of the emergency, late in 1960, allowed the leaders the opportunity of regrouping their scattered forces. The process began early in the Eastern Cape, particularly Port Elizabeth, long an A.N.C. stronghold.(2) Secret meetings were called in response to a directive of the national executive committee of the African National Congress, now in hiding, explaining how the organisation was now to function.(3)

The meetings ran very much to pattern. At each the convener announced that he had been appointed the chief steward of the zone, and that all those present were appointed cell stewards. Because the organisation was now underground, public meetings could no longer be called. Communications with Africans outside the A.N.C. were to be kept open by leaflets and through ostensibly 'social' gatherings such as tea parties. The zone itself, with its own chief steward, was to consist of a number of streets, each street having its own cell. The cell stewards, in turn, were to recruit seven additional members each, whose identity would not be known to any other cell. Secret meetings would then be held by each cell, the venue alternating among the houses of the members to prevent detection.(4)

In addition to linking the cells of his zone, the chief steward was the link with the higher bodies of the underground organisation, the regional committees. He would apprise those below of the decisions of the leaders, and would convey to the leaders both what was done and what was felt by the rank-and-file. He was not, however, to have direct access to the leadership. This was to be done through another man, termed the 'contact'; (5) the regional committees in turn were linked by other 'contacts' to the national executive committee.

Various steps were taken at all levels to ensure that the organisation should remain secret. Old membership cards of the A.N.C. were to be destroyed, and no new ones issued. Instead of cards, members paying their dues would be issued a receipt with a bird emblem, which gave no name and only the house number.(6) The receipts were issued against new, higher membership fees, which had been raised from about 4s. 2d. per annum to 2s. 4d. per month. This sum, small as it seems, was a large one for Africans, and was intended both to provide financial resources and to induce among the members a greater sense of purpose and organisational effort.(7)

This plan had been mooted since the 1950s, although a serious effort to put it into effect was something new. Named the 'M-Plan' after its originator, Nelson Mandela, it was intended to frustrate police vigilance and to prevent the breaking up of the organisation by the police. It was only meagrely implemented while the A.N.C. was still lawful, and was largely ignored by the branches in the country as a whole.(8) As the plan, by setting up a cell system, would virtually end the operations of formal branches, it was resisted by A.N.C. men, whose strength lay in the branches they had organised largely by virtue of their own authority and personality.

As formulated, the M-Plan was to replace the structure of branches, provincial committees, and annual conferences by the system of cells, zones and regional committees briefly outlined above.

After the organisation was banned and driven underground, it seemed that the M-Plan might be put into effect.(9) 'Contracts' recruited chief stewards, who in turn found others willing to be cell stewards. All officials were now to be appointed in terms of the plan. In its days of legality, the A.N.C. had been a highly democratic organisation, in principle. All officers were elected and, while the elections often left much to be desired, 'packed' meetings and intimidation frequently being used, election to office was still the rule. Now all office holders had to be appointed from above, being advised of their appointment by the official one rank higher. However much the men of the A.N.C. may have deplored this method, it was the only one practicable for a secret organisation. Appointment as, say, a chief steward could not be refused, according to some court witnesses; but refusal was unlikely in the event, as the appointees felt honoured by the appointment.(10) Once appointed, the 'contacts' told the chief stewards how to go about implementing the M-Plan in their zones.(11) Appointments from above meant that those above had powers of removal also. A chief steward who, for instance, failed to make his receipts tally with what he sent on to headquarters could be reduced to cell steward, and this seems to have happened more than once.(12)

With the appointment of chief stewards, the building up of cells seems to have stagnated. The cell stewards failed to find more members, so that they themselves became, in effect, the lowest-ranking members of the organisation, the ordinary members, while the chief stewards were, in effect, cell stewards. Few new members joined the ranks of the underground A.N.C. after it had been initiated.(13)

Chief stewards were not the only officers appointed at the zone level; there was, in addition, a prime steward, whose exact duties have been only vaguely delineated by various witnesses. He was above the chief steward in some things, it seems, but not in others. Some said that the prime stewards were really in charge of the A.N.C. volunteers, a body that had sworn to undertake anything, including murder, for the Congress. Others again said that the prime steward was mainly responsible for organising fund-raising functions, such as the tea parties referred to above.(14) The only firm conclusion is that, where the underground organisation became increasingly concerned with violence, the prime steward was the man in charge. In other areas, however, he remained under the chief steward.

The change to the M-Plan was not accepted without demur. The officers of the old organisational entities resisted the change. Those of the Youth League in Port Elizabeth, for example, on hearing of the directive to disband, visited their counterparts in Grahamstown, an important inland centre of the Eastern Cape, in the hope of gaining their support in rejecting the M-Plan. This, however, proved futile. The Youth League in Grahamstown had apparently been convinced, and were already beginning to implement the plan.(15) As a result, those who resisted the innovation were isolated, and sometimes dropped out of the A.N.C. altogether. This meant, in the long run, that those likely to prove 'weak-willed' in the matter of violence were weeded out.

The aim of the underground, at the outset, was to avoid arrest at all costs. Meetings were rotated among the homes of the different members of what was termed the zone but was in effect a cell. An additional precaution was that each zone (or cell) held its meeting on a different night of the week, though each zone retained the same night. Thus, if Zone G, say, met on Tuesdays, it would always meet on Tuesdays, while Zone B might meet on, say, Wednesdays. This practice would be observed until the cell was broken by the police.(16) The meetings themselves little resembled the social gatherings so dear to Africans. Coming singly or in small groups, members would assemble, hear the information given by the chief steward, ask questions if need be, and the meeting would disperse. The idea, as one witness put it, was to get it over quickly, before the police arrived.(17)

Attendance at cell meetings was compulsory, and such members as could not attend had to make their excuses to the chief steward—who could order disciplinary punishment—besides finding out from others in the cell, or from the chief steward himself, the house where the next meeting was to be held. This was only announced at the meeting itself, again for the sake of secrecy.(18) The prolonged absence of any member was viewed as tantamount to defection, unless excused, while attendance was accepted as membership. The small size of the group made it unnecessary to keep formal membership records, and absences stood out. Although no compulsion was exerted on members to remain in the movement, any who left were suspect, being considered already as informers—as indeed was often the case.(19) Sometimes the fears backfired. One man, for instance, who had already informed the police, but whose actions were not known to his fellows, continued attending meetings for fear of discovery and retribution.(20)

Perhaps the most astonishing thing about the underground A.N.C. was that, despite the unhappy situation of Africans in South Africa, recruitment was so slow and new recruits so few. And it should be borne in mind that, in speaking of recruitment for an illegal organisation, one must think in tens rather than in hundreds or thousands. That the movement remained largely with the original cell stewards might thus seem strange. Part of the explanation may be that those who joined the underground initially were mostly those who had come to the movement in the militant fifties and, even of these, not all came back. Once the hard core of the A.N.C. was thus exhausted, there was little else for the organisation to draw on. Where new recruits were added—and there seem to have been only a few instances of this—there were not more than one or two for each cell.(21)

Recruitment involved another problem, that of 'vetting' the new members. From what witnesses said later, it would appear that recruits were not selected by any particular process, nor were they subjected to any tests.(22) The individual cell stewards were free to recruit whom they pleased except government employees; as one witness humorously put it, 'We did not go around recruiting *them.*'(23) A newly recruited member was simply brought to the meeting, introduced to the others as a comrade, and that was that. His *bona fides* were unquestioningly accepted. This allowed, as can be imagined, for police penetration. Indeed there are cases of non-commissioned officers in the police being accepted into cells virtually on their first day in a town.(24) Possibly the question of accepting all recruits arose out of their scarcity value. Members felt that only the hot-headed would seek A.N.C. membership, and that this was in itself a guarantee of good faith.(25) Self-selection would thus replace more formal processing.

The time has now come to speak of two further series of meetings which also determined the course of urban revolt in South Africa.

THE RISE AND FALL OF *UMKONTO WE SIZWE*

The change from a policy of non-violence, espoused by the A.N.C. since its foundation, to one of violence was bound to be instituted only after much heart-searching. The break with the past was made in June 1961, when it was decided that the A.N.C., with its allies, and with the Communist Party particularly, would create a new organisation, to perform sabotage and to be the nucleus of a future military force.(26) This was to be called *Umkonto we Sizwe*, whose members were *Madelakufe*—those who despise death. *Umkonto* became a part of a larger plan, named 'Operation *Mayebuye*' (literally 'Operation Come Back', meaning that South Africa should 'come back' to the hands of the Black people). Operation *Mayebuye* was intended to have three stages: first of all, the building up of the underground; then a sabotage campaign, to be carried out concurrently with the sending of men abroad for guerrilla training; finally, a full-scale guerrilla war, of the sort envisaged by Che Guevara, was to be launched. Indeed, Guevara's book, *Guerrilla Warfare*, was a standard text among the *Madelakufe*.

The A.N.C. leaders hoped, of course, that it would not be necessary to put all stages of Operation *Mayebuye* into effect. The sabotage campaign, directed mainly against government buildings, and not intended to involve loss of life, would, it was hoped, frighten Whites into making concessions in favour of Africans. Only if the sabotage campaign did not work out as planned, was the guerrilla campaign to be launched, and violence to be unlimited. In such a case, outside aid, both arms and funds, was to be actively solicited. Once Operation *Mayebuye* was well and truly launched, an invasion of foreign troops would be procured from sympathetic countries, particularly the Soviet Union or other East European powers.(27) The second phase was clearly the most crucial. It was then the fate of the insurrection would be determined. To ensure success, arrangements were made with a number of African states for the training of saboteurs and guerrilla fighters. The idea was that the men so trained would return to South Africa and train others in their turn.(28)

The plan involved a complete *volte face* for the A.N.C. leaders. For years they had been preaching non-violence to their members. Now they had to persuade the same members to assist in implementing the new policy. The change was made known in stages. First, meetings were called in the major centres in June 1961 and at later times elsewhere. Members were told then that non-violence was no longer enjoined on them. Then, at later meetings, at the beginning of 1962, the formation of *Umkonto* and its relationship to the A.N.C. was made known.

Fears that the A.N.C. leaders would lose their following by espousing violence were quickly belied. The new policy was received happily, for as one member put it, they felt that they would now get their freedom.(29) The first announcement, in 1961, was limited in its scope. Violence was to be used against police officers who tried to break up cell meetings or who tried to prevent the distribution of leaflets. To this end, members were urged to arm themselves with any weapons they could find, devise, or steal. 'Revolvers, swords, or even axes' should be employed.(30) Police were not the only ones to be singled out. Africans who collaborated with the police or who refused to participate in Congress campaigns were also to be attacked.(31)

Intimidation was, of course, nothing new to the A.N.C. It had taken place even when the organisation was officially committed to non-violence. Reviewing the story of the A.N.C., it would seem that at all times they were more concerned with non-violence against Whites than against their own people. As so often happens with radical movements, more brickbats are hurled among the faithful than are hurled at the foe in front.

Violence took place when attempts were made to mobilise the African population behind some A.N.C. campaigns. One example was the 'National Day of Mourning', held on 26 June 1962. On that day Africans were told not to use municipal buses (the only ones serving the townships of Port Elizabeth), but to walk to work. Other municipal services were also to be boycotted, such as electricity; people should use candles to illuminate their homes. No one should listen to the government-controlled radio. Many Africans complied, either because they believed in the cause of the A.N.C., or through fear; but many did not. As a result, fights broke out among supporters and non-supporters of the A.N.C., and buses were stoned, passengers coming home from work attacked, and many injured on both sides.(32) Typically, the picketing of the bus stops was not done systematically but was haphazard. No zone had apparently been told to picket any particular bus stops, so pickets were mounted in piecemeal fashion. Nevertheless, the boycott was fairly effective, though it is hard to say just how effective it was. If death is a measure, it can be said that numbers were killed.

The directive to resist the police was also put into effect. The most serious result was the killing of Major O. Kjelvie, District Commandant of Police for Port Elizabeth, who was stabbed to death when attempting to stop a group of A.N.C. volunteers on the night before the 'Day of Mourning'. Major Kjelvie's death brought forth a show of force from the police, and the arrest of over 100 A.N.C. volunteers. (33) As the investigating officer for Port Elizabeth put it in evidence, things were absolutely abnormal in the Eastern Cape from 1961, and reached a peak in 1962, during which time Africans did all in their power to impede the police. Barricades of petrol drums were improvised, as well as of large stones and other heavy objects. Nails to puncture the tyres of police vehicles were thrown in the streets. Only the arrest of some 800 Africans in the following year, according to this officer, restored the situation to norma.(34)

Such was the atmosphere among Africans when *Umkonto* was announced in 1962. A few words about this formation might be in order here. After the national executive of the A.N.C. had given its members permission to undertake violent acts, intermittent incidents took place in August 1961. This was a dress rehearsal, it would seem, for the main campaign launched in December of that their forbears over the Zulu chieftain Dingane, a concerted series of bomb explosions took place in three of the principal South African cities—Johannesburg, Durban, and Cape Town. At the same time a manifesto was distributed in the townships and pasted up on walls and telegraph poles in the White areas, announcing the formation of *Umkonto*. It was, it said, 'the front line of the people's defence . . . . the fighting arm of the people against the Government in its policies of race suppression . . . the striking force of the people for liberty, rights, and their final liberation'.(35)

As far as can be determined, *Umkonto* was to be run separately from the A.N.C. and from the Communist Party, although its multi-racial leadership was to be drawn from both. There was at that time a considerable overlapping between the leadership of the Communist Party and the A.N.C., as many African leaders turned to the Communists from conviction or despair. There were other reasons also. For one thing, the Communist Party had, since the 1920s, been the only South African political party which had admitted Africans to all ranks and offices, and invited their participation. Banned in 1950 and reconstituted in 1953, the party had come out in its own colours in 1960. It continued its tactics of working for African support and penetrating and manipulating African organisations. As a result, when *Umkonto* was brought into being, its leaders, White and African, were either card-carrying members of the party, or so close to the party position as made no difference. Those who were not of such mind were frozen out of *Umkonto*. Indeed, the close affiliation of that organisation with the Communist Party was to cause considerable friction between the A.N.C. and *Umkonto* at the regional level. At the same time the rise of *Umkonto*, and the transfer of the most active leaders to it, deprived the A.N.C. of much of its strength, and it declined in such efficacy as it possessed and interest as it retained.(36)

In its structure *Umkonto* paralleled the A.N.C. in many particulars, though the names given to the different organisational elements were not the same. There was, for instance, a National High Command, determining over-all policy, and regional high commands, charged with the selection of targets for attack, subject to the approval of the national body. The actual work of sabotage would be done by the platoons and sections into which the A.N.C. volunteers were to be organised. A Volunteer-in-Chief in each zone would take his orders from the 'contact', who in turn received these from the regional high command. The way things were to be organised on the local level is less clear. It seems that *Umkonto* was organised into sections, each consisting of three men and a leader; four of these sections made up a platoon.(37)

In Port Elizabeth the men for the platoons and sections were recruited from among the members of the A.N.C. cells. In general, from the evidence, it seems that assignment to *Umkonto* was an honour. There would, on occasion, be a speech in praise of the man selected for service, one of which went like this: 'This man, you will not see him again, he is leaving us. You may see him off and on, perhaps at one meeting now and at a later meeting. He is leaving us. He is going into this other organisation, namely *Umkonto we Sizwe*, that is, the soldiers' organisation.(38) It was pointed out to the members of branches that those called on to serve should not refuse to do so, because men were needed. The members of *Umkonto* might still attend A.N.C. meetings, and sometimes did.

In any one area *Umkonto* in fact drew its members from several zones, and in a typical group one man might be drawn from one zone, two from another, and so on. No specific pattern was followed.(39) Indeed, men who had not been part of the A.N.C. cell structure were also recruited. Being a member of the A.N.C. did not automatically make one a member of *Umkonto*, and vice versa. In all, however, the membership of the A.N.C., the Communist Party, and *Umkonto* tended to overlap, and membership of all three was by no means rare.(40)

The A.N.C. members included not only young people but also old and unfit men and women. These were clearly unsuited to be either saboteurs or soldiers of a guerrilla army. So the policy was to recruit the most fit and active young men who were willing to join, train them, and send abroad those suitable for military training.(41) A good source of trainees was sometimes found among the socially rejected. In Natal, for instance, Bruno Mtolo writes of recruiting a contingent of pickpockets, who because of their hard life were considered ideal material.(42) In all, at least 300 men were sent overseas, particularly to Ethiopia and Algeria, but others as far afield as Communist China.

Those recruited to *Umkonto* were trained in practical methods of sabotage, and these were put to use. In the Eastern Cape, one of the most active of the regions, 63 acts of sabotage were undertaken, these being almost a third of the 193 acts for the country as a whole, recorded to 1964. Training was under the control of a series of specialised committees, the most important of which was the Technical Committee, charged with procuring the raw materials for bombs and with training members of *Umkonto* in making and handling them.(43) Members of the Communist Party, mostly Whites, were sent to the different centres to show how bombs could be made, and to urge members of *Umkonto* to steal explosives from government stocks.(44)

Although the organisation of the underground A.N.C. and of *Umkonto* represented considerable achievements under extreme pressure from a vigilant Government, its actual effects were considerably less than its leaders had hoped. The individual acts of sabotage, with few exceptions, were minor and did insignificant damage. The average monthly value of the damage done was about £90, and for the Eastern Cape it was about £5,800 in all. If the reported and unreported values of sabotage for the country as a whole are computed, they come to little more than £62,000 at the outside.(45) This is hardly enough damage to shake a modern industrial economy, particularly one whose budget runs to some £50 million. In other words, for all the courage and resourcefulness of the men who undertook sabotage, the damage they did had little more than nuisance value. It was certainly not on a scale either to shake the South African Government or to frighten the Whites into surrendering their privileged position. Doubtless, had the authorities not reacted so quickly to the sabotage, the intensity and scale of the attacks could well have increased. Indeed, without this, Operation *Mayebuye* might have become a reality.

Another factor that must be taken into account is that a number of the acts of sabotage included in the above totals were directed against Africans by *Umkonto*. There were some 16 attacks on informers, real or suspected, and on men who supported the Government's policy of separate development. There may have been more such attacks which went unreported, but there is no way of assessing this. These attacks often had tragic consequences. In one case two young girls, asleep in their uncle's house, were badly burned by a petrol bomb, one being fatally injured. But there were other cases where informers were not attacked at all, and continued to live among the friends and relatives of those they had betrayed. There is no clear pattern to the terrorism employed. Like much in the A.N.C. and *Umkonto*, action against men and against property seems to have been random and ill organised. It would be a mistake to think of all members of *Umkonto* as textbook insurgents, dedicated and efficient. On the whole they were poorly trained, scarcely directed, and often badly frightened. Although there are many instances illustrating this argument, the story of two men may serve as an example.(46)

The two men, Magwayi and Ngoza, were defendant and witness in one of the trials of *Umkonto* members. According to their evidence, after having been assigned to *Umkonto*, they were afraid to come to ordinary A.N.C. meetings as they feared betrayal. They were taught to make bombs by a member of the technical committee, and decided to use this knowledge to set fire to the premises and one of their former places of employment, a timber yard. This would, on the face of it, seem an excellent and inflammable target, but the saboteurs proved inept even at this. Their efforts led to no more than minor damage, as some of the bombs did not go off, and at least one petrol bomb was thrown without igniting. Their skill did improve subsequently, but was never very high.

What is significant is not only the level of skill, but the freedom of choice that saboteurs enjoyed, despite the supposed existence of a chain of command. Targets were supposedly to be cleared with the regional high command, but there is ample evidence that saboteurs made their own selections.(47) The local man largely decided, with his Volunteer-in-Chief, what was to be blown up or burned down. What was generally attacked was what lay most conveniently to hand. This, however, was not always the kind of target whose destruction would most harm the Government.

Military training was one of the main objectives of the *Umkonto* command. The men sent abroad were to be a nucleus of instructors, each of whom was to train another 20 men. Many of them were arrested on their return either to Rhodesia or to South Africa; again, the evidence of one might be taken to illustrate their general experiences. The man in question, one Metshane, had fled to Dar es Salaam, and was sent to Communist China for some two to three months. He returned to South Africa via Dar, and once back in Johannesburg regularly met the A.N.C. leaders, who paid him a salary of about £ 29 per month—a handsome sum for an African by South African standards. He had no particular duties, and did nothing much to earn the money. After a few months of this restful existence, Metshane was ordered to take a number of young African recruits to Bechuanaland, from where they would leave for training abroad. He undertook this task, but was arrested with his charges at the border.(48)

The motives of those who were recruited emerge in the court cases. Some state quite openly that they went because they wanted to fight for their freedom, to 'fight the Whites'.(49) Others went out of a sense of adventure. Others, again, were lured abroad with promises of education or scholarships. But there were others who had become so enmeshed in the toils of South Africa's racial laws that illegal exit was the only solution. The case of Mokgoro can serve to show what is meant. He existed in a kind of legal 'no-man's land', for he was forbidden to live in Johannesburg, his home town, and was ordered to go back to his birthplace, Kimberley. As it happened, he could not return there either, as he had been ordered to leave by a magistrate for some other offence. He was therefore instructed to go back to the rural site of his tribe, where he had not been before, knew nobody, and did not believe that he could make a living. Having no place to go, and having been a member of the A.N.C. Youth League, he turned to them. They told him he would only be helped if he was willing to go for military training abroad. Mokgoro was reluctant, but there seemed no alternative. Witnesses said he had made plain his intention of reneging on this promise as soon as he could in Bechuanaland. He never reached Bechuanaland, however, being arrested on the frontier with Metshane's party.(50)

The local branches of the A.N.C., during all this time, continued with their activities, though on a diminishing scale. In the main, their task was to support *Umkonto* financially through tea parties and concerts, and through strikes and boycotts. They also tried to keep open channels of communication with the African public by distributing leaflets. They did not, however, function very long after the launching of *Umkonto*. Many were discovered and their members arrested. The arrests usually began with a single member, who frequently gave evidence with little pressure. Asked why they had given information, they later said that the police seemed aware of everything that was going on, down to the details; it was evident, therefore, that someone else had talked, and there was little further point in silence.(51) Nothing could be gained, and for the individual everything could be lost, by not giving evidence. This attitude, needless to say, was encouraged by police interrogators. Another justification was that the leaders themselves had given evidence when brought to trial.(52)

Although most activity was shut down from 1964, there have been reports from time to time of a revival of the A.N.C. cells. Most of the activity of the A.N.C. has, however, been based on the building up of an army of 'Freedom Fighters' in Tanzania and Zambia. These have been making incursions into Rhodesia and South Africa, which are on the whole little reported. According to one report, however, there was great discontent among the recruits brought to Dar es Salaam from South Africa, who were told that they were being given educational bursaries, and who were expected to undertake military training instead.(53) It is difficult to know how much credence can be given to this report. All in all, however, it is apparent that nothing much is happening which can seriously threaten the stability of the South African state at this time.

WHY DID THE REVOLT FAIL?

There is much that potential revolutionaries can learn from the South African experience, and some of the lessons have already been emphasised elsewhere. The first is that it takes more than an act of will to launch a successful revolt. Che Guevara learnt this among the Bolivian peasants, and the A.N.C. in the African townships. The second is that a government is as capable of learning as are the revolutionaries. They are as able to alter their methods of attack as their opponents. They need not, as many revolutionaries believe, simply repeat their blunders on an ever-growing scale.

Clearly, there are several unique aspects of the situation in South Africa. Racial stratification has created what are, in effect, several co-existing nations. David Rapoport in a recent article has suggested that a distinction should be made between 'public' and 'population'. The 'public' in South Africa would be the Whites, who, in response to a disturbance in the 'non-public sphere', would be drawn together just as they would be against a foreign foe. The threat would be a threat to all. 'In their most mutinous days the Janissaries would meet a Christian disturbance as resolutely as a White army in South Africa is likely to deal with a Black uprising.'(54) The distinction provides the key to much of what has happened in South Africa. It explains why that country has so successfully repressed incipient revolution. In part this was due to very efficient police work and the errors and weaknesses of their opponents. But this does not explain all. The South African Government was able to act against the revolutionaries because it controlled a still relatively open 'public' polity, whereas for most of the 'population' the system was as closed and as rigid as human ingenuity could make it. Registration requirements and the web of restrictive laws, together with some limited economic rewards, served to keep them damped down, and allowed for the maximum control of dissidence.

Given the social set-up in South Africa, the Government could and would take any step, legal or administrative, to ensure internal peace. White society was efficiently organised, with little reason to defect. The administrative structure, drawn from the 'public', in whose interests it operated, was unlikely to be prey to corruption on any scale. Thus, despite the underground achievement of the A.N.C.

and the Communists, their organisation could only be of a rudimentary kind. Anything more complex was speedily broken up. The members of *Umkonto*, in many cases, were ready to go to any lengths to gain the freedom they prized, but they could never build up an organisation which could mount a campaign of sufficient strength to effect the desired changes. And they had to work in the shadow of police efficiency, never knowing who was in the pay of the police or who was betraying them for other reasons. The movement could not be expanded because of these factors. Fear of betrayal, the knowledge that the police were vigilantly investigating the organisation, and the problems of approaching others inhibited the growth of *Umkonto* and contributed to the speed with which it was discovered and destroyed.

NOTES

Since the full titles of the court cases are fairly long and difficult to abbreviate, they will be cited in the footnotes by the surname of the first accused, e.g. Bongco, Gcquabi, and the year of the trial concerned. An index of these surnames, in alphabetical order, giving full details of each case title and the place where it was heard, appears below:

Bongco: *State vs Washington Bongco and four others; Grahamstown.*

Gcquabi: *State vs Joe Gcquabi, SH J 241/63; Pretoria.*

Hlekani: *State vs Stanford Hlekani, RC 8/65; Addo, E. Cape.*

Khayingo: *State vs Ndodomzi Khayingo and Elliott Lloyd, RC 6/65; Addo, E. Cape.*

Makinane: *State vs Diliza Johnson Makinane and three others, RC 25/65; Humansdorp, E. Cape.*

Mapolisa: *State vs Joyce Mapolisa, RC 12/65; Addo, E. Cape.*

Magwayi: *State vs Magwayi and two others, RC 28/65; Humansdorp, E. Cape.*

Mbolompo: *State vs Willie Mbolompo and 44 other, RC 240/64; Cape Town.*

Mgalunkulu: *State vs Mountain Mgalunkulu and eight others, RC 26/65; Humansdorp, E. Cape.*

Mtalana: *State vs Douglas Mtalana and Maki Maxaki, RC 11/65; Humansdorp, E. Cape.*

Siwundla: *State vs Abner Themba Siwundla and five others, RC 20/64; Port Elizabeth.*

Tangala: *State vs Johannes Shadrack Tangala and George Mokgoro, 562/65; Johannesburg.*

Tshela: *State vs Clement Tshela and six others, RC 14/65; Humansdorp, E. Cape.*

Tsishela: *State vs Rosie Tsishela, RC 11/65; Humansdorp, E. Cape.*

In addition there is the Rivonia Trial, which is properly styled *State vs Nelson Mandela and nine others; Pretoria.*

All these handwritten, verbatim court records are available on microfilm from Microfile Ltd, Box 5425, Johannesburg.

(1) Judgement, Gcquabi (1963), p. 4.

(2) Africans live in separate 'locations', at some distance from the White suburbs. A description of life in these townships in the late 1950s and early 1960s can be found in a series of books published by Oxford University Press: D.H. Reader, *The Black Man's Portion* (London, 1961); P. Mayer, *Townsmen or*

Tribesmen (London, 1961); B.A. Pauw, *The Second Generation* (London, 1963); and Monica Wilson and Archie Mafeje, *Langa* (London, 1963). There are also interesting contemporary newspaper reports on the townships, for example the *Eastern Province Herald* (Port Elizabeth), 8 August 1966.

(3) Komani and Mashinyana in Kondoti (1964), pp. 196, 214, and 226; Magidwana in Tshela (1965), pp. 43-6; and Ngoza in Magwayi (1965), pp. 48-50.

(4) Joxo in Mtalana (1964), pp. 39-40; Tshume in Bongco (1964), pp. 172-5.

(5) Petros in Makinane (1965), pp. 44-6; Mashinyana and Mdube in Bongco (1964), pp. 231 and 362.

(6) Gulwa in Mapolisa (1965), pp. 8-9; Petros in Makinane (1965), pp. 33-4; Ngoza in Mgawayi (1965), p. 2; Mcblwana in Tsishela (1963), p. 30; Ngoza in Magwayi (1965), pp. 49-50; Gulwa in Mapolisa (1965), pp. 3-4; and Qumpula in Hlekani (1965), p. 1.

(7) Qumpula in Hlekani, p. 1; Magidwana in Tshela, p. 43; Petros in Makinane, p. 32; Ngoza in Magwayi, pp. 1-2 and 49-50; Dondashe in Mgalunkulu, p. 13; and Gulwa in Mapolisa, pp. 3-4. All these cases were heard in 1965.

(8) Mbanjwa in Mbolompo (1965), pp. 755-6 and 774.

(9) Ibid. p. 769.

(10) Dondashe in Mgalunkulu (1965), pp. 25-6.

(11) Tshume and Kumani in Bongco (1964), pp. 176, 196-9, and 214; Petros in Makinane (1965), pp. 45-6.

(12) Gulwa in Mapolisa (1965), pp. 3-4.

(13) Dondashe and Kulele in Mgalunkulu (1965), pp. 19, 50, 64-5, and 81; Petros in Makinane (1965), p. 49.

(14) Gulwa in Mapolisa, pp.3-4; Petros in Makinane, pp. 46-8; and Dondashe in Mgalunkulu, p. 30 (all heard in 1965).

(15) Njikalana in Siwundla (1964), pp. 16-23.

(16) Petros in Makinane (1965), pp. 82-3; Ngoza in Magwayi (1965), pp. 1-2; and Zepe in Mtalana (1964), pp. 20-3.

(17) Joxo in Mtalana (1964), p. 54; Gulwa in Mapolisa (1965), p.7.

(18) Gulwa in Mapolisa (1965), pp. 10-11; Zepe in Mtalana (1964), pp. 20 and 34.

(19) Kulelo in Mgalunkulu (1965), pp. 77 and 81; Mhlawuli in Mapolisa (1965). p. 23; Neingane in Makinane (1965), p. 118; and Tanana in Bongco (1964), p. 351.

(20) Mali in Magwayi (1965), pp. 114-17.

(21) Mtoloko and Mali, ibid. pp. 92 and 117-18; Zepe in Mtalana (1964), p. 47; and Pandashe and Kulelo in Mgalunkulu (1965), pp. 19 and 82.

(22) Ncingane in Makinane (1965), pp. 175-6; Zepe in Mtalana (1964), p. 37.

(23) Zepe, ibid.

(24) *Golden City Post* (Johannesburg), 23 August 1964.

(25) Kulelo in Mgalunkulu (1965), p. 82.

(26) See, for instance, Nelson Mandela, *No Easy Walk* (New York, 1965), p. 169.

(27) Mgemuntu in Mbolompo (1965), p. 13; Gungulu in Khayingo (1965), p. 17; and Mashinyana in Bongco (1964), p. 247.

(28) Tollie and Senna in Tangala (1965), pp. 93-5 and 196-7.

(29) Zepe and Joxo in Mtalana (1964), pp. 13 and 41-3; Magidwana in Tshela (1965), p. 47.

(30) Gulwa in Mapolisa (1965), pp. 5-7; Ngoza in Magwayi (1965), pp. 53-5. It is interesting to compare the instructions given by Lenin, who called for combat groups in the 1905 revolution to arm themselves with 'bombs, knives, knuckle-

dusters, sticks, rags soaked in kerosene for starting fires'. V.I. Lenin, *Collected Works* (Moscow, 1962 edn.), vol. xix, p. 420.

(31) Zepe in Mtalana (1964), pp. 12-13; Gulwa and Mhlawuli in Mapolisa (1965), pp. 5 and 23; Petros in Makinane (1965), pp. 33 and 56; and Ngoza and Mtloko in Magwayi (1965), pp. 3-4, 52, and 66.

(32) Ngoza in Magwayi (1965), pp. 15-16 and 33-7.

(33) Ngoza, Mali, and du Preez, ibid. pp. 3-4, 124-6, and 141-4.

(34) du Preez, ibid. p. 146.

(35) Quoted from *New Age* (Johannesburg), 21 December 1961.

(36) Bruno Mtolo, *Umkonto we Sizwe: the road to the Left* (Durban, 1966), pp. 25-9.

(37) Mbanjwa in Mbolompo (1965), pp. 751-4; Mashinyana and Mdube in Bongco (1964), p. 231.

(38) Joxo in Mtalana (1964), p. 46.

(39) Ibid. p. 12.

(40) Mbeki in Rivonia Trial (1963-4), p. 380; Mbanjwa in Mbolompo (1965), p. 756.

(41) Mbanjwa, ibid. p. 759.

(42) Mtolo, op. cit. pp. 78-88.

(43) Nyombo in Mbolompo (1965), pp. 647-51; Ngoza in Magwayi (1965), pp. 39-43.

(44) Mtolo, op. cit. pp. 30-4.

(45) My figures are calculated from Rivonia Trial, Annexure A, which sets out the list of acts of sabotage done by *Umkonto*.

(46) Ngoza in Magwayi (1965), pp. 39-43. This is the only case where the evidence of the accused has been drawn upon (cf. p. 56, above).

(47) Ibid, p. 44.

(48) Metshane in Tangala (1965), pp. 178-86.

(49) Makamba in Gcquabi (1963), p. 4.

(50) Mokgoro in Tangala (1965), p. 53-5.

(51) Ngoza, Mtloko, and Mali in Magwayi (1965), pp. 13, 72, and 112; Joxo in Mtlana (1964), pp. 59 and 65-7; Mtolo in Rivonia Trial (1963-4), pp. 235-6; and Dondashe in Mgalunkulu (1965), pp. 52-4.

(52) Mali in Magwayi (1965), p. 113; Zepe in Mtalana (1964), p. 31.

(53) *Sunday Times* (Johannesburg), 26 January 1969.

(54) David Rapoport, 'The Political Dimensions of Military Usurpation', in *Political Science Quarterly* (New York), LXXXIII, 4, December 1968, pp. 560-1 n.

This selection is reprinted from the *Journal of Modern African Studies* 8, 1 (1970) pp. 55-72.

document

THE MEANING OF APARTHEID

Hendrik F. Verwoerd

. . . The question is, therefore: What is apartheid? And now I hope that hon. members on the opposite side of the House really want to know and will genuinely accept it if I try to explain to them by quotation from several documents what it is—in other words, what they want to know. The impression that has been created up to now is that on this side we can simply say what we please, but that all they do is to stop up their ears and prove that they really want to know nothing. I want to say in the first place that there is nothing new in what we are propagating, nor have we made any claim that there is anything new in it. The claim that we have made is that we are propagating the traditional policy of Afrikanerdom, the traditional policy of South Africa and of all those who have made South Africa their home—that we want to apply that traditional policy to the full; that is our claim. Our claim is that, whether it is called segregation or by the clear Afrikaans name 'apartheid', our claim is that the traditional policy must be put into effect, otherwise South Africa will really land in a position which not we, but members on the other side of the House apparently want.

Nobody has ever contended that the policy of apartheid should be identified with 'total segregation'. The apartheid policy has been described as what one can do in the direction of what you regard as ideal. Nobody will deny that for the Native as well as for the European complete separation would have been the ideal if it had developed that way historically. If we had here a white South Africa in the sense in which you have a white England and a white Holland and a white France, and if there had been a Native state somewhere for the Natives, and if this white state could have developed to a self-supporting condition as those European states have developed by themselves, then we should certainly not have had the friction and the difficulties which we have today. Surely it would have been an ideal state of affairs if we had not had these problems. If the Native had not had anything to do with the whites, if he were capable of managing his own affairs, it would also have been an ideal state of affairs for him. And if that is the case, then surely it cannot do any harm to see it and to state it; it can do only good. If you appreciate that you are saddled with a complicated situation, a highly complicated situation, you must have the direction in which you wish to move to solve your problems clearly in mind. In every field of life one has to fix one's eyes on the stars, to see how close one can come to achieving the very best, to achieving perfection. For that reason I say this: keep in view what promises to be the best for your country and try to approach it within the realm of what is practical. . . .

This is what the Minister of Lands, the leader of the National Party in the Transvaal, wrote, among other things:

> As far as territorial segregation is concerned, 'total segregation', as you call it in your letter of 31/10/42 addressed to the secretary of our party on the Rand, would have been the ideal solution, but in practice it is incapable of being carried out, because quite apart from all the other difficulties, our own people, our farmers and thousands and tens of thousands of others, who use the services of the Natives and coloured people as labour, would never agree to it. For that reason, as far as 'territorial segregation' is concerned, we have adopted as a policy mainly the following: 1. That Natives should not be allowed to own land among white people, but that so far as the ownership of land is concerned they should be confined to the various Native reserves; 2. that Natives and coloured people in our towns and villages should not live in European residential areas, but that there should be separate residential areas for them, that is to say, separate Native and coloured villages; and 3. that in our factories, etc., Europeans and non-Europeans should not be allowed to work among one another, but separately, and that certain sorts of work should be reserved for the Europeans.

In connection with that I myself have stated up to now, I want to draw attention to the fact that he says in it precisely what was said above, total segregation may be the ideal but that is not practicable, and that what can be put into effect are these forms of territorial segregation, among other things. (Naturally, political segregation as well.) That is what Mr. Strydom wrote in 1942. He went on to refer to hospital and medical services for Natives, and then he wrote *inter alia* of:

> . . . the fact that we use the Natives as labourers in our businesses, in our industries and in many cases in our homes. . . .

The fact that he used that sentence serves to prove further that having the Native everywhere was within the scheme which he envisaged. Then he went on and remarked:

> Now so far as trading activities and so on in the Native areas and also in the Native residential areas of our cities are concerned. It is clear to me that if segregation is to mean anything we Europeans, except for necessary officials, should stay out of the Native areas. Shops and so on should in my opinion be in the hands of Natives in those areas. For the same reasons we Europeans will have to keep out of the Native residential areas in our cities, just as we want to keep the Natives out of the European residential areas, except for those who have to come in there daily to work.

We are therefore applying the same principle on both sides, and it is indicated here how the Natives will be everywhere and how they will be separated from the whites.

Mr. President, I also have here in my possession a number of documents which are general knowledge. They have been spread far and wide. In them is set out the colour policy of this side of the House in unequivocal terms. In the first place the basis on which it is founded is to be found in the programme of principles of the party. Here it is as it appeared in the Transvaal as the programme of principles of the party. In each of the provinces the relevant clause is exactly the same:

> The party accepts the Christian trusteeship of the European race as the basic principle of its policy in regard to the non-European races. In accordance with this it desires to afford the non-European races the opportunity of developing themselves in their own fields, according to their natural ability and capacity, and it desires to assure them of fair and just treatment in the administration of the country, but it is emphatically opposed to any mixture of blood between the European and the non-European races.
>
> It further declares itself in favour of the territorial and political segregation of the Natives, as well as in favour of the separation between Europeans and non-Europeans in general in the residential and, in so far as it may be practicable, also in the industrial field.
>
> Further, it desires to protect all sections of the population against Asiatic immigration and competition, among other things by prohibiting further intrusions into their fields of activity, as well as by an effective scheme of Asiatic segregation. . . .

Two things again emerge very clearly everywhere, that the non-European worker will be there to assist in the economic progress of the country; and that there will be protection for one group as well as for the other. It has also been stated, and we are propagating it, that there must be a worthwhile wage for European labour. It has also been stated that there must be enough non-European labour for the country districts. That has been propagated openly. When we come to 'Social Welfare and Public Health', you find that it is stated here:

> There must be separate residential areas for Europeans and non-Europeans, and as far as possible this principle of apartheid must also be applied to the various non-European racial groups in their relationships towards one another, such as coloured people, Indians and Natives.

They must also as far as possible be separated from one another: the Indian, the coloured people and the Natives. The Natives must be separate, the Indians and the coloured people each separate too. Now that almost tens of thousands of these documents have been spread throughout the country it is still said that our apartheid policy has never been defined and is not clear. That is an unimaginable idea. There is another pamphlet which was distributed in tens of thousands through the country. All in all close on 100,000 must have been circulated throughout the country. In regard to the first one might say: There is the economic scheme, and to read no further, but here he cannot say that he has not read anything more, that he therefore has an excuse for not knowing. Here you have clearly 'The Colour Policy of the Nationalist Party', 'Maintenance of European Civilisation as the Prime Task'. In it the various aspects of the matter are worked out extensively. The United Party must know of them. I am only going to make a few quotations. Under the heading 'General Basis' you find:

> The party believes that a determined policy of separation between the European race and the non-European racial groups, and the application of the principle of separation between the non-European racial groups as well, is the only basis on which the character and the future of each race can be protected and made secure and enabled to develop in accordance with its own national character, abilities and destiny.
>
> In their own areas the non-European racial groups will be afforded a full opportunity of development and they will be able to develop their own institutions and social services, and in that way the abilities of the more progressive non-Europeans will be enlisted in the advancement of their own people.

Under 'Policy toward the Natives' we find the following:

> The policy will aim at concentrating in so far as it is possible the main ethnical groups and sub-groups of the Bantu in their own separate territories, where each group will be able to develop into a self-sufficient unit.

That is not an effort to exploit differences between the races, this is not an effort to stir them up to hostility towards one another—an effort to divide and rule! As the nations of the world each in its own territory accomplishes its own national development, so also the opportunity will be given here to the various Native groups each to accomplish its own development each in its own territory. To each of them, from the tribal chief to the ordinary Native, the chance is being given to accomplish a fair and reasonable development within his own national group. That has come from those who are stigmatised by the other side as oppressors of the Natives.

Under 'Native Land' we find here:

> The principle of territorial segregation between Europeans and Natives is generally accepted. Further, land will only be allocated under the 1936 Act in a sensible way and after a careful investigation, while a determined policy for the rehabilitation of the land and a campaign against overcropping, in which the assistance of the Natives themselves will be enlisted, will be carried out.

A body of experts to bring about the proper use of land in the Native territories will be brought into being. Then further, and, indeed, under the heading 'Native Reserves', it is stated:

> The Native reserves must become the true fatherland of the Natives. It is there that his educational institutions should be, and it is there that these improved services for the Natives should be made available, in contrast to the present policy which is to make them available in urban locations. Prestige and respect must be accorded to the Natives in all fields in the reserves, so that they may set a standard and act as the mouthpiece of the Bantu.

Is that oppression?

A greater variety of economic activities will gradually be brought into being so as to bring about greater productivity and stability for the Native reserves, and for this purpose planning committees will be instituted.

Is that oppression? Then, under the heading *Natives in Towns':*

The Party appreciates the danger of the influx of Natives into the towns and undertakes to preserve the European character of our towns, and to take energetic and effective measures for the safety of persons as well as of property and for the peaceful life of urban residents.

All Natives must be placed in separate residential areas, and their concentration in our urban areas must be counteracted. The Native in our urban areas must be regarded as a 'visitor', who will never have the right to claim any political rights or equal social rights with the Europeans in the European areas.

Let me just interpolate something here and make a statement to Hon. Senators as to what, for example, happens in other countries where a great trek of workers from one country to another takes place. It is known that so far as France is concerned about three million labourers come in there from Italy every year; they are seasonal workers. Those three million seasonal workers who come from Italy do not obtain any civil rights in France; they are regarded as visitors. And the same thing will apply to the Native in the European areas, though, at the same time we are now going to give him civil rights in his own territories such as he enjoys nowhere at present. That will be the place in which to achieve his ideals. The Native who becomes a lawyer, or the Native girl who becomes a nurse or teacher or whatever the case might be, will in the first place be able to provide his services there in his own community. However, as soon as the Native comes into an area of a European community, then he will have no such political rights there, there in the white man's country. But the reverse is also true. If there are Europeans who have to go into the Native territories, and they will only go there because they have to in order to help the Natives, they will not enjoy any political rights there. Then I read on further:

The number of detribalised Natives must be frozen. After that the coming of the Natives into the towns and their regular departure will be taken under control by the State on a country-wide basis, in co-operation with the urban authorities. The Native territories must be placed under effective efflux policy and the towns under an influx policy. All surplus Natives in the towns will have to be sent back to the country districts or to the Native reserves or to wherever they came from.

The Hon. the Leader of the Opposition became so worried yesterday about the use of the word 'frozen', as if one were dealing with people who became bodily frozen so tight in the plains of the South Pole that they could not get away again, for he asked whether it meant that the Natives would be placed in concentration camps. We hope that some of those Natives who become able to serve their own people actually will migrate to the reserves. They should be dealt with in such manner that they will go there. What will happen is that in that sense the numbers in the cities will be frozen to such an extent that no more Natives will be allowed to come in from outside other than the Natives who have the full residential right to stay there; let only those who are there retain that right. That is not unreasonable. Freezing therefore means that we are not going to permit any new influx as happened under the previous Government, and, indeed, to such an extent that Johannesburg and the Witwatersrand and the whole of that neighbourhood has become one vast breeding-place of injustice and crime, of unemployment and all sorts of misery, of poverty and of mutual oppression. Within and outside that city the position has become impossible. It is also stated here that all surplus Natives in the towns should be sent back to the country districts or to the reserves from which they came. They must be away from the misery of those hovels, away from those sacking villages, away from starvation, of little boys who run about and perish and degenerate, and go back to places where some care can be taken of them again. So 'freezing' in this case has not the meaning as in the interpolation of the Hon. Senator. I am reading further:

> Natives from the country districts and the reserves will in the future be allowed to enter the white towns and villages only as temporary workers, and on the termination of their service contracts they will regularly have to go back to their homes.

That must also be well understood. The Natives who remain behind in the towns are one group. But a further influx into the towns will be allowed only in the form of such temporary labour. That is very fair, and it is very important that it should be carried out if we want to ensure them, too, the happiness to which they are just as much entitled as we are, namely to be linked to their own community and their liberties. The pamphlet also says:

> The principle of apartheid will be carried out so far as it is possible in practice in factories, industries and workshops. The Natives must be induced to build up his own social, health and welfare services in his own reserves. His own capabilities must be enlisted for that purpose.

Social and welfare services take place within the perspective and policy of this side of the House and best by providing for the Native through the Native himself. The hand that gives must be drawn from the people to whom the services are given. That is the first principle of all welfare services. The same applies to self-management. As to its own management I read the following:

> The party is in favour of an individual system of local government, more or less on the basis of the Bunga (the Transkeian Territories General Council) system, in which the Native chiefs will be completely incorporated and which will at the same time present the educated Native with an opportunity of enlisting himself in the service of his own people. Such a council will be brought into being for every reserve, and they will be able to develop into separate central councils for the various ethnic groups and sub-groups.
> The Native Representative Council will be abolished. In the urban locations councils will be instituted which will, however, never be able to develop into independent bodies.

Those two points must be clearly understood. Even the Natives who are going to get their residential areas within or rather near the towns and who will be able to achieve a great deal of local government within those residential areas, those Natives will not be able to go any further within the European area than the obtaining of local government. If they have ambitions in the direction of full citizenship, then they have to go back to the areas that are theirs; but if for their own selfish interests and their own economic gain they want to stay in the Native residential areas within the European areas, then the greatest share in government which they can achieve will be local government. That is giving them more than what for instance those Italians are able to achieve in France.

This selection is comprised of excerpts from a speech delivered in the South African Senate on September 3, 1948.

BIBLIOGRAPHY

There exists excellent literature on South Africa and the different dimensions of the apartheid problem. A general but lucid treatment is to be found in Hepple (7). Van den Berghe, a well-known student of South Africa, has analyzed the society from broad sociological perspectives. His focus is on conflict, contradiction and dysfunction. For the historical treatment, the best source is the history of the Republic edited by Wilson and Thompson (10). Carter (2) has concentrated on the crucial period after the Nationalist party came into power in 1948. Her approach is within the framework of the conventional political theory. Carter et al (3) and Hill (8) deal with the policy of Bantustans. Adams (1) whose subject is the modernization of race relations, has taken the position that neither guerrilla warfare nor outside intervention would generate the desired changes. He suggests that a multi-racial society would emerge out of economic realities in South Africa. United Nations viewpoint has been reflected in the work of Cruz (4), and one interested in resolutions adopted by that distinguished body would find it rewarding. Those interested in the contemporary struggles against the minority rule in South Africa are advised to read the relevant section from Gibson (5).

(1) Adam, Heribert. *Modernizing Racial Domination.* Berkeley: University of California Press, 1971.

(2) Carter, Gwendolen M. *The Politics of Inequality.* London: Thames and Hudson, 1958.

(3) Carter, Gwendolen M., Thomas Karis and Newell M. Stultz. *South Africa's Transkei: The Politics of Domestic Colonialism.* Evanston: Northwestern University Press, 1967.

(4) Cruz, Herman S. *Racial Discrimination.* New York: United Nations, 1971.

(5) Gibson, Richard. *African Liberation Movements: Contemporary Struggles Against White Minority Rule.* London: Institute of Race Relations, Oxford University Press, 1972.

(6) Hahlo, H.G. "A European-African Worker Relationship in South Africa." *Race,* (July, 1969), pp. 13-34.

(7) Hepple, Alex. *South Africa.* New York: Frederick A. Praeger, 1966.

(8) Hill, Christopher R. *Bautustans.* London: Institute of Race Relations, Oxford University Press, 1964.

(9) Van den Berghe, Pierre L. *South Africa: A Study in Conflict.* Middletown: Wesleyan University Press, 1965.

(10) Wilson, Monica and Leonard Thompson (eds.). *The Oxford History of South Africa, Volume I: South Africa to 1870.* Oxford: Clarendon Press, 1969. *Volume II: South Africa 1870-1966.* Oxford: Clarendon Press, 1971.

VI.
THE
CENTRAL
AMERICAN
CASE
STUDY

INTRODUCTION

In this section, we are concerned with race relations in Indo-America,(1) that region that stretches from Mexico along the Andean backbone of South America through Ecuador, Colombia, Peru, and Bolivia and into Northern Chile. Before the Spanish arrived in this region, several economically and politically complex societies lived there with a relatively high population density. Unlike the Indians in Portuguese America, the indigenous population along the continental coast was familiar with mining, and when the Spanish arrived, they found an experienced labor force.

Like the Portuguese in Africa and the East, the Spanish were more interested in conquest and commerce than in colonization.(2) They wanted to acquire the gains from plunder and trade, and at first they were not interested in restructuring the internal order of the societies they found. The Spanish did have a theory of empire, including roles for conquered peoples. When they failed to find societies in the New World as commercially advanced as those in the East, they soon began to change them. They simply replaced the indigenous Indian societies with Spanish ruling classes who assumed control of and redirected the labor of the native population towards imperial gain.

In some areas, the Spanish efforts to obtain control over Indian labor, deaths from epidemics, and the casualties of warfare destroyed the indigenous population. Hispaniola, estimated to have 300,000 Carib Indians when Columbus landed in 1492, had only 500 Indians in 1548.(3) On the Indo-American mainland, the Spanish impact was catastrophic but did not completely obliterate the population. In New Spain, population declined from about thirteen million at the time of the Conquest to approximately two million at the end of the sixteenth century.(4) The population of Peru was reduced by a half to two-thirds as a result of the Conquest.(5) Yet the Indian population of Spanish America did survive; after reaching a nadir after 150 years of Spanish rule, it stabilized and began to recover. Thus, despite the importation of many Africans and even some Filipinos into Spanish America, Indian labor remained vital.

The *encomienda* system guaranteed Spanish control over all this labor. Under the system, a Spaniard received a grant entitling him to take charge of a certain number of Indians. Spaniards also received "grants of land . . . in the same spirit as grants of Indians: as an incentive to private action so as to pave the way for the Conquest and produce a surplus for the benefit of the Crown. Land, in itself, was not an attraction. However, given the demand for agricultural products, it could become the source of a surplus to be extracted from the population ceded to the *encomendero*."(6) The early control of land and labour through the *latifundio* or large landed estate or through the *minifundio* or Indian community was the basis for an agrarian structured society that has endured to the present. By the mid-seventeenth century, debt peonage and reclamation of land by the *latifundio* guaranteed Spanish control over Indian labor even after the end of the institution of the *encomienda*.

The Roman Catholic priests who came with the Spanish conquerors are often seen as defenders of the Indians, and in fact they did incur the wrath of the settlers and the Crown. The priests and the settlers both argued that the cultural level of the Amerindian peoples was low, that guided assimilation under Spanish direction was desirable, and that the main Indian function was to provide labor for the ruling group. However, the freedom the priests were willing to give the Indians was narrowly defined; it was paternalistic and did not include the freedom to reject Christianity or the encroachments (defined as progress) of Spanish institutions.

Although the system of forced labor in Spanish America was generally similar to that in other parts of the New World, the outcome in terms of race relations was distinct. Few Spanish immigrants, a predominantly male Spanish population that did immigrate, a constant relationship with the Amerindian population due to a demand of labor, and perhaps the Spaniards' previous experience with darker skinned Moors all combined to produce a racially mixed population. Initially, attempts were made to classify people according to their presumed percentage of Spanish blood, but over a long period of time, this kind of classification proved impossible. However, racial mixing did gradually result in the emergence of a *mestizo* or *Ladino* population and the establishment of a system of social race. Distinctions here were determined largely by socio-cultural characteristics rather than by ancestry, as in North America, or by physical appearance, as in Brazil. The essential difference between classification by socio-cultural characteristics and ancestry can be summarized as follows: in the latter system, children produced by a black and a white are classified as non-white, thus continuing the system; children produced by an Indian and a mestizo produces a mestizo, thus breaking down the system.

In the nineteenth century, race relations were consolidated with the Indian population in a subordinate position. The Wars of Independence in the first quarter of the century were not fought to end Indian oppression, nor did the Indian population emerge as an independent political force. During the rest of the century, the Spanish penetrated into the countryside to break up Indian communal holdings, thereby contracting further the Indians' land base. The introduction of crops like coffee produced new migratory labor patterns and several revolts, but the main function of the Indians, under Spanish rule, was as a labor resource.

The Mexican Revolution of 1910-1917 signalled the beginning of a new set of race relations in Indo-America which is still uncompleted. Debt peonage was abolished, and land was redistributed especially under the Lázaro Cárdenas government in the 1930's. As its focus, Mexican land reform was based on the communal Indian landholding or *ejido* system that had been largely destroyed by the development of commercial agriculture. However, the peasant-worker thrust of the Revolution was blunted, and power, race, and class relations were not radically changed.(7)

In Guatemala, debt peonage lasted until 1934 when it was officially replaced by the Vagrancy Laws which effectively controlled Indian labor. The 1944 overthrow of Ubico resulted in the repeal of the Vagrancy Laws, and Indians were allowed to form rural unions. Considerable progress was made in race relations until a counter-revolution under Castillo Armas was sponsored in 1954 by the United States. Meanwhile, in Bolivia, the Indians participated in the 1952 revolution which resulted in land reform and modified the old system of exploitation. Throughout Indo-America, however, the liberation of the Indians remains incomplete.

The first two readings in this section provide an historical overview of the Indians in Indo-America. André Gunder Frank, citing a variety of sources, argues persuasively that the Indians have never been outside of the political and economic structure of Spanish conquered Indo-America. To him, the problem is not Spanish or Indian integration into a national society but is the transformation of that society. Magnus Mörner sketches the decline of the Indian population under the impact of the Conquest and provides a concise account of the emergence of the *mestizo* in Latin America.

In "Haciendas and Plantations in Yucatan," Arnold Strickon details the impact of the world market on Indian villages and brilliantly demonstrates the vulnerability of apparently isolated and autonomous areas to the system of national and international stratification. In a study of what he calls a plural society, Pablo González-Casanova outlines one of the earliest developments of the internal colonial model. The selection by Rudolfo Stavenhagen is an excerpt from a long essay in which he places the post-conquered Indian history in Meso-America within the framework of internal colonial analysis. His ability to incorporate a variety of empirical material on the region indicates the powerful explanatory potential of this kind of analysis.

NOTES

(1) Charles Wagley, "Plantation America: A Cultural Sphere," Vera Rubin (ed.), *Caribbean Studies: A Symposium*, (Seattle, Washington: University of Washington Press, 1960), pp. 3-13.

(2) E.E. Rich, "Colonial Settlement and Its Labour Problems," E.E. Rich and C.H. Wilson (eds.), *The Cambridge Economic History of Europe*, Vol. IV, *The Economy of Expanding Europe in the Sixteenth and Seventeenth Centuries*, Cambridge, England: Cambridge University Press, 1967, p. 304.

(3) *Ibid.*, p. 319.

(4) Keith Griffin, *Underdevelopment in Spanish America: An Interpretation*, London: George Allen and Unwin Ltd., 1969, p. 46.

(5) *Ibid.*, pp. 46-7.

(6) Celso Furtado, *Economic Development of Latin America: A Survey from Colonial Times to the Cuban Revolution*, Cambridge, England: Cambridge University Press, 1970, p. 14.

(7) James D. Cockcroft, "Special and Economic Structure of the Porfiriato: Mexico, 1877-1911," in James D. Cockcroft, Andre Gunder Frank and Dale Johnson, (eds.), *Dependence and Underdevelopment: Latin America's Political Economy*, Garden City, New York: Anchor Books, 1972, p. 47.

ON THE 'INDIAN PROBLEM' IN LATIN AMERICA

André Gunder Frank

The "Indian problem" in Latin America is in its essence a problem of the economic structure of the national and international capitalist system as a whole. Contrary to frequent claims, the problem is not one of the Indian's cultural isolation, still less one of economic isolation or insufficient integration . . .

. . . The problem of the Indian lies in his economic relationship to the other members of the society; and this relationship has been in turn determined by the metropolis-satellite structure and development of capitalist society as a whole since the Indian's incorporation into it by the conquest. Stavenhagen suggests that "the colonial system operated, in fact, on two levels. The economic restrictions and prohibitions that Spain imposed on its colonies (and which would generate the independence movements) were repeated, only many times worse, in the relations between the colonial society and the Indian communities. The same commercial monopolies, the same restrictions of production, the same political controls that Spain exercised over the colony, the latter imposed on the Indian communities. What Spain was for the colony, the latter was for the Indian communities; a colonial metropolis. From then on, mercantilism penetrated the most isolated villages of New Spain" (Stavenhagen 1963: 91).

Thus the supposedly isolated "folk" society or rather community popularized by Redfield (1941, 1960) and the corporate Indian community, far from being original in Latin America or traditional to it, in fact developed or, better, underdeveloped as a product of the development of capitalism in Latin America in the colonial period and also in the national period . . .

After simple slavery, the principal institution through which the Spanish entrepreneurs recouped their investment was the *encomienda*, which permitted them to exact tribute and labor from the Indian population. José Miranda summarizes the "economic function" of the *encomenderos*—those to whom the *encomiendas* were granted—as follows:

Although the continental *encomendero* has much of the feudal lord, European style . . . he seems to have no real interest in his feudal-style position or function. No; the *encomendero* is above all a man of his time, moving by desire for profit and pursuing the goal of wealth. Among his contemporaries, the *encomendero* is the man of action in whom the ideas and anxieties of a new world take strongest root. . . . For this reason, he does not, like the feudal lord, limit himself to the mere enjoyment of tribute and service; but he converts the one like the other into the principal base of several business enterprises. . . . He will do the same as any entrepreneur from that time till now: use his own and others' resources and the work of others in the pursuit of his own wealth and well-being. Thus the *encomendero* gives place of pride to the capitalist grant element of the *encomienda*, which is the only one which can bring him what he pursues with vigor: riches. . . .

The business which the *encomendero* establishes to take economic advantage of the *encomienda* are, therefore, of three kinds: mining (for the extraction of gold, at first), livestock, and agricultural (the agricultural ones, at first, being limited almost exclusively to the production of wheat). . . . With respect to the first one, he would extract from his *encomienda* for his businesses, gold, means of subsistence, slaves, clothing, etc. These goods would be used by him: the gold, in the most necessary investments, like the purchase of tools, and where necessary, in the payment of Spanish workers (miners and helpers) and the purchase of food; the means of subsistence in the maintenance of his slaves, *encomienda* Indians, and other workers, and livestock raising; the slaves, in the mining work, where they were the main source of labor, and in agriculture and livestock raising. . . . We often see the *encomendero* caught up in a complicated net of economic and legal relationships; he participates in various mining companies, established before a notary public; he is owner of a herd of swine or sheep, which he grazes on the range of another *encomendero*—with whom he has entered into an economic contract for the purpose—and which are under the care of a Spaniard whose services he has obtained through some contract or payment; and all this after having conferred general powers to some relative, friend, or employee to administer his *encomiendas* and after having conferred special powers to other people so they might administer his haciendas or livestock ranches, his shops or sugar mills, or to take care of his interest wherever it may be necessary. (Miranda 1947: 423-424, 427, 446).

Thus the expansion and development of capitalism incorporated the Indian population into its exploitative monopoly structure immediately upon conquest, and the capitalist and his fast-growing cattle and sheep herds appropriated the Indian's land. The new capitalism penetrated the Indian economic organization so quickly and profoundly that ten years after the conquest of Mexico "due, undoubtedly, to the increase in money and the large demand for consumer goods, some Indian villages, especially those near the capital and important cities, came to prefer paying their tribute in money and asked that their payments in goods or labor be commuted to gold or silver. Ramírez de Fuenleal informed the King of this turn of events and asked him to remove the legal obstacles to the payment of tribute in money . . . "it seems that now some villages prefer to keep their corn and blankets for trading, and would rather give gold; because through their trading they earn enough to pay their tribute and to provide for their subsistence' " (Miranda 1952: 204). Like all those in a capitalist economy who must pay, in times of inflation the Indians preferred to pay in devalued money.

The immediate consequences of capitalist penetration of the Indian society were the decimation of the Indian population and the transformation of his society and culture. In Mexico, the Indian population dropped from 11 million at the time of conquest in 1519 to a low of 1.5 million in 1650 (Borah 1951: 3). At the same time, as Miranda notes, "the heavy load of tribute caused important changes in the distribution of the population: on the one hand, the population decline due to death or absence; and on the other hand, the spread of many Indians to the less populated areas, the settlement of uninviting or inaccessible places, and the change of residence or transfer of home from one village to another. Some villages died out or declined; new settlements were born, some of which became small towns with the passing of time; and some places grew. Many of the Indians who did not wish to pay the excessive tributes adopted the only way to evade them, that is, abandoned their place of residence, either to go to live where the Spaniards could not bother them or to go to live somewhere else where the weight of tribute was lighter" (Miranda 1952: 216-217). The Indian settlements of later times, at least of all their structure and relation to the larger society, are not then survivals of pre-conquest times. They are, on the contrary, the underdeveloped product of capitalist development. Since then and still in our day, insofar as the corporate Indian community has been isolated at all, this reflects the self-chosen retreat which is the Indians' only available means of protection from the ravages and exploitation of the capitalist system . . .

. . . In its incorporation of the Indian, then, no less than of anybody else, the development of capitalism generated the institutional forms appropriate to its changing needs at different times and places. This capitalist development and its institutions transformed the entire fabric of Indian society from the very beginning, and it has continued to determine the manner and quality of Indian life ever since . . .

. . . As we already noted in our review of Chile, the seventeenth century witnessed the decline of mining production in the colonies, brought depression to the metropolis, and isolated the two from each other more than they had been in the previous century or would again be in the later ones. Urban-rural polarization in the colonies seems to have increased. Urban population, manufacturing and demand for rural products increased in the face of the continued population decline (Borah 1951: 30). In response to this urban development and to the decline of both the output and profitability of mining, agricultural production also grew in importance and was increasingly concentrated in the Spanish hacienda rather than the Indian village. The students of this process in Mexico have interpreted it as the involution of an economy which was turning in upon itself due to an economic depression (Chevalier 1956, Borah 1951, Wolf 1959). I have argued elsewhere that this is a misinterpretation of these events (Frank 1965a). The growth and consolidation of the monopolistic hacienda and the associated decline of small-scale, in this case Indian, agricultural production in Mexico was then and has always been due to the increase of demand for and price of agricultural products, just as in the cases of Chile and Brazil which are reviewed in this book and in the clear cases elsewhere in Latin

America of Argentina and the West Indies (Frank 1965b). The seventeenth century, then, witnessed the development of the principal rural institutional forms which, in the hacienda and the Indian community, have persisted in most of Indian Latin America to this day; but these institutions themselves have been flexible enough to adapt to the world and national economic fluctuations and transformations since that time . . .

. . . The relations between Indians and others then are many; but, as all the writers cited here agree, they are never relations of equality. The Indian is always exploited.

Alejandro Marroquín notes that "traditionally, the Indian in the Tzeltal-Tzotzil region is exploited in two ways: he is exploited as a worker at the service of the landowners and *hacendados* who use Indian labor and pay low wages for each day of work; and he is exploited in his capacity as a small producer; the Indian produces goods which are sometimes very much in demand in the national market" (Marroquín 1956: 200) . . .

. . . It is hard to find many Indians, even in Mexico after its land reform, who own enough land to permit them to lead a life worthy of their integral membership in human society. It is a generally acknowledged fact that the Indians have been robbed of their lands by legal and illegal means over the course of history, often not so much because others wanted the land in itself as because they sought to render the Indians dependent by denying them ownership of the resources necessary for their independent survival.

Contemporary land tenure studies in various countries of Latin America show that the Indians are still losing their lands, not to speak of the lands' fertility. This shortage of land is undoubtedly the key to their status of inferiority, exploitation, poverty, lack of culture, in a word the status of underdevelopment of the Indians and of many others who participate all too fully in the social progress of capitalist development. It is for this reason that Stavenhagen can claim that "from the point of view of the global economic structure, the self-subsistence community plays the role of a labor reserve; . . . private land-ownership benefits the *ladinos* and is prejudicial to the Indians . . . the accumulation of land on the part of the *ladinos* serves them to obtain and control a cheap labor force . . . the Indian is always the serves them to obtain and control a cheap labor force . . . the Indian is always the employee and the *ladino* always the employer" (Stevenhagen 1963: 71, 75, 77). Little wonder that Indians value the corporativeness of their community which affords them some protection against outside encroachment on their land through its communal ownership and through strong social sanctions against the sale of individually owned land to outsiders.

Obviously it is their lack of land which forces the landless Indians and ex-Indians to contribute their labor for very low wages and sometimes for none at all to landowners and others in order to obtain a little piece of land of low fertility, a leaky roof over their heads, a little corn or wheat or beer, a few pesos. But it is also the shortage of land among those who have a little of it which forces the communal Indians and other small owners, in order to obtain bread for their children and grass for their animals, to submit to the exploitation of the *ladinos* and others who are fortunate enough to have stolen, extorted or inherited enough land and capital from the Indians and others to enable them now to live off their exploitation.

The organization of this exploitation takes all sort of forms, like being born, working as an ordinary laborer, and dying on the same hacienda; or working as a half-share cropper on such a hacienda—if you are fortunate enough to obtain even half of what you produce for yourself; of leaving your own small plot in the hands of your family while you go to work on the neighboring hacienda; or coming down hundreds of miles from the mountains every year to harvest other people's coffee—especially if it is these others who own "your" land in the mountains; or migrating as a *bracero* thousands of miles to California to serve as a supply of cheap labor; or combining these activities with some minor trading and any kind of occasional labor if you can find it in the provincial small towns; or emigrating to the provincial or national capital, there to become an occasionally employed slum dweller; in any case, becoming wholly integrated in a capitalist metropolis-satellite economic, social, and political structure which takes all possible advantage of your short, sad life without ever also integrating you into the benefits which this same social structure generates.

The Indians and others, besides being exploited as laborers, as Alejandro Marroquín notes, are also exploited as small producers, both as sellers and buyers in the local, regional, and national market. The Indian's "limited familiarity with the laws of supply and demand inhibit him from placing the proper value on the goods he brings to the urban market; it is thus that the Indian becomes an instrument in the hands of monopolists who take his products away from him and pay ridiculous prices only to sell the same goods later at relatively high prices" (Marroquín 1956: 200). . . .

These commercial relations take on a multitude of forms. Marroquín summarizes some of these in his study of *La Ciudad Mercado (Tlaxiaco)* [The Market Town (Tlaxiaco)]:

> The function of distribution consists in the job which the weekly market of Tlaxiaco does in distributing the multitude of goods brought from Puebla, Oaxaca, Atlixco, or from Mexico. . . . The function of concentration is the inverse: the weekly market concentrates a series of regional goods in Tlaxiaco so that they may then be sent to the major centers of consumption; on the other hand, the two foregoing functions are accomplished mainly through the function of commercial exchange, that is, through the growing activity of buyers and sellers, which leaves an excess of profit for the professional merchants. The function of monopolization is a higher stage of the function of concentration and consists in the monopolizing work of the buying agents of the big merchants principally from Puebla and Mexico, who try to control the production of those Indian goods which are in great demand in the most important centers of consumption of the country. . . .
> The Indians who produce straw hats belong to the economically most backward villages. . . . Parents as well as children are engaged in the production of hats in very long workdays which exceed 18 hours daily. The cultural backwardness of these Indians leaves them completely at the mercy of the buyers who, relying on their economic power, fix the prices of their hats entirely at their own will and with no other limit than that which they fix among themselves through competition. Even in the Indian villages there are one or two monopolists who buy many hats in order to take and sell them in Tlaxiaco on Saturday. They assure themselves of profit buying the hats

produced by the Indians at very low prices which these sell in their village, forced perhaps by some economic need. . . .

The buying agents try to get a corner on particular Indian goods in order to send them to the urban centers where there is a big demand for these goods. The buying agents depend on important commercial centers like Mexico, Puebla, or Oaxaca, etc. and keep in perfect touch with the market fluctuation in these places. In accord with these fluctuations, they determine the prices of the Indian products. The Indian products in greatest demand by the buying agents are eggs, chickens and turkeys, avocados and coffee. . . . The work of the buying agencies is eased through a typical network of middlemen to gather up the Indian products through small purchases and then deliver them to their respective agents in large quantities. These middlemen are all native to Tlaxiaco. . . . Seven pairs of hands have introduced themselves between the producer and the consumer and have caused the price [of eggs] to rise from 16 cents to 50 cents, more than 300 percent. The Indian products reach Tlaxiaco in order then to spread out to the major urban centers of the country; but in their brief passage through Tlaxiaco they have contributed to strengthening the commercial sector of the city. This profit, parasitically extracted from the hunger and misery of the Indian, consolidates the power and the concentric force of Tlaxiaco as the fundamental nucleus of the Mixtecan economy.

Summarizing, we may note the following as the general characteristics of the urban market of Tlaxiaco: 1. the total predominance of the mercantile capitalist system. 2. intense competitive fighting, as in any capitalist economic system. 3. powerful influence of the distributive monopolies. 4. a dense network of middlemen which weighs heavily on the Indian economy. 5. the parasitic aspect of the economy of Tlaxiaco which is based on the exploitation of the devalued work of the Indian. . . . All of which shows that Tlaxiaco is not a producing center but a distributive center which depends mainly on outside production. Tlaxiaco is the base around which take place the weekly markets of the villages which are subordinated to the orbit of the head city (Marroquín 1957: 156-163).

It should be especially emphasized that the shortage of resources and low bargaining power which puts the Indians in a very disadvantageous position in the market is heightened by the frequent and large fluctuations in demand, supply, and price which for speculative ends are often monopolistically generated by the merchants themselves. . . .

. . . The development of capitalism, then, generates ever more underdevelopment in the Indian community just as it does in most others. Thus the "problem" of the Indian and his community, from his point of view, is one of constant struggle for bare survival in a system in which he, like the vast majority of other people, is the victim of uneven capitalist development within a fully capitalist metropolis-satellite structure. It is a losing battle the Indian has fought for over four centuries. He is still losing. And, like millions of others, he will continue to lose until he can overthrow the system, a task which no one is prepared to do for him. . . .

. . . The "Indian problem" therefore does not lie in any *lack* of cultural or economic integration of the Indian into society. His problem, like that of the majority of people, lies rather in his very exploitative metropolis-satellite *integration* into the structure and development of the capitalist system which produces underdevelopment in general.

REFERENCES

Borah, Woodrow, 1951. "New Spain's Century of Depression." *Ibero-Americana*, (Berkeley), No. 35.

Chevalier, Francois, 1956. "La formación de los grandes latifundios en México." *Problemas Agrícolas y Industriales de México*, January-March, published in English.as, *The Growth of the Latinfundium in Mexico*, Berkeley: University of California Press, 1965.

Frank, Andrew Gunder, 1965a. "Services Rendered." *Monthly Review*, (New York), Vol. 17, No. 2, June. Also "El costo de importaciones en América Latina," *Presente Económico* (Mexico), June 1965 and "?Sercicios Extranjeros o Desarrollo Nacional?" *Comercio Exterior*, (Mexico), Vol. XI, No. 2, February 1966.

Frank, Andrew Gunder, 1965b. "Brazil: One Year from Gorillos to Guerrillas." *The Minority of One*, (Passaic, N.J.), VII, No. 7 (68), July, 1965.

Marroquín, Alejandro, 1957. *La ciudad mercado* (Tlaxiaco). México, Universidad Nacional Autónoma de México,.Imprenta Universitaria.

Marroquín, Alejandro, 1956. "Consideraciones sobre el problema económico de la región Tzeltal-Tzotzil." *América Indígena* (Mexico), XVI, No. 3, June.

Miranda, José, 1947. "La función económica del ecomendero en los orígenes del regimen colonial: Nueva España (1521-1531)." *Anales*, Instituto Nacional de Anthropología e Historia, Vol. 2, México, Secretaría de Educación Publica. Republished in book form by Universidad Nacional Autónoma de Mexico, 1965.

Miranda, José, 1952. El tributo indígena en la Nueva España durante el siglo XVI. Mexico: Colegio de México.

Redfield, Robert, 1941. *The Folk Culture of Yucatan*. Chicago: University of Chicago Press.

Redfield, Robert, 1960. *The Little Community and Peasant Society and Culture*. Chicago: University of Chicago Press.

Stavenhagen, Rodolfo, 1963. "Clases, colonialismo y aculturación: Ensayo sobre un sistema de relaciones interétnicas en Meso-américa." *América Latina* (Rio de Janeiro), Vol. 6, No. 4, October-December.

Wolf, Eric R., 1959. *Sons of the Shaking Earth*. Chicago: University of Chicago Press.

This selection is abridged from André Gunder Frank, *Capitalism and Underdevelopment in Latin America: Historical Studies of Chile and Brazil.* Monthly Review Press, New York, 1967, pp. 123, 124, 125-128, 130, 131-132, 135-139, 141, 142.

THE INDIAN POPULATION OF LATIN AMERICA

Magnus Mörner

In a way, the Spanish Conquest of the Americas was a conquest of women. The Spaniards obtained the Indian girls both by force and by peaceful means. The seizure of women was simply one element in the general enslavement of Indians that took place in the New World during the first decades of the sixteenth century. Indian slavery was finally prohibited categorically in the New Laws of 1542. It then gradually disappeared, at least in most areas of Spanish America.(1) But Schmidel tells us about a campaign in Gran Chaco in 1547 that rendered him no fewer than fifty slaves: men, women, and children.(2) In Chile, where the Spaniards faced the stubborn resistance of the warlike Araucanos, the enslavement of the Indians, including that of their women, was once again made legal in 1608.(3) Bernal Díaz, that remarkable eyewitness of the conquest of Mexico, presents a lively account of the actual enslavement of women. Cortés had decided that all the slaves taken by the soldiers should be branded, so that the Royal fifth (the Crown's share) and his own share of the human booty could be taken. When the soldiers returned the following day to recover the remaining slaves, they discovered to their dismay that Cortes and his officers had "hidden and taken away the best looking slaves so that there was not a single pretty one left. The ones we received were old and ugly. There was much grumbling against Cortes on this account. . . ."(4) Military campaigns have no doubt always been accompanied by rape and other brutalities against the defenseless. It seems, however, that violence possesses special characteristics during warfare between peoples representing widely different civilizations. Critical, then, is the lack of common ethical norms,(5) as in the wars between Christians and Moslems in the Iberian Peninsula, and also during the Conquest of the Americas.

Perhaps the element of violent rape should not be overemphasized. Though prematrimonial virginity was highly considered by certain tribes, the opposite was true among others. Probably the Indian women very often docilely complied with the conquistadores' desires.(6)

The Spaniards also obtained women in the form of gifts and as tokens of friendship from the Indian *caciques*. This kind of hospitality has existed in many other environments and ages. Bernal Díaz tells us how the Cacique Xicotenga offered Cortés his virgin daughter and four other pretty girls to his captains. Similar episodes abound in the chronicles of the times.(7) From Paraguay, Rui Díaz de Guzmán reports that the Guaraní caciques considered the gift of women to be an excellent means of allying themselves with the Spaniards. "They called all of them brothers-in-law. This is the origin of the existing custom of calling the Indians entrusted to you *Tobayá* which means brother-in-law. And it so happened that the Spaniards had many sons and daughters with the Indian women they received."(8) Once confirmed by the gift of women, the alliances between Spaniards and Indians were likely to be strong and lasting. This could very well be of greatest importance for the success of a small group of conquistadores. As Inca Garcilaso de la Vega puts it, "as soon as the Indians saw that a woman had been begotten by a Spaniard, all the kinsfolk rallied to pay homage to the Spaniard as their idol and to serve him because they were now related to him. Such Indians were of great help during the Conquest of the Indies."(9)

Another way of obtaining women was provided by the *encomienda*, the famous institution by which Indians were distributed among Spaniards who were granted their tribute. In his turn, the recipient of an encomienda was supposed to protect and civilize his Indians and see to it that they were Christianized. At least until the New Laws (1542), the Indians usually paid their tributes to the *encomendero* in days of work. It is not surprising that the encomenderos often asked for female domestic servants. As Bishop Juan de Zumárraga of Mexico observed, in his well-known letter to Emperor Charles in 1529, such servants were used as concubines more often than not. Near Cuenca in present Ecuador, Cieza de León reports, the Indians sent their wives and daughters to carry the Spaniards' luggage, while they stayed at home. The chronicler remarks that these women were "beautiful, and not a little lascivious, and fond of the Spaniards."(10) It also happened that the Indians paid their tribute in slaves, men or women. Slavery already existed among many Indian tribes on different cultural levels. The Indians also occasionally sold female slaves to the Spaniards. This traffic was prohibited by the New Laws.(11)

However the Spaniard and the Portuguese of the early sixteenth century had obtained them, by force, purchase, or gift, he lived surrounded by Indian women. Sometimes they were his slaves or the kind of serfs called *naborias* in the Caribbean and *yanaconas* in Peru; sometimes they were, theoretically, free servants. This way of life often produced the impression of a real harem, though some accounts of contemporary observers seem exaggerated, perhaps because they were shocked or too enthusiastic. We should not take as a statistically verified fact the report that in Paraguay, called the Paradise of Mohammed, every Spaniard had an average of twenty to thirty women.(12)

The Church, of course, by no means approved of this situation, but it was certainly not easy to do anything about it. The Bishop of Santo Domingo wrote to the Emperor in 1529 that when his Spanish parishioners were living in sin the concubines were their own Indian servants "and nothing can be found out about it." Furthermore, the results of such unions were often born in faraway places. As another report from Santo Domingo during the same period put it: "there are a great many mestizos here, sons of Spaniards and Indian women who are usually born in *estancias* and uninhabited places.(13) The civil authorities during the

Conquest were often satisfied with having the Indian women baptized prior to coition. Thus, the commander of an expedition in Cartagena in 1538 was instructed that he should see to it that "no soldier slept with any Indian who was not a Christian."(14) The conquistadores themselves seem to have taken the reproaches for being promiscuous very lightly, whether they were aware of fulfilling a "civilizing" mission or not. Accused by the Inquisition of a great many blasphemous utterances, the old conquistador Francisco de Aguirre, governor of Tucumán, confessed among other things to having declared that "the service rendered to God in producing mestizos is greater than the sin committed by the same act."(15)

There can be no doubt that casual intercourse and concubinage accounted for most of the crossing during the Conquest.(16) And polygyny was more frequent. But it should not be forgotten that marriage also brought about race mixture. Intermarriage was explicitly permitted by the monarch in 1501. Two years later Governor Ovando of Santo Domingo was instructed to see to it that "some Christians [i.e., Spaniards] marry some Indian women and some Christian women marry some Indian men, so that both parties can communicate and teach each other and the Indians become men and women of reason." We shall discuss this decree in its legal context later. Here, we are interested in how such a policy was received in the American environment. The colonial authorities were far from enthusiastic about it, but there were always some churchmen around who put pressure on them to permit or even promote intermarriage. Spanish-Indian couples living in concubinage should be persuaded to marry. According to a chronicler, Governor Ovando ordered the Spaniards in Santo Domingo either to marry their Indian partners or to part company: "In order not to lose their authority over the Indian women and their services they married them."(17) But even with such methods rather little was achieved. A census taken in Santo Domingo in 1514 revealed that only 171 of the 689 Spaniards living there were married. The wives of 107 were Spanish (5 of them having been left behind in Spain), and only 64 were natives. Those married to Indian women usually belonged to the lowest social stratum.(18) The policy of the Crown also vacillated a great deal with regard to intermarriage. By its orders, numbers of white female slaves were sent to the Indies. The Royal decree of 1514 explained that the very lack of women there was such that it had caused some Spaniards to marry Indian women, "people far from possessing reason."(18) And many Spaniards preferred to marry a white prostitute rather than a native woman. This is why Cervantes called the Americas the "great lure of licentious women."(20) As soon as Spanish women were available, the Spaniards were likely to reject their Indian spouses or favorites. This also happened to "princesses," such as the mother of Inca Garcilaso de la Vega. The famous writer himself sadly states: "In Peru there have been few who have married in order to legitimize their natural offspring enabling them to inherit."(21)

It seems fair to draw two conclusions on the basis of what we know about race mixture during the Conquest. In the first place, the color of the sexual partner was of no importance, as well stated by Juan de Carvajal, a conquistador in Venezuela. When accused of promiscuity he flatly replied: "No one in these parts who has a homestead can live without women, Spanish *or* Indian."(22) Second, it is obvious that the Spaniards preferred to marry Spanish women, above all, probably because of their desire to provide their descendants with a good lineage.

To the Indian women, association with the conquistadores offered many advantages, even though they were not allowed to marry. But many seem to have become aware of their inferiority to their white rivals. Chronicler Gonzalo Fernández de Oviedo tells a pathetic story of how Indian girls tried to bleach their skin. The Indian women could hope that the children they had with the whites would be accepted as free "Spaniards."(23)

In the beginning, such expectations seemed to be fulfilled. As a rule, the first generation of mestizos was accepted as "Spaniards." This is easy to understand for mestizos born in marriage, but, as we have pointed out, these were not at all frequent. On the other hand, during this early period many mestizos were recognized by their fathers. The process of legitimization seems to have been frequently used at this time both in Spain and Portugal.(24) A very tolerant attitude, indeed, was that of a certain Diego de Ocaña in sixteenth-century New Spain. In his will he confesses that the Indian servant Antonica had been his mistress. Since she also lived with an Indian, however, he did not know for sure who was the father of her child, even if the color made it likely that it was Diego. Be this as it may, he found he had better recognize the child and ask his legitimate children to instruct him and to take good care of him.(25) In another will, that of Domingo Martínez de Irala, a famed conquistador of Paraguay, the list of children sired with seven Indian women comprises tnree boys and six girls. Whereas six of the mothers were servants of Irala himself, the seventh was "the servant of Diego de Villalpando." Irala had married his daughters to other conquistadores, providing them with the best possible dowry, he declares.(26)

Mestizos of this accepted and well-treated category must, as a rule, have felt strong solidarity with the paternal group. In the beginning, mestizo sons were even able to inherit the grant of an encomienda from their Spanish fathers.(27) And the first generation of mestizos took an active part in the last stages of the Conquest. In the River Plate region it was Juan de Garay and his fellow mestizos from Asunción who founded Santa Fé and, finally, Buenos Aires in 1580. In Chile the mestizos were active in the struggles against the Araucanos. In an interesting letter from the governor of Chile to the king in 1585, the former acknowledges receipt of a royal decree restricting the rights of the mestizos. Barely able to suppress his anger, the governor refers to the fact that there are 150 mestizos in the army, most of them sons to the conquistadores. Without them Chile would have been lost, he exclaims: "I should pray to God that there were as many good people among those sent to us from Spain as there are among those Mestizos."(28) In Brazil, it is well known that two shipwrecked Portuguese, "Caramurú" and João Ramalho, with their numerous progeny, helped Governor Tomé de Souza to found the settlements of Baía and São Vicente respectively. The Governor wrote to the king that Ramalho had so many children that he did not dare to put down the number. "Caramurú," for his part, is said to have had at least sixty. However savage and primitive were the Brazilian mestizos ("mamelucos," as they were called), the future explorers of the inland, they obviously remained loyal to the cause of their fathers.(29)

But there were exceptions from the general solidarity of the early mestizos with the paternal group. Some mestizos of the first generation chose to stay with the maternal group, or, later in life, came to join it. Most of the "Spanish deserters" who went over to the Araucanos in Chile were probably mestizos. But this phenomenon was not confined to mestizos. Quite a few Spaniards, some of them involved in shipwreck or captivity, also switched sides, and were assimilated with the Indians. As distinguished from "Caramurú" and Ramalho, some could not revive their original loyalty even by direct contact with compatriots later on. Thus we have the pathetic Francisco Martin, a member of an expedition of conquest in Venezuela, who "went native" after almost incredible adventures and hardships. Years later he was found by a group of compatriots and was forced to return to "civilization" with them. He soon fled to join his Indian tribe and family but was fetched away for a second time and exiled to New Granada. Chronicler Fernández de Oviedo says that "his love for the wife and children he had in captivity was such that he lamented and wept for them. The Indian ceremonies and customs were also so deeply ingrained in him that by carelessness he sometimes made use of them among Spaniards.(30) Another interesting story is that of the two Spaniards, Jaime Aguilar and Gonzalo Guerrero, who had been taken prisoner in Campeche. When Cortes arrived at Cozumel years later he got to know about them, and forwarded to Aguilar the ransom required to set both of them free. Aguilar, who had come to be more than happy, went to Guerrero to break the news. But the latter replied: "Brother Aguilar, I am married and have three children, and they look on me as a *Cacique* here, and a captain in time of war. Go, and God's blessing be with you. But my face is tattooed and my ears are pierced. What would the Spaniards say if they saw me like this? And look how handsome these children of mine are. . . ." And Guerrero's wife angrily added, storyteller Bernal Díaz says: "Why has this slave come here to call my husband away? Go off with you, and let us have no more of your talk."(31) As an example of acculturation and assimilation, Aguilar was the "misfit," the man incapable of assimilation, whereas Guerrero had been successful in assimilating. In fact, the poor sailor had climbed the social ladder, becoming chieftain and captain of war.

To return to the mestizos of the first generation, we have seen that, obviously, most were absorbed by the paternal group, whereas others joined the Indians. Certainly there were also those who led a marginal existence between the two groups without being accepted by either. But this phenomenon was to occur on a large scale only later on. It is a simple sociological fact that persons of mixed origin tend to be absorbed by either parental group when they are few in number. When they are numerous, though, they are likely to form a group of their own.(32)

DEMOGRAPHIC DISASTER

. . . We can be rather sure that the relatively small groups of Europeans and Africans who arrived in the Indies during the first half of the sixteenth century carried on miscegenation as extensively as was feasible, and the opportunities were certainly present. Since most of the offspring joined their fathers and the other Europeans, this dynamic biological activity also opened the way for acculturation and assimilation into the Western civilization. But the advance of the mestizaje during the Conquest would have been much less conspicuous if the Indian masses had remained as numerous as they evidently were prior to contact with the Europeans. In order to assess the importance of the mestizaje during the sixteenth century, we must see it against the background of the terribly rapid decline in the Indian populations.

Even the very cautious calculations made by Angel Rosenblat imply that the aboriginal population of the Americas was reduced from 13.3 million to 10.8 million between 1492 and 1570. As for the whites, Negroes, and mixed population,

Rosenblat assesses their number as no more than 3.5 percent of the population in 1570 (19 per cent in 1650).(33) The very detailed calculations prepared by the Berkeley school team of historians and demographers show an infinitely more dramatic curve than that of Rosenblat for Central Mexico:

1519	25,200,000
1532	16,800,000
1548	6,300,000
1568	2,650,000
1580	1,900,000
1595	1,375,000
1605	1,075,000

Even though the figure for 1519 is admittedly hypothetical (based on an average of 4.5 persons per family), the following figures, especially from 1568 onward, seem to be better documented, based as they are, above all, on fiscal records.(34) At the same time, Woodrow Borah, one of these scholars, thinks that the so-called Spanish population in the same region increased from about 57,000 in 1570 to 114,000 in 1646. Another American scholar, Henry Dobyns, suggests that it is most likely that the Central Andean Zone underwent a similar disastrous demographic decline, but the topic remains to be studied with serious methods.(35) Scattered evidence from other parts of the Americas also indicates a sharp downward trend after "contact." An investigation of the Quimbaya tribe in present Colombia shows that the number of Indians liable to tribute dropped from 15,000 in 1539 to only 69 in 1628.(36) The demographic disaster was obviously the keynote of sixteenth-century Latin American history, though our knowledge so far is very incomplete. "Like the baroque altars soon to arise in the colony, the splendor and wealth of the new possessions but covered a grinning skull," as Eric Wolfe expresses this tragic reality.(37)

The primary causes of the demographic decline were the imported diseases: smallpox, typhus, measles, and influenza. Isolated from the rest of the world as they had been, the Amerindians had developed no resistance at all against these diseases. Smallpox, introduced into Mexico by a sick Negro participant of Narváez' expedition in 1520, spread havoc among the Indians not yet reached by the Spaniards. In a similar way European diseases reached Peru in the 1520's, ahead of the conquistadores themselves. The striking discrepancy between the demographic figures for New Spain in 1568 and 1580 resulted from the epidemic of *matlalzáhuatl*, probably a variety of typhoid. Malaria, trachoma, and yellow fever seem to have been brought to the Americas from Africa by Negro slaves, who themselves often fell victims to dysentery.(38)

In attributing the horrible mortality primarily to these imported diseases I am not ignoring the fact that great numbers of Indians were victims of violence and cruel treatment inflicted by the conquistadores. But I think it is obvious that quantitatively such causes were infinitely less important. We cannot reasonably attribute casualties as heavy as might be expected in atomic war to sixteenth-century warfare techniques. . . .

"MESTIZO" AND "INDIAN" BECOME SOCIAL CONCEPTS

. . . The demographic surplus of mestizos was not channeled toward the pueblos de indios alone. There was another flow toward the haciendas. There had always been mestizos who served as foremen and in other positions of trust. But it is interesting to notice the steady increase in the number of mestizo tenants. In New Spain we find the *rancheros* renting outlying portions of the haciendas in exchange for services rendered to the hacendados.(39) In New Granada there were both Spanish and mestizo tenants, some very poor, others relatively well off.(40) The only study of any depth referring to this social category seems to be that made by Mario Góngora on central Chile. According to the traditional view, the *inquilino*, the characteristic rural proletarian of Chile, derived from a category of Indian workers of the post-encomienda period. But Góngora convincingly shows that, instead, the inquilino developed from a form of non-Indian tenancy. Within the pastoral economy of seventeenth-century Chile, the landowners let out land to other Spaniards and mestizos as *préstamos de tierras* (loans of land), in exchange for an almost symbolic rent and some easily performed services. But, during the eighteenth century, the number of tenants increased at the same time as the growing wheat export to Peru caused a remarkable rise in land values. Thus, as we would expect, the rents were increased considerably. Toward the end of the century many tenants found themselves obliged to pay their rent by day labor, which lowered their social status. Now they were called inquilinos, and their pieces of land grew smaller. But, as Góngora sees it, their real transformation into a miserable proletariat took place during the nineteenth century, a process mainly to be explained by their increasing numbers.(41)

The agrarian phenomenon may be compared with an interesting parallel phenomenon that has been studied in the mining district of Norte Chico in the northern part of central Chile. Employers were able to attract workers by offering them "loans of veins" to exploit on their own account. Later, thanks to the debt service, they were able to restrict the movements of these workers. This device, which, as we have seen, was often used with the Indians on the haciendas, in the mines, and in the workshops, was found equally expedient for people of Spanish or mixed origin. The study of Norte Chico labor indicates that 49 per cent of the mine workers from 1720 to 1750 were "whites," 21 per cent "mestizos," and 30 per cent "Indians." For the years 1750-1800, the author states that no less than 79 per cent were classified as "whites," 14 per cent as "mestizos," and only 7 per cent as "Indians."(42) A similar breakdown of hacienda labor probably would have shown a similar trend. It is rather obvious that the criterion of ethnic classification had become more generous both for mestizos who wanted to pass as "whites" and for Indians who wanted to pass as "mestizos."

On the eve of emancipation, the designation "Indian" had already, in the rural sector, become mainly a social instead of a racial concept. The "Indian" was generally a member of an Indian community that functioned in accordance with the Hispano-Indian norms set down in the Laws of the Indies. He was a full-fledged member of that community, as distinguished from the Spanish or mestizo vecinos, who lived among the Indians but did not share their legal status.

If he left his native community and his district for good, the way was open for the enterprising Indian to change his status. In the central parts of the South American Andes, the vague and transitory name *cholo* helped to bridge the gap between "Indian" and "mestizo"; that is, between community peasant and the mestizo farmers and artisans.(43). When the legislators and administrators of the era of emancipation introduced the new word "indígena," this step reflected their awareness that the division between the rural groups had become social rather than racial. It was also an attempt to remove the disdain attached to the designation "Indian." Near the end of the nineteenth century, similar efforts, with the same basic motivation, were made by replacing "indigena" with "poor peasant" *(labrador, pobre, campesino)*.(44) . . .

THE INDIAN POPULATION IN THE NINETEENTH CENTURY

. . . In the early years of the nineteenth century there were more or less numerous Indian populations almost everywhere in Spanish America.(45) Toward the end of the century only Mexico, Guatemala, Ecuador, Peru, and Bolivia housed Indian populations of any great size. Evidently these countries also had the most numerous Indian populations at the beginning of the century. But it might be expected that the acculturation and assimilation that were so advanced late in the colonial period would have much reduced the Indian sector in the five countries during the nineteenth century. Whereas the Indians were absorbed in the countries where they already were in the minority, acculturation and assimilation in the five countries where they formed the majority actually slowed down in the nineteenth century. When we consider the integrationist aims of Latin American liberalism, this fact is indeed paradoxical. George Kubler shows that the province of Huánuco in the Peruvian highlands had a mestizo majority in 1796 but had reverted to an Indian majority at some time before 1854. Kubler thinks that this and other retrogressions were caused by the isolation and bad economic conditions in the early national period, when many improverished mestizos in outlying parts lost their status.(46) As for the Indian communities, the economic depression of the early national period and the civil wars probably made them more isolationist, more closed against the outer world, and more marginal.(47) When the economic situation changed in the latter half of the nineteenth century, the vitality and capitalist dynamics of the national society made the retrogression of the surviving Indian communities even more striking. The place assigned by the new society to the Indians within its economic class structure was the lowest of them all. From then on, Indians who had lost their lands, formerly the key to their social identity, tended to remain Indians. In the Guatemalan municipality of Jilotepeque, about 95 per cent of the Indians in our day have to rent their lands from the mestizos.(48) In such cases conditions prevailing during the colonial period have become completely reversed. The racism pervading nineteenth-century Western civilization strengthened the traditional criollo and mestizo disdain for the "Indian dogs." This attitude helped to keep them apart in an extremely depressed proletarian situation.

Although mestizaje, in the strict sense of the word "miscegenation," had reached practically all the populations in Latin America on the eve of the twentieth century, acculturation and assimilation were delayed or even halted in some parts of the immense region. Whereas the multiracial structure of the decaying Régimen de Castas of the late colonial period was rather fluid in practice, the "Indo-American countries" of the nineteenth century brought into being an artificial ethnic dualism between "indígenas" and national citizens. It was a dichotomy with a strong taint of class exploitation.

But let us read a summary of the situation, written by Francisco Pimentel, a perspicacious Mexican intellectual, in 1865:

The white is a proprietor, the Indian a proletarian. The white is rich, the Indian poor, and miserable. The descendants of the Spaniards have all the knowledge of the times within their reach . . . the Indian is ignorant of everything . . . the white lives in the city in a splendid house, the Indian lives in isolation in the countryside in a miserable hut . . . There are two peoples in the same territory. What is worse, these peoples are to a certain degree mutual enemies.(49)

NOTES

(1) Richard Konetzke, 1949, "La esclavitud de los indios como elemento de la estructuración social de Hispanoamérica," *Estudios de Historia Social de España*, I (Madrid).

(2) Richard Konetzke, 1946a, "Documentos para la historia y crítica de los registros parroquiales en las Indias," *Revista de Indias*, VII (Madrid), 19.

(3) Alvaro Jara, 1956, *Legislación indigenista de Chile*, Mexico (Instituto Indigenista Interamericano), 205-207.

(4) Bernal Díaz del Castillo, 1955, *Historia verdadera de la conquista de la Nueva España*, I-II, Mexico, I, 428.

(5) Franklin Frazier, 1957, *Race and Culture Contacts in the Modern World*, New York, 46.

(6) Virginia Gutiérrez de Pineda, 1963, *La familia en Colombia*, I, Bogota, 67ff.

(7) Bernal Díaz del Castillo, 1955, *op. cit.*, 222.

(8) Richard Konetzke, 1946b, "El mestizaje y su importancia en el desarrollo de la población hispanoamericana durante la época colonial," *Revista de Indias*, VII (Madrid), 24-25.

(9) José Varallanos, 1962, *El cholo y el Perú*, Buenos Aires, 45.

(10) C.E. Marshall, 1939, "The Birth of the Mestizo in New Spain," *The Hispanic American Historical Review*, XIX, 173; Pedro de Cieza de León, 1945, *La crónica del Perú*, Buenos Aires, 145.

(11) Recopilacion de leyes de los Reinos de las Indias, Madrid VI-I-6, 1680; Bernal Díaz del Castillo, 1955, *op. cit.*, 387-388.

(12) Alberto M. Salas, 1960, *Crónica florida del mestizaje de las Indias: Siglo XVI*, Buenos Aires, 189ff.

(13) Richard Konetzke, 1946b, *op. cit.*, 22-23; Manoel de Nóbrega, 1955, *Cartas do Brasil e mais escritos . . . com introducão e notas históricas e criticas de S. Leite*. Coimbra, *passim*.

(14) Virginia Gutiérrez de Pineda, 1963, *La familia en Colombia*, *I*. Bogota, 183; Manoel da Nóbrega, 1955, *op. cit.*

(15) José Toribio Medina, *Los Aborígenes de Chile*, Fondo Histórico y Bibliográfico, Santiago, Chile, 1952, 85.

(16) The assertion of J.M. Ots Capdequi, 1957, *El estado español en las Indias*, 3rd edition, Buenos Aires and Mexico, 80, that most Spanish-Indian concubinages ended in marriage, seems to be completely groundless.

(17) CDFS, *Colección de documentos para la formación social de Hispanoamérica*, 1493-1810, I-III:2 (Madrid 1953-1962), I, 12-13; Richard Konetzke, 1946a, *op. cit.*, 215-216.

(18) Richard Konetzke, 1946b, *op. cit.*, 218.

(19) Richard Konetzke, 1946b, *op. cit.*, 235.

(20) Miguel de Cervantes Saavedra, 1949, *Obras completas*, ed. A. Valbuena Prat. Madrid, 902.

(21) Inca Garcilaso de la Vega, 1959, *Comentarios Reales de los Incas*, Buenos Aires and Lima, I:2, ch. I.

(22) Juan Friede, 1961, *Los Welser en la conquista de Venezuela*, Caracas, 405.

(23) Quoted by Alberto M. Salas, 1960, *op. cit.*, 57.

(24) Virginia Gutiérrez de Pineda, 1963, *La familia en Colombia*, I. Bogota, 160-161.

(25) Herbert I. Priestley, 1929, *The Coming of the White Man, 1492-1848*, New York, 111-112.

(26) R. de Lafuente Machain, 1939, *El gobernador Domingo Martínez de Irala*, Buenos Aires, 560-561.

(27) J.M. Ots Capdequi, 1957, *op. cit.*, 125-126.

(28) CDIHCh. III, *Colección de documentos inéditos para la historia de Chile*, Ed., by J.T. Medina, 2nd series, III, Santiago, 1959, 268/269.

(29) On Ramalho see also Manoel da Nóbrega, 1955, *op. cit.*, 183-184.

(30) Juan Friede, 1961, *op. cit.*, 198-202; Juan Friede, 1965, "La extraordinaria experiencia de Francisco Martín (1531-1533)," *Fundación John Boulton, Bouletín Histórico*, No. 7 (Caracas), 33-46.

(31) Bernal Díaz del Castillo, 1955, I, *op. cit.*, 98.

(32) UNESCO (1956), 315.

(33) Angel Rosenblat, 1954, *La población indígena y el mestizaje en América*, I-II, Buenos Aires, New ed. of the preceding item, 88, 102.

(34) Woodrow Borah, 1951, *New Spain's Century of Depression*, Berkeley, 18 and *passim*; S.F. Cook and W. Borah, 1960, *The Indian Population of Central México*, 1531-1610, Berkeley, and other studies by these two scholars. Whereas Borah places the demographic nadir around 1650, José Miranda, 1962, "La población indígena de México en el siglo XVII," *Historia Mexicana*, XII, on the basis of additional sources, suggests that demographic recovery in Central Mexico set in between 1620 and 1630. When tracing the demographic evolution of Chile, 1540-1620, Rolando Mellafe, 1959, *La introducción de la esclavitud negra en Chile: Trafico y rutas*, Santiago, 212-226, place the nadir around 1600.

(35) Henry F. Dobyns, 1963, "An Outline of Andean Epidemic History to 1720," *Bulletin of the History of Medicine*, XXXVII.

(36) Juan Friede, 1963, *Los quimbayas bajo la dominación española: Estudio documental*, Bogota, 253-254.

(37) Eric R. Wolf, 1962, *Sons of the Shaking Earth*, Chicago, 195.

(38) F.D. Ashburn, 1947, (ed.) *The Ranks of Death: A Medical History of the Conquest of America*, New York.

(39) Francois Chevalier, 1956, *La formación de los grandes latifundios en México*. Mexico (Problemas agrícolas e industriales de Mexico). The American edition unfortunately lacks the scholarly apparatus, 226:

(40) Orlando Fals Borda, 1957, *El hombre y la tierra en Boyacá: Bases sociológicas e históricas para una reforma agraria*, Bogota, 84.

(41) Mario Gongora, 1960, *Origen de los inquilinos en Chile Central*, Santiago, *passim*.

(42) Marcelo Carmagnani, 1963, *El salariado minero en Chile colonial: su desarrollo en una sociedad provincial: El Norte Chico*, 1690-1800, Santiago, 52-64.

(43) George Kubler, 1952, *The Indian Caste of Peru, 1795-1940: A Population Study Based upon Tax Records and Census Reports*, Washington, D.C., 36-37.

(44) See, *e.g.*, *Métodos, 1954, Métodos y resultados de la política indigenista en México*, Mexico 1954 (Memorias del Instituto Nacional Indigenista, VI), 118-119. The president of Guatemala in 1876 decreed that the indigenas of San Pedro de Sacatepequez who from 1877 onwards used ladino dress would "for legal purposes be declared to be ladinos"! J. Skinner-Klee, 1954, (ed.) *Legislación indigenista de Guatemala*, Mexico (Instituto Indigenista Interamericano), 33, 117-118.

(45) The different grades of mestizaje and acculturation in the interior of Argentina in the early nineteenth century are described well by the Swedish traveler J.A. Graaner, 1949, *Las provincias del Río de la Plata en 1816*, Buenos Aires, 33-34. See also IPGH, 1961, *El mestizaje en la historia de Ibero-América*, Mexico 1961 (Instituto Panamericano de Geografia e Historia), 96. It is calculated that there were still 48,000 Indians in central Chile by 1813, in addition to those in the border region. Alvajo Jara, 1956, *op. cit.*, 14-15.

(46) George Kubler, 1952, *op. cit.*, 39-42 and *passim*. Moisés Sáenz, 1933, *Sobre el indio peruano y su incorporación al medio nacional*, Mexico, 262, gives another earlier example. The governor of Quijos, Peru, reported in 1754 of a village with thirteen mestizos and only two Indian families that "the Mestizos no longer differ from the Indians in color or way of life, for despite being a mixture of whites and Indians, they have retroceded. . . ." According to the governor it was due to their having married Indians, which was probably only a partial explanation.

(47) Rodolfo Stavenhagen, 1963, "Clases, colonialismo y acculturación," *America Latina*, VI (Rio de Janeiro), 92. Kubler, 1952, *op. cit.*, 65, concludes: "The colonial attitudes toward passage from Indian to non-Indian caste may be described as more relaxed and more permissive than (it has been) since Independence . . . The governing factors in the process are probably economic and ideological and in no case biological. . . ."

(48) Rodolfo Stavenhagen, 1963, *op. cit.*, 74.

(49) F. Gonzalez del Cossío, 1958 (ed.) *Legislación indigenista de Mexico: Recopilación*, Mexico (Instituto Indigenista Interamericano), 151. It is amusing to find that the Maya Indians also cling to a dualist terminology, the criterion being the place of birth rather than "race." The opposite of the *mazehualob* (natives) are the *dzulob* (aliens). Robert Redfield, 1941, *The Folk Culture of Yucatan*, Chicago, 60.

This selection is from Magnus Mörner, *Race Mixture in the History of Latin America*, pp. 22-29, 31-33, 101-102, and 107-109. Copyright © 1967 by Little, Brown & Co., (Inc.). Reprinted and edited by permission.

HACIENDAS AND
PLANTATIONS IN YUCATAN

Arnold Strickon

Almost a quarter of a century ago Robert Redfield published *The Folk Culture of Yucatan*, a comparative study of four Yucatecan communities (Redfield 1941). In this book, and in a number of other books and articles which preceded and followed it (Redfield 1934; 1947; 1950; Redfield and Villa Rojas 1934) Redfield stepped over a threshold around which the anthropological profession had been milling for some years. The work of Redfield and his associates in Yucatan was far from the first study of so called "peasant" cultures. It was, however, the most influential pioneering attempt to construct a body of anthropological concepts specifically to deal with cultures which were part of modern, complex, social systems. This, of course, is not meant to imply that the ideas expressed by Redfield were completely original with him. Redfield himself expressed the intellectual debt he owed to Park, Durkheim, and Wirth.

Redfield's concepts, the folk society as a type, and the folk-urban continuum as a framework for the comparative study of "the little community" in complex systems, triggered a series of discussions (i.e. Redfield 1947; Miner 1952; Foster 1953; Mintz 1953). These discussions ultimately led to the replacement of Redfield's original concepts (or, perhaps, refinement of them) by more sophisticated typological categories and analytical frameworks.

The folk-urban construct was originally applied to order the data collected by Redfield, Hansen, and Villa Rojas on the distribution of cultures, or more accurately, the distribution of community types, on the peninsula of Yucatan. It sought to explain this distribution in terms of differential exposure of Maya agriculture communities to "urban" influences.

The present article is also concerned with the distribution of community types on the peninsula of Yucatan. It seeks to explain this distribution, however, in terms of the changing adaptations of various types of rural communities to a number of specific habitats and cultural-ecological niches. These cultural-ecological niches of Yucatan were part of a larger encompassing socio-economic system. This system, in turn, was itself changing over time. I believe that by considering these changing local adaptations as well as shifts in the total system it will be possible to integrate the materials presented by Redfield with aspects of Yucatecan culture with which he did not concern himself.

It was widely recognized, as soon as *The Folk Culture of Yucatan* appeared, that Redfield had all but ignored the henequen plantations of the northern peninsula. In terms of the economic role of the henequen industry for the whole peninsula, and in terms of the proportion of the Yucatecan population which was directly or indirectly dependent upon it, this zone and these plantations constituted the most important sector of the Yucatecan economy, society, and polity. It is my contention that the henequen estates of Redfield's time were critical to an understanding of Yucatecan culture as Redfield saw it. The article goes a step beyond this, however. I shall argue that the whole development of Yucatecan culture ever since the contact period has been tied to the agricultural estate in one of its typological guises. Not only is modern Merida inseparable from the plantation, but so are Dzitas, Chan Kom, and even the most "isolated" of Redfield's communities, Tusik. . . .

. . . In the development of Yucatecan culture the agricultural estate played a crucial economic, social, and political role. In the earlier periods of Yucatecan history it was devoted to cattle, later to sugar, and later still to henequen. Each of these stages, and the two major changes in crop, were critical to the evolution of Yucatecan community types up to the moment that Redfield saw them in the nineteen-thirties. It is this moment in time which is the bench mark of this analysis. Later developments in Yucatan are not considered.

The Maya agricultural village community itself played a rather passive role in the massive changes experienced by Yucatan in its post-conquest history. In periods and places where estate agriculture had no great labor demands the agricultural village was permitted to go its own way as long as a minimum of goods, labor and taxes were delivered to the superordinate groups. In those times and places where the superordinate economic and political interests needed the reserves of land and labor to be found within the Maya communities these resources were incorporated into the larger system and the village community was displaced. At various times and places the reverse also occurred. Estates surrendered both land and personnel which were reconstituted as "traditional" Maya village communities. Chan Kom is a result of this latter process. The driving force of this interaction between estate and village came from the estate and not the village.

In discussing the state systems in Yucatan I have chosen to follow the terminology of Eric Wolf and Sidney Mintz (1957) and speak about "haciendas" and "plantations". The "hacienda" is the capital extensive estate type where one of the primary concerns is to maintain a subsistence base for owners and workers, and a solid base for the elevated status position of the owner. The "plantation" is the capital intensive, often mechanized, estate which is corporately owned and which has as its primary function the provision of profits on the investment of its stock holders. The distinction between these two types of estate systems essentially parallels those made by Wagley and Harris (1955) between *engheno* and *usina* plantation types, and by Steward (1956) when he distinguishes between family and corporate plantation types.

In its organization this article begins with a brief outline of the environment of Yucatan. It then proceeds to discussions of the *encomienda* period, the cattle hacienda, the sugar plantation and the War of the Castes, the henequen plantation, and the emergence of the distribution of cultures as reported by Redfield. . . .

. . . At the time of Redfield's study three major zones could be delineated on the basis of rainfall, soils, natural cover, and agricultural use. 1. *The Northern Zone.* This is an arid area of thin soils characterized by a low scrub as its natural vegetation. The production of henequen for export today centers in this zone and has centered here since the eighteen-sixties. Throughout the Colonial and Early Republican periods, however, this area was the center of the livestock industry. 2. *The Central-Eastern Zone.* An area of moderate rainfall, deeper but still thin soils, and tall forest cover. The chief agricultural product in the nineteen-thirties was maize which served as both a subsistence and cash crop for its producers. At various times in the past, however, this zone has been one of subsistence maize production by Indians seeking refuge from Spanish or Mexican control, the climax area of the Yucatecan sugar industry, and a peripheral area of production of the henequen industry. 3. *The South-Eastern Zone.* A wet area of deep soils and rain forest. The primary agricultural product is maize which, at least up to the time of Villa's study, was produced for subsistence purposes only. Throughout the post-conquest history of Yucatan this had been a refuge area and has never been directly involved in agricultural production for export. At the time of Villa's study some chicle was collected for cash. More recently commercial lumbering operations have begun in the area (Villa Rojas 1962). This latter development, however, is beyond the concern of this paper. . . .

. . . During the years following the Conquest the basic social categories of the population emerged in Yucatan in a way paralleling that of the rest of Latin America. It was a three category division (variously described as class and/or caste, a distinction which need not concern us here) which closely correlated with the division of labor within the society. At the top were the Spanish and creoles who held the major social, political, and economic roles in the society. These people resided chiefly in Merida and Valladolid with occasional forays to their rural properties. Below these people were the mestizos who were the soldiers, overseers, artisans, *etc.* They were to be found both in the towns and in the countryside. At the bottom were the Indians who were the farmers and laborers. They were, for the most part, concentrated in the rural areas (Orosa Diaz 1945: 35; Chamberlain 1948: 240).

The Indians, for the most part, lived in their own villages which were separate from the Spanish and creole settlements. The Spanish institutions which administered these villages were distinct from those which administered Spanish, creole, and mestizo affairs. The direct administration of the Maya villages, however, was in the hands of Mayas confirmed by the Spanish in these roles. As long as minimum economic, political, and religious requirements set by the conquerors were met the villages were left to their own devices. (Cline 1950b: 26; Scholes 1937: 2; Chamberlain 1948: 339).

The degree of control of the Spanish and creoles over the Maya villages was not uniform over the entire peninsula. Effective control weakened as one moved south and east from Merida to Valladolid. Valladolid marked the Spanish-Free Maya frontier. Beyond this frontier were independent Maya villages which though similar to the ones held in encomienda were free of the labor and tribute obligations imposed by the Spanish on the northern Maya. From the mid-sixteenth century the area south and east of Valladolid was a refuge area for those escaping from or avoiding Spanish (and later Yucatecan and Mexican) rule. The border region between the refuge and Spanish areas became a breeding ground for revolt whenever the territorial and structural *status quo* between the "Euro-Mexicans" and the Free Maya was threatened (Villa Rojas 1945: 10-19; Cline 1945: 171).

In 1785 the encomienda period in Yucatan was brought to an end. The major institutions of that system, however, were carried forward in the cattle hacienda. . . .

THE CATTLE HACIENDA

. . . The production of cattle for export was the chief source of cash for the Yucatecan hacendado. Beef and cattle products were marketed in Cuba (Cline 1947: 50-51; Chamberlain 1948: 331). Maize was also an important product of the hacienda system in Yucatan but not, apparently, for export purposes. It was the chief source of subsistence for all parts of the population, Indian and non-Indian alike (Chamberlain 1948: 330).

The cattle hacienda stressed self-sufficiency. Transportation was poor and the seller could never be sure he could get his animals to market (Camara 1936: 13). Commodity imports were limited by the scarcity of cash and the same problem of transportation. It is characteristic of this kind of estate system that imports were chiefly luxury items for the owners and those things not produceable upon the estates themselves (Cline 1950a: 68).

After the encomienda system was outlawed tenure by the hacendados over the land they controlled underwent a legal change. Under the old system the encomendero had direct control over the Maya labor force and through them over the land they worked.

With the end of the encomienda system the hacendados tended to purchase outright the core area (the *planta*) of the old encomienda grant. Upon this core area stood the *casa de hacienda* and its attendant outbuildings, barracks, shops, etc. (Cline 1950b: 107; Stephens 1841 II: 402-403; Stephens 1868 I: 143 *passim*). The majority of the productive land which the hacienda needed, *milpa* for its maize and grazing land for its cattle, were usually state-owned public lands. These lands were rented at very low cost and even the low rents were only sporadically collected (Cline 1950b: 391-396). . . .

. . . The labor force on the haciendas was divided into two categories based upon residence or non-residence on the estate. The resident workers (*peones acasillados* or *asalariados*) consisted of foremen, cowboys, clerks, shopkeepers, policemen (if the hacienda were large enough), and others who carried out the day to day jobs on the "core" of the estate. These workers tended to be mestizos. Most of the resident workers were in fact cowboys *(vaqueros)* (Camara 1936: 19). These resident workers lived on hacienda property and received a regular salary and permanent employment. The rate of remuneration was, however, lower than that received by the non-resident *peon*. Both categories of workers, of course, were bound to the estate by the system of debt peonage. (Mendez 1921: 155-158).

The non-resident peons, or *luneros*, constituted the largest category of hacienda labor (Cline 1950b: 399). The term *"lunero"* is derived from the fact that one day a week the Indians of this class of labor had to work on estate lands. Customarily this was done on Monday, in Spanish, "lunes", hence lunero. These workers were Mayas.

These people lived on land owned, controlled, or peripheral to the hacienda. But where the resident workers lived in or near the hacienda headquarters, the non-residents lived in their own villages. They obtained their water from the wells or cisterns of the hacienda. In return for the use of the water and debts incurred by the Indian to the hacendado the Indians had to perform work on hacienda land. They had to clear and till about an acre of previously untilled land and another acre of land previously cleared. If for some reason a man could not put in his day's work he had to pay a fine of one *real* in silver. In addition to the work in the hacienda's fields the Indian had to work around the estate's great house carrying out a variety of drudge tasks for several hours on Saturdays.

Aside from his work as a lunero and the weekend work, the Indian tended to his own land from which his subsistence was derived. Depending upon local conditions, the lunero may have obtained this land from the estate, from public lands, communal lands, or it may have been privately owned. Whether the land was his or not, the Maya probably received tools and seed from the estate as well as credit at the estate store (Mendez 1921: 155-158; Stephens 1841 II: 414). . . .

. . . More so than their northern opposites, the Maya of the frontier region were independent of Creole controls. The Indian to white ratio was larger than in the northern zone and state power was not immediately available to the estate owners.

In the first half of the nineteenth century the Maya could generally be divided into four broad categories in Yucatan (Cline 1950a: 79-80). *a)* The City Maya who were highly acculturated and were, in fact, on the verge of becoming Mestizos; *b)* The Hacienda Maya who were the dwellers in the Maya villages and part-time laborers on the estates; *c)* The Free Maya of the frontier regions who, like the Hacienda Maya, depended for their subsistence upon the production of maize. They lived in their own villages but they were not tied as laborers and debtors to the haciendas; *d)* The *Huites* who were semi-sedentary Maya similar to the Lacandones. These lived on the far side of the frontier.

The Hacienda Maya and the Free Maya represented an essentially similar way of life. They were differentiated chiefly by the relative freedom of the latter from hacienda obligations. The Caste War was begun by "Huites" and Free Maya but they succeeded in recruiting to their cause a large number of Hacienda Maya.

The parents of the people of both Chan Kom and Tusik were derived from the "*b*" and "*c*" categories. The differences between these communities in the mid-nineteen-thirties can be attributed to different influences which were at work on two segments of what had originally been an essentially similar population.

After the initial shock of the contact situation the conditions to which the Maya communities had to adapt were in many ways a good deal simpler than those experienced by other peoples of the High Civilizations of the New World. The basic crop remained what it had always been . . . maize. The Spanish accepted this as their subsistence crop and could not demand (as they did in parts of the Andean Highlands) the production of European subsistence crops. There was no major shift necessary in the traditional Maya agricultural cycle. Unlike areas of Mexico and Peru in which mineral wealth existed, the Maya villagers did not have to supply masses of laborers for the mines.

On the contrary! The basic cash product on which the Spanish depended was cattle, and cattle production for beef and hides is labor extensive. Not enough livestock were raised to even begin to put a strain on the population's capacity to supply the necessary labor. The Spanish and their creole heirs, in fact, had more labor than they could utilize for money producing purposes.

This relatively enviable situation for the Maya was to come to an end. The livestock hacienda with its labor, land, and capital extensive patterns was to be replaced by the plantation with its intensive use of these resources. The European attack on the basic subsistence patterns of the Maya, which had not occurred in 1547, was finally to occur three hundred years later when sugar would demand the intensive use of Maya labor which livestock had not.

THE SUGAR PLANTATION AND THE CASTE WAR

The transition from hacienda to plantation did not occur all over Yucatan. Rather the sugar plantations tended to fill the deepsoiled, more humid regions which lay along the border of the Creole-Free Maya frontier, an area which had been marginal as far as European settlement was concerned prior to this time.

The emergence of sugar production as a major and large scale cash crop in Yucatan dates roughly from the removal of Spanish control over Mexico in 1821. When this happened the Major Yucatecan exports, beef and related products, lost their market in Havana which, of course, remained under Spanish rule. Later when Yucatecan hacendados tried to recapture this market they discovered that their place had been taken by Argentine producers who could sell the same goods at a lower price (Cline 1947: 50-51). Similar displacements and losses of markets occurred in relation to lumber from Campeche. The same process that had led to these market losses led as well to the cutting off of Yucatecan imports of sugar and rum from Cuba (Regil 1852: 275).

Cut off from their traditional markets, and from their source of supply for sugar and rum, investment capital was diverted into sugar production on the peninsula. This process was supported by State preferential tax policies (Cline 1950b: 518-520). . . .

. . . The sugar plantations were quite different from the maize and cattle haciendas to the north. Whereas in the haciendas an identical labor cycle was required on both hacienda and Maya maize plots, the cycle and pattern of work on the plantations was different, and probably conflicted with the needs of the individual Maya's milpa. Sugar requires almost instantaneous processing after it is cut. The period during which it may be harvested is rather limited. Therefore, large amounts of labor are needed during the harvest period and during this period the laborer, at least ideally, should be available full time. Because sugar must be processed by relatively expensive and complex machinery before it is marketable, it is necessary for both field and mill functions on a sugar plantation to be closely integrated.

The semi-sedentary slash and burn agriculture upon which the Maya depended for their subsistence was not compatible with the closely integrated and controlled work patterns required by commercial sugar production. Milpa agriculture came under the attack of Yucatecan economists and publicists as an inefficient and primitive means of production. They attacked as well those Indians who sought escape from the estates by retreating further into the bush as the "sugar frontier" advanced (Regil 1852: 296, 299-300; Mendez 1923: 165-166). In an effort to control the exodus of actual or potential Maya estate laborers the Yucatecan government enacted laws which sought to bring the Maya under effective control of the government and (incidentally) of the estates (Yucatan 1849 I: 296; Yucatan 1849 III: 75). The laws bring to mind the reduction laws of the early Conquest period.(1)

The need for relatively large amounts of labor, and the kind of labor which the sugar estates required as compared to that needed on the old haciendas, changed the order of relationship between owner or manager and laborer. In Cline's words (Cline 1950b: 555-556):

> The direction that changes took was less towards direct suppression of habitual native ways than the extension of new enterprises which were predicated on somewhat different relationships between the Maya and creole than was usual in the early days. Colonial economy rested on Maya labor and effort, but more or less accepted the fact that Indians were permitted to go their own way, so long as tribute goods appeared at the designated time. The newer doctrines, however, began a conscious or unconscious drift toward the native as a human tool, as part of a disciplined and fixed labor force necessary for operation of large scale commercial enterprises.

Those Indians who, for whatever reason, refused to attach themselves to the sugar plantations (or were lucky enough to avoid being rounded up) found themselves being pushed further into the bush with each passing year. As the plantations took over the best lands of the rich frontier region the Maya's position was becoming more and more desperate. It was these Maya who initiated the Caste War of 1847 and together with the hacienda and plantation Maya who were recruited to their cause, finally brought to an end the sugar industry of Yucatan (Cline 1950b: 355, 369, 526).

The Caste War, which began in 1847, was the last (and most successful) Indian uprising in Yucatan. Although the Indians provided the manpower for the rebellion, the leadership was clearly mestizo (Cline 1950b: 333; see also Ancona 1889: 16-18; Baqueiro 1878 II: 233-237; Orosa Diaz 1945: 30). The high point of the rebellion came in the spring of 1848 when the rebels held some four-fifths of the peninsula. Only Merida and some coastal roads remained in creole hands. In general from this point on Maya fortunes ran downhill (Baqueiro 1878 II: 358; see also Reed 1964).

The Indians trekked south into what is now Quintana Roo. This is the genesis of the Maya of the X-Cacal subtribe of east-central Quintana Roo, the people of Tusik (Villa 1945: 22, 40, 127). These Maya kept up some military activity until as late as 1901. During this long period practically their only peaceful contacts with outsiders were with the British at Belize who sold them arms. Under almost constant stress for almost seventy-five years the Santa Cruz Maya developed a highly integrated political, religious, and military pattern while carrying on the same basic milpa subsistence pattern as most other Maya (Villa 1945: 118). Both the people of Tusik and Chan Kom derive from the same body of hacienda and plantation Maya. The chief difference between them date from the Caste War and its aftereffects.

The War of the Castes set the stage for the next major shift in Yucatecan estate agriculture. The family and sugar plantations had been burned and sacked from

Hopelchen in the west to Valladolid in the east. The loss in population was great and the thriving sugar industry was choked off. The continuing fear of raids by the Santa Cruz Maya caused the abandonment of much of the old frontier zone (Cline 1950a: 135).

The saving grace was henequen:

> In more ways than one the plant saved Yucatan. Its plantations formed a protective belt . . . around Merida making inrushes of raiding Mayas more difficult. Railroads and other communications connected Merida to its newly formed port of Progreso, and at the same time extension of communication networks made a compact unit of the north and northwest section of the Peninsula, leaving Merida's hegemony unchallenged . . . now henequeneros ruled much like colonial encomenderos. (Cline 1950a: 137; see also Baqueiro 1881 II: 117). . . .

HENEQUEN

. . . Although the expansion of henequen as a major crop for export began prior to the War of the Castes this expansion was based primarily upon the essentially Maya technology for utilizing the plant. Some attempts had been made to perfect a mechanical rasper for freeing the valuable fiber from the leaves but these were, for the most part, failure.

The War of the Castes paralyzed henequen production on the peninsula and prices on the world market soared (Camara 1936: 15). The war also deprived the northern estates of their labor force either because the workers had run off to join the rebels or because they were rounded up by the government to fight against those who had. After the northern region had been cleared of rebels the northern estate owners began lobbying in order to "get at" the large numbers of soldiers who were being held in the north by the government as a strategic reserve. After a great deal of effort by the henequeneros these reserves were removed from direct military control and went to work on the northern plantations (Camara 1936: 22-26).

The provision of a renewed labor supply, however, did not solve all the problems of the estate owners. The increasing demand for henequen fiber in the world market made it clear that the volume of fiber that was necessary to even begin to meet the demand could not be supplied by the manual technology of the Mayas. A new technology was needed oriented to a large scale of production. Once the technology was developed capital to equip the estates with it would also have to be found. Answers to both problems, of course, were found. A mechanical rasper was invented by Solis (a Yucatecan) in 1857. It was originally operated by human or animal power but steam was applied to it in 1861. Capital came from the estate owners themselves and from the United States (Camara 1936: 26-28).

The interest of United States' capital in the Yucatecan henequen industry was based upon the growing mechanization of North American agriculture spurred by the invention of the mechanical reaper by McCormick. It was found that henequen fibers made the best twine to bind the sheathes of wheat as they were cut and bundled by the McCormick reaper. As the use of this machine spread in North America so the demand for henequen fiber increased. This was especially so in the decade of the eighteen-eighties (Cline 1950b: 543).

By the eighteen-fifties and sixties the modern henequen industry based upon fixed labor, commercial capital, and the mechanical rasper had emerged from the old pre-war "mixed hacienda" of corn, cattle, and small-scale henequen production (Cline 1950b: 552). The change-over was not effected overnight. Part of this can be attributed to the high cost of capitalizing the new type of plantation. It is estimated that it took about $130,000 (U.S.) to set up an average sized plantation of the new type and keep it going until a return was realized (Cline 1948: 34). This problem was met by shifting slowly from old to new production procedures (and crops) and using already producing henequen plots to supply the funds for the capital investment necessary for the expansion of the new styles of production (Cline 1950b: 535; see also Ober 1884: 88). By this means mixed plantations could be changed over to primarily modern henequen production. Ober, (1884: 65-66), while travelling through Yucatan in 1881, mentions seeing great fields of hemp on the plantation at Uxmal. Less than forty years before Stephens had noted only small plots for local use on the same estate. . . .

. . . By the turn of the century the henequen industry was more or less confined to the northern arid regions of the peninsula. This was the situation as Redfield saw it during his work. Until the eighteen-eighties and nineties, however, the crop was cultivated over a much wider area.

The modern commercial henequen plantation (at least up to the third decade of this century which is our primary concern) is an agricultural factory which exists for the primary reason of growing and processing henequen fiber for the world market. Unlike the hacienda of old there is no longer an attempt at self-sufficiency; food, clothing, and other necessities are brought in from the outside (Cline 1950b: 377).

I shall not enter here into a detailed description of the general structure of these plantations.(2) Worth noting, however, are the differences in the kinds of labor in the new plantations as compared to those of the old haciendas. Yucatan, which before the Caste War and the sugar episode had been a region of labor "surplus" was now one of labor shortage. The deficiency was made up by the importation of foreign workers and by the cooperation of the Diaz government in providing Indians from other areas of Mexico. Turner reports (1910: 15) that on one plantation of 1,500 workers thirty were Koreans, 200 were Yaquis, and the rest were Maya. He estimated that on all the henequen plantations there were 8,000 Yaquis, 3,000 Chinese and Koreans, and 100,000 to 125,000 Mayas.

This labor force was bound by the traditional system of debt peonage (Turner 1910: 34, 37) and the payment of wages in plantation scrip (Cline 1950b: 197). These were reinforced by estate controls (or attempts at control) over the marriage of their workers (Turner 1910: 22) and by the liberal use of physical punishment (Turner 1910: 24).

Under the old hacienda system most of the labor force consisted of part-time laborers who were still able to look after their own milpas and communal affairs off the estate's planta. On the henequen plantations of the period of the Mexican Revolution the majority of workers were full-time residents who dwelled either in barracks, if single, or in separate huts with their families if married. The quota of leaves to be cut for married men was generally set higher than that for single men so that their families would have to work in the fields with them (Turner 1910: 25, 27, 30; Edwards 1924: 7). In addition to the resident laborers there were some part-timers who came from settlements around the estate. These men, apparently, were resident upon the estate while under contract to it (Turner 1910: 30-31; Tannenbaum 1929: 112). . . .

THE EMERGENCE OF THE SAMPLE COMMUNITIES

... The four communities that Redfield and his party studied may now be examined within the matrix of the changing structure of the estate system in Yucatan.

Prior to the War of the Castes Merida was, in Cline's (1950b: 187) words, "an overgrown Spanish village". Its chief function was to serve as the administrative center for Yucatan and as the place of at least part-time residence of the area's hacendados.

With the coming of the henequen boom, however, Merida started to become more a commercial center and its "sleepy Spanish village" aspects began to be submerged. The old port of Merida, Sisal, was replaced, concurrent with the early henequen boom, with the deep water port of Progreso. The very name the local leaders chose for the new port is probably a measure of their changing orientation.

As henequen money began to pour into the area some of it was invested in providing the city of Merida with the surface trappings of a "modern" city, such as paved and lighted streets and public transportation (Redfield 1941: 34-35).

The growth of Merida was not to be measured in the increasing numbers of public facilities alone. In the period from 1895 to the first third of the century the population of the State of Yucatan increased by thirty per cent (297,088 to 384,790) while the population of Merida increased by seventy per cent (50,000 to 85,000) (Hansen 1934: 134). The emergence of Merida from the state of being a pre-industrial administrative center is literally inseparable from the henequen industry which tied the economy of the area into the industrial economy of the northern hemisphere.

At the time of Redfield's study the henequen plantations were concentrated in the arid northern zone of the State. When the henequen boom started after the end of the Caste War, however, commercial cultivation of the plant had occupied the more humid and deeper soiled zones along the old pre-war frontier as well.

The desire to put land into henequen practically submerged maize for a time. In 1845 (prior to the outbreak of the Caste War) 610,000 acres (94.9 per cent of the total acreage in major crops) was devoted to maize. In 1881 only 36,400 acres were in maize, twenty-three per cent of the total acreage. Even as late as 1930, although the total acreage devoted to maize had gone far over the 1881 figure (there were in 1930, 151,000 acres in maize), the proportion of acreage devoted to maize had actually decreased (to 20.4 per cent) due to the massive increase in henequen acreage (Cline 1950b: 380-381; see also Ober 1884: 27, 87; Redfield 1941: 8).

Paralleling the expansion of henequen into the southern and eastern areas was the spread of a railroad network whose chief business was to service the henequen estates. A major junction of this railroad network to the south and east of Merida was established at the town of Dzitas. Although Dzitas became more important after this, it tended to maintain, as do most provincial towns in Latin America (Wagley 1955: 438), many customs and practices which were characteristic of larger population centers in earlier years, and thereby provide an apparent "link" between Merida and Chan Kom in Redfield's analysis. Unlike pre-henequen Merida, however, the importance of Dzitas did not lay in any administrative functions which may have centered there which had been Merida's earlier function. Rather, its importance depended upon its role in the railroad network.

The expansion of henequen into the relatively rich-solid interior played an important role in the emergence of Chan Kom as well as Dzitas. By the last decade of the nineteenth century increasing production in the arid northern region had placed the interior producers in a marginal position. The richer soils and heavier rainfall of the interior meant a more luxurious growth of weeds as compared with the northern estates. This resulted in higher labor costs due to the effort necessary in keeping the weeds down (Edwards 1924: 2). The interior producers also had higher transportation costs in moving their product from the estates to the port of Progreso. As greater acreage was converted to henequen production in the north and as the northern producers were better able to meet the total demand for henequen the higher production and transportation costs of the interior producers forced them to operate on a shrinking margin of profit. Ultimately they had to withdraw from production.

As more land in the northern zone was devoted to henequen this climax area became less capable of feeding itself. As the lands in the central and eastern areas were withdrawn from henequen they were turned back to maize by the former workers on the estates. By the end of the nineteenth century the northern area had become completely dependent upon the maize of the old frontier zone (Cline 1950b: 379, 555). The production of maize for the northern estates was not carried out on plantations. Rather maize was raised for subsistence purposes by the Maya who lived, once again, in their own villages. The surplus of maize that they produced was sold to travelling merchants who came to the market towns. The merchants, in turn, sold the maize to the commercial establishments of the north. The railroads which were originally meant to carry henequen from the interior to the port were now carrying maize from the interior to the arid zone estates.

As this "niche" in the Yucatecan ecology opened up the Maya started to drift back into what had been a no-man's-land since the Caste War as well as into those areas abandoned by the interior estates. It was in this region, around a cenote, that Chan Kom was founded (Redfield and Villa 1934: 2).

The southern zone, Quintana Roo, did not take part in the explosive growth of the henequen industry either directly or indirectly. The interest of Mexico and the rest of the world in it was limited. The Santa Cruz Maya, the people of Tusik, were permitted to live relatively uninvolved with the larger economy and polity in an area that no one else wanted. These Maya raised maize for their own use and retained intact the military and religious structures they had developed in response to the pressures of the Caste War. They may have lost some of their pugnaciousness but very little of their suspicion of outsiders as they filled a niche, that of refugees, which had been an ongoing part of Yucatecan culture ever since Spain and the estate system appeared on the peninsula. . . .

NOTES

(1) "Indians and other people who live furtively in the countryside are obliged to be admitted within thirty days to some village, *rancho*, or *hacienda* . . . and that the *alcalde* in whose jurisdiction these people are found comply with the order and within ten days of the said terminal date send to the chief of his district a count [of such people]." (Yucatan 1849 I: 296. The translation is my own. A.S.)

(2) The only source available to me, and the only one that I know of, that contains a description of life on the henequen plantations of Yucatan in the period

between the turn of the century and the nineteen-thirties is John K. Turner's-*Barbarous Mexico* (1910). This is a political propaganda piece designed to convince readers in the United States to avoid American interference in the Mexican Revolution. The general structure and institutional situation that Turner describes, however, fits nicely with the descriptions we have in other areas of the world about the organization of highly capitalized plantation systems. There are some works which in varying detail treat of the henequen plantation since Redfield's time (Villa Rojas 1962; Deshon 1959; Chardon 1961).

BIBLIOGRAPHY

Ancona, Eligio, 1889: *Historia de Yucatán, desde la época más remota hasta nuestros días*, 2nd ed. Barcelona: Jaime Jepus Roviralta, vol. II.

Baqueiro, S., 1878: *Ensayo Histórico sobre las Revoluciones de Yucatán desde el año de 1840 hasta 1864.* Mérida: Manuel Heredia Argüelles, 2 vols.

Camara Zavala, Gonzalo, 1936: *Reseña Histórica de la Industria Henequenera de Yucatán.* Mérida: Imprenta Oriente.

Chamberlain, R., 1948: *The Conquest and Colonialization of Yucatan: 1517-1550.* Washington, D.C.: Carnegie Institution of Washington, Pub'l. 582.

Chardon, Rolan, E.P., 1961: *Geographic Aspects of Plantation Agriculture in Yucatan.* Washington, D.C.: National Academy of Sciences, National Research Council.

Cline, Howard F., 1945: "Remarks on a Selected Bibliography of the Caste War and Allied Topics." *The Maya of East-Central Quintana Roo,* by Alfonso Villa Rojas. Washington, D.C.: Carnegie Institution of Washington, Pub'l. 559. 1947: The "Aurora Yucateca" and the Spirit of Enterprise in Yucatan, 1821-1843. *The Hispanic-American Historical Review,* vol. 27. 1948: The Henequen Episode in Yucatan. *Inter-American Economic Affairs,* vol. 2. 1950a: "Related Studies in Early Nineteenth Century Yucatecan Social History." *Microfilm Collection of Manuscripts on Middle American Cultural Anthropology,* No. 32. Chicago: University of Chicago Library. 1950b: "Regionism and Society in Yucatan, 1825-1847: A Study of 'Progressivism' and the Origins of the Caste War." *Microfilm Collection of Manuscripts on Middle American Cultural Anthropology,* No. 32. Chicago: University of Chicago Library.

Deshon, Shirley K., 1959: *Women's Position on a Yucatan Henequen Hacienda.* Ann Arbor: University Microfilms.

Edwards, H.T., 1924: *Production of Henequen Fiber in Yucatan and Campeche.* Washington, D.C.: United States Department of Agriculture, Department Bulletin No. 1278.

Foster, George M., 1953: What is Folk Culture? *American Anthropologist,* vol. 55.

Hansen, Asael T., 1934: "The Ecology of a Latin American City." *Race and Culture Contacts,* E.B. Reuter (ed.). New York: McGraw-Hill Book Co.

Mendez, Santiago, 1921: "The Maya Indians of Yucatan in 1861." *Reports on the Maya Indians of Yucatan,* Marshall H. Saville (ed. and trans.) Indian Notes and Monographs, vol. 9, No. 3. New York: Museum of the American Indian.

Menéndez, Carlos, 1923: *Historia del Infame y Vergonzoso Comercio de Indios: Vendidos a los Esclavistas de Cuba por los Politicos Yucatecos desde 1848 hasta 1861.* Mérida: Talleres Gráficos de "La Revista de Yucatán."

Miner, Horace, 1952: The Folk-Urban Continuum. *American Sociological Review,* vol. 17.

Mintz, Sidney W., 1953: The Folk-Urban Continuum and the Rural Proletarian Community. *The American Journal of Sociology*, vol. 59.

Ober, Frederick, 1884: *Travels in Mexico and Life Among the Mexicans*, Boston: Estes and Lauriat.

Orosa Díaz, J., 1945: *Yucatán, Panorama Histórico, Geográfico y Cultural*, México: Secretaría de Educación Pública.

Redfield, Robert, 1934: Culture Changes in Yucatan. *American Anthropologist*, vol. 36. 1941: *The Folk Culture of Yucatan*, Chicago: University of Chicago Press. 1947: The Folk Society. *The American Journal of Sociology*, vol. 52. 1950: *A Village That Chose Progress: Chan Kom Revisited*. Chicago: University of Chicago Press.

Redfield, Robert and Alfonso Villa Rojas, 1934: *Chan Kom, A Maya Village*, Washington, D.C.: Carnegie Institution of Washington, Pub'l. 448.

Reed, Nelson, 1964: *The Caste War of Yucatan*. Stanford: Stanford University Press.

Regil, José M. and Alonso M. Peón, 1852: Estadística de Yucatán. *Boletín de la Sociedad Mexicana de Geografia y Estadistica*, vol. 3.

Scholes, F.V., 1937: *The Beginnings of Hispano-Indian Society in Yucatan*, Washington, D.C. Carnegie Institution of Washington, Supplementary Publications No. 30.

Stephens, John L., 1841: *Incidents of Travel in Central America, Chiapas, and Yucatan*, vol. II. New York: Harper and Brothers. 1868: *Incidents of Travel in Yucatan*, 2 vols., New York: Harper and Brothers.

Steward, Julian, et al., 1956: *The People of Puerto Rico*. Urbana: University of Illinois Press.

Tannenbaum, Frank, 1929: *The Mexican Agrarian Revolution*. New York: The Macmillan Co.

Turner, John K., 1910: *Barbarous Mexico*. Chicago: Charles H. Kerr and Co.

Villa Rojas, Alfonso, 1945: *The Maya of East-Central Quintana Roo*. Washington, D.C.; Carnegie Institution of Washington, Pub'l. 559. 1962: Notas sobre la Distribución y Estado actual de la Población Indígena de la Península de Yucatán, México. *America Indigena*, vol. 22.

Wagley, Charles and Marvin Harris, 1955: A Typology of Latin American Subcultures. *American Anthropologist*, vol. 57.

Wolf, Eric and Sidney Mintz, 1957: Haciendas and Plantations in Middle America and The Antilles. *Social and Economic Studies*, vol. 6.

Yucatan, State of, 1849: *Collección de Leyes, Decretos y Ordenes, o Acuerdos de Tendencia General del Poder Legislativo del Estado Libre y Soberano de Yucatán*, Alonso Aznar Pérez (ed.). Mérida: Rafael Pedrera. 3 vols.

This selection is abridged from Arnold Strickon, "Haciendas and Plantations in Yucatan: An Historical-Ecological Consideration of the Folk-Urban Continuum in Yucatan," *America Indigena*, Vol. 25, No. 1, Jan. 1965, pp. 36-37, 39-40, 41-42, 42-43, 44-45, 45-46, 47-48, 49, 50-52, 54-55, 56-57, 58-60.

INTERNAL COLONIALISM IN MEXICO

Pablo González-Casanova

Marginal national development, lack of participation in economic, social, and cultural development, a large sector of have-nots—these are characteristics of underdeveloped societies. Not only do underdeveloped societies have an unequal distribution of wealth, income, culture, and technology, but, as is the case in Mexico, they often contain two or more socio-cultural aggregates, one which is highly participating and another which is quite marginal; one which is dominant—be it called Spanish, Creole, or Ladino—and another which is dominated—be it called native, Indian, or indigenous.(1)

These phenomena—marginality and non-participation in the growth of the country; dual or plural society; cultural, economic, and political heterogeneity which divides the country into two or more sectors with different characteristics—are interrelated. They are in turn linked to the much deeper problem of *internal colonialism*, or the domination and exploitation of certain groups by others. "Colonialism" does not, as is commonly believed, pertain only to relationships between nations. It also pertains to relationships within a nation, insofar as a nation is ethnically heterogeneous and certain ethnic groups become the dominant groups and classes and others become the dominated. Despite the long years of revolution, reform, industrialization, and development, inheritances from the past—marginality, plural society, and internal colonialism—persist in Mexico today in new forms. Those factors determine the characteristics of the society and the national polity.

Marginality can be measured in various ways. Mexican censuses gather general and specific data which are quite useful for analysis of marginality. They register the illiterate population. They estimate the size of the population which does not eat wheat bread because it eats only corn or oats neither, a distinction closely linked to standards of living and marginality. They enumerate the population which does not wear shoes because it wears sandals or no footgear at all, the school-aged population which does not attend school, the population which does not drink milk, and that which does not eat meat or fish.

Some of these indicators of marginality have been traced in all the censuses since the beginning of the century; some have not. From those that have been, we can get an idea of the problem as it is today and how it evolved.

Although marginality occurs in the cities in forms characteristic of slum life, it is a phenomenon which nonetheless tends to become closely associated with rural life. Marginal society is predominantly rural.

According to the 1960 census, Mexico has a population of 27,980,000 aged six or over. Of these, 17,410,000 are literate and 10,570,000 are illiterate. Among the urban population the number of literate individuals is 10,750,000, whereas that of illiterate individuals is 3,430,000. Among the rural population the number of literate individuals is 6,660,000 and that of illiterate individuals is 7,150,000. Whereas in urban areas 76 per cent of the population is literate, in rural areas only 48 per cent is literate, and whereas the urban population only has 24 per cent illiteracy, the rural population has 52 per cent.

According to the same 1960 census, of a total population of 33,780,000 aged one or over, 23,160,000 ate wheat bread, and 10,620,000 did not. Among the urban population 14,940,000 ate wheat bread and 2,180,000 did not. Among the rural population 8,220,000 ate wheat bread, and 8,430,000 did not. Whereas in urban areas only 13 per cent did not eat wheat bread, in rural areas 51 per cent did not.

In 1960, according to the census, 25,630,000 Mexicans one year of age or over had one or more of the following foods—meat, fish, milk and eggs—whereas 1,840,000 did not have any of these foods. Among the urban population 14,970,000 inhabitants ate one or more of those foods, and 2,160,000 ate none. Among the rural population 10,660,000 inhabitants ate one or more of these foods, whereas 5,990,000 ate none. That is, of the urban population, 87 per cent ate meat, fish, milk, or eggs, whereas 13 per cent ate none; of the rural population 49 per cent ate these foods, whereas 51 per cent ate none.

In 1960, 21,040,000 inhabitants of one year of age or more wore shoes, 7,910,000 wore sandals, and 4,830,000 went barefoot. That is, 12,740,000 did not wear shoes. Of the urban population, 14,450,000 wore shoes, and 2,680,000 did not. Of the rural population, 6,590,000 wore shoes, and 10,060,000 did not. Thus, 84 per cent of the urban population wore shoes and 16 per cent did not, whereas of the rural population only 40 per cent wore shoes and 60 per cent did not. With respect to the population that goes barefoot, 1,010,000 persons go barefoot in cities, and 3,750,000 in the countryside, that is, 6 per cent and 23 per cent, respectively.

The statistical analysis, then, reveals that illiteracy, not eating wheat bread, meat, fish, milk, or eggs, and going barefoot are more usual in rural life. They also occur in cities, but not to the same extent.

Analysis of the same data also reveals that those who do not eat bread are often those who do not drink milk. Those who do not drink milk are often those who do not wear shoes, those who are illiterate, those who do not eat wheat bread, and so on. There is a kind of integral marginality. The population which is marginal in terms of one factor is highly likely to be marginal in terms of all the factors. Thus there is an immense number of Mexicans who have nothing of nothing.(2)

Despite the fact that the percentage of marginal population has decreased in the past fifty years—this demonstrates a process of national integration—the marginal population has increased in absolute numbers, and should present trends continue, it will increase in the future. . . .

... The integration of the country, the relative decrease of the marginal population, and the absolute increase of the participant population amount to an absolute increase of the marginal population. That is, if the percentage of marginal population in Mexico today, for example, is smaller, in absolute figures there is nonetheless a greater number of marginal Mexicans. They constitute a national economic, cultural, and political problem of magnitude. Our integral marginal population, which lacks all the minimum products of development, is the most vigorous challenge to the development of the nation and of the national policy. It is one part of a social structure which is divided into two large sectors, the one of Mexicans who participate in development and the other of those who are marginal in terms of development. Here we see the internal dynamics of inequality, one of the two major national problems.

MARGINALITY AND PLURAL SOCIETY

The dual or plural society in Mexico is made up of the Ladinos and Indians. The Indians constitute the super-marginal population; they almost have the attributes of a colonial society. The division between the two Mexicos—participant and marginal, haves and have-nots—scarcely indicates the existence of a plural society, but reveals the residue of a colonial society. The relationships between the Ladinos and the Indians exemplify far more precisely the problems of plural society and internal colonialism. Unfortunately, when we analyzed these phenomena we found very few correlations. For the analysis of plural society we have a single indicator, language. For the analysis of internal colonialism, we have only indirect indicators, which reveal the existence of semi-colonial discrimination and exploitation.

The percentage of Mexicans aged five or over who speak no Spanish but an indigenous language or dialect was 8.4 per cent in 1930; 3.8 per cent in 1940; 3.6 per cent in 1950; 3.8 per cent in 1960. In absolute numbers, these figures are 1,190,000 in 1930; 1,240,000 in 1940; 800,000 in 1950; and 1,104,000 in 1960.

The population which speaks an indigenous language or dialect, also "gibbers" some Spanish and is predominantly Indian in culture. It is not integrated with the national culture, and was of these percentages: 7.6 per cent in 1930; 7.5 per cent in 1940; 7.6 per cent in 1950; and 6.4 per cent in 1960. In absolute numbers, the figures are: 1,070,000 in 1930; 1,250,000 in 1940; 1,650,000 in 1950; and 1,930,000 in 1960.

The monolingual and bilingual indigenous population is in simple, conservative terms, the indigenous population which is not integrated with the national culture. Its percentage of the total population aged five and over has varied as follows: 16 per cent in 1930; 14.8 per cent in 1940; 11.2 per cent in 1950; and 10 per cent in 1960. In absolute numbers the figures are: 2,250,000 in 1930; 2,490,000 in 1940; 2,450,000 in 1950; and 3,030,000 in 1960.

Meanwhile, the population which represents the national culture constituted 83.9 per cent of the total aged five and over in 1930; 85.1 per cent in 1940; 88.8 per cent in 1950; and 90 per cent in 1960. In absolute figures, 11,790,000 people in 1930; 14,300,000 in 1940; 19,370,000 in 1950; and 25,970,000 in 1960.

We should note that the percentage of monolingual indigenous population decreased from 1930 to 1950, and increased from 1950 to 1960. The total of the monolingual indigenous population remains practically the same during those thirty years. In absolute figures it decreased only between 1940 and 1950, but it increased from 1950 to 1960; in 1960 it was practically identical to what it had been in 1930.

The percentage of the bilingual indigenous population remained practically unchanged from 1930 to 1950 and decreased between 1950 and 1960. In absolute figures, there was a sustained increase decade by decade throughout the period.

The percentage of the monolingual and bilingual population—that is, the total indigenous population—decreased in every decade throughout the period 1930-60. In absolute figures, it increased from 1930 to 1940, decreased from 1940 to 1950, and increased again in 1960.

The population representing the national culture increased in absolute terms, both by decades and throughout the whole period. The character of this change will become evident if we analyze the rates of growth of the national population and those of the indigenous population, as shown in the following chart.

RATES OF GROWTH OF THE NATIONAL AND INDIGENOUS POPULATION
(1930–40)

Rates of growth of the population	1930–40	1940–50	1950–60
Total	18.73	31.22	35.40
Rural	15.84	16.07	16.27
Monolingual	4.36	− 35.72	26.47
Bilingual	17.66	31.79	16.52
Monolingual-bilingual	10.66	− 1.73	23.80
National culture	18.42	35.49	34.04

These figures lead us to several conclusions. For the monolingual population and the total of the monolingual and bilingual populations, the rates are only negative—and therefore imply an absolute decrease—between 1940 and 1950. It is unlikely that during that decade there was a decrease in birth rates or an increase in death rates among the Indians, so it seems that this is the only decade in which the absolute number of Indians who learned Spanish and became integrated with the national culture increased. Or there may have been an underestimation of the monolingual population in the 1950 census. Both changes may also have taken place simultaneously. During 1940-50 the bilingual population and the national population reached their highest rates of growth. This is particularly significant with respect to the bilingual population, insofar as it seems to grow at the expense of the monolingual population, because it indicates that large groups of Indians learned Spanish and still maintained their own languages and dialects. Among the rural population, in the decade from 1950 to 1960, the monolingual group grew at a much faster rate, the monolingual-bilingual group grew at a faster rate, and the bilingual group had the same rate of growth as did the total rural population. . . .

. . . All these estimates are conservative; they are based only upon census data and linguistic criteria. The facts reach far beyond. As the anthropologists Isabel H. de Pozas and Julio de la Fuente noted: "It is frequently found that census data regarding language highly differ from reality, and that the decrease of the monolingual Indian population is only apparent, since Indians who hardly speak a few words of Spanish are registered as speaking that language." Using the linguistic criterion, the Indian population was 10 per cent of the total in 1960; using other indicators, such as the awareness of belonging to a community which is different and isolated from the national culture or to the tribal or pre-Hispanic spiritual and material culture,(3) we find that the percentage of Indians is between 20 and 25 per cent, and thus numbers between 6 and 7.5 million.(4)

This problem is far more significant and pervasive than has been previously thought. It is not merely an Indian problem, but a problem of national structure. As such it explains not only the behavior and condition of the Indians, but also that of Mexicans generally, and with far greater precision than a simple analysis of the nation's class structure.

PLURAL SOCIETY AND INTERNAL COLONIALISM

The ideology of liberalism, which considers all men to be equal before the law, is a great advance from the racism prevailing in colonial times. Similarly, the ideology of the Revolution is a no less important advance over the social Darwinist and racist ideas of *porfirismo*. Today the Indian problem is approached as a cultural problem. No Mexican scholar or ruler believes that this is an inborn, racial problem. Social and political mobility in Mexico has allowed Indians to occupy the highest positions and to achieve the highest social status in Mexican society since Independence, and particularly since the Revolution. Even national history and its pantheon of heroes have viewed Cuauhtémoc, the leader of the resistance against the Spaniards, the Juárez, the Indian President and builder of modern Mexico, with highest regard.

The same equality has been recorded at national and local levels by anthropologists. Indians who participate in the national culture are able to achieve the same status as mestizos or whites in economic, political, and interpersonal and family relationships. An Indian participating in the national culture is in no way an object of racial discrimination. He may feel the consequences of discrimination because of his economic status, his occupational role, or his political role. But that is all. For these reasons, Mexican anthropology views the Indian problem as a cultural problem. This affirmation represents an ideological advance over the racism prevailing in the social sciences of the Porfirian period. From a scientific point of view, the statement corresponds to reality. Yet it does not explain all the basic characteristics of this reality.

The Indian problem is essentially one of internal colonialism. The Indian communities are Mexico's internal colonies. The Indian community is a colony within the national territory, and it has the characteristics of a colonized society. This fact has not been recognized by the nation. Resistance has been multiple and will be powerful. The habit of thinking of colonialism as an international phenomenon has caused people to overlook internal colonialism. The habit of viewing Mexico as an ex-colony or a semi-colony of foreign powers, and of seeing Mexicans generally as subjected to foreign colonialization, has blocked the development of the view that Mexicans are colonizers and colonized. The past and present national struggle for independence is a factor in this problem, and it has made the men involved in this struggle national heroes. Another fact which has contributed to obscuring the situation is that both internal and international colonialism manifest their more extreme characteristics in typically colonial regions far from the metropolis. Although in the city there are no colonial prejudices or struggles, but rather democratic and egalitarian styles of life, quite the opposite obtains in the outlying areas. Here we find prejudice, discrimination, colonial types of exploitation, dictatorial forms, and the separation of a dominant population, with a specific race and culture, from a dominated population, with a different race and culture. This is what occurs in Mexico. In the conflict areas, in those regions in which both Indians and Ladinos live, we find prejudice, discrimination, colonial types of exploitation, dictatorial forms, and the racial cultural alignment of dominant and dominated populations. From a social point of view, the most striking difference from international colonialism is the fact that a few members of the Indian communities can physically and culturally escape from these internal colonies. They can go to the cities and find a job, and they have the same chances of mobility as the members of the lower classes who have no Indian cultural background. Yet this mobility has limitations and does not end internal colonialism. Internal colonialism exists wherever Indian communities are found. Research done by Mexican anthropologists reveals the existence of a way of life that corresponds to that of the historical definition of colonialism. This is true among the Amuzgos, Coras, Cuicatecos, Chatinos, Chinantecos, Choles, Huaxtecos, Huaves, Huicholes, Mayas, Mayos, Mazahuas, Mazatecos, Nahoas, Mixes, Mixtecos, Otomíes, Popolocas, Tarahumaras, Tarascos, Tepehuanos, Tlapanecos, Tojolabales, Totonacas, Tzeltales, Tzotziles, Yaquis and Zapotecos—that is, among several million Mexicans.

One form assumed by internal colonialism is when what anthropologists call the "ruling center" or "metropolis" (San Cristóbal, Tlaxiaco, Huauchinango, Sochiapan, Mitla, Ojitlán, Zacapoaxtla) exercises a monopoly over Indian commerce and credit, with relationships of exchange unfavorable to the Indian communities. This is manifest in a permanent decapitalization of the Indians at the lowest levels. The commercial monopoly isolates the Indian community from any other center or market, promoting monoculture and dependence.

Another form of internal colonialism is the exploitation of the Indian population by the different social classes of the Ladino population. This exploitation, as is the case in all colonies of modern history, is a combination of feudalism, capitalism, slavery, forced and salaried labor, share farming and peonage, and demand for free services. The despoliation of Indian lands performed the same two functions it fulfilled in the colonies: it deprived the Indians of their land, and it transformed them into peons or salaried workers. The exploitation of one population by another manifested itself in different salaries for the same jobs (in mines, sugar refineries, coffee plantations); in the over-all exploitation of Indian craftsmen (workers with wool, *ixtle*, palm, willow, ceramics); social, verbal, and dress discriminations; and, as we shall see, juridical, political, and trade-union discriminations. Such discrimination demonstrated colonialist attitudes on the part of local and even of federal functionaries, and of course on the part of the Ladino leaders of political organizations.

Still another form of internal colonialism is shown by cultural differences and differences in standards of living according to whether the population is Ladino or Indian. Observable differences, however, are not sharply divided between people speaking Indian languages and those who do not, because a large sector of the nearby non-Indian peasant population has standards of living as low as those of the Indian populations.(5)

Indian communities have the following characteristics: a predominantly subsistence economy, with minimal money and capitalization; lands unsuitable for crops or of low quality, unfit for agriculture because of hilly terrain, or of good quality but in isolated locations; deficient crop-growing and cattle-breeding because of low quality seeds and inferior animals smaller than the average of their kind and pre-Hispanic or colonial techniques of land exploitation; a low level of productivity; standards of living lower than those of peasants in non-Indian areas, exemplified by poor health, high rates of mortality, including infant mortality, illiteracy, and the presence of rickets; lack of facilities and resources, such as schools, hospitals, water, and electricity; promotion of alcoholism and promotion of prostitution by hookers and Ladinos; aggressiveness among communities, which may be overt, or expressed through games or dreams; magic-religious culture; economic manipulation through the imposition of taxes and a status-bound economy; and political manipulation.

All these conditions are basic to colonial structure and are found in the definitions and explanations of colonialism from Montesquieu to Myrdal and Fanon. They are also mentioned in the works of foreign writers and anthropologists of Mexico. Together they demonstrate the existence of internal colonialism, which is characteristic of those regions where Indians and Ladinos coexist. Internal colonialism is *also* characteristic of the *national society*, in which there is a continuum of colonialism from groups exhibiting the entire range of colonial characteristics to regions and groups in which only traces are visible. Internal colonialism affects an estimated 3 million Indians using the criterion of language, 7 million using the criterion of culture, and almost 12 million according to the Index of Contemporary Indocolonial Culture created by Whetten.(6) In fact, internal colonialism encompasses the whole marginal population and penetrates the entire culture, society, and polity of Mexico in different ways and intensities, depending on the groups and regions.

The Indian problem is one of national scope; it defines the nation itself. It is the problem not of a small sector, but of many millions of Mexicans who do not share in the national culture and also of those who do participate in the national culture. The concept of internal colonialism explains the national structure as a whole better than the concept of social classes in a pre-industrial society, in terms of ideology, political affiliation, and class consciousness. . . .

NOTES

(1) Cf. Pablo González Casanova, "Sociedad Plural y Desarrollo: El caso de México," *América Latina* (Centro Latinoamericano de Pesquisas em Ciéncias Sociais), October-December 1962, No. 4, pp. 31-51.

(2) Isabel H. de Pozas and Julio de la Fuente, "El problema indígena y las estadísticas," *Acción Indigenista* (Mexico: Instituto Nacional Indigenista, December 1957).

(3) A. Caso, "Definición del indio y de lo indio," *Indigenismo* (Mexico: Instituto Nacional Indigenista), 1958

(4) *Ibid.*

(5) Cf. Julio de la Fuente, "Población Indígena" (unpublished); Alejandro D. Marroquín, "Problemas Económicos de las Communidades Indígenas de México" (mimeographed course program), Mexico, 1956; Miguel O. de Mendizábal, "Los problemas indígenas y su más urgente tratamiento," *Obras Completas IV* (Mexico, 1946); Moisés T. de la Peña, "Panorama de la Economía Indígena de México,"

Primer Congreso Indígena Interamericano (Pátzcuaro, 1946); Jorge A. Vivó, "Aspectos Económicos Fundamentales del Problema Indígena," *Revista América Indígena*, Vol. III, No. 1, January 1947; Gonzalo Aguirre Beltrán and Ricardo Pozas, *Instituciones Indígenas en el México Actual* (Mexico: Instituto Nacional Indigenista, 1954).

(6) Cf. Nathan L. Whetten, "México Rural," *Problemas Agrícolas e Industriales de México*, Vol. V, No. 2 (Mexico, 1953), pp. 245 ff.

CLASSES, COLONIALISM, AND ACCULTURATION

Rodolfo Stavenhagen

This article will analyze the ethnic relations which characterize the intercultural regions of *Altos de Chiapas* in Mexico and Guatemala. It is not my intention to add new data presently unknown to experts in the area. My purpose is both more modest and more ambitious. I will recognize known data into a scheme of interpretation differing from those which are currently used in anthropology. I believe that a conceptual scheme based on the role of internal colonialism in inter-ethnic relations will help in clarifying some historical and structural problems in the formation of national societies of Mexico and Guatemala.

The conceptual frame of reference of the analysis of social classes is more adequate to understanding relationships between economy and society than the frames of reference generally employed by researchers. I shall use some concepts that are sometimes ambiguous. In each case I will try to specify their meanings, but this will not always be possible. In such cases, these concepts will have to be understood in their more common-sense use. The sources cited are merely illustrative, not exhaustive. Many of the facts analyzed are sufficiently well known so as to require no further documentation. The choice of the region, which includes areas of Mexico and Guatemala, is justified because of cultural and historical similarities of the Indian region on both sides of the border. Political and economic differences between the countries, especially in the course of the last few years, do not seem to have substantially modified the quality of inter-ethnic relationships; particularly is this the case on the analytical level at which the essay is written.

The Maya region of Altos de Chiapas and Guatemala is peculiar in that each local community constitutes a cultural and social unit which is distinguished from other similar communities, and its limits, furthermore, coincide with those of modern political-administrative units called municipalities or municipal agencies. Thus, the Indian population of every municipality (or municipal agency) can be distinguished from others through its clothing, dialect, membership, and participation in a religious and political structure of its own. This usually also involves economic specialization and a developed feeling of identity with other members of the community, reinforced by a somewhat generalized endogamous system. Aside from being an administrative unit integrated in Mexican and Guatemalan national political structures, the municipality in this region represents the sphere of the Indian population's social unit, which has been called "tribe" by some ethnologists, and which others have even termed the germ of the "nation."(1)

This coincidence of modern municipal institutions with traditional Indian structures, resulting from the particular historical evolution of the region, has allowed the survival of the traditional structures within the framework of the modern national state.

INDIANS AND LADINOS

In the entire region and in almost all the local communities there coexist two kinds of populations, two different societies: Indians and Ladinos. The problem of the relationships between these two ethnic groups has been studied in different ways by anthropologists.(2) Only a few of them, nonetheless, have attempted an interpretive analysis of the total society.(3) In these pages, I intend to offer some elements for such an analysis.

It is well known that biological factors do not account for the differences between the two populations; we are not dealing with two races in the genetic sense of the term. It is true, of course, that in a general way the so-called Indian population has biologic traits corresponding to the Amerinds and equally, that the so-called Ladino population has the biologic traits of the Caucasoids. But even though Ladinos tend to identify with whites, in fact they are generally mestizo. It is the social and cultural factors that distinguish one population from the other. . . .

THE DYNAMICS OF INTER-ETHNIC RELATIONS

. . . Colonial society was the product of mercantilist expansion: of the dawning of the bourgeois revolution in Europe. Its structure still retained much of the feudal era, especially in the character of human relationships. Some researchers even affirm that feudalism grew stronger in America after it had begun to decline in Spain, and that America "feudalized" Spain once again.(4) Exploitation of the Indian population was one of the main goals of colonial economic policy. In order to maintain this labor reserve, it was framed by a complex of laws, norms, restrictions, and prohibitions which kept accumulating during three centuries of colonialism, and which resulted in the corporate "folk" communities. All things were determined for the settler's benefit: the land tenure of the Indian community, its local government, technology, economic production, commerce, residential pattern, marriage norms, education, dress styles, and even its idiom and use of language. In Spain, nobles, landowners, commercial bourgeoisie and petty bourgeoisie were at times fighting, at times cooperating in the struggle for their respective interests. But in Spanish America a rigid social hierarchy based upon centralization of political and economic power and validated in the *Legislation of Indias* kept the natives in the position of inferiority with respect to all of the other social levels.

The colonial system worked on two levels. The restrictions and economic prohibitions which Spain imposed upon her colonies (and which were to forment the independence movements) were repeated, often aggravated, in the relations between the colonial society and the Indian communities. As Spain was to the Colony, so the Colony was to Indian communities: a colonial metropolis. Since then mercantilism penetrated even the most isolated villages of Spanish America.

The social groups in Spanish America which took part in the processes of economic production and distribution which sustained the Spanish empire also participated in the class structure of the colonial system. In the same way the Indian population participated in the class structure of the Colony. Colonial relationships and class relationships underlay ethnic relationships. In terms of *colonial relationships*, the Indian society as a whole confronted colonial society. Primary characteristics of the *colonial situation* were ethnic discrimination, political dependence, social inferiority, residential segregation, economic subjection, and juridical incapacity. In the same way, class structure was defined in terms of labor and property relations. These relations were not defined in ethnic, political, social, or residential terms. Only juridical coercion (supported by military power) as well as other economic and extra-economic pressures intervened in the establishment of labor relations. Labor relations were not between two societies, but only between two specific sectors within them. Colonial and class relationships appear intermixed throughout this period. While the former primarily answered to mercantilist interests, the latter met the capitalist ones. Both kinds of relationships were also opposed to each other: the development of class relationships came into conflict with the maintenance of colonial relationships. Indian communities were constantly losing members to the developing national society. Despite tutelary legislation, the biologic and cultural mixing was a constant process which kept producing new problems for colonial society. Those Indians who for various reasons were absorbed by the larger society, therefore, quit the colonial relationships to become integrated simply in a class structure. In consequence, they were no longer Indians. . . .

. . . Contemporary inter-ethnic relations partly result from colonial policy. They also represent the disintegration of that policy and are a function of present economic and class structures. As has been shown by various economists, underdeveloped economies tend to polarize into areas of growth and structurally related areas of stagnation. The Maya region of Chiapas and Guatemala constitutes such an area, as do other Indian areas of Mexico. The marginal populations inhabiting these areas are growing in absolute numbers, despite national economic development.(5) If this happens in Mexico, despite accelerated economic growth in recent years, then in Guatemala where there has been no such development, it must surely happen with greater intensity. During the colonial period, *colonial relations* in the Indian region served the interests of a well defined tructurally related areas of stagnation. The Maya region of Chiapas and Guatemala constitutes such an area, as do other Indian areas of Mexico. The marginal populations inhabiting these areas are growing in absolute numbers, despite national economic development.(5) If this happens in Mexico, despite accelerated economic growth in recent years, then in Guatemala, where there has been no such development, it must surely happen with greater intensity. During the colonial period, *colonial relations* in the Indian region served the interests of a well defined dominant class which in turn subdued the colonial society as a whole to its own interests, insofar as relations with Spain would permit. In the situation of *internal colonialism* (which might be called the *endo-colonial situation*) class relationships within the whole society are more complex. The regional dominant class, represented by Ladinos, is not necessarily the dominant one in the national society. In Guatemala, since the defeat of the nationalist bourgeoisie in 1954, these two groups became identified. There is no contradiction between landowners, commercial bourgeoisie (particularly coffee-growers) and foreign capital.(6) In Mexico the situation is different. National power is held by a bureaucratic, "developmentist" bourgeoisie, a product of the 1910 Revolution. This bourgeoisie has displaced latifundists on a national level, but in more backward regions, such as Chiapas, it tolerates them while seeking the support of a new rural bourgeoisie composed of traders, neo-latifundists and public employees.(7) In both Mexico and Guatemala the regional dominant class is composed of "power brokers"—to use Wolf's term(8)—of mestizo origin who have come to fill the power vacuum left by the old feudal landowning aristocracy. In Guatemala the endo-colonial situation is stronger than in Mexico, where latent contradictions between the "developmentist" bourgeoisie in power and its weak shadow in the Indian hinterland contribute to a rapid development of class relationships to the detriment of colonial relationships, and have allowed the development of a structural development-underdevelopment dichotomy. Thus, inter-ethnic relations at the level of total society may be considered as a function of the development-underdevelopment structural dichotomy (in its social aspect of internal colonialism), and of the dynamics of national class structure.

For purposes of analysis, four elements may be isolated in the inter-ethnic situations: colonial relationships, class relationships, social stratification, and the acculturation process. These four elements constitute interdependent variables and with them we may attempt to build a hypothetic model of inter-ethnic relations.

COLONIAL RELATIONSHIPS

These relationships are a function of the structural development-underdevelopment dichotomy, and they tend to be in force for as long as the dichotomy persists. As long as there are areas performing as internal colonies in underdeveloped countries, the relationships characterizing their inhabitants tend to take the form of colonial relationships. These are strengthened where there exist, as in the Maya region, marked cultural differences between two sectors of the population, leading to a rigid stratification. There exists an obvious interest on the part of the dominant ethnic group (Ladinos) in maintaining colonial relations, especially when their predominance depends on the existence of cheap and abundant labor. This is the case when possibilities of expansion of the economy are few, when agriculture has a low level of productivity and when the labor-capital relation in agriculture is high, when local or regional industrialization is weak or non-existent; and when the region's internal market is poorly developed. Therefore the maintenance of colonial relations is rather a function of the degree of development of national economy than of local or regional decisions.

In contrast to Ladinos, the Indians—the subordinate ethnic group—derive no benefit from the colonial situation and may try various forms of reaction to it. The first is withdrawal into the corporate community, both physically and socially. As Wolf pointed out, this has happened on various occasions in the history of the region, and it represents on the part of the Indian ethnic group a latent tendency which becomes manifest when the economic and political situation allows it. In association with this withdrawal, the Indians also react to the colonial situation in terms of nationalism. This form of reaction may have as its objective the strengthening of the Indian government (regional council), and possibly the struggle for the Indians' national political representation. It also becomes manifest through an extreme anti-Ladinism and resistance to ladinization. Here there also intervene other counter-acculturative factors such as messianism and, on certain occasions, armed upheavals and other violent manifestations. Finally, there is a third form of reaction to the colonial situation, and this is assimilation. It is an individual process which, as has been seen, represents a separation from the corporate structure of the community. From a cultural point of view it represents ladinization. From a structural point of view it means that the individual becomes integrated to the class structure, no longer as an Indian (that is, a colonized person), but simply due to his relationship to the means of production. Ladinization, as we have seen, may be the result of upward mobility in the scale of socio-economic indices. But generally it only means the proletarianization of the Indian.

Of the three main forms of reaction to the colonial situation, the first, simple withdrawal, does not seem to have many adherents at present. Among those who are still clinging to it we find a few traditionalist elders. But other members of the community know that there are better ways to combat the harmful effects which colonial relations have upon Indians. The reaction which we have called "nationalism" (for lack of a better term) assumes diverse shapes. Some of them are spontaneous and circumstantial (such as armed upheavals and messianic movements); others have been induced by external agents (such as education in the Indian language); and still others may be the consequence of a political consciousness of Indian communities (such as the election of a person participating in corporate civic-religious political structure, to a position in the constitutional municipal government). At present, the main forms of nationalistic reaction are promoted—at least in Mexico—by the national government's specialized agencies. Measures such as literacy in the Indian language and adequate political representation of the Indians show that those responsible for Indianist policy are conscious of the colonial character of inter-ethnic relations, despite the fact that the problem has never been formulated in those terms by the ideologists of *indigenismo*. Yet paradoxically, these measures are only taken as a means to an end which represents its absolute negation, that is, the incorporation of the Indian to Mexican nationality, in other words, the disappearance of the Indian as such. The paradox, nonetheless, has a practical justification: national integration can only be achieved if contradictions inherent in colonial relations are overcome. This can be done either by suppressing one of the terms of the contradiction, or by a qualitative change of content in that relation. By encouraging measures of a nationalist kind, Indianist policy is committed to the second of these alternatives. Yet if the contradiction inherent to the colonial relation between Indians and Ladinos is solved, there would be a greater contradiction resolved at the same time: that which exists between those colonial relations and national integration (since the existence of the former represents an obstacle to the latter). In other words, national integration may be achieved, not by eliminating the Indian, but only by eliminating him as a colonized being.(9) Mexican Indianism has admitted this timidly and not without some ambiguities. But in this respect it is much more advanced than the rest of the national society. Indianism certainly does not escape the contradictions of national society when, for instance, it is stated that literacy in the Indian language in Chiapas only serves to facilitate the teaching of Spanish, and a series of "assimilationist" measures (particularly the action of "acculturation agents" or "promoters of cultural change") are simultaneously put into practice.

CLASS RELATIONSHIPS

We cannot over-emphasize that the class character and colonial character of inter-ethnic relations are two intimately related aspects of the same phenomenon. They are separated here only for the purpose of our analysis. Class relationships have developed parallel to and simultaneous with colonial relations and tend to displace them more and more. But the colonial character of inter-ethnic relations impresses particular characteristics upon class relations, tending to stop their development. In this context, class relations mean mutual interactions between persons holding opposed economic positions, independent of ethnic consideration. These relations develop together with the region's economic development. As agricultural production increases, as the market for industrial product expands, as monetary economy develops, and as the labor market expands, colonial relations lose their importance and give way to the predominance of class relations. The latter's development also depends, to a great degree, upon structural factors of national economy and is not the result of decision-making at the regional or local level. At any rate, this development tends to impress upon the class relations between Indians and Ladinos a characteristic mark while the feudal or semi-feudal aspects, so frequently indicated in the literature, tend to disappear.

Consequently, measures for local or community development such as improvement of agricultural techniques, establishment of production, cooperatives, etc., may change colonial relations into class relations, but not necessarily so. This transformation can only take place if such developments are accompanied by parallel development of the regional economy as a whole, and particularly of its Ladino metropolis. If such is not the case, the likelihood is that the fruits of local development will enter the traditional socio-economic circuits without modifying the regional structure.

It has already been seen that on certain occasions Ladinos are interested in maintaining colonial relations. There also exist circumstances in which they are interested in strengthening class relationships to the detriment of colonial relationships. This happens particularly with the development of the productive forces: when Ladinos are presented with new opportunities of investment, when they need seasonal labor which can only be obtained through monetary incentives, or when they require non-agricultural labor (for certain manufacturing industries or for construction work in the cities or on the roads) ; finally, when they need to develop new regional markets and the strengthening of the Indians' demand for manufactured products. The Ladinos' interest in the development of class relations also arises when the agrarian reform manages to really break the land monopoly and when the possession of his own land can turn the Indian back to subsistence farming. In this case, class relations develop particularly through the marketing of crops and the agricultural credit structure.

Under certain circumstances Ladinos may have an interest toward curbing the development of class relations: for instance, when their interests are affected by the establishment of plantations by foreign companies, which modify the status quo by attracting a certain amount of labor and paying higher wages than those which are usual in the region, etc. This has happened in Guatemala. Or, for example, when economic development of the region contributes to the liberation of labor, thus increasing its emigration or at the least its capacity to demand higher salaries, in which case the Ladino latifundists are forced to invest a greater amount of capital in agriculture, and this capital they do not possess.

Indians are also interested in the development of class relationships because these imply the existence of better economic opportunities and of wider alternatives for action. On the other hand, they may be interested in curbing the development of class relations because they tend to destroy the subsistence economy, because they contribute to economic and psychological insecurity and encourage proletarianization and disintegration of Indian culture.

The development of class relations involves new forms of sociability and social organization; there emerge new social categories and new groupings and social institutions. The development of these relations tend to destroy the rigidity of social stratification, to modify its bases (from ethnic characteristics to socio-economic indices) and to encourage ladinization of the Indian.

SOCIAL STRATIFICATION

Insofar as the regional system of social stratification has only two strata based essentially on ethnic characteristics it tends to maintain the appearance of a colonial situation. At the same time, it tends to change into a clearly defined socio-economic stratification. The already existing stratification among Ladino ethnic groups tends to become extensive to both ethnic groups. Perhaps the day will come when both ethnic groups—independent of their cultural characteristics—will be included into a single stratification system, based exclusively on socio-economic criteria. The old stratification system, based on ethnic characteristics (sometimes called *castes*) tends to conflict with the development of class relations and the socio-economic stratification based on them. Thus, for instance, an Indian trader or landowner receives discriminatory treatment from Ladinos who are in a socio-economic situation inferior to their own, while Indian day laborers tend to receive smaller wages than the Ladinos who are in the same position. Among the Ladinos there exists an obvious concern over maintaining the bases of ethnic stratification; especially among the lower strata of the Ladino population, who in this way avoid competing with mobile Indians. This is the same phenomenon as that of the poor whites in the south of the United States and other such cases in other parts of the world.

Social stratification, as we have seen, comprises two aspects: inter-ethnic stratification reflects its colonial past, while Ladino socio-economic stratification, in which Indians are increasingly participating, reflects the development of new class relations, devoid of their ethnic content. The Indians' upward vertical mobility in the socio-economic scale is accompanied by a certain degree of ladinization, but, as has already been pointed out, not all of the aspects of Indian culture change at the same rate. Development of class relations tends to facilitate the Indian's upward mobility, since an ascent in the socio-economic scale renders the conservation of a low status based upon exclusively ethnic criteria more precarious. Upward mobility, as much in the socio-economic scale, as in the shift from the Indian to the Ladino ethnic group, is a function of the transformation of the colonial situation into a class situation.

LADINIZATION

This process of acculturation of the Indian is hard to place in a structural analysis, since it is used in the literature to refer to processes which are highly varied in content. In a general sense it means the adoption of Ladino cultural elements by individuals or groups (communities) of the Indian ethnic group. Thus, the change in dress, the substitution of folk medicine by scientific medicine, and the change of occupation, to take only three examples, are all part of the process of ladinization. Yet the structural significance of these three examples, taking each by itself, is very different. Without considering for the moment the motivational determinants leading to a change in dress, this by itself has no consequences for the social structure; except if, carried out collectively by the Indians, it should lead to certain changes in the value systems of both ethnic groups, which in turn might influence the systems of mutual action and interaction, thus affecting social structures. But this kind of chain argument does not lead to a better understanding of the phenomena being studied. Of the preceding examples, the second—the shift from traditional medicine to modern medicine—does not by itself represent a structural change in either. But it may lead to demographic consequences which will have important structural results. Change of occupation, on the contrary, can only be understood within the frame of a structural analysis. The above shows that the concept of ladinization may mean anything from a simple change in the daily use of an object (using a spoon instead of a tortilla to eat soup), up to a complete change of the Indians' life and world view. Within the limits of this essay, concern over the process of ladinization is only meaningful insofar as it has immediate structural implications.

NOTES

(1) Sol Tax, "The Municipios of the Midwestern Highlands of Guatemala," *American Anthropologist*, Vol. 39 (1937); Henning, Siverts, "Social and Cultural Changes in a Tzeltal (Mayan) Municipio, Chiapas, Mexico," Proceedings of the 32nd International Congress of Americanists, Copenhagen, 1956.

(2) By *ethnic group* we understand a social group whose members participate in the same culture, who may sometimes be characterized in biological or racial terms, who are conscious of belonging to such a group and who participate in a system of relations with other similar groups. An *ethnia* may be, depending upon circumstances, tribe, race, nationality, minority, caste, cultural component, etc., according to the meaning given to these terms by different authors.

(3) The global society is the widest operational social unit within which the studied relations take place and which is not a part of the immediate experience of the actors in the social system. It includes the community, the municipality, the region, the ethnic group, etc., and their diverse systems of interrelation. It is sociologically structured. The global society has been termed a macroscopic group embracing the functional groupings, social classes and conflicting hierarchies. Generally, in this essay, it is identical to the nation (or to the Colony), but it sometimes also refers to the wider economic system, in which the nation participates. See Georges Gurvitch, *La Vocation Actuelle de la Sociologie*, Paris, 1950, p. 301, *passim*.

(4) Angel Palerim, "Notas sobre la Clase Media en México," *Ciengias Sociales* (Washington), No. 14-15 and 16-17 (1952). (Reproduced in *Las Clases Sociales en México*, Mexico, s.f., 1960.)

(5) *Cf.* Pablo González Casanova, "Sociedad Plural y Desarrollo: el Caso de México," *América Latína*, Year 5, No. 4 (1962).

(6) Jaime Díaz Rozzotto, *El Carácter de la Revolución Guatemalteca*, Mexico, 1958. Also see Richard N. Adams, "Social Change in Guatemala and U.S. Policy," in *Social Change in Latin America Today*, New York, (1960).

(7) *Cf.* Rodolfo Stavenhagen, *"La Réforme Agraire et les Classes Sociales Rurales au Mexique,"* Cahiers Internationaux de Sociologie, 34, 1963.

(8) *Cf.* Eric Wolf, *Sons of the Shaking Earth*, Chicago, 1959.

(9) The term "national integration" is very ambiguous. The way it is used by Myrdal, for example, referring to its economic aspects, it simply means equality of opportunities *(Cf.* G. Myrdal, *Solidaridad o Desintegración*, Mexico, 1956). When Aguirre Beltrán, in *El Proceso de Aculturación*, speaks of "intercultural integration" at the regional level, he rather refers to the homogenization of the cultural differences between Indians and Ladinos, that is, to the predominance of the mestizo culture, which is Mexico's national culture. In the preceding paragraph the term has been used in the sense given by Myrdal, which is why we affirm, differing from Aguirre Beltrán, that national integration may be achieved without the disappearance of the "cultural" Indian.

BIBLIOGRAPHY

Further reading is recommended in Morner (8) who summarizes a vast amount of research on the changing situation of both the Amerindian and the African population of Latin America. This work also contains an extensive bibliography. Wagley and Harris (10) provide both a background and a historical outline of the varying situations of minorities in the New World. Gibson (5) provides a solid summary of Mexican colonial society from the conquest to independence. The relationship between Indian labor and Mexican development is treated by Chevalier (2) for the same period. Kubler (7) examines the Indian population in another area of Andean America. His work can serve as a background for the personal account by Blanco (1) of the struggle of the Indian peasantry for control over their land. Hobsbawm (6) provides an account of the area in Peru which was an important locus of peasant insurgencies during the early 1960's. The article by Cotler (3) develops a theoretical model of subordination and domination for the group relations in Peruvian society. Pearse (9) provides an account of the uprisings of the Indian peasantry during the last century in still another Andean nation. Dessaint (4) analyzes the devastating impact of large scale agriculture on the Indian population of Guatemala.

(1) Blanco, Hugo. *Land or Death: The Peasant Struggle in Peru.* New York: Pathfinder Press, 1972.

(2) Chevalier, Francois, (trans.) Alvin Eustis. *Land and Society in Colonial Mexico: The Great Hacienda.* Berkeley, California: The University of California Press, 1970.

(3) Cotler, Julio. "The Mechanisms of Internal Domination and Social Change in Peru." *Studies in Comparative International Development,* Vol. 3, No. 12, 1967-68.

(4) Dessaint, Alain Y. "Effects of the Hacienda and Plantation Systems on Guatemala's Indians." *American Indigena,* Vol. 22, No. 4, October, 1962.

(5) Gibson, Charles. *The Aztecs Under Spanish Rule: A History of the Indians of the Valley of Mexico, 1519-1810.* Stanford, California: Stanford University Press, 1964.

(6) Hobsbawm, E.J. "A Case of Neo Feudalism: La Convencion, Peru." *Journal of Latin American Studies,* Vol. 1, No. 1, May 1970.

(7) Kubler, George. *The Indian Caste of Peru, 1795-1940: A Population Study Based on Tax Records and Census Reports.* Washington, D.C.

(8) Morner, Magnus. *Race Mixture in the History of Latin America.* Boston: Little, Brown and Company, 1967.

(9) Pearse, Andrew. "Peasants and Revolution: The Case of Bolivia." *Economy and Society,* Vol. 1, Nos. 1 & 2, August and November, 1972.

(10) Wagley, Charles and Marvin Harris. *Minorities in the New World.* New York: Columbia University Press, 1958.

VII.
RACE, COLOR, AND
WORLD STRATIFICATION

INTRODUCTION

In Section II, we argued that the historical origins of modern race relations lay in the expansion of the white world in Western Europe and later, in the United States. This expansion remade the societies of non-white peoples as subordinated strata in empires dominated by whites. At the same time, ideologies justifying the domination of non-white peoples by white conquerors matured. From the fifteenth to the nineteenth centuries, a world-wide system of racial stratification was therefore established.

During the last twenty-five years, some contradictory trends in this system of modern race relations seem to have appeared. Even before World War II, racial ideologies had begun to lose legitimacy throughout the most of the world, although a few nations and some social groups within nations publicly advocated racial ideologies. Most racial arguments were silenced by the experience of Nazi racism in World War II and by the winning of independence by large numbers of non-white peoples. Further, even those nations that construct racial ideologies for domestic uses are loathe to explain their foreign policy and trade in these terms. The decline in legitimacy of racial thought in the last three decades is striking. The world seems to have taken a big step towards the obliteration of a major form of inhumanity.

Yet there is an apparent paradox, for there is a continuation and even solidification of the international structure of racial stratification produced by the expansion of the white, Western world. The powerful and wealthy are, with the exception of Japan and perhaps China, white; the weak and the poor are generally the non-white nations. The resolution of the paradox is that the function of the earlier era of white expansion and racial ideologies was the creation of a system that consolidated the power and privilege of the white world. No longer is there a need for the white administrator, plantation owner, or entrepreneur. The international system of racial domination and subordination can now reproduce itself without the violence of colonial conquest. In the place of conquest is the silent violence of malnutrition, infant mortality, and substandard living conditions to define reality for many non-white peoples. Structural violence has replaced overt violence.

The reality of continuing differential structural violence by skin color is regularly overlooked by international observers. Statistics are usually colorless, and it is easy to forget the simple human meaning, much less the racial differentiation, involved in the aggregate facts of international wealth and poverty. More important, the standard analysis of gains and losses from the operation of the international system of racial stratification does not make apparent the linkages between those who gain and those who lose, because those who analyze international dynamics use the nation-state as the primary unit of analysis. The world is conceived as being composed of approximately a hundred nations. While some are larger and more powerful than others, each moves independently in the international arena. Further, what happens within one nation is thought to be basically independent of the desires and actions of groups in other nations. Perception of the world in terms of East-West, communist-democratic, in spite of *detente*, further reduces the visibility of the structural violence of racial subordination. Finally, and perhaps most surprisingly, even those critics who have been most aware of the vulnerability of hinterland social structures to manipulation by metropole interests have usually failed to include the fact of color in their international analyses. The purely economic model of dependency can mask race as effectively as the statistical yearbooks of the United Nations.

Although the system of domination that is the basis for modern race relations has been shaken in recent decades, much of it is still intact. It is the defining reality for most of the world's population. Consequently, the readings in this section focus on the mechanisms and contemporary structure of that international system rather than its dissolution. The first selection by Ronald Segal examines the statistics of international poverty in human terms and builds an analysis of current world politics in terms of color. The selection by Tilden J. LeMelle and George W. Shepherd, Jr., is a systematic discussion of the forces leading to changes in white dominance systems. Especially worth noting is their emphasis on the link between internal racial structure and foreign policy.

The next two selections, by Johan Galtung and Dale Johnson, outline a model of domination and some of the mechanisms by which dominance is preserved. Neither author explicitly treats the question of color, but in Galtung's terminology, the centers, with the exception of Japan, are white, while the peripheries are nonwhite. Galtung's analysis is particularly interesting since he suggests ways that metropolitan elites may retain power through linkages with (non-white) elites in hinterland nations. His article provides a useful corrective to the overly optimistic conclusions about the end of colonialism often found in the literature on international relations. Johnson focuses on one of the most stable of the international linkages, that between the United States and Latin America, although the former's dominance has lessened in recent years.

Edward Shils, writing from a conservative perspective, recognizes many of the same facts of metropolitan dominance. His belief that dominance will gradually wither away and that a general acceptance of "Western values" will ensue is perhaps questionable. At the very least, the process is unlikely to be as smooth as he suggests and will entail some modification of those Western values, one of which has been racial domination.

THE COLOR OF WANT

Ronald Segal

British politicians, when occasion requires them to praise the Commonwealth, are given to describing it as a family of nations which represents, in its variety of races and cultures, an image of the world. Leaving aside the 'family' platitude, which has no application to the past of most members and little enough to the present, the surviving claim has some validity; the Commonwealth resembles the world, and in the variety not only of its races and cultures but also of its economic circumstances. In the scale of *per capita* annual income, Canada exists at one end, with £570, and Malawi at the other with £12½, or just over 2 per cent of that amount. The Commonwealth, like the world, is less a single home than a street, with the rich residing behind high windows and the poor struggling for life in the gutters below.

If a *per capita* annual income of £170 is the frontier of wealth,(1) only five Commonwealth countries—Canada £570) Australia (£544), New Zealand (£452), Britain (£448), and Cyprus (£193)—have crossed it, and if they encompass only 88 million people, or some 11 per cent of the 790 million in the whole association. India, with 471 million people, has a *per capita* income of £24; Pakistan, with 106 million, one of £25; and Nigeria, with 55 million, one of £35. The overwhelming mass of the people in the Commonwealth—some 89 per cent—are poor, and so poor as to find mere survival the proper object of hope. Moreover, wealth and want have different skins. The five countries that have crossed the economic frontier are all 'white,' while with the tiny exception of Malta (342,000 people and a *per capita* income of £140), all those still behind it are 'coloured.'(2)

It is this correspondence of colour and poverty that gives the Commonwealth its fundamental meaning. For the whole world is similarly divided into the rich who are nearly all white, and the poor who are coloured, with the poor and the coloured in a massive majority. The regions of relative wealth—North America, Europe and the Soviet Union, Australasia and Japan—contain some 1,000 million people, with only Japan and her 100 millions providing a significant exception to the rule of income and race. Across the remaining map of mankind, some 2,250 million people or 70 per cent of the total, almost all of them coloured, live in general want.

Figures for *per capita* annual income are, of course, in themselves commonly misleading. They emerge only through a corridor of distorting mirrors—currency exchange rates; the guesswork of economists on the value of subsistence agriculture; the necessary reduction to averages. The existence of vast discrepancies in income between members of the same society makes the condition of the poor even worse than the *per capita* figures may suggest. A relatively few merchants, managers and professional men—not infrequently involved in the operations of expatriate companies—produce by the contribution of their own large incomes an average which, however low, is still above, sometimes far above, that attained by the mass of society.

The available figures for *per capita* national income are useful as no more than crude guides to the enormous differences in standard of living between the rich countries and the poor ones. It says something about the world that the average Australian has an income more than twenty-two times as great as that of the average Indian. And the difference is not one of a capacity to purchase luxuries. It is a difference of no less than the capacity to survive. The poverty of the world's poor is hunger, malnourishment, illiteracy, needless disease and early death. At least 500 million people go hungry every day of their lives, at least another 1,000 million are seriously undernourished, and the numbers increase every moment. More meaningful for a measure of the distance between the rich white peoples and the poor coloured ones than any figures for cash income can be, are the statistics for infant mortality and life-expectancy.

Country	Population 1964 Estimates	Infant Mortality (per 1,000)	Life Expectancy Male	Female
Sweden	7,661,000	13·6	71·32	75·39
Australia	11,136,000	19·5	67·14	72·75
Japan	96,906,000	20·4	67·21	72·34
Czechoslovakia	14,058,000	22	67·21	72·83
France	48,440,000	23·4	67·2	74·1
United States	192,119,000	25·2	66·6	73·4
U.S.S.R. (1963)	224,764,000	30·9	65	73
Spain	31,339,000	37·9	67·32	71·9
Mexico	39,643,000	67·7	55·14	57·93
Colombia	15,434,000	88·2	44·18	45·95
Senegal	3,400,000	92·9	— 37	—
India	471,627,000	139	41·89	40·55
Morocco	12,959,000	149	— 49·6	—
Brazil	78,809,000	170	39·3	45·5
Haiti	4,551,000	171·6	— 32·61	—
Tanganyika	9,990,000	190	— 35 to 40	—
Burma	24,229,000	193–300	40·8	43·8
Zambia	3,600,000	259	— 40	—

What is finally terrifying is not so much that the gap between the rich and the poor is so wide already but that it is widening yet farther all the time. Possessed of the capital and skills necessary to increase the yields of agriculture and industry, the rich societies steadily grow richer, saving more than their generally low birth-rate adds to their consumption, and so enabled to invest more in the production of capital and skills. Like the rich man who spends steadily less than his income and so swells his capital and the income from it by merely standing still, the rich nation prospers on the very momentum of money. The poor, by the same rule, grow poorer as they stand still. Without the capital and skills necessary to develop their economies, and with a generally high birth-rate adding constantly to the pressure on their resources, they have less and less to spend, until their very survival is threatened.

While the population of the world increased by 2 per cent in the year 1963-4, food production in the poor, hungry countries increased at a generally lower rate or not at all. The important gains were made in those very areas—like North America (4 per cent) and Australasia (3 per cent)—where food surpluses already existed. (Indeed, in several areas of the world, *per capita* food production today is less than it was thirty years ago, during the depression of the thirties.) Yet how can the poor afford to buy food from the rich? India herself, with a seventh of all humanity inside her borders, has escaped widespread famine during the past few years by importing food from the United States, on terms made easy by political—and so demonstrably undependable—considerations.

The hunger of the poor is, however, only the most obvious attribute of their poverty. They are weakened, when not killed, by diseases which more or better food, sanitation and medical services would prevent or cure; they can seldom read or write; those who escape the stagnation of the countryside live in burgeoning city slums, sometimes not even in shanties but on streets in the shelter of a wall; millions have no work at all, and many more, much less work than their time and surviving energies could accommodate. Such poverty is self-defeating. The sick, the ignorant, the idle do not need any the less to be fed and clothed and housed, but they give correspondingly little to help the society sustain them. Like children they are potentially productive, but meanwhile more obviously mouths than hands.

The pat explanation for the persisting poverty of the poor is their high birth-rate. If only, like the rich, they would have less children, they could save more of their income for investment in their future, instead of having to spend all that they earn on keeping alive their enlarging families. Certainly, despite the much higher death-rate among the poor, the accomplishments of modern medicine have enabled them to increase their numbers much faster than the rich apparently choose to do.

| | Rate of Population Increase (%) | |
Area	1958-63	1960-63
World	1·8	1·9
Europe	0·9	0·9
U.S.S.R.	1·6	1·6
North America	1·6	1·6
Asia	1·8	1·9
Africa	2·3	2·5
Latin America	2·7	2·8

By the middle of 1965, the population of the world had reached 3,308 million, and the U.S. Population Reference Bureau reported in early 1966 that if the present growth rate continues, the world's population will top 7,000 million by the year

2000. In 1965 there were 125 million births and 60 million deaths, and not one of the 'developing' or poor countries, the Bureau declared, had yet achieved an effective reduction in the traditionally high fertility.

A cheap and easy contraceptive is the cry of the rich to the murmuring of the poor. It is altogether too glib. The rich themselves do not commonly limit their families in dedication to the economic advance of their societies, or because amenable forms of contraception are more available to them than to the poor. In France, where the annual population increase is only 1.1 per cent, the government has long encouraged larger families by financial benefits, periodic exhortation, and the pious outlawing of contraceptives widely used in near-by countries. In India, where the population increase is twice as high, government encouragement of birth-control meets steady resistance from those who see in many sons (and daughters, after all, arrive despite the most fervent prayers) help in the labour of the fields, support in old age, and the consolation of ritual at and after death. How can the state contradict the commandments of tradition by the mere distribution of pills, loops and advice? The hard truth is that societies seem to reduce their fertility less with the advance of contraceptive methods than with the rise in general income and education. The dilemma is complete: the poor are likely to become rich by limiting their numbers, and only likely to limit their numbers by becoming rich.

The rich could, of course, help the poor by providing them with the huge amount of capital necessary for dynamic development. But they are far more concerned in promoting a yet higher rate of economic growth for themselves; in, sometimes, attempting to eradicate the islands of poverty and human waste in their midst; in protecting the strength of their national currencies; and, perhaps above all, in ensuring their military power. The defence budget of the United States alone is now almost $60,000 million a year, while the total expenditure on defence by all the rich societies is well over twice that figure, or enough to reshape the future for hundreds of millions of the poor. Indeed, in the estimate of Senator Fulbright, Chairman of the United States Senate Foreign Relations Committee, the single war in Vietnam cost the United States in 1965 some $15,800 million,(3) or more than three times the foreign economic aid given to India in the twelve years from August 1949 to December 1961.

The total net flow of capital from the rich to the poor is about $6,000 million a year, or something like the sum spent each year just by Britain on defence. And this sum of $6,000 million—which represents no more than 0.6 per cent of the collective gross product achieved by the industrial countries—is itself far from a donation. Much of it is made up by private investment for dividend return, and much of it by loans bearing a high annual interest. George Woods, President of the World Bank, recently claimed(4) that the service on debts incurred by the underdeveloped countries now stands at more than a tenth of foreign exchange earnings, and that when amortization, interest and dividends are considered together, the poor are losing half of what they gain each year from the rich in new capital.

The aid given by the communist rich, while often more efficient, more productive, and when in the form of loans, more generous than that provided by the capitalist rich—the Communists charge on the whole half the interest rate required by many Western sources—is, in its extent, scarcely impressive. In the period 1954-64 annual aid from the communist countries—mainly, of course, the Soviet Union—to the non-aligned poor ran at $665 million, a tiny fraction of the aid provided by the West and of the Soviet Union's own national income. And when, in

1964, communist aid rose sharply to $1,700 million, it was largely the result of intervention by the Chinese; China—competing for influence against the Soviet Union—provided a quarter of the total, while the Eastern European states were responsible for another quarter, and the Soviet Union for half. It says little for the seriousness with which the Soviet Union regards her obligation to help promote the economic progress and political independence of the poor that she should be providing, under the provocation of the Sino-Soviet dispute, only twice the aid that China, so much poorer and herself in need of aid, seems ready to supply.

The fact is that public opinion in the rich countries is even less enthusiastic than officialdom about paying to alleviate the anguish of the alien poor. After the harsh years of the Stalinist era, the people of the Soviet Union want some of the so-long-promised recompense for their suffering, and Stalin's successors, their command of power less secure, are more concerned with securing popular approval than Stalin felt it necessary to be. Furthermore, the unrest that culminated in the Hungarian revolt of 1956 revealed the dangers of allowing popular disaffection in Eastern Europe to develop beyond apathy, and such subventions from Soviet wealth as the Soviet leadership has considered it possible to spare have, since then, increasingly been devoted to nourishing support with the European bloc.

In the West itself, where individual enrichment and conspicuous consumption are the objects of common endeavour, the needs of the poor have recommended themselves to attention, when at all, only as irritating threats of communist advance, and military intervention where necessary has appeared a more effective method of containing communism than has economic aid. The de Gaulle government in France, provoked less by compassion for the poor than by an anachronistic dedication of national grandeur, has devoted a higher proportion of national income to economic aid than has the government of any other Western state, and has come under mounting public criticism for such extravagance. Indeed, whether reflecting the moral indifference of British prosperity after the austere years of the war and its immediate aftermath, or the moral materialism of the Yankee which sees poverty as the natural desert of laziness or stupidity, Western public opinion has admitted no real obligation to help the poor of the world escape their condition. And its inattention or opposition has been fed by the apparent inability of the poor to practise those same virtues of voluntary individual sacrifice for the common good, the eradication of personal privilege, and the emphasis on human rather than on national advantage which the rich themselves have for so long so cheerfully ignored. Costly clashes among the needy, like the war between India and Pakistan in 1965, are proclaimed as proving the pointlessness and even damage of economic aid, although the rich have themselves promoted the purchase of military equipment—by offering far easier terms of payment for aeroplanes and tanks than for combine harvesters and trucks—and it is the impossibility of getting anywhere near sufficient aid for significant economic advance that has encouraged many of the poor to seek distraction in nationalist adventures.

Indeed, the value of aid has, far from merely failing to increase, been actually diminishing. The flow of funds from the rich world as a whole remained virtually unchanged from 1961 to 1965, though inflation steadily eroded its purchasing power, and the largest donor of all, the United States, had recently made substantial cuts in its contributions. The 1965 American programme was the lowest since 1948 and worth less than half the programmes of 1951, 1952 and 1953.(5) And the programme for 1966 promises yet further cuts. The total of $2,469 million requested by the President for economic aid was $235 million lower than his 1965 request, and represented less than 0.4 per cent of the country's gross national product. The largest single item in the programme—$550 million—was for South Vietnam, as part of the war effort there; aid for all Latin America, under the much advertised Alliance for Progress, was to be $543 million (from $580 million in 1965); and an amount of $665 million was recommended for development loans to countries—mainly India, Pakistan, Nigeria, Turkey, and Korea—with a total population of over 700 million. Moreover, the President made no effort to conceal the strings attached. Aid was to go to countries which not only gave 'solid evidence that they are determined to help themselves,' but which were 'not hostile to us' (a criterion subject to wide differences of interpretation).

Ths condition of the poor is even more desperate, however, than their too rapidly increasing numbers, capital hunger and accumulated indebtedness suggest. It has for several years been a buyer's market in the very commodities that the poor produce for sale to the rich. The price of natural products like cocoa, sugar, rubber, cotton, coffee, tea, and of most important base metals has fallen, so that the most strenuous efforts at increasing yields have led to little or no rise, sometimes even a drop, in overall income. By heavy capital investment in disease and pest control, new acreage and plants, Ghana and Nigeria enormously increased their production of cocoa within a decade.

Country	Year	Cocoa Crop	Approximate Earnings
Ghana	1954-55	210,000 long tons	£85,500,000
	1964-65	590,000	£77,000,000
Nigeria	1954-55	89,000 long tons	£39,250,000
	1964-65	310,000	£40,000,000 (6)

Together Ghana and Nigeria, therefore, tripled their production of a commodity crucial to their economies and saw their earnings from the sale of it abroad fall from a combined £125 million to £117 million. In the looking-glass world of the poor, one must run very fast to stand still.

Britain's National Institute of Economic and Social Research has revealed a major decline since 1947 in the export prices received by primary producers.

Year		Total Index Figure	Food	Non-Food
1957		100	100	100
1958		90·4	95	83·1
1959		90·7	90·8	90·6
1960		91·2	88·8	95·2
1961		84·7	84·2	85·7
1962		82·7	82·9	82·2
1963	I	87·7	88·6	86·2
	II	95·1	99·9	87·3
	III	92·3	96·4	85·8
	IV	99·9	105·8	90·4
1964	I	101·9	108·2	92
	II	98·6	104·4	89·3
	III	94·9	99·5	87·6
	IV	91·9	96·4	84·8
1965	I	89·7	94·3	82·5
	II	90·2	94·4	83·4 (7)

Such price declines have eaten away at, and even altogether swallowed the effects of aid for economic development; the supply of United States aid to Latin America, for instance, has long been offset by the overall fall in the price of major Latin American commodities. Furthermore, the very instability of prices makes it impossible for the poor societies properly to plan economic development, and put their available resources to the most productive use.

While the products of the poor have fallen in price, however, the products of the rich have risen, steadily widening the gap between what the poor must pay and what they manage to earn. The average cost of machinery and transport equipment exported by the West to the poor societies, products necessary for the economic progress of the poor, has increased year by year, rising over 45 per cent in little more than a decade. With an index figure of 100 in 1958, prices stood at 73 in 1950, and rose to 80 in 1951; 85 in 1952; 88 in 1953 and 1954; 89 in 1955; 91 in 1956; 96 in 1957; 101 in 1959; 103 in 1960; 105 in 1961; and 106 in 1962.(8)

Nor is the profit appetite a concern only of the capitalist West. The Cuban government, selling sugar to the Soviet Union in exchange for manufactured goods, found the price of such manufactures frequently higher than that ruling on the world market, and only after repeated representations achieved an agreement by which Soviet prices would be cut wherever it could be shown that similar goods from other industrial countries cost less. Between the buyer's market for natural products and the seller's market for manufactures, the trading position of the poor persistently deteriorates. Overall, average unit prices of commodity exports from the poor countries were 12 per cent lower in 1962 than they had been in 1955, while average unit prices of imports from the rich countries to the poor rose over the same period by 16 per cent.(9)

Production Indices of Natural and Synthetic Raw Materials

	Natural Fibres		Synthetic Fibres			Natural	Synthetic
Year	Cotton	Wool	Rayon	Non-Cellulosics	Total	Rubber	Rubber
1952	100	100	100	100	100	100	100
1953	104	101	118	123	118	97	106
1954	103	103	126	151	128	101	82
1955	109	109	142	204	147	107	124
1956	106	116	149	237	155	105	138
1957	104	113	154	314	166	106	144
1958	112	120	142	323	156	108	142
1959	118	126	157	446	179	114	186
1960	118	126	162	549	191	111	214
1961	119	128	168	648	204	117	225
1962	125	127	179	835	228	118	255

SOURCE: Report of the U.N. Food and Agriculture Organization, quoted in *The Times*, 5 October, 1964.

Even the ultimate consolation of the poor, that their products are necessary to the industrial economies of the rich, has diminishing validity with the development of manufactured substitutes for agricultural commodities. Synthetic fibres increasingly compete with cotton, wool, jute and sisal, while synthetic rubber is displacing not only natural rubber but even leather. In the period 1959-61 world exports of such synthetics—almost entirely from the rich industrial nations, of course—totalled in value some 24 per cent of world agricultural trade. Indeed, the extent to which the growth in the production of synthetic raw materials is outstripping the growth in the production of natural ones threatens the poor societies with the loss of one market after the other.

How may the poor hope to compete except by industrializing themselves? And how can they industrialize when the cost of industrialization constantly rises? Year by year the price of effective technology rises, capital requirements are higher, and the established producers, by accumulating skills and resources, make commercial competition from others all the more difficult and unlikely. Having achieved their lead in history—not without the assistance of conquest, subjugation and pillage—the rich are not merely maintaining but steadily increasing it. According to George Woods, president of the World Bank,(10) *per capita* income in the poor world may rise, if present trends continue, from $120 (£43) today to $170 (£61) by the year 2000. In the United States *per capita* income will increase from $3,000 (£1,270) today to $7,500 (£2,685) in the same period. Such predictions, however, suggest that the rate of growth, both among the rich and among the poor, will stay as it is. But whereas the rich will probably increase their rate of growth, with their command of skills and capital, the poor show every sign of having their already low rate yet further reduced. In 1950-54, the rate of increase in gross national product among the poor as a whole was around 5 per cent. In 1955-60, this rate dropped to 4½ per cent, and in 1960-64 to 4 per cent. With the population increasing as well, with mounting loan charges and debt repayment, this meant for many poor countries no rise in *per capita* income at all, or even a fall.

Since the rich show no sign of effectively helping the poor—indeed, their own problems of liquidity, with the weakness of crucial trade currencies, make further reductions in foreign aid more likely than any increases—the poor must depend on their own efforts to secure economic progress and even the reasonable prospect of survival. From their very want they must squeeze capital, for investment in machines, power, transport, education; if they consume little, they must learn to consume less, and if they are already saving much, they must learn to save more. The demands of change are high. 'Economists fix a level of about twelve to fifteen per cent of national income as the range needed to cover all possible increases in population, some increase in consumption, and a high expanding level of investment.'(11) When national income is already inadequate for the proper sustenance of life, the saving is something like an eighth is more than exceptional effort; it becomes organized suffering. . . .

NOTES

(1) *The Rich Nations and the Poor Nations*, by Barbara Ward (Hamish Hamilton, 1962), p. 35.

(2) Figures in the *Guardian*, June 17, 1965.

(3) *The Times*, February 5, 1966.

(4) *The Times*, December 17, 1965.

(5) 'A New Look at Trade and Aid,' by Susan Strange, in *International Affairs*, Vol. 42, No. 1, January 1966.

(6) *Neo-Colonialism*, by Kwame Nkrumah (Nelson, 1965), p. 10. The figures for 1964-5 are estimates.

(7) *The Times* Supplement on the Food and Agriculture Organization, October 16, 1965.

(8) *United Nations Statistical Yearbook*, 1964, p. 499.

(9) S. Strange, ibid.

(10) Reported in *The Times*, December 17, 1965.

(11) B. Ward, op. cit., p. 46.

RACE IN THE FUTURE OF
INTERNATIONAL RELATIONS

Tilden J. LeMelle & George W. Shepherd Jr.

Although Western scholarship has largely failed to recognize its importance, race has become the central problem of international politics. Disciplined analysis has lagged behind events, and little systematic attempt has been made to relate the racial factor to theories of international relations. In sum, no consistent analysis has been applied to the problems of international racial conflict and integration.(1) However, the impact of race may well revolutionize international studies as we come to understand how racial stratification influences national behavior and sets a world pattern of conflict. This article will suggest a conceptual framework of racial stratification and examine some of the future problems of international race relations.

Racial stratification exists when the availability and distribution of individual choices in society are determined by membership in a particular racial group, and is, in effect, racial discrimination against a subordinate racial group. Thus, in a racially stratified system, class stratification is a function of racial stratification and the boundaries of the two are highly coterminous.(2) Racial stratification systems have many variations, but we are primarily concerned here with white dominance systems. In these systems dominant groups have a high color consciousness and a high technical capability with which they subordinate other groups perceived as non-white.(3) White dominance social systems are found in high capability Euro-American societies which perceive themselves to be dominant internationally. These societies have manifested a history of Darwinian imperialism which reached its peak in the colonization of Asia, Africa, and Latin America. The conflicts and wars of the first half of this century were in large measure the result of rivalries between white dominance powers; the revolutions of the second half are primarily the result of the colonized asserting their identity and refusing to accept a continued status of servility.(4)

THE FUNCTION OF RACE IN WHITE DOMINANCE SYSTEMS

All racially stratified systems tend toward dysfunction. In such systems race functions initially as the basis for establishing and regulating dominant and subordinate relationships by means of subjection and/or pseudo-assimilation.(5) In this stage race acts as a system-wide *centripetal* force drawing together all racial components under the assumed superiority of the dominant (and solely legitimate) racial group. With the breakdown of subjection and pseudo-assimilation, race functions as a divisive factor leading to open inter-racial conflict. At this stage race acts as a *centrifugal* force fragmenting the system along its already racially stratified lines. Thus, in a white dominance system, race is not only the rationale for and a continuing cause of discrimination, but it is also the catalyst for eventual violence between dominant and subordinate racial groups and for societal disintegration. These general principles are applicable to the analysis of international as well as national race relations.

WHITE DOMINANCE CENTRIPETAL SYSTEMS

Prior to the emergence of non-white nationalism in the mid-20th century, race functioned as a regulative force for maintaining stability both in white-dominated states and in the white-dominated international system. Inter-race relations were a matter of white control over subordinate racial groups either through subjection or emanation(6) or a combination of both. Patterns of racial stratification remained relatively stable and racial discrimination (a function of the convergence of racism and power) served as an instrument for regulating mobility, power, and the distribution of values in inter-race relations.

The centripetal white dominance system is best characterized by its value assumptions which are messianic and ethnocentric. Virtue is assumed to exist primarily in what is white and Western, and evil is equated with blackness and the assumed irreligious ways of non-white societies. These values, which blend color and culture, have explicitly justified slavery, the color bars of the Southern U.S., apartheid in South Africa, and even the discriminatory laws regulating Indian lands and non-white immigration.

The organization of power in the centripetal system enthroned and perpetuated the white dominance system. Violence was used to conquer the non-white and was then legalized as police and vigilante power to protect the privileges of those who controlled the land and production as well as the government. Police force and military power were the ultimate weapons by which the stratification pattern was enforced. Affection for the law and the lawmaker was taught as a special virtue, but for those non-whites who broke the law there was little justice, *only* swift punishment.

Limited mobility within this general centripetal system was available only to those non-whites who rejected their own heritage and race—in short, who became assimilated.(7) Historically, the extent of mobility has varied with the depth and intensity of non-white culture, with the perceived economic threat which mobility represented to the white man, and with the level of production and job opportunities.

Thus, the centripetal pattern of white dominance held together as long as dominant and subordinate groups accepted assimilationist values, respected and feared discriminatory legal and police powers, and hoped that limited mobility could lead to a better life. At different times and places in the 20th century this centripetal race system has been broken and reversed. In some states it still continues. The historic breaking point has varied greatly. In the U.S. it was the rise of Black Power in the 1960's; in the United Kingdom, the colonial rebellion begun by Gandhi in the 1930's, fostered the black immigration and demands of the post-war period; the French fought bloody colonial wars against Asians and Arabs in the 1940's and 1950's and today confront angry Algerian workers in the streets of Paris. South Africa and Australia employed discriminatory and repressive devices which came under stringent attack from non-white indigenous populations. White dominance responses have varied from civil rights laws in the U.S. to colonial immigration barriers in the U.K. and brutal suppression in South Africa. Yet all have failed, despite temporary compromises, because the centripetal white dominance system, giving up subjection and insisting upon assimilation as the price of equality, has denied non-whites full equality.

CENTRIFUGAL WHITE DOMINANCE SYSTEMS

The basic new pattern in white dominance systems is a centrifugal or conflict pattern in which race no longer serves as an adequate regulatory device but rather designates lines of open conflict between white and non-white within and between nations. Increasingly race is being transformed from a suppressive or assimilationist device into a rallying point for self-determination by non-white groups which have become self-conscious and power motivated. The promise and denial of equality by white dominance systems have been the contradictory thesis and anti-thesis which have spurred subordinated racial groups to reassert their selfhood and cultural pride.

Conflict rather than assimilation or integration is characteristic of this phase. Within nations this means the formation of interest and political groups along racial lines, the strengthening of racial community consciousness, and the growth of counter-racist attitudes among subordinate and dominant groups. Riots and rebellion are frequently the product of the self-determination drive of non-whites, and in irreconcilable situations the ultimate conflict, racial war, arises. A state of mind which Manfred Halpern has called *incoherence*(8) develops in the white and non-white groups due to the breakdown in assimilationist, consensual goals and in communication. Riots in U.S. urban centers, uprisings of Africans and riots of colored in South Africa, clashes with police in London and Paris, Black Power demonstrations against whites in the Caribbean, and aboriginal demonstrations in Australia all dramatize the emergence of a centrifugal conflict pattern of race relations. These patterns are not uniform; different levels of violence exist; and various national and regional policies have attempted to minimize conflict.

CHANGING PATTERNS OF INTERNATIONAL RACE RELATIONS

Because of the breakdown of subjection and assimilation as regulative factors in international race relations, the tendency is toward intensification of racial conflict and *increasing* transnational racial ties. Since Europeans united in a common bond of whiteness to dominate the black, brown, and yellow peoples of the world, men have been attempting to join in the bond of color across national lines to pursue racially justified (if not always racist) causes. The Pan-African Movement, formed after black African resistance had failed to curb white intrusion into Africa, is probably the best-documented transnational racial grouping organized to counter white dominance. Black men of different nationalities and cultures, and speaking different languages, joined in pan-Negro organizations to win humane treatment, then equality, and finally independence for their black brothers in Africa. Out of this movement grew the race-conscious philosophies of Negritude and the African Personality—philosophies of color which black men had never before felt a need to formulate.

Although political independence has been won by most black African states, the influences of white dominance still linger in varying degrees. Economic dependence, in particular, is a major point of continuing conflict as indicated by the tensions over nationalization of Euro-American foreign investments.

The 1955 Bandung Conference of African and Asian peoples was the first international meeting explicitly called to unite "peoples of color" against white domination and oppression. Specifically referring to racial differences, China successfully kept the U.S.S.R. out of the Bandung meeting, making it an international conference of non-white peoples. The policies of racial discrimination in South Africa and the U.K. increasingly are causing Indians and other Asians in those countries to refer to themselves as black—black symbolizing a transcendence of nationality, religion, culture, and sex—in order to combat white dominance. History also provides much evidence of transnational white collaboration in support of white domination over non-white peoples.

TRENDS

The centripetal racial system was not conducive to transnational linkages between subordinate racial groups. Its domestic assimilationist thrusts minimized attempts at transnational racial ties which were largely rejected by non-whites, e.g., Marcus Garvey and his "back to Africa" movements in the U.S. As a consequence, the foreign policies of states with these types of systems unabashedly reflected the racist assumptions and interests of their white dominant groups; for example, President Woodrow Wilson and Jan Christian Smuts, Prime Minister of South Africa, joined together at Versailles to defeat the Japanese plea for a covenant on racial equality.

In contrast, the centrifugal stage of domestic race relations tends to encourage outside intervention as subordinate groups seek aid for their rebellion or secession. The incipient pattern of racial pluralism that characterizes the centrifugal stage encourages non-white transnational movements to strengthen the identity ties and cultural accomplishments of their group. Illustrative of this is the Mexican-American of the Southwest whose militant groups increasingly identify with the nationalist movements of Puerto Rico and Latin America. The foreign policy response of white dominance states to this phase is more accommodating, since they both fear and respect the new forces that have become domestically important.

A central proposition is that *centripetal (assimilationist) racial patterns have had a strong influence on the development of expansionist and imperialistic foreign policies while centrifugal pressures promote revolution against white dominance.* Obviously, additional factors such as economic exploitation may produce imperialism. But the relationship of racial stratification to the development of social Darwinism in the 19th century is substantiating evidence of the development of racism as a rationale for imperialism. The "primitiveness of non-white races" and the "superiority of Euro-American religious and political forms" are notions related to the motive and rationale for colonization which found their zenith in the Victorian era.(9) The "civilizing mission" of the British, French, and Germans was, in the eyes of the European upper classes, a justification for the subjection of Africa in the 19th century. And the U.S. sense of Manifest Destiny in the Pacific was an important influence in the acquisition of the Philippines.(10) The origins of these racist ideas can be traced to the dominant white Western elites. Black men did serve in empires, as in the case of the French Governor of Senegal, Blaise Diagne, prior to World War I. However, these were assimilated Africans, or what South Africans would call "honorary whites," because they accepted the values and practices of dominant whites. The fact was that the ruling elites were white and Western and arrogantly confident of their mission to bring order, commerce, Christianity, and their particular culture to the "inferior peoples."

This historic expansion of the U.S.S.R. in Asia is a pattern of white assimilationist imperialism. Today this plays a part in the Sino-Soviet conflict along with ideological and geographical factors. There is much evidence that the U.S.S.R. today exhibits what we would describe as a disintegrative conflict pattern toward its own minorities, despite claims to non-racialism and multi-nationalism. The treatment of its Jewish minority is the outstanding example of this centrifugal pattern of incoherence.(11) Marxist states, despite their theoretical elimination of the class struggle, do not always abolish the racial struggle with their class revolution, but do create severe internal and external tensions by their mythology of multi-nationalism which intensifies the drive of subordinate groups for genuine self-determination. The Sino-Soviet conflict within the international communist movement is in large part the result of white dominance of the non-white world now in revolt over values and power distribution.

South Africa is in a stage of transition from a centripetal racist system to a centrifugal one. The power of subjection is so great that racial identification is still regulative rather than disintegrative. Until they were banned, the nationalist movements were highly European-oriented and non-racial in values. They sought a common citizenship for all races based on Euro-American principles of government. This attitude still predominates among most non-whites, but given the influence of Black Power spokesmen and secessionist movements, this attitude is changing.(12)

In South Africa the separate development policy of the government has projected deceptive multi-national goals, such as the establishment of separate nationhood through Bantustans, and the granting of nominal independence to Lesotho, Botswana, and Swaziland. This independence is a myth. The reality for the vast majority of non-whites, whose numbers are growing very rapidly, is continued subjection to the industrialized economy and marginal assimilation into the consumption patterns of urban life, while the standard-of-living gap grows.

Despite subjection of the masses, there has begun, among a minority of black South Africans, secessionist movements which are strong precipitating forces for revolution and racial war. Thus, Bantustan leaders, such as Chief Buthelezi, hope to achieve independence, and exiled revolutionaries gather in increasing numbers on the boundaries to attack South Africa from without and organize resistance within.

South Africa's foreign policy reflects the transitional movement from a centripetal to a centrifugal pattern of race relations. Ruled since the 1950's by the blatantly racist Afrikaners, an imperialistic South Africa has acquired territory

(Namibia) and used financial power to penetrate markets in the independent African states. The country's military boundaries have been extended recently into the Portuguese territories and into Rhodesia.(13) An active program of seeking client African states ready to accept South African loans and trade by a policy of "dialogue" and "contacts" has begun. In addition, South Africa has sought closer military ties with Euro-American powers through arms purchases.

While her imperialistic expansion is characteristic of centripetal systems, the rapid expansion of South Africa's military forces is indicative of the fears characteristic of the centrifugal pattern. Euro-American powers have needed far greater military power in this defensive process than during imperialistic expansion. South Africa's attempts to join the NATO alliance further indicate her desire for white assistance. At the same time a low level of racial war has begun along her extended boundaries where African states support liberation movements. South Africa also seeks to assist Portugal and Rhodesia in defeating the black liberation movements. Continuous treason trials at home and desperate attempts to organize multi-national Bantustans are all indicators of the conflict and incoherence that now characterize the domestic politics underlying South Africa's foreign relations.

Under the centrifugal pressures of non-white resistance, the assimilationist system becomes incoherent and this in turn develops a new set of foreign policy pressures. Threatened by a significant secessionist movement which promises civil war, a state becomes especially sensitive to the dangers of foreign intervention. This shifts the emphasis from expansionism to an inwardly-directed militarization. Efforts are made to placate those who might intervene on behalf of the racial secessionists, and external military assistance is sought to suppress rebellion. This pattern persists where white domination of non-white people continues and becomes more rigid because of non-white centrifugal pressures and white failures to reform or compromise.

The best example of a white dominant system which has reached the secessionist stage can be found in Portuguese Africa, where the claim over the "Portuguese Provinces of Africa" is widely disputed by the rebellions of liberation forces in Guinea-Bissau, Angola, and Mozambique. Through NATO, Portugal has obtained outside assistance to repress the secessionists and actively seeks diplomatic support from Latin American and Asian states. Its racially-based *assimilado* policy for Africans is producing the same reaction which the French assimilation policy produced in Indochina and Africa:(14) increased rebellion and growing outside intervention.

Secessionist conflicts arising from the centrifugal stage of incoherence are very dangerous in the modern world, particularly if great powers sometimes utilize them either to maintain their presence in an area or to dislodge an antagonist. As the South African and Rhodesian racial patterns move directly into the disintegration phase of irreconcilable conflict, they become prime targets for interventionary cold war tactics. Here lies one of the gravest dangers to world peace.

The U.S. has also moved into the centrifugal conflict phase. Racist war abroad and minority rebellion at home have created a major racial crisis in which domestic and foreign policy cannot be distinguished clearly. During the centripetal period of domestic assimilation and Darwinian colonial expansion abroad, the U.S. attempted to build a *Pax Pacifica*. Pre-World War II rivalries with Japan, the post-war intervention of the U.S. in the Chinese civil war, and the two wars the U.S. has fought in Korea and Vietnam have been influenced by domestic racial assimilationist attitudes and external paternalistic power patterns originally structured in the 19th century. The post-World War II assumption that peace depended upon American political and military presence on the Asian mainland and the islands of the Pacific has a racial dimension closely akin to the imperialistic rule of the British Raj. Early involvement in the Indochina War arose out of the power vacuum caused by French decolonialization. The U.S. leadership believed this would be filled by the Communists. However, the attempt to launch a crusade against Communism for Asian self-determination reflected the same kind of racist assumption that underlay the concept of the "white man's burden" in the League's Mandate system—a system first suggested by President Wilson.

The racial aspects of the Vietnam conflict clearly emerged as a form of genocide as the war expanded. American militarists refused to believe that "coolies" could stand up to saturation bombing and pressed for a victory despite humanitarian protests. Indisputable proof of the racial paranoia of American society which sustained these policies was the widespread outcry of support for Lt. Calley when even the Army sought to condemn him to life imprisonment for his "wasting" of Vietnamese civilian lives.

The centrifugal phase in American society and foreign policy has only begun as a result of the rise of minority militancy which has been greatly accelerated by the Vietnam disaster. Black and Chicano movements have been joined by young Asians in protesting the "white man's war" and the particular "racist" exploitation of minorities to fight it. The growing disaffection of these minorities has already had a considerable impact upon the expansionist policies of the U.S. American white dominance leadership is sensitive to the penetration possibilities of foreign adversaries, as J. Edgar Hoover's remarks concerning the security threat of immigrant Chinese demonstrated. And the white urban middle class is increasingly anxious to quell the restlessness of the ghettos. Therefore, the political power of those advocating disengagement and reduction of American power abroad has been enhanced by the disenchantment of non-white minorities with the melting pot myth and with their tendency to identify with non-whites abroad in clashes against American power. It is too early to predict whether this will set in motion forces capable of finally curbing the considerable American corporate interests in Latin America and Southern Africa, but the revolutionary black workers of Polaroid have surfaced a conflict of interests with explosive potential in American politics and foreign policy.

Resolution of major domestic racial issues would mean the movement from centrifugal disintegration and conflict into a pluralistic consensus in which race was no longer a significant stratification indicator. This can begin either as a result of an equalitarian revolution, which removes white dominance, or secession, which establishes a uni-racial state. There are no pure societies of this type in the world today, but they may well emerge out of the centrifugal conflict era.

In pluralistic societies centripetal imperialism would be non-existent, and the tendency toward the militarism and paranoia of the centrifugal race pattern would also disappear. By removing discrimination at home, such societies would also contain a high level of respect and recognition for non-white cultures and peoples. This would tend to strengthen the humanistic factors in foreign policy as against the corporate and security factors which have predominated to date. Much less certain would be the consequences of secession since such new states might carry with them the seeds of racial imperialism from which they had escaped.

Sweden, where only the Lapps are affected adversely by racial status, is moving in the direction of racial pluralism. A great asset for Swedish foreign policy is its long history of neutrality and imperial abstention. The Swedes have directly assisted liberation movements in Africa, an important new departure for a white dominance system. Perhaps this is indicative of a relationship between non-racialism at home and anti-apartheid abroad.

SUBSYSTEMS AND RACE

Since the early 1950's, at the regional subsystem level,(15) centrifugal forces in racial patterns have injected conflict which contributes to colonial wars and secessions. European nations have granted independence to African states rather than fight protracted colonial wars. More recently the identification patterns of subordinate minorities have emerged, cutting across national lines, particularly among the blacks within the Atlantic subsystem which is a prime example of a racially stratified white dominant system.(16) The white NATO powers (excluding Greece and Turkey) form its core group and dominate the system, while non-NATO white powers such as those in white dominated Southern Africa comprise the peripheral area of the subsystem. The Atlantic subsystem demonstrates a high degree of integration in terms of standard interaction variables as well as race.(17) In fact, racial stratification patterns account in large measure for the coordination of political and economic policies within the subsystem and explain in part the magnitude of mutual support between white states in the North and South Atlantic to the exclusion of the non-white.

In the modern centrifugal era, the racial factor alienates and even precipitates rebellion against the prevailing policies of the dominant powers in the Atlantic subsystem. The growing alignment of subordinate black groups within the system with sympathetic outside states, both African and communist, is indicative of potential conflicts in the future. The link-up with rebellious groups is not limited to states outside of the subsystem. There is a growing identification between Black Power and colored dissidence within the core group of states, including the revolutionary forces of Southern Africa on the periphery.

The effect of the growth of this black identity bloc in close proximity to the U.S. and cutting across U.S. relations with Latin America, may have significant implications for future relations. The growth of Black Power movements in the Caribbean is a trend that may greatly affect the future.

THE GLOBAL SYSTEM

Race thus operates as a stratification device for the entire world system in which the powerful white dominant nations have long predominated. Eastern Europe is joined with the white Atlantic regional subsystem to create a world racial pattern of white dominance. The attitude of the white states of the world is in part a reflection of their own internal stratification problems. There appears to be a direct relationship between the severity of these internal racial problems and the defensiveness or openness of a white nation's policy toward the non-white world, as reflected by support for human rights conventions and international collective action to abolish discriminatory practices within and between nations.(18)

International racial stratification can be seen in terms of international mobility and opportunity. Here, poverty statistics, development trends, population growth, and international migration all point to a very rigid global system of distribution. Race is the most important factor determining the life chances of any child born into this world. This, coupled with the militaristic and conflict-prone policies of white dominance states, projects conflict, not stability.

The formation of the U.N. and other world organizations has enabled the non-white peoples to gain greater participation within the international system. Yet even an Afro-Asian majority within the U.N. does not change the realities of international stratification in the distribution of rewards. The basic decisions regarding the world economy are still made by the white dominance nations, as the GATT conferences have clearly shown. Communist China's hostility to the current Euro-American domination of the U.N. and the world system is not simply ideological, but is also a protest, with power, on behalf of the colonized majority whose color has been for centuries a sign of weakness. The racial stratification pattern which maintains power and control in the hands of the white dominance nations of the world is bound to be a source of hostility and conflict.

And modification of this racial basis of international conflict in the future probably will be achieved best by the development of racial pluralism in white dominance powers. These states might then be able to lead an attack upon international racial inequities provided time has not run out.

The lack of determination by the most powerful nations of the world to reform the international system significantly through economic development programs or changes in trade patterns has frequently been attacked. There is a remarkable decline in international aid while GNP rises in the U.S. and other white dominance systems—an indication of their inability to sympathize with the "have-not" nations. It may be that fear is a more compelling stimulus to reform than empathy, and that real redistribution and reform will come about only with the growth of revolutionary racial conflict.

The racially pluralist pattern is clearly the ideal for the international system, as well as individual state systems. Guidelines for redirection can be taken from this pattern, which must create mobility and real life chances for all, as well as redistribute power. Any prospect for preventing growing racial conflict is linked to radical changes within the white dominance systems themselves. The questions of time and pace are acute. Dominant groups, however, tend to lack either the vision or the determination to turn the disastrous possibilities into more hopeful prospects.

NOTES

(1) See George W. Shepherd, Jr., "The Study of Race in American Foreign Policy and International Relations," *Studies in Race and Nations*, Vol. 1, No. 4 (1970), Center on International Race Relations, Graduate School of International Studies, University of Denver. For a detailed analysis of U.S. "integration" as colonial-type assimilation, see Tilden J. LeMelle, "Ideology of Blackness, African-American Style," *Africa Today*, Vol. XIV, No. 6 (December, 1967), pp. 2-4. Also see Karl Deutsch, "Research Problems on Race in Intranational and International Relations," in George W. Shepherd, Jr. and Tilden J. LeMelle, eds., *Race Among Nations* (Lexington, Mass.: Heath Lexington, 1970), pp. 123-152. Only a few earlier and prophetic analysts, such as W.E.B. DuBois, Richard Wright, and

Gunnar Myrdal, have identified the significance of race in transnational relationships.

(2) See G.W. Shepherd, Jr., "Comparative Policy in White Dominance Systems," paper for a Conference of U.N. Institute for Training and Research (UNITAR) and the Center on International Race Relations on Public Policy and Racial Discrimination, Aspen Institute, 1970.

(3) See T. Shibutani and K. Kwan, *Ethnic Stratification, a Comparative Approach* (New York: Macmillan, 1965). Richard Schermerhorn's work, a conflict analysis of dominant-subordinate group relations is important. His modification of an earlier conflict model of group relations is found in *Comparative Ethnic Relations: A Framework for Theory and Research* (New York: Random House, 1970), pp. 22-25.

(4) A.R. Preiswerk, "Race and Colour in International Relations," *The Yearbook of World Affairs*, Vol. 24 (1970), London Institute of World Affairs, p. 58.

(5) Cf. Tilden J. LeMelle, "Black Power and the Integration/Assimilation Myth," in Lenneal J. Henderson, Jr., *Black Political Life in the U.S.* (San Francisco: Chandler, forthcoming).

(6) The concepts of "subjection" and "emanation" are used in the same sense as that employed by Manfred Halpern in "Applying a New Theory of Human Relations to the Comparative Study of Racism," *Studies in Race and Nations*, Vol. 1, No. 1 (1969), Center on International Race Relations, GSIS, University of Denver. Emanation in this case means the acceptance of the legitimacy of white rule by subordinate groups.

(7) Slavery, the U.S. color bar, and apartheid were aversive-suppressive and subjective rather than assimilationist. See Joel Kovel, *White Racism: A Psychohistory* (New York: Pantheon, 1970).

(8) Halpern, *op. cit.*, p. 14.

(9) Ali Mazrui, "Post Imperial Fragmentation: The Legacy of Ethnic and Racial Conflict," *Studies in Race and Nations*, Vol. 1, No. 2 (1969), Center on International Race Relations, GSIS, University of Denver.

(10) William A. Williams quoted William Jennings Bryan as saying, "The Filipinos cannot be citizens without endangering our civilization," in *The Tragedy of American Diplomacy* (Cleveland, Ohio: World Publishing Co., 1959), p. 36. Americans therefore had to civilize them.

(11) Edy Kaufman, "The Jews in Russia," *Race Today* (March, 1970), pp. 67-75.

(12) Newell M. Stultz, "The Politics of Security: South Africa under Verwoerd, 1961-66," *The Journal of Modern African Studies*, Vol. 7, No. 1, pp. 3-21. See also Gwendolen Carter, "Multi-racialism in Africa," *International Affairs*, Vol. 34, No. 4, pp. 437-463.

(13) Richard Stevens, "South Africa and Independent Black Africa," *Africa Today*, Vol. 17, No. 3 (May-June, 1970), pp. 25-32.

(14) See "Allies in Empire," *Africa Today*, Vol. 17, No. 4 (July-August, 1970).

(15) Michael Banks, "Sub-systems and Regional Studies," *International Studies Quarterly* (Winter, 1970).

(16) L. Centori and S. Spiegel in *The International Politics of Regions: A Comparative Approach* (New York: Prentice-Hall, 1970). Their model included Europe but did not develop it as an Atlantic system including the U.S.

(17) Unpublished paper by G.W. Shepherd, Jr., "The White Atlantic Subsystem and Black Southern Africa," delivered to a UCLA symposium in April, 1970.

(18) While the ratification of human rights conventions by the small non-white powers leaves much to be desired, it is a substantially superior record to the U.S. and South Africa. See "Acceptance of Human Rights Treaties," UNITAR, A/Conf 32/15, March 28, 1968, Annex 11.

A STRUCTURAL THEORY OF IMPERIALISM

Johan Galtung

This theory takes as its point of departure two of the most glaring facts about this world: the tremendous inequality, within and between nations, in almost all aspects of human living conditions, including the power to decide over those living conditions; *and* the resistance of this inequality to change. The world consists of Center and Periphery nations; and each nation, in turn, has its centers and periphery. Hence, our concern is with the mechanism underlying this discrepancy, particularly between the center in the Center, and the periphery in the Periphery. In other words, how to conceive of, how to explain, and how to counteract inequality as one of the major forms of *structural violence.*(1) Any theory of liberation from structural violence presupposes theoretically and practically adequate ideas of the dominance system against which the liberation is directed; and the special type of dominance system to be discussed here is *imperialism.*

Imperialism will be conceived of as a dominance relation between collectivities, particularly between nations. It is a sophisticated type of dominance relation which cuts across nations, basing itself on a bridgehead which the center in the Center nation establishes in the center of the Periphery nation, for the joint benefit of both. It should not be confused with other ways in which one collectivity can dominate another in the sense of exercising power over it. Thus, a military occupation of B by A may seriously curtail B's freedom of action, but is not for that reason an imperialist relationship unless it is set up in a special way. The same applies to the *threat* of conquest and possible occupation, as in a balance of power relationship. Moreover, *subversive* activities may also be brought to a stage where a nation is dominated by the pin-pricks exercised against it from below, but this is clearly different from imperialism . . .

DEFINING 'CONFLICT OF INTEREST'

. . . 'Conflict of interest' is a special case of conflict in general, defined as a situation where parties are pursuing incompatible goals. In our special case, these goals are stipulated by an outsider as the 'true' interests of the parties, disregarding wholly or completely what the parties themselves say explicitly are the values they pursue. One reason for this is the rejection of the dogma of unlimited rationality: actors do *not* necessarily know, or they are unable to express, what their interest is. Another, more important, reason is that rationality is unevenly distributed, that some may dominate the minds of others, and that this may lead to 'false consciousness'. Thus, learning to suppress one's own true interests may be a major part of socialization in general and education in particular.

Let us refer to this true interest as LC, *living condition.* It may perhaps be measured by using such indicators as income, standard of living in the usual materialistic sense—but notions of *quality of life* would certainly also enter, not to mention notions of *autonomy.* But the precise content of LC is less important for our purpose than the definition of conflict of interest:

> There is *conflict,* or *disharmony of interest,* if the two parties are coupled together in such a way that the LC *gap* between them is *increasing;* there is *no conflict,* or *harmony of interest,* if the two parties are coupled together in such a way that the LC *gap* between them is *decreasing down to zero.*

Some points in this definition should be spelled out.

First, the parties have to be coupled together, in other words *interact.* A difference between mutually isolated parties does not in itself give rise to problems of interest. There was neither harmony, nor disharmony of interest between the peoples in Africa, Asia, and America before the white Europeans came — there was *nothing.*

Second, the reference is to *parties,* not to actors. In the theory of conflict of *interests,* as opposed to the theory of conflict of *goals,* there is no assumption that the parties (better: categories) have crystallized into actors. This is what they may have to do after they see their own situation more clearly, or in other words: the conflict of interest may have to be transformed into a conflict of *goals.* Thus, if in a nation the center, here defined as the 'government' (in the wide sense, not the 'cabinet') uses its power to increase its own LC much more than does the rest of the nation, then there is disharmony of interest between government and people according to this definition. This may then be used as a basis for defining the government as illegitimate—as opposed to the usual conception where illegitimacy is a matter of opinion, expressed in the legislature or in the population. The trouble with the latter idea is that it presupposes a level of rationality, an ability of expression and political consciousness and party formation that can only be presupposed at the center of the more or less vertical societies in which human beings live. It is a model highly protective of the center as a whole, however much it may lead to rotation of groups within the center, and hence protective of vertical society.

Third, there is the problem of what to do with the case of a *constant gap.* The parties grow together, at the same rate, but the gap between them is constant. Is that harmony or disharmony of interest? We would refer to it as disharmony, for the parties are coupled such that they will not be brought together. Even if the *grow* parallel to each other it is impossible to put it down as a case of harmony, when the distribution of value is so unequal. On the contrary, this is the case of disharmony that has reached a state of equilibrium.

Fourth, this definition has the advantage of enabling us to talk about *degrees of harmony and disharmony* by measuring the angle between the two trajectories, perhaps also taking speed into account. Thus we avoid the difficulty of talking simplistically in terms of polar opposites, harmony vs. disharmony, and can start talking in terms of weak and strong harmony and disharmony.

Fifth, there is an implicit reference to *time* in the two terms 'increasing' and 'decreasing.' We have not been satisfied with a time-free way of operationalizing the concept in terms of static LC gaps. It is much more easy with conflict of *goals*, as we would then be dealing with clearly demarcated actors whose values can be ascertained, and their compatibility or incompatibility likewise: there is no need to study the system over time. To understand conflict of *interest* it looks as if at least a bivariate, diachronic analysis should be carried out to get some feel of how the system operates.

Table I. Four types of harmony/disharmony of interest

		gap decreasing	gap increasing
gap	narrow	A	C
	wide	B	D

But we should obviously make a distinction between the *size* of the gap, and what happens to the gap over time. If we only had access to static, synchronic data, then we would of course focus on the magnitude of the gap and talk about *disharmony of interest if it is wide, harmony of interest if it is narrow or zero.*

As a first approximation this may not be too bad, but it does lead us into some difficulties. Thus, how do we rank these combinations in terms of increasing disharmony of interest? (Table I). As we see from the Table, the only doubt would be between combinations B and C. We would favor the alphabetical order for two reasons: first, becoming is more important than being (at least if the time-perspective is reasonably short), and second, the diachronic relationship probably reveals more about the coupling between them. For example, the gap in living conditions between Norway and Nepal in 1970 is not significant as an indicator of any imperialism. If it keeps on increasing there may be a bit more basis for the suspicion, but more evidence is needed to state the diagnosis of imperialism. The crucial word here is 'coupling' in the definition. The word has been put there to indicate some type of social causation in interaction relation and interaction structure which will have to be demonstrated, over and above a simple correlation.

Let us conclude this discussion by pointing out that a gap in living condition, of at least one important kind, is a necessary, if not sufficient, condition for conflict or disharmony of interest. If in addition the gap can be observed over time, a more satisfactory basis for a diagnosis in terms of imperialism may emerge.

And then, in conclusion: it is clear that the concept of interest used here is based on an ideology, or a *value premise of equality.*(2) An interaction relation and interaction structure set up such that inequality is the result is seen as a coupling not in the interest of the weaker party. This is a value premise like so many other value premises in social science explorations, such as 'direct violence is bad,' 'economic growth is good,' 'conflict should be resolved,' etc. As in all other types of social science, the goal should not be an 'objective' social science freed from all such value premises, but a more honest social science where the value premises are made explicit.

DEFINING 'IMPERIALISM'

We shall now define imperialism by using the building blocks presented in the preceding two sections. In our two-nation world, imperialism can be defined as one way in which the Center nation has power over the Periphery nation, so as to bring about a condition of disharmony of interest between them. Concretely, *Imperialism* (3) is a relation between a Center and a Periphery nation so that 1. there is *harmony of interest* between the *center in the Center* nation and the *center in the Periphery* nation, 2. there is more *disharmony of interest* within the Periphery nation than within the Center nations, and 3. there is *disharmony of interest* between the-*periphery in the Center* nation and the *periphery in the Periphery* nation.

Diagramatically it looks like something like Fig. 1. This complex definition, borrowing largely from Lenin,(4) needs spelling out. The basic idea is, as mentioned, that the center in the Center nation has a bridgehead in the Periphery nation, and a well-chosen one: the center in the Periphery nation. This is established such that the Periphery center is tied to the Center center with the best possible tie: the tie of harmony of interest. They are linked so that they go up together and down, even under, together. How this is done in concrete terms will be explored in the subsequent sections.

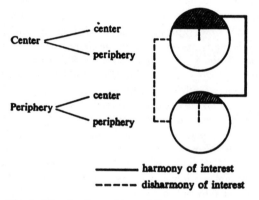

Fig. 1. The structure of imperialism

Inside the two nations there is disharmony of interest. They are both in one way or another vertical societies with LC gaps — otherwise there is no possibility of locating a center and a periphery. Moreover, the gap is not decreasing, but is at best constant. But the basic idea, absolutely fundamental for the whole theory to be developed, is that *there is more disharmony in the Periphery nation than in the Center nation.* At the simplest static level of description this means there is more inequality in the Periphery than in the Center. At the more complex level we might talk in terms of the gap opening more quickly in the Periphery than in the Center, where it might even remain constant. Through welfare state activities, redistribution takes place and disharmony is reduced for at least some LC dimensions, including income, but usually excluding power.

If we now would capture in a few sentences what imperialism is about, we might perhaps say something like this:

In the Periphery nation, the center grows more than the periphery, due partly to how interaction between center and periphery is organized. Without necessarily thinking of economic interaction, the center is more enriched than the periphery — in ways to be explored below. However, for part of this enrichment, the center in the Periphery only serves as a transmission belt (e.g., as commercial firms, trading companies) for value (e.g., raw materials) forwarded to the Center nation. This value enters the Center in the center, with some of it drizzling down to the periphery in the Center. Importantly, there is less disharmony of interest in the Center than in the Periphery, so that *the total arrangement is largely in the interest of the periphery in the Center.* Within the Center the two parties may be opposed to each other. But in the total game, the periphery see themselves more as the partners of the center in the Center than as the partners of the periphery in the Periphery — and this is the essential trick of that game. Alliance formation between the two peripheries is avoided, while the Center nation becomes more and the Periphery nation less cohesive — and hence less able to develop long-term strategies.

Actually, concerning the three criteria in the definition of imperialism as given above, it is clear that no. 3. is implied by nos. 1. and 2. The two centers are tied together and the Center periphery is tied to its center: that is the whole essence of the situation. If we now presuppose that the center in the Periphery is a smaller proportion of that nation than the center in the Center, we can also draw one more implication: *there is disharmony of interest between the Center nation as a whole and the Periphery nation as a whole.* But that type of finding, frequently referred to, is highly misleading because it blurs the harmony of interest between the two centers, and leads to the belief that imperialism is merely an international relationship, *not a combination of intra- and inter-national relations.* (5)

However, even if the definition given above purports to define the pure case of imperialism, we may nevertheless fruitfully think in terms of degenerate cases. Thus, the first point in the definition about harmony between the two centers is obviously the most important one. If the second point does not hold, and consequently not the third point either, it may still be fruitful to talk about imperialism. But in this degenerate case the two peripheries may more easily find each other, since they are now only kept apart by geographical distance (assuming that the two nations are nation states, often even located far apart), not in addition by disharmony of interest. Thus, if the relationship between the two peripheries and their centers should become more similar, periphery alliance formation might easily be the result, and the two centers would have to resort to more direct means of violence rather than, or in addition to, the delicate type of structural violence that characterizes the pure type of imperialistic relationship.

But what if there is no distinction between center and periphery in the two nations, what if they are completely horizontal societies? In that case, we should not talk about the dominance relationship whereby the Center nation extracts something from the Periphery nation as an imperialistic one, but rather as something else — looting, stealing, etc. Where there is no bridgehead for the Center nation in the center of the Periphery nation, there cannot be any imperialism by this definition.

From this an important methodological remark may follow. Imagine we now start from the other end and discover that over time some nations increase their living conditions more than other nations — the 'increasing gap' so often referred to today — and that there seems to be some kind of structure to this, some kind of invariance. As mentioned, this does not in itself constitute proof of any diagnosis in terms of imperialism, but should prompt the researcher to look for data in that direction. More particularly, we should try to study the precise nature of the interaction between the nations or groups of nations, and see whether the nations can be differentiated in terms of centers and peripheries that relate to each other in the way indicated. But to do this is at all a concrete manner, we must make our definition of imperialism much less abstract. To this we now turn, in successive stages, exploring two *mechanisms*, five *types*, and three *phases* of imperialism.

THE MECHANISMS OF IMPERIALISM

The two basic mechanisms of imperialism both concern the *relation* between the parties concerned, particularly between the nations. The first mechanism concerns the *interaction relation* itself, the second how these relations are put together in a larger interaction structure: 1. the principle of *vertical interaction relation*, and 2. the principle of *feudal interaction structure*.

The basic point about interaction is, of course, that people and nations have different values that complement each other, and then engage in exchange. Some nations produce oil, other nations produce tractors, and they then carry out an exchange according to the principles of comparative advantages. Imagine that our two-nation system has a prehistory of no interaction at all, and then starts with this type of interaction. Obviously, both will be changed by it, and more particularly: a gap between them is likely to open and widen if the interaction is cumulatively asymmetric in terms of what the two parties get out of it.

To study whether the interaction is symmetric or asymmetric, on equal or unequal terms, *two* factors arising from the interaction have to be examined: 1. *the value-exchange between the actors* — *inter*-actor effects, and 2. *the effects inside the actors* — *intra*-actor effects.

In *economic* relations the first is most commonly analyzed, not only by liberal but also by Marxist economists. The inter-actor flow can be observed as flows of raw material, capital, and financial goods and services in either direction, and can literally be measured at the main points of entry: the customs houses and the national banks. The flow both ways can then be compared in various ways. Most important is the comparison in terms of *who benefits most*, and for this purpose intra-actor effects also have to be taken into consideration.

In order to explore this, the interaction budget indicated in Table II may be useful. In the Table the usual exchange pattern between a 'developed' nation A and a 'developing' nation B, where manufactured goods are exchanged for raw materials, is indicated. Whether it takes place in a barter economy or a money economy is not essential in a study of exchange between completely unprocessed goods like crude oil and highly processed goods like tractors. There are negative intra-actor effects that accrue to both parties, indicated by the terms 'pollution' for A and 'depletion' for B, and 'exploitation' for either. So far these negative spin-off effects are usually not taken systematically into account, nor the positive spin-off effects for A that will be a corner-stone in the present analysis.

It is certainly meaningful and important to talk in terms of unequal exchange or asymmetric interaction, but not quite unproblematic what its precise meaning should be. For that reason, it may be helpful to think in terms of three stages or types of exploitation, partly reflecting historical *processes* in chronological order, and partly reflecting types of *thinking* about exploitation.

Table II. An interaction budget

	A ('developed')		B ('developing')	
	inter-actor effects	intra-actor effects	inter-actor effects	intra-actor effects
positive (in)	raw materials	spin-offs	manufactured goods	little or nothing
negative (out)	manufactured goods	pollution, exploitation	raw materials	depletion, exploitation

In the first stage of exploitation, A simply engages in looting and takes away the raw materials without offering anything in return. If he steals out of pure nature there is no human interaction involved, but we assume that he forces 'natives' to work for him and do the extraction work. It is like the slave owner who lives on the work produced by slaves — which is quantatively not too different from the land owner who has land workers working for him five out of seven days a week.

In the second stage, A starts offering something 'in return.' Oil, pitch, land, etc., is 'bought' for a couple of beads — it is no longer simply taken away without asking any questions about ownership. The price paid is ridiculous. However, as power relations in the international systems change, perhaps mainly by bringing the power level of the weaker party up from zero to some low positive value, A has to contribute more: for instance, pay more for the oil. The question is now whether there is a cut-off point after which the exchange becomes equal, and what the criterion for that cut-off point would be. Absence of subjective dissatisfaction — B ways that he is now content? Objective market values or the number of man-hours that have gone into the production on either side?

There are difficulties with all these conceptions. But instead of elaborating on this, we shall rather direct our attention to the shared failure of all these attempts to look at *intra*-actor effects. Does the interaction have enriching or impoverishing effects *inside* the actor, or does it just lead to a stand-still? This type of question leads us to the third stage of exploitation, where there may be some balance in the flow between the actors, but great differences in the effect the interaction has within them.(6)

As an example let us use nations exchanging oil for tractors. The basic point is that this involves different levels of processing, where we define 'processing' as an activity imposing culture on Nature. In the case of crude oil the product is (almost) pure Nature; in case of tractors it would be wrong to say that it is a case of pure Culture, pure *form* (like mathematics, music). A transistor radio, an integrated circuit, these would be better examples because Nature has been brought down to a minimum. The tractor is still too much iron and rubber to be a pure case.

The major point now is the *gap in processing level* between oil and tractors and the differential effect this gap will have on the two nations. In one nation the oil deposit may be at the waterfront, and all that is needed is a derrick and some simple mooring facilities to pump the oil straight into a ship — e.g., a Norwegian tanker — that can bring the oil to the country where it will provide energy to run, among other things, the tractor factories. In the other nation the effects may be extremely far-reaching due to the complexity of the product and the connectedness of the society.

Table III. Intra-actor effects of interaction across gaps in processing levels

Dimension	Effect on center nation	Effect on periphery nation	Analyzed by
1. Subsidiary economic effects	New *means of production* developed	Nothing developed, just a hole in the ground	Economist
2. Political position in world structure	Central position reinforced	Periphery position reinforced	International relationists
3. Military benefits	*Means of destruction* can easily be produced	No benefits, wars cannot be fought by means of raw materials	
4. Communication benefits	*Means of communication* easily developed	No benefits, transportation not by means of raw materials	Communication specialists
5. Knowledge and research	Much needed for higher levels of processing	Nothing needed, extraction based on being, not on becoming	Scientists, specialists
6. Specialist needed	Specialists in *making*, scientists, engineers	Specialist in *having*, lawyers	Sociologists of knowledge
7. Skill and education	Much needed to carry out processing	Nothing needed, just a hole in the ground	Education specialists
8. Social structure	Change needed for ability to convert into mobility	No changed needed, extraction based on ownership, not on ability	Sociologists
9. Psychological effects	A basic psychology of self-reliance and autonomy	A basic psychology of depenence	Psychologists

There may be ring effects in all directions, and in Table III we have made an effort to show some types of spin-off effects. A number of comments are appropriate in connection with this list, which, needless to say, is very tentative indeed.

First, the effects are rather deep-reaching if this is at all a correct image of the situation. And the picture is hardly exaggerated. It is possible to set up international interaction in such a way that the positive intra-actor effects are practically nil in the raw material delivering nation, and extremely far-reaching in the processing nation.(7) This is not in any sense strange either: if processing is the imprint of Culture on Nature, the effects should be far-reaching indeed, and strongly related to development itself.

Second, these effects reinforce each other. In the nine effects listed in Table III, there are economic, political, military, communications, and cultural aspects, mixed together. Thus, the nation that in the international division of labor has the task of providing the most refined, processed products — like Japan with its emphasis on integrated circuits, transistors, miniaturization, etc., (or Eastern Europe's Japan: the DDR, with a similar emphasis) — will obviously have to engage in research. Research needs an infra-structure, a wide cultural basis in universities, etc., and it has obvious spill-over effects in the social, political, and military domains. And so on: the list may be examined and all kinds of obvious types of cross-fertilization be explored.

Third, in the example chosen, and also in the formulations in the Table, we have actually referred to a very special type of gap in processing level: the case when one of the nations concerned delivers raw materials. But the general point here is the *gap*, which would also exist if one nation delivers semi-finished products and the other finished products. There may be as much of a gap in a trade relations based on exchange between textiles and transistors as one based on exchange between oil and tractors. However, and this seems to be basic: we have looked in vain for a theory of economic trade where this gap is meaningfully operationalized so that the theory could be based on it. In fact, *degree of processing*, which is the basic variable behind the spin-off effects, seems absent from most thinking about international exchange.

This, and that is observation number *four*, is not merely a question of analyzing differences in processing level in terms of what happens inside the factory or the extraction plant. It has to be seen in its social totality. A glance at the right-hand column of Table III immediately gives us some clues as to why this has not been done: academic research has been so divided that nowhere in a traditional university set-up would one come to grips with the totality of the effects of an interaction process. Not even in the most sophisticated inter-, cross- or trans-disciplinary research institute has that type of research been carried so far that a meaningful operationalization has been offered. Yet this is indispensible for a new program of trade on equal terms to be formulated: *trade, or interaction in general, is symmetric, or on equal terms, if and only if the total inter- and intra-actor effects that accrue to the parties are equal.* (8)

But, and this is observation number *five*: why has the idea of comparing the effects of interaction only at the points of exit and entry been so successful? Probably basically because it has always been natural and in the interest of the two centers to view the world in this way, not necessarily consciously to reinforce their position in the center, but basically because interaction looks more like '*inter*-action only' to the center. If the center in the Periphery has based its existence on being rather than becoming, on ownership rather than processing, then the inter-action has been very advantageous to them. What was formerly Nature is through the 'beneficial interaction' with another nation converted into Money, which in turn can be converted into many things. *Very little effort was needed:* and that this was precisely what made the exchange so disadvantageous, only became clear after some time. Japan is, possibly, the only nation that has really converted the absence of raw materials into a blessing for the economy.

Some implications of the general principle of viewing intra-actor in addition to inter-actor effects can now be spelled out.

One is obvious: *asymmetry cannot be rectified by stabilizing or increasing the prices for raw materials.* Of course, prices exist that could, on the surface, compensate for the gap in intra-actor effects, convertible into a corresponding development of subsidiary industries, education industry, knowledge industry, and so on (although it is hard to see how the psychology of self-reliance can be bought for money). Much of this is what raw material producing countries can do with the money they earn. But this is not the same. One thing is to be *forced* into a certain pattern of intra-actor development *in order to* be able to participate in the inter-actor interaction, quite another thing to be free to make the decision without having to do it, without being forced by the entire social machinery.

The second implication is also obvious, but should still be put as a question to economists. Imagine that a nation A gives nation B a loan L, to be repaid after n years at an interest rate of p % p.a. There is only one condition in addition to the conditions of the loan: that the money be used to procure goods at a high level of processing in A. Each order will then have deep repercussions in A, along the eight dimensions indicated, in addition to the direct effect of the order itself. The value of these effects is certainly not easily calculated, but in addition A also gets back from B, if B has not gone bankrupt through this process in the meantime, $L(1+p)^N$ after n years. If procurement is in terms of capital goods rather than consumer goods (usually for consumption by the center in the Periphery mainly) there will also have been intra-actor effects in B. In all likelihood the intra-actor effects of the deal in A are more far-reaching, however, for two reasons: the effects of the interaction process enter A at a higher level of processing than B, and A has already a socio-economic-political structure enabling it to absorb and convert and re-direct such pressure for maximum beneficial impact.

Imagine now that n is high and p is low; the loan is said to be 'on generous terms.' The question is whether this generosity is not deceptive, *whether it would not have paid for A to give L for eternity, at no interest,* i.e., as a grant. Or even better: it might even have paid for A to persuade B to take on L with negative interest, i.e., to pay B for accepting the loan, because of all the intra-actor effects. The situation may be likened to a man who pays some people a certain sum on the condition that they use the money to pay for an article on, say, imperialism. By having to produce, by having obligations to fulfill, the man is forced to create and thereby expand, and consequently forced to enrich himself.(9)

In short, we see vertical interaction as the major source of the inequality of this world, whether it takes the form of looting, of highly unequal exchange, or highly differential spin-off effects due to processing gaps. But we can also imagine a fourth phase of exploitation, where the modern King Midas becomes a victim of his own greed and turns his environment into muck rather than gold, by polluting it so strongly and so thoroughly that the negative spin-off effects from processing may outstrip all the positive effects. This may, in fact, place the less developed countries in a more favorable position: the lower the GNP, the lower the Gross National Pollution.

But this phase is still for the (near?) future. At present what we observe is an inequality between the world's nations of a magnitude that can only be explained in terms of the cumulative effect of *strong* structural phenomena over time, like the phenomena described here under the heading of imperialism. This is not to deny that other factors may also be important, even decisive, but no analysis can be valid without studying the problem of development in a context of vertical interaction.

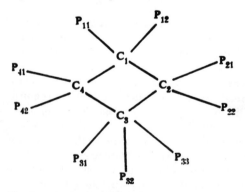

Fig. 2. A feudal center-periphery structure

If the first mechanism, the *vertical interaction relation,* is the major factor behind inequality, then the second mechanism, the *feudal interaction structure,* is the factor that maintains and reinforces the inequality by protecting it. There are four rules defining this particular interaction structure(10): 1. interaction between Center and Periphery is *vertical.* 2. interaction between Periphery and Periphery is *missing,* 3. multilateral interaction involving all three is *missing,* and 4. interaction with the outside world is *monopolized* by the Center, with two implications: Periphery interaction with other Center nations is *missing,* and Center as well as

Periphery interaction with Periphery nations belonging to other Center nations is *missing.*

This relation can be depicted as in Fig. 2. As indicated in the Figure, the number of Periphery nations attached to any given Center nation can, of course, vary. In this Figure we have also depicted the rule "if you stay off my satellites, I will stay off yours.'

Some important *economic* consequences of this structure should be spelled out.

First and most obvious: the *concentration on trade partners.* A Periphery nation should, as a result of these two mechanisms, have most of its trade with 'its' Center nation. In other words, empirically we would expect high levels of *import concentration* as well as *export concentration* in the Periphery, as opposed to the Center, which is more free to extend its trade relations in almost any direction — except in the pure case, with the Periphery of other Center nations.

Second, and not so obvious, is the *commodity concentration:* the tendency for Periphery nations to have only one or very few primary products to export. This would be a trivial matter if it could be explained entirely in terms of geography, if, e.g., oil countries were systematically poor as to ore, ore countries poor as to bananas and coffee, etc. But this can hardly be assumed to be the general case: Nature does not distribute its riches that way. There is a historical rather than a geographical explanation to this. A territory may have been exploited for the raw materials most easily available and/or most needed in the Center, and this, in turn, leads to a certain social structure, to communication lines to the deposits, to trade structures, to the emergence of certain center groups (often based on ownership of that particular raw material), and so on. To start exploiting a new kind of raw material in the same territory might upset carefully designed local balances; hence, it might be easier to have a fresh start for that new raw material in virgin territory with no bridgehead already prepared for imperialist exploits. In order to substantiate this hypothesis we would have to demonstrate that there are particularly underutilized and systematically underexplored deposits precisely in countries where one type of raw materials has already been exploited.

The combined effect of these two consequences is a *dependency* of the Periphery GNP for the Periphery, the trade between them is a much higher percentage of the GNP for the Periphery and with both partner and commodity concentration, the Periphery becomes particularly vulnerable to fluctuations in demands and prices. At the same time the center in the Periphery depends on the Center for its supply of consumer goods. Import substitution industries will usually lead to consumer goods that look homespun and unchic, particularly if there is planned obsolescence in the production of these goods in the Center, plus a demand for equality between the two centers maintained by demonstration effects and frequent visits to the Center.(11)

However, the most important consequence is political and has to do with the systematic utilization of feudal interaction structures as a way of protecting the Center against the Periphery. The feudal interaction structure is in social science language nothing but an expression of the old political maxim *divide et impera,* divide and rule, as a strategy used systematically by the Center relative to the Periphery nations. How could — for example — a small foggy island in the North Sea rule over one quarter of the world? By isolating the Periphery parts from each other, by having them geographically at sufficient distance from each other to impede any real alliance formation, by having separate deals with them so as to tie them to the Center in particularistic ways, by reducing multilateralism to a minimum with all kinds of graded membership, *and* by having the Mother country assume the role of window to the world.

However, this point can be much more clearly seen if we combine the two mechanisms and extend what has been said so far for relations between Center and Periphery *nations* to relations between center and periphery *groups* within nations. Under an imperialist structure the two mechanisms are used not only between nations but also within nations, but less so in the Center nation than in the Periphery nation. In other words, there is vertical division of labor within as well as between nations. And these two levels of organization are intimately linked to each other (as A.G. Frank always has emphasized) in the sense that the center in the Periphery interaction structure is also that group with which the Center nation has its harmony of interest, the group used as a bridgehead.

Thus, the combined operation of the two mechanisms at the two levels builds into the structure a subtle grid of protection measures against the major potential source of 'trouble', the periphery in the Periphery. To summarize the major items in this grid: 1. the general impoverishment of pP brought about by vertical division of labor within the Periphery nation, and particularly by the high level of inequality (e.g. differential access to means of communication) and disharmony of interest in the Periphery nation; 2. the way in which interaction, mobilization, and organization of pP are impeded by the feudal structure *within* Periphery nations; 3. the general impoverishment of the Periphery nation brought about by vertical division of labor, particularly in terms of means of destruction and communication; 4. the way in which interaction, mobilization, and organization of the Periphery nations are impeded by the feudal interaction structure *between* nations, making it difficult to interact with other Periphery nations 'belonging' to the same Center nations, and making it even more difficult to interact with Periphery nations 'belonging' to other Center nations; 5. the way in which it is a fortiori difficult for the peripheries in Periphery nations to interact, mobilize, and organize intra-nationally because of 1. and 2., and inter-nationally because of 3. and 4., in addition: because the center in the Periphery has the monopoly on international interaction in all directions and cannot be counted on to interact in the interest of its own periphery; 6. the way in which pP cannot appeal to pC or cC either because of the disharmony of interest.

Obviously, the more perfectly the mechanisms of imperialism within and between nations are put to work, the less overt machinery of oppression is needed and the smaller can the center groups be, relative to the total population involved *Only imperfect, amateurish imperialism needs weapons; professional imperialism is based on structural rather than direct violence.*

THE TYPES OF IMPERIALISM

We shall now make this more concrete by distinguishing between five types of imperialism depending on the *type* of exchange between Center and Periphery nations: *economic, political, military, communication, and cultural.*

The order of presentation is rather random: we have no theory that one is more basic than the others, or precedes the others. Rather, this is like a Pentagon or a Soviet Star:(12) imperialism can start from any corner. They should all be examined regarding the extent to which they generate interaction patterns that utilize the two *mechanisms* of imperialism so as to fulfill the three *criteria* of imperialism, or at least the first of them.

The most basic of the two mechanisms is *vertical* interaction, which in its modern form is conceived of as interaction across a gap in processing level. In other words, what is exchanged between the two nations is not only not the same things (which would have been stupid) but things of a quite different kind, the difference being in terms of where the most complex and stimulating operations take place. One tentative list, expanding what has been said previously about economic interaction, might look like Table IV. The order of presentation parallels that of Table III, but in that Table cultural imperialism was spelled out in more detail as spin-off effects from economic imperialism.

Table IV. The five types of imperialism

Type	Economic	Political	Military	Communication	Cultural
Center nation provides	processing, means of production	decisions models	protection means of destruction	news, means of communication	teaching, means of creation – autonomy
Periphery nation provides	raw materials, markets	obedience, imitators	discipline, traditional hardware	events, passengers, goods	learning, validation – dependence

The vertical nature of this type of *economic* interaction has been spelled out in detail above since we have used that type of imperialism to exemplify definition and mechanisms. Let us look more at the other types of vertical interaction.

The *political* one is clear: the concept of a 'mother' country, the Center nation, is also an indication of how the decision-making center is dislocated, away from the nation itself and towards the Center nation. These decisions may then affect economic, military, communication, and cultural patterns. Important here is the division of labor involved: some nations produce decisions, others supply obedience. The decisions may be made upon application, as in 'bilateral technical assistance', or in consultation — or they may simply emerge by virtue of the model-imitator distinction. Nothing serves that distinction quite so well as unilinear concepts of 'development' and 'modernization', according to which Center nations possess some superior kind of structure for others to imitate (as long as the Center's central position is not seriously challenged), and which gives a special aura of legitimacy to any idea emanating from the Center. Thus, structures and decisions developed in the 'motherland of liberalism' or in the 'fatherland of socialism' serve as models by virtue of their place of origin, not by virtue of their substance.

The *military* implications or parallels are also rather obvious. It cannot be emphasized enough that the economic division of labor is also one which ensures that the Center nations economically speaking also become the Center nations in a military sense: only they have the industrial capacity to develop the technological hardware — and also are often the only ones with the social structure compatible with a modern army. He who produces tractors can easily produce tanks, but he who delivers oil cannot defend himself by throwing it in the face of the aggressors. He has to depend on the tank-producer, either for protection or for acquisition (on terms dictated by the Center). And just as there is a division of labor with the Center nation producing manufactured goods on the basis of raw materials extracted in the Periphery nation, there is also a division of labor with the *Center nations processing the obedience provided by the Periphery nations into decisions that can be implemented.* Moreover, there is also a division of labor with the Center providing the protection (and often also the officers or at least the instructors in 'counter-insurgency') and the Periphery the discipline and the soldiers needed — not to mention the apprentices of 'military advisors' from the Center.

As to the fourth type, *communication* imperialism, the emphasis in the analysis is usually turned towards the second mechanism of imperialism: the feudal interaction structure. That this largely holds for most world communication and transportation patterns has been amply demonstrated.(13) But perhaps more important is the vertical nature of the division of labor in the field of communication/transportation. It is trivial that a high level of industrial capacity is necessary to develop the latest in transportation and communication technology. The preceding generation of *means of communication/transportation* can always be sold, sometimes second-hand, to the Periphery as part of the general vertical trade/aid structure, alongside the *means of production* (economic sector), the *means of destruction* (military sector), and the *means of creation* (cultural sector). The Center's planes and ships are faster, more direct, look more reliable, attract more passengers, more goods. And when the Periphery finally catches up, the Center will already for a long time have dominated the field of communication satellites.

One special version of this principle is a combination of cultural and communication exchange: *news communication*. We all know that the major agencies are in the hands of the Center countries, relying on Center-dominated, feudal networks of communication.(14) What is not so well analyzed is how Center news takes up a much larger proportion of Periphery news media than vice versa, just as trade with the Center is a larger proportion of Periphery total trade than vice versa. In other words, the pattern of partner concentration as something found more in the Periphery than in the Center is very pronounced. The Periphery nations do not write or read much about each other, especially not across bloc borders, and they read more about 'their' Center than about other Centers — because the press is written and read by the center in the Periphery, who want to know more about that most 'relevant' part of the world — for them.

Another aspect of vertical division of labor in the news business should also be pointed out. Just as the Periphery produces raw material that the Center turns into processed goods, *the Periphery also produces events that the Center turns into news*. (15) This is done by training journalists to see events with Center eyes, and by setting up a chain of communication that filters and processes events so that they fit the general pattern.

The latter concept brings us straight into *cultural* imperialism, a subtype of which is scientific imperialism. The division of labor between teachers and learners is clear: it is not the division of labor as such (found in most situations of transmission of knowledge) that constitutes imperialism, but the location of the teachers, and of the learners, in a broader setting. If the Center always provides the teachers and the definition of that worthy of being taught (from the gospels of Christianity to the gospels of Technology), and the Periphery always provides the learners, then there is a pattern which smacks of imperialism. The satellite nation in the Periphery will also know that nothing flatters the Center quite so much as being encouraged to teach, and being seen as a model, and that the Periphery can get much in return from a humble, culture-seeking strategy (just as it will get little but aggression if it starts teaching the Center anything — like Czechoslovakia, who started lecturing the Soviet Union on socialism). For in accepting cultural transmission the Periphery also, implicitly, validates for the Center the culture developed in the center, whether that center is intra- or inter-national. This serves to reinforce the Center as a center, for it will then continue to develop culture along with transmitting it, thus creating lasting demand for the latest innovations. Theories, like cars and fashions, have their life-cycle, and whether the obsolescence is planned or not there will always be a time-lag in a structure with a pronounced difference between center and periphery. Thus, the tram workers in Rio de Janeiro may carry banners supporting Auguste Comte one hundred years after the center of the Center forgot who he was. . . .

. . . In science we find a particular version of vertical division of labor, very similar to economic division of labor: the pattern of scientific teams from the Center who go to Periphery nations to collect data (raw material) in the form of deposits, sediments, flora, fauna, archeological findings, attitudes, behavioral patterns, and so on for data processing, data analysis, and theory formation (processing, in general) in the Center universities (factories), so as to be able to send the finished product, a journal, a book (manufactured goods) back for consumption in the center of the Periphery — after first having created a demand for it through demonstration effect, training in the Center country, and some degree of low level participation in the data collection team.(16) This parallel is not a joke, it is a *structure*. If in addition the precise nature of the research is to provide the Center with information that can be used economically, politically, or militarily to maintain an imperialist structure, the cultural imperialism becomes even more clear. And if to this we add the *brain drain* (and body drain) whereby 'raw' brains (students) and 'raw' bodies (unskilled workers) are moved from the Periphery to the Center and 'processed' (trained) with ample benefits to the Center, the picture becomes complete.

Table V. Three phases of imperialism in history

Phase	Period	Form	Term
I	Past	*Occupation*, cP physically consists of cC people who engage in *occupation*	Colonialism
II	Present	*Organization*, cC interacts with cP via the medium of international *organizations*	Neo-colonialism
III	Future	*Communication*, cC interacts with cP via international communication	Neo-neo-colonialism

THE PHASES OF IMPERIALISM

We have mentioned repeatedly that imperialism is *one* way in which one nation may dominate another. Moreover, it is a way that provides a relatively stable pattern: the nations are linked to each other in a pattern that may last for some time because of the many stabilizing factors built into it through the mechanism of a feudal interaction structure.

The basic idea is that the center in the Center establishes a bridgehead in the Periphery nation, and more particularly, in the center of the Periphery nation. Obviously, this bridgehead does not come about just like that: there is a phase preceding it. The precise nature of that preceding phase can best be seen by distinguishing between three phases of imperialism in history, depending on what type of concrete method the center in the Center has used to establish the harmony of interest between itself and the center in the Periphery. This is enumerated in Table V.

From the Table we see that in all three cases, the Center nation has a hold over the center of the Periphery nation. But the precise nature of the grip differs, and should be seen relative to the means of transportation and communication. No analysis of imperialism can be made without a reference to these means that perhaps are as basic as the means of production in producing social dynamics.

Throughout the overwhelming part of human history, transportation (of human beings, of goods) did not proceed at a higher speed than that provided by pony expresses and quick sailing ships; and communication (of signals, of meaning) not at higher speed than that provided by fires and smoke signals which could be spotted from one hilltop to another. Precise control over another nation would have to be exercised by physically transplanting one's own center and grafting onto the top of the foreign body — in other words, colonialism in all its forms, best known in connection with 'white settlers'. According to this vision, colonialism was not a discovery of the Europeans subsequent to the Great Discoveries: it could just as well be used to describe great parts of the Roman Empire that through textbooks and traditions of history-writing so successfully has dominated our image of racial and ethnical identity and national pride.(17)

Obviously, the quicker the means of transportation could become, the less necessary would this pattern of permanent settlement be. The break in the historical pattern came when the steam engine was not only put into the factory to provide new *means of production* (leading to conditions that prompted Marx to write *Das Kapital*) but also into a vessel (Fulton) and a locomotive (Stephenson): in other words, *means of transportation* (the book about that is not yet written). This gave Europeans a decisive edge over peoples in other regions, and colonialism became more firmly entrenched. Control could be accurate and quick.

But decolonialization also came, partly due to the weakening of cC, partly due to the strengthening of cP that might not challenge what cC did, but want to do so itself. Neo-colonialism came; and in this present phase of imperialism, control is not of the direct, concrete type found in the past. It is mediated through the means of transportation (and, of course, also communication) linking the two centers to each other. The control is less concrete: it is not physical presence, but a link; and this link takes the shape of international organizations. The international organization has a certain permanence, often with physical headquarters and a lasting general secretary in the mother country. But above all it is a medium in which influence can flow, with *both* centers joining as members and finding each other. Their harmony of interest can be translated into complete equality within the international organization, and vice versa. Their identity is defined relative to the organization, not to race, ethnicity, or nationality. But with differential disharmony *within* nations, this actually becomes an instrument of disharmony *between* nations.

These organizations are well-known for all five types of imperialism. For the economic type, the private or governmental multinational corporations (BINGOs) may serve;(18) for the political type, many of the international governmental organizations (IGOs); for the military type, the various systems of military alliances and treaties and organizations (MIGOs?);(19) for communication the shipping and air companies (CONGOs?), not to mention the international press agencies, offer ample illustration; and for cultural imperialism, some of the international nongovernmental organizations (INGOs) may serve as the conveyor mechanisms. But this is of course not to say that international organizations will necessarily serve such purposes. According to the theory developed here, this is an empirical question, depending on the degree of division of labor inside the organization and the extent to which it is feudally organized.

Next, the third phase. If we now proceed even further along the same line of decreasingly concrete (but increasingly effective?) ties between the two centers, we can envisage a phase where even the international organizations will not only go into disrepute, but dissolve. What will come in their place? *Instant communication.*

whereby parties who want to communicate with each other set up ad hoc communication networks (telesatellites, etc.) that form and dissolve in rapid succession, changing scope and domain, highly adjustable to external circumstance, guided by enormous data-banks that permit participants to find their 'opposite numbers' without having them frozen together in a more permanent institutional network that develops its own rigidities.(20)

In other words, we envisage a future where very many international organizations will be threatened in two ways. First, they will be exposed to increasing criticism as to their function as a tie between two centers, communicating and coordinating far above the masses in either country, which will in itself lead to a certain disintegration. Second, this does not mean that the centers, if they are free to do so, will cease to coordinate their action, only that they will do so by other means. Instead of going to ad hoc or annual conventions, or in other ways instructing a general secretary and his staff, they may simply pick up their videophone and have a long distance conference organized, where the small group of participants can all see and talk to each other — not like in a conference, but in the more important adjoining lobbies, in the coffee houses, in private quarters — or wherever they prefer to carry out communication and coordination.(21)

FROM SPIN-OFF TO SPILL-OVER

. . . We have now presented a theory of imperialism based on *three* criteria, *two* criteria, *two* mechanisms, *five* types, and *three* phases. In the presentation, as is usually done in any presentation of imperialism, economic imperialism was used for the purpose of illustration. However, we tried to carry the analysis further: for economic imperialism, exploitation was not only defined in terms of unequal exchange because A gives less to B than he gets from B, but also in terms of differential intra-actor or spin-off effects. Moreover, it is quite clear from Tables III and IV that these spin-off effects are located in other areas in which imperialism can also be defined. Vertical economic interaction has political spin-offs, military spin-offs, communication spin-offs, and cultural spin-offs; and vice-versa, as we shall indicate.

For that reason we shall now make a distinction between *spin-off* effects and *spill-over* effects. When a nation exchanges tractors for oil it develops a tractor-producing capacity. One possible spin-off effect is a tank-producing capacity, and this becomes a spill-over effect the moment that capacity is converted into military imperialism, for instance in the form of *Tank-Kommunismus* or *Tank-Kapitalismus*. Of course, this does not become military imperialism unless exercised in cooperation with the ruling elite in the Periphery nation. If it is exercised against that elite, it is a simple *invasion* — as distinct from an *intervention* that is the product of cC—cP cooperation.

A glance at Tables III and IV indicates that the road from spin-off to spill-over is a short one, provided that there are cooperating or even generalized elites available both in the Center and the Periphery nations. It is not necessary for the same person in Center and Periphery to be on top on both the economic, political, military, communication, and cultural organizations — that would be rather superhuman! Many would cover two or three such positions, few would command four or five. But if the five elites defined through these five types of exchange are *coordinated* into generalized upper classes based on a rich network of kinship, friendship, and association (not to mention effective cooperation), then the basis is laid for an extremely solid type of *generalized imperialism*. In the extreme case there would be rank concordance in both Center and Periphery, which means that there would not even be some little disequilibrium present in either case to give some leverage for a revolutionary movement. All groups would have learned, in fact been forced, to play generalized roles as dominant and dependent, respectively.

For this rank concordance to take place, gains made from one type of imperialism should be readily convertible into the other types. The analytical instrument here could be what we might call the *convertibility matrix*, given in Table VI.

	Economic	Political	Military	Communication	Cultural
Economic	1	2	3	4	5-9
Political					
Military					
Communication					
Cultural					

The numbers in the first row correspond to the spin-off effects for vertical division of labor in economic transactions, as indicated in Table III. A more complete theory of imperialism would now try to give corresponding spin-off effects, convertible into spill-over effects, for the other four types with regard to all five types. We shall certainly not engage fully in this taxonomic exercise but only pick one example from each row.

Thus, it is rather obvious how political imperialism can be converted into economic imperialism by dictating terms of trade, where the latter are not seen so much in terms of volume as trade composition.(26)

Correspondingly, military imperialism can easily be converted into communication imperialism by invoking the need for centralized command over communication and transportation facilities. It is no coincidence that the capital in so many Center countries is located inland and well protected, whereas the capital in most Periphery countries is a port, easily accessible from the Center country, and with a feudal interaction network inland facilitating the flow of raw materials to the capital port and a trickling of consumer goods in the other direction (most of it being absorbed in the capital port itself). Precise command of territory may be necessary to establish a communication network of this type, but once established, it is self-reinforcing.

Similarly, to take another example: communication imperialism may be converted into cultural imperialism by regulating the flow of information, not only in the form of news, but also in the form of cheaply available books, etc. from the Center country.

Finally, cultural imperialism is convertible into economic imperialism in ways very commonly found today: by means of technical assistance processes. A technical assistance expert is not only a person from a rich country who goes to a poor country and stimulates a demand in the poor country for the products of the rich country.(27) He is also a man who goes to the poor country in order to establish a routine in the poor country, reserving for himself all the benefits of the challenges of this entrepreneurial activity. He *writes* the SOP (Standard Operating Procedure); it is for his 'counterpart' to *follow* the SOP. That this challenge is convertible into more knowledge (more culture) and eventually also into economic benefits upon the return of the technical assistance expert is hardly to be doubted in principle, but it is another question whether the Center country understands this and fully utilizes the resource.

Convertibility could now be studied at two levels: the extent to which the nation as such can use such spin-offs from one type and direct them towards consolidation of another type, and the extent to which an individual may do so. If an individual can, the result is some type of rank concordance; if the nation can, we might perhaps talk of imperialism concordance.

But the only point we want to make here is that the convertibility matrix seems to be complete. It is hard to imagine any cell in Table VI that would be empty in the sense that there could be no spill-over effects, no possibility of conversion. If everything can be bought for money, obtained by political control, or ordered by military imposition, then that alone would take care of the first three horizontal rows. Correspondingly, most authors would talk about economic, political, and military imperialism, but we have added the other two since they seem also to be primordial. Perhaps the first three will build up more slowly along the lines established by division of labor in communication and cultural organizations, but it is very easy to imagine scenarios as well as concrete historical examples.

The completeness of the convertibility matrix, more than anything else, would lead us to reject the assumption of one type of imperialism as more basic than the others. It is the mutual reinforcement, the positive feedback between these types rather than any simple reductionist causal chain, that seems the dominant characteristic. If economic, political, and military imperialism seem so dominant today, this may be an artifact due to our training that emphasizes these factors rather than communication and cultural factors. Belief in a simple causal chain is dangerous because it is accompanied by the belief that imperialism can be dispensed with forever if the primary element in the chain is abolished, e.g. private capitalism. The more general definition of imperialism presented here directs our search towards the two mechanisms as well as the particular criteria of exploitation within and between nations.

In order to talk about imperialism, not only economic equality but also political, military, communication, and cultural inequality should be distributed in an inegalitarian way, with the periphery at the disadvantage. Are they? We think yes. The not-so-blatantly-unequal access to acquisite power, to some *political* power through voting, to some control over the *use of violence* (through political power, through civilian control of the military and through equality of opportunity as to access to ranking positions in the military), to *communication* (usually via access to acquisitive power, but also via denser, less feudal communication networks linking periphery outposts more directly together in Center nations), and to *cultural* goods (through widespread literacy and equality in access to educational institutions)—all these are trademarks of what is referred to as a liberal democracy. And that form of socio-political life is found in the Center rather than the Periphery of the world.

This leads to an important point in the theory of imperialism. *Instead of seeing democracy as a consequence or a condition for economic development within certain nations, it can (also) be seen as the condition for exercising effective control over Periphery nations.* Precisely because the Center is more egalitarian and democratic than the Periphery, there will be more people in the Center who feel they have a stake in the present state of affairs, since the fruits of imperialist structures are more equally shared on the top than on the bottom. And this will make it even less likely that the periphery in the Center will really join with the periphery in the Periphery against the two centers. Rather, like Dutch workers they will oppose the independence of Indonesia, and like U.S. workers they will tend to become hard-hats over the Indo-China issue.

It is now relatively clear what would be the perfect type of imperialism. In perfect imperialism, regardless of phase, we would assume all three criteria, both mechanisms, and all five types to be completely operative. This would mean complete harmony between the centers, with the elites in the Periphery nations almost undistinguishable from the elites in the Center nations where living conditions are concerned; much better distribution in the Center nations than in the Periphery nations; a perfectly vertical division of labor along all five types of exchange, and a perfectly feudal interaction network.

Where in the world, in space and/or time, does one find this type of relations? The answer is perhaps not only in the colonial empires of the past, but also in the neo-colonial empires of the present using international organizations as their medium. To what extent it is true is an empirical question, and all the factors mentioned above can be operationalized. In other words, what is often called 'positivist' methodology can be brought to bear on problems of structuralist or even marxist analyses. A crude and limited exercise in this direction will be given in the following section.

Suffice it here only to say that no system is perfect, and no system is a perfect copy of some ideal-type model. It may be that the neo-colonial empire United States had in Latin America in the 1950's and into the 1960's was a relatively perfect case,(29) and that this also applies to the relation between the EEC countries and the Associated States.(30) But it does not apply to the United States in Western Europe, nor to the Soviet Union in Eastern Europe, to the Soviet Union in the Arab World or to Japan in Southeast Asia. This is not to deny that United States in Western Europe and Soviet Union in Eastern Europe are at the summit of military organizations that seem to satisfy all conditions, although the parallel is not entirely complete. But both of the super-powers are peripheral to the communication networks, their cultures are largely rejected in Western and Eastern Europe respectively, and where economic penetration is concerned there is a vertical division of labor in favor of the United States relative to Western Europe, but in favor of Eastern Europe (in general) relative to the Soviet Union—with Soviet Union as a provider of raw materials for, for instance, high level processing in the DDR. But it may then be argued that what the Soviet Union loses in economic ascendancy it compensates for in a political organization with strong feudal components.(31)

Similar arguments may be advanced in connection with the Soviet Union in the Arab World, and with Japan in Southeast Asia. Where the latter is concerned there is no doubt as to the economic imperialism, but there is neither political, nor military, nor communication, nor cultural ascendancy.(32)

And this, then, leads to the final conclusion in this section. Imperialism is a question of degree, and if it is a perfect instrument of structural violence. When it is less than perfect something must be substituted for what is lost in structural violence: direct violence, or at least the threat of direct violence. This is where the military type of imperialism becomes so important, since it can be seen as a potential to be activated when the other types of imperialism, particularly the economic and political types, show important cracks in the structure. This does not, incidentally, necessarily mean that direct violence only has to be applied in Periphery nations; it may also be directed against the periphery in Center nations if there is a danger of their siding with the periphery in the Periphery. The structural conditions for this would be that criterion no. 2 in the definition does not hold, in other words that there is not less, but possibly even more, inequality in the Center than in the Periphery. . . .

So far we have operated with a simple scheme involving two nations and two classes; time has now come to break out of that limitation. Here we shall only offer some remarks in that connection, not carry the analysis through in detail.

Thus, the introduction of a middle class between the center and the periphery would be entirely consistent with thinking in most social science schools. Whether the center is defined in terms of economic, political, military, communication, or cultural interaction, a strict dichotomy between center and periphery will often be too crude. The alternative to a dichotomy may be a continuum, but on the way towards that type of thinking a trichotomy may also be useful. Strict social dichotomies are usually difficult to obtain unless hedged around by means of highly visible and consensual racial, ethnic, or geographical distinctions. A country composed of three races may therefore provide a stable three-class structure; if there is only one race, the continuous model may be more useful.

However, it is difficult to see that this should significantly affect our theory. Whether there are two or three classes or a continuum from extreme center to extreme periphery does not invalidate descriptions of the nation in terms of averages (such as GNP/capita) and dispersions (such as Gini indices). Nor will it invalidate the comparisons between the nations in such terms. In fact, there is nothing in this theory that presupposes a dichotomous class structure since the theory is not based on a dichotomy like owner vs. non-owner of means of production.

More interesting results can be obtained by interspersing a third nation between the Center and Periphery nations. Such a nation could, in fact, serve as a go-between. Concretely, it would exchange semi-processed goods with highly processed goods upwards and semi-processed goods with raw materials downwards. It would simply be located in between Center and Periphery where the degree of processing of its export products is concerned. Moreover, such go-between nations would serve as an intermediate layer between the extreme Center and the extreme Periphery in a feudal interaction structure. And needless to say: the intra-national centers of all three nations would be tied together in the same international network, establishing firm ties of harmony of interest between them.

In another version of the same conception the go-between nation would be one cycle behind the Center as to technology but one cycle ahead of the Periphery; (40) in line with its position as to degree of processing. This would also apply to the means of destruction and the means of communication.

If the United States is seen as *the* Center nation in the world (with Japan as an extremely dangerous competitor precisely in terms of degree of processing), then several such chains of nations suggest themselves, as shown in Table VII.

Just as for the generalization of three classes, this could also be generalized to a continuous chain which would then serve to make for considerable distance between the extreme Center and the extreme Periphery.

So far all our thinking has been within one empire, except for passing references to countries outside the empire that the Periphery is prevented from interacting with. But the world consists of more than one empire, and any realistic theory should see an empire in its context—especially since direct violence is to relations between empires what structural violence is within empires.

Clearly, relations between empires are above all relations between the centers of the Centers; these relations can be negative, neutral, or positive. Two capitalistic empires may be in competition, but they may also sub-divide the world between them into spheres of interest so perfectly that the relations become more neutral. In this first phase one empire may fight to protect itself in the competition with another capitalist empire, but in a second phase they may join forces and more or less merge to protect not this or that particular capitalist empire, but the system of capitalism as such. And we could easily imagine a third phase where non-capitalist empires join with capitalist empires in the pattern of 'united imperialism', for the protection of imperialism as such.

Center	Go-Between	Periphery
USA	Western Europe	Eastern Europe
USA	Canada	Anglo-America (Trinidad, etc.)
USA	Mexico Argentina Brazil	Central America
USA	Japan	Southeast Asia
Japan	South Korea Taiwan	Southeast Asia (and North America)
Western Europe	Eastern Europe	Soviet Union

All this is extremely important from the viewpoint of the Periphery nations. A world with more empires, which above all means a world with more Center nations, is at least potentially a world with more possibilities. To explore this in more detail, let us assume that we have Center and Periphery nations, vertically related to each other. For each type of nation there are three cases: one nation alone, two nations either very low on interaction or hostile to each other, and two nations in so friendly cooperation as to constitute one actor. The result is shown in Fig. 3, which permits us to recognize many and politically very important situations (the arrows in Fig. 3 stand for relations of vertical interaction).

Here, situations *a*, *b*, and *c* take place within one empire and lead to a situation with a certain element of defeudalization: horizontal interaction has been established between the two Periphery nations.

In situations *d*, *e*, and *f* Periphery nations are able to interact with more than one Center nation, possibly even play one against the other because of their hostile relationship. In this situation the Periphery will have a vested interest in protracting the Center conflict, and may even join forces (model *f*) to make optimum gains from the conflict.

In situations *g*, *h*, and *i* it is the Center side that cooperates, for instance by establishing a 'consortium' whereby several rich nations join together to help one or more poor nations, singly or combined.(41)

Importantly, none of these strategies will lead to any changes in the vertical interaction *relation*, only to some changes in the feudal interaction *structure*. As such they attack only one aspect of imperialism, not the other, possibly more important aspect. And if we look more closely at model *i*, this is nothing but model *a* writ large, as when EEC rather than France alone stands in a relationship of vertical interaction with 18 Associated States rather than with one of them alone. It is difficult to see that imperialistic relationships become less imperialistic by being established between super-Center and a super-Periphery rather than between the original Center and Periphery nations (we should add that h rather than i is a more correct model of the relationship between EEC and the Associated States).

	Center nations		
	one alone ◯	**two, neutral** ◯ ◯	**two, positive** ◯—◯
Periphery nations			
one alone ◯	*a*	*d*	*g*
two, neutral ◯ ◯	*b*	*e*	*h*
two, positive ◯—◯	*c*	*f*	*i*

This factor notwithstanding, there is no reason to deny that a multi-empire world not only creates more bargaining possibilities, but also is a more realistic model of the world in which mankind lives—at present.

NOTES

(1) For an exploration of this concept, see Galtung, J. 1969: Violence, Peace and Peace Research, *Journal of Peace Research 6* pp. 167-91.

(2) This equality premise may be formulated in terms of distribution, or redistribution, of values generated by the society in liberal theory, or as absence of exploitation in marxist theory. The two approaches have in common the idea that a party may have an interest even if it does not proclaim that it has this interest, but whereas the liberal approach will keep the social structure but carry out some redistribution along the road, the marxist approach will change the social structure itself. In both cases one may actually also make a further distinction as to whether harmony is to be obtained by equalization of what the society produces of material and spiritual value, or equalization when it comes to the power to decide over what the society produces. But imperialism as a structure cuts across these distinctions and is, in our view, based on a more general concept of harmony and disharmony of interests.

(3) No attempt will be made here to explore similarities and dissimilarities between this definition of imperialism and that given by such authors as Hobson, Luxemburg, Lenin, Hilferding and very many others. This definition has grown out of a certain research tradition, partly inductively from a long set of findings about international interaction structures, and partly deductively from speculations relating to structural violence in general and the theory of inequality in particular.

(4) Particularly one aspect of Lenin's conception of imperialism has been picked up in our definition: the general idea of a labor aristocracy. Lenin quotes Engels when he says that '—quand aux ouvriers, ils jouissent en toute tránquillite avec eux du monopole colonial, de l'Angleterre et de son monopole sur le marche mondial'. (L'imperialisme: Stade supreme. du Capitalisme, Moscow, 1969, p. 139). The same idea is expressed by L.S. Senghor: 'les proletaires d'Europe ont beneficie du regime colonial; partant, ils ne s'y sont jamais rellement, je veux dire efficacement, opposes'. (Nation et voie africaine du socialisme, p. 51.) And T. Hopkins in Third World Modernization in Transnational Perspective (The Annals, 1969, pp. 126-36) picks up the other angle of this: '. . . there are strong indications that in most Third World Countries, internal inequality is increasing. The educated are markedly more advantaged; urban workers are relatively well-off; unemployment is high and increasing; rural populations are poor'.

(5) Thus, international statistics should not be given only for national aggregates since this conceals the true nature of the relations in the world. It would be much more useful if statistics were given for the four groups defined in our definition. In general we would assume such statistics over time to show that cC and cP grow most quickly and more or less together, then follows pC and at the bottom is pP that is not only located much below the other two, but also shows very little growth or none at all. The more numerous the group, the lower the growth: it is the accumulated work from these vast masses that permits the growth of the dominating minorities. One highly stimulating analysis in this direction is given by Th. E. Weisskopf who tries to disaggregate the growth rates and is led to the conclusion that the growth in the developing countries has taken place in the upper and middle strata of the population, in the secondary sector of economic production, and in the urban areas. The growth rates in these parts of the developing nations are not too different from growth rates in corresponding parts in developed nations, but due to the absence of mechanisms for redistribution this leaves the vast periphery of the developing nations with close to zero or even negative growth. Weisskopf, T.E.: Underdevelopment, Capitalistic Growth and the Future of the Poor Countries, World Order Models Project, 1970.

(6) The argument is carried much further for the case of interindividual rather than international interaction in Galtung, J.: Structural Pluralism and the Future of Human Interaction, paper presented at the Second International Future Research Conference, Kyoto, April, 1970, and Galtung, J.: Perspectives on Development: Past, Present and Future, paper presented at the International Sociological Association Conference, Varna, September, 1970.

(7) The basic point here is that a demand generates a chain of demands. Economists have made some estimates in this connection. For instance, H.B. Chenery and T. Watanabe conclude, 'In the four industrial countries studied here (United States, Japan, Norway, and Italy), between 40% and 50% of total domestic demands for goods and services comes from other productive sectors rather than from final users' (International Comparisons of the Structure of Production, Econometrica, 1958, p. 504). The more connected the economy of a country, the more will a demand proliferate. Other social scientists should have tools corresponding to the input-output analyses of the economists in order to study the degree of connectedness of a society. Characteristic of a traditional society is precisely the low level of connectedness: the spread effect into other branches of economic activity and into other districts is much lower. Also see Stirton-Weaver, F.: Backwash, Spread and the Chilean State, Studies in Comparative International Development, vol. V. no. 12, and Hirschman, A.O.: The Strategy of Economic Development (New Haven: Yale Univ. Press, 1958), especially his discussion of backward and forward linkages (pp. 100-119).

(8) It is this equality that we stipulate to be in the interest of both parties, both for the exploiter and the exploited. Obviously, there are two approaches: the

interaction structure can be changed so that the inter- and intra-actor effects are equal, and/or redistribution can take place. But if this interaction structure has been in operation for a long time and has already generated considerable differences in living conditions then both methods may have to be used, a point to be further elaborated in section 10 below. For highly stimulating discussions of unequal elaborated subsequently. For highly stimulating discussions of unequal exchange, see Casanova, P.G.: *Sociologia de la Explotacion* (Mexico: Siglo Veintiuno, 1969); and Arghiri Emmanuel: *L'exchange inegal* (Paris: Maspero, 1969).

(9) What we have in mind here, concretely, is of course all the various forms of development assistance based on the idea that grants are given to poor countries on the condition that they use them to procure capital goods in developed countries. In an excellent article, 'Prospectives for the Third World', S. Sideri summarizes much of the literature showing how well development assistance pays. However, these analyses are by no means complete since only some aspects of the economic spin-off effects are considered, not all the others that may also, incidentally, be convertible into economic effects, at least in the long run.

(10) For an analysis of social status systems using feudal interaction as the basic concept, see Galtung, J.: Feudal Systems, Structural Violence and the Structural Theory of Revolutions, in *Proceedings of the IPRA Third General Conference, I* pp. 110-188. Van Gorcum, Assen, 1970.

(11) For a penetrating analysis of the relation between dependency and development, see Cardoso, F.H. & Faletto, E.: *Dependencia y desarrollo en America Latina* (Mexico: Siglo Veintiuno, 1969). One important difference between that book and the present analysis lies in the warning the authors give against generalization beyond the concrete case. While sympathetic to this, we nevertheless feel there is considerable virtue in general theory, as a baseline for understanding the concrete case.

Another basic analysis of this type of relationship is, of course, Frank, A.G.: *Capitalism and Underdevelopment in Latin America* (N.Y.: Monthly Review Press, 1967). The basic key to Frank's analysis is the structure that 'extends from the macrometropolitan system center of the world capitalist system 'down' to the most supposedly isolated agricultural workers, who, through this chain of interlinked metropolitan-satellite relationships, are tied to the central world metropolis and thereby incorporated into the world capitalist system as a whole' (p. 16), and he goes on (p. 17) to talk about 'the exploitation of the satellite by the metropolis or—the tendency of the metropolis to expropriate and appropriate the economic surplus of the satellite'. All this is valid as general formulas, but too little emphasis is given to the type of exploitation referred to here as 'asymmetric distribution of spin-offs' and the special organization referred to as 'feudal interaction structure'. And economists with no Marxist inclination at all are certainly not helpful when it comes to reflecting imperialistic types of relations. Thus, in Jan Tinbergen, *The Design of Development* (Baltimore: Johns Hopkins, 1966), development is discussed throughout the book as if the government in a developing country is free to make its decisions. And in T. Haavelmo, *A Study in the Theory of Economic Evolution* (Amsterdam: North-Holland Publ. Co., 1954) it is difficult to see that any theory at all based on *relations* between nations is offered to explain the tremendous disparities in this world; just to mention two examples. And even Myrdal's *Asian Drama* has little to say on international relations, as pointed out by Lars Rudebeck in an excellent review article *(Cooperation and Conflict* 1969, pp. 267-81).

(12) One book that gives a fairly balanced account of Soviet dominance patterns is *The New Imperialism* by Hugh Seton-Watson (N.Y.: Capricorn Books, 1961). Andre Amalrik's analysis *Will the Soviet Union Survive Until 1984* (N.Y.: Harper & Row, 1970) also deserves reading, not so much for its apocalyptic scenario as for its penetrating analysis of the internal dominance system. The question of whether the total Soviet system should be referred to as imperialism remains open, however,

among other reasons because the Soviet Union does not enjoy spin-offs from processing of raw materials and because the internal inequality is hardly lower than in dependent countries. But the elite harmonization criterion will probably hold to a large extent mediated through the cooperation between party elites. Comparative studies of imperialistic structures, in the tradition of Helio Jaguaribe, comparing different types of empires in this century as well as long-time historical comparisons bringing in, for instance, the Roman Empire, would be highly useful to shed more light over this particular international structure. At present this type of exercise is hampered by the tendency to use 'imperialism' as an abusive term, as a category to describe the other camp. We have preferred to see it as a technical term, which does not mean that he who struggles for peace will not have to struggle against imperialism regardless of what shape it takes.

(13) For an analysis of international air communication, see Gleditsch, N.P.: Trends in World Airline Patterns, *JPR* 1967, pp. 366-408.

(14) For an analysis of the role of the international press agencies, see Ostgaard, E.: Factors Influencing the Flow of News, *Journal of Peace Research 2*, pp. 39-63.

(15) For an analysis of this, see Galtung, J. & Ruge, M.H.: The Structure of Foreign News: The Presentation of the Congo, Cuba and Cyprus Crises in Four Norwegian Newspapers, *Journal of Peace Research 2*, pp. 64-91.

(16) For an analysis of this, see Galtung, J.: After Camelot, in Horowitz, I.L. (ed.): *The Rise and Fall of Project Camelot* (Cambridge, Mass.: M.I.T. Press, 1967).

(17) As one example, and a very explicit one, may serve the following quotation: '. . . can we discharge our responsibility to God and to man for so magnificent, so populous a proportion of the world? — Our answer is off hand ready and simple. We are adequate. We do discharge our responsibilities. We are a conquering and imperial race. All over the world we have displayed our mettle. We have discovered and annexed and governed vast territories. We have encircled the globe with our commerce. We have penetrated the pagan races with our missionaries. We have innoculated the Universe (sic!) with our institutions. We are apt indeed to believe that our soldiers are braver, our sailors hardier, our captains, naval and military, skilfuller, our statesmen wiser than those of other nations. As for our constitution, there is no Briton at any hour of the day or night who will suffer it to be said that any approaches it.' From Lord Boseberry; Questors of Empire 1900, in *Miscellanies, Literary and Historical, vol. II* (London: Hodder & Stoughton, 1921). I am indebted to Fiona Rudd for this remarkable reference.

(18) This is extremely clearly expressed in Report of a U.S. Presidential Mission to the Western Hemisphere (The Rockefeller Report): '. . . Just as the other American republics depend upon the United States for their capital equipment requirements, so the United States depends on them to provide a vast market for our manufactured goods. And as these countries look to the United States for a market for their primary products whose sale enables them to buy equipment for their development at home, so the United States looks to them for raw materials for our industries, on which depend the jobs of many of our citizens. . . .' (Quality of Life in the Americas, Agency for International Development, August, 1969, pp. 5-113.) The paragraph is as if taken out of a textbook on imperialism, emphasizing how the Center countries provide capital equipment and manufactured goods, and the Periphery countries raw materials and markets. The only interesting thing about the quotation is that it is still possible to write like this in 1969.

(19) One example is the Brezhnev Doctrine: 'Speaking in Warsaw on November 12, 1968, to the V Congress of the Polish United Workers Party Brezhnev emphasized the need for "strict respect" for sovereignty of other socialist countries, and added: "But when internal and external forces that are hostile to Socialism try to turn the development of some socialist country towards the restoration of a capitalist regime, when socialism in that country and the socialist community as a

whole is threatened, it becomes not only a problem of the people of the country concerned, but a common problem and concern of all Socialist countries. Naturally an action such as military assistance to a fraternal country designed to avert the threat to the social system is an extraordinary step, dictated by necessity." Such a step, he added, "may be taken only in case of direct actions of the enemies of Socialism within a country and outside it, actions threatening the common interests of the Socialist camp." ' *(Keesing's Contemporary Archives*, 1968, p. 23027). Its similarity to the Monroe doctrine has often been pointed out, but there is the difference that the U.S. sometimes seems to be acting as if they had a Monroe doctrine for the whole world.

Without implying that the following is official Soviet policy, it has nevertheless appeared in *International Affairs* (April, 1970): 'The socialist countries, united in the Warsaw Treaty Organization, are profoundly aware that the most reliable guarantee that their security will be preserved and strengthened is allround cooperation with the Soviet Union, including military cooperation. They firmly reject any type of anti-Soviet slander and resist attempts by imperialism and the remnants of domestic reaction to inject into the minds of their people any elements of anti-Sovietism, whether open or veiled.

With the two worlds—socialist and capitalist—in global confrontation, any breach of internationalist principles, any sign of nationalism, and especially any toleration, not to say use, of anti-Sovietism in policy turns those who pursue such policies into an instrument of imperialist strategy and policy, regardless of whether their revisionist slogan is given a Right or ultra-Left twist, regardless of the subjective intentions of the advocates and initiators of the course. And whether it is very big or very small, it remains nothing but an instrument in the hands of imperialism and in either case retains its ignominious essence, which is incompatible with truly revolutionary socialist consciousness'. (V. Razmerov: Loyalty to Proletarian Internationalism; Fundamental Condition for Success of All Revolutionary Forces). What this quotation says is in fact that not only hostile deeds, but also hostile words are to be ruled out. It is also interesting to note that the types of attitudes that are not to be expressed are referred to as 'anti-Soviet'. In other words, the reference is to the Center country in the system, not even to the masses of that country, nor to anti-socialism.

(20) In general, international contacts between ministries seem to become increasingly transnational. Where the minister of defense in country A some time ago would have to use a channel of communication involving at least one embassy and one ministry of foreign affairs to reach his opposite number in country B, direct telecommunication would now be the adequate channel. What this means in terms of cutting out filtering effects and red tape is obvious. It also means that transnational ties may be strengthened and some times be posted against the nation state. Obviously, this sytem will be expanding, for instance with a system of telesatellites available for elite communication between Center and Periphery countries within a bloc. For the Francophone countries the projected satellite Symphonie may, perhaps, be seen as a step in this direction, although it is targeted on audiences rather than on concrete, specific persons. The NATO satellite communication system is another example.

(26) This is a major difference between liberal and structuralist peace theory. It is hardly unfair to interpret liberal peace theory as somehow stating that 'peace' is roughly proportionate to the volume of trade, possibly interpreted as an indicator of the level of interdependence, whereas structural peace theory would bring in the factor of equality and ask for the composition as well as the volume of trade. If structural theory is more correct and if the present world trade structure is such that only the Center nations can enjoy both high level of interdependence and high level in equality of exchange, then 'peace' is one extra benefit that will accrue to the Center layer of the world.

(27) Another concept would be the frequently quoted saying that 'technical assistance is taken from the poor man in the rich country and given to the rich man in the poor country'. The model of the world implied by the dominance theory would certainly not contradict this quite elegant statement: technical assistance is to a large extent paid for by taxpayers' money, not to mention by the surplus produced by the masses working in the rich countries, and given via public channels for investment in infrastructures in poor countries, often for the benefit of the layers in the poor countries that have a consumption structure compatible with a production structure that the rich countries can offer.
can offer.

(28) Galtung, J.: International Relations and International Conflicts: A Sociological Approach, *Transactions of the Sixth World Congress of Sociology* (International Sociological Association, 1966), pp. 121-61.

(29) E.g. Magdoff, H.: *The Age of Imperialism,* (N.Y.: Monthly Review, 1969).

(30) Research on this is currently in progress at the International Peace Research Institute, Oslo.

(31) But it is still an open question whether this should really be referred to as imperialism, since so many of the criteria do not seem to be fulfilled. Once more this seems to bring up the importance of seeing imperialism as a special case of a wider set of social relationships, conveniently lumped together under the heading 'domination'.

(32) Relations between Soviet Union and the Arab World and Japan and Southeast Asia are being explored at the International Peace Research Institute, Oslo, by Tormod Nyberg and Johan Galtung, respectively.

(33) This type of structural reasoning seems particularly important in the Soviet case. It can hardly be claimed that the Soviet periphery participates more in the decision-making made by the Soviet center than the Czech periphery participated in the decision-making made by the Czech center in the months prior to the invasion in August 1968. On the contrary, the opposite hypothesis seems more tenable. And if this is the case the Soviet center could no longer necessarily count on the allegiance of its own periphery, particularly not the Ukranian periphery, bordering Czechoslovakia not only geographically, but also linguistically and culturally (and apparently listening attentively to broadcasts). This means that what happened in Czechoslovakia became a threat to the Soviet center, perhaps more than to the Soviet Union as a Center nation. . . .

This selection is abridged from *Journal of Peace Research,* 1971, No. 2, pp. 81-117, published by UniversitetsForlaget, Oslo, Norway.

THE INTERNATIONAL SYSTEM AND NATIONAL CLASS AND POWER STRUCTURES

Dale Johnson

The literature on the impact of colonial domination in Asia and Africa shows much more clearly how colonialism shapes social structures than does the literature (which has generally suffered from a severe economic bias) on Latin America. A recent example of such analyses of experiences in other underdeveloped regions is Barrington Moore's book *Social Origins of Dictatorship and Democracy*, which contains chapters on India, China, and Japan. Although colonialism is not his focus (and I believe he underestimates its impact) Moore manages to show how British colonial policy and practice undermined the development of an Indian national bourgeoisie while creating strong landlord and moneylender classes. Thus, India was left with a social structure which, combined with its new neocolonial status and severe internal problems, probably condemns this unhappy nation to perpetual underdevelopment. While China escaped India's fate of total colonization—and the traditional ruling class, independently of the obstacles placed by imperialism, helped to keep the lid on industrialization—the effects of imperialist encroachment were no less effective in shaping the direction of development and the structure of classes. Specifically, imperialism created a merchant *comprador* class, strengthened and made alliances with decrepit bourgeois warlords, and prevented the emergence of a national bourgeoisie.

> After the conclusion of the Opium War in 1842, the *compradores* spread through all the treaty posts of China. These men served in a variety of capacities as intermediaries between decaying Chinese officialdom and the foreign merchants. ... By shady methods they could accumulate great fortunes to live a life of civilized ease. . . .
> Not until 1910 did the Chinese business class begin to show some definite signs of emerging. . . . But the whole indigenous commercial and industrial impulse remained puny. By the end of the Imperial regime, there were said to be some 20,000 "factories" in China. Of these, only 362 employed mechanical power.
> Thus China, like Russia, entered the modern era with a numerically small and politically dependent ideology of its own as it did in Western Europe. . . .(1)

. . . Latin America is another case. Historically, the situation in the region may be described, in Frank's terminology, as a process of the "development of underdevelopment." This is a sociological as well as economic process. Underdevelopment is *structured* by the patterns of historical movement of the international economy; underdevelopment is cemented by the dependent position of national oligarchies in international stratification. Claudio Veliz explains the manner in which this process occurred in late nineteenth-century Chile, a process repeated with variations elsewhere in Latin America. According to Veliz, Chile was dominated by the "three legs of the national economic table":

> In the first place, there were the mining exporters of the north of the country; then there were the agricultural and livestock exporters of the south; and finally there were the large import firms. . . . These three pressure groups were in entire agreement about what economic policy the country should follow . . . and the three totally dominated national life, from the municipal councils to diplomatic representation, economic legislation and the horse races. . . .
>
> The mining exporters of the north of the country were free traders. This policy was not fundamentally due to reasons of doctrine—though they also had these—but rather to the simple reason that these gentlemen were blessed with common sense. They exported copper, silver, nitrates, and other minerals of lesser importance to Europe and the United States, where they were paid in pounds sterling or dollars. With this money they bought equipment, machinery, manufactures, or high quality consumer goods at very low prices. It is hard to conceive of an altruism or a far-sighted or prophetic vision which would lead these exporters to pay export and import duties with a view to the possible industrialization of the country.
>
> The agricultural and livestock exporters of the South were also emphatically free traders. They sent their wheat and flour to Europe, California and Australia. They clothed their cowboys with ponchos of English flannel, rode in saddles made by the best harnessmakers of London, drank authentic champagne and lighted their mansions with Florentine lamps. At night they slept in beds made by excellent English cabinet-makers, between sheets of Irish linen and covered by blankets of English wool. Their silk shirts came from Italy and their wives' jewels from London, Paris and Rome. For these *hacendados* who were paid in pounds sterling, the idea of taxing the export of wheat or of imposing protective duties on imports was simply insanity.
>
> The big import houses of Valparaiso and Santiago also were free traders. Could anyone imagine an import firm supporting the establishment of high import duties to protect national industry!
>
> Here, then, is the powerful coalition of strong interests, which dominated the economic policy of Chile during the past century and part of the present century. None of the three had the least interest in Chile and industrialization. They monopolized the three powers at all levels: economic power, political power, and social prestige; and only in a few instances did they see the absolute control they exercised over the nation endangered.(2)

The table toppled when it lost two of its legs: foreign capital displaced national capital in northern mining and the *hacendados* of the South lost their export markets. In the twentieth century, incipient industrialization transpired and reshaped the social structure. But the contemporary situation in Chile (until 1970 at least) and elsewhere in Latin America is still characterized by national class and power systems that mesh smoothly with the international system. The new urban-based oligarchies and national bourgeoisies, though essentially dependent, even client or *comprador* classes, profit from the structure of the international system and from their close financial and political relations with multinational corporations and those who hold power internationally. The Latin American middle classes, strengthened by industrialization at one time, played vaguely nationalist and progressive roles as classes in ascendance. Now they engaged in what Claudio Veliz terms "the politics of conformity"(3) and have developed a close ideological affinity with the precepts of the political and social thought promoted by established interests within the international system and national oligarchies.

Modern imperialism systematically generates and shapes dependent national class and power structures. The extreme of this situation in Latin America was perhaps found in pre-revolutionary Cuba. The unusual clarity and drama of the analysis make Edward Boorstein's words concerning Cuba worth quoting at some length.

> The class structure of Cuba was not just a matter of the traditional division into bourgeoisie, proletariat, and peasantry, but also of relations with imperialism. Cutting across the traditional divisions was the line between those who benefited from imperialism and those who suffered from it. The richest, most powerful groups derived their wealth and power from imperialism. Those groups which did not enjoy the favors of imperialism tended to be poor and weak.
>
> All but a small part of Cuba's upper classes were dependent on activities tied to the United States. There were the magnates of the sugar industry, owners of the sugar centrals and *latifundia*. The big importers, the core of the urban oligarchy, had a magnificent source of income in the hundreds of millions of dollars worth of goods imported each year. The bankers depended for most of their business on the export of sugar and tobacco and on imports. The real estate operators depended on the oligarchy and the government for most of their business and on the United States for equipment and many construction materials.
>
> Most retail stores other than the small ones in wooden shacks, depended on imports.
>
> For whom did the financially successful professionals work in Cuba? Where were the jobs and the money? The most expensive lawyers worked for the big companies, the big importers and commercial speculators, the real estate operators. The engineers and chemists worked for the large foreign-owned or foreign-oriented sugar companies, manufacturing plants, or mines. The architects worked for the real estate companies, the rich, or the government. And the doctors, dentists, and nurses served the rich and middle classes, most of whose income was tied directly or indirectly to imperialism.
>
> Many employees and even some workers in the foreign companies got salaries and wages which by Cuban standards were high. In the capital-intensive, automated plants the cost of granting good pay was small. Many of these employees and workers developed a strong interest in their own favored position.
>
> Now let us cross the imperialist divide in Cuban society. What can be considered a national bourgeoisie was weak and small; it did not have enough of a base in national industry and commerce on which to rest. The owners of the little—often family-operated—shops and factories turning out bread, shoes, dresses, furniture, etc., were not really in the same class as the sugar magnates, the big importers and the bankers. And there were not enough of them to make up for their individual weakness, to make them in the aggregate into a force that could worry imperialism and its local partners.

There were thousands of small retail enterprises in Cuba—in wooden shacks or outdoor stalls and stands. Many of them had lower incomes and a more precarious economic position than the higher-paid workers in the foreign plants.

Most city workers, in the cottage industries and small shops, on the docks, and in the transportation system received much smaller wages than the elite in the large foreign companies. Nevertheless, they were better off than the vast majority of those engaged in agriculture.

About two-thirds of Cuba's farmers were tenants, sharecroppers, and squatters. Historically, the peasants had been thrown off the land when the cattle ranches and sugar estates were formed. They had an interest in land reform, in the expropriation of the large estates, including the choice lands of the large foreign sugar companies.

Finally there was the largest, most homogenous, and poorest bloc of the Cuban proletariat: the workers in the cane fields—a proletariat created by the sugar industry. Although the workers in the cane fields and those in the electric power industry were both proletarians, their positions differed greatly. The electric power workers enjoyed privileges which the foreign corporations had found it expedient to grant in order to soften the opposition to imperialism. But there could be no privileges for the sugar workers. The profits of the large companies and the functioning of the sugar industry required that they be kept in misery.(4)

Of course, Cuba was an exceptional case. Perhaps only Puerto Rico and the Dominican Republic (and the client states of Asia such as South Korea, Taiwan and Thailand) approximate the status of full-fledged economic colony and political protectorate that once characterized Cuba. The extreme case, however, serves to accentuate the fundamental forces at work in the various countries of Latin America. Each Latin American dependence has specific qualities and dimensions; each nation has developed underdevelopment according to unique economic, social-cultural, and political factors and events in their separate histories. But the unique qualities, factors, and events should not be allowed to obscure the fundamental conditioning situation of dependence. Under present circumstances, dependent states under control of local oligarchies and their allies among the military and middle classes can only negotiate the conditions of dependence.

In the case of the industrialized countries of Latin America, several general and specific aspects of class relations across national frontiers have already been discussed in the examination of dependence and foreign investment. In subsequent studies, special attention will be given to the role of nationalist ideology and support for national development policies among the national bourgeoisies and middle classes of Latin America. Generally speaking, the middle classes and the national bourgeoisies are not nationalist in orientation, while the structure of dependence has been a critical factor in determining the political shift (and the support that these classes have lent to the shift) toward a politics of conformity everywhere and a politics of reaction especially notable in key countries like Brazil and Argentina. It remains here to seek to clarify the issue of whether or not international *gran capital* has usurped the position of dominant class from the oligarchies.

The degree to which the presence of multinational corporations in countries such as Brazil, Argentina, Uruguay, and Mexico, and increasingly Chile, Peru, Colombia, and Venezuela, has caused a shift in the internal structure of the dominant classes, is difficult to analyze in the absence of careful empirical research.

What is certain in the most industrialized countries is that national oligarchies are in close interconnection with foreign industrial and finance capital and that the wealth and power of both the core of national oligarchies and foreign businessmen are now primarily based upon finance and industry (rather than the earlier base of primary production and export-import). Theotonio dos Santos has argued that the extreme significance and economic weight of large enterprise in basic industries which are subsidiaries or otherwise integrated with multinational corporations, has brought those in control, *"gran capital,"* to the position of the dominant core of the class holding the reins of economic power, and ultimately of political power. Dos Santos takes Brazil as the case in point, but argues that the same process is occurring in other industrialized or industrializing countries in Latin America. Perhaps dos Santos' case is overstated. Undoubtedly, international *gran capital* is an influential interest group within the uppermost circles of national class and power structures. But it seems more likely that the national multisector oligarchies happily accede the larger and more risky investments to the multi-national corporation and cooperate with foreign capital in joint ventures, while still retaining control of key sources of national economic and political power.(5)

It is not that foreign businessmen form a corporate group exercising power as an enormously influential interest group in Latin American societies, which is certainly the case of national oligarchies. Nor is it that foreign businessmen are integrated into the social circles and political intrigues of national oligarchies. As Baer and Simonsen observe of the American business community in Brazil,

> United States executives and their families do not expect to settle there permanently; often the man sees his period of work in Latin America as simply one rung in a ladder of success most of which is to be climbed elsewhere, and his family are not necessarily the most willing camp followers. They do not learn Portuguese, the children do not attend local schools, the parents keep to their own clubs and social activities.(6)

On the other hand, what Norman Bailey has referred to as "neo-liberal groups"(7) (conservative propaganda and action organizations of businessmen) active in various countries have the financial backing of the U.S. capital and participation by American executives in Latin America. In Brazil, the Instituto de Pesquisas Estudos Sociais (IPES), which played an important role in creating the conditions for the Brazilian military coup of 1964, had the participation of 297 U.S. firms operating in Brazil.(8)

The case seems to be that at the international level *gran capital* is dominant; at the national level, *gran capital* is highly integrated into national structures; but national oligarchies are dominant in most institutional spheres. If indeed national oligarchies still retain predominant control of the economy and the principal social and political institutions within Latin American societies, then the development alternatives and the political choices that they can make with this power are defined and circumscribed. This is evidently the case when development takes place within a context in which the Latin American economies are integrated into a dependent position in the world economy, and national power is subordinated in the international stratification of power.

The points of articulation between the interests in the imperial Center reside in their position at the apex of structures of wealth, privilege, and power, in distinct yet closely interrelated worlds, neither of which could continue to exist without the other. Imperialism could not sustain itself as a dominant force in the world, were it not for support among client classes in underdeveloped countries. And oligarchies would fall one by one to national revolutions if they did not get international backing.

NOTES

(1) Barrington Moore, Jr., *Social Origins of Dictatorship and Democracy: Lord and Peasant in the Making of the Modern World* (Boston: Beacon Press, 1967), pp. 176-77.

(2) Claudio Veliz, "La mesa de tres patas" *Desarrollo Economic* III, No. 1-2 (Seb.-Abril 1963), pp. 237-42.

(3) Claudio Veliz (ed.), *The Politics of Conformity* (New York: Oxford University Press).

(4) Edward Bookstein, *The Economic Transformation of Cuba,* New York: Monthly Review Press, 1968, pp. 12-14.

(5) The Editors of *Monthly Review* suggest: ". . . while multi-national corporations do not, as so often claimed, internationalize their managements, they do *de*nationalize a section of the native bourgeoisies in the countries they penetrate. This of course weakens these native bourgeoisies and makes it that much harder for them to resist demands and pressures emanating from more powerful countries." "Notes on the Multinational Corporation," *Monthly Review* XXI (October 1969), p. 6.

(6) Werner Baer and Mario Henrique Simonsen, "American Capital and Brazilian Nationalism," in Marvin D. Bernstein (ed.), *Foreign Investment in Latin America* (New York: Knopf, 1966), p. 279.

(7) Norman Bailey, "The Colombian 'Black Hand': A Case Study of Neo-liberalism in Latin America," *Review of Politics* XXVII (October 1965); Theotonio de Santos, *El nuevo caracter de la dependencia (op. cit.)* offers some evidence of the direct political role of U.S. capital located in Brazil.

(8) Theotonio dos Santos, La crisis de la teoria del desarrollo y las relaciones de dependencia en America Latina (Santiago: Boletin del Centro de Estudios Socio-Economicos, No. 3, 1968, Universidad de Chile), p. 63.

This selection is reprinted from *Dependence and Underdevelopment* by James D. Cockcroft, Andre G. Frank and Dale L. Johnson, (eds.) New York: Anchor Books, Doubleday and Company, 1972, pp. 102-111.

COLOR, THE UNIVERSAL
INTELLECTUAL COMMUNITY, AND
THE AFRO-ASIAN INTELLECTUAL

Edward Shills

In itself color is meaningless. It is not like religion, which is belief and entails either voluntary or hereditary membership in a community of believers and therewith exposure to an assimilation of a tradition of beliefs. It is not like kinship, which is a tangible structure in which the individual has lived, which has formed him, and to which he is attached. It is not like intellectual culture, which is belief and an attitude toward the world (or particular parts of it). It is not even like nationality, which is a superimposition of beliefs about a community of culture upon a common primordial existence of that community in a given territory. The designation of a person as being of a particular religious community or of a particular school of thought or even of a given nationality is a statement about that person's mind, about the pattern of meaning by which he interprets reality. His participation in the interpretation of reality according to that pattern of meaning might be hypocritical; it is undoubtedly intermittent and vague. All this notwithstanding, the involvement of the mind is a major though not the sole component in the definition of the person in question. It is not this way with color.

Color is just color. It is a physical, a spectroscopic fact. It carries no compellingly deducible conclusions regarding a person's beliefs or his position in any social structure. It is like height or weight—the mind is not involved. Yet it attracts the mind; it is the focus of passionate sentiments and beliefs. The sentiments color evokes are not the sentiments of aesthetic appreciation. Nor does color have any moral significance; color is not acquired or possessed by leading a good or a bad life. No intentions are expressed by color; no interpretations of the world are inherent in it; no attachments are constituted by it. The mind is not at work in it, and it is not a social relationship. It is inherently meaningless.

Why, then, has this inherently meaningless property of man come to assume such great importance in the self-image of many human beings? Has only a historical accident of an unequal distribution of power and wealth between two differently pigmented aggregates of human beings led to this cleavage between those called white and those called colored? Or have sentiments of injury and anger implicated in the consciousness of being colored developed because those called white have so often used their greater power to injure those called colored in ways beyond what is intrinsic in the exercise of power?

One of the simplest and most obvious reasons why color is a focus of passionate sentiments is that it is an easy way to distinguish between those from periphery and those from the center of particular societies and of the world society. Differences of pigmentation symbolize or indicate contemporaneous differences between present wealth and power and present poverty and weakness, between present fame and present obscurity, between present eminence in intellectual creativity and present intellectual unproductiveness. It is correlated with past events too—above all, with past events of humiliation, injury, and insult. Military conquest and alien rule, cultural derogation and individual affront, political suppression, military repression, and almost every other kind of coercion form an important part of the history of the colored peoples resident in the once-colonial countries or descended from them, and they are bitterly remembered. Color is the shorthand that evokes all these griefs and grievances. Is it more than that?

Conquest and maltreatment were not first brought to Asia and Africa by the European imperial powers. Long before, Asians had conquered other Asians; Arabs had exploited and enslaved black Africans, often with the aid of other black African rulers. Still, it is the European conquest that is remembered. It is remembered most vividly because it is the most recent, extending well into the memory of all living adults and many young people. It is also remembered because it was experienced more painfully than previous imperial conquests. The greater painfulness stems, in part, from the vividness of freshly remembered events. Moreover, this more recent dominion—imperial and internal—inculcated moral, political, and intellectual standards for its own criticism, a practice previous imperial rulers had not employed. The acquisition of the standards implicit in the religious and political culture that the whites brought to Asia and Africa and that they preached and partly observed in their own countries made the discrepancy between those standards and their own action and presence in Asia and Africa and their conduct toward colored peoples in their own countries uncomfortable to bear.(1) There seem to be some other reasons as well. The European conquerors came from far off, they were not expanding neighbors, and they were of a different color.

Tyranny is always painful, but tyranny exercised by the ethnically alien, whose ethnic alien-ness is underscored by the most easily distinguishable color difference, is especially repugnant. In Asia and Africa, the illegitimacy of an ethnically alien tyranny is almost all gone now. Why does it still rankle so much in the hearts of Afro-Asian intellectuals? They are no longer being exploited, maltreated, or insulted by white men in their own countries. Why do they still feel the slights directed against their fellow-colored in the few parts of the world still under colonial rule or in the United States or in the United Kingdom?(2)

Their feeling of being excluded from the center, of being treated contemptuously as inferiors, of having their weakness "rubbed in" comes to a tormenting focus in their awareness of the differences in color between themselves and the "white" men at the center. The injurious actions explicit in policy and custom, the studied insults implicit in policy, and the random results of individuals are wounding to those who experience them and to those who identify with the wounded.

There is certainly much truth in the explanation of color identification that points to the coincidence of patterns of color distribution and patterns of the distribution of power and wealth. The coincidence of color with inferior positions in the various distributions in colonial societies, in predominantly white societies, and in world society reinforces—some would say, generates—the interpretation of "color identity" as a variant of "class identity." There is truth also in the proposition that color identification arises in part from the assimilation by the colored periphery of the dominant white center's use of the categories "whiteness' and "coloredness." But these hypotheses, valuable though they are, do not provide an exhaustive explanation. Another element should be mentioned not as an exhaustive alternative explanation, but as a complementary one that deals with a vital phenomenon otherwise excluded from consideration. It is this: self-identification by color has its origins in the sense of primordial connection with which human beings find it difficult to dispense.

The prominence and ubiquity of self-identification by kinship connection and territorial location are well known, but they tend to be taken for granted and even neglected in the study of modern society. Because they are taken for granted, they are seldom reduced analytically to man's need to be in contact with the point and moment of his origin and to experience a sense of affinity with those who share that origin. The need for connections or relationships of a primordial character will be endemic in human existence as long as biological existence has a value to the individual organism. Ethnic identification, of which color identification is a particular variant, is a manifestation of this need. Traces of the sense of affinity and of shared primordial properties occur also in the phenomenon of nationality.

Self-identification by color seems to entail some reference to a common biological origin that is thought to establish ties of affinity, sometimes obligation and solidarity among those who share it, and of separation from those who do not. In its crudes form, it denies the membership of those of other colors in the same species.

There are great interindividual differences in this sense of affinity with those who share a putatively common origin, just as there are great interindividual differences in the need for contact with divinity. The need, where it is weak, is often powerfully reinforced by the cultures and social structures generated by color identification and by those that parallel it. A weak disposition toward color identification can be strengthened by class—or national—identifications that are congruent with color boundaries.

Decrease in the dominance of primordial attachments of kinship and locality has been accompanied by an increase in the importance attributed to ethnicity and color. The latter two represent a broadening of the scope of particularistic primordial identification. Ethnicity in numerous cases—color in very few—has yielded precedence in many respects to nationality, which verges toward civility while retaining much of a primordial, often pseudo-ethnic basis.

In nationality, the primordial element begins to recede. It yields to an "ideal" or 'ideational" element—a "spirit," an "essence"—that is recognized as involving the mind. It is not accidental that a common language—the most widely shared of cultural objectivations—has so often been regarded as a crucial element in nationality.

The primordial is one focus of man's disposition to attribute sacredness to particular entities or symbols. It was a great accomplishment of the human race to have relocated the sacred from the primordial to the ideal, from biological and territorial properties of the self and the kinship-local group to entities apprehensible by thought and imagination. But it has done so only very falteringly. Its failure to accomplish it entirely is a source of many of mankind's miseries. The shift occurred in both Judaism and Buddhism, although the Jews retained the primordial ethnic element in a central position. It reached a high development in Christianity and in Islam. Nevertheless, in none of the cultures in which these religions have become established has the sacredness of the primordial been anything more than diminished. Still, it has been displaced to some extent, as the development of religion and politics testifies. The sacred—both primordial and "ideal"—is capable of attenuation and dispersion—with numerous relapses into intensification and concentration. There is, however, a major primordial property that has been very reluctant to yield its sacredness to attention. This is color.

The self-identification by color common among Asians and Africans of wide horizon—and the Afro-Asian intellectuals, in particular—is not attributable exclusively to its primordial quality. Nor is color the sole or always dominant criterion of this self-identification. Color plays a considerable, if indeterminate, part in their self-identification because it symbolizes many other properties of the Africans' and Asians' position in their own societies—both in colonial times and in the world since independence. For intellectuals, additional factors—such as their position in the world-wide intellectual community and their own societies, and the relation of these societies to those of the once-ruling imperial powers and the other advanced countries—coincide with the color self-identification and accentuate its force. When these other factors diminish, the intensity of the total self-identification by color will diminish too. But what of the primordial root of the color-identification? Will color yield some of its power in the formation of the self-image of Asians and Africans? Will it yield some of its power over the intellectual's self-image and its influence on his response to intellectual things?

I should now like to turn away for a moment from color as a focus of self-identification and consider possible changes that might enter into the self-identification of intellectuals—literary men, journalists, scientists, and scholars. First of all, their focus on nationality and civility might grow if the new states become consolidated internally as integrated national societies. They might also identify themselves as members of intellectual communities which transcend the boundaries of states and the limits of regions and continents.

The intellectual community, in its territorial scope and its criteria of admission, is the most universal of communities. Its adherents are scattered over the world's surface. To be a member of it, a person must either be engaged in intellectual activities or be in the state of mind that intellectual actions express and engender. In principle, no primordial properties, such as connections of kinship, locality, tribe, or territory, are valid in the assessment of the qualifications for membership in any of its constituent institutions or for advancement in its corporate or honorary hierarchies. (Of course, in practice, primordial properties are sometimes operative in governing admission to membership in particular corporate institutions, but those who apply them know that they are contravening the rules of the intellectual community—unarticulated and amorphous though these are.) The intellectual community is universalistic because it applies criteria of universal validity, criteria generally acknowledged throughout the world as true and relevant by those who have been exposed to them by education and training. Sometimes the intellectual community might seem to have no reality, to be only a figurative name for a class of actions and states of mind, to be, in fact, no community at all. It certainly lacks a corporate structure, although it has many subsidiary corporate structures, such as international scientific and professional associations. It lacks a formal structure of authority, although it has many subsidiary structures of authority, such as universities, research institutions, periodicals, and professional associations. It lacks formal articles of faith, but it has many quite specific actions and beliefs that define membership. Indeed, as a single community, it scarcely exists, and yet it would be excessively and prejudicially tough-minded to deny its existence altogether. Its subsidiary, more specialized spheres certainly have more reality; they are more easily apprehensible.

The world scientific community is one of these. It is the community of those who do scientific research, the real science that is practiced with efficacy in teaching and research in many parts of the world. Its members communicate easily with one another—partly because the subject matter of each substantively specialized subsector is common to all its members wherever and whoever they are, partly because the symbols and notations used are universally uniform, and partly because science, particularly scientific research, uses one or a few common written languages.

The international scientific community has three major lines of internal differentiation. The first, differentiation by substantive spheres of knowledge, is so pronounced that members of some sectors are frequently unable to communicate about their substantive interests and results very efficiently with members of other sectors, even those within the same country or university. The second, differentiation according to the quality of individual and collective performance, results in an approximation of a hierarchy of individuals and institutions (departments, universities, laboratories). The third, which follows from the second, is a territorial differentiation and hierarchy within a larger territory; it is intranational and international. In the international intellectual community, entire countries become the units for assessing the merit of performance on the basis of the average of accomplishment of particular intranational institutions. (In both, the assessment of the merit of collectivities is a precipitate or average of the assessment of the work of individuals; as a result, the ranks of particular individuals, their institutions, and their countries are only imperfectly correlated with one another.)

Yet despite these vertical and horizontal lines of differentiation and separation, the international scientific community does exist. Specialized scientists, blocked from communicating with one another about what they know best by the specialization of their knowledge, regard one another as "scientists." They consider themselves as having very important, although ordinarily unspecified, things in common. Regardless of their special subjects, they have the same heroes—Galileo, Newton, Darwin, Mendel. They believe that they belong to a common group because they perform and are committed to the performance of certain types of action and to the maintenance of certain states of mind that bring them together and set them apart from other human beings. They accept in common the discipline of scientific procedure, the unconditional value of truth, and the worthwhileness of striving for it. From this mutuality grows an attachment to one another, not as persons but as the bearers of an outlook.

The members of the scientific community are, of course, members of other communities as well, many of them authoritatively elaborated, with specific and specifiable obligations. Citizens of states and municipalities, administrators of laboratories and university departments, they are also members of political parties, churches, clubs, and civic and professional associations. They have different nationalities and religious beliefs. None of these properties or characteristics is, however, allowed in principle to contaminate the obligations scientists acknowledge themselves to have as scientists or to impair the affinity they sense among all scientists. In assessing the results of another scientist's research, a scientist permits none of these other obligations to stand in the way of his overwhelmingly preponderant obligation to observe, to think, and to judge as a scientist. In activities that are more secondary within the scientific community, these other obligations and loyalties sometimes play a greater part, although there, too, it would ordinarily be denied that this is so in particular cases, and it would be emphatically denied in principle.

In the social sciences, with the exception of economics, there is much less common culture among the practitioners. Whereas economic theorists and economists speak to one another out of a knowledge of a common set of problems and a common body of literature, sociologists and political scientists diverge markedly after sharing but a few common elements in their disciplines. They have relatively fewer common symbols and notations. The data of the various social sciences, being largely descriptive of particular situations, are more intimately related to the various territories in which they were gathered and from which the social scientists come. The problems many social scientists study are, moreover, more intimately involved in their own particularistic attachments, even though they seek and often attain a high degree of detachment. Insofar as this detachment becomes more or less articulated in a general theory or in specific techniques, it gives them a common universe of discourse and thereby confers membership in an international community. Nevertheless, the international communities of social scientists are not as unified as those of the natural scientists. The social scientist's self-identification is more affected by his particularistic attachments than is that of the natural scientist.

The humanistic disciplines, except for general linguistics and certain classical subjects, are even more parochial than the social sciences. Much of the work of the humanistic disciplines is concerned with the establishment, precision, and interpretation of the national or regional (continental or otherwise territorial) cultural inheritance in the form of history, modern languages, literary, religious, philosophical, and artistic works. Much of the work done in these fields is only of interest to nationals of the countries in which it is done, and this not primarily because of linguistic barriers. Some of the scholarship in history and sociology is part of the consensus and dissensus of the various national societies in which it is carried on, and it entails relatively little transnational self-identification.

The practice of the social sciences and the humanistic subjects has nonetheless a considerable internationality. For one thing, the study of the society and the culture of a particular country is not confined to nationals of that country. Oriental and African studies—history, religion, society, literature, and languages—link European and American social scientists and humanistic scholars with scholars indigenous to the countries being studied. These studies, too, have their disciplined techniques, their heroes, and their classics, which are commonly shared by scholars wherever they are. The world communities of scholars in the social sciences and humanities are patchier and less integrated than the world community of natural scientists, but they are international intellectual communities nonetheless.

Literature has not the common institutional (largely academic) foundation, nor the compact, systematically unfolding tradition of the academically cultivated branches of science and scholarship. The diversity and lack of connections among traditions are greater. Nevertheless, the novel in both English-speaking and French-speaking Africa is and must be viewed in the larger context of the English and French literary traditions. Independent oral and written literary traditions enter into the creative work of Asian and African prose writers, but the great European models toward which the novelists outside Europe orient themselves help to form and guide the work of novelists in the Asian and African countries. Poetic creation shows these latter characteristics to an even greater extent. Shakespeare, Hugo, Yeats, T.S. Eliot, and Rimbaud are influences all over the world and create a sense of unity among poets.

The worldwide intellectual community is neither dense, continuous, nor highly organized. Its coverage is very imperfect, and it does not have a complete consensus. Nonetheless, members of the various communities in the major areas of intellectual life evaluate intellectual performance with little or no reference to nationality, religion, race, political party, or class. An African novelist wants to be judged as a novelist, not as an African; a Japanese mathematician would regard it as an affront if an analysis of his accomplishment referred to his pigmentation; a British physicist would find it ridiculous if a judgment of his research referred to his being "white."

Every community has a center in which its highest values are symbolized and represented, from which authority is exercised on behalf of these values, and to which deference is given. Intellectual communities are no different from primordial communities and communities of religious belief in this regard. The centers of the modern intellectual communities are largely in the West—in the United Kingdom, Western Europe, and North America. The Soviet Union has recently become more of a center than Tsarist Russia was—except in literature—and Japan is beginning to become one. These two newer centers are handicapped because their languages are not so widely known outside their borders as those of the Western European and North American centers. They have also come forward more recently, and they have not entered so much into the modern cultures of Asia and Africa as have the older centers. The metropolitan cultures are still the centers for much of the modern intellectual life of the new states for such obvious reasons as the facility offered through the language introduced by the former ruler and the relatively low cultural productivity, in modern works, of the new states. The increased demands for intellectual products in the new states—books, periodicals, services of intellectual institutions, results of research and scientific surveys—have placed a burden on local or indigenous intellectual powers which they cannot yet accommodate.(3) The result is dependence on the most easily available source—which is, in most cases (except Indonesia), the culture of the former ruler. Pride, realism, and the competition of the great powers in seeking the approval of the new states have altered the pattern somewhat, but not fundamentally.

The institutional structure was organized on the assumption—by both parties—that the colonies were, insofar as they had a modern intellectual life, peripheral to the metropolitan centers. Where they had universities, they were formed on the metropolitan pattern. Many who taught in them, indigenous and expatriate, were trained in the metropolitan universities. The books on sale in bookshops came from the publishers in the metropolitan countries, since the publishers were organized to supply the colonial market, such as it was; the same was true for periodicals. The young men who were trained either in the metropolitan universities or in the governmental or missionary institutions acquired the culture of the metropolis. If they became creative and productive, they did so as members of an intellectual community that had its center in the metropolis.

With relatively small differences, these conditions still exist in the new states of Asia and Africa. One of the constitutive differences between the center and the periphery in the intellectual community is that the scholars and the scientists of the center are more widely known. Exceptional individuals at the periphery are accepted as equals at the center because of their accomplishments and regard themselves more or less as equals. They share the standards of the metropolis and judge themselves in that light; they appreciate that their own accomplishments put them in a position equal to that of the leading persons at the center and superior to that of the more mediocre practitioners at the center. The weight of the awareness of peripherality or provinciality persists, however, even among those who have become creative, because their accomplishment has not yet been attended by an intellectual infrastructure of institutions and products. They have not yet succeeded in changing the map that members of the intellectual communities in their own country and abroad carry in their minds.

This might not make much difference within a single country with a common language and culture. When center and periphery are located in different countries, however, it is quite another matter. The intellectual centers are more powerful economically and militarily, more famous, and more populous intellectually. The volume of their production is richer and is taken more seriously, not only because it is superior intellectually but also because the countries in which it is produced are more powerful and more famous. Moreover, the metropolitan cultures are the cultures of the former rulers or of those who are somehow associated in the minds of those on the periphery with their former rulers. All this strains the self-esteem of the intellectuals at the periphery. At the same time, the modern culture of the countries at the periphery of the international intellectual community is discontinuous with the indigenous culture of the peripheral areas.

As if to symbolize the whole thing, the inhabitants of the countries at the periphery are of a different color from those at the center.

With an intranational intellectual community, there are strains of inferiority and superiority. It is not pleasant to adjudge oneself to be mediocre, and be intellectually dependent on others, and to see the world's praise directed toward them. Yet in addition to the usual mechanisms that preserve failures and near-failures from extremes of distress, belonging to a culture with a high position in the intellectual hierarchy also reduces the stress of failure—just as membership in a common nationality alleviates to some extent the distress of inequality.

The situation is more complicated and less favorable for the intellectuals of Asia and Africa. They are not members of this international community of cultures of the center. They have their own national and regional cultures in which their own dignity is involved and which they do not share with their intellectual confreres of other nationalities and countries. This cuts them off to some extent from those intellectual confreres and reduces the solidarity of the ties of intellectual affinity. Their own national and regional cultures are, furthermore, like all human creations, subject to assessment. The criteria for the assessment of a complex culture of many strands and a long history are more qualified and more ambivalent than are the criteria of individual accomplishment in the intellectual communities. Given the particularistic attachments that individuals have to their own cultures, bound up with them as they are through kinship ties and early experience, judgments about them are likely to be more "relativistic" than those about accomplishments in the various fields of modern culture, where the criteria are more consensual. Nonetheless, intellectuals in the new states are affected by the order of worth assigned to their culture by those at the centers of the intellectual communities. They feel this way, although the centers' preeminence within any particular field of intellectual work does not qualify them for comprehensive preeminence.

Cultures are assessed, in part, on grounds of their "modernity." Since the criteria of intellectual worth, being so vital to modernity, form such a large ingredient in the criteria of national worth, there is a tendency for national cultures as a whole to be ranked very roughly and approximately in accordance with the level of intellectual eminence.

In the more delimited realms of modern science and scholarship, the present-day nullity of the traditional inheritance of the African and Asian countries seems unchallengeable.(4) This consensus between center and periphery breaks down, however, when attention is shifted to the broader fields of culture, to religion and ethos. There is something substantially contemporaneous in these realms; societies have lived by them over long stretches of time, reaching into the present. They have become incorporated into works of thought and art, some of which have held the attention and aroused the admiration of the center in ways unparalleled by anything else in the social structures and cultures of the African and Asian countries.(5) They are, moreover, objects of genuine primary attachment for many intellectuals in these countries. Even where they are not, they are something to fall back on as evidence of past creativity, of greatness in human accomplishments and quality. They are thereby, worthy of respect before a universal audience; by that token, they enhance the dignity of those who participate in or are otherwise associated with them and who are also part of a worldwide intellectual community and share some of its standards. The indigenous traditional cultures offer the simulacrum of an alternative center to which the intellectuals of Asia and Africa are drawn.

The need for a countercenter has a widely ramified origin. The Asian and African intellectuals are more than intellectuals participating in some manner in the universal intellectual community. They are members also of territorially limited but more than local societies, delimited nationalities, and a subspecies of the human race with pigmentation different from that of those in ascendancy.

Their conscious identification of themselves by these classifications is partly a product of their assimilation into the worldwide intellectual community. They came to transcend the narrowly local and ascended to the national, regional, and continental through participation in the universal intellectual community. Through modern education and training at home, through experience with the metropolis while being educated and trained in metropolitan institutions or in domestic institutions formed on their model, through sojourns in the metropolis, they became aware that they were something different from what they had been and what they were becoming. They became aware that they belonged to the colonial peoples, that they belonged to distinctive continents; they came to perceive themselves as having nationality, which they defined as coterminous with the area over which the authority they rejected ruled. The self-definition was a negative one; it was the product of a process of distinguishing the self from the powerful, oppressively dominating center.

One major primordial property symbolizes through its concentration of all differences their differences from the metropolis. This is skin color. The awareness of differences in skin color heightens awareness of other differences. It does so not just by symbolizing those differences, but by serving as a focus of self-identification as a member of a species with a distinctive biological origin and separateness.

The conflict between the primordial realm and the realm of the mind is especially pronounced in the intellectual, who—by virtue of what he is—is, in a way, the custodian of things of the mind for his society. Intellectual activity is the cultivation of the "ideational" realm. A change in the African or Asian intellectual's relations to the center of the international intellectual community might diminish the intensity of his color identification. The provinciality of his present position in the intellectual community is one of the distractions from which he suffers. This is only aggravated by the structural handicaps, both institutional and social, of his own country and the world.

When many more African and Asian intellectuals become productive and creative in the natural and social sciences, in humanistic scholarship, and in literature, their position will begin to change, and so will their self-identification by color. As individuals in the universities and towns of Africa and Asia begin to produce works that commend themselves to the intellectual appreciation of their colleagues at the centers in other parts of the world, and as they begin to produce some of their own succession, they will emerge from provinciality to centrality. This has already happened in certain fields and in certain places—for example, in statistics and economic theory in Calcutta and Delhi. Once these achievements begin to take deeper root by reproducing themselves and expanding their influence within India, the diminuation of Indian intellectual peripherality will be under way. Similar processes are readily imaginable for other parts of Asia and Africa. They are not likely to occur in a very short time, but as they do, the strain of an inferior position in the international intellectual community will be reduced. A sense of genuine equality will then join to the sense of shared standards an awareness of shared accomplishment.

In emerging as new centers in the network of creative centers of the international intellectual community, African and Asian intellectuals will cease to feel so urgently the need for a countercenter, of which color is one of the foci of identification. The argument for a countercenter is only a large contrived surrogate for the real thing. The countercenter could never be successful in attaining the end these intellectuals seek—the dignity of creative achievement.

The impetus to the "revolt against Western values" will weaken. The values will cease to be Western, except in the sense that in their more recent history they have not been most cultivated in the West. They will become more fully what they are already patchily and unevenly—the universalistic values of a worldwide intellectual community.

The enhancement of the quality of civility in their societies will likewise work to diminish the force of the color identification. The closely connected sense of nationality will differentiate the "world of color," and will thereby reinforce the factors shifting the need for "serious" attachments away from color to alternative foci of *la vie serieuse.*

As these changes occur—and it is reasonable to expect them to occur—the primordial attachment to color will still remain, but it will be deprived of its extraneous supports; it will no longer act so powerfully on the sentiments. Like ethnic, kinship, and local primordial attachments, it will survive but not so strongly as to deflect the intellect and imagination from their appropriate activities. Just as the rule of law and political equality have become established in areas once dominated by primordial attachments and the particularistic standards they dictated, so will the intellectual communities and their universalistic standards constrict the loyalties nurtured by the self-identification of color. This identification will become fainter and fainter. . . .

NOTES

(1) Cf. the dedication of Nirad C. Chaudhuri's great book, *The Autobiography of an Unknown Indian* (New York, 1951).

(2) In a statement concerning the recent British legislative restrictions on Commonwealth immigration, a great Indian public servant, one of the most rational

and modern of men without the slightest trace of xenophobia, demagogy, or revivalism in his mental make-up, wrote:

> Sadly it must be recorded that Britain, the mother of parliaments, the originator of democracy and the rule of law, the home of liberty and fair play, the refuge of the persecuted and the oppressed, has fallen far below her high degree. She has now publicly declared herself a country riddled with color consciousness. She needs constant replenishment of her labour force but she will take care to see that most of the new workers have white skins. They need not belong to the Commonwealth. Better by far total strangers politically, Portuguese and Greeks and Spaniards and South Irish than West Indians and Nigerians and Indians. . . .

The Labour politicians, whatever and however strong their moral convictions in this matter, have discovered, perhaps to the dismay of some of them, that the voter, the ordinary Briton, feels strongly on this subject. He does not like the coloured man, black or brown, and he does not want them near him. They fear the political party which will not keep the coloured out will lose votes, and what after all are principles, moral or other, in comparison with votes? . . . A party led by a statesman and with a few statesmen in it might well have resisted the electorate rather than give way to its prejudice, but the last British statesman was Churchill, and puny are the men of Westminster today.

So much for the British side. More important for us, our proper attitude to this declaration of national dislike. Not a few of us have come across some instance of colour-prejudice on our visits to England. (The writer can remember experiences on his first visit in 1921 and his last in 1962). We have however put them down to aberrations on the part of an individual or a small section. No indictment most of us have felt like drawing up was against the British people as a whole. But now proposals in Parliament put forward by Her Majesty's Government in all seriousness and with all solemnity assure us that we were wrong, that the whole British people cannot tolerate us because of the colour of our skins. This is a serious situation and the answer to it from us must be equally serious.

Since it is obvious that no self-respecting person thrusts himself into company where he is not wanted, all brown and black people should refrain from going to Britain for any purpose whatever. This may entail some loss in the matter of education, but there are many countries now in which quite as good, or even better, training can be obtained than in Britain. Business connections with Britain should be reduced as much as possible, nor should undue friendliness be shown toward British officials and businessmen in black and brown countries. After all, reserve in place of cordiality is the least retort to deadly insult. A special effort must be made to refrain from looking at the world through British eyes, a practice to which educated Indians are in particular addicted. There is no real reason for regarding what happens or is thought in Britain as specially important to us, for keeping up with life there through the *Times*, the *Guardian*, the *New Statesman*, etc. Britain after all today is a small island off the West Coast of Europe, not the centre of the world.

We wish Britain no harm; in the hearts of those of us who knew the best of her people and hold many of her sons and daughters our friends, there will always be a warmth for them and her, but the clear implication of the measures her government proposes we much realize. No special relationship is possible, no special cordiality can be sustained, with those to whom the colour of your skin is anathema. Let the coloured doctors and nurses, so notably welcomed because so emphatically useful, remember this. They are sought as mercenaries. Will they be mercenaries, sell their souls for a mess of pottage to those who scorn the people of their colour, but have no objection to using for their own benefit, as the Roman patrician used the Greek physician slave, the skill they in particular have acquired at the cost of the people of that colour?

("Alas for Britain," *Opinion* (Bombay), vol. 6, no. 15 (August 17, 1965), pp. 3-4).

(3) Indeed there is no good reason why local resources or persons should be expected to provide all that is needed when it is available from abroad; to do so would not only be wasteful of scarce resources but also beyond the powers of the underdeveloped countries.

(4) The situation is quite different as regards the remotely past accomplishments of India, China, and the Islamic Middle East in science and mathematics.

(5) It is interesting to speculate on the influence of Max Muller and other Western Indologists on the renewal of Hinduism in the last part of the nineteenth century, and of the European appreciation of African sculpture on African self-esteem in the twentieth century.

Reprinted by permission from *Daedalus*, Journal of the American Academy of Arts and Sciences, Boston, Massachusetts, Vol. 96, No. 2 (Spring, 1967), *Color and Race*.

BIBLIOGRAPHY

Further reading is recommended in Segal (9) for an interpretation of current history in terms of world-wide structure of racial conflict. The essays collected in *Daedalus*(2) examine some of the same phenomena from a more traditional viewpoint. Schiller(8) extends the analysis of the mass media and cultural dependency outlined in the selection chosen for this reader. Jalee (6) presents a large amount of empirical data of the dimensions of dependency in the post World War II period. The special issue of the *Review of Radical Political Economics* (7) represents an effort on the part of a group of economists to provide a conceptual framework for the information presented by Jalee. Fanon (3) remains the classic treatment of the race relations of colonialism and dependency in the African situation. The essays by Cabral (5) are an analysis by a recently assassinated revolutionary leader of the development of the class structure in a colonized society. Frank (4) is one of the seminal works in the new interpretation of Latin American history and development which have appeared in the last few years. The selection of essays in Cockcroft, Frank and Johnson (1) extend this new mode of analysis.

(1) Cockcroft, James D., Andre Gunder Frank and Dale Johnson. *Dependence and Underdevelopment: Latin America's Political Economy*. Garden City, New York: Anchor Books, 1972.

(2) *Daedalus*. Journal of the American Academy of Arts and Sciences. Vol. 96, No. 2, 1967.

(3) Fanon, Frantz. *The Wretched of the Earth*. New York: Grove Press, 1968.

(4) Frank, Andre Gunder. *Capitalism and Underdevelopment in Latin America: Historical Studies of Chile and Brazil*. New York: Monthly Review Press, 1967.

(5) Handyside, Richard (ed.). *Revolution in Guinea: Selected Texts by Amilcar Cabral*. London: Stage 1, 1969.

(6) Jalee, Pierre. *The Third World in the World Economy*. New York: Monthly Review Press, 1969.

(7) *Review of Radical Political Economics*. Special issue on "Imperialism and Dependency," Vol. 4, No. 1, April 1972.

(8) Schiller, Herbert. *Mass Communications and American Empire*. Boston: Beacon Press, 1971.

(9) Segal, Ronald. *The Race War*. New York: Bantam Books, 1967.

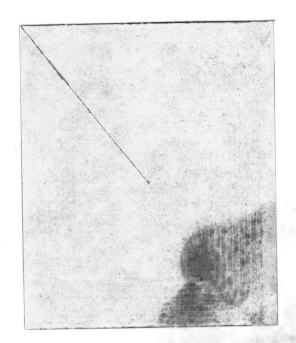